D1000301

Glinka's Life in Music
A Chronicle

Russian Music Studies, No. 20

Malcolm Hamrick Brown, Series Editor

Chairman, Musicology Department
Indiana University

Other Titles in This Series

Glinka's Life in Music
A Chronicle

by
Alexandra Orlova

Translated by
Richard Hoops

U·M·I Research Press

Ann Arbor / London

WITHDRAWN
ITHACA COLLEGE LIBRARY

Copyright © 1988
Alexandra Orlova
All rights reserved

Produced and distributed by
UMI Research Press
an imprint of
University Microfilms Inc.
Ann Arbor, Michigan 48106

Library of Congress Cataloging in Publication Data

Orlova, Aleksandra Anatol'evna, 1911-
   [Letopis' zhizni i tvorchestva M.I. Glinki. English]
   Glinka's life in music : a chronicle / by Alexandra Orlova ;
translated by Richard Hoops.
      p. cm—(Russian music studies ; no. 20)
      Translation of: Letopis' zhizni i tvorchestva M.I. Glinki.
      Includes index.
      ISBN 0-8357-1864-6 (alk. paper)
      1. Glinka, Mikhail Ivanovich, 1804-1857—Chronology.
   2. Composers—Soviet Union—Biography.   I. Title.   II. Series.
   ML410.G460813   1988
   780'.92'4—dc19
   [B]   88-4870
                                                                    CIP
                                                                     MN

British Library CIP data is available.

Glinka in the Spring of 1852
Daguerreotype by Sergey Levitsky.

Contents

Translator's Preface

The translation of Alexandra Orlova's *Glinka's Life in Music* was undertaken nearly three years ago when Professor Malcolm Brown, general editor of the series *Russian Music Studies,* first approached me concerning this project. I frankly had no idea of the magnitude of the undertaking, though the effort required to bring this work to completion has been liberally rewarded by the richness of the material and the satisfaction of working with the author. *Glinka's Life in Music* is a magisterial example of scholarship, conducted, as the author describes in her Introduction, over a period of nearly four decades. In fact, her work continued as I was translating and as she received new information, which is included in the present version of the text. I received the work in essentially two parts, the first of which, through the year 1843, had been published in the Soviet Union (Muzyka, 1978) before the author's emigration to this country. Numerous changes were made to this text by means of marginal annotations in the book and letters to me. The second part, which would have been published as a second volume had Mme Orlova not applied for emigration, only existed in typescript. This too was amended by the author's written comments and corrections. Thus this translation not only represents the first complete publication of Orlova's new chronicle, but it also reflects the most current scholarship regarding Glinka's life and works. There is no comparable work on Glinka in any language.

Some explanatory notes are essential to assist the reader in understanding how the book is organized and how I have gone about the task of translating it. I have transposed to this Preface the directions concerning matters of dating and source material that Orlova originally included in her Introduction. First, however, the matter of transliteration, for which I have relied upon J. Thomas Shaw's *Transliteration of Modern Russian for English-Language Publications* (University of Wisconsin Press, 1967). For Russian names, Shaw's System I has been used throughout, including the index and source citations. His System II has been used for "words as words." Insofar as Russian names are concerned, this practice is fairly consistent, although there are some names which I have rendered in their more customary Western spellings. Problems arise with the names of people of non-Russian origin who settled in Russia and effectively became naturalized, of people of unknown origin, or of native Russians whose family backgrounds, and thus their names, were Western European. In such cases, I have attempted only to be consistent, if no common practice existed to guide me. Likewise troublesome are those examples of non-Russian names that only appear in Russian sources. Once again, consistency has been the rule, though I have tried to obtain the most appropriate spellings (for example, of the names of many of Glinka'a acquaintances abroad).

Most of the in-text bibliographical citations appear in the form of *sigla,* a list of which appears at the front of this volume. Most of these sources appear in the text in abbreviated Russian with a translation in brackets normally on first appearance. Other frequently appearing items which I have abbreviated are also explained along with the list of sources. Some of these, in fact most, I have simply adapted from Orlova's usage in the original Russian text. Very few translator's notes appear in the text. Those notes that do occur are typically efforts to clarify matters of translation and appear in brackets.

Deviating from common practice, I have presented most song titles in Russian with an English translation appearing in the text on first occurrence. Translations are provided for all works in the index, and I have tried to reconcile these with the available translations in other English-language sources so that the reader may easily be able to locate discussions of a work elsewhere. Since so few of Glinka's songs and romances are available in translation or in any English-language publications, this seemed to me to be the preferable course of action. This is also consistent with my handling of bibliographic sources, in particular, periodicals and newspapers (which are rendered in abbreviated Russian), since anyone who wishes to refer to the original sources will be obliged to acquaint himself with the Russian language.

Initially it was intended to include any non-Russian quotations in their original languages (which include German, French, Spanish, and Italian), but the sheer bulk of the text eventually precluded this possibility. Most non-Russian texts appear in the form of personal letters which could claim no real justification for being distinguished from texts written in Russian, hence I have included only occasional phrases in languages other than English. A parenthetical note, however, identifies the language of those passages not originally in Russian. Concerning the issue of non-Russian texts, I think it important to say that the original texts were not always available to me. When they were, they provided the basis for my translation; otherwise I was obliged to rely solely upon Orlova's Russian version of the original text.

In keeping with the nature of the chronicle genre, *Glinka's Life in Music* is based entirely upon original documents cited as excerpts and quotations, or, more rarely, as short summaries. Glinka's aesthetic opinions are quoted as fully as possible. Glinka's *Zapiski* [Memoirs], letters, and other autobiographical materials housed in archives in Moscow and Leningrad have been checked by the author against the original documents. All the composer's letters are quoted in accordance with the authorized, "academic" edition of his correspondence and writings (*Polnoe sobranie sochinenii,* Moscow, 1973–77). No citations are provided for material quoted from this source, except for information first printed in the editorial commentary, in which case the appropriate volume is cited. Likewise, there are no citations identifying autographs kept in the Glinka Archives of the manuscript department of the Leningrad Public Library, with the exception of archival materials initially published in the first edition of Orlova's Chronicle (*Letopis' zhizni i tvorchestva M. I. Glinki,* Moscow, 1952). In all instances where Orlova's research led to conclusions at variance with those presented in the authorized edition of Glinka's writings, the author has provided an explanation of the issue. Such matters, along with other editorial commentary, appear in small print. Reminiscences of Glinka by his friends and contemporaries are quoted from another volume published by Orlova (*Glinka v vospominaniiakh sovremennikov* [Glinka in the reminiscences of his contemporaries], Moscow, 1955), also based upon carefully verified texts. References to this volume are abbreviated thus: first the name of the memoirist and then, *Vosp.* [i.e., "Memoirs"]. All other sources and references are identified by *sigla.* If material is printed in succession from a single source, the source is indicated with the last reference.

All dates are presented in the old style current in Russia before 1918, except in those instances where the document was written abroad. In such cases the old-style date is presented first, followed by the new, or Western, date. All dating has been meticulously verified by the author, though in some instances, when an exact date could not be determined, an approximate date is given. For the dating of printed publications in cases where no date is given, the date of the censor's authorization has been supplied.

Within any given text, all markings except brackets and ellipses belong to the author of the document. An ellipsis signifies a break in the text; bracketed material belongs to either the editor or the translator. With rare exceptions, words or phrases crossed out in the autographs have not been restored.

I am grateful to Professor Malcolm Brown for the considerable assistance he gave me in the preparation of this translation, but I am much more grateful to him for the opportunity he provided me to do the work in the first place. His encouragement and advice have been invaluable.

The author herself, however, has been my most important collaborator in this effort, and I am gratified that I could participate in making available to lovers of Russian music the work on which she labored for so many years. She has been of unfailing help to me whenever I needed it and has patiently endured the snail's pace at which I was obliged to work.

Finally, a sincere word of thanks to my wife, Sarah Paulk, without whose constant support and self-sacrifice this work would never have been completed.

Introduction

Glinka's Life in Music is the third book on a subject of musicological interest written in a biographical genre that is quite widespread in Soviet literary studies. The first of these was Georgy Orlov's biographical chronicle of Musorgsky. At the same time, a group of writers, myself among them, started an analogous work on Tchaikovsky. Since then, the genre of biographical chronicle has held a secure position in Soviet musicological writing.[1]

In the introduction to *Musorgsky's Days and Works,* I commented on the advantages of research of this sort, and I consider it worthwhile to touch on the matter once again.[2] The chronicle approach opens up many possibilities in reconstructing an artist's creative and intellectual biography. The great range and variety of documents combined with direct quotations from the "hero" himself minimize the need for conjecture and possibly arbitrary interpretation, since everything is based upon strictly verifiable facts and authentic sources and is thus maximally reliable. Comparison of the documents and their reciprocal illumination allow us to peer more deeply into the past and to view things from a new perspective. This is the essence of the genre.

The chronicle not only provides an opportunity to view the subject's personality more fully and realistically, it allows insight into the relation between the artist's external activities and his work. This, in turn, facilitates understanding of the psychology of creativity, allowing us to imagine the creative mind "from within."

The biographical chronicle is a unique kind of scholarly writing based entirely on materials contemporary with its subject. Memoirs are the only "posthumous" materials employed. Herein lies the specific character of such a work, reflected in the strictly chronological arrangement of the materials. Such a study is intended to reflect the characteristic details of the composer's personality and to show the conditions which, one way or another, had an effect on his work. Thus nothing is too humble or too exalted for inclusion. Both life and people are shown as they were, in all the complexities and contradictions of their characters and interrelations. Not everything gets described as fully as it might, for at times the materials are insufficient; and the author of a chronicle has no right to interpose things of his own, since this would violate the objectivity of the account.

Of course there is no place in a chronicle for exhaustive descriptions of historical and cultural background or of the musical life that the subject of the book both participated in and witnessed. This emerges implicitly from the material itself, from which the reader is able to see the real conditions in which the composer lived and worked.

The organizational principles of a biographical chronicle depend upon its materials. In some cases, when material is abundant, documents must be used selectively within certain established limits (this applies, for example, in the cases of Tchaikovsky and Rimsky-Korsakov). In other cases (such as Glinka and Musorgsky) everything must be taken account of, even references of seemingly little significance, so long as the composer's biography and the history of his works still include so much that is unclear or unknown. In such instances, any detail is potentially valuable in clarifying some matter or filling a gap.

Glinka has long been acknowledged as the creator of Russian classical music. His contemporaries, and—even more—his successors, recognized unconditionally that he had established the models for the further development of Russian music. Tchaikovsky, Musorgsky, Borodin, Rimsky-Korsakov, and succeeding generations of composers, including the giants of contemporary music, Stravinsky and Shostakovich, esteemed Glinka as their progenitor. Nor was his historical role or musical genius less appreciated by the great music critics, beginning with Odoevsky, Serov, Laroche, and Stasov, and ending with the academician Boris Asafiev.

At the same time, a virtually institutionalized denigration of his character took root. A prejudice towards his intellect arose in the nineteenth century among both Soviet and Western musicologists and continued through the 1930s. Glinka was seen as an anomaly: though supposedly a man with little education or intellect, a dilettante composer of trifles during his youth, he abruptly created a work—the opera *A Life for the Tsar*—which, in Tchaikovsky's words, placed him on the same level as Mozart and Beethoven. In truth, is there not something improbable about this?

Actually no such miracle occurred in Glinka's development as a composer. This was simply the legend that evolved, facilitated in part by his own *Memoirs*, in which he appears intentionally to misrepresent himself. The impression one gets of Glinka here is quite different from that which one receives from his letters or from the accounts of his contemporaries. If one reads between the lines of his *Memoirs*, it becomes apparent that he is far from being the simpleton he makes himself out to be.

Apropos of this, Asafiev writes:

Glinka's mind has remained stubbornly concealed. With a sort of dull, importunate obstinacy he has been perceived as everyone's boon companion. Every aspect of his "conviviality" has been scrutinized and underscored with a certain malicious intent, while everything positive has either been hushed up or concealed. Modestly and timidly there have been occasional efforts to draw out the real Glinka who composed *Ruslan* and whose intelligence and sensitivity are imprinted on the daguerreotype of 1842.[3]

Asafiev was the first to turn his attention toward this contradiction and eventually to refute the legend of Glinka's personality, which had been current for nearly a century. The information available to him was scant, and he realized that it abounded in voids and incongruities. The basic material available to Asafiev were Glinka's *Memoirs,* with tendentious commentary by Andrey Rimsky-Korsakov (1930), and a very incomplete edition of the composer's letters, published without commentary by Nikolay Findeyzen (1907).[4] Nonetheless, Asafiev's intuitions proved correct. Equipped with a profound appreciation of Glinka's music and its intonational world, Asafiev read the *Memoirs* again. The result was an article entitled *"Na poliakh Zapisok Glinki"* [In the margins of Glinka's *Memoirs*], from which the quotation above was taken. It was this article that reversed traditional perceptions.

Unfortunately this essay was not included in Asafiev's *Collected Works.* Published during World War II in a collection entitled *Sovetskaia muzyka* (the journal of the same name had ceased publication during the war), it probably did not come to the attention of Western musicologists. For Soviet scholars, however, Asafiev's insight became a lodestar, which is why I feel I must dwell on it in greater detail.

Speaking of his own study of Glinka's artistic development and creative methods, Asafiev remarks: "By virtue of [Glinka's] artistic intelligence, the scholar is increasingly drawn toward the personality of a great and inimitable master. In any fragment of Glinka's music one perceives his individual touch, but at the same time his music never sounds like the fanciful whims of a subjective imagination." Asafiev points to the sources of Glinka's music, which is "rooted in the classical past of Western European music and in its present," i.e., in the music of Glinka's own time. At the same time, it "stands far ahead of its time, for [Glinka's music] . . . is profoundly national," and extends beyond the mere quotation of folk sources. Asafiev observes that he has "managed to clarify the exceptional intelligence, clarity, and aptness of Glinka's musical opinions . . . [and moreover] to guess the significance of many things in Glinka's creative laboratory and compositional method." Asafiev emphasizes that in his music "Glinka's profound intelligence is everywhere apparent, as is his ability to efficiently select and assimilate the 'nourishing influences' of the past and the present. Everywhere there is present an inborn sense of artistic proportion as well as a profoundly organized and creatively active sense of hearing. In a word," the author concludes, "his is the mind of the Russian enlightenment's most intelligent epoch, the epoch of the Decembrists and of Pushkin."

Further on Asafiev states that

> if one does not fail to take account of the *most important* thing in his life, namely his music, or to read the *Memoirs* and materials about him critically, one has to conclude that the composer of such intelligent, fresh, and interesting music (interesting in the sense of conscious craftsmanship), was a totally different person from the Glinka described in false rumors spread by his detractors, even though, with the arch cunning and characteristic spite he showed toward those around him, he to some extent encouraged them. Glinka was not at all like the legend portrays him. He could not have written what he wrote—he simply would not have had the time to do it. He would not have had the time during the mere twenty years of intensive work, including all his greatest music, if one only considers the hours of physical labor, just writing the music down as he was accustomed to. He did not compose "instinctively," nor did his sensible, intelligent, and skilled judgments spring "from within." On the contrary, they required prolonged, patient acquaintance with the musical phenomena. Moreover, Glinka also had a profound understanding of literature and the other arts. . . .

Asafiev refers to Glinka's *Memoirs* as an "Aesopic" document "because of the character of the language, the understatment, and his alleged occasional 'forgetfulness.'" As Asafiev asserts, Glinka's *Memoirs*

> are characteristic for their period and represent a psychologically valuable document because of their clever use of Aesopic language. . . . Even in the conversations with Serov, Glinka is a different person, but in the *Memoirs* he subtly encodes his own working secrets from the gaze of the curious as he tosses out the rare pearls of his musical opinions. Glinka does not lie in his *Memoirs,* but he does recall things "selectively" and encode them, withholding from the reader the opportunity . . . to guess what he really knows.[5]

Several years before the publication of his article on Glinka's *Memoirs,* that is, at the end of 1940, Asafiev suggested that I begin collecting materials for a "chronicle" of the great Glinka's life and activities. He was convinced that if documents from Glinka's time could be published and systematized, they would help draw a truer picture of the composer and the events of his creative life. At that time Asafiev did not share his thoughts and assumptions with me. He simply said, "Be unbiased in your search, and hold no preconceived notions. Let the material itself be your guide."

Following his advice, I not only was able to fill a number of voids but also could confirm how correct Asafiev was in proposing an entirely new approach to the study of Glinka's biography. He was not altogether accurate in all of his conclusions. For example, at the beginning of the forties, Asafiev relied upon one of the then basic documents in the study of Glinka's biography (I am referring to Kukolnik's "Diary"), which in the mid-forties the Moscow musicologist Boris Shteynpress proved to be a forgery.[6]

The war interrupted my work on the chronicle, since all valuable archival resources had been evacuated from Leningrad. Meanwhile, during the blockade, Asafiev continued to work on his monograph about Glinka, and after moving to Moscow and assuming leadership of a group of musicologists there, he continued to search for and study documents pertaining to Glinka. Discoveries emerged as if from a cornucopia. One only had to glance in the archives and press of Glinka's time for more and more new material to come to light. At the end of 1944, returning to Leningrad after the evacuation, I again took up my work on the chronicle. It became fully apparent to me that Asafiev was right, for his assessment of Glinka's personality and creative work found corroboration in the source materials, documents, and testimony of his contemporaries.

When I began collecting material about Glinka, I had at my disposal only his *Memoirs* (which, as I have said, were published in incomplete and inaccurate form with tendentious commentary that disparaged the composer's intellect), very carelessly published letters, and scattered recollections of him in various periodicals. I must make it clear, however, that in referring to the incompleteness and carelessness of early publications of Glinka's written legacy, I do not mean to criticize my predecessors for deliberate negligence. They labored hard and persistently. Still, in the nineteenth century and even during the first quarter of the twentieth century, textual criticism in Russia was primitive compared to today's standards.

During the 1950s, a number of musicologists contributed to the enrichment of Glinka studies, which in time became a specialized branch of theoretical and historical musicology.[7] Just what the difference amounted to between the state of Glinka studies at the beginning of the 1940s and the end of the 1950s can be shown by the introductions to two books. In the introduction to his monograph about Glinka, Asafiev wrote: "There are many, many things about his life that are unclear, and gaps abound in his biography. Concerning his music, more has been said than done. Soviet theoretical and historical musicology shows little interest in Glinka. There is no authoritative edition of his music. The manuscripts have been naively described but not studied." This was written in 1947.[8] Not ten years had passed when this assertion was made: "'Glinkiana' is one of the most worked-over areas in Soviet musicology."[9]

It is not my task to provide a survey or critical assessment of what has been written about Glinka during the last several decades. I only wish to stress that every scholar involved in this effort provided additions, elaborations, and corrections to research that had been published earlier. This was only natural. Because of the wealth of new information, our knowledge grew in both breadth and depth. New discoveries provided opportunities for further investigations, which in turn were accepted as immutable fact. It was quite natural that in the excitement of discovery scholars were sometimes given to exaggeration or error. Sometimes it happened that a casual and seemingly insignificant hint allowed one to fill a gap, to establish a precise date, or to arrive at an important conclusion. Thus events proceeded during my collection of materials for this chronicle, as they also had during the preparation of other works.

It must be said that many discoveries were initially received with hostility, at sword's point, as they say, by those of conservative thinking. For example, after careful study of the press accounts of Glinka's time, I proposed that the accepted account of the failure of *Ruslan and Lyudmila* was false; that it was not a fiasco; that the affair was quite complicated; and that it appeared more appropriate to speak of the opera's success. This raised a regular furor. There was an organized filibuster against me after reading my paper on this subject at a conference of the Institute of Theater and Music. Several years later, with great difficulty, my article was published; a definitive version appears in Evgenia Gordeeva's collection, *M. I. Glinka: k 100-letiiu so dnia smerti* [M. I. Glinka on the 100th anniversary of his death] (Moscow, 1958). Now, however, not only have musicologists accepted this view, but, without any reference to the controversy it first caused, it appears in the textbooks of Russian music history.

One must also consider that in the years immediately following the war many archives in the Soviet Union had not yet been able to systematize or describe their resources. For all intents and purposes, this work began after World War II. As a case in point, the very rich collection of autographs of the Insititute of Russian Literature of the Soviet Academy of Sciences (the Pushkin House in Leningrad) was not only not catalogued, but even the inventory listings did not reflect their complete holdings. Frequently one could only grope one's way with the hope of clearing a path for future research. Under such circumstances, lacking essential facts and often proceeding at random, scholars unwittingly made false moves and committed mistakes. It goes without saying that subsequent research rectified their errors.[10]

I must also note that at the end of the 1940s and beginning of the 1950s, certain new information could only be published fragmentarily for reasons of censorship. As an example, the documents I found describing Glinka's divorce case were not permitted to be printed at all. Even now the subject of Glinka's numerous love affairs is carefully avoided in print. Such subjects are deemed unworthy of a classical composer!

In order to sum up the work of an entire generation of scholars and to eliminate the accumulated errors, an authorized edition of Glinka's works was a necessity. For our purposes, most important are the two volumes of his letters and writings, with their detailed commentary. This edition summarizes the work of at least four decades in the area of Glinka studies.

Still, even in such an edition, it proved impossible to answer all questions, and inaccuracies are to be found in it. I doubt that the time will come when it will be possible to say that all the gaps have been filled. Apparently much material is irretrievably lost. The publication of the two volumes of Glinka's letters and writings signifies only an important stage in the area of Glinka studies, though this in no way reduces the importance of the commentaries contained in them. Glinka studies cannot cease, for it is still too early to put a halt to the study of sources concerning his life and work.

In the Russian edition of my chronicle of Glinka's life, newly published and forgotten documents predominated, but the attainments of Glinka studies since have changed the character of the present edition, the point of which is to sum up the research in primary sources. My purpose has not been to replenish "Glinkiana" with new materials, since for the present the academic edition of his letters and writings may be considered complete, but to compile the documents which have already been found and to clarify certain facts. I must emphasize that not everything can be established with certainty. Given the present condition of archives, some things do not yield themselves to definitive dating, and some questions must simply be resolved on the basis of what is presently known. This book represents an effort to consolidate well-known and authenticated information obtained from all available resources, including foreign repositories and private collections. Thus one may trace the life and creative activity of the founder of Russian classical music in the greatest possible detail.

Alexandra Orlova
Leningrad, 1978
Jersey City, New Jersey, 1985

Notes

1. Georgy Orlov, *Letopis' zhizni i tvorchestva Musorgskogo* [A chronicle of Musorgsky's life and work] (Moscow, 1940). Several months later the following book was also published: *Dni i gody Chaykovskogo; letopis' zhizni i tvorchestva* [Tchaikovsky's days and years, a chronicle of his life and work], compiled by E. Zaydenshnur, V. Kiselev, A. Orlova, N. Shemanin, and edited by V. Yakovlev (Moscow, 1940).

2. Alexandra Orlova, *Musorgsky's Days and Works: A Biography in Documents,* trans. and ed. Roy J. Guenther (*Russian Music Studies*, No. 4, Malcolm Hamrick Brown, series editor [Ann Arbor: UMI Research Press, 1982]).

3. *Sovetskaia muzyka* [Soviet Music], coll. 2 (Moscow, 1944), p. 14.

4. M. I. Glinka, *Zapiski* [Memoirs], ed. A. Rimsky-Korsakov (Leningrad, 1930); *Pis'ma M. I. Glinki* [M. I. Glinka's letters], collected and published by N. Findeyzen (St. Petersburg, 1907).

5. *Sovetskaia muzyka,* coll. 2, pp. 11–13.

6. Boris Shteynpress, "Kukolnik's Diary as a Source for Glinka's Biography," in the collection *M. I. Glinka: Issledovaniia i materialy* [M. I. Glinka, studies and materials], ed. A. Ossovsky (Leningrad-Moscow, 1950), pp. 88–119.

7. A complete bibliography of "Glinkiana" up to this time is published in the anthology *M. I. Glinka: k 100-letiiu so dnia smerti* [M. I. Glinka on the 100th anniversary of his death], ed. E. Gordeeva (Moscow, 1958), pp. 662–89.

8. Boris Asafiev, *Glinka* (Moscow, 1947), p. 7.

9. Gordeeva, *M. I. Glinka: k 100-letiiu so dnia smerti*, p. 5.

10. It must be emphasized that almost no one working in the search for sources concerning Glinka avoided mistakes of this sort. So as not to name any of my former colleagues, I will use one of my own blunders as an example. During the second half of the 1940s, while looking for materials about Glinka in the manuscript collections of the Pushkin House, I stumbled upon material among documents of the Tsarskoye Selo Lyceum about the existence of a boarding school associated with the Lyceum called the Lyceum Boarding School for Nobility. In an account of students of the school (published in 1817), a certain Mikhail Glinka is mentioned. Insofar as the composer Glinka spent only four years in a St. Petersburg boarding school out of a five-year term of study, I concluded that Glinka spent one year in the school at Tsarskoye Selo. I also found other information, which, as I calculated, supported this idea. I reported my find in an article entitled "Glinka's School Years" in a collection edited by Aleksandr Ossovsky (see note 6 above), which also contained valuable fragments I had also found in the Pushkin House from Nikolay Markevich's "Memoirs." This mistake almost found its way into the first edition of my chronicle. But to my relief (I cannot deny it!), a colleague of mine working on another subject in another repository discovered at the beginning of 1952 archival materials concerning the Tsarskoye Selo Boarding School which included a list of its students. This list revealed that the student in Tsarskoye Selo was the son of a St. Petersburg police official, whereas the father of the composer was a landowner in the province of Smolensk. In other words, they were two different people sharing the same name. Thus this error did not enter my chronicle.

Abbreviations

Arnold—Yury Arnold, *Vospominaniia* [Memoirs], part 2, Moscow, 1892

Attestat Glinki—Glinka Certificate, see *Sovetskaia muzyka* [Soviet Music], 1954, no. 6

Bib-ka dlia chteniia—Biblioteka dlia chteniia [Library for Reading], periodical

Biographical Note—*Biograficheskaia zametka Glinki* [Glinka biographical note], in M. I. Glinka, *Complete Works,* Literary Works and Correspondence, vol. 1, Moscow, 1973

coll. *Dargomyzhsky—A. Dargomyzhsky. Vospominaniia i pis'ma* [A. Dargomyzhsky. Reminiscences and letters], ed. N. Findeyzen, Petrograd, 1921

coll. *Glinka—M. I. Glinka. Issledovaniia i materialy* [M. I. Glinka. Studies and materials], ed. A. Ossovsky, Leningrad, 1950

coll. *Glinka 1958—Glinka. Sbornik statei* [Glinka. Collection of articles], ed. E. Gordeeva, Moscow, 1958

coll. *Pamiati Glinki—Pamiati Glinki, 1857–1957* [To the memory of Glinka, 1857–1957], Moscow, 1958

d.c.a.—date of censor's authorization

EIT—Ezhegodnik imperatorskikh teatrov [Yearbook of the Imperial Theaters], periodical

Findeyzen *Glinka 1*—Nikolay Findeyzen, *M. I. Glinka. Ego zhizn' i tvorcheskaia deiatel'nost'* [M. I. Glinka. His life and creative activity], vol. 1, part 1, SPb., 1896

G 1—Glinka, *Complete Works,* Literary Works and Correspondence, vol. 1, Moscow, 1973

G 2-A—*Ibid.,* vol. 2-A, Moscow, 1975

G 2-B—*Ibid.,* vol. 2-B, Moscow, 1977

GIALO—see LGIA

GPB—Leningrad Public Library

Grigoriev—V. V. Grigoriev, *S-Peterburgskii universitet v techenie pervykh 50 let ego sushchestvovaniia* [SPb. University in the first 50 years of its existence], SPb., 1870

IRLI—Institute of Russian Literature of the Soviet Academy of Sciences (Pushkin House), manuscript department (Leningrad)

ITMK—Institute of Theater, Music, and Cinematography, section for manuscript studies (Leningrad)

IV—*Istoricheskii vestnik* [Historical Bulletin], periodical

Kann-Novikova 1, 2, 3—E. Kann-Novikova, *M. I. Glinka. Novye materialy i dokumenty* [M. I. Glinka. New materials and documents], parts 1–3, Moscow, 1950–55

Karamziny—*Pushkin v pis'makh Karamzinykh, 1836–1837* [Pushkin in letters of the Karamzins, 1836–1837], Moscow, 1960

Khudozh. gaz.—*Khudozhestvennaia gazeta* [Newspaper of the Arts], periodical

L.—A. Orlova, *Letopis' zhizni i tvorchestva M. I. Glinki* [Chronology of the life and work of M. I. Glinka], ed. B. V. Asafiev, Moscow, 1952

LGIA—Leningrad State Historical Archive (formerly State Historical Archive of the Leningrad District [GIALO])

LGK—Leningrad State N. A. Rimsky-Korsakov Conservatory, Department of Manuscripts

LNG 1, 2—*M. I. Glinka. Literaturnoe nasledie* [M. I. Glinka. Literary legacy], ed. Bogdanov-Berezovsky, vols. 1 & 2, Leningrad, 1952–53

Lit. gaz.—*Literaturnaia Gazeta* [Literary Gazette] (19th century) periodical

Lit. supp.—literary supplement

Livanova, Protopopov, *Glinka*—T. Livanova & V. Protopopov, *Glinka. Tvorcheskii put'* [Glinka. Creative path], vols. 1 & 2, Moscow, 1955

M.—Moscow

MN—*Muzykal'noe nasledstvo* [Musical Legacy], periodical anthologies

Mokritsky—*Dnevnik A. N. Mokritskogo* [Diary of A. N. Mokritsky], Moscow, 1974

Mosk. nabliudatel'—*Moskovskii nabliudatel'* [Moscow Spectator]

Mosk. telegraf—*Moskovskii telegraf* [Moscow Telegraph], periodical

Mosk. ved.—*Moskovskie vedomosti* [Moscow Gazette], newspaper

Muz. let.—*Muzykal'naia letopis'* [Musical Annals], parts 1 & 2, Petrograd, 1922–23

Nikitenko—*Diary of A. V. Nikitenko*, SPb., 1893

Ob ekzamenakh—*Ob ekzamenakh i otkrytom akte v Blagorodnom pansione S.-Peterburgskogo universiteta* [On the examinations and public ceremonies of the SPb. University Boarding School for Nobility], SPb., 1820

Otech. zap.—*Otechestvennye zapiski* [Notes of the Fatherland], periodical

Panteon—*Panteon russkogo i vsekh evropeiskikh teatrov* [Pantheon of the Russian and All European Theaters], periodical

RA—*Russkii arkhiv* [Russian Archives], periodical

RMG—*Russkaia muzykal'naia gazeta* [Russian Musical Gazette]

Repertuar—*Repertuar russkogo teatra* [Repertory of the Russian Theater], periodical

Repertuar i Panteon—*Repertuar russkogo i Panteon vsekh evropeiskikh teatrov* [Repertory of the Russian Theater and Pantheon of All European Theaters], periodical

Rus. invalid—*Russkii invalid* [Russian Invalid], newspaper

Rus. starina—*Russkaia starina* [Russian Antiquity], periodical

Rus. vestn.—*Russkii vestnik* [Russian Herald], periodical

Sev. pchela—*Severnaia pchela* [The Northern Bee], newspaper

Soch.—*Sochineniia* [Works]

Syn otechetsva—[Son of the Fatherland], periodical

Sollogub—*Memoirs* of V. Sollogub, Leningrad, 1931

Soloviev—D. N. Soloviev, *Piatidesiatiletie pervoi peterburgskoi gimnazii* [Five decades of the first Petersburg grammar school], SPb., 1880

Sov. muzyka—*Sovetskaia muzyka* [Soviet Music], periodical

SPb.—St. Petersburg

SPb. univ. 1—*S.-Peterburgskii universitet v pervoe stoletie ego deiatel'nosti* [SPb. University in the first century of its activity], vol. 1, 1819–35, ed. S. Rozhdestvensky, Petrograd, 1919

SPb. ved.—*S.-Peterburgskie vedomosti* [SPb. Gazette], newspaper

SPb. vestnik—St. Petersburg Messenger

Stasov, *Izbr.*—V. V. Stasov, *Izbrannye sochineniia* [Selected works], 3 vols., Moscow, 1952

TsGALI—Central State Archives of Literature and Art (Moscow)

TsGIA—Central State Historical Archives (Leningrad)

Glinka's Life in Music:
A Chronicle

1802

30 May

Village of Novospasskoe, Smolensk Province, Elninsk district. Wedding of Ivan Nikolaevich Glinka and his second cousin Evgenia Andreevna Glinka (sister and ward of Afanasy Andreevich Glinka, landlord of the neighboring village of Shmakovo). (Shestakova, *Vosp.,* p. 31; entry in the registry of births; Findeyzen, *Glinka 1,* p. 16).

1803

Aleksey, son of Ivan and Evgenia Glinka, is born and dies the same year (Shestakova, *Vosp.,* p.31).

1804

20 May

6 o'clock a.m. Mikhail Ivanovich Glinka is born. "According to Mother's story, after the baby's first cry, they heard in the thick foliage of a tree directly under her bedroom window the clear call of a nightingale with its enchanted trilling" (Shestakova, *Vosp.,* p. 31; copy of Glinka's birth certificate in *RMG,* 1901, no. 47).

1805

Glinka's sister Pelageya is born (*Zap.*).

1806

Glinka's grandfather Nikolay Alekseevich dies (Shestakova, *Vosp.*, p. 32).

1809

11 August

Glinka's sister Natalia is born (Findeyzen, *Glinka 1*, p. 18).

1804–1810

Glinka spent these years in his grandmother's quarters. "I was a child with a weak constitution, scrofulous, and very high strung. . . . In the room . . . where I stayed . . . it was never less than 20 degrees Réaumur. Despite this I always wore a coat. Very rarely was I allowed outside in the fresh air, and then only when it was warm. There can be no doubt that my initial upbringing had a strong influence on my physical development. . . . My grandmother indulged me to an incredible degree. . . ."

"One of my favorite activities was to crawl on the floor drawing trees and churches in chalk. My musical talent at that time expressed itself as a passion for the pealing of bells. I listened avidly to these sharp sounds, and I was able, using two brass wash basins, to imitate a bell-ringer quite aptly. Whenever I was sick, little bells were brought into the room for my amusement."

"While he lived at his grandmother's there were no friends or companions for him, and he grew up completely alone. . . . A second nurse, Avdotya Ivanovna, assistant to Tatyana Karpovna, was a cheerful young woman, who knew many different stories and songs (Shestakova, *Vosp.*, p. 32).

Ca. 1809–1810

"Having learned to read *extremely* early, I often moved my grandmother and her friends by reading from sacred books."
[Glinka's first teacher of reading and writing was the priest of the village of Novospasskoe, Ioann Stabrovsky (N. Findeyzen, *Glinka. Biograficheskii ocherk* [Glinka. Biographical essay], 1903, p. 5).]

1810

Death of Glinka's grandmother, Fyokla Aleksandrovna. "After my grandmother's death, my way of life changed somewhat. My mother catered less to me and even tried to accustom me to the fresh air, but her efforts were for the most part unsuccessful." Glinka was brought up together with his sister Pelageya. In addition to my first nurse, "another nurse was hired, the widow of a surveyor, Irina Fedorovna Meshkova, who arrived with her daughter."

"Glinka had no other childhood companions except these two girls" [his sister Polenka and Katya Meshkova] (Shestakova, *Vosp.*, p. 33).

2 September

Glinka's sister Elizaveta is born (Findeyzen, *Glinka 1*, p. 18).

1811

Ivan Glinka, along with several other people, purchased the right to collect liquor taxes in the villages of Bely, Dorogobuzh, Dukhovshchina, and Elnya, Smolensk province, for the years 1811–15.

1812

Ivan Glinka's business was disrupted as a result of the invasion of the French (G 2-A, p. 59).

August

Relocation to Orel during the French invasion. "The landlord and church warden of the village [Novospasskoe], Captain Glinka, along with his large household, withdrew to another province as the enemy advanced. . . . They travelled in ten carriages pulled by their own horses . . . and returned the same way in 1813" (A. Shchukin, "Heroic Deed of the Priest of the Village of Novospasskoe," *Rus. vestnik,* 1817, no. 23/24; ltr. from L. Shestakova to N. Findeyzen, 14 May 1894, in *L.*, p. 15).

Orel. The Glinka family took up residence in the house of a wealthy merchant (ltr. from L. Shestakova to N. Findeyzen, 14 May 1894, in *L.*, p. 15).

"My musical sensitivities remained undeveloped and crude . . . I listened to the sound of bells with the same avidity as I had before and could distinguish the bells of each church. I intently imitated their sound on my brass wash basins."

30 August

Attack by the French on the church of Novospasskoe, which was defended by the peasants under the leadership of Stabrovsky. "The scoundrels, with no hope of breaking into the church, took to pillaging the landlord's house" (Shchukin, "Heroic Deed of the Priest of the Village of Novospasskoe," *Rus. vestnik,* 1817, no. 23/24; an account of this document appears in a book by V. Voronovsky, *Otechestvennaia voina 1812 goda v predelakh Smolenskoi gubernii* [The war of 1812 in Smolensk Province]).

1813

Novospasskoe. Return of the Glinka family from Orel. "Although many buildings had been destroyed, since the French passed through very near us, all our possessions were hidden and protected by the peasants. They liked father . . . He not only treated them like human beings but he recognized their needs willingly and helped them" (Shestakova, *Vosp.* p. 33).

Glinka's sister Maria is born (Findeyzen, *Glinka 1,* p. 17).

A French governess, Roza Ivanovna, was appointed to Glinka and his sister Pelageya. An architect living in the house taught Glinka drawing. "I caught on quickly." "Above all, a distant relative, inquisitive, cheerful, and of pleasant disposition, loved to tell me stories about foreign places, primitive peoples, and the climate and customs of tropical countries. He brought me a book called *O stranstviiakh voobshche* [On travelling in general], published during the reign of Catherine II, which I eagerly set about reading and from which I began to make excerpts. This secured the basis of my passion for geography and travel."

1813 and After

"Because I was always surrounded by women and played only with my sister and my nurse's daughter, I was not at all like the other boys of my age. Furthermore, my passion for reading, travel pictures, and drawing, which I was getting perceptibly good at, often distracted me from children's games. As before, I was a quiet and mild-mannered child."

On Glinka's parents' namedays and on holidays, musicians from Afanasy Andreevich Glinka's orchestra would come to Novospasskoe. They "would stay for several days, and when the dances were over after the guests' departure, they would customarily play several pieces."

1814

Ivan Glinka submitted a petition to the Ministry of Finance requesting that he be awarded damages for his tax losses. His petition, however, was rejected, and instead of reimbursement, a large sum was exacted for wine not selected during the period from state stores, for undeposited amounts from Bely, and for arrears in Dorogobuzh, Dukhovshchina, and Elnya. Since Moscow tax-farmers had received certain privileges in similar cases, Glinka tried to get the same, though he nonetheless paid the required sum (G 2-A, p. 59).

1814 or 1815

One time Glinka's uncle's musicians "played a Crusell quartet with clarinet. This music made an inscrutable, new, and delightful impression on me. For an entire day I remained in a feverish condition. I was immersed in an inexplicable and agonizingly sweet state and was absent-minded the following day during my drawing lesson. At the next lesson my absent-mindedness had increased, and my teacher . . . repeatedly took me to task. Finally, however, guessing what was the matter, he said to me . . . that he had noticed how I was thinking about nothing but music. *'What can I do,'* I answered. *'Music is my soul.'* And truly, from that moment I had fallen in love with music. For me my uncle's orchestra was the source of the keenest delights. Whenever they played for dances—ecossaises, matradours, quadrilles, and waltzes—I picked up a violin or piccolo and tried to play along with the orchestra, it goes without saying, by means of the tonic and dominant. During supper they usually played Russian songs transcribed for two flutes, two clarinets, two French horns, and two bassoons. These tender and melancholy, but to me easily accessible sounds, pleased me immensely (I could hardly bear harsh sounds, even the French horn's low notes if played loudly). Perhaps these songs which I heard in my youth were the earliest reason why I later began to work with Russian folk music."

1815

1 March

Glinka's brother Evgeny is born (Petersburg Necropolis).

A new governess, Varvara Klammer, was appointed to Glinka. She was a graduate of the Smolny Insititute. She "set about teaching us Russian, French, German, geography, and music. In succession there followed grammar, conversation (*dialogues*), short descriptions of lands and cities, etc. All of this we were required to learn by heart. . . . Although she also taught us music, i.e., playing the piano and reading music, in a mechanical way, I nonetheless learned quickly." Klammer "had a board fitted over the keys in such a way that playing was still possible though you could not see your hands or the keys. From the very beginning I got used to playing without looking at my fingers."

In *Rus. vestnik* (part 1, no. 3), there is an article by F. G. [Glinka], entitled "On the Inborn Talent of Russians for the Fine Arts": ". . . Music from time immemorial has visited itself on our fatherland. . . . The whistling of the wind and sounds of the forest have never extinguished the sensitivity of the Slav and his descendants. He sang in the shadow of the one-hundred-year-old trees of his frozen native wilderness, and what delightful music he bestowed upon us. Find, if you will, anything similar in countries more caressed by the sun! There the children of plenty create their splendid melodies *out of their imaginations*. Here, the Russian child of the north creates his simple tune out of sounds drawn straight from the heart, and show me a heart that would not be charmed by it! . . . But can a *foreigner* sing the Russian's praise with such genuine rapture, with such zealousness, as the Russian's countryman? . . . How can he know what is *dear to the Russian heart?*" In the conclusion a program is suggested: Russian music must become a reflection of Russian folk life, of the struggles and glory of the people. "The echoes of this, scattered throughout *our authentic folk songs,* only a truly Russian musician could imagine collecting."

1816

17 November

Glinka's sister Lyudmila is born (V. Stasov, "Biographical Note about Lyudmila Ivanovna Shestakova," in *EIT,* 1893, p. 459).

One of the first violinists in Afanasy Andreevich Glinka's orchestra began to teach Glinka violin. "Unfortunately he did not play in tune himself, and his bowing was very stiff, which he passed on to me."

1815–1817

"Although I liked music without even thinking, . . . I nonetheless preferred pieces which were accessible to my musical understanding at the time. In general I liked orchestral music better than anything else, and of the orchestral pieces, after Russian songs, I preferred overtures: *Ma tante Aurore* of Boieldieu; *Ladoiska* of Kreutzer; and *Les deux aveugles* of Méhul. These last two I liked to play on the piano, besides several sonatas by Steibelt, especially the rondo *L'orage,* which I played quite neatly. Gyrowetz (the Czech) I did not care for at all, in part because I found his sonatas too long and intricate, but even more because they were so badly printed. . . . My understanding of this music was poor, for which reason I frequently caught a pencil across my knuckles."

1817

Beginning of the Year

The Ministry of Education announces the opening of an educational institution for the privileged classes called Boarding School for Nobility, Affiliated with the Main Pedagogical Institute. By regulation the boarding school was to 1) provide its pupils with a general education which would equip them for further study in various specialties, and 2) prepare young people for government service" (Soloviev, p. 67).

Glinka develops a passion for birds. "By the year we left the country for Petersburg, I already had birds flying about in my room."

1 September

Ceremonial opening in Petersburg of the Boarding School for Nobility, Affiliated with the Main Pedagogical Institute (Markevich, *Vosp.,* p. 119).

Beginning of winter

Glinka, along with his mother, his uncle Afanasy Glinka, his sister, and Miss Klammer leave for St. Petersburg. "The trip was undertaken in order to place me in the newly opened Boarding School for Nobility, Affiliated with the Main Pedagogical Institute."

Petersburg. Arrival. ". . . the sight of the huge well-proportioned buildings and streets had a magical effect on me, and for a long, long time I remembered my impressions of delight and astonishment."

Glinka in 1817 with His Mother and His Sister Pelageya
Miniature by an unknown artist on an ivory snuffbox.

1817–1818

December or January (?)

Ivan Glinka arrived and "once he had been introduced to the school's inspector, Lindkvist, and found out everything, he got down to business."

1818

January–February

"Upon our arrival in St. Petersburg I began studying piano with the famous Field, but unfortunately I only had three lessons with him before he moved to Moscow. . . . In the *three* lessons I took with him I studied his second Divertissement (E major) and received his flattering approval. . . . Although I did not hear him many times, I can still remember well his strong, sensitive, and distinct playing. It seemed that he did not strike the keys but that his fingers fell on them like great drops of rain or like pearls scattered on velvet."
[This is dated according to the period of Field's stay in St. Petersburg.]

2 February

Glinka is enrolled in the Boarding School for Nobility, located on the Fontanka at Kalinkin Bridge, Otto's house, now Fontanka no. 164 (*Istoriia SPb. universiteta* [History of St. Petersburg University] 1, P., 1919).

14 February

By tsarist decree the Boarding School for Nobility, Affiliated with the Main Pedagogical Institute was accorded status equal to a lyceum. (A. Voronov, *Istoriko-statisticheskii obzor SPb. uchebnogo okruga* [Historical and Statistical Survey of the St. Petersburg Educational Region], SPb., 1849, p. 117).

28 March

Glinka attended a concert of the Philharmonic Society and heard the singers Elizaveta Sandunova, Grigory Klimovsky, and Yanovsky in Müller's oratorio *The Archangel Michael* (G 1, p. 369). "At that time I did not understand serious singing well at all, and what I liked most were the orchestra and instrumental soloists."

"My father did not spare me expenses and therefore placed me with three other pupils of my same age and a special tutor (Wilhelm Karlovich Kuechelbecker) on the mezzanine floor of the same building. There was even room there for a piano, which was shortly later exchanged for a grand piano built by Tischner." "Kuechelbecker . . . was instructor of Russian language and literature. . . . He was the noblest, kindest, and most unsullied of beings and was loved and respected by all the students" (*Zap.;* Markevich, *Vosp.,* p. 126).
[Kuechelbecker was appointed instructor at the Boarding School at the beginning of the 1817/1818 school year (application dated 19 August 1817, examination lecture 28 August, GIALO, archives of the Main Pedagogical Institute). Two of the pupils were the brothers Andrey and Aleksey Tyutchev. Who the third was has not been established; perhaps it was Lev Pushkin.]

The administrator of the Boarding School was Sergey Uvarov, the Director, Dmitry Kavelin. "He was inaccessible, quite severe toward any fault, and short on rewards. The dreadful looking Inspector was much better, more cordial and kinder than Kavelin. He was Andrey Andreevich Lindkvist, who was only three years younger than the immortal Schiller, with whom as a schoolmate he sat on the same bench. . . . He was a kind and noble man, possessed of a bright mind and kind heart beneath a rough and even harsh exterior" (Markevich, *Vosp.,* pp. 126, 122).

"Among the instructors of the lower classes one encountered originals, and there were such amusing characters among the tutors that my school colleagues still preserve memories of them" (*Zap.*). ". . . But there were three principal ones whose looks were engraved in the memories of all my classmates. First was the Frenchman Deline, a clever, Russified dandy who had wormed himself into Russian society. . . . He was a glib, smiling, dependable administrator who, to be sure, was required to mete out justice and was famous for his floggings. . . . There was the long-nosed German Goek, who was ugly and as dumb as an empty bottle. Finally, there was that utter fool, the broad-shouldered Englishman, Bitton, who was built like a stocky bulldog. All three were disloyal, bored by their posts, and considered their profession an unendurable bore" (Markevich, *Vosp.,* p. 123). "*Gospodin, monsieur,* Mister Bitton . . . was a crude Englishman (apparently once a sailor) who was extremely fond of rice pudding. On those days when it was served, he selected several sacrificial victims from among the youngest students. . . . In the evening after dinner the tutor Savely would take all the portions of rice pudding withheld from those being punished to the dormitory to *Gospodin, monsieur,* Mr. Bitton, who greedily devoured his take that night" (*Zap.*).

"The idea of freedom and a constitution was in the air. Kuechelbecker advocated them from the chair of Russian language. Pushkin wrote his ode *"Vol'nost' "* [Liberty], *"Kinzhal"* [The dagger], and *"Derevnia"* [The village], all of which I got through Kuechelbecker and Lev Pushkin" (Markevich, *Vosp.,* p. 134).

"At the beginning . . . I applied myself diligently . . . I made such rapid progress in arithmetic and algebra that I was made a tutor in the latter. . . . Our good Assistant Inspector Ivan Ekimovich Kolmakov was our consolation; whenever he was around we were always put in a cheerful mood. His amusing pranks, accompanied by grimaces and strange looks, were known to many who did not know him personally. . . . For Ivan Ekimovich learning was a genuine pleasure, his towering passion. He knew everything, remembered everything, would willingly substitute for an absent professor, and would explain anything to a student at the slightest provocation. . . . With his help I read excerpts from Ovid's *Metamorphoses,* and I am indebted to him first of all for my acquaintance with Latin literature."

"Glinka had so assimilated Kolmakov's comic personality that even ten years after [Kolmakov's] death he could still imitate his old teacher with striking exactness and recreate what Kolmakov might have said or done in one situation or another" (Panaev, *Vosp.,* p. 145).

In the Boarding School Glinka began to take violin lessons from Franz Boehm (Melgunov, *Vosp.,* p. 159). Boehm "played accurately and distinctly. However he did not possess the gift of being able to impart his own understanding to others" (*Zap.*).

1819

"My favorite subjects were languages: Latin, French, German, and English."

8 February

With the establishment of the university, the Boarding School was renamed Boarding School for Nobility, Affiliated with St. Petersburg University (Soloviev, p. 48).

End of March

"We pupils were struck by the news of Kotzebue's death, which many in Petersburg were talking about. Aleksandr Pushkin then penned an epigram addressed to Strudza:

Bondsman of a crowned soldier,
Be grateful for your fate:
You deserve the fame of Herostratus
And the celebrated death of Kotzebue.
(Markevich, *Vosp.*, p. 138)

[The German dramatist August Kotzebue, a secret agent of Alexander I, was killed by a German patriot, the student Karl Sand. Pushkin sang of Sand's deeds in the poem "The Dagger."]

"Already at the Boarding School he was an excellent musician. He was a student of Field at the time and played the piano delightfully. His improvisations were already exquisite. He was small, even diminutive, somewhat unkempt, with a head large for his body and intelligent, penetrating eyes. I nicknamed him 'Glinochka.' . . . I spent many, many wonderful days with him (Markevich, *Vosp.*, p. 130).

Glinka takes a melody from Catterino Cavos's song *"Dusha l' moia, dushen'ka"* [My dear, my little darling] for Sobolevsky's poem "Assistant Inspector Kolmakov Educates Fools."

June

Glinka receives a certificate of merit for his examinations.

July

Novospasskoe. Glinka spent his vacation in the country. "Despite the fact that I had not progressed far [on the violin] I was able to play in my uncle's orchestra. My uncle's orchestra had improved and was augmented by several boys sent by my father to learn so that he could have his own dance music."

1818–1820

Petersburg. Glinka stayed in the home of relatives of N. Melgunov "and through the sons their fathers got to know each other. . . . The young people became such good friends that Glinka's father almost let Glinka go abroad with the Melgunovs" (A. Kirpichnikov, *"Mezhdu slavianofilami i zapadnikami,* N. A. Melgunov" [Between Slavophiles and Westerners, N. A. Melgunov] in *Rus. starina,* 1898, v. 96, no. 11, p. 303).

"When Field left, his student Aumann took me on as a pupil and began with Field's Concerto No. 1 in E-flat. After him Zeuner improved my technique somewhat further and to a certain extent even my style. . . . However the teach-

ing of theory, *especially intervals and their treatment,* wasn't so successful.
Zeuner demanded that I learn his lessons *by heart,* and this I hated."

"The varied and continuous activities of life at the school did not distract him
from his favorite art. . . . Even then, during long winter evenings, or in the
Petersburg summer twilight . . . after dry recitations . . . he gave himself over
to flights of free improvisation to rest from mentally taxing activities and students' concerns. In these sounds, vibrating with emotion, he expressed his
youthful dreams, his languid sorrow, and living joy. If anyone saw him sitting
at the window on a moonlit summer night with Arseniev's geography or his
favorite Cuvier in his hands, or if one saw how his eyes wandered from the
book to the moon and back again, then surely one would have said: 'Here is a
diligent, zealous student, but learning is not his calling. He was born to be an
artist' "(Melgunov, *Vosp.,* p. 159).

Pushkin "used to come to the school to visit his brother" (*Zap.*).

"Many things from the outside world reached us inside the Boarding School
walls. The wonderful songs of that eternally carefree and melodious Frenchman
[Beranger] . . . soared to our school benches. . . . The grandson of those scoundrels the Lyudoviks, the disgusting Bourbons, the basest breed of men, Lyudo-
vik XVIII . . . conspirator and intriguer, lounged on his vile throne. . . . One
more name, not to mention Goethe, resounded throughout Europe at the time.
We did not have true, accurate translations of his works, but their echoes
reached us and found a response in every heart of noble birth and feeling. . . .
That was Lord Byron. At that time he was travelling about in southern Europe,
and wherever the proud singer's song was heard, there shortly afterwards flew
the flag of freedom."

There were literary and political debates in the Boarding School for Nobility.
According to Markevich, for his contemporaries the poetry of Delvig was "dull,
jaded, and insipid. It is significant that Kuechelbecker was always of the same
opinion as I on this point. When I uttered the foregoing judgment to him, he
agreed with me and kissed me for my 'praise' of the two Lyudoviks. . . . Lyovik
Pushkin and Mikhaylo Glinka shared my opinions. Besides music, Glinka was
also a good judge of poetry and did not sympathize with any Bourbon." The
students started several societies in secret from the teachers and instructors.
"The first of them was called 'Society of *Guards*'. . . . Then they took it into
their heads to rename it 'Society of Lovers of Freedom.'" Markevich "started
an '*Amusements* Society'" and later "two others, the *Mineralogical* Society and
Botanical Society." The main society was the "*Little Russian* Society. Every
Little Russian was eligible to enroll, unless he was a spy or informer, in which

case neither birth nor homeland could help him. . . . Whoever kept wine excluded himself from the rolls of the Little Russian. Then they decided to receive into the 'Little Russian' good and honest people whatever their nationality. . . . Lyovik, because Aleksandr Sergeevich was his brother, and Vasily Lvovich his uncle; Glinka, for music; Shipilov, because he was the nephew of Konstantin Petrovich Batyushkov; and so forth" (Markevich, *Vosp.*, pp. 138, 140, 132). "I can recall the general excitement of my colleagues when the instructor of Russian language and literature, K-r [Kuechelbecker], brought . . . a little book 'for a few' from Zhukovsky and how we read these exquisite lines until we knew them by heart" (N. Markevich's explanations regarding letters to him, in *Moskvityanin*, 1853, v. 3, no. 12, part 2, p. 13).

1820

"The professors of the upper classes were men of learning and culture, who, for the most part, had finished their education in German universities. . . . Among them were the well-known Raupach, professor of German literature; Arseniev, professor of geography and statistics; and Kunitsyn, law" (*Zap.*). "Raupach, a European celebrity and German author of tragedies, was professor of German, French, Latin, and Greek languages, as well as professor of history. He was a man with an uncommon gift for words, even in Russian, and was serious, intelligent, and thoughtful" (Markevich, *Vosp.*, p. 125). "So far as K. I. Arseniev was concerned, in addition to his work in general history and Russian statistics, there was the service he rendered to Russia and humanity through his influence on the issue of the abolition of serfdom, which he exercised through his students by cultivating in their minds the thought of its realization" (Grigoriev).

> To Kunitsyn, a gift of heart and wine,
> He created us, he ignited our flame.
> He laid the corner stone,
> He kindled the pure light.
> (Pushkin, "19 October" [1825]—draft)

"Quick of mind, penetrating, possessed of great breadth of knowledge, [Kunitsyn] was distinguished by a steadfast and noble character" (P. Pletnev, *Otchet SPb. universiteta* [Account of SPb. University], p. 75). "Zembnitsky was instructor of natural history. . . . Galich . . . professor of logic . . . was a pedant. Chizhov, professor of mathematics. . . . Bessonov, instructor of drawing . . . was a very cheerful character. . . . Vysotsky, guitarist and piano teacher. . . . Boehm, a musical celebrity, violinist. He was a small person and fond of me because I always attended the lessons he gave to Masalsky, Glinka, and Gervais with such obvious enthusiasm. Cavos, the maestro, teacher of singing . . . Dutac [dancing teacher] . . . Severbrik, fencing teacher" (Markevich, *Vosp.*, p. 125).

"The required four-year course (at the Boarding School) was increased by one year" (Soloviev, p. 49).

Kuechelbecker's *"Poety"* [Poets], in which he speaks of Pushkin's exile, is printed in the journal *Sorevnovatel' prosveshcheniia i blagotvoreniia* [Advocate for Enlightenment and Philanthropy], no. 4.
[Before its publication, Kuechelbecker read the poem before the Free Society for Lovers of Russian Literature in connection with Pushkin's exile to the south.]

4 June

Kuechelbecker was denounced for his poem *"Poety"* by the publicist Karazin (*Rus. starina*, 1899, v. 98, no. 5, p. 277).

21 June

"Open examination of the students began in the presence of their relatives and outside clerical and civil representatives." The students were examined in logic, ethics, Russian language and literature, and scripture. Before the examinations began "one of the older students, Mikhaylo Glinka, delivered . . . a speech of his own composition to those present." The first day the examinations lasted from seven until ten in the evening.

22 June

"During the examinations, which lasted from six until ten o'clock in the evening, students from different classes demonstrated their progress in the following subjects: mathematics, physics, military science, and natural history."

23 June

"Beginning at the same time and continuing until ten o'clock, there were examinations of various classes in the following subjects: German, Latin, Greek, and French languages; geography, statistics, and history."

24 June

"Examinations began at six o'clock and continued until nine in the evening. The students demonstrated their ability in music, singing, dancing, and fencing."

28 June

Graduation ceremonies at the Boarding School.
["Upon the arrival of the Minister of Religious Affairs and Popular Education, His Honor Prince Aleksandr Nikolaevich Golitsyn, 1) The student M. Glinka plays a concerto by Mr. Zeuner on the piano. 2) The guests are shown examples of the students' progress in drawing and penmanship. 3) Director of St. Petersburg University and of the Boarding School for Nobility, Actual State Councillor Kavelin, concludes the examinations . . . with a speech. 4) Then the names of students entitled to advance to the next class are read, following which His Honor the Minister . . . hands out awards to pupils distinguished for good behavior and progress in their studies. . . . At the conclusion of the ceremonies the guests are invited to a special hall for supper" (*Ob ekzamenakh* [Concerning the Examinations], pp. 1–5).]

Glinka, who was passed from the third class to the second, received a Certificate of Merit No. 5 and a drawing for his progress in the art of drawing (*Ob ekzamenakh,* attachments A and B).

End of June

Kuechelbecker writes to Zhukovsky: "The young people who matured in my presence, whom I taught to think and to feel, left my class and passed on to the next" (*L.,* 28).
[The letter is dated on the basis of its contents.]

July

Novospasskoe. Glinka spent the vacation in the country, where he played music with his sister's governess's husband, Karl Gempel, son of an organist from Weimar (he "was a fine musician"). In his free time he travelled to Shmakovo and heard his uncle's orchestra.

The Italian Todi lived with the Glinka family, where he instructed Glinka's sisters in singing. He "was just as poor a musician as all the other singing birds of his kind" (*Zap.*).

Beginning of August

Petersburg. Glinka returns to school.

13 August

Kuechelbecker applies to be released from the Boarding School for Nobility because of illness (*Lit. nasledstvo,* vol. 59, M., 1954, p. 509).

[It was not because of illness but in anticipation of reprisal for his poem *"Poety."* With the help of influential friends, Kuechelbecker fled abroad and avoided punishment there.]

1817–1821

"When we lived at Kalinkin Bridge . . . there was a large garret belonging to the mezzanine where we lived where we raised a variety of pigeons and rabbits. . . . What prompted the development of my passion for zoology more than anything else were our visits to the natural history museum under the direction of Professor Zembnitsky, who explained these subjects to us."

1820 (?) 1821 (?)

On one of his trips to Petersburg, Ivan Glinka took his son to the "Lvovs' Academy," "and the tender sounds of Aleksey Fedorovich's sweet violin engraved themselves deeply in my memory."

Persian was added to Glinka's language studies. "Having had geometry, I gave up mathematics altogether, probably because in the upper classes the number of subjects increased considerably." "As a teacher . . . I took Karl Meier, who in time became my friend. He contributed to the development of my musical talent more than the others."

1821

Before 13 January

Protest over Peninsky's teaching, organized by Lev Pushkin, and demanding the return of Kuechelbecker.
[Peninsky was the new instructor of language and literature who had replaced Kuechelbecker.]

13 January

Lev Pushkin's dismissal from the school (Director's Journal, 26 February 1821, in *L.*, p. 28).

20 January

Kavelin's report to Uvarov on the disorders at the school.

7 February

In instructions from the Minister A. Golitsyn to Uvarov it says: "We cannot consider this disorder as only temporary and accidental, for it clearly shows the weak direction provided by this establishment's administration in allowing so harmful a spirit to take root among the students that it has finally erupted in obviously disorderly conduct. . . . The Inspector of the school, Lindkvist, who has demonstrated his weakness in this episode . . . should be given a strict reprimand."

2 March

In his written statement to Golitsyn, Uvarov states: "Continual relations of the children with their parents and their weekly release from school not only to see their parents but even relatives is without doubt the main source of disorder. Therefore necessity demands that these relations be curtailed as much as possible if not stopped altogether" (*SPb. univ. 1*, p. 131).

5 March

Talyzin, instructor of logic, and the tutors Goek and Yakukevich apply for release from the school. The school administration grants Talyzin's request but transfers Goek and Yakukevich to instruction in German and Latin.

19 March

The following items were presented before a meeting of the school's administration: request from instructor Peninsky for his transfer following the conflict with the students and "a proposal by His Honor the Administrator . . . for the dismissal of Ordinary Professor Kunitsyn from teaching at the Boarding School for Nobility altogether. The proposal was approved" (Director's Journal, 19 March 1821, in *L.*, p. 29).
[Professor Kunitsyn was dismissed because his book *Estestvennoe pravo* [Natural law] was considered "critical of true Christianity and leading to the destruction of all family and civil ties" (Soloviev, p. 50).]

After 19 March

"V.I. Krechetov began to teach Russian language and literature. He was one of the young ones, or as Professor Tolmachev called them, *liberal*-instructors. The students always loved to hear his lectures, especially since they were forbidden fruit for them. He brought along and always with the greatest approval read and discussed the works of Pushkin, reading of which was strictly forbidden among the students. . . . [Krechetov] . . . developed in his listeners a strong love of reading" (Soloviev, p. 40).

6 April

Lindkvist was dismissed from his duties. In his place Ordinary Professor Tolmachev was named Inspector of the school (Director's Journal, 8 April 1821, in *L.*, p. 29). "His former pupils retained very warm memories" of Lindkvist (Soloviev, p. 51).

14 May

The student Petr Sergeev was named instructor of law and political economy for the upper class (Director's Journal, 14 May 1821, in *L.*, p. 30).

29 June

As an award for having successfully completed his examinations, Glinka received a Bible with the inscription: "From the St. Petersburg University Boarding School to Mikhail Glinka, for good conduct and achievment in scripture, Russian language and literature, statistics, mathematics, and Latin. June 29, 1821." (The Bible is preserved in ITMK, coll. 6; *L.*, p. 30).

July

Novospasskoe. Glinka continued to play music with Gempel and to travel to hear his uncle's orchestra. "I admit to my ignorance at that time. Since I was already somewhat familiar with the overtures of Cherubini and Méhul, I listened to the overtures of Rossini with great satisfaction. Of these I liked *La Cenerentola* so much that Gempel and I transcribed it for piano four-hands and often amused ourselves playing it."

Fall

Petersburg. Glinka's uncle Afanasy arrived from the country, and Glinka "took advantage of a mild illness to stay with him" at Vasily Vasilievich Engelgardt's (*Zap.*).

8 October

"Received for the son Mikhail of Captain Glinka 750 rubles for the period from 2 August [1821] to 2 February 1822" (Director's Journal, 8 October 1821, in *L.*, p. 30).

3, 4, 7 November

Special meetings at the University as a result of a statement made by the Director of the St. Petersburg educational district D. Runich to the administration of the University that philosophy and history were being taught in a spirit contrary to Christianity. Professors Arseniev, Galich, German, and Raupach were called to account (M. Sukhomlinov, *Materialy dlia istorii obrazovaniia v Rossii pri Aleksandre I* [Materials on the History of Education in Russia During the Time of Alexander I], vol. 2, St. Petersburg, 1886, p. 90).

30 December

The administration of the school received the following directive: "1. Introduction of the book *Readings from the Evangelists and Acts of the Apostles* in place of the book *On the Responsibilities of Man and the Citizen;* 2. Surrender to the Department of Public Education of all copies on hand of the books *On the Responsibilities of Man and the Citizen* and likewise *Course in the Philosophical Sciences* by Yakob, also withdrawn from use in all educational institutions" (Director's Journal, 31 December 1821, in *L.*, p. 30).

"Undoubtedly I might have attained a certain degree of accomplishment in drawing, but the academics Bessonov and Sukhanov bored me to tears with their arrogance. Their demands for slavish imitation, line for line, led to the point where I simply gave up in their lessons. I lost interest in mathematics when it turned to analysis. Criminal law and Roman law I did not like at all. I was poor in dancing, just as I was in fencing. . . . Overall I did the best in languages. I learned German in half a year to the astonishment of the professor. Latin with I. E. [Kolmakov] and Persian with Professor Dzhiafar went well. Geography I knew well and history decently. Natural sciences, especially zoology, I loved passionately."

1817–1822

"While I was at the Boarding School from the moment I arrived in Petersburg, my parents, relatives and friends of theirs took me to the theater. Opera and ballet were indescribably exciting for me. . . . I saw the operas *Les deux journées*

by Cherubini, Méhul's *Joseph, Jaconde* by Nicolo Isouard, and *Le Petit Chaperon rouge* by Boieldieu. The tenors Klimovsky and Samoylov and the bass Zlov were truly remarkable singers. Although she no longer sang in the theater, our well-known singer Sandunova participated in large concerts, and I heard her in oratorios.
[Sandunova retired from the stage in 1823.]

1818–1822

Glinka's friendship with his cousin Sofia Ivanovna (daughter of his uncle Ivan Andreevich Glinka), "a girl of excellent education, nice, attractive, and also fond of music and books." Glinka played piano duets with his uncle, who "was a fine musician. He had a large supply of various pieces, mainly overtures for piano duet . . . by Cherubini, Méhul, Mozart, Righini, Spontini, Paer, and Rossini. We played all these things quite well and entertained our acquaintances. I never missed an opportunity to attend concerts. Every week I was taken to P. I. Yushkov's, where they played and sang. The orchestra, though incomplete, played well."

1821/1822

Winter

"Every time I succeeded in obtaining leave from the school for a little while I was extremely happy: the old general [Engelgardt] regarded me with favor."

1822

January

Golitsyn's conclusions regarding the Arseniev affair: ". . . The adjunct Arseniev's understanding of religion and government is absurd to the extent of demonstrating an attitude of impertinence toward his country's government. . . . Under the guise of statistics, history, and philosophy dangerous teachings are being disseminated" (*Materialy po istorii SPb. universiteta* [Materials for the History of St. Petersburg University], vol. 1, P., 1919).

Winter

Glinka lived at the home of his uncle Afanasy Andreevich Glinka.

January or March

"One day my uncle Afanasy Andreevich took me to see the famous Hummel. . . . He graciously listened as I played him the first solo section of his A-minor concerto. Then he improvised for us. He played delicately and distinctly as if he were playing a piece he had already composed and learned by heart."

[Dated according to Hummel's appearances in Petersburg on 18 January and 16 March (in the interval he travelled to Moscow).]

Beginning of Spring

Glinka "became acquainted with an attractive young lady. She played the harp well, but above all she possessed an exquisite soprano voice. Her voice did not resemble any instrument. It was a natural, silvery clear soprano, and she sang naturally and very nicely. Her excellent qualities and the tenderness with which she treated me (she called me nephew, and I called her my aunt) stirred my heart and inspired my imagination. She loved music, and often for hours at a time she would sit next to the piano as I played with my uncle and would sing along at her favorite places in her silvery clear voice. Since I wished to serve her, I had the idea of composing a set of variations on a favorite theme of hers from Weigl's opera *Die Schweizerfamilie*. After that I wrote the Variations on a Theme of Mozart (E-flat major) for harp or piano and then a waltz of my own invention for piano (F major). . . . These were my first efforts at composition, even though I did not yet know thorough bass. . . . I first became acquainted with the harp then, an exquisite instrument, if used at the right times."

Glinka's *Thème de Mozart varié pour pianoforte ou harpe par M. Glinka (composé l'an 1822) S.P. bourg* dates from this period. The first edition includes three variations on the theme of the orchestral accompaniment to the chorus and dance of the slaves from Act I of the opera *Die Zauberflöte*. To this period also belongs the composition of *Variations sur Thème composé par M. Glinka "dediés à . . . ich werde es nicht sagen."* The ellipsis appears in the dedication.

2 May

Glinka writes to his parents: "I would not dare blame the institution in which according to your wishes . . . I acquired that little education which may pave the way to greater learning. Speaking truthfully, however, I must admit that the teaching here is in a state of complete collapse. . . . All our people, that is the

Lindkvists, Ivanovsky, *etc.*, thank heaven, are well and convey their regards to you.. Without fail I must see you in July."

May (?)

"Some time before graduation I delved into science, counting on my memory, but catching up with my colleagues was impossible. Mathematics I had long since given up on."

End of June

Examinations at the Boarding School. "Since I had only studied one case in criminal law, I did not answer the question the professor asked at all, but I answered so cleverly that the examiner, Professor Zyablovsky, was well satisfied, despite the poorly concealed anger of the professor of law. In a word, partly because of my former merits, partly because of my clever subterfuges, it happened that . . . I was graduated first, with entitlement to a tenth-class rank."
[Glinka graduated second in his class from the University Boarding School: first, Stanislav Petrovsky; second, Glinka; third, Stepan Palitsyn; fourth, Aleksandr Kraevsky; fifth, Ivan Yakovlev; sixth, Vasily Gudim-Levkovich; seventh, Gavriil Vulf; eighth, Boris Vrevsky; ninth, Nikolay Krasno-Miloshevich; tenth, Karl Didrikhs (Soloviev, appendix).]

3 July

On the day of graduation from the Boarding School Glinka played Hummel's Concerto in A Minor publicly. Karl Meier accompanied him on a second piano. Aleksandr Stepanov "was at the ceremonies . . . and was delighted with . . . our relative Glinka's . . . piano playing" (P. Stepanov, *Vosp.*, p. 183).
[Aleksandr Petrovich Stepanov, the father of Glinka's future friends Petr and Nikolay Stepanov, was in Petersburg before he left for Krasnoyarsk, where he had been appointed governor of Enisey province.]

4 July

In *Syn otechestva*, part 79, no. 28, there is an account "of the examinations at the Boarding School for Nobility of St. Petersburg University," which reports that Glinka performed Hummel's Concerto (d.c.a.).

July

In "Register of the Department of Public Education," no. 7, there is a report about the graduation ceremony at the Boarding School for Nobility.

Summer

Novospasskoe. Glinka lived with his parents.

Fall

Petersburg. On his return from the country, Glinka did not enter the civil service immediately. His father wanted him to serve in the foreign service. Glinka took rooms not far from Lindkvist, where he "ate lunch and dinner for a set price" (*Zap.*).

[After Lindkvist's dismissal from his position of Inspector at the Boarding School (in 1821), Glinka continued to maintain his friendship with him and his family. Lindkvist lived on Italyanskaya Street (now Rakov Street, no. 31). Where Glinka lived at the time has not been established.]

21 December

Glinka attended a concert of the Philharmonic Society in a performance of Haydn's oratorio *The Creation,* in which Sandunova, Zeibich, and Shreyntser participated (G 1, p. 369).

1822 and later

"Soon after graduation from the Boarding School" Glinka "worked out ideas using Russian themes" (*Zap.*).

1822/1823

Winter

Glinka studied French diplomatic language with Lindkvist. "Our work went badly, however. This language was not at all poetic to me, and it seemed crude and would not stick in my mind. With Meier and even Boehm on the other hand, I made rapid progress. . . . I took several lessons with Fuchs" [the theorist].

1823

Glinka often visited Rimsky-Korsak and other young school friends. "His serious face, with its dark southern coloring and wandering, or more accurately, absent-minded looking eyes, always grew animated during conversation. If his black frock coat was conspicuous among our regular ones, then the peculiar liveliness of his movements, his clear voice, and his bold, energetic speech stood out even more. Sometimes his abrupt, almost convulsive movements would startle us. He might suddenly stop, put his arm around the waist of one colleague or another, or stand on tiptoe and fervently whisper something to each in turn, as intense people often do. In stature he was between small and medium, and for the most part he was well-proportioned. Even at that time he did not appear to fit the behavioral norm of most people. His affection for his schoolmates and their affection for him left an indelible impression on me" (Strugovshchikov, *Vosp.*, p. 186).

"During this latter part of my stay in Petersburg, Meier developed my musical taste considerably. By requiring distinct and *natural* playing of me, he did not just limit himself to things contrary to refined and elegant styles of playing, but, so far as I was able to understand then, he explained to me naturally and without pedantry the value of pieces, distinguishing classical pieces from good ones and the latter from bad ones."

Beginning of March

Glinka received an offer from his father to take a trip to the Caucausus "to take the waters."

March

Departure for Novospasskoe with his uncle Ivan Andreevich Glinka and his daughters Sofia and Evgenia. "The trip was pleasant. I was already friends with Sofia Ivanovna, and Evgenia Ivanovna, who had just graduated from the Ekaterininsky Institute, was a very pleasant and amusing girl. The slightest adventure was a cause for laughter and genuine pleasure."

On the road from Petersburg to Novospasskoe (400 versts from Petersburg). "Our wagon got stuck in half-melted snow . . . and we had to send for help. Fortunately we found help not far away from a wealthy landowner, Zherebtsov, who sent us beautiful horses with carriages and then put us up for several days and entertained us with incomparable cordiality. . . . He had a private theater. . . . At a rehearsal of Kauer's *Rusalka* there were actors, house-serfs, who appeared in the most fantastic costumes, each corresponding to his duties or occupation."

April

Novospasskoe. Glinka stayed in the country "until the last days of April."

End of April

Departure for the Caucasus accompanied by his Uncle Ilya and his cook Afanasy.

End of April to the Beginning of May (before the 10th)

Road from Novospasskoe to Kharkov. "After several days, near Orel, the first warm winds of spring began to blow, and crossing the Oka, I found myself in a new, unfamiliar southern region."

10 May

Kharkov. Glinka arrived in Kharkov, where he was to meet his fellow-traveller Petrovsky-Murovsky, an acquaintance of his father.

After 10 May

Glinka made the acquaintance of the music store owner Vitkovsky. "I made such a pleasant impression playing the first solo section of Hummel's Concerto in A Minor that I was immediatly introduced to the musical family of my host, and even before the expected arrival of my colleague they entertained me with music."

Middle of May (?)

Kharkov-Pyatigorsk. "Finally my colleague arrived with his brother, and we travelled on. Soon the endless steppe replaced the picturesque Ukraine. We crossed the Don at Oksai and found ourselves in Asia."

Second Half of May (?)

"Before our arrival at the sulphuric waters (today Pyatigorsk), we saw nothing very picturesque. On the contrary, there was almost nothing to be seen except the boundless steppe, overgrown with dense, high, aromatic grass."

Second Half of May (?)

Pyatigorsk. Arrival. "Today's Pyatigorsk had a fantastic appearance at that time, but it was still magnificent. There were not many houses, and there were no churches and gardens at all. But then, as now, there was the magnificient expanse of the Caucausus mountain ranges covered with snow. Likewise the

Podkumok wound like a ribbon along the valley, and eagles in great numbers soared in the clear sky. My colleagues and I settled into a modest little house. . . . I was happy there."

Summer

Life and treatment in Pyatigorsk. "I saw the dancing of Circassian girls and the games and horse races of the Circassian men."

28 July

Glinka's brother Andrey was born in Novospasskoe (Petersburg Necropolis).

End of the Summer

Zheleznovodsk. After treatment in Pyatigorsk, Glinka proceeded "to ferrous waters" (Zheleznovodsk). "The site of these waters is wild and extremely picturesque." Feeling a deterioration of his health after a few baths, he left for Kislovodsk.

End of the Summer

Kislovodsk. "The site of Kislovodsk is more cheerful than Pyatigorsk, but when I was there, there were as yet few houses and no trees at all. Here one had to drink and bathe in the Narzan waters. . . . Things went as badly here as in the ferrous waters."

Second Half of August

Departure.

Kharkov. Glinka parted from Petrovsky-Muravsky.

Orel. "Upon arrival in Orel [Glinka] . . . fell ill with a fever. In a few days the illness passed on its own. . . . They guessed that I had been radically cured, but they were completely wrong."

16 September

Novospasskoe. Return after a four-month-long absence (Shestakova, *Vosp.*, p. 34).

"During the trip . . . I only had a piano available to me in Kharkov, and I played violin very unsatisfactorily."

September

"Having rested, I returned to music with new fervor. . . . The irritating effect of the mineral waters and the abundance of new impressions stimulated my imagination."

Fall, Winter

Glinka raised birds at home. He often lay on the couch listening to the twittering and singing of the birds. "Always after he had been around the birds for a while, he would return to his room, sit down at the piano, and play for a long, long time" (Shestakova, *Vosp.*, p. 35).

"Every time that the musicians arrived (which was approximately twice a month, and they usually stayed several days or even a week), in order to achieve the most precise performance, I went through each musician's part with him before any full rehearsals (though not with some of the better ones) until there was not one wrong note or even a doubtful one. Thus I took account of the best orchestral composers' instrumentation. (Gluck, Handel, and Bach I only knew by hearsay.) Afterwards I listened to the overall effect of the piece, having carried out the first play-throughs together—I myself conducted the orchestra, playing the violin. When the piece finally went well, I stepped back some distance and thus followed the effect of the instrumentation I'd already studied." The repertoire of the orchestra at Novospasskoe was as follows: Cherubini's overtures to *Médée, L'hôtellerie Portugaise, Faniska, Lodoiska, Les deux journées*—"the first two were my favorites"; Méhul's overtures to *Joseph, Le trésor supposé,* and *L'irato;* Mozart's overtures to *Don Giovanni, The Magic Flute, La Clemenza di Tito,* and *Marriage of Figaro;* Beethoven's *Fidelio* (E major); and overtures by Bernhard Romberg (E-flat major) and Maurer (E-flat major). "The viola part was missing from the latter, and spreading all the other parts out in front of me . . . I wrote out a viola part, faultlessly, I believe. We had three symphonies": Haydn's B-flat major, Mozart's G minor, and Beethoven's Second Symphony. "The last I liked especially well. We did not play Rossini overtures yet."

1823–1824

Glinka began to write "first a septet and then an adagio [andante cantabile] and rondo for orchestra." "My understanding of composition overall, or of figured bass, counterpoint, and the other conditions of correct writing was so vague that I took pen in hand without knowing how to begin or where to go." Two overtures for orchestra in G minor and D major come from this period (G 1, p. 370).

1824

14 April

In the journal *Mnemozina* [Mnemosyne], bk. 2, there is an article by Kuechelbecker entitled "On the direction of our poetry, especially lyrical, during the last decade": "It is not enough . . . to appropriate to oneself the treasures of foreigners. For Russia's glory let us write poetry which is genuinely Russian. Let there be a Holy Rus' of supreme power not only in the secular but also in the moral world! Our ancestors' beliefs and our native customs, chronicles, folk songs, and tales are the finest, purest, and most reliable sources for our literature. May we begin to hope that our writers, several younger ones of which are endowed with true talent, will finally throw off their German chains and wish to become Russians." In "Letter XVII—Travel Excerpts," Kuechelbecker tells of a meeting in Dresden in October, 1820, with Melgunov, ". . . who was one of my dearest Petersburg pupils" (d.c.a.).

April

Glinka's departure for Petersburg (Shestakova, *Vosp.*, p. 35). Glinka was accompanied by two serf musicians, the Netoev brothers Aleksey (a violinist) and Yakov (cellist), and also his uncle Ilya (*Zap.*).

Zhukovo. En route Glinka stayed for a week with A. Gerngross and arranged daily concerts. Gerlichko played first violin; Glinka, second; Yakov Netoev, cello; and Aleksey Netoev, viola (according to A. Netoev, in *Bayan,* 1888, no. 34).

Petersburg. On his return Glinka settled in Kolomna (address unknown). Aleksey Netoev "was taken as a student by the first violinist of P. I. Yushkov's orchestra." I began practicing the piano and violin with renewed ardor."
[The first violinist in Yushkov's orchestra was the serf Ivan Grigorievich.]

7 May

Glinka accepted the post of assistant to the secretary in the office of the Council for Communications with an annual salary of 1000 rubles (General List of Civil

Glinka in 1824
Portrait by M. Terebenev.

Servants in Posts Under the Jurisdiction of the Chief Administration of Communications Serving in 1827, bk. 37, p. 5, in *L.*, p. 38). "This circumstance had an important influence on my future. First, I had to be in the office only five to six hours per day. I was not assigned work at home, and I had no real duties or responsibilities. Consequently, all the rest of my time I could devote to my favorite activities, especially music. Second, in a short time my work associations gained me acquaintances who were very beneficial musically."

Glinka met a senior member of the Council for Communications and hero of the War of 1812, Count Egor Sivers, who was a music lover and "what was still better, loved good classical music." Glinka began to visit in his home. "Countess Sivers sang lead soprano and had a reliable, clear, and pleasant voice." Glinka also sang at the Sivers' musical evenings. "Besides singing, other pieces were sometimes performed": quartets, quintets, and other chamber ensembles.

Besides Count Sivers, "where I was received very cordially, I had many other acquaintances, who took me to the home of the chief of our office, Aleksandr Nikolaevich Bakhturin."

Spring

Meier refused to give Glinka lessons. He once said, "You are too talented to take lessons from me. Just come see me every day, and we will make music together." From that time Glinka visited Meier almost daily. "He lived with his mother and sisters. With the older of them, Henriette (later Mme Garegnani), I frequently played duets. As before Meier would give me various pieces, sometimes his own, but more often Hummel's. He would always look over my efforts at composition patiently and explain to me, so far as he could, the rules of art, though he never imposed himself or his style of writing on me. On the other hand, Mozart, Cherubini, Beethoven, and other classics he displayed as models of perfection. At the time the well-known contrapuntist Müller was in Petersburg, but somehow I never managed to meet him. How is one to know? Perhaps that was best. Strict German counterpoint does not always agree with ardent fantasy."

Summer

Glinka moved to Faleev's house in Kolomna (Kanonerskaya Street, no. 2). Aleksandr Kiprianov, husband of a cousin of his, moved in with him. [He was] "an extremely intelligent man, well-educated, and pleasant. Seeing the furious passion with which I applied myself to composition, he tried to dissuade me from what in his opinion was a baneful tendency. He insisted instead that the talent to play the piano and violin, besides my own satisfaction, might certainly gain me pleasant and beneficial acquaintances, but from composition, he said, I could hope for nothing but envy, disappointment, and distress."

Fall, Before 7 November

Glinka composed the romance *"Moia arfa"* [My harp] to words of Bakhturin. This was "my first unsuccessful attempt at composition with a text."
[Glinka's first idea for an opera on the subject of Sir Walter Scott's poem "Mathilda Rokeby" is connected with this romance. Fragmentary sketches of the proposed opera are preserved (O'Neil and Mathilda's duet and Bertram's theme). The romance "My Harp," written again from memory in 1855, Glinka jokingly referred to as having been written "before the flood," that is, the flood of 7 November 1824.]

7 November

Glinka was a witness to the flood. "The water, which had reached the threshhold of my apartment, began to recede."

Fall, Winter

Glinka "soon became convinced of the necessity of being able to dance and began taking lessons from Golts. I studied with him about two years and advanced to steps then executed by the stylish dandies. I did not like the company of men then but preferred the society of ladies and young women who were attracted by my musical talent."

The artist Terebenev did Glinka's portrait in water colors (V. Stasov, *"Pamiati M. I. Glinki"* [To the memory of M. I. Glinka], SPb. , 1892, p. 19).
[The portrait is in the Tretyakov Gallery.]

"About that time or a little bit later . . . I met the Italian singer Belloli and began to study (Italian) singing with him. My voice was hoarse, somewhat nasal, and inderterminate, that is, neither tenor nor baritone. . . . Although my ear was excellent, in the first months I sang out of tune because I was unaccustomed to listening to myself. Belloli taught well and still possessed an adequate voice, so that he could sing everything he taught me. I soon began to perform *buffa* music quite tolerably."

1824–1825

"Despite my frequent sessions with Meier, his explanations and the constant profound exertions under which I labored in composition all came to naught. . . .

At that time I wrote a quartet for two violins, viola, and cello (D major), but this effort was as unsuccessful as previous ones."
[The manuscript of the quartet is preserved in incomplete form.]

1825

Beginning of the Year

Glinka met the Khovansky family and especially befriended Yury Khovansky, who was educated in the Lyceum at Tsarskoe Selo (*Zap.*).

16 April

By order of the Senate, Glinka was confirmed for the rank of tenth class (*Attestat Glinki* [Glinka Certificate]).

Tsarskoe Selo. Glinka frequently visited the Khovanskys and played music with their domestic music teacher Liegle (from Vienna), who "was an excellent sight reader . . . and accompanist. I played primarily piano four-hand versions of Haydn quartets, Haydn and Mozart symphonies, and even a few pieces by Beethoven with her. . . . I often went there for several days. My appearance was always a pleasure for everyone, because they knew that where I was there would be no boredom. . . . I was able at the time (a pleasant time) to amuse my acquaintances in various ways, especially with apt performances of scenes from opera *buffa*."

Petersburg. Glinka met Elena Demidova, who "justifiably was considered one of the best amateur singers of the capital. She possessed an extremely powerful contralto voice, but she could also perform soprano parts. Liegle usually accompanied her singing on the piano, and Belloli very often sang duets by various masters with her. . . . I am much indebted to the musical exercises that took place in Demidova's house."

Composer's dating on an autograph title page: *"Sonata pour le pianoforte avec accompagnement d'alto-viola ou violon. Composé l'an 1825."*

Glinka composed the first allegro of the Sonata in D Minor for Piano and Viola. "This piece was tidier than the others. I performed this sonata with Boehm and Liegle. With the latter I played viola. The adagio was written later [1828], and the rondo, the theme for which was of Russian origin . . . I did not try to complete. . . . Recently I used it [the rondo] in a children's polka." The composition of the romance to Baratynsky's words, *"Ne iskushai menia bez nuzhdy"*

[Do not tempt me needlessly] appears to date from this period. This was "my first successul romance" (*Zap.*).

[Two undated autographs are preserved. The romance was first published by the firm of Petz (with no date).]

Glinka met Petr Stepanov at the home of Fedor Kashtalinsky, "our common grandfather" (P. Stepanov, *Vosp.*, p. 54).

End of Summer

Glinka moved to Zagorodny Prospect, house of Nechaeva (the wooden wing of house no. 42 has not been preserved), into an apartment with Aleksandr Rimsky-Korsak, "a boarding school colleague from the same district. Our apartment, which was very cozy, was located on the second floor . . . of a small wing looking onto the courtyard. It had a garden . . . and in the garden was a summer house with an edifying inscription: *'Ne poshto daleche, i zdes' khorosho'* [It's pointless to look further when things are fine here]."

Fall (?)

Glinka wrote a French quadrille for a party at the Khovanskys. The rehearsal he arranged at his apartment on Zagorodny Prospect. Glinka's friends "gathered to listen to it and were enthralled." Glinka's French quadrille was performed at a party at the home of Count Khovansky. "The music began, couples began to move, conversations began. The ladies listened only to their partners and not to the music, which passed unnoticed. Nonetheless Glinka was very satisified. For the first time he had appeared before the public, and we were proud of him" (P. Stepanov, *Vosp.*, p. 54).

End of the Year (Fall [?])

Glinka met "with some of his former colleagues," one of whom, Mikhail Glebov, tried to persuade Glinka to join a secret society. He subsequently "was divested of his rank and nobility and was exiled to Siberia in 1826" (*Zap.*).

[The name Glebov has been established by collation of the list of students at the Boarding School for Nobility with the list [*Al'favit*] of Decembrists. The second colleague was Stepan Palitsyn (*L.*, p. 40).]

"Among the rebels were people very well known to me."

[These people included first Kuechelbecker, then his former school colleagues Glebov and Palitsyn, and finally a coworker in the Council for Communications, Aleksandr Bestuzhev (Marlinsky).]

"As a young man Glinka fell into a select society of Petersburg youths, some of whom paid dearly after the thoughtless revolt for their sacrilegious patriotism" (Sollogub, p. 561).

During the course of the twenties "the revolutionary verses of Ryleev and Pushkin could be found in the hands of young people in the farthest reaches of the empire. There was not a single well-educated lady who did not know them by heart, not a single officer who did not carry them in his field kit, not a single son of a priest who did not make a dozen copies of them. . . . A whole generation fell under the influence of this fervent youthful propaganda" (A. Herzen, *Sobr. soch.*, vol. 7, M., 1956, p. 198).

1 December

Glinka was reckoned to be on leave from this date (*Attestat Glinki*).

14 December

In the morning Lindkvist's oldest son came to see Glinka. Glinka went with him and Rimsky-Korsak "to the square and saw the sovereign come out of the palace. . . . We stayed at the square for several hours. Then, compelled by hunger (since I hadn't eaten breakfast), I went to Bakhturin's. Perhaps this apparently unimportant circumstance saved me from death or maiming: we soon heard the sounds of gun fire directed against the rebels."
[The Moscow Regiment arrived at Senate Square ca. 11 o'clock. We may assume that Glinka and his friends, arriving after the Moscow Regiment (their route from Zagorodny Prospect by way of Gorokhovaya Street to Senate Square coincided), appeared at the place of the uprising at about 11 o'clock. Apparently, like the crowd which filled the Palace and Senate Squares, Glinka walked about and did not stay in one place. This allowed him to see Nicholas I up close. At about 11:30 the tsar came out of the Winter Palace into Palace Square and began to read to the assembled crowd the manifesto concerning his accession to the throne. Insofar as Glinka remembered leaving not long before the buckshot, he was a witness to the cavalry attack on the mutinous regiments as well as the firing of the insurgents and the participation of the crowd in defense of them (the crowd threw stones and pieces of firewood). At about 4:15 Nicholas gave the order to fire on the insurgent regiments with buckshot. By this time it had already gotten dark. (See M. Nechkina, *Dvizhenie dekabristov* [The decembrist movement], vol. 2, M., 1955, pp. 271, 279, 295, passim).]

Second Half of December

Glinka was summoned at night to an interrogation before the chief of the Council for Communications, Duke Würtembergsky, in connection with the search for Kuechelbecker, who had disappeared (*Zap.*). "And then the arrests began: 'they have taken so-and-so,' 'so-and-so has been seized,' 'they have brought so-and-so from the country.' Frightened parents shuddered in fear for their children. Dark clouds obscured the sky" (A. Herzen, *Sobr. soch.* [Collected works], vol. 8, M., 1956, p. 57).

End of December

Glinka leaves for the country with Rimsky-Korsak (*Zap.; Attestat Glinki*).

Novospasskoe. Glinka's arrival for the engagement of his sister Pelageya with Yakov Sobolevsky (Shestakova, *Vosp.*, p. 35).

Glinka's sister Olga was born during this year (Findeyzen, *Glinka 1*, p. 18).

1822–1826

To this period belong the Septet in E-flat for oboe, two violins, bassoon, cello, bass, and French horn; the Quartet in D; the Symphony in B-flat; and the overtures in G minor and D major.

1826

January

Smolensk. Glinka arrives with his parents in Smolensk, where they stay at the home of a relative, Aleksey Andreevich Ushakov. For [Ushakov's] daughter Elizaveta, Glinka wrote the Variations in E-flat on the romance *"Benedetta sia la madre."* This was Glinka's first published composition (*Zap.*). On the manuscript there is this inscription: *"Dedié à Mademoiselle Lise Ouschakoff par Michel Glinka, L'auteur"* (ITMK, coll. 6).
[Shortly afterwards Elizaveta's sister, Ekaterina Ushakova, married the *agent provocateur* Sherwood. Elizaveta married after 1847 (married name Mitskaya). In the printed edition of the Variations the dedication is missing. In the autograph it is struck out, apparently by Glinka himself.]

At the request of General Apukhtin, Glinka wrote music to "Prologue on the Death of Alexander I and Accession to the Throne of Nicholas I." "The words for the composition were written in French by the tutor in the General's home. . . . Karl Gempel played the piano and sang the high tenor part in the chorus in C minor. I sang the B-flat major aria . . . dressed like a spirit. Despite several clumsy places . . . and the incongruity of the keys of C minor and B-flat major, I consider this cantata my first successful effort at vocal composition on a large scale. . . . The music expresses the text quite accurately.
[The tutor in Apukhtin's house was the French immigrant Count Olidor.]

End of January

Novospasskoe. Marriage of Pelageya Ivanovna Glinka to Yakov Sobolevsky, "a kind and cultured man." Glinka was his sister's best man (*Zap.;* Shestakova, *Vosp.*, p. 36).

Beginning of February

After his sister's wedding Glinka and his immediate family made several trips to close relatives who lived in the area (Shestakova, *Vosp.*, p. 36).

Between 21 and 28 February

Smolensk. Glinka went to Smolensk "to celebrate Shrovetide." "I played in General Apukhtin's domestic theater" (*Zap.;* Shestakova, *Vosp.*, p. 36).

Glinka sent a certificate of illness to his office with a request for extension of his leave (*Zap.; Attestat Glinki*).

Beginning of March

Novospasskoe. Glinka returned to the country, where he "acquired birds of various kinds; there were as many as 16."

March–May

"In the evenings and at dusk I loved to dream at the piano. Zhukovsky's sentimental poetry pleased me very much and moved me to tears. (Generally speaking, in my youth I was a boy of romantic disposition and loved to shed the sweet tears of emotion.)" At this time Glinka wrote "two melancholy . . . romances," *"Svetit mesiats na kladbishche"* [The moon shines on the cemetery] and *"Bednyi pevets"* [The poor singer] to words by Zhukovsky.

Second Half of May

Glinka returns to St. Petersburg.

End of May

Petersburg. Glinka returns from the country (*Zap.*).

1 June

Glinka "was on leave during 1825 from 1 December through 1 March 1826, appeared on 1 June, having overstayed his leave on account of sickness, for which he presented a doctor's certificate" (*Attestat Glinki*).

17 June

In a supplement to *Sev. pchela,* no. 72, the "Report of the Investigative Committee" on the Decembrist case was published.

22 June

In a supplement to *Sev. pchela,* no. 74, a "list" was published "of individuals associated with secret societies of criminal intent who have given themselves up . . . to the criminal court."

13 July

Execution of Ryleev, Pestel, Muraviev-Apostol, Kakhovsky, and Bestuzhev-Ryumin. Civil punishment and banishment to penal servitude of other participants in the Decembrist uprising. "The hanged have been hanged; but penal servitude for 120 friends, brothers, and colleagues is terrible" (ltr. from A. Pushkin to P. Vyazemsky, 14 August 1826, in Pushkin, *Soch.* [Works], vol. 13, p. 291).

Summer

"I suffered from sleeplessness. . . . No doubt I was busy with music . . . but what in particular I was working on, I do not remember at all."

Glinka's acquaintance with Anton Delvig through Mikhail Yakovlev. "I often visited him."
[Glinka mistakenly dates his acquaintance with Delvig to 1828. Delvig visited at Glinka's and Rimsky-Korsak's when they lived at Nechaeva's on Zagorodny.]

Glinka's acquaintance with Anna Kern in Yussupov's garden, where, while walking with his superior General Bazen, he met her accompanied by Lev Pushkin. When he arrived at Bazen's, Glinka improvised for those present on a Ukrainian song (chosen by Bazen), *"Navarila, napekla, ne dlia Gritsya, dlia Petra"* [She boiled and baked, not for Gritse but for Petr]. "One can imagine, but to describe my amazement and pleasure is difficult! . . . Such suppleness and facility, such feeling in the sounds, and such a complete absence of virtuosity I had never encountered in anyone! With Glinka the keys sang at the touch of his small hands, and the sounds they emitted flowed together as if they were bound together by affection. He had so expertly mastered the instrument that he could express any subtlety he desired. . . . He played, first of all, the theme of the song Bazen had sung, and then improvised wonderful variations on the tune in a brilliant and fascinating way and performed it all amazingly. In the sounds of his improvisations one could hear both the folk melody and Glinka's own individual tenderness, playfulness, and dreaminess. We listened afraid to stir, and when he was finished we remained in a wonderful state of distraction" (A. Kern, *Vosp.*, p. 147).

September–October

In Moscow Pushkin read his tragedy *Boris Godunov* at Venevitinov's (12 October), Vyazemsky's, and Sobolevsky's.

October

Moscow. Glinka arrived in Moscow, "attached to Melgunov and Sobolevsky more than others, and music joined us" (M. Pogodin, *Vosp. o S. P. Shevyreve* [Reminiscences of S. P. Shevyrev], in *ZhMNP*, 1869, v. 141, p. 405).
["Who knows but that these exhilarating days and hours, spent caught up in the enthusiasm of a whole crowd of Moscow intellectuals for *Boris Godunov*, and Glinka among them, might have been the first and secret reason for conceiving the idea of *A Life for the Tsar*.!? Note also the proximity of the periods of time: in the drama it is the end of Tsar Boris; in the opera it is the beginning of the time of Tsar Michael. Perhaps Pushkin was also the father of *A Life for the Tsar*, like he was the father of *Dead Souls* and *The Inspector General*, even though Zhukovsky pointed out the subject for *A Life for the Tsar*" (ltr. from V. Stasov to Findeyzen, 26 May 1893, in coll. *Glinka*, p. 243).]

End of the Year

Petersburg. Glinka makes the acquaintance of Vladimir Odoevsky.

In a humorous letter addressed "to the office of the publisher of the *Moskovskii vestnik* [Moscow Herald] from its St. Petersburg division, a most humble report from D. Venevitinov and Odoevsky," Odoevsky writes to Sobolevsky: "Not long ago I met your schoolmate Glinka, a splendid fellow. A musician, the likes of which there are few. Not a monster like you" (N. Barsukov, *Zhizn' i trudy M. Pogodina* [Life and Works of M. Pogodin], bk. 2, p. 67).

Ivan Glinka arrived and moved in with his son. "He loved me and all of his children very much, and he treated me like a colleague. He confided his own secrets and intentions to me and did not hide his joys and sorrows."

Composer's manuscript dating: *"Air russe, Sredi doliny rovnyia* [In the gentle valley]. *Varié pour le pianoforte composé l'an 1826"* [Variations on a Russian theme].

To this period also belong the romance *"Akh ty, dushechka, krasna devitsa"* [You darling, beautiful maid], variations on a theme from the opera *Faniska* by Cherubini, and the romance *"Pamiat' serdtsa"* [Heart's memory] on Batyushkov's poem *"Moi genii"* [My genius].
[In his *Zapiski* [Memoirs] Glinka mistakenly places the composition of this romance in 1828.]

1824–1827

To this period belongs a fragment of a letter from Glinka to Melgunov (?), in which he says that he cannot go with the latter to the museum, since that evening he must meet with Meier, and during the day he wishes to take advantage of a "moment of complete freedom in order to work for an hour or so with music. . . . You say that I am wasting my time. But what's one to do? I love music, and you know that it is my passion. Perhaps one year I will realize that I should have found a better use for my poor talent, but for now I cannot resist the temptation."
[This dating has been established on the basis of Glinka's service in the office of the Council for Communications, since the letter speaks of his desire to take advantage of a "moment of complete freedom." The letter was published for the first time in Italian in Enrico Carozzi's book *Michele Glinka. Appunti critico biografici* (Milan, 1874, on the occasion of a performance of the opera *A Life for the Tsar* at La Scala). The addressee is *"Sereno Tobolsky,"* (which sounds nonsensical). However, the content of this letter, and especially a second letter (spring 1834, from Berlin), allow one to suppose that the addressee is most likely Nikolay Melgunov. I first presented this suggestion in an article entitled "Letter to an 'Unknown' Friend," published in *Sovetskaia muzyka* [Soviet Music], 1957, no. 2. Probably the letter was written to Melgunov at the time of one of his trips to St. Petersburg. It is not clear which museum Glinka is talking about, most likely the *Kunstkammer,* since the Hermitage was not open to the public then, and the Rumyantsev Museum first opened in 1831.]

1826 or 1827

Glinka's acquaintance with the Tolstoy brothers. "There were four of them; the youngest, Feofil Matveevich (Rostislav) possessed a very lovely tenor voice."
[At the time of Glinka's acquaintance with the Tolstoys, there were six brothers. With which of them besides Feofil Glinka was acquainted is not known.]

1827

Beginning of the Year

"Since the apartment . . . in Nechaeva's house on Zagorodny Prospect had begun to seem small to us, we moved at the beginning of 1827 to Torgovaya Street on Theater Square into Piskarev's house (today a section of house no. 8 on the Union of Printers Street).

Glinka frequently saw his boarding school colleague Lukyanovich. "He was a cheerful, entertaining, and nice person. He loved literature and with Korsak wrote several articles. Even I, poor sinner, sometimes took up the pen, enticed by their example."

The composition of the poem *"Al'sand"* belongs to this time as well as Glinka's acquaintance with Evgeny Shterich, which turned into friendship. "He . . . possessed rare mental qualities and played the piano respectably."

End of Winter, Before Shrovetide

Glinka makes the acquaintance of Sergey Golitsyn ("Firs"). This "had an important influence on the development of my musical abilities. He was a nice, cheerful, and at times entertaining young man, who knew music well and sang very agreeably in a beautiful deep bass. At the time I was extremely shy. He was able to reassure me and introduced me to the society of young people of a higher caliber. . . . He had a knack for inciting me to work. He wrote verses for me and gladly performed my compositions."

Between 6 and 12 February (Shrovetide)

Glinka participated in a performance in the home of the president of the State Council, Viktor Kochubey (Fontanka no. 16). In a scene from Mozart's *Don Giovanni* Glinka played the part of Donna Anna, "with a white mantilla and a woman's wig with long curls . . . he sang the contralto part very well." In the divertissement Glinka, dressed as a peasant girl, danced the polonaise with a tall Englishman as his partner (N. Golitsyn, *Vosp.*, p. 143).

Beginning of Spring

Ivan Glinka received a proposal from State Councillor Vasily Pogodin to undertake a joint business venture which subsequently resulted in a large profit by releasing the Glinka estates from any debts (*Zap.*). This is the period of Ivan

Glinka's complaint to the tsar over the improper assessment of his liquor business (G 2-A, p. 59).

Glinka's father left for the country for a while. "I stayed with Korsak."

Spring

Glinka wrote "several individual scenes for voice and orchestra for the theater, namely: a duet with recitative for bass and tenor (A major), a chorus on the death of a hero (C minor), and an aria for baritone (A-flat). The Adagio of the latter I used for the canon in the finale to Act I of the opera *Ruslan and Lyudmila*. There was also a *'Molitva'* [Prayer] in three parts in F major for the theater." As a result of an unsuccessful infatuation for a young girl named Katenka, he also wrote a romance to words of Rimsky-Korsak, *"Ia liubliu, ty mne tverdila"* [I love, you assured me]. "Subsequently Prince Golitsyn supplied a French text to this music, and the romance is now known as *'Le baiser.'*" Glinka also wrote the aria for soprano *"Mio ben, ricordati"* at the same time. [Subsequently it was rewritten for two voices. It was first published in the "Lyrical Album for 1829."]

Glinka frequently held musical gatherings in his apartment. "Varlamov assisted me in the vocal parts." Count Devier, who played the violin well, would get musicians from the wind orchestra of the Horse Guards regiment. Varlamov brought the singers. "Thus I was able to hear the effect of what I had written."

Acquaintance and lessons with the violinist Remi, "who in a few lessons corrected my right arm."

Summer

Pavlovsk. Glinka frequently visited at the dacha of Evgeny Shterich, where he "normally was either silent or joked like a seminarian. Often he sat down at the piano and so immersed himself in his playing that he neither saw nor heard what was going on around him." Then Glinka sang: "His voice was hollow, weak, and unappealing. At first he whispered, speaking [the words] with expressive nuances, which I . . . began to understand only later. Gradually he became more animated, almost frenzied, and cried out the high notes, straining furiously, even painfully. Then he stood up, laughed merrily, put his hands in his waistcoat and, throwing back his head, be began to strut about the room like a rooster, asking: 'And how was my chest B-flat?' . . . Whoever heard Glinka knew that he could have been a stupendous singer, without possessing any of the physical attributes." Glinka's appearance at the time " was distinguished by his shortness and individual build, which was certainly not unattractive or unappealing. He had dark hair, a short, round, straight nose and a protruding chin. He was always throwing his head back, nose in the air, by instinct wishing to appear taller. Then with a characteristic gesture he would thrust his finger behind the slit of his waistcoat under his arm, which would straighten him out even more. The most striking thing about him were his eyes, now immovable and thoughtful, now sparkling, now wide open and profoundly solemn under the spell of a supernatural inspiration" (Sollogub, p. 204).

Glinka meets Zhukovsky and becomes good friends with Mikhail Vielgorsky (*Zap.*).

21 August

Petersburg. Glinka along with Sergey Golitsyn and the Tolstoy brothers arranged a serenade on the Little Chernaya River. "At about nine o'clock in the evening a launch decorated with blazing torches appeared on the quiet waters of the Little Chernaya River. The hosts and the piano were situated under an umbrella. On the prow were the musicians of the Horse Guards Regiment. Boats with fireworks followed behind. The banks of the river on the side of the settlement and Countess Stroganova's gardens were crowded with people. A chorus accompanied by piano sang Russian songs, French romances, and theatrical arias in turn. In the intervals between the singing, trumpets played, and at the same time Roman candles, fountains, wheels, and rockets would illuminate groups of listeners. . . . The serenade continued until midnight." Glinka accompanied on the piano and directed the chorus (*Sev. pchela,* 27 August 1827).
[Glinka indicates that there were two launches: "we sat on one, and on the other were the trumpeters of the Horse Guards Regiment."]

27 August

In *Sev. pchela,* no. 103, there is an article by F. B. [Bulgarin] entitled "Petersburg Notes. On entertainment in the capital. Letter to Aleksandr Nikit. Peshchurov in Libovo," which includes a description of the serenade on the Little Chernaya River on 21 August.

24 December

Glinka was present on Holy Evening at Sollogub's grandmother's, E. Arkharova's, where "he played, I believe, a Mozart sonata" (Sollogub, p. 205).

Composer's dating on the manuscript of *"Chto, krasotka molodaia"* [Why do you cry, young beauty?], a Russian song to words by Delvig, and *"Russkaia pesnia" (Gor'ko, gor'ko, mne, krasnoi devitse)* [Russian song ("I am grieved, beautiful maid")] to words by Rimsky-Korsak: "Composed in 1827."

In this year Glinka's uncle Afanasy Andreevich Glinka died (Shestakova, *Vosp.*, p. 37).

In the general register of civil servants in positions under the jurisdiction of the Directorate of Communications serving in 1827, book 27, p. 5, under the heading "assistants to the secretaries" appears the record reproduced opposite.

A later addition reads: "Released 23 June 1828" (*L.*, p. 48).

In the course of the year Glinka wrote the following: a serenade to Italian words supplied by Feofil Tolstoy (*"O mia dolce, mia carina"*); a quartet in F major for soprano, alto, tenor, and bass, accompanied by two violins, viola, and cello (*"Come di gloria al nome"*); and a quartet for the same voices and instruments in G minor (*"Sogna chi crede d'esser felice"*). "These two pieces were performed at Demidova's, and the first (F major) subsequently also at Lvov's." He also composed romances to words by Sergey Golitsyn *"Pour un moment"* and *"Skazhi, zachem"* [Tell me, why].

The second version of the Variations in E-flat on a Theme by Mozart (taken from the orchestral accompaniment to the chorus and dance of the slaves from the finale to Act I of the opera *The Magic Flute*) dates from this period. In this version there are five variations.
[Published during Glinka's life by Stellovsky.]

The Trio in D for alto, tenor, and bass, with piano accompaniment, on a text by an unidentified author, *"Bozhe sil, vo dni smiaten'ia"* [God, preserve our strength in days of distress], was composed during this year.

1827/1828

During the course of the winter and spring of 1827/1828, Pushkin was at Delvig's "almost every evening" (V. Gaevsky, *"Del'vig,"* in *Contemporary* [*Sovremennik*], 1854, vol. 47, no. 9/10, p. 12).

Pushkin read *Boris Godunov* in Delvig's home.

From the General Register of Civil Servants, 1827

Beginning date of period						
In Service	In Current Grade	In Dept. of Communications	In Current Position	Position, Rank, Name	Annual Salary	Location of Civil Servant & Other Remarks
1824 May 7	1824 May 7	1824 May 7	7	Titular Counselor, 10th class, Mikhail Ivanov Glinka	1000	Retired (1 word illegible) since 12 March 1828 (illegible)

"At about this time I was often in the company of our most illustrious poet Aleksandr Sergeevich Pushkin . . . and enjoyed his acquaintance until his death."

1828

12 March

Departure for Novospasskoe (*Zap.; Attestat Glinki*).

Second Half of March to the Second Half of April

Novospasskoe. Glinka stayed with his parents. "I saw my oldest sister then . . . for the last time."

Second Half of April

Departure for Moscow to meet with Melgunov (*Zap.*).

Ca. 20 April

Moscow. Arrival in Moscow.

24 April

The "Musical Album for 1828" compiled by Varlamov and Glinka was presented to the Moscow censorship committee and approved. The censor was Sergey Aksakov (coll. *Glinka,* 1958, p. 388).
[The edition was never printed.]

On the same day, the censor's approval was granted for publication of a "Russian song with variations, set to music" [Variations on a Russian theme, "In the gentle valley"?] (Ibid.).

Ca. 20 April–9 May

Glinka is in Moscow. At Melgunov's Glinka met Stepan Shevyrev. While he was at Melgunov's, Glinka wrote the B-flat adagio of the Sonata in D Minor for viola and piano: "the counterpoint in this piece was quite clever."

9 May

"At daybreak" Glinka left for Petersburg "by post chaise" (*Zap.*).

12 May

Petersburg. On his arrival Glinka went to stay with his "fellow student from the boarding school, Chirkov," in Barbazan's house on the corner of Nevsky and Vladimirskaya (today no. 49/2). "He arrived at the end of his leave" and "returned to his official duties" (*Zap.; Attestat Glinki*).
[Two Chirkov brothers studied with Glinka in the boarding school, Nikolay and Nikanor. It is unknown which one is referred to here.]

21 May

Order of the Senate promoting Glinka to the rank of Titular Councillor "with seniority from 7 May 1827."

1 June

Glinka "is released from the Council for Communications by his own request in order to attend to other matters" (*Attestat Glinki*).

May, and later in the Summer

Priyutino. At the Olenins' dacha a circle gathered which included representatives of the upper aristocracy as well as writers, artists, and musicians. Pushkin, Krylov, and Glinka frequently appeared in this circle. "Between games the young writers often read their works, and M. I. Glinka performed his compositions" (P. Ustimovich, "A. A. Andro," in *Rus. starina* [Russian antiquity], 1890, v. 67, part 8, p. 389).

Mid-May–6 June

Glinka "spent nearly an entire day" with Aleksandr Griboedov. "He was a very good musician and showed me the theme of a Georgian song to which A. S. Pushkin soon thereafter wrote the romance *'Ne poi, volshebnitsa, pri mne'* [Sing not, enchantress, in my presence]."
[It is possible that this meeting with Griboedov occurred at the Olenins' dacha in Priyutino. On 6 June, Griboedov left Petersburg.]

8 June

Glinka's oldest sister Pelageya Ivanovna Sobolevskaya died in Novospasskoe (Shestakova, *Vosp.*, p. 37).

12 June

Pushkin wrote the poem *"Ne poi, volshebnitsa, pri mne"* (first version).
[Glinka wrote a romance on the first and third verses of this version. The word *krasavitsa* [beauty], instead of *volshebnitsa* [enchantress], Glinka inserted in the romance after he became acquainted with the second version of the poem in 1829.]

23 June

Glinka is released from the office of the Council for Communications ("Register of civil servants in positions under the jurisdiction of the Directorate of Communications serving in 1827," book 37, p. 5, in *L.*, p. 52).

28 June

Glinka was issued a certificate for his period of service in the office of the Council for Communications from 7 May 1824 to 1 June 1828, signed by the Director Bakhturin (*Attestat Glinki*).
[This certificate, apparently, served Glinka as a residence permit (cf. 1 May 1835).]

18 July

Note in the diary of A. Olenina (in Priyutino): "Pushkin and Kiselev are the heroes of my present novel. Sergey Golitsyn (Firs), Glinka, Griboedov, and especially Vyazemsky are more or less interesting personalities" (Pushkin, *Issledovaniia i materialy* [Papers and materials], v. 2, M., 1958, p. 264).

Acquaintance with the tenor Nikolay Ivanov and lessons with him. "Subsequently he participated frequently in our domestic musical gatherings."

Tsarskoe Selo. Glinka participated in a performance in which "my serenade and couplets with chorus *"Lila v chernoi mantii"* [Lila in the black mantle] (words by Count S. Golitsyn) were performed. Ivanov sang the couplets, and the court singers, the chorus" (*Zap.*).
[*"Lila v chernoi mantilla"* is apparently the Barcarolle (G 1, p. 376).]

Petersburg. Glinka participated in some "mischief" in which ghosts were represented on the Little Chernaya River.

Marino. Journey of 10 days to Countess Stroganova. "I participated in the performance of several scenes from Rossini's *Il barbiere de Siviglia*" and played the part of Figaro. Sergey Golitsyn was Bartolo, and Feofil Tolstoy, Almaviva.

"After this they entertained us there for several days" (*Zap.*; F. Tolstoy, *Vosp.*, in *Rus. starina*, v. 3, part 4, p. 426).

11 August

Priyutino. On A. Olenina's birthday many guests arrived: "lovely Sergey Golitsyn, Krylov, Gnedich, the Zubovs, and dear Glinka, who after dinner played wonderfully and on Wednesday will come to give me my first singing lesson. Pushkin came as usual."

15 August

Glinka began to give voice lessons to Olenina (*L.*, p. 53).

Summer

Petersburg. Glinka made the acquaintance of Maria Szymanowska and from that time frequently attended her salon, where he met Adam Mickiewicz. "I was the maestro at Szymanowska's musical matinees. Sometimes I even performed my own music."

1 September

Pushkin writes to Vyazemsky: "We have all dispersed now. Kiselev, they say, is already in the army; 'Junior' [A. A. Olenin] is in the country; Golitsyn spends his time with Glinka and arranges aristocratic family occasions for celebration. I was allowed in society because I was homeless" (Pushkin, *Soch.*, v. 14, p. 26).

29 September

Glinka's poem *"Al'sand"* was printed in the eighth issue of the journal *Slavyanin* (d.c.a.).

After 7 October

From this time Glinka often visited at Delvig's, who for Glinka's music reworked the song *"Akh ty, noch' li, nochen'ka"* [Oh, night, dark night]. Also at that time Glinka wrote a romance to Delvig's verse *"Dedushka, devitsy raz mne govorili"* [Grandfather, maids once told me]. "M. L. Yakovlev sang this song very well" (*Zap.*).

[The dating of Glinka's visits to Delvig is defined by the period of Delvig's absence from Petersburg (from February to 7 October).]

"Among my acquaintances Glinka called on the Pushkins and was at Bazen's
... and Baron Delvig's." At Delvig's, "a great lover of music and admirer of
Glinka," he "often delighted our entire circle with his marvelous inspirations.
At times he was joined by Prince Sergey Golitsyn or M. L. Yakovlev, and
sometimes as a chorus we all would sing some fashionable bravura romance or
a barcarolle" (A. Kern, *Vosp.*, p. 148).

Mid-November

Pushkin (from Malinniky) writes to Delvig: "My sister requests my *"Voron"*
[Raven] for her *"Golubchik"* [Little dove]. What do you think? Let my brother-in-
law engrave it, and you print it" (Pushkin, *Soch.*, v. 14, p. 36).
[The "little dove" was Nikolay Pavlishchev. The conversation is about the publication of Mikhail
Vielgorsky's song *"Voron k vorony letit"* [The raven flies to the raven] in the "Lyrical Album for
1829," which Glinka and Pavlishchev prepared.]

1 November

At Pavlishchev's "were many musicians, among them Glinka, who, they say,
composes better than he plays, although he is extremely skillful in the latter"
(A. Vulf, *Dnevnik* [Diary], in *Pushkin i ego sovremenniki* [Pushkin and his
contemporaries], vols. 21–22, P., 1915, p. 23).

End of the Year

Glinka became ill (*Zap.*).

11 December

In *Sev. pchela,* no. 148, there is an anouncement of the forthcoming publication
before the new year of a "Lyrical Album for 1829," edited by Glinka and
Pavlishchev.

12 (?) December

Publication of "'Lyrical Album for 1829,' edited by M. Glinka and N.
Pavlishchev. St. Petersburg, Beggrov's Lithographers, Nevsky Prospect, 52."
[Contents: 1. *"Vospominanie"* [Recollection], romance with words by Zhukovsky and music by
Nikolay Norov; 2. *"Voron k voronu letit"* [The raven flies to the raven], song, words by Pushkin,
music by Count Vielgorsky; 3. *"Vilia,"* song from Mickiewicz's poem *"Wallenrod,"* music by Mme
Szymanowska; 4. *"Pamiat' serdtsa"* [Heart's memory], romance, words by Batyushkov, music by
Glinka; 5. *"Chernaia shal', pesnia"* [The black shawl, song], words by Pushkin, music by Count
Vielgorsky; 6. *"Mio ben, ricordati,"* duettino per tenore e contralto dal S. M. Glinka; 7. Stances

tirées de Lamartine. Mise en musique par N. Noroff; 8. *"Skazhi, zachem"* [Tell me, why], romance, words by Count Golitsyn, music by Glinka. In an appendix to the "Lyrical Album": 1. Waltz, composed by M. Rubets; 2. Mazurka, by V. Dabry; 3. Cotillon, composed by M. G. [Glinka]; 4. Cavalry Trot, by Prince A. Golitsyn; 5. Waltz, by M. Rubets; 6. Mazurka, by M. G. [Glinka]; 7. Waltz, by Pavlishchev; 8. Waltz, by Shterich.]
[Prince A. Golitsyn is a misprint; it should be L. (Lev Grigorievich, brother of Sergey) (G 1, p. 378).]

13 December

In the *Journal de St.-Pétersbourg,* no. 149, there is an announcement of the publication of the "Lyrical Album." "Messrs. M. Glinka and N. Pavlishchev have joined forces to present the public with this musical New Year's gift, which, we feel, is distinctive for content as well as elegant format and beautiful printing. The collection consists of unpublished works: two songs by Pushkin with music by Count Vielgorsky; verses of Lamartine and a romance of Zhukovsky with music by N. Norov; and, finally, three pieces of M. Glinka, a young composer, whose efforts promise the addition of a great name to the annals of our native music. Wishing to satisfy all tastes, the editors have added an appendix containing a collection of dances for piano, by various composers."

During the year, after a lapse of several years, Glinka met Petr Stepanov again at the home of Ekaterina Kosheleva, "the daughter of a relative of ours. After dinner Glinka sat down to play, and, after he had performed several pieces and fantasies, he said, 'If you wish, I will sing you my romance,' and he sang *"Ne iskushai menia bez nuzhdy"* [Do not tempt me needlessly]. Since that day every note of the song lives in my memory" (P. Stepanov, *Vosp.,* p. 55).

During this year Glinka and Feofil Tolstoy studied Italian with Marochetti. From the son of the famous *buffo* of the Italian opera, Zamboni, Glinka "took lessons in composition. He would give me an Italian text and have me write arias and recitatives as well as two-part fugues without words. I cannot boast about these latter exercises, even though I was already somewhat familiar with Sebastian Bach's *Clavecin bien tempéré.*"

Glinka wrote these romances on Italian texts: Canzonetta in A major, Canzonetta in G minor, *"Mi sento il cor traffigere"* (C minor), *"Tu sei figlia,"* *"Ho perduto il mio tesore"* (G minor), *"Pur nel sonno"* (G major), as well as *"Molitva"* [Prayer] and *"Iako do tsaria"* ['Twas to the tsar].

"At that time we preferred to study Italian with Zamboni's daughter, who performed the contralto part in *Forty Thieves* charmingly" (F. Tolstoy, *Vosp.,* in *Rus. starina,* 1871, v. 3, part 4, p. 423). "When after two months of daily excercises at Langer's, we had barely learned to read and speak a few words. . . .

Mikhail Ivanovich already spoke quickly and fluently with a surprisingly nice Italian pronunciation and no foreign accent" (A. Kern, *Vosp.*, p. 156).

Glinka "managed to cook up a canon . . . on the following words by Prince Golitsyn: 'In this holy dwelling place'" (*Zap.*).

Composer's manuscript dating: *"Nocturne pour piano ou harpe, composé l'an 1828."*

Glinka's poem "Question (to Princess Ukhtomskaya)" was written during this year. (It was first published in coll. *Shchukinsky,* inst. no. 4, M., 1905, p. 244).
[There is no basis for refuting Glinka's authorship, as was done in G 1 (cf. *Sov. muzyka,* 1974, no. 9, p. 126).]

1829

9 February

Censor's authorization for the literary miscellany *Podsnezhnik* [Snowdrop], in which Glinka's romance on Delvig's words *"Dedushka, devitsy raz mne govorili"* was published under the title *Russkaia pesnia* [Russian song]. The poem also appeared separately.
[A second version of this song was published later by the firm "Odeum" (and later still, it was reprinted by Stellovsky).]

12 February

Sev. pchela, no. 19, contains a review of the "Lyrical Album for the Year 1829. Edited by M. Glinka and N. Pavlishchev": "For some time the passion for music has developed almost exclusively from the noble sentiments of society's higher circles. . . . The publishers of the 'Lyrical Album,' apparently, wished to satisfy these very needs, and we can easily say that they fully achieved their goal. The selection of poetic works which makes up the Album and the names of the composers who have set these works to music serve already as a guarantee of the pleasure which this beautiful collection of musical pieces will give the music lover. Those who were lucky enough to have heard all or some of these pieces before are sure of the publishers' success and that their Album will receive a flattering reception from the public here."

18 March

There is an announcement in a supplement to *SPb. ved.*, no. 65, that the "Lyrical Album for the Year 1829," edited by Glinka and Pavlishchev, is available in Glazunov's store.

5 April

In a supplement to *SPb. ved.*, no. 81, there is an announcement that the miscellany *Snowdrop*, in which Glinka's romance *"Dedushka, devitsy raz mne govorili"* was printed, is on sale in I. Slenin's bookstore.

April

There is a review of the "Lyrical Album for the Year 1829" in *Mosk. telegraf* [Moscow Telegraph], no. 7, part 26, in the section headed "Russian Literature. Contemporary Bibliography. Books for 1829": "This collection of pieces, published in the form of an album, is distinguished by the beauty of the selection and the beauty of the publication."

May–June

Glinka is sick (*Zap.*).

28 June

Glinka and Rimsky-Korsak leave for Vyborg on their way to Imatra, following the Delvigs, Orest Somov, and Anna Kern (O. Somov, (?) "Four Days in Finland," in *Sev. pchela,* 12 Sept. 1829).

29 June

Vyborg. They stayed in the hotel of a Signor Motti. "When we returned to the hotel we realized that our company had increased by two more companions. M. I. Glinka, the well-known amateur musician, whom you probably know from his beautiful musical compositions, caught up with us in Vyborg and had with him a cheerful colleague whom we all knew." Departure for Imatra that same day (*Sev. pchela,* 17 Sept. 1829; A. Kern, *Vosp.*, p. 150).
[The building in Vyborg where Glinka stayed still stands. There is now a memorial plaque on the building.]

Sitola. During the trip Glinka "completely forgot that he was melancholy."

Imatra. Trip to the waterfall. "Various names had been written on some of the rocks on the shore, and one of them was dearly known to us all, E. A. Baratynsky. Following suit, we wrote our own names there also" (A. Kern, *Vosp.*, p. 151). Between 10 and 12 o'clock that evening they took a second trip to the waterfall. "Dreams crowded . . . my imagination, thoughts gave way to thoughts like waves following upon waves. . . . My main, overriding thought was that I saw before me something enormous and living that moved, that was in a state of unrest, and that moaned in its passion like a living creature. Such was the uneasiness this caused me that nothing has ever suppressed it. Centuries will pass over Imatra, and every moment, changeless and never silent, will be filled by this stormy surging, boiling, roaring, and thundering. . . . It was nearly midnight when we returned to our lodging for the night."

Sitola. They spent the night in Sitola.

30 June

Imatra. "The remaining hours of the morning we spent in Imatra. . . . We left Imatra slowly and unwillingly" (O. Somov, "Four Days in Finland," in *Lit. gaz.* [Literary Gazette], 1830, no. 34).

Sitola. They set out on their return trip. "Glinka sat with Somov in the cart."

Ikhandola, Bentgila. They passed two stations. "Our driver . . . sang Finnish songs; he was in a cheerful mood and on occasion conversed with us in Russian, despite his limited knowledge of the Russian language. 'What's your name, friend?' I asked him. 'Simka, or as you would say Simon Yakovlevich'" (O. Somov, "Four Days in Finland," in *Sev. pchela*, 21 and 26 Sept. 1829).

Bentgila. While they were changing the horses, "we noticed that he [Glinka] was standing with a pencil and piece of paper in his hand next to a half-torn-down shed writing something, while our driver standing in front of him sang some song. Having committed to paper what he needed to, he led the Finn to us and had him sing his song" (A. Kern, *Vosp.*, p. 153). "At our last stop in Bentgila, Simon Yakovlevich parted company with us. . . . For the whole trip he had been invariably cheerful, except for that minute when he said good-bye to us. He sang us Finnish songs, one of which pleased us all with its attractive melody. One of our colleagues, a music lover, recorded the tune" (*Lit. gaz.*, 1830, no. 35).

["You had to have heard then how Glinka played this tune with variations and what he made of these few primitive, melancholy notes!" (A. Kern, *Vosp.*, p. 153). Finnish Song for piano was attached to this issue of *Lit. gaz.*. In 1838 it was used for Finn's ballad in the opera *Ruslan and Lyudmila*.]

Vyborg. Arrival at seven o'clock in the evening. They saw the sights of the city and the garden of Baron Nikolay.

Night of 30 June/1 July

Between twelve and one o'clock, they leave for Petersburg.

Lillpero, Gotaka, Kiuriulia, Pampala, Kivinebb, Raiyaiokki. The return route to Petersburg.

1 July

Beloostrovka. Inspection of their baggage by a customs official for contraband.

Petersburg. "We came into the city on the evening of July 1 like homeless wanderers, since, on the pretext of having gone for a walk, we were not able to get into our apartment immediately" (*Lit. gaz.*, 1830, no. 36).

Beginning of July

On their return from Imatra, Glinka and Rimsky-Korsak "successfully entertained the Delvigs, Kern, and Somov with Kolmakov and Oginsky."
[According to Glinka, Assistant-Inspector Kolmakov of the Boarding School for Nobility and the instructor Oginsky played comical scenes at times in the company of friends (*Zap.*).]

Summer

Glinka wrote the romance *"Noch' osenniaia, noch' liubeznaia"* [Gentle autumnal night] to words of Rimsky-Korsak.

Glinka frequently visited the Delvigs, who lived at their dacha at Krestovsky Ferry, and "often heard Naryshkin's horn music on the Neva. Szymanowska's piece *'Vilia,'* which consisted solely of arpeggios, had a particularly magical effect on me."

Delvig wrote the words for Glinka's song *"Ne osennii chastyi dozhdichek"* [Not the frequent autumnal rains]. "I subsequently used the music to these words for Antonida's romance *"Ne o tom skorbliu, podruzhen'ki"* [It is not that which I lament] in the opera *Ruslan and Lyudmila*."

The following works belong to this period: song with chorus on words by Delvig, *"Drugi, drugi (Zastol'naia pesnia)"* [Friends, friends ("Drinking song")]

(The autograph of the choral parts is on the reverse side of the score for the chorus of the song *"Ne osennii chastyi dozhdichek."*); the score *Valse tirée d' "Oberon" par Stéritch arrangé pour les 2 Violons, Basse, Flûte, 2 Clarinettes, 2 Cors, Trompette, Trombone et Timbales;* and a revision of the "Finnish Song" for piano.

10 August

Censor's authorization for "Odeum's" edition of the romances *"Bednyi pevets"* and *"Svetit mesiats na kladbishche"* (under the title *"Net ego! Na tom on svete"*).

End of the Summer

Oranienbaum. Pleasure trip with Anna Kern and the Delvigs to see Olga Pavlishcheva (A. Kern, *Vosp.,* p. 155).

19 September

Petersburg. Glinka's romance to Zhukovsky's words *"Svetit mesiats na kladbishche"* was published in a musical supplement to the *Nevskii al'manakh* [Nevsky almanac] for 1830 (d.c.a.).

Between 4 August and October

At Evgeny Shterich's home Glinka had a Persian song performed by the secretary to the Persian Prince Khozrev Mirza. "This melody served me for the chorus *"Lozhitsia v pole mrak nochnoi"* [The gloom of night lies over the field] in the opera *Ruslan and Lyudmila."*
[Khozrev Mirza arrived in Petersburg on 4 August 1829, in the capacity of an ambassador with "apologies" and expensive gifts for Nicholas I after the brutal execution of Griboedov in Teheran. The song written by Glinka is a folk song "which throws the Persians into a frenzy" (A. Gangeblov, *Vosp.,* in *Rus. archiv,* 1886, part 2, inst. 6, p. 244).]

September (?)

"At about this time, pain, especially in my tonsils, became so intense that I rolled on the floor in agony and bit myself because of the unbearable torment." Glinka notified his parents of his condition.

Fall

Glinka "was at the Lvovs," where his quartet in F major *"Come di gloria al nome"* was performed (*Zap.*).

At a party at Rimsky-Korsak's, Glinka urged Kolmakov and Oginsky to do their comic antics for Delvig's amusement (I. Panaev, *Vosp.*, p. 145).

Glinka often visited the Pavlishchevs. The tenor Ivanov, Mickiewicz, Zhukovsky, Delvig, and Kern also frequented their home. Glinka gladly sang and played (A. Yatsevich, *Pushkinskii Peterburg* [Pushkin's Petersburg], Leningrad, 1930).

Glinka continued to participate in gatherings of a small circle of friends from the Boarding School (A. Podolinsky, *Vosp.*, in *Rus. archiv*, 1872, v. 1, insts. 3–4, p. 859).

Glinka "began to think about travelling abroad." He read a book about a trip to Spain and "from that very moment I dreamed about this absorbing country" (*Zap.*).

Before October

Glinka met Nikolay Titov, who showed Glinka his romance *"Sharf goluboi"* [The sky-blue scarf]. Glinka approved of the romance and made several corrections in it (M. Blinova, "Nikolay Alekseevich Titov," ITMK, manuscript).

Beginning of October

Evgenia Andreevna Glinka arrived with her daughter Natalia and took Glinka to Novospasskoe (*Zap.*). Apparently, during the time that Evgenia Andreevna was in St. Petersburg, Ivan Glinka's complaint concerning the improper assessment of his liquor revenues was given to the tsar for the second time (G 2-A, p. 59).

Middle of October

Novospasskoe. Upon his arrival in the country, Glinka asked his father's permission to travel abroad. His refusal "distressed [me] to the point of tears."

Before 27 October

Glinka composed "several small pieces, . . . the romance *"Golos s togo sveta"* [A voice from the other world] to words by Zhukovsky . . . and six [seven] contralto études for my sister Natalia Ivanovna" (*Zap.*).

27 October

Glinka sends the publisher Bernard his song on Rimsky-Korsak's words *"Noch' osenniaia, liubeznaia"* and the romance on Zhukovsky's words *"Golos s togo sveta."* "I shall not fail to provide you with a few more pieces of my composition. I am fully convinced that you will see to it that they are printed carefully. I attach great importance to this. In my opinion, accuracy is worth more than luxury" (ltr. to M. Bernard, 27 October 1829; Fr. original).
[The romance *"Noch' osenniaia, liubeznaia"* was first published in *SPb. vest.*, 1831, no. 22.]

Fall–Winter

Glinka "learned Hummel's Septet and immediately performed it with accompaniment. I perfected my piano playing by steady practice of the études of Cramer and Moscheles and sometimes even worked on Bach. I composed several minor pieces, which are in the green notebook" (*Zap.*).
[The following compositions by Glinka are included in the "Green Notebook": Prologue on the death of the Emperor Alexander I and the accession of Nicholas I (the manuscript has no title); Etudes for N. I. Glinka (untitled): *Trot de cavalerie* in D, *Trot de cavalerie* in C, *Fugue à 3 voix* in E-flat, *Fugue à 3 voix à 2 sujets* in A minor, *Fugue à 4 voix* in D; a Georgian song and postscript to it; a Russian song (*Akh ty, dushechka*); *"Bednyi pevets"*; a "Song" (*"Dedushka, devitsy raz mne govorili"*); *"Zabudu l' ia?"* [Shall I forget?]; a "Song" (*"Akh ty, noch'"*); *"Golos s togo sveta"*; *"Pour un moment"*; *"Le baiser"*; *"Svetit mesiats"*; and *"Ne iskushai."* The minor pieces apparently are the Cavalry trots and the fugues.]

Winter

Glinka instructed his sister Lyudmila in music and geography. "In a room for my younger sisters and brother I constructed a little hill out of boards, which they could ride on in brass wash basins" (*Zap.*). "My brother taught me music and played easy overtures with me in versions for piano duet, but he wanted me to play 'Don Giovanni' with him just as fast as he played it. I wasn't able to at all, and he announced to me that I should not come back to him until I had learned to play it as he wished. What could I do? Despite the fact that I was only 13 years old, I managed to fulfill his wishes. Whenever we played this overture together, he would say to me, 'You see, patience and hard work overcome all things'" (L. Shestakova's ltr. to E. Napravnik, 21 February 1894, in *L.*, p. 60).

Glinka compiled notes on geography for his sister Lyudmila.
[Five small pages have been preserved. (In the 1890s Shestakova gave away individual pages of the notes as gifts. Some carry attributions and dedicatory inscriptions.)]

End of the Year

The regimental doctor Spindler arrived in Novospasskoe. After examining Glinka, he announced to his father that Glinka had "a whole quadrille of illnesses" and he recommended going abroad for "not less that three years. . . . Thus my trip to Italy and Germany was decided."

To this year belongs the composition of a French quadrille for piano (the year of composition is given on Stellovsky's edition).

1822–1830

Whenever Glinka came to visit his parents, who knew his fondness for folk dances and songs, they placed a large room at his disposal in which country banquets were held in Glinka's presence. There were singing, dancing, and games, in all of which Glinka took part (according to words of Aleksey Netoev, in *Bayan,* 1888, no. 34).

1830

24 February

In *Sev. Merkury* [Northern Mercury], no. 24, there is an announcement about the "Nevsky Almanac for 1830," in which Glinka's romance *"Svetit mesiats na kladbishche"* is printed.

28 February

Glinka's application addressed to the office of the ruling civil governor of Smolensk, Vice Governor and Knight Gavriil Korneevich Selastennik, for the issuance of a passport for a trip to Italy and Germany "for a period of three years for medical treatment." "The matter concerning provision of a passport to Titular Councillor Mikhail Glinka for a journey to foreign parts" begun on this date was concluded on 19 April 1830 (RMG, 1907, no. 24/25). The governor of Smolensk made a written statement to the Governor General, Prince Khovansky, about granting Glinka's leave. To the statement were attached certificates "from noble persons having no objections to M. I. Glinka's leaving to travel abroad," a description of Glinka's features, a signed statement by Glinka concerning his obligation to return to Russia his father's house serf Ulyanov, and 1 ruble, 50 kopeks for the passport. The governor reported that in view of the guarantees of "the aforementioned noble persons" he found no obstacle to Glinka's leave.

[In the "Case concerning provision of a passport to Titular Councillor Mikhail Glinka for a journey to foreign parts" there appears the following description of his features: "age, 25; of small stature—2 arshins to 2 1/2 at the most in height; forehead medium; hair dark; eyebrows black; eyes brown; nose moderate, oblong; mouth moderate; chin moderate; face white; particular features: on the left temple a small wart and a forelock on the right side of the head" (RMG, 1907, no. 24/25). The testimonies of eight people, Glinka's guarantors, are attached to this document. Among those signing are Ivan Glinka, Sergey Glinka, Prince Grigory Drutskoy-Sokolinsky, A. Zagryazhsky, Roman Gerngross, and others (G 2-B).]

15 March

Nikolay Ivanov makes application to the Director of the Court Chapel, Fedor Lvov, to be sent to Italy in order to perfect himself in singing: "Regarding this very matter I beg to submit that the musician Mr. Glinka, who is known to your excellency for his talent and knowledge, is departing for Italy in May of this very year and has offered me his companionship, which for the attainment of my goal would be most beneficial" (*RMG,* 1903, no. 47).

17 March

Approval by the Governor-General (No. 1466) of Glinka's leave to travel abroad (*RMG,* 1907, no. 24/25).

[On this date Glinka was issued a foreign passport for a period of three years "from the date cited below" (G 2-B).]

18 March

F. Lvov writes the Minister of the Court, P. Volkonsky, in support of Ivanov's petition: "To fulfill Ivanov's intentions a most convenient circumstance has presented itself, for a certain landowner from Smolensk, Mikhail Glinka, a Titular Councillor on leave of absence and a passionate music enthusiast who is very learned in this field, offers him his companionship. This coming May, Glinka is travelling from Russia to Ems in order to take the cure there and thence to Naples or Milan to study music at the academy" (*RMG,* 1903, no. 47).

19 April

Conclusion of the procedure for obtaining Glinka's foreign passport.

22 April

In *Sev. pchela,* no. 48, in the section "Miscellany," there is a notice about the publisher Bernard's tasteful presentation of *Hommage à la jeunesse de St.-Pétersbourg:* "look, for example, at the vignette on the title page of Mr. Glinka's beautiful romance '*Svetit mesiats.*'"

March–April

Glinka's health "went from bad to worse" (*Zap.*).

Beginning of April (?)

Glinka composed the Quartet in F for strings: "My sickness at the time is reflected in it."

Ca. April 20

Nikolay Ivanov's arrival in Novospasskoe for the trip abroad with Glinka (*Zap.*).

Before 25 April

Composer's dating on a transcription of the quartet in F for piano duet: "1830, *avril.*"

25 April

Glinka's and Ivanov's departure, along with Evgenia Andreevna Glinka, who accompanied them as far as Smolensk.

Beginning of May

Smolensk. Departure.

Smolensk to Brest-Litovsk. "From Smolensk to Brest-Litovsk my brother-in-law (*beau-frère*) Yakov Mikhaylovich Sobolevsky and his servant Aleksey (a violinist) accompanied us. . . . It was cold and snowing."

Brest-Litovsk. "We said good-by to the old fellow and Aleksey here and . . . the two of us set out for Warsaw."

Warsaw. "We left in a carriage for Dresden with three confectioners from Grazbinden."

First Half of May

Dresden. Glinka consulted with a doctor who recommended "first the waters at Ems and then those at Aachen. From Dresden we travelled to Leipzig."

20 May

In Petersburg the "Finnish Song, transcribed by M. I. Glinka" was published in the form of an addendum to Orest Somov's article "Four Days in Finland" (*Lit. gaz.,* 1830, no. 35).

May

Ems. Over the course of three weeks Glinka drank waters which "considerably weakened" him. After that he left for Leipzig.

From Leipzig to Frankfurt-am-Main. They travelled "in a carriage for a long time. A student travelled with us . . . who sang bass. Every time we stopped for dinner or the night's lodging, if we found a piano, we tried to sing together: Ivanov, first, and I, second tenor, and the student sang the bass part of well-known excerpts from operas: the chorus and trio from the first act of *Freischütz* (*Terzett und Chor*) went especially well, and Germans in the small towns gathered to listen to us."

From Frankfurt to Mainz. "From there by steamer on the Rhine; short of Koblenz, we went ashore and walked around in Ems."

25 June

There is an announcement in *Lit. gaz.,* no. 36, of the forthcoming separate publication of Somov's article "Four Days in Finland" with the "Finnish Song" as an addendum.

End of June

Aachen. Glinka took the waters. "In a very short time I felt . . . significant benefit," but drinking the water and bathing to excess had a baneful effect on his health (*Zap.*).

Beginning of July (?)

In Petersburg, separate publication as a small booklet of Somov's essay "Four Days in Finland," with six scenes drawn by V. Langer, and the music of the "Finnish Song" (*Lit. gaz.*, 25 June 1830).

11 July

In a letter (from Novospasskoe) to Nikolay Pavlishchev, Ivan Glinka asks that he send him 2 copies of the "Lyrical Album for the Year 1829" (*Mus. letopis'* [Musical Annals], 1925, coll. 3, p. 131).

July

"In an Aachen theater . . . a troupe of good German singers en route from Paris was performing." Glinka and Ivanov heard *Fidelio*. "The first time . . . we did not understand, but the second performance brought us to tears." In addition they heard *Freischütz* and Spohr's *Faust*. "The soprano roles were sung quite precisely by Mme Fischer. At that time Haizinger and Eichberger were justifiably considered the best tenors in Germany."

Beginning of August

Ems. Arrival in order to meet Shterich (*Zap.*).

9/21 August

Stepan Shevyrev reports in a letter (from Rome) to Sergey Sobolevsky: "Poor Glinka (the musician) died on the way to Italy" (*L.*, p. 63).

18/30 August

Sobolevsky writes (from Turin) to Shevyrev: "I feel pity for the married Pushkin . . . even more so for those married to Ushakovs, but most of all I am sorry for my poor Glinka, who has died" (*Rus. arkhiv*, 1909, bk. 2, inst. 7, p. 486).

August

Schlangenbad. Arrival of Glinka and Ivanov with Shterich and his mother.

Frankfurt. Arrival of Glinka and Ivanov with Shterich and his mother. "We saw the famous statue of Ariadne and in the theater heard Cherubini's opera *Médée.* I confess that I only understood the overture, which was performed excellently. The rest I could not make out at all."
[The statue of Ariadne was done by the German sculptor Heinrich von Dannecker (1758–1851).]

From Frankfurt, Glinka and Ivanov travelled by stagecoach to Basel.

Basel. Glinka and Ivanov met the Shteriches here and headed the next day by way of Solothurn, Bern, and Lausanne, to Geneva. "With the Shteriches we admired the splendid sights of Switzerland."

Geneva. "The Shteriches in their own carriage and we in the stagecoach travelled together to Milan by way of Simplon."

Beginning of September (O.S.)

Milan. Arrival in Milan. "We stayed temporarily in the Albergo del Pozzo, which was not far from the famous Domo di Milano."
[Albergo del Pozzo is the name of a hotel.]

Glinka was enthralled with the sight "of the splendid white marble cathedral and of the city itself." Soon they found a permanent apartment, and "we moved into the *Corso di porta Renza (orientale)* across from the column of *Leone della porta Renza* and the church of *S-ta Babilla,* at no. 626. . . . Our apartment consisted of one large room with three windows on the street." The landlady was Guiseppa Abbondio.

"Among our neighbors I must mention a young girl of pleasant appearance. Her name was Adelaide, *Didina* as they say in Milan. We were first brought together by the sounds of our piano and then got in the habit of seeing each other often. She lived in the same house with us" (*Zap.*).

6 September

In Petersburg Ivan Glinka's case regarding his liquor license was submitted to the Senate for consideration (G 2-A, p. 59).

October

Turin. Glinka arrived in Turin to visit Shterich, who was attached to the Russian consulate at the Sardinian court (*Zap.;* ltr. from S. Sobolevsky to S. Shevyrev, 8/20 November 1830, in *L.,* p. 64).

"In Turin I heard a beautiful performance of the opera *buffa Gli cantatrici villani*. The prima donna Unger sang excellently and played her part very naturally. I also heard Duprez there. His voice at that time was clear but not strong. Even then he sang somewhat in the French style, that is, *il relevait chaque note avec affectation*."

Beginning of November

Milan. Return from Turin. Ivanov began to take singing lessons from Eliodoro Bianchi, and Glinka began lessons with the composition teacher and director of the Milan Conscrvatory, Basili. "He had me work with four parts in the following fashion: one voice proceded in whole notes; another in half notes; the third in quarter notes; and the fourth in eighth notes. . . . My ardent imagination could not submit itself to such dry and unpoetic labors. I did not study long with Basili and soon gave up lessons with him."

8/20 November

Sobolevsky (from Turin) writes Shevyrev: "Apropos of Glinka's death, I will tell you the news: the musician Glinka was here ten days ago and now, in perfect health, has gone to Milan. Notify those who told you of his death on the way to Italy of this" (*Rus. arkhiv,* 1909, bk. 2, inst. 7, p. 492).

13/25 November

By way of informing Sobolevsky of his long-range plans (winter and spring to be spent in Milan and the following fall to travel to Naples) and of his impressions of Milan's theaters, Glinka writes: "It is entirely understandable to me why you find Italy foolish and boring. One has to be an artist in order to grasp her fascination."

24 November/6 December

Glinka writes to Sobolevsky: "Probably the news has reached you that I came abroad not only to restore my health but also for other *secret* reasons which drove me to become an artist. . . . I intend . . . to fully devote myself to art."

Reporting on how he is spending his time, he writes: "In my opinion I am living very agreeably. Until 1 o'clock in the afternoon I am so busy that I do not have time to be bored. Moreover . . . Ivanov lives with me. . . . In all respects Italy is a second homeland for me. Here for the first time after long suffering I am beginning to put my life in order."

November–December

"In the evenings" around Glinka and Ivanov "there soon formed . . . a company of third-rank singers both old and young, male and female, who lived in the vicinity."

Glinka began to study Spanish with the musician Quatrini (*Zap.*).

11/23 December

Sobolevsky arrived to see Glinka.

13/25 December

Sobolevsky writes Shevyrev: "I am definitely leaving from here on the 3rd of January. I am now in Milan to see Glinka for two days" (*Rus. arkhiv,* 1909, bk. 2, inst. 7, p. 495).

14/26 December

At the season's opening performance in the Carcano Theater, Glinka heard the Donizetti opera *Anna Bolena*. "The performance was like magic for me. Rubini, Pasta (who performed the role of Anna Bolena exceptionally well, especially the last scene), Galli, and Orlandi, et al. participated. . . . I wallowed in pleasure, especially since at that time I was not yet indifferent to *virtuosité*."

31 December 1830/11 January 1831

Ivanov writes to Fedor Lvov: ". . . I continue to be engaged with Mikhail Ivanovich Glinka and am beginning now to understand him somewhat" (*RMG,* 1903, no. 47).

End of the Year

In Petersburg the romance *"Gor'ko, gor'ko mne"* (subtitled "Russian Song") is published in "'Musical Album for the Year 1831,' Assembled and Dedicated to the Fair Sex by I. Romanus."

1830/31

Winter

In the Carcano Theater Glinka heard Rossini's *Semiramide,* Zingarelli's *Romeo e Giulietta,* and Meyerbeer's *Il crociato.*

Glinka "enjoyed the use of our envoy at the Sardinian court Count Vorontsov-Dashkov's box *d'avant scène.*"

1831

End of January to the Beginning of February

Milan. Glinka "came to life with the appearance of the lovely Italian spring, and my imagination began to stir. . . . I began to work . . . beginning with variations on a theme from Donizetti's *Anna Bolena,* which I dedicated to Shterich. Then I wrote Variations on two themes from the ballet *Chao-Kang.* These I dedicated to Count Vorontsov-Dashkov. . . . That same spring I wrote a Rondo on a theme from Bellini's *Montecchi e Capuleti* [*Rondino brillante*] and dedicated it to the daughter of the Marchesa Visconti."

3/15 February

The manuscript of the *"Variazoni brillanti* on a Theme from the Opera *Anna Bolena* by Donizetti for pianoforte" was given to the publisher Ricordi for engraving (coll. *Glinka,* 1958, p. 396).
[The complete title of Glinka's variations is *"Variazioni brillanti per pianoforte composte dal sig-re M. Glinka sul motivo dell'aria "Nell veder fua costanza" cantata del celebre sig-re G. B. Rubini nell'Anna Bolena dell M-o Donizetti dall'autore dedicate al suo amico Eugenio Steritch gentiluomo di camera di sua majesta di tutto le Russie."*]

Ca. 16/28 February

"Finally at the end of carnival there appeared Bellini's long-awaited *Sonnambula.* . . . The opera had a tremendous effect. . . . Pasta and Rubini . . . sang with great vitality. In the second act they actually cried and caused the audience to do the same. . . . Shterich and I, in the envoy's box, embraced one another and shed a flood of tears from emotion and joy. When we returned home after every opera, we picked out the sounds that helped us to recall our favorite places. In a short time Ivanov was quite successfully able to sing Rubini's scenes from *Anna Bolena* and subsequently did the same with *Sonnambula* as well. I accompanied him at the piano and, moreover, imitated Pasta very aptly by playing her arias on the piano, much to the surprise and satisfaction of our landlady, neighbors, and acquaintances."

25 February/8 March

The manuscript of the Variations on Two Themes from the Ballet *Chao-Kang* was given to the publisher Ricordi for engraving (coll. *Glinka,* 1958, p. 396).
[The autograph is in the USA in the music library of Stanford University. The complete title is *Due ballabile nel balletto Chao-Kang variati per pianoforte e dedicati a sua eccelenza il sig-re conte Woronzow-Daschkow dal sig-r M. Glinka.* Shortly afterwards the piece was issued in Paris under the title *Deux airs de ballet. Pas de clochettes et Danse du mariage de Chao-Kang, ballet chinois, varié pour le piano par Glinka* (*Gazette musicale de Paris,* publisher Maurice Schlesinger) (G 1, pp. 381-82).]

Glinka visited with the Ricordi family (ltr. to Ricordi, 12 October 1833).

Glinka underwent treatment with Dr. Filippi. He visited Vorontsov-Dashkov and was introduced there to the amateur singer Count Pompeo Belgiojoso (bass) and his cousins Prince Emilio Belgiojoso and Count Belgiojoso, the latter two of whom "possessed beautiful tenor voices." At that time he also met the musical amateur Marchesa Visconti "and after that many minor artists and music enthusiasts."

Glinka was introduced to the compositions of Pollini "and soon thereafter to Pollini himself. In my opinion, he was one of the most remarkable Italian artists. . . . By rights the invention of a new style of piano playing belongs *to him and to no one else.* . . . Could Pollini have imagined that in time abominable hackwork for piano would be written as a result of his discoveries?"

2 March

In *SPb. vestnik,* no. 18, Glinka's song *"Akh ty, noch' li, nochen'ka"* was published (d.c.a.).

March

Turin. Trip to Shterich.

Spring

Como, Varenna, Lecco, Brianza, Monza. Glinka in the company of Ivanov, his Italian teacher, and Eliodoro Bianchi "set out for three days' travel in the environs of Milan" (*Zap.*).

12 May

Milan. Censor's authorization for the romance *"Ne poi, krasavitsa, pri mne"* in Petersburg (published by "Odeum").

Beginning of June (N.S.)

Turin. Trip to Shterich. He meets with Sobolevsky and makes the acquaintance of Elim Meshchersky (*Zap.*).

3/15 June

Glinka wrote the *Proshchal'nyi val's* [Farewell waltz], subsequently published by Varlamov (*Eolova arfa* [Aeolian Harp], 1834, No. 6).

June

Milan. "When I returned to Milan the intense heat increased," which Glinka could not endure. "Warm baths and doses of opium, prescribed by de Filippi, had no effect."

June

Ansano. Glinka "availed [himself] of an invitation to visit a family [he] knew . . . in Ansano. This village is not very far from the well-known valley *pian d' Erba,* which is located between Como and Lecco" (*Zap.*).

7/19 June

The *Rondino brillante* on a theme from the opera *I Capuleti ed i Montecchi* by Bellini was given to the publisher Ricordi for engraving (coll. *Glinka,* 1958, p. 396). The complete title is *Rondino brillante per pianoforte nel quale e intro-*

dotto il motive "La tremende ultrice spada" del M-o Bellini. Composto e dedicato a donna Teresa Visconti d'Arragona da M. Glinka.

8/20 July

Milan. Sobolevsky arrives in Milan to see Glinka.

9/21 July

Glinka met with Sobolevsky.

11/23 July

Glinka passes the time with Sobolevsky (Sobolevsky's diary, in *L.*, p. 69).

July

Trescore, near Bergamo. On the advice of Dr. Filippi, Glinka went with Ivanov to take the sulphuric waters, which "completely destroyed [Glinka's] nerves."

Milan. Return from Trescore to Milan, from which "the unbearable heat once more drove me out."

Trescore. Second trip, but Glinka "did not take the waters this time but only took advantage of the wonderful, pure mountain air. There was pleasant company there as well as dancing and walking."

Bergamo and Brescia. Trips from Trescore which "gave me considerable pleasure."

Before 29 July/10 August

Milan. Glinka returns to Milan (Sobolevsky's Diary, 29 July/10 August 1831, in *L.*, p. 69).

29 July/10 August

Sobolevsky writes to Shevyrev: "We are in a state of bliss here. We have Rubini and the superb Ferlotti, though she is perfectly ugly" (*L.*, p. 59).

July or August

One day Sobolevsky brought Mendelssohn to see Glinka. "After much persuasion he played a rondo of an easy sort, from which it was impossible for me to judge the extent of his talent."
[Dated according to Mendelssohn's stay in Milan.]

Beginning of Fall (before September)

Glinka "often visited friends, Pini and Besana, the latter of whom possessed a beautiful baritone voice." At this time Glinka also made the acquaintance of Josef Dessauer (*Zap.*).

Fall

A year after Glinka's arrival in Milan "passersby who met him stopped, and they spoke with one another with all the liveliness of Italians, accompanying their words with gestures. 'Look, look, there's the Russian maestro!' Actually our *maestro* had already become like a native to Milan. His works were played and sung at almost all the concerts. . . . A Russian composer in Italy, a foreigner who had caused people to talk about him in the land of music! You must agree that this is something new" (Melgunov, *Vosp.*, p. 160).

22 September

In Petersburg, censor's authorization for the "Lyrical Album for the Year 1832," edited by Ivan Laskovsky and Nikolay Norov. The lithographer was I. Beggrov.
[The contents include these romances by Glinka: on page 1, *"Zabudu l' ia"* (words by Golitsyn) and on page 28, *"Golos s togo sveta"* (words by Zhukovsky). In an appendix are two waltzes by Griboedov.]

27 September/9 October

Glinka and Ivanov leave Milan for Turin (*Zap.*; ltr. from N. Ivanov to F. Lvov, 26 September/8 October 1831, in *RMG*, 1903, no.47).

Ivanov writes to Lvov: "Tomorrow I set out from Turin by steamer via Genoa to Naples" (*RMG*, 1903, no. 47).

Turin. Arrival at Shterich's (*Zap.*).

Departure, accompanied by Shterich, to Genoa (*Zap.;* ltr. from N. Ivanov to F. Lvov, in *RMG*, 1903, no. 47).

Beginning of October (O.S.)

Genoa. Arrival in Genoa, where "we spent two days and looked at everything worthy of comment." To Glinka the city seemed to be "a realization of a description of Babylon with its hanging gardens. . . . When the day of our departure came, Shterich accompanied us in the launch to the steamer. It was my last meeting with him."

Livorno. Arrival the next day by steamer. "The weather was splendid. This was at the beginning of October."

Civitavecchia. Arrival by steamer, and "from there to Rome."

Beginning to the Middle of October (O.S.)

Rome. They spent "about two weeks" in Rome. Meeting with Shevyrev, who served in the capacity of mentor to the son of Zinaida Volkonskaya. Shevyrev showed Glinka "all the sights with commentary. I failed to be convinced of the value of the church of St. Peter, apparently because . . . I prefer Gothic and Byzantine churches to all others."

In Rome Glinka met Zinaida Volkonskaya, her sister M. Vlasova, Count Ricci, Bruni, Rozhalin, and Marietta (Copalti?) (ltr. to Z. Volkonskaya, 11/23 February, 1832).

At a party at Villa Medici held by the Director of the French Academy, Horace Vernet, Ivanov performed Glinka's romances "delightfully." Berlioz was present at this party. Glinka's romances impressed him because of their lovely melodic style, which was different from anything he had heard before (Berlioz, "Michel Glinka," in *Journal des débats*, 1845, 4/16 April; reprinted in *Mosk. ved.* in translation from the French, 1845, vol. 50, 26 April).

Ca. 20 October/1 November

Departure for Naples by stagecoach: "I was particularly captivated on this journey by the palms in Terracina and the cactuses between Itri and Fondi."

20 October/1 November

Naples. Arrival in Naples. Glinka "was in complete ecstasy and for a long time gazed to my heart's content at the unusual, splendid beauty of the sites: the transparency of the air, the clear holiday-like light—all this was new to me and fascinatingly beautiful."

In Naples the wife of the minister of the court "S. Volkonskaya . . . took us under her special patronage" (ltr. to S. Shevyrev, 29 October/10 November, 1831).

29 October/10 November

Glinka writes to Shevyrev: "Here . . . once again I am beginning to succumb to indifference to everything, even to nature's charms, for there is no one with whom to share my feelings. . . . Naples, despite the marvelous beauty of the place, is *antipatico* to me—in part because of its resemblance to Petersburg, which I hate, and in part because I find little that is Italian in the city."

10/22 November

Glinka writes to Shevyrev that Naples irritates him because of its orderly appearance of freshly painted houses and all the full-dress uniforms. "It all seems to me like I am in Petersburg. . . . My only pleasure is taking walks in the Villa and the environs of the city."

26 November/8 December

Shterich writes (from Turin) to Sobolevsky: "Our *amico* Glinka has written me long mournful epistles from Naples. The poor fellow is groaning and complaining there at the foot of Vesuvius and is considering returning to Milan" (Sobolevsky's diary, in *L.*, p. 71).

"Did I compose anything in Naples? I don't remember. It seems that I memorized some piece or another for a concert for some Englishmen."

November–December

Glinka's meeting with Karl Bryullov. Acquaintance with Bellini and Donizetti. Dinners at Sofia Volkonskaya's.

ITHACA COLLEGE LIBRARY

Glinka attended the theaters. "In the Fondo I heard Tamburini in Rossini's *Turco in Italia*. He sang and acted very well. In the S-Carlo the singer was Ronzi de Begnis, a fine artist, though her voice was already spoiled. . . . Basadonna (the tenor) was fine. My favorite theater in Naples was the little theater of S-Carlino, in which they performed in Neapolitan dialect (*vago dialetto napolitano*). The actors there were outstanding. All the well-known tragedies took on a Neapolitan character with the assistance of Pulcinella. . . . At one of the theaters, I believe the Teatro nuovo, the comic opera *Il ventaglio* was performed at that time in Neapolitan dialect. It was a rather amusing piece. . . . I . . . found it vacuous and made no attempt to meet its composer, Raimondi. Now it turns out that this same Raimondi was a very remarkable contrapuntist."

Ivanov began to take lessons with the well-known voice teacher Nozzari. His "scales from a low B-flat to the highest . . . were amazingly even and clean, that is, in his way they were just as superb as were Field's scales on the piano." Glinka met regularly with Nozzari and Josephine Fodor-Mainvielle ("simply Fedorova"). "I am more indebted to Nozzari and Fodor for my understanding of singing than I am to all other masters."

"Having at that time an opportunity to observe the style which Ivanov acquired through his lessons, he [Glinka] applied every effort toward learning the difficult and capricious art of mastering the voice and of writing according to the peculiarities of different voices. With this goal he listened attentively to the most famous singers and amateurs. In this respect Nozzari and Mme Fodor were his best assistants" *Biograficheskaia zametka* [Biographical note]).

4 December

In *Sev. pchela,* no. 276, there is an announcement of the forthcoming publication of the "Lyrical Album for the Year 1832," edited by Laskovsky and Norov, containing compositions by Glinka.

Middle of December

Glinka and Ivanov climb Vesuvius (*Zap.*).

19 December

In Petersburg, censor's authorization for the "Northern Musical Album for the Year 1832." On p. 29, it contains the song *"Noch' osenniaia, liubeznaia"* to words by Rimsky-Korsak and on p. 42, the song *"Akh, ty, noch' li, nochen'ka"* to words by Delvig.

The first version of the song *"Akh ty, noch' ..."* was published here. The second version was printed later by Stellovsky.

21 December

Melgunov writes (from Moscow) to Shevyrev: "Besides the fact that you sent me good news about yourself, you let me know about Glinka, about whom I no longer knew what to think. I had even begun to doubt whether or not he was fully alive. Now I am relieved. Yes, you were right. He is a marvelous, fine fellow. His spirit, like a full chord, cannot live without consonance. It is too bad that you did not spend much time together. You would have provided him wholesome, reliable support. From his few lines to me I can see that he is still susceptible to attacks of depression, which could ruin him more than illness. He, like all people whose emotions gain the upper hand over all their other strengths, must live by means of someone else's good sense. I talked to him about this several times and once even wrote and tried to convince him to seek out your confidence and friendship. I am sincerely happy that my wishes were realized" (*L.*, p. 72).

1832

19 January

In *Molva* [Rumor], no. 6 (Moscow), in the section headed "Musical News," there is a notice of the publication of the "Lyrical Album," edited by Laskovsky and Norov. Of the vocal works in the anthology, it states that "Glinka's romance *'Zabudu l' ia?'* and Vielgorsky's *'Quel est cet amant?'* are particularly noteworthy."

29 January

There is a notice in *Sev. pchela*, no. 23, that the "Musical Album" published by Bernard has "for a short time," i.e., recently, become available. Its contents include the following romances and songs: three by Titov, three by Glinka, one by Makarov, and two by Bernard. It also mentions among the dances a mazurka and waltz by Sterich [Shterich]. "Since the names of these composers are well known for their beautiful music, we are relieved of the obligation of praising their compositions. All music lovers have already prepared a place for Mr. Bernard's Album on their pianos."

11/23 February

Glinka thanks Zinaida Volkonskaya for her letter and invitation "to play in the philharmonic," but with his worsening health he is unable to do it, since he has "completely abandoned" playing the piano. "Nonetheless I hope that the desire to please you will make up for my lack of *savoir-faire,* if only for the few days that I can spend in Rome, and allow me to participate in the good music which is performed under your patronage" (Fr. original).

Between 10/23 and 17/29 February

Glinka "felt an unbearable depression" and decided to leave Naples. Ivanov remained behind. "I advised Ivanov at the time not to request an extension of his leave but to return to Russia and then, after spending a year there, to take leave again and return to Italy. He disregarded my advice. . . . When we parted company in Naples all relations between us came to a stop" (*Zap.;* ltr. to Z. Volkonskaya, 11/23 February 1832).

After 11/23 and Before 17/29 February

Glinka leaves for Rome (*Zap.; RMG,* 1903, no. 47; ltr. to Z. Volkonskaya, 11/28 February 1832).

17/29 February

Ivanov writes (from Naples) to Fedor Lvov about Glinka, saying that "the volcanic air here became too irritating, for which reason he found it necessary to leave Naples" (*RMG,* 1903, no. 47).

End of February (O.S.)

Rome. Glinka "did not remain long" in Rome.

Beginning of March

Bologna. Glinka arrived by stagecoach from Rome via the Marche d'Ancona. He stayed there twenty-four hours and looked at the picture gallery and the Campo Santo.

Parma, Modena, Piacenza. Glinka travelled through these cities to Milan.

Milan. Upon his arrival in Milan, Glinka took his "former apartment." "Spring renewed me, and I set to work on a serenade on themes from *Sonnambula* for piano, two violins, viola, cello, and bass." The full title of the work is *Divertimento brillante per Pianoforte con accompagnemente di due violini, viola, violoncello e contrabasso sopra alcuni motivi dell'Sonnambula del M-o Bellini composto e ridotto per pianoforte principale e pianoforte a quatro mani da M. Glinka.* The autograph is not known in Russia. Published by Ricordi in Milan in 1832.

18 March

In the "Miscellany" section of *Sev. pchela,* no. 64, there is an announcement that compositions received from Italy by Italian composers are on sale at Bernard's. "We recommend the Rondino, *Les variations,* and *Due Ballabili* of our countryman Mr. M. Glinka, who under Italy's sunny skies has developed his rare talent even further. A charming waltz, composed by Shterich, is also worthy of the attention of those who enjoy graceful dance music."

March (?)

"This spring an acquaintance of Sobolevsky presented me . . . with the words for two romances: *"Pobeditel'"* [The victor] by Zhukovsky and *"Venetsianskaia noch'"* [Venetian night] by Kozlov. I set them to music immediately." Composer's dating on the romance *"Venetsianskaia noch'"*: "Composed in Milan in 1832."

Glinka composed Variations on a Theme from the Opera *I Capuleti ed i Montecchi (L'amo, l'amo è a me pui cara)* and dedicated them to the amateur singer Countess Cassera (*Zap.*). The full title is *Variazioni per il pianoforte sull'aria del tenore nell'opera del M-o Bellini I Montecchi e Capuleti composte de M. Glinka e da lui dedicate alla nobile madamigella la signora contessina Angiola Cassera dilletanta distinita.*

Glinka heard Bellini's *Norma* at La Scala. "The singers included Pasta, Donzelli, and Giulietta Grisi," who was "remarkably fine, though she sang a bit 'cat-like,' that is, wanting to soften every phrase and miaowing somewhat through the nose. I liked *Otello* [by Rossini] better, both as music and as drama. In the last scene Donzelli was so superb that he was frightening to look at."

After several "artificial sulphuric-ferrous baths," Glinka "felt a rush of blood in my head, which later erupted in such strong nervous attacks, that my doctor de Filippi considered it necessary to get me out of Milan, where it was already becoming too hot."

Luinate. Glinka stayed with Doctor Branca in the village of Luinate near the small town of Varese between lakes Maggiore and Como. De Filippi's married daughter lived here. She "played the piano so well that even the finest artists visited her, for example Chopin."

Glinka "often called on de Filippi's daughter, for the similarity of our education and our passion for the same art had to attract us to each other."

21 April/3 May

For Filippi's daughter Glinka began writing the *Gran sestetto originale* for piano, two violins, viola, cello and bass, "taking account of her strong piano playing" (*Zap.*; composer's dating).
[The complete title is *Gran sestetto originale per pianoforte, due violini, viola, violoncello e contrabasso composto e dedicato a M-lla Sofia Medici de' Marchesi di Marignano da M. Glinka*.]

23 April/5 May

The Variations on a Theme from the Opera *I Capuleti ed i Montecchi* by Bellini for piano was given to the publisher Ricordi for engraving (coll. *Glinka*, 1958, p. 396).

9/21 June

Composer's dating on the fourth page of the manuscript of the Sextet: "Luinate, 3 *di maggio*—21 *guigno*."

Milan. "Whenever I was in Milan I frequently visited Pollini, who had taken a liking to me. . . . At his home I often met Bellini, with whom I became friends to a certain extent. . . . We often talked about German composers, though he was not well acquainted with them. He wrote according to his feelings, trying primarily to move the hearts of the ladies."

"I began working on a serenade on themes from Donizetti's *Anna Bolena* after I had become acquainted with the family of the attorney Branca, whose oldest daughter, Cyrilla Cambiaggio, played the piano beautifully and whose second daughter, Emilia, played the harp quite well.

11/23 June

Varese. Glinka began writing the Serenade on Themes from the Opera *Anna Bolena*. There is an inscription on the score: *Serenata sopra in motivi dell' Anna Bolena*, which is dated at the beginning: *Varese il 23 guigno*. The manuscript is in the Département de la Musique of the Bibliothèque Nationale in Paris (G 1, p. 383).

17/29 June

Varese. Glinka thanks Sobolevsky for his "invitation to roam" with him "in Milan's beautiful environs," but since "circumstances do not permit [him] to hop over to Milan," he invites Sobolevsky to come to Varese. "You will find me in the *casa del dottore Branca*, who will show you everything."

20 June/2 July

Glinka informs Sobolevsky that he has received his letter. He writes that he is sick (fever and spasms).

22 June/3 July

Glinka asks Sobolevsky to inquire at the Turin post office if he has gotten any letters and to give him Shevyrev's address.

24 June/6 July

The *Divertimento brillante* on themes from the opera *Sonnambula* by Bellini for piano, two violins, viola, cello, and bass, as well as for piano with accompaniment of a second piano four-hands, are given to the publisher Ricordi for engraving (coll. *Glinka*, 1958, p. 398).

11/23 July

Glinka completes the Serenade on Themes from the Opera *Anna Bolena*. "*Terminato il 23 luglio*" (G 1, p. 383).

In a letter to Sobolevsky, Glinka asks if there has been no news from Turin. He invites him [Sobolevsky] to Varese. "I'll not write further, for my uniform way of life doesn't make for very interesting news."

July

Milan. The *Divertimento brillante* on themes from the opera *Sonnambula* was "performed outstandingly" by a student of Pollini's (the young girl to whom Glinka dedicated the piece), "accompanied by the best musicians in Milan."

Milan. The Serenade on themes from the opera *Anna Bolena* was performed on the terrace of the home of the attorney Branca. "We had hoped for a grand effect, but we had not counted on the poor acoustics, and the sound was scattered in all directions. Despite this, during the rehearsal the piece went well. It was played by the principal artists of the Teatro della Scala. When I heard for the first time the viola solo of my piece played by the celebrated Rolla, tears welled up in my eyes because of the cleanness and accuracy of the playing, but still he asked for my advice."

May–August

During this period Ricordi published the following works by Glinka: *Variazioni sull' Aria "L'amo, ah! l'amo" nell' Opera I Capuletti e Montecchi del Maestro Bellini* and *Divertimento brillante per Pianoforte con accompagnemento di due Violini, Viola, Violoncello e Contrabasso sopra alcuni motivi della Sonnambula,* and the same works for piano accompanied by second piano four-hands (*Sov. muzyka,* 1954, no. 6, p. 95).

Summer

Because of the forced separation from Filippi's daughter, Glinka composed the romance to words by Felice Romani *"Ah, se tu fossi mecco"* (*Zap.*).

8/20 August

In a letter to Sobolevsky, Glinka thanks him for his troubles. He reports that he is suffering from fever and nerves and that "in order to drive away the depression which recently has subdued" him, he is travelling "from Milan to Varese and back." Glinka leaves this day for Milan, "probably . . . until the first of September."

1/13 September

The manuscript of the Serenade on Themes from the Opera *Anna Bolena* was given to the publisher Ricordi to be engraved.

12/24 September

The manuscript of the *Impromptu en galop* on the barcarolle from the Donizetti opera *L'elisir d'amore* for piano four-hands is given to the publisher Ricordi to be engraved (coll. *Glinka, 1958*, p. 398).

Beginning of Fall

Milan. Glinka meets with Feofil Tolstoy and spends 10 days with him. Tolstoy found that during his stay in Italy, Glinka "had changed a great deal physically. . . . His face had grown somewhat thin, and his eyes had lost some of their customary brightness. In general it was apparent that he was very depressed." In conversation with Tolstoy, Glinka "laid out in detail the plan for a large five-act national opera which he had conceived. . . . The story was thoroughly national with a strong patriotic coloring and was rather gloomy. . . . He was already able to play . . . the theme of *'Kak mat' ubili'* [How mother was killed], and he pointed with pride to the counterpoint in *'Vse pro ptenchika, moi Vanya'* [Everything for my nestling, my Vanya]. 'What do you think of the double counterpoint?' he kept asking, singling out first the left and then the right hand of the phrase which is so well known today. Nothing was said at that time about words and speeches, but the thought of embellishing the simple folk melody by, as he expressed it, all the *devices of musical wisdom*, was already fully matured in Glinka's mind. 'The themes will remain as they are,' he would say in his peculiar language, 'and the cut of the sarafan or caftan will not change, but what happens so far as accessories are concerned, that will be compliments of me! And I'll not be niggardly about it!'" (F. Tolstoy, *Vosp.*, p. 106).

15/27 September

Como. Glinka and Sobolevsky visit Giuditta Pasta "on her name day at her private villa" (*Zap.*).
[Giuditta Pasta's name day may have been (according to the new calendar) 6 May, 29 June, or 27 September. In his *Zapiski* Glinka places the trip in the spring of 1833, but on the 6th of May the theater season was not yet over, and Glinka himself mentions attending a performance of *Norma* at La Scala in which Pasta sang at approximately this time. On the 29th of June (N.S.) Glinka wrote to Sobolevsky and invited him to travel to Varese. Thus the most probable date is 15/27 September (cf. also S. Sobolevsky's ltr. to S. Shevyrev, 2/14 November 1832).]

End of September to the End of October (N.S.)

Tramezzo. Glinka visited at the villa of his acquaintance Giulini "in the middle of Lake Como. . . . It was the last indisputably pleasant period which I spent in

Italy. . . . Early in the morning . . . after a short walk, I continued work on the sextet, for which I was writing a Finale. Before dinner everyone got together, sometimes to sing, sometimes to talk. After dinner . . . we went for a walk. A month was hardly adequate in which to see the beautiful, immediate environs."

20 September/2 October

Composer's dating on the manuscript of the beginning of the third movement (finale) of the piano score of the Sextet: *"2 ottobre."*

5/17 October

Composer's dating on the draft manuscript of the sextet: *"Terminato a Tramezzo il 17 ottobre."*
[Because of gossip about Glinka's friendship with Filippi's daughter, he had to dedicate the sextet to her friend Sofia Medici (*Zap.*).]

Glinka wrote the trio for piano, clarinet, and bassoon and expressed "the deep despair" brought on by illness in it. On the title page of the piano score is Glinka's inscription: *"Trio pathétique pour Pianoforte, clarinette et basson par M. Glinka."* Below is the epigraph: *"Je n'ai connu l'amour que par les peines qu'il cause."*
[The following note is attached to an excerpt of the autograph manuscript of the trio: *"Fragment du Trio pathétique (Re-min) pour piano, clarinette en si min. et basson composé par M. Glinka à Tramezzino sur le lac de Côme en 1832"* with the same epigraph (*L.*, p. 76).]

18/30 October

Varese. In a letter to Ricordi, Glinka requests one copy of each of his works published by Ricordi to be sent to him by way of Sobolevsky.
[By this time Ricordi had published the following works of Glinka: *Variazioni brillanti per pianoforte composte dal sig-re M. Glinka sul motivo dell'aria "Nell veder la tua costanza" cantata del celebre sig-re G. B. Rubini nell' Anna Bolena dell M-o Donizetti* (1831); *Due ballabile nel balletto Chao-Kang variati per pianoforte* (1831); *Rondino brillante per pianoforte nel quale e introdotto il motive "La tremende ultrice spada" del M-o Bellini;* at the end of 1832 the *Serenata sopra alcuni motivi dell'opera Anna Bolena* for piano, harp, French horn, bassoon, viola, cello, and bass was printed.]

October

Glinka composed an exit aria for the singer Tosi for her debut in Donizetti's *Fausta,* "successfully, I believe, i.e., very much in the style of Bellini." Tosi, however, requested that changes be made, and Glinka "could not satisfy her at all. I got so sick of this *pretentiousness* that I vowed not to write for Italian prima donnas."

2/14 November

Milan. Sobolevsky writes to Shevyrev: "I ate hazel grouse all fall with Glinka on Lake Como. Glinka, by the way, sends his regards to you all. He has begun to think that he is recovering and is preoccupied with music. His printed compositions stand in high regard here, and he has many musical projects in mind for when he returns. It would not hurt anything to blow his horn a bit in the newspapers. Ricordi told me that he considers Glinka to be on a par with Bellini and Donizetti, but *more learned* than they in counterpoint. Herald him, for it will be beneficial to him in the future and sweet to our ears. Musically he recoils somewhat from the Germans and acknowledges that our national [music] must more resemble the Italian, just as you had thought about poetry" (*L.,* p. 76).

November

Glinka's sextet was performed at the home of Sofia Medici, whose performance of the piano part was "unsatisfactory, though the piece was carried by the excellent musicians who accompanied her."

End of Fall

Glinka composed a cavatina for the opera *Beatrice di Tenda* [to words by Pini].

Fall–Winter

Glinka attended the theaters. "They were then performing the outstanding fantastic ballet *Masquerade.*"

September–December

During this period Ricordi published the following compositions by Glinka: *Impromptu en galop pour P.F. à 4 mains sur la Barcarolle de Donizetti dans L'Elisir d'amore* and *Serenata sopra alcuni motivi dell' Opera Anna Bolena* (*Sov. muzyka,* 1954, no. 6, p. 96).

9 December

In *Molva* (Moscow), no. 99, there is a notice entitled "News from Italy" by Melgunov: "M.I. Glinka, well known for his music, left for Italy with our renowned singer Ivanov and has acquired great fame and prominence in the classical land of music. Ricordi, Europe's premier music publisher and a great connoisseur of music himself, acknowledges that Mr. Glinka is the equal in composition of Italy's two best composers—Messrs. Pacini and Donizetti, and in counterpoint he acknowledges Mr. Glinka's superiority."

26 December/8 January 1833

The aria for soprano, *"Pronto giunga il fatal momento"* [in its Russian edition, *"Smertnyi chas ko mne podkhodit"* (The hour of death approaches)] was given to Ricordi to be engraved (coll. *Glinka,* 1958, p. 385). Its full Italian title continues *Aria per voce di soprano composta per Sig-na Luigia Giulini egregia diletante da M. Glinka.*

End of the Year

In a letter to Feofil Tolstoy, Glinka recalls a conversation with him in Milan and promises to translate into sounds a picture of the southern night.

December

Glinka performs the *Trio pathétique.* "My friends, artists of the theater *della Scala,* Tassistro, clarinet, and Cantú, bassoon, accompanied me, and at the conclusion of the Finale the latter said in amazement, '*ma questo e disperazione!*'"

1833

15/27 January

In a letter from Novau, Maria Coursel (the marchesa Paulucci by marriage) invites Sobolevsky to visit and also to convey her invitation to Glinka: ". . . Tell him that we will pamper him even more than Serafima Ivanovna [Shterich] (*L.,* p. 77).

Before 20 February/4 March

Glinka "decided to travel to Venice for diversion, hoping that a trip, as had often been the case, would improve my health. De Filippi approved of my intentions."

20 February/4 March

Glinka asks Sobolevsky if he is not going. "If not, then provide me with a passport, and if it will not be too much trouble for you, a ticket on tomorrow's stagecoach." He asks him to come.

[The note is marked "Monday." When published it was dated "Italy, 1832." The remark regarding his departure ("tomorrow's stagecoach") corresponds to Glinka's indication in the *Zapiski* that he left for Venice by stagecoach. His next letter is dated 23 February/7 March, 1833. This allows for the specific dating of the fragment of 20 February/4 March 1833.]

21 February/5 March

Departure for Venice (*Zap.*).

[The date of his departure is confirmed based upon Glinka's letters to Sobolevsky on 20 February/4 March and 23 February/7 March 1833.]

23 February/7 March

Venice. Glinka tells Sobolevsky of his arrival that same day and shares with him his first impressions of Venice, which, "unlike the Milanese . . . I like very much." He asks Sobolevsky to give him the "address of Ninetta Zampo. Shterich always said she was very good looking."

Between 23 and 28 February/7 and 12 March

Glinka heard Pasta in Rossini's *Tancredi* and remarked that "her low notes were almost inaudible." During this period Glinka spent his time "in the theater with Bellini and company . . . at rehearsals. I only attended the theater once in the evening. . . . Except for the theater, I go out little, since the weather is so bad."

28 February/12 March

Glinka writes to Sobolevsky: "I still have not decided on anything. Today I have a consultation about the baths. In any case, I would like to remain here. Just like at school, I do not want to return to Milan very badly. . . . If I decide to stay here, then I will move from here in Leoné, which is expensive and not very convenient." He writes of acquaintances in society and of theatrical intrigues.

Between 28 February/12 March and 3/15 March

Glinka "received a letter from Russia—all is well—leave of absence for another year—here there are new troubles, where and how to kill it?"

3/15 March

Glinka writes to Sobolevsky: "I am sad, but there is nothing to be done. The weather is terrible, my nerves are exhausted, and the theater for now is awful and does little to entertain me. . . . I found Ninetta Zampo . . . but I did not find the affectionate reception which you had predicted—*mezzo fiasco* (this adventure is being postponed to a more favorable time)."

Glinka is present at the dress rehearsal of *Beatrice di Tenda*. "For no obvious reason I fear for Bellini. The music is fine, but God only knows what the foolish audience wants, it's difficult to please them" (ltr. to S. Sobolevsky, 3/15 March 1833).

4/16 March

Glinka attends the premiere of Bellini's opera *Beatrice di Tenda*. "Despite all Pasta's efforts in the part of Beatrice, the work was not a success."
[The aria which Glinka had written for this opera was a monolog for the heroine denouncing treachery and violence, but apparently it was not performed.]

Beginning of March

Glinka "saw the sights of the city."

First Half of March

Como. Trip to Lake Como, where Glinka "met Sobolevsky" (*Zap.*).

16 March

Evgeny Shterich's funeral in St. Petersburg (Nikitenko, *Dnevnik*, p. 310).

Middle of March

Glinka's health worsened. He returned to Milan quite ill. "In the stagecoach were Ricordi and a lady acquaintance of his who was a little over 40. They looked after me with concern."

Milan. "When I arrived in Milan, de Filippi found my pulse in such a condition that he immediately ordered blood let from my left arm, which, however, was of no significant benefit."

17/29 April

The manuscript of the *Gran sestetto originale* for piano, two violins, viola, cello, and bass is given to Ricordi to be engraved (coll. *Glinka,* 1958, p. 398).

Second Half of March to the End of April

Glinka is seriously ill. "In the intervals between attacks, my suffering became *duller.* I sat at the piano and involuntarily elicited strange sounds in which were reflected the irrational feelings which troubled me. This extreme disorder of my nervous system had an effect, however, not only on my *imagination.* My indeterminate and somewhat hoarse voice was suddenly transformed into a strong, clear, high tenor."

End of April

De Filippi sent Glinka to Varese to Dr. Branca.

May

Varese. "Living there was difficult for me. . . . The doctor . . . had me walking without mercy, though sometimes I took a cabriolet . . . and even rode horseback a little."

Milan. Glinka "sometimes" travelled to Milan, "but only for short periods."

Varese. "The feelings that tormented me caused me deep depression, and the latter, nostalgia (*Heimweh*)."

Beginning or Middle of July (N.S.)

Glinka received news from home that his sister Natalia Ivanovna and her husband N. Gedeonov had left for Berlin. "This news ignited my desire to travel there myself."

End of July (N.S.)

Glinka "left Italy."

1830 to July 1833

A sketch for an Italian symphony dates from the period of Glinka's stay in Italy. On the last page of the autograph appears the initial sketch of Ratmir's aria, *"Chudnyi son"* [Lovely dream], composed 10 years later.

This is how Glinka summed up his stay in Italy: "Frequent contact with first-and second-class singers as well as amateurs of both genders gave me a practical understanding of the capricious and difficult art of mastering the voice and writing aptly for it. . . . My work as a composer I consider less successful. It cost me no little effort to imitate the Italian *sentimento brillante,* as they call the feeling of well-being which is the result of being happily established under the beneficent influence of the southern sun. We, dwellers of the north, feel things otherwise. Impressions either do not touch us at all or they deeply imprint themselves in our souls. We experience either frenzied gaiety or bitter tears. Love, that entrancing feeling, the universal life-giver, with us is always connected with sadness. There is no doubt that our doleful Russian song is a child of the north, which was somehow transmitted to us by the inhabitants of the east, for their songs are also doleful, even in happy Andalusia. . . . All the pieces which I wrote to oblige the people of Milan and which have been very nicely printed by Giovanni Ricordi, have only convinced me of the fact that I was not following my own path and that I could not *sincerely* be an Italian. Yearning for my native land led me gradually to the resolve of writing in Russian."

1833

July

Como, Varenna, Tirol, Innsbruck, Salzburg, Linz. En route to Vienna.

Vienna. Arrival. "After Italy, Vienna seemed gloomy to me, particularly on account of the foul weather. I heard the orchestras of Lanner and Strauss often and with pleasure.

31 July/12 August

Glinka consulted with Dr. Johann Malfatti, who sent him to the baths at Baden (*Zap.;* G 2-B).

31 July/12 August

Malfatti issued Glinka a medical certificate attesting to the necessity of treatment in the Baden mineral waters. Glinka sent this certificate to Russia for an extension of his passport ("Case concerning the issuance of a new foreign passport to Glinka," in G 2-B).

31 July/12 August

Glinka writes to Ricordi that, because of the condition of his health (which "is now so bad"), he has decided not to travel to Karlsbad, but to stay in Baden, near Vienna. He asks therefore that his published compositions be sent to Vienna *poste restante*.

August

Baden. Glinka was treated in the Baden mineral waters, which completely wrecked his nerves.

End of August

Once while walking, Glinka dropped in on "a Catholic priest, who had a piano. I began to improvise, and apparently very mournfully, because the priest asked me with surprise, 'How is it possible at your age to play so sadly?' I answered, 'What can I do? It is not easy, you know, to be sentenced to death in the flower of one's youth,' and I briefly told him of my sufferings." The priest recommended returning to homeopathy, which Glinka "took for ridicule." Continuing in his efforts to persuade Glinka, the priest asked him, "Isn't it one and the same in that case whether you die from allopathy or homeopathy?"

Glinka's condition worsened, and he was taken to Vienna (*Zap.*).

15 September

Correspondence is initiated among Nikolay Khmelnitsky, Prince Khovansky, and Count Benkendorf concerning the issuance of a new foreign passport to Glinka or extension of the old one (G 2-B).

Vienna. Glinka returned to homeopathy, which improved his condition.

Glinka moved to Kärtner Strasse and "began to read Schiller for diversion. . . . I rented a piano and memorized Herz's variations on various themes. After listening to Lanner and Strauss, I tried several times to compose . . . and invented the theme which served for the krakowiak in *A Life for the Tsar*.

September

Pavel and Sofia Engelgardt, as well as Glinka's cousin Natalia Ivanovna and her husband Petr Kirillovich Ryndin, were en route through Vienna: "I spent several pleasant days with them." Soon after their departure, Glinka's brother-in-law's brother, Fedor Gedeonov, arrived.

30 September/12 October

Glinka writes to Ricordi that "finally" he is leaving Vienna, and thanks him for "all the kindnesses you have shown me." He asks that one copy of all the works published by Ricordi be sent to him via the Russian embassy.

5/17 October

Departure with Fedor Gedeonov (*Zap.;* Ya. Prokhaska, "Glinka in Czechoslovakia," in *Sov. muzyka,* 1954, no. 10, p. 64).

7/19 October

Prague. Arrival. They stayed in the Black Horse Hotel.

8/20 October

Departure for Berlin at three o'clock (*Prager Zeitung,* 22 October 1833, reprinted in *Sov. muzyka,* 1954, no. 10, p. 64).

10/22 (?) October

Berlin. Arrival and meeting with his sister Natalia Gedeonova and brother-in-law. Address: Jägerstrasse no. 10.

October

Meeting with his boarding school comrade Chirkov and with the voice teacher Gustav Teschner.
[It is not known which Chirkov is being referred to, Nikolay or Nikanor.]

Teschner introduced Glinka to his pupil Maria, who was "very beautiful and resembled a madonna to a certain extent. . . . I began to teach her singing and wrote études for her (from one of them I later arranged the *"Evreiskaia pesnia"* [Hebrew song] for Kukolnik's drama *Prince Kholmsky).* I saw Maria almost daily and imperceptibly began to feel an attraction for her, which, I believe, she shared."

Acquaintance through Teschner with Siegfried Dehn, "without question the premiere musical *sorcerer* in Europe."

28 October/8 November

Glinka's studies with Dehn begin. "There is no doubt that I am more indebted to Dehn than to any other of my masters. He . . . not only brought order to my knowledge but to my ideas about art in general. As a result of his lectures I began to work gropingly no longer but with understanding" (*Zap.;* an inscription in his notebook of contrapuntal exercises). "Dehn was gifted with great perceptiveness, which enabled him to guess his student's inclinations. In his teaching he dispensed with all pedantry and unnecessary dryness and had the student practice writing three-and four-voiced fugues, which hastened the development of his taste and brought order to his theoretical understanding of music" (*Biograficheskaia zametka*).

5 November

The correspondence among Khmelnitsky, Khovansky, and Benkendorf about issuing Glinka a foreign passport is concluded. A new passport is issued with permission "to remain [abroad] until recovery" (G 2-B).

19 November/1 December

Glinka writes to Sobolevsky that "although my poor health persists, I am beginning to get used to it and do not cry out that I am dying as I did before. Here they are treating me with cold showers . . . and for now, it seems, not without effect."

23 November/5 December

Glinka began to write the Variations on Alyabiev's Romance "The Nightingale." The composer's dating on the first page of the manuscript reads: *"Berlin, 5 Decembre 1833"* (*L.*, p. 82).

17/29 December

The Variations on Alyabiev's "The Nightingale" were completed. The composer's dating on the title page of the manuscript reads: "*'Solovei.' Romance d'Alabieff variée pour le Pianoforte par M. Glinka. Berlin, le 29 decembre 1833*" (*L.*, p. 82).

During the year Glinka's *Gran Sestetto originale* was published in Milan by Ricordi with parts (coll. *Glinka,* 1958, p. 396).

1833/1834

Winter

"Once [Dehn] gave me a theme consisting of eight bars on which I was to write the skeleton of a fugue by my next lesson. The theme more resembled a recitative than a melody suitable for a fugue, and I vainly labored over it. At the next lesson he once again asked me to work with this theme, and once again I struggled with it in vain. At the third lecture Dehn appeared with a huge book containing a fugue by Handel on the very theme which I could not master. On looking at it, I realized that the entirety of the great composer's development was based on the eighth bar, while the first seven bars only rarely appeared. With this realization I grasped what is meant by fugue."

"Besides my lessons with Dehn and Maria's lessons, I worked some at composition. I wrote two romances: *"Dubrava shumit"* [The leafy grove howls] (Zhukovsky) and *"Ne govori, liubov' proidet"* [Do not say that love passes] (Delvig), variations on Alyabiev's 'The Nightingale' for piano, and a Potpourri on several Russian themes for four hands. In the latter, *pretensions* to counterpoint are apparent. I also wrote a study for an overture-symphony on a *krugovaia* (a Russian [dance] theme), which, however, was worked out in the German manner."

"The idea of national music (I am not speaking yet of opera) became clearer and clearer. I composed the theme '*Kak mat' ubili*' (the orphan's song from *A Life for the Tsar*) and an allegro first theme for an overture."

1834

3 January

In *Mosk. ved.*, no. 1, there is an announcement of the publication of the romance *"Dubrava shumit."*

Beginning of the Year, January or February (?)

Composer's dating on the manuscript (part written by Glinka, part by an unknown hand) of the Capriccio on Russian themes for Piano Four-hands: *"Capriccio sopra alcuni motivi Russi per Cembalo a 4 mani composto dal Sr. M. Glinka. 1834"* (L., p. 85).

[The themes are of the songs *"Ne bely snegi"* [Not the white snows], *"Vo sadu li v ogorode"* [In the garden or in the orchard], and *"Ne tesen terem"* [The tower is not crowded]; the fourth theme is in the character of the *bytovoi* romance. Two variants of the Potpourri on Russian songs have been preserved. In the autograph the overture-symphony is called *Sinfonia per orchestra sopra due motivi Russi.* The introductory part is based upon the theme of the song *"Ia ne znala ni o chem v svete tuzhit' "* [I did not know what to grieve for].]

4/16 March

Ivan Glinka died in Novospasskoe (date on the tombstone; Shestakova, *Vosp.*, p. 38).

5/17 March

Glinka writes to Sobolevsky. "My state of mind is improving, gloomy thoughts very rarely bother me, and I'm able to work. I am taking advantage of this situation to acquaint myself with the German school of music and the cleverness [*khitrost'*] of German counterpoint. Above all, I have collected and prepared productive material for a number of pieces, especially in a national vein. Please pass this on to Melgunov and embrace him as a friend for me. Ask him to pardon my silence. I promise to write as soon as my health permits."

26 March/7 April

Glinka attends a performance of *Der Freischütz* (G 2-B, p. 292).

After 26 March/7 April

Glinka writes to Melgunov (?): "You unjustly complain about my silence. A friend does not forget his friend. You are always with me, you are always close to my heart." Further on he tells of his work with Dehn and shares his plans for the future: "I will not remain here long, and I impatiently await the moment when I may embrace you. I have a project, an idea . . . but I do not wish to be too candid. Perhaps if I were to disclose everything to you, you would look at me with a smile of disbelief, I'm afraid. Still perhaps, when you yourself embrace me soon, you will notice in me some kind of change. Perhaps you will find more in me than you could have imagined or suspected before my departure from Petersburg. Shall I disclose what's on my mind to you? . . . I think that even I may be able to give our theater a work worthy of it. It will not be a grand thing. I am the first to grant that, but nonetheless it will not be all that bad either. What do you think? Most important is to find the subject. In any case, I want it all to be national, first of all the subject, but also the music, so that my dear fellow countrymen will feel at home, even though abroad they did not consider me a braggart or imposter dressed up in strange feathers. . . . Who knows if I shall keep the promise I have made to myself!"

[Dated in relation to the letter to Sobolevsky of 5/17 March 1834. This letter was written later, but before receipt of the news of his father's death. The original of this letter is unknown.]

End of March

"Thus we lived quietly and agreeably until the end of March. Once I travelled with Chirkov to Charlottenburg, and on our return I learned from my brother-in-law that Father had died. The news staggered me. . . . We decided to return home."

1830 to the Beginning of April 1834

"In the course of the three-and-one-half years which he spent in Italy and then in Germany, his name was mentioned several times in French and German papers . . . placing him higher than Mercadante, Ricci, and other contemporary Italian composers and saying that only three were not inferior to him: Bellini, Donizetti, and Pacini. In the Leipzig musical press he was also referred to with terms of praise. Many of his piano pieces published in Milan were favored with the dubious honor of being reprinted in Paris" (Melgunov, *Vosp.*, p. 160).

Beginning of April (O.S.)

Berlin. Glinka's departure for Novospasskoe with his sister Natalia Gedeonova, her husband, and their maid Luisa (*Zap.*).

2 April

In Petersburg Pushkin wrote in his diary: "Several days ago . . . I had dinner at Prince Nikolay Trubetskoy's with Vyazemsky, Norov, and Kukolnik, whom I saw for the first time. He appeared to be a very decent young person. I don't know if he has talent. I did not finish reading his 'Tasso' and did not see his *'Ruka'* [Hand], etc. He is a fine musician. Vyazemsky said of his piano playing: *'Il brédouille en musique comme en vers.'* Kukolnik is writing 'Lyapunov,' as is Khomyakov. Baron Rozen possesses greater talent" (Pushkin, *Soch.*, v. 12, p. 323).

9 April

In Petersburg the State Council reviewed the report of the provisional general meeting of the Senate on the case of Ivan Glinka's business affairs and resolved to submit it to the Minister of Finance, Kankrin, for review (G 2-A, p. 59).

Poznan, Königsberg, Tilsit, Yurburg, Kovno, Vilno, Minsk, Smolensk: the route of Glinka's return trip.

End of April

Novospasskoe. Glinka's arrival (*Zap.*).

1/13 May

The romance *"Il desiderio"* is given to the publisher Ricordi in Milan to be engraved (coll. *Glinka,* 1958, p. 385).

14 May

The Senate passed a resolution to repay Ivan Glinka a part of the sum due him of 136,618 rubles 38 1/2 kopecks (G 2-A, p. 59).

End of April to the Beginning of June

Glinka stayed in the country, where he "led a quiet and rather pleasant life."

Glinka wrote the romance *"Ia zdes', Inezil'ia"* [I am here, Inezilla] to words by Pushkin.
[In his *Zapiski* Glinka gives the time of composition of this romance as "Winter 1834," but on the 15th of June, Melgunov mentions an *"Ispanskii romans"* [Spanish romance] in the paper *Molva* as

if it were already known. That means that the romance was composed not later than the spring of 1834.]

Beginning of June

Trip to Moscow "in order to see my friend Melgunov."

Moscow. Glinka stayed with Melgunov, who lived "in . . . his own house near Novinsky. I was assigned rooms in which all who stay there, Melgunov said to me with a smile, immediately get married. . . . Pavlov lived on the mezzanine. . . . He gave me his romance *'Ne nazyvai ee nebesnoi'* [Do not call her heavenly] . . . which I set to music right in his presence."

9 June

In Petersburg, the Minister of Finance, Kankrin, declined to grant Ivan Glinka's petition on grounds of the remoteness of the time and from apprehension that it would arouse others in the same business to similar demands (G 2-A, p. 59).

10 June

In a note to Praskovya Barteneva, Glinka states that his musical evening has been postponed until Tuesday.

12 June

In the morning Glinka visits Barteneva. In the evening Glinka's musical gathering took place in Melgunov's house (ltr. to P. Barteneva, 10 June 1834; *Zap.*).

Glinka's entry in Praskovya Barteneva's album of a piece for violin (?) belongs to this period (?) (GPB, coll. 48, no. 2, leaf 16).
[First published in 1952 for violin and piano with the title *"Listok iz al'boma"* [Page from an album], edited by Izrail Yampolsky.]

15 June

In *Molva*, no. 24, there is an article by Melgunov (without signature) entitled "Moscow Notes, the Music of Glinka." "You know the music and Delvig's song *'Akh ty, noch' li, nochen'ka,'* or *'Dedushka, devitsy'*; you will recall the music album published in Petersburg some five years ago; and perhaps you have heard the 'Spanish Romance' or *'Akh ty, dushechka,'* etc., etc. Is it not true that you were delighted with this music? Be glad! . . . Glinka, the composer of this music, of these romances, recently arrived in Moscow . . . and several days ago he played for several acquaintances and amateurs two large pieces for piano with quintet, which he wrote and had published in Italy. We would not wish after only one hearing to offer a definitive judgment of these musical compositions by Glinka. It does seem to us, however, that these works appear to combine the various qualities of contemporary music: brilliance, melody, and counterpoint, which are combined in such a manner that they comprise one inseparable and highly original whole. One can recognize Glinka's music within the first eight bars. His originality consists in the inexpressible grace of his melodies and the clarity, or so to say, the transparency of his style!" The article also refers to the publication of songs and romances by Glinka in an edition *"exclusively* by Melgunov," the first volume of which will appear by September (d.c.a.).

Before 20 June (?)

"The thought of a Russian opera had become implanted" in Glinka's mind. "I had no words, but the idea of *'Mar'ina roshcha'* [Marina's grove] turned around in my head. At the piano I played several excerpts from scenes which partially served me in *A Life for the Tsar*."
[A story by Zhukovsky, *"Mar'ina roshcha. Starinnoe predanie"* [Marina's grove, an ancient legend] (written and published in 1809).]

In Melgunov's house "several families gathered who belonged to Moscow's highest social circle. . . . Bravura and Kireeva (née Alyabieva)." Besides these, Glinka "got to know the composer Gebel and repeatedly heard his quintets and quartets well performed. I also saw Genishta . . . [and] Barteneva, who went through my romances with me. In general I spent my entire stay in Moscow very happily."

Glinka "happened to be at a concert given by Genishta. It consisted entirely of classical pieces: Mozart, Beethoven, and Handel" (ltr. to K. Bulgakov, 23 July 1855).

Before 26 June

Novospasskoe. Glinka returns to the country.
[Glinka's return from Moscow is dated according to his receipt of an order from the Elninsk district court to submit a new application for a foreign passport.]

26 June

Through the Elninsk district court Glinka received "instructions from the civil governor of Smolensk to submit a new application for a trip . . . to Germany and Italy" (Glinka's application to N. Khmelnitsky for issuance of a foreign passport, July [undated] 1834, in G 2-B).

First Half of July

Glinka made application for a foreign passport to the governor of Smolensk, Khmelnitsky, for a period "of three years," and indicated: "I am going *abroad alone,* and none of our servants will be accompanying me" (*Zap.;* the application, July [undated] 1834, in G 2-B).

[Glinka made application no later than 15 July, since on the 16th, Khmelnitsky began the "procedure" for issuing a passport.]

"My intention was to travel directly to Berlin in order to see Maria. I had been in continual correspondence with her and her family."

25 July

In Moscow, censor's authorization for the sixth issue of the journal *Eolova arfa* [Aeolian Harp], published by Varlamov. On p. 13 are Glinka's Mazurka and *Farewell Waltz* for piano (composed in 1831).

Upon receiving news of the serious illness of Glinka's brother, Evgeny Ivanovich, who was a student in the Artillery School, Evgenia Glinka and her daughter Elizaveta left for St. Petersburg (*Zap.*).

14 August

Censor's authorization for the seventh issue of the journal *Aeolian Harp,* in which Glinka's romance *"Il desiderio"* is printed on p. 2 and his Mazurka for Piano on p. 7.

Middle of August

Glinka received permission for his trip abroad (*Zap.*).

23 August

Evgenia Glinka (in Petersburg) submitted a petition "to His Imperial Majesty" to review the case of Ivan Glinka's tax farming (G 2-A, p. 59). Despite receipt of a positive response shortly thereafter, Evgenia Glinka could not secure return of the money. The affair dragged on until the end of 1841.

End of August

Glinka left for Smolensk accompanied by Yakov Netoev and Natalia Gede-onova's maid, Luisa Lange (who was to be taken to Berlin).

Smolensk. Glinka stayed with his sister Maria Stuneeva. Because of a misunder-standing over Luisa Lange's passport, Glinka was obliged to return with her to Petersburg. " . . . I still hoped to be able to reach Berlin before winter. Fate decided otherwise."

3 September

Glinka's brother Evgeny dies in St. Petersburg (Petersburg Necropolis).

6 September

Petersburg. Glinka's arrival. He stays at the home of Aleksey Stuneev, married to Sofia Petrovna, née Ivanova (*Zap.; SPb. ved.*, 16 September 1834).
[The Stuneevs lived on the fourth floor of a house adjoining the School of Guards Cadets on Voznesenskaya Street (today part of bldg. no. 14 on Mayorov Prospect; the house itself has not been preserved).]

7 September

Glinka's meeting with Sofia Stuneeva's sister, Maria Petrovna Ivanova.
[The basis for this date is that Glinka told Shestakova that he first saw Maria Petrovna on the first Friday after his arrival in Petersburg.]

16 September

In a supplement to *SPb. ved.*, no. 215–16, Glinka ("from Smolensk") is men-tioned among those arriving in Petersburg during the period 4–6 September.

September and Later

"Imperceptibly I began to be captivated by Maria Petrovna's prettiness and inborn grace, and I was in no hurry to leave."

1 October

"Snow fell, and winter's course established itself," but Glinka "persisted in staying in Petersburg."

Beginning of October and Later

Glinka receives treatment from various doctors upon the recommendation of Aleksey Stuneev (*Zap.*).

2 November

In *Molva* (Moscow), no. 44, in the section headed "Announcements," there is a notice about the publication of Glinka's first book of romances and songs, including the romance *"Ne nazyvai ee nebesnoi"* (d.c.a.).

12 November

The State Council passes a resolution about the Senate's inquiry into the case of the destroyed wine, the refusal to pay for wine taken for the army, and payment to the Glinkas for wine which they did not receive from the government (G 2-A, p. 59).

21 November

Mosk. ved., no. 93, contains an announcement that the romance *"Ne nazyvai ee nebesnoi"* is available in Gresser and Müller's music store.

30 November

The following announcement appears in *Sev. pchela*, no. 273: "Several days ago the fourth issue of I. V. Romanus's *Melodikon* was published. This issue includes 1) a waltz by K. Meier; 2) a romance by M. Glinka; 3) a mazurka by A. Rheingold; 4) a waltz for [piano] three-hands by J. Weirauch; and 5) a French quadrille by the publisher."
[The romance by Glinka was *"Pour un moment."*]

Fall

The director of the Court Chapel, Fedor Lvov, called on Glinka and showed him "unusual attention" (*Zap.*).

Melgunov writes (from Moscow) to Yanuary Neverov: "I am publishing some romances by Glinka. Two parts have been published and are on sale in SPb. at Pets and Bernard's. Recommend them to anybody and everybody. Glinka is now [in Petersburg] and is sick" (coll. *Glinka,* p. 134).

Fall–Winter

"Little by little lovers of singing began to call on me," among them Nikolay and Matvey Volkov, Ivan Andreev, and others. "I was a stay-at-home then, and more so since I was becoming more and more attracted to Maria Petrovna."

8 December

The following entry appears in the diary of Apollon Mokritsky: "I had dinner at Kazadaev's, and Mme Glinka was there. She invited me to see her and requested a portrait of Sofia Aleksandrovna" (Mokritsky, p. 37).
[The people referred to are Evgenia Andreevna Glinka and Sofia Aleksandrovna Galagan, the daughter of Aleksandr Kazadaev.]

Winter

The firm "Odeum" publishes the romance *"Ia zdes', Inezil'ya"* (N. Sinyavsky and M. Tsyavlovsky, *Pushkin v pechati* [Pushkin in print], *1814–1837,* M., 1914).
[The first publication of Glinka's romance is also the first publication of Pushkin's poem, which during the poet's life was not published separately from the music.]

"Mother and my sister returned to the country, while I stayed on at Stuneev's, who gave me his study."
[Glinka mistakenly places his mother's departure at the end of September (cf. 8 December).]

At this time Glinka "always attended Vasily Andreevich Zhukovsky's gatherings. He lived in the Winter Palace, where each week an elite company of poets, writers, and people favorable to the arts gathered. . . . A. S. Pushkin, Prince Vyazemsky, Gogol, and Pletnev were always in attendance. . . . Prince Odoevsky, Vielgorsky, and others were often there as well. Sometimes instead of reading there was singing or piano playing. Ladies were present at times likewise, but only those receptive to the fine arts" (*Zap.*).

A sketch for a national hymn, *motif de chant national,* dates from this period (N. Findeyzen, description of the manuscript in *RMG,* 1895, no. 7).

"When I expressed my desire to work on a Russian opera, Zhukovsky . . . suggested the subject of Ivan Susanin to me. The scene in the forest engraved itself on my imagination. I found many things in it which were original and characteristically Russian. Zhukovsky wanted to write the words himself, and for a test he composed these well-known lines:

> *Akh, ne mne, bednomu,*
> *Vetru buinomu*
>
> [Oh, not me, poor one,
> Wild wind]

(From the trio with chorus in the epilog)."
[Glinka undoubtably has in mind the "scene in the forest" from Ryleev's *duma* [ballad] "Ivan Susanin." In Zhukovsky's opinion, "Tsar Michael and the danger to him, Susanin and his self-sacrifice . . . represented something exceptional" (ltr. from V. Zhukovsky to M. Zagoskin, 1830. *Raut,* historical and literary collections, part 3, M., 1854, p. 303).]

Glinka "began to work, and completely backwards, that is to say, I began with what others end with, namely the overture, which I wrote for piano four-hands, including indications of the instrumentation. . . . The Adagio . . . I changed later."
[There were three versions of the overture: The first was written in orchestral score without the slow introduction (there was simply the allegro). In the second version an introduction was added based on the first theme [of the allegro]. The final (third) variant was composed not long before the premiere of the opera. Glinka changed the slow introduction, introducing in it Vanya's theme from the epilogue. The Allegro also underwent changes. The piano four-hands transcription which is preserved is based upon the last version (Vladimir Protopopov, *Ivan Susanin: Muzykal'no-teoreticheskoe issledovanie* [Ivan Susanin: research in music theory], M., 1961).]

"Themes for various places in the opera, often with contrapuntal development, I wrote down in a special notebook as they were invented."
[This notebook has not been discovered.]

30 December

Date on a watercolor portrait of Glinka done by Nikolay Volkov: "30 December 1834." According to the composer's words, Volkov painted his portrait "very successfully."

1834/1835

Winter

In Demidova's concert Glinka sang "Rubini's part" in the finale of Bellini's *Il Pirata*.

Glinka composed the romance *"Tol'ko uznal ia tebia"* [I had but recognized you] to words by Delvig—"this latter for Maria Petrovna" (*Zap.*).

Feofil Tolstoy came to consult with Glinka after he had written a one-act opera, *Le médecin malgré lui,* and had received an offer to stage it from the Minister of the Court, P. Volkonsky. "Glinka carefully looked over the score and then uttered the following words, which I will never forget: 'It is not fitting that our brother, the Russian composer, should go before the public with such *trifles* (he actually said this). We have a serious mission, which is to cultivate our own individual style and to pave the way for Russian operatic music. . . . Lay your operetta aside, my dear friend, this cosmopolitan little work, and continue to write romances. Perhaps you will come across some kind of new forms for our chamber music which break with our German leaders and better suit our indigenous native song'" (F. Tolstoy, *Vosp.,* p.110).
[Tolstoy's operetta *Le médecin malgré lui* was performed in the fall of 1835 in the Mikhaylovsky Theater and after three performances was withdrawn from the repertoire.]

1835

3 January

In *Mosk. ved.,* no. 1, there is an announcement that Glinka's romance *"Dubrava shumit"* to words by Zhukovsky is available (without indication of who the composer is).

16 January

In *Mosk. ved.,* no. 5, there is an announcement stating that the second series of Glinka's romances and songs is available in Lengold's music store.

Beginning of the Year (January?)

Glinka took to Odoevsky "a sheaf of individual pages of music . . . which constituted the embryo of *Ivan Susanin,* or *A Life for the Tsar.* The greater part of the opera had been written *before the words.* . . . The entire work, in its main features, was already in his head. . . . He wanted to confine himself to three scenes: the scene in the country, the Polish scene, and the concluding celebration. From the very first he played through the entire opera for me in this form, told me its contents, and hummed or improvised what was not written down. I could not but be struck by the originality of his melodies, the freshness of the ideas, and the depth of his harmonic combinations. . . . Glinka and I went to see Vasily Andreevich Zhukovsky. When I showed him the meters which the composer required, Zhukovsky burst out laughing . . . and began right then to drive verses into this framework. . . . To fill in the metric scheme he inserted nonsense words, and we laughed to the point of exhaustion. But meanwhile, a joke's a joke, and work is work. The matter at hand had to do with the fact that without words there would be no opera" (Odoevsky, *Vosp.,* p. 166).

"Obligations would not allow" Zhukovsky "to fulfill his intentions" and write the libretto for Glinka's opera (*Zap.*).
[Zhukovsky only wrote the text for the epilog of the opera.]

Apparently the plan for the opera was prepared during this time, though only the plan of the first three acts has been preserved. In this plan the opera is entitled "Ivan Susanin. Patriotic heroic-tragic opera in five acts or parts."

Odoevsky "brought together" Glinka and Vladimir Sollogub. "The subject had already been selected. . . . Much to my surprise I found out that the scenario was established and that even the music was in large measure composed, although without words. Glinka only needed someone to tidy up words to already composed music. . . . Glinka . . . asked only that words be added to the music. I wrote the first two choruses very poorly, then Antonida's aria, while Glinka remarked: 'Write what you like as long as there is always an "a" or "i" under the high notes. . . .' My collaboration with Glinka did not continue very long. We parted over the second act. To my question, what the act consisted of, Glinka answered that there would be a polonaise, a mazurka, a krakowiak, and a chorus in it. 'Pardon me,' I remarked, 'that is no act but a divertissement. . . .' But Glinka just smiled . . . 'I will change nothing,' he said flatly" (Sollogub, p. 562).

"Glinka was a person who was inflexible in his convictions, and I experienced this myself when I began to write the libretto to *A Life for the Tsar* for him. The music had been written prior to the words. I declined the honor of being his collaborator because of the Polish act, which he envisioned, it seemed to me, as an intermezzo, whereas I wished to introduce action" (ltr. from V. Sollogub to F. Tolstoy, 20 December 1870, in *Rus. starina,* 1871, v. 3).

19 February

In a supplement to the first issue of the *Moskovskii nabliudatel'* [Moscow Observer], Glinka's romance *"Venetsianskaia noch'"* is printed (d.c.a.).

Middle of February

Glinka asks his mother's permission to marry Maria Petrovna (ltr. to his mother, 9 March 1835).
[This letter by Glinka has not been found.]

February

Glinka was introduced to Nestor Kukolnik. "He was prepared to write the words for me, but he left for Moscow and sent me a sample of a scene from there. From this I could see that it would be impossible to work by correspondence, particularly since the greater part of the music was already finished, and it would be necessary to accommodate words to it."

Glinka tries to obtain a post with the Directorate of Imperial Theaters (ltr. to his mother, 9 March 1835).

In a memorandum addressed to the Director of Imperial Theaters, forwarded to Odoevsky, Glinka writes that he "requests that the position of *Chief of Repertoire* be renamed . . . to something else, for example, the official for the section on enhancing artistic standards," and that he "is not concerned about salary," but wants "only to introduce for opera's benefit the practical knowledge of art acquired by him," and also "improved methods in singing the leading roles, seeking voices for the theater and even recruiting them in Little Russia."

Before 4 March

Glinka received his mother's consent to marry Maria Petrovna.

5 March

Glinka officially proposed to Maria Petrovna. Her mother, Luisa Ivanova, accepted "my proposal . . . very well."

Before 8 March

Evgenia Glinka's petition to the Governor of Smolensk concerning issuance of Glinka's "Certificate" (passport). The resolution reads: "Issue 8 March 1835" (G 2-B).

9 March

Glinka thanks his mother for her permission to get married and tells her that he has proposed. Maria Petrovna writes to Evgenia Glinka: "Having the good fortune of becoming a member of your most respected family, I regard it as the pleasantest duty to submit to your kindred favor. Knowing your kind heart, I comfort myself with the hope that I will find in you a solicitous, kind-hearted, and tender mother" (*L.*, p. 94).

12 March

Glinka returns "the Beethoven symphony" to Odoevsky and asks him "to let [me] know when it has been arranged to meet with Rozen. Without him it will be impossible to proceed." He tells Odoevsky that he is fasting but that "after Mass [he is] free all week."

[The undated note is marked "Tuesday." Work with Rozen was initiated in 1835. On the 13th of March that year the Allegretto of Beethoven's Seventh Symphony was performed. If Glinka is returning the score of this symphony to Odoevsky, then the letter was written 12 March, which corresponds to the fourth week of Lent, when Glinka may have been fasting.]

In a supplement to *SPb. ved.*, no. 58, there is an announcement of Romberg's concert (13 March) in the Mikhaylovsky Theater, in which Glinka is to appear and participate in the performance of his Serenade on themes from the opera *Anna Bolena* by Donizetti (for piano, harp, cello, bassoon, and horn).

13 March

In the Mikhaylovsky Theater, Romberg "will have the honor of presenting a new concerto for violin of his own composition. Moreover, Mmes. Karatygina and Vorobieva will sing, and Glinka will play a new serenade for piano, harp and many instruments. Mendelssohn's octet will be performed twice, and the first allegro of Beethoven's great Symphony in A Major" (*SPb. ved.*, 12 March 1835; *Sev. pchela*, 13 March 1835).

Zhukovsky's note to Odoevsky (undated) probably dates from this time: "I will be calling on you in order to go see Glinka. Thence to Rozen" (*Rus. arkhiv,* 1900, no. 3, inst. 9, p. 54).

To this period belongs Zhukovsky's note to Pushkin with an invitation to come "around ten o'clock today" for "a little conference" with Glinka, Odoevsky, and Rozen. "Your presence is necessary" (Pushkin, *Soch.,* v. 16, p. 100).
[In Pushkin's *Works* the letter is incorrectly dated "January–March 1836 (?)," but in 1836 such a "conference" no longer had any meaning.]

For preparation of the libretto, Zhukovsky "handed" Glinka "over to Baron Rozen, a diligent writer of German extraction who at the time was secretary to His Imperial Highness the Tsesarevich" (*Zap.*).
["Even the Emperor himself, Nicholas I, had thought about Russian opera in 'folk style.' In conversation on the subject with Zhukovsky he had even indicated that Rozen might be the person to carry out such a project. 'Even though he is German,' the Emperor said, 'he has a fine command of Russian, and he can be confided in.' This is why Zhukovsky recommended Rozen and not someone else as Glinka's collaborator. The Baron himself did not want to at all and did not wish to become another librettist" (M. Ivanov, *Muzykal'nye nabroski* [Musical sketches], in *Novoe vremia* [New Time], 1900, no. 8913).]

"My imagination, however, forestalled the industrious German. As if by some magical act, both the plan for the entire opera and the thought of contrasting Russian and Polish music suddenly materialized. Finally, many themes and even details of their development all flashed at once into my head."

Odoevsky "would take a melody Glinka had written, one voice or polyphonic, and, according to his intentions, place accents over the notes in an effort to give the meter shape and to try to preserve all the melodic nuances. In a word, I dealt with the music as if it were some rare flower, whose every petal, pistil, and speck of pollen were precious. Baron Rozen wrote the greater part of the verses found in the opera to correspond to these meters and the thought expressed in the music. He only wrote a few scenes before the music" (Odoevsky, *Vosp.,* p. 167).

March, First Half (?)

A friend of Glinka, Captain Kopiev, "a music lover, who had a pleasant bass voice and had composed a few romances," introduced Glinka to "a little man in a light blue frock coat and red waistcoat who spoke in a squeaky soprano. When he sat down at the piano, it turned out that this little man was a very lively pianist and subsequently the very talented composer Aleksandr Sergeevich Dargomyzhsky" (*Zap.*).

[The time of Glinka's introduction to Dargomyzhsky is based upon Dargomyzhsky's claim that when they met Glinka was already engaged (M. Pekelis, *Aleksandr Sergeevich Dargomyzhsky i ego okruzhenie* [Dargomyzhsky and his milieu], v. 1, M., 1966, p. 168).]

29 March

Glinka was at Zhukovsky's where he performed excerpts from the opera ". . . (he is composing an opera called *Ivan Susanin* based upon Russian themes) and romances: '*Svetit mesiats.*' It seemed terribly oppressive to me [Nadezhdin] . . . and the heart-rending music completed my torment. But then we heard bright, ceremonial chords: '*Sto krasavits svetlookikh*' [One hundred bright-eyed beauties] . . . Sweet harmony overflowed in my soul." Besides this Glinka sang "*Tol'ko uznal ia tebia.*" "Glinka sang this romance with special feeling: he is engaged to be married this spring himself" (ltr. from N. Nadezhdin to E. K., in *Rus. arkhiv*, 1885, no. 2, inst. 8, p. 579; Journal of the Ryazan Archival Commission, meeting of 30 March 1885, p. 14).

3 April

In *Mosk. ved.*, no. 27, there is an announcement of the arrival at Glazunov's store of three small volumes of Glinka's romances and songs: v. 1) "*Ne nazyvai ee nebesnoi*" to words of N. Pavlov; v. 2) "*Pevets*" [The singer] and "*Uteshenie*" [Consolation] to words by Zhukovsky; and v. 3) "*Chetyre russkie pesni*" [Four Russian songs] to words by Delvig.

5 April

In *Molva*, no. 14, "Literary Chronicle," there is a reference to Glinka's romance "*Venetsianskaia noch'* " (without title), which was printed in *Mosk. nabliudatel'*. "Mr. Glinka's music is fascinating" (d.c.a.).

Spring, First Half

Glinka was at Zhukovsky's: "Gogol read his '*Zhenit'ba*' [Marriage] to me."
[Dated according to when Gogol completed the first version of the comedy.]

March and Before 26 April

"During the course . . . of April and March he [Rozen] prepared the words for the first and second acts according to my plan. He was faced with considerable work: most of the themes as well as the development of individual pieces had been done, and he had to match words to music which sometimes required very strange meters. Baron Rozen was up to the mark. Whatever sort of meter you might order, whether it was duple or triple or even odd ones, made no difference to him. The next day he would have it ready. Zhukovsky and others jokingly said that Rozen had prefabricated lines tucked away in his pockets, and I only had to say what sort, i.e. meter, and how many I needed, and he would pull out as many of each sort as were necessary, each from a special pocket. Whenever the meter and thought corresponded to the music and agreed with the progress of the drama, then things turned up in my poetry with stubborn obstinacy. He defended every one of his lines with stoic heroism. For example, to me these lines from the quartet did not seem altogether apt:

> Thus for my earthly life,
> My future little wife, etc.

Somehow these words struck me as objectionable: *griadushchaia* [future] seemed Slavonic, even Biblical, and *zhenka* [little wife] seemed rural and peasantlike. I battled long but vainly with the stubborn Baron. There was no possibility of persuading him of the correctness of my observations. He talked heatedly. . . . He ended our dispute with the following words: '*You do not understand, this is the best poetry.*' "

Glinka sent notes to Rozen with directions for work on the opera's libretto (Arnold, inst. 2, p. 184).
[According to the testimony of Yury Arnold, Rozen had kept "a whole bundle of Glinka's notes," which he showed to Arnold. After Rozen's death, his brother Pavel destroyed all the poet's papers as "unnecessary manuscript rubbish" (M. Ivanov, "Musical Sketches," in *Novoe vremia*, 1900, No. 8913; Ivanov refers to the testimony of E. Rozen's daughter, Yuzikova).]

Glinka's visits to Rozen, who lived on Konnaya Square, were combined with visits to his fiancée and her mother, who lived not far from Rozen on the Sands (*Zap.*).

March–26 April

Glinka's meetings with Dargomyzhsky. "We played duets a lot and analyzed the symphonies of Beethoven and overtures of Mendelssohn in score" (Dargomyzhsky's Autobiography, coll. *Dargomyzhsky*, p. 4).

"The idea for the well-known trio '*Ne tomi, rodimyi*' [Do not despair, dear one] was the result of my insane love at the time. Even a minute without my fiancée seemed unbearable to me, and I actually felt what was expressed there."

26 April

Glinka's wedding takes place in St. Mikhail's Church in the Engineering Castle. The Archpriest Malov performed the marriage ceremony. Glinka's proxy father was Aleksandr Kazadaev. "The groom's guarantors for the ceremony were Staff-Captain Petr Aleksandrov[ich] Stepanov of the Regiment of Chasseurs Life-Guards and Captain Yury Alekseev Kopiev of the Izmaylovsky Regiment. For the bride: Saulov of the Cuirassiers Regiment Life-Guards and Dmitry Stepanov Ryndin of the Guards Company (Excerpts from the birth register, in *L.*, p. 95). "There were not many who attended the wedding. I invited no one but family, but since over the last several days I had told many of my acquaintances of my marriage, some of them came to the church to pray for my happiness" (ltr. to his mother, 1 May 1835). After the marriage ceremony Malov gave a speech of welcome. "'Incidentally,'" he said, 'Mikhail Ivanovich, your wife is so young. She is a flower which has barely blossomed. Protect her. A cold wind or excessive heat could destroy her.' It is too bad that he did not say something along the same lines to Maria Petrovna" (P. Stepanov, *Vosp.*, p. 55). About 12 people came out of the church—"only the proxy fathers and mothers, their best men, and closest relatives."

After the wedding Glinka and his wife settled on the Sands not far from his mother-in-law. "The apartment is very nice, comfortable, spacious, and cheerful. . . . We have lived together now for several days, and it has been so quiet and cheerful. . . . I confess that despite the bliss of being forever united with one's beloved, I was terrified of the future and the various kinds of misfortune which often befall married life."

1 May

Glinka writes to his mother that he is happy and adds: "I am sure that you will like her. She has returned your son to you. Going to Berlin would have destroyed me. Now my heart has been restored, I can feel and pray, be happy and cry. My muse has been resurrected, for all of which I am indebted to my angel, Maria. I do not know the words to use to express my gratitude to Providence for this good fortune."
[Glinka had planned to travel abroad to marry his pupil Maria "with a face like a madonna." He would have been "destroyed," because it would have cut him off from his family.]

Maria Petrovna writes to Evgenia Glinka: "With true joy and delight I take up my pen to thank you for all the maternal favors which you have shown me, as well as for the beautiful diamonds which my dear Michel put on me himself. I am made even happier by the thought that I shall soon have the pleasure of thanking you personally and of covering your little hands with kisses, as I try to repay, my dear, kind little mother, your totally unmerited attention and kindness, which I already enjoy" (postscript to a letter by Glinka, 1 May 1835, in *L.*, 96).

Annotation in the Glinka *Attestat:* "Herein referred to Titular Councillor Mikhaylo Ivanov Glinka, 26 April 1835, married, to the daughter of deceased Lt. Colonel Petr Ivanov, the maiden Maria, both, according to the custom and rule of the Greco-Eastern church, for the first time, to this I certify. They were married in the church of the Engineering Castle by the Archpriest, Master, and Knight Aleksey Malov. The sexton was Pavel Petrov."

Beginning of May (?)

Together with Kukolnik, Glinka began to visit at Fedor Tolstoy's (M. Kamenskaya, *Vosp., L.,* p. 96).

16 May

Glinka's note to Ludwig Maurer about the orchestral parts for the overture to *Ivan Susanin.*
[The year has been established according to the calendar (in the letter it says "Thursday, 16 May") and the contents.]

Between 12 and 17 May

Melgunov's arrival from Moscow (*SPb. ved.,* 22 May 1835).

Between 18 and 24 May

On one of these days, apparently, the second version of the overture to *Ivan Susanin* was performed with orchestra (V. Protopopov, *Ivan Susanin,* p. 91; ltr. to L. Maurer, 16 May 1835).

Spring, Before 24 May

"Almost every day there appeared [at Glinka's] the golden-haired Feb, Baron Rozen, the librettist for *A Life for the Tsar,* a man who was always excited, who had never learned to speak Russian, but who wrote Russian poetry, and sometimes not badly" (P. Stepanov, *Vosp.,* p. 55).

24 May

In a letter directed to Shevyrev via Glinka Melgunov writes: "This evening Glinka will be coming to see you and will bring his wife and his opera. His wife is a kind, naive half-German; the opera is an original work in every sense of the word. But you will see the one and hear the other."

Night of 24/25 May

Glinka with his wife and mother-in-law depart for Moscow (ltr. from N. Melgunov to S. Shevyrev, 24 May 1835, in *L.*, p. 97). "We went to Moscow to meet with relatives of my wife. I had the words for two acts with me."

27 May (?)

Beyond Novgorod. "In the carriage" Glinka "quickly . . . composed the chorus in $\frac{5}{4}$ meter, '*Razleleialas*' " for *A Life for the Tsar* (*Zap.*).

From 29 May

Glinka's visit in Moscow for several days (ltr. from N. Melgunov to S. Shevyrev, 24 May 1835, in *L.*, p. 97).

First Half of June

Novospasskoe. Glinka's arrival with his wife and mother-in-law (Shestakova, *Vosp.*, p. 38; ltr. from N. Melgunov to S. Shevyrev, 24 May 1835, in *L.*, p. 97).

11 July

Stepan Shevyrev writes (from Moscow) to Yanuary Neverov: "I am sending you a little note from Melgunov, in which you are asked to fetch Glinka's books from the censorship committee. However, I do not think that they will give them back without a warrant" (according to Yanuary Neverov; ltr. from S. Shevyrev, in *Rus. arkhiv*, 1909, no. 2, inst. 5, p. 91).

Beginning of June to the Beginning of August

Glinka "worked assiduously, i.e., *scored* what had already been prepared and worked ahead. Every morning I sat down at the table in the big, cheerful hall of our house in Novospasskoe. This was our favorite room. My sisters, mother, my wife, in a word, the entire family spent their time there, and the livelier their conversations and laughter were, the faster my work went. It was a beautiful time. Often I worked with the door to the garden open and drank in the clean balsam air. At first I wrote '*Ne tomi, rodimyi,*' in $\frac{2}{4}$ and in A minor, but then I thought that there may be too much duple division of the bar in the first act. For example, the introduction, Antonida's aria, and Susanin's recitative with chorus. . . . Not wanting . . . to be found at fault for uniformity, I wrote the same melody in $\frac{6}{8}$ and in B-flat minor, which undoubtedly better expresses the tender languor of love.''

Karl Gempel spent "considerable time" as Glinka's guest and "was genuinely pleased with the successful progress of my work."

July

At Aleksey Netoev's wedding, Glinka "wanted a real celebration and opened the ball himself with the new bride and then played with the musicians" (A. Netoev's comments to the editor of *Smolensk. vestn.*, A. I. Elishev, 22 May 1885, in P. Veymarn's book *M. I. Glinka, Biograficheskii ocherk* [Biographical sketch], M., 1892).

9 (?) August

Departure with his wife and mother-in-law for Petersburg (*Zap.*).

13 or 14 August

Petersburg. Arrival from the country (*SPb. ved.*, 17 August 1835). They settled "on Konnaya Square in a special house which we occupied alone."
[The square no longer exists, nor has the house been preserved.]

17 August

In *SPb. ved.*, no. 186, Glinka is named among those arriving in the "capital city of St. Petersburg" on 13 and 14 August.

August, Second Half

"Soon my mother-in-law moved in with us. . . . Aleksey Stuneev did not approve of this and said to me several times, 'Now, Michel, do not take your mother-in-law into your home. . . .' Partly out of independence, partly out of the artist's peculiar laziness when it comes to domestic annoyances, but also to please my wife, I allowed my mischievous mother-in-law into my home."

27 August

Composer's dating on the title page of the Introduction to *Ivan Susanin* (Act I): "St. Petersburg, 27 August 1835."

Beginning of September (?)

Glinka wrote the *Mazurque dédiée à M-me Marie de Glinka par son sincère ami M. Glinka* in F major.

12 September

Olga Pavlishcheva writes (from Pavlovsk) to her husband: "Michel Glinka is married to a girl named Ivanova, a young being without means or education, who is not at all pretty and hates music to boot. That, however, has not prevented Glinka from composing an exceptionally lovely piece of music for her, which I heard performed at Mme Pushkin's (always *l'ex Ennings*), performed by young Dargomyzhsky. . . . It was he who told me of his friend's notorious marriage." In the same letter: "Twenty copies of your 'Lyrical Album' turned up at my brother's [Aleksandr Pushkin]. I wanted to exchange them for books, but no one will even give me *Ledianoi dom* [The ice house, by Lazhechnikov], and it costs only one ruble with pictures, and all together they are worth less than a ruble" (*Pushkin i ego sovremenniki* [Pushkin and his contemporaries], inst. 17–18, SPb., 1913, pp. 167, 171; Fr. original).

17 September

Entry in Apollon Mokritsky's diary: "I went to the old man Kazadaev . . . and received an invitation to do Mme Glinka's portrait from him."

5 November

Mokritsky arrived at Glinka's: "The artist received me with due attention. At first we spoke about the portrait and then about a picture by Bryullov. I left with the hope of doing a portrait of his wife" (Mokritsky, pp. 43, 50).

24 November

In a letter to Ekaterina Lazareva in Nikolaev, Kukolnik writes: "A true marvel in music is being prepared here. It is Glinka's music for *Ivan Susanin*. It is exceptionally Russian music and unusually engrossing. Our other composers are silent, excusing themselves on the grounds that there are no suitable subjects" (*L.*, p. 100).

30 November

In a letter to Aleksandr Turgenev, Vyazemsky writes: "Glinka is writing a new opera, that is Glinka the musician, a Russian national opera called *Ivan Susaniñ*. The poem is being written by Baron Rozen ... a Revel-Russian poet with talent" (*Ostaf'evskii arkhiv kn. Viazemskikh* [Ostafiev Archive of the Princes Vyazemsky], v. 3, SPb., 1899, p. 279).

Fall

"Work went well. Every morning I sat down at the table and wrote six pages of the score in small script. . . . In the evenings, sitting on the sofa among family or sometimes a few good friends, I took little part in what was going on around me. I was totally immersed in work, and though much was already written, there still remained much to consider, and these considerations demanded no little attention. Everything had to be adjusted for there to be a well-balanced whole."

Beginning of Winter

In a letter to Rozen, Glinka gives instructions about the character of Susanin's scene in the forest: "The languour of death, the first two lines are a sort of appeal to God; then again anguish, the last line is torment" (*Novoe vremia*, 1901, no. 8986).

"I wrote Susanin's scene in the forest with the Poles during the winter. Before I began to write, I often read the entire scene aloud with feeling and became so carried away by the situation of my hero that my hair stood on end and my skin crawled. Baron Rozen gets full credit for the development of this scene according to my plan."

On Rozen's manuscript of the libretto alongside Susanin's words

> I have led you
> Where even the grey wolf
> Has not strayed!
> Where even the black raven
> Has not carried its bones!

is Glinka's note: *c'est à Michel Glinka.*

"Everything went well, and so well, that my friend Stepanov, who often visited us, said to me once: 'My soul is glad to see your happiness, I congratulate you.' I answered, 'I will truly thank you if you can congratulate me 10 years from now.'"

Before 20 December

Glinka was a guest at Anna Kern's, where he met Pushkin and Pavlishcheva. "Glinka was there. He is presenting his opera 'Susanin'" (ltr. from O. Pavlishcheva to N. Pavlishchev, 20 December 1835, in *Istoricheskii vestnik* [Historical Bulletin], 1888, v. 34., p. 576).

Winter

The beginning of Glinka's friendship with Kukolnik (N. Kukolnik, *"Muzykal'nyi vopros"* [A musical question], in *SPb. ved.,* 1862, no. 52).

1835/1836

Winter

"During the course of my work I was obligated in no small way to the advice of Prince Odoevsky and somewhat to Karl Meier. Odoevsky was extremely pleased with the theme which I had gotten from the Luga cart driver's song:

He advised me to recall this theme, which introduces Susanin's part in his last scene in the forest with the Poles. I was able to do this. After the words 'I have led you where even the grey wolf has not strayed, Where even the black raven has not carried its bones,' there is a fragment of the theme which the driver gave me:

While composing the beginning of Susanin's answer to the Poles, I had in mind our famous robbers' song, *"Vniz po matushke, po Volge"* [Down Mother Volga], making use of the beginning of it in diminution in the motion of the accompaniment:

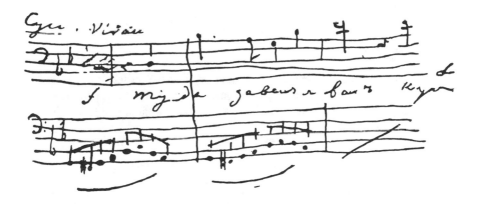

Sometimes I consulted with Karl Meier about orchestration, particularly in fortissimo passages. I also recall that he suggested the figure in the accompaniment of the mazurka to me:

This figure is repeated by various instruments in different keys and does not have a bad effect."

Glinka often saw Zhukovsky and Pushkin at this time (*Zap.*).

Glinka gave Dargomyzhsky the five notebooks of the course in counterpoint which he had taken with Dehn in Berlin (Dargomyzhsky's Autobiography, coll. *Dargomyshsky,* p. 5).

1836

New Year's Eve

Glinka welcomed in the New Year at Odoevsky's. Also present were Pushkin, Ivan Kireevsky, Krivtsov, Zhukovsky, Sobolevsky, and others. (A pencil sketch, signed by V. Odoevsky, portraying the sitters around a table is in coll. *Glinka,* 1958).

Beginning of January

Shevyrev writes (from Moscow) to Odoevsky, that a sheaf of papers which Melgunov left for Glinka was taken by the latter "en route through Moscow. What was in the package, I do not know, though I think it was music and plates" (*L.,* 101).

18 January

Gogol reads his comedy *Revizor* [The inspector general] at Zhukovsky's (*Ostafiev Archive of the Princes Vyazemsky,* SPb., 1899, p. 285).

"Praskovya Arsentievna Barteneva was in Petersburg. Through her or her brother-in-law, D. I. Naryshkin, an orchestral rehearsal of the first act of my opera was arranged in the home of Count Yusupov."

20 January

A note from Glinka to Dargomyshsky about the rehearsal "tomorrow."

22 January

Glinka listened to Count Yusupov's orchestra: "It's not all that bad."

23 January

Letter from Glinka to Dargomyzhsky about preparations for the rehearsal: "The important thing is to have a good bass and cello—you have seen to this. . . . If you can, stop by this evening. . . . If we can get Memel, then it's in the bag."

29 January

Glinka informs Dargomyzhsky that, since the contrabassist Memel is busy, "the rehearsal of the first act of *Ivan Susanin* is being postponed from 31 January to 1 February" (Fr. original).

In a supplement to *Mosk. ved.*, no. 9, there is an item announcing the sale of the journal "Aeolian Harp" (published in 1834) at Gresser and Müller's, the sixth part of which includes the *Farewell Waltz* for piano, and the seventh, an Italian romance (*"Il desiderio"*) and a Mazurka for piano.

1 February

In a letter to Feofil Tolstoy, Glinka invites him to the rehearsal of the first act of *Ivan Susanin*. The orchestral rehearsal took place at the palace of Prince Yusupov. "Even though the orchestra was poor, it nonetheless performed quite well. Iogannis conducted. . . . The choruses were not performed, though Bartenev, Volkov, and I sang in places. Nonetheless the effect of the orchestration seemed satisfactory."
[The Yusupov Palace is on the Moyka Embankment (today no. 94).]

28 February

Glinka went to Mikhail Vielgorsky and asked him to assist in arranging the performance of *Ivan Susanin* at the Bolshoi Theater. The count promised his assistance and asked [Glinka] to return in a few days (according to A. Komovsky, in *Istoricheskii vestnik,* 1885, v. 19, p. 367).

February (?)

Glinka moved to Schlothauer's house (later Merts's) on Fonarny Lane, today, number 3/8 (S. Sobolevsky's ltr. to A. Pushkin, 11 March 1836, in Pushkin, *Soch.,* v. 16, p. 91).

5 March

In a letter to Dargomyzhsky, Glinka asks him if he will be able to attend "the rehearsal of my opera" at the Vielgorskys' "on Tuesday of next week." He asks for assistance in getting a piano. "Staben . . . has taken back my former piano, which he made. The one I took subsequently is so bad that it has never been possible to play on it. My servant, Yakov, was at Staben's yesterday. . . . and found that he had pianos. . . . Make him see reason, for I'll be lost without a piano."

7 March

On the day of the premiere of Beethoven's Symphony No. 9, Glinka attended the dress rehearsal at 10 o'clock in the morning (arranged for music lovers) for the Philharmonic Society's concert in Engelgardt Hall. "We were sitting on the steps near the windows which looked out on the constant flow of traffic on the Nevsky Prospect. . . . After the allegro Glinka said: 'Let's sit down lower, it's more becoming,' and he sat on the green cloth covering the steps. . . . During the scherzo Glinka exclaimed, hiding his face in his hands, 'It's simply perfect! Oh, it's impossible!' and he cried. I realized that I could not have had a greater artist at my side" (W. Lenz, *Beethoven et ses trois styles,* v. II, SPb., 1852, p. 189).

10 March

The second private rehearsal of Act I of *A Life for the Tsar* took place in Mikhail Vielgorsky's apartment (Mikhaylovsky Square, house of Golenishchev-Kutuzov, later of Yakovlev, now Square of the Arts, number 3), "for which he [Vielgorsky] deserves eternal *thanks* . . . artists sang the various roles. I do not remember who was in the chorus, only that they were not members of the court choirs. Gedeonov was at this rehearsal, as was my mother. The rehearsal was quite adequate. Count Vielgorsky made two sensible comments. There was no ending (coda) to the introduction, and as he suggested, I then added a coda. In No. 3, Susanin's scene, the main theme of which I had taken from a Russian song I had heard not far from the city of Luga (St. Petersburg province), the chorus was only heard off stage before the entry of the bridegroom. The Count recommended that I add an on-stage chorus, ending fortissimo after a crescendo, which I brought off successfully, and the bridegroom's appearance became incomparably more ceremonial because of it."

Glinka writes to Sobolevsky: "Zhukovsky will be here Friday at nine o'clock—I hope that you also will come. You would do me a favor if you took the responsibility of inviting Pushkin on my behalf. As you know, I am not a great writer, and besides I am preoccupied with things to do because of my mother's imminent departure."

11 March

Composer's dating on the title page of the manuscript of an aria with chorus for the drama *The Moldavian Girl and the Gypsy Girl* by Konstantin Bakhturin: "Aria with chorus for the drama *Moldavanka i tsyganka, ili Zoloto i kinzhal* [The Moldavian girl and the Gypsy girl, or gold and the dagger]. Composed by M. Glinka, 11 March 1836" (*L.*, p. 104).
[The words "gold and the dagger" were written in pencil by another hand. The words "Moldavian girl and gypsy girl" are crossed out in ink. "To Mr. Bryansky," "To Mr. Bakhturin," and "For Glinka" are written in pencil at the top of the title page in an unknown hand.]

Sobolevsky writes to Pushkin: "The musician Glinka, who lives at Schlothauer's, invites us for Friday *à 9 heures*" (Pushkin, *Soch.*, v. 16, p. 91).
[This note is dated in relation to [Glinka's] letter to Sobolevsky on 10 March. In Pushkin's *Works* the date is indicated approximately: "February, first half of March, 1836."]

13 March

In the morning "Zhukovsky . . . gave me . . . his fantasy *"Nochnoi smotr"* [The night review], which he had just written. By evening it was ready." That same day, at 9 o'clock in the evening, Glinka was visited by Pushkin, Zhukovsky, and Sobolevsky. Glinka performed the ballad *"Nochnoi smotr,"* which he had just written. Evgenia Glinka was also present (*Zap.;* ltr. to S. Sobolevsky, 10 March 1836).
[In his *Zapiski*, Glinka mistakenly dates this event to the winter of 1836/37. From comparison of various documents and facts (Glinka's ltr. to Sobolevsky and Sobolevsky's to Pushkin; Glinka's mother's stay in St. Petersburg; Glinka's address; the time of Pushkin's death; the times of composition and publication of Zhukovsky's ballad) Pushkin's visit to Glinka may be dated 13 March 1836.

The date of composition of the ballad *"Nochnoi smotr"* has been confirmed accordingly. In the *Zap.* it mistakenly says 1837 (*Sov. muzyka,* 1937, no. 6; G 2-A, p. 63).]

After 13 March

Evgenia Glinka left for the country. After her departure, Maria Petrovna "fell ill and then contracted pneumonia." The doctor "was able to save her, but her recovery was slow. . . . My wife's illness shook my faith in marital happiness. Her capriciousness after her illness completely destroyed this faith."
[Glinka mistakenly dates this to 1837, even though he himself indicates his address at the time as Merts house on Fonarny Lane, whereas in 1837 he was already living in the Court Chapel building.]

15 March

In a letter to Nikolay Golitsyn, Dargomyzhsky reports that he "has thought of an opera" and that "after much searching and the advice of Glinka and others" he has decided on "Lucretia Borgia" (Dargomyzhsky, *Izbr. pis'ma* [Selected letters], inst. 1, p. 20).

March

"During Lent the rumor went about in the backstage world that a Russian composer named Glinka had appeared and had written a grand opera on the subject of *A Life for the Tsar.* Of course this was of interest to us all" (Petrova-Vorobieva, *Vosp.,* p. 169).

"After the rehearsal at Count Vielgorsky's there was trouble and rumors. I had to get my opera accepted for performance. I was assured that the conductor Caterino Albertovich Cavos, who had at one time written successful music for an opera entitled *Ivan Susanin,* was actively intriguing against me. Time revealed otherwise, for he more than anyone else convinced the Director to do my opera, and later he conducted the rehearsals with diligence and integrity."

The Directorate of Imperial Theaters commissioned Caterino Cavos "to look at the new work," and Cavos, "despite the fact that his own opera *Ivan Susanin* . . . was then in the repertoire, truthfully and nobly recognized the superiority of Glinka's work" (Yury Arnold, "On the Possibility of the Establishment of an Independent Russian National School of Music," *Bayan,* 1888, no. 22).

"Still there were ill-intentioned people who tried to make Glinka believe that his opera would not be accepted because Cavos would intrigue against him. . . . Unaware of what kind of man Cavos was, Glinka believed this gossip. Finally, after he had examined and evaluated the new opera, Cavos appeared before the Director, Gedeonov, and said that *A Life for the Tsar* possessed unquestionable value, both musically and dramatically, and that it should be accepted and preparations for staging it be undertaken immediately. . . . Cavos announced that if *A Life for the Tsar* were staged, he would not allow his own opera to be produced" (Petrova-Vorobieva, *Vosp., p. 171).

Glinka made the acquaitance of Osip Petrov and Shemaev "and then of other performers from the Russian Opera, and little by little I began to familiarize them with my opera. . . . Lomakin, whom I met at that time, assisted me in my work. He brought in the singer Belikov (soprano) to try the aria *'Ne o tom skorbliu'* [It is not that which I lament] the ritornello of which Tikhmenev played on the flute."

Mikhail Vielgorsky expressed his opinion of the opera: "It is a *chef d'oeuvre!* . . . Glinka's . . . opera is remarkable for its originality. From beginning to end its character is exclusively Russian and Polish. This is no trifle. Moreover, the finale and the final romance are works of genius."

Glinka began to visit the Vielgorskys regularly. He once got into a conversation with "a painter who had worked at Vielgorsky's and said the following: 'I always envy the painter. I see how he gradually comes to enjoy his work and how solid the enjoyment is. If the mood is the same, the pleasure is the same, whereas one does not always receive pleasure from music. To savor it one has to have the patience necessary to hear the entire piece. Often individual parts are not especially distinctive, while the whole turns out to be a marvelous gift and excellent work. In painting, on the other hand, one may admire every stroke, and that stroke is forever and unchanged, while in music everything depends on the performance.'" On another occasion at Vielgorsky's Glinka said: "I would not believe in eternal bliss if I had not seen these three arts—music, painting, and sculpture—here on earth. They are the representatives of a greater happiness. A person in ecstasy because of them forgets the world. He is in a state of bliss, and at that moment he is completely happy, because his spirit requires nothing higher or greater. This is the point at which we stop in our desire and striving for something better. This is the point of true happiness" (according to A. Komovsky, in *Istoricheskii vestnik*, 1885, v. 19, p. 368).

Maria Petrovna complained to Petr Stepanov with tears in her eyes that Glinka did not love her and had betrayed her "for his detestable opera, with which he spends all his time. He has cast me aside and abandoned me. . . . it is a misfortune in married life when the wife begins to get bored" (P. Stepanov, *Vosp., p.*

55). Maria Petrovna "complained to my aunt (my father's sister), Maria Nikolaevna Zelepugina, that I wasted money on music paper" (*Zap.*).

A note to Sobolevsky belongs to this period (?): Glinka asks for a loan to pay the rent. "My wife is sick, and expenses for the doctor and other things have completely exhausted my treasury."

8 April

In a request addressed to the Director of Imperial Theaters, Aleksandr Gede-onov, Glinka writes: "I have the honor of submitting an opera of my own composition, which, if it be worthy, I most humbly request you accept for the theater here. Any conditions I submit exclusively to Your Honor's considera-tion, though I feel it necessary to bring to your attention that this opera . . . may only be given in the theater in St. Petersburg, for, while writing it, I took into account the voices of the singers of this troupe. I am therefore obliged to make a most humble request that Your Honor petition the highest authorities to grant that the opera which I have presented belong exclusively to the repertoire of the St. Petersburg theaters. The management of the Moscow theaters would not be able to manage it without my direction" (ltr. registered among the cases of the Directorate of Imperial Theaters, 8 November 1837, in G 2-B).

First performance in the Aleksandrinsky Theater of the *The Moldavian Girl and the Gypsy Girl* (*SPb. ved.*, 8 April 1836).

After 8 April

"I was bound by a signed statement not to demand any kind of payment for the opera. I gave such a statement to Gedeonov's secretary, A. Nevakhovich, at Nestor Kukolnik's apartment in Gavrilova's house near Siny Most" (today Moyka, 70) (*Zap.*). . . . "I made an agreement with the Director of Theaters to deliver the opera to him one act at a time" (ltr. to his mother, 1 May 1836).

14 April

Kukolnik writes to A. M. Bakunina in Rome: "A genuine musical marvel is being prepared here, M. I. Glinka's opera entitled *Ivan Susanin*. It is charming, marvelously folklike, full of variety, splendid. We will see it on the stage not earlier than September. Hardly another nation may boast of such a folklike opera. Except for *Freischütz* nothing even comes close to it."

14/26 April

Melgunov writes (from Hanau) to Shevyrev: "Besides an article about my trip, in a few days I will be sending Glinka an article about him with a request that it be printed in the *Nabliudatel'* [Observer]. The article is free, for I gave it to Glinka as a gift. It will be necessary before the appearance of the opera, which is already being put on" (*L.*, p. 106).

First Half of April

Glinka was present at an evening given by the Empress. "I was in good voice and sang well" (ltr. to his mother, 1 May 1836).

24 April

In *Sev. pchela*, no. 92, in a feuilleton signed "P. M.," entitled "The St. Petersburg Theaters," there is a review of the drama *The Moldavian Girl and the Gypsy Girl*, which is sharply critical of the play and the music. "Vorobieva played the role of the slave girl. . . . But how was one to recognize her? Instead of the brilliant armor of the military commander Semiramide, she was dressed in the paltry costume of an obscure slave girl, and the prima donna gets confused with the members of the chorus. Instead of the inspired cavatinas of Rossini, she must sing poor lines set to weak music."

29 April/11 May

Melgunov (from Hanau) sent Yanuary Neverov his article "Glinka and His Music" along with a letter to Glinka in which he entrusts the article to him and advises that it be printed in any journal. "Your name is still too little known *du gros public* in Russia. Things have to be prepared if your name is to buzz in their deaf ears. Print it wherever you wish in some paper which everyone reads, but if it's in *Sev. pchela*, then *only without my name*. If you send it to *Nabliudatel'*, then my name may be used. . . . But don't tarry. It's necessary that the article be published before the first performance if audiences are to be prepared. After the performance, ask Odoevsky to write a detailed critique of the opera and to put it in both the Petersburg and Moscow papers" (*Vosp.*, p. 375).

Melgunov writes Neverov that simultaneously he is sending him an article about Glinka, which "he had promised him [Glinka] as soon as his opera was accepted," and a letter to Glinka. "Read the article and letter through . . . and print them as an official letter or simply as they are. Give them to him personally from me. I would like for him to allow you to come to rehearsal so that you can write me your opinion and other things" (*Rus. arkhiv,* 1909, part 2, inst. 5, p. 82). Melgunov informs Shevyrev: "I have sent an article about Glinka to him so that he may look it through and send it on to you" (*L.,* p. 106).

Before 1 May

Glinka presented Gedeonov with the first act of the opera (ltr. to his mother, 1 May 1836).

1 May

Glinka complains to his mother about his health and difficult financial circumstances. He writes that the copying of the second act "is proceeding very slowly because of illness."

Beginning of May

Glinka received the article "Glinka and His Music" from Melgunov. "To express the lyrical aspect of Russian folk character in all kinds of music, particularly opera, is the goal which Glinka has set for himself. His understanding of the words *Russian music* and *Russian opera* differs from that of his predecessors. He is neither more nor less limited to strict imitation of folk melody. He has studied the deep structure of Russian songs performed by the people themselves— these cries, the sharp changes from grave to lively, from loud to soft, the shading, surprises of every sort, and finally, the unique harmony and development of musical phrases, which are not based on accepted rules. In a word, he has opened up an entire system of Russian melody and harmony which is drawn from folk music itself and does not resemble any earlier school. His first large-scale effort, the opera *Ivan Susanin,* proves the extent to which he has realized his idea and dream" (*Vosp.,* p. 159).

[Melgunov's article was not published during Glinka's lifetime, since the composer, apparently, feared that Melgunov's "panegyric" "might appear too immodest" (Strugovshchikov, *Vosp.,* p. 197).]

13 May

Dargomyzhsky writes to Nikolay Golitsyn: "Apparently Glinka's opera will be produced. He had the good fortune to sing and play excerpts at one of Her Majesty the Empress's evenings, which certainly won him Gedeonov's favor. Evidently he feels obliged to accept the opera for performance, even though it is a little contrary to his own wishes. Glinka, whom I see often, as before, said to me that his appearance at the court was a crushing blow to our court musical

monopolists" (A. Dargomyzhsky, *Izbrannye pis'ma* [Selected letters], inst. 1, M., 1952, p. 18; Fr. original).
[By musical monopolists Glinka is apparently referring to the Lvovs (father and son) and to Feofil Tolstoy.]

27 May

Entry in Mokritsky's diary: "Worked a little on my *Raznoschik* [Pedlar] and the lithograph of Koltsov but wanted to draw Glinka."

28 May

Mokritsky was at Glinka's and "drew his head" (Mokritsky, p. 77).
[This portrait is not extant.]

Spring

Glinka's wife and mother-in-law moved to Peterhof. "I found the sea air hard to tolerate and for that reason rarely visited my wife in Peterhof."

"Zhukovsky, Pushkin, Gogol, and other men of letters" were present at a literary evening at Ivan Kozlov's. "The conversation was about Russian opera and Russian composers. Pushkin said that he would like to see a lyrical opera in which all the marvels of choreography, music, and the decorative arts were combined" (*SPb. ved.*, 25 October, 1852).
[Dated in connection with Gogol's departure from St. Petersburg on 6 June.]

Glinka was at the home of the Russian Opera prima donna Stepanova, where he met Vorobieva, who expected "someone extraordinary" and had counted on "meeting someone proud and majestic." Instead she saw "a very small man, somewhat thin and dark. His face was pale, his hair dark and straight . . . he had small eyes, though there was a sparkle in them. . . . After the usual introductions, Glinka sat down at the piano and sang Antonida's romance '*Ne o tom skorbliu, podruzhen'ki*,' and I was immediately captivated. His voice was not big, but it was pleasant, and it was apparent he possessed great feeling and ability. He had mastered his voice marvelously, and I thought then what an incomparable teacher he would be. After the romance he asked Stepanova to look through the beginning of the first aria with him. To me it seemed very new, original, and completely Russian in spirit. After the aria Glinka turned to me with the following words: 'M-lle Vorobieva, I must admit to you that I am an enemy of Italian music. At every step in it I hear insincerity. Since my arrival in St. Petersburg, I consequently have not been to the Russian Opera once, though I know that you recently did *Semiramide* with great success. I hear from everyone that you possess a true contralto voice and great depth of feeling. In view of this, I would like to ask you to sing the song I brought from my opera *without any feeling.*' This surprised me somewhat, and I said to him: 'Mikhail Ivanovich, I would very much like to do as you wish, but on the stage I am accustomed to taking clear account of why I sing some piece one way and not another, and therefore I must ask you to explain to me what in this song provokes Vanya to such apathy?' To which he said to me: 'I will explain it to you thus, Anna Yakovlevna: Vanya is an orphan who lives with Susanin. He is sitting alone in the cottage over some light work singing a song to himself, giving no thought at all to the words but only to his work.' This was sufficient for me. I sang the song through, and Glinka said, 'It is beginning to go beautifully . . .' Afterwards Glinka asked me what my free range was on stage. I answered, two octaves, from 'G' to 'G.' 'And can you go higher and lower?' 'Yes, up to 'A' and down to 'F,' but only as passing notes.' It seemed as if the young composer were feeling out my capabilities. . . . He wanted naturalness and simplicity and not Italian melodrama by any means." Glinka brought the singers separate numbers from the opera, "and little by little we studied our roles under his direction. In very clear and brief terms he explained what he wanted from the performers. He was a great master at explaining his intentions, and sometimes in two or three words he could express what he wanted, while we, like experienced hands on the stage, caught his remarks on the fly. . . . At the time Glinka was very satisfied with the artists" (Petrova-Vorobieva, *Vosp.*, p. 170).

"It was necessary . . . to complete study of the individual roles and begin study of the choruses, to finish the dances and re-do several of them under the guidance of the ballet master, Titus. Besides the polonaise, krakowiak, mazurka, and *pas de quatre* (in A major), I incidentally prepared two more dances [*pas*], one in E, in which there was a solo for Boehm, and another in C for oboe and cello."

Quartet rehearsals of *Ivan Susanin* began in the hall of the Aleksandrinsky Theater, while Cavos held rehearsals with individual groups of instruments to better acquaint the orchestra with the score. "Cavos conducted the rehearsals with his accustomed diligence, though he typically did not observe nuances. In particular pianissimo sections almost never came through, or they were more like mezzo-forte. Similarly he somehow was unable to find the right tempo and always took things either too slow or too fast" (*Zap.*). "Just to give an idea of how far this man [Cavos] was from any kind of intrigue or envy, which are so common in the theater world, I recall . . . Cavos's selfless participation in the performance of Glinka's opera *A Life for the Tsar*" (*Zapiski* of P. Karatygin, in *L.*, p. 110).

"The orchestra was good, but not entirely. In comparison, the second violins were much worse than the first; there were few violas; not all the basses were very good, except for the first chair, Memel. Among the winds, not all the horns played in tune, nor did some of the other second chair players. On the other hand, there were fine artists among the first violins. There were four or five excellent cellists. Among the woodwinds, the clarinettist Bender had an exceptionally full sound, and the flutist Zusman was without argument one of the best, if not the best, artist in Europe" (*Zap.*).

Spring or Summer (?)

The writer Elena Gan writes to her parents: "Now here is a novelty! They are preparing a purely Russian opera, *Ivan Susanin,* a dramatic opera, with a libretto by Kukolnik and music by a young student of the Russian musical school, Glinka. It is entirely in the Russian manner, and from all quarters I hear abundant words of praise for it. Everyone is excited about this national music. A new Russian contralto named Vorobieva has appeared here. They say she possesses a marvelous voice. God forbid . . . she will debut as a boy in this opera" (*Rus. starina,* 1887, v. 53, part 3, p. 741).

Spring–Summer

"Although Zhukovsky did not actually write the libretto, he nonetheless participated faithfully in my work. He explained to the technician and the painter Roller how to do the final scene in the Kremlin effectively, and he went with me to Roller's atelier. Zhukovsky observed things attentively and asked questions. The matter was crowned with success. In the last scene the various groups of people in the distance, which had been cut from cardboard, created an excellent optical illusion, which appeared to be an extension of the real crowd of people standing on the proscenium."
[Two of Zhukovsky's pencil sketches for the epilog of Glinka's opera have been preserved among Odoevsky's papers (*GPB*).]

10 July

Entry in Mokritsky's diary: "Today we once again had dinner for Bruni. . . . Bryullov and Horace Vernet were likewise invited to dinner. After dinner we all went to Kukolnik's, where the composer Glinka, Petrov, and Vorobieva were already gathered. The evening passed very pleasantly. Artists adorned our company, all of whom with unfeigned pleasure extolled the artists who adorned the stage of our theaters and did honor to our fatherland. That evening, under the roof of one private home, about 17 people more or less well known in Europe had gathered" (Mokritsky, p. 83).

11 July

Shevyrev writes to Neverov about the music for Glinka which Melgunov had sent him (*Rus. arkhiv,* 1909, part 2, inst. 5, p. 91).

26 July

Neverov writes to Shevyrev: "According to Melgunov's note, I went to the foreign censorship committee and did not find there any parcel either for myself or for Glinka. Accordingly, it will have to be looked for in customs. . . . It would be rather difficult for me to go to customs and other places completely unknown to me. Glinka is in Petersburg himself. . . . Tomorrow I will give him Melgunov's note, so that he may track down his things himself, since I believe they must be in customs. There is nowhere else they could be" (*GPB,* coll. 850).

Summer

After bathing in the sea in Peterhof, Glinka once again "began to suffer severely, initially a nervous disorder. . . . Soon a fever developed." He began to undergo treatment with a homeopathist.

End of Summer

In Kukolnik's apartment, Glinka wrote the trio with chorus *"Akh, ne mne, bednomu"* [Oh, not me, poor one] "taking Vorobieva's capabilities and talents into account. . . . There were about 15 of us gathered there. . . . I wrote, or rather, composed, this moving scene amid the noise and conversation of my partying friends. At first I wrote the accompaniment to the trio for violas and cellos, but then on the advice of Prince Odoevsky, for only four cellos and one bass. It was he who led me to the idea of using violins *divisi* in four and three parts in the introduction to the trio *'Vse ta zhe toska'* [Always the same yearning], etc."

12 September

In an announcement about the establishment of Snegirev's publishing company in *Sev. pchela,* no. 209, it says that the firm "has acquired the rights to Mr.

Glinka's new Russian opera, which has been impatiently awaited by the public and by connoisseurs, who may be somewhat familiar with its individual beauties."
[Leonty Snegirev undertook the first incomplete edition of *Ivan Susanin* comprising separate numbers in transcription for voice and piano done by Glinka and, without voice, by Karl Meier (in the edition the names of the composers are not indicated everywhere). According to Glinka's words, Kukolnik helped him to sell the opera to Snegirev.]

End of September

"Through the good offices of Gedeonov, I received permission to dedicate my opera to His Majesty the Emperor, and instead of *Ivan Susanin* it was called *A Life for the Tsar*."
[There is no dedication either in the manuscripts or in the printed scores. Glinka's wording ("it was called") emphasizes that the renaming of the opera occurred independently of him.]

September

"Glinka introduced us, that is, Stepanova, Leonov, Petrov . . . and me, to his young wife and his relatives. Sometimes we rehearsed in his house, that is, we sang the trios, duets, and quartet. This was done at home, since rehearsals in the theater had not yet begun except for the chorus and orchestra learning their parts" (Petrova-Vorobieva, *Vosp.*, p. 171).

2 October

The Directorate of Imperial Theaters forwarded Glinka's opera *A Life for the Tsar* to the censor (*L.*, p. 111).

6 October

The Third Section returns "the piece entitled *A Life for the Tsar*, approved for performance" to the office of the Imperial Theaters, and asks that "this piece be once again submitted to the Section after the alteration of several annotated places" (Proceedings for Russian and German Dramatic Works, 1836–1840, in *L.*, p. 111; Leningrad Kirov Theater of Opera and Ballet collection, *L.*, 1940, p. 74).

8 October

The manager of the office of the Imperial Theaters, Aleksandr Kireev, asks Glinka to change several "places" in *A Life for the Tsar*, "made note of by the Third Section," and "to submit [it] once again for examination" (ibid., p. 72).

13 October

The libretto for *"A Life for the Tsar* is published: *"A Life for the Tsar: Opera in three acts. Written by Baron Rozen.* Music by M. I. Glinka. SPb., 1836" (d.c.a.).

From the second half of October. Rehearsals were transferred to the Bolshoi Theater—at first choral rehearsals and then rehearsals with orchestra, first in the hall and then on the stage (Petrova-Vorobieva, *Vosp.*, p. 172). "In order to check out the acoustic properties of the hall of the Bolshoi Theater, the quartet was performed there . . . *'Milye deti, bud' mezhdu vami mir i liubov' '* [Dear children, may there be love and peace among you]" (*Zap.*). "The musicians played and listened very carefully to the music of the overture and the first numbers of the opera, but when they began to play the rowers' chorus, in which the orchestration of the string instruments so naturally imitates the playing of several balalaikas, the musicians became indescribably excited and expressed this to the composer with an outbreak of applause. The krakowiak likewise made a strong impression" (Petrova-Vorobieva, *Vosp.*, p. 171). "I confess that this approval satisfied me more than all the public's expressions of satisfaction" (*Zap.*).

20 October

The Directorate of Imperial Theaters sent to the Third Section the changes made in the libretto of *A Life for the Tsar* by Glinka and Rozen (memorandum from the Third Section to the Directorate of Imperial Theaters, 21 October 1836, in the book *Teatr opery i baleta im. Kirova* [The Kirov Theater of Opera and Ballet], p. 73).
[In the autograph score of *A Life for the Tsar* the changes in the text have been made partly by Glinka and partly by Rozen.]

21 October

The Third Section returned to the Directorate of Imperial Theaters "the approved piece entitled *A Life for the Tsar,* with changes made by the authors themselves" (*The Kirov Theater of Opera and Ballet,* p. 72).

24 October

Glinka held a musical evening attended by a "large company" including Kukolnik, Mokritsky, and others.

27 October

Glinka attended Nestor Kukolnik's nameday celebration, which also included Bryullov, Petr Karatygin, Mokritsky, Heydenreich, Yanenko, and Kireev. "Having spent the evening pleasantly, we returned home" (Mokritsky, p. 87).

4 November

Report from the stage manager of the Russian Opera troupe, Lebedev, to the office of the Imperial Theaters concerning dispatch and distribution of parts for the opera *A Life for the Tsar* to the chorus of the Preobrazhensky Regiment. The chief of the office of the Imperial Theaters, Kireev, writes to the office of the Lifeguard of the Preobrazhensky Regiment on the same subject (TsGIA, coll. 497, no. 7251).

6 November

Aleksandr Karamzin writes to Andrey Karamzin in Paris: "There is a lot of talk now about Glinka's opera, with which the Bolshoi Theater is opening. It has been remodelled, and they say it is very beautiful. Vielgorsky speaks passionately about this opera as something very beautiful. Unfortunately, they say it will be impossible to get seats for the first performance, which is taking place at the end of the month" (*Karamziny,* p. 133).

9 November

In *Sev. pchela,* no. 257, there is an announcement, which reads: "An original Russian opera, *A Life for the Tsar,* composed by M. I. Glinka, with text by Baron E. F. Rozen, is being performed at the Bolshoi Theater, which will open in a short time. Rehearsals for the opera are drawing to a close, and the first performance probably will follow at the end of this month."

11 November

In *Rus. invalid,* no. 286, there is this notice about *A Life for the Tsar:* "Rehearsals for the opera are drawing to a close, and the first performance probably will follow at the end of this month."

17 November

Neverov writes to Shevyrev: "There is much news here, however not literary. We are impatiently awaiting Glinka's opera *A Death for the Tsar, or Susanin,* with which the Bolshoi Theater is opening. The finishing touches, as they say, have been wonderfully done."

Before 20 November

Melgunov (from Hanau) writes to Shevyrev that he is surprised that no one is writing him, "if only about Glinka's opera" (*L., p.* 113).

22 November

Konstantin Bulgakov writes to his father: "The opening of the Bolshoi Theater is not far off, and Glinka's opera, *A Life for the Tsar*, otherwise known as *Ivan Susanin*, will be given. As Count Mikhail [Vielgorsky] says, the music is charming, but more importantly, it is completely national in spirit" (G 2-A, p. 68; Fr. original).

20–29 November

"The outstanding oboist, Brood, arrived for the final rehearsals. He played his parts on both oboe and English horn exceptionally well" (*Zap.*).

The last rehearsals of *A Life for the Tsar* took place "amid the thumping of workers lounging in the boxes of the Bolshoi Theater. Outwardly Glinka showed great composure in the face of this and everything else, but inwardly he was deeply distressed by such disregard both toward art in general and toward himself personally. He surmised that under such circumstances *A Life for the Tsar* would not last three performances. I admired his firmness and iron patience and remarked that he, like Vanya, faced "service to a great truth," for, new directions in art aside, *A Life for the Tsar* also had a political meaning. It would counteract the painful memory which was still alive in people's minds of the mischief of the Arakcheevs and Magnitskys, who had done so much harm to people's most sacred beliefs because of their arbitrariness and contempt for law" (Odoevsky, *Vosp.*, p.104).

"At one of the orchestral rehearsals our tenor Leonov sent a note saying that because of illness he would not be at the rehearsal. Mikhail Ivanovich was there on the stage, and recognizing the problem, he said, 'No matter, I will sing in his place.' They began the rehearsal, and Glinka wandered about the stage rubbing his hands. At last came Sobinin's entrance. Glinka very valiantly approached the footlights and opened his mouth to sing the first phrase, '*Radost' bezmernaia*' [Boundless joy], but he stopped after pronouncing the syllable '*Ra.*' The orchestra also stopped. Everyone looked at him in disbelief. I said to him, 'Mikhail Ivanovich, what is the matter? Go on.' Disconcerted, he answered, 'I can't, I'm afraid. . . . Hell, I never expected it to be so frightening to sing on these boards'" (Petrova-Vorobieva, *Vosp.*, p. 172).

25 November

Glinka was not present at the dress rehearsal of *A Life for the Tsar* "because of illness." "The theater was full." After the rehearsal Odoevsky told Glinka that it went well and assured him by "insisting that the success of the first performance was beyond doubt" (*Zap.*).

27 November

The following announcement appears in *Sev. pchela,* no. 272: "On Friday the 27th of November, in the Bolshoi Theater for its opening after being remodelled, *A Life for the Tsar,* opera in three acts, with words by Baron E. F. Rozen and music by M. I. Glinka; scenery by Messrs. Roller, Kondratiev, and Gonzago; dances by Titus; costumes by M. Baltieu." Then in the "Miscellany" section of the same issue: *"A Life for the Tsar,* an original Russian opera with music by Mr. Glinka and words by Baron Rozen, which has been impatiently awaited by many music lovers to whom parts of it were known, is finally being performed on the stage and will be presented today. If it makes the same impression on the general public as many excerpts from it have made on connoisseurs who have heard them, we sincerely congratulate our young composer for the success of his first large work after many charming, original small pieces of his which everyone loves." There is also a notice here of the publication "today" of *"Pesnia siroty"* [The orphan's song], and within the next few days, the overture and mazurka from the opera *A Life for the Tsar.* "This is not all: the opera's composer has put together some charming French quadrilles from several themes, and without doubt these will soon be played on every piano and by all our large orchestras."
[There is a copy of Glinka's published quadrille on themes from *A Life for the Tsar* in ITMK, coll. 6.]

Announcement in *SPb. ved.,* no. 271: "Today . . . at the Bolshoi Theater for its opening after reconstruction, the premiere of *A Life for the Tsar,* an original opera in three acts."
[There is a comparable announcement in *Rus. invalid,* no. 301.]

A poster: "Today, Friday, November 27, the premiere of *A Life for the Tsar* will be presented at the Bolshoi Theater by actors of the Russian court. Original, grand opera in three acts with epilog, choruses, and dances. Music by M. I. Glinka. Scenery for the first act (the village Domnino on the river Shacha) by

A. Roller; hall by G. Petrov; in the second act, a peasant hut, by P. Gonzago; in the third act, a dense forest covered in snow, by A. Kondratiev; in the epilog, Red Square, with a view of the Kremlin, by Andrey Roller. Dances by the balletmaster Titus. Costumes by Baltieu. Main curtain by Andrey Roller. The dancers will be Pimenova, the middle Semyonova, Andreyanova II, and Smirnova. The characters: Ivan Susanin, a peasant from the village Domnino, sung by Mr. Petrov; Antonida, his daughter, by Mme Stepanova; Bogdan Sobinin, her fiancé, by Mr. Leonov; Vanya, an orphan and ward of Susanin, sung by Mme Vorobieva; leader of the Polish detachment, Mr. Baykov; leader of the Russian detachment, Mr. Efremov; the Polish courier, Mr. Makarov; the Russian people, Polish troops. Curtain at seven o'clock."

Aleksandr Turgenev writes in a letter to Aleksandr Bulgakov: "Today they are presenting a new opera by Glinka. Everyone is trying to get seats, which have been taken long ago" (*Pis'ma Aleksandra Turgeneva Bulgakovym* [Letters of Aleksandr Turgenev to the Bulgakovs], M., 1939, p. 196). Entry in A. Turgenev's diary: "Dinner at the Vyazemskys' with Zhukovsky. With Pushkin in the theater. *Semeystvo Susaninykh* [The family of Susanins]; opening of the theater, the audience. Repeat of the same" (*Pushkin v vospominaniiakh sovremennikov* [Pushkin in the reminiscences of his contemporaries], vol. 2, M., 1974, p. 171). "To get tickets to the premiere of *A Life for the Tsar* without influence was rather difficult" (N. Kulikov, "A. S. Pushkin and P. V. Nashchokin," in *Rus. starina,* 1881, v. 31, part 8, p. 614).

That evening the first performance of the opera *A Life for the Tsar* took place. "It is impossible for me to describe my feelings that day, especially before the performance began. I had a box on the second tier. The first was completely occupied by members of the court and dignitaries with their families. My wife and relatives were in the box. . . . The opera was a complete success, and I was in a state of intoxication" (*Zap.*). Pushkin was present at the performance. He sat in the eleventh row of the parterre near the aisle. "During intermissions members of cultured society from the first rows approached him with praise for Glinka. In general the opera had a brilliant success" (N. Kulikov, "A. S. Pushkin and P. V. Nashchokin," in *Rus. starina,* 1881, v. 31, part 8, p. 614).

"The renovated theater opened with a new work by an original Russian talent, M. I. Glinka's opera *A Life for the Tsar,* with text by Baron E. F. Rozen." The Tsar and his family were present, as well as "the most distinguished members of St. Petersburg society . . . and members of the diplomatic corps with their families, including representatives of the embassy of the Khanate of Bukhara." "All were enthralled with the sounds of the native, Russian national music. Everyone showed complete accord in the expression of enthusiasm which the patriotic content of the opera aroused. . . . At the conclusion of the opera the composer was unanimously called to the stage" (*SPb. ved.* and *Rus. invalid,* 4 December 1836; cf. also *Sev. pchela,* 3 December 1836; reprinted in *Mosk. ved.,* 11 December 1836).

"The opening of the Bolshoi Theater (which is very beautiful) has taken place. Glinka's *Ivan Susanin* was presented in the presence of the court, the diplomatic corps, and all the state dignitaries. I was there with good Mrs. Shevich in a box on the second tier (naturally, we were not able to get such seats ourselves). Many arias of the opera are lovely, but on the whole it seemed to me to be written in a mournful tone, all much the same, and insufficiently brilliant. It is all based on Russian themes and is in minor keys. In the last scene the depiction of the Kremlin is splendid. The crowd of people painted on canvas blended with the faces and seemed to extend into infinity. As usual here, the reception was chilly; the applause died down and seemed to be restored with reinforcements" (ltr. from S. Karamzina to Andrey Karamzin, 28 November 1836, in *Karamziny,* p. 143).

After the performance Glinka "was called to the side of the Imperial box. First His Majesty thanked me for my opera, remarking that it was not good that Susanin should be killed on the stage. I explained to His Majesty that, since I had not been at the dress rehearsal because of illness, I was unable to know how this would be dealt with, but according to my program the curtain was to be immediately lowered during the Poles' attack on Susanin and his death announced by the orphan in the epilog. After the Emperor, the Empress thanked me, and then the great princes and the princesses who were in the theater."

"At the first performance someone in one of the boxes on the dress circle said of the opera, '*C'est mauvais.* You can hear the likes on any street, *dans tous les cabarets*' " (V. Odoevsky, "The New Russian Opera, *A Life for the Tsar*," in the literary supplement to *Rus. invalid,* 30 January 1837).

Leaving the theater, Bulgarin said to Vigel "that it was a kind of potpourri. I just answered him with a bitter smile" (ltr. from F. Vigel to V. Odoevsky, 29 November 1836, in *Vosp.,* p. 401).

After the performance Kukolnik wrote this couplet:

> With him, the dawn of Russian music first emerged,
> He will not be forgotten, like *A Life for the Tsar*.
> (ltr. from V. Engelgardt to V. Afanasiev, 30 May 1908, *L.,* p. 116)

On being asked what he had to say about the new opera, D. P. Tatishchev responded: "I can say nothing. The experts assure me that one must hear it through several times in order to understand and appreciate its good qualities. I, however, was so overtaken by boredom at the first performance that I, obedient servant though I am, will not be enticed to a second" ("Excerpts from an old notebook begun in 1813," in *Rus. arkhiv,* 1873, part 2, inst. 11, p. 2159).

Ivan Turgenev attended the premiere of *A Life for the Tsar:* "I candidly admit that I did not understand the meaning of what was taking place before my eyes ... *A Life for the Tsar* simply bored me. ... But I must have understood Glinka's music all the same" (I. Turgenev, "Literary and Everyday Reminiscences," in *Sobr. soch.,* v. 10, M., 1956, p. 268).

An entry by K. N. Lebedev: "I have just returned from the Bolshoi Theater. There were thousands of spectators, the aristocracy, stars, brilliance, and beauty— all the finest in St. Petersburg. They gave *A Death for the Tsar, Ivan Susanin,* a national opera including prolog and epilog with music by Glinka and words by Baron Rozen. It is a small opera written with successful tunes as it were and a desire to speak or sing apothegms for Petrov, especially for him. It is not a work of art at all. There are motifs from Russian songs, and in abundance. The composer selects a tune for his beginning, adds an ending, and puts together his score. Petrov performed Susanin's part in the forest beautifully, namely his aria to the sunrise, but then Petrov performs everything beautifully. The sets are brilliant, the scenery is by Roller. It seems there were three things on which the composer's understanding of national music was based (this is its source): Russian songs (either in full, or reworked, or half and half with his own fantasies); liturgical music (mostly in the choruses); and that characteristic trait so explicitly and distinctly expressed in our songs—the exchange of grief and joy, festive gaiety, fluidity, and briskness. He made use of these means. Will the experts judge it good? These are just the external signs, however, and not the thing itself. It's still young and green! It's a child who cries 'wolf,' when it's only a bearskin coat" (From the notes of Senator K. N. Lebedev, in *Rus. arkhiv,* 1910, part 2, inst. 7, p. 377).
[Dated according to its content.]

Returning late in the evening from Petr Klodt's, Mokritsky and Karl Bryullov "dropped in for a minute on Vasily Ivanovich Grigorovich. It was nearly 12 o'clock. The man had just then arrived from the theater and enthusiastically told us about the successful premiere of Glinka's opera, *Ivan Susanin*" (Mokritsky, p. 94).

"During the first few years the chorus dampened the effect of the action in our lovely opera *A Life for the Tsar*. A crowd of men makes its entrance, sings some chorus, and carelessly disperses without action" (R. Zotov, "My Reminiscences of the Theater," in *Repertuar*, 1840, part 9, p. 58).

28 November

In a letter to his mother Glinka tells her of the opera's success: "Yesterday evening finally fulfilled my desires, and my long labor was crowned with the most brilliant success. . . . I must give Gedeonov his due for producing the opera with exceptional taste and splendor. . . . Now, because of guests and well-wishers, I do not have a minute alone."

"The day after the premiere, I [Konstantin Bulgakov] went to see Glinka, and he asked me to tell him what specifically I did not like about the opera. I told him, and he agreed with me completely that the libretto was poorly done and that on such a good story it should have been possible to write something much better than what Baron Rozen wrote" (ltr. from K. Bulgakov to A. Bulgakov, 1 December 1836, in G 2-A, p. 68).

Petr Vyazemsky shares his impressions of *A Life for the Tsar* in a letter to Aleksandr Bulgakov: "Yesterday was the opening of the Bolshoi Theater and Glinka's opera. . . . We will speak another time about the opera, when I have heard it two or three times. Overall there are no effective places. Nothing is immediately striking to the ears or hearts of us laymen like in the operas of Rossini, Bellini, Meyerbeer, and others. Therefore one has to listen intently with a sharp ear and become familiar with the music in order to judge the opera. Generally it was well accepted. Glinka was called out. The libretto was rather cold and pale, so consequently it was more difficult for the musician to embroider a pattern on its design" (*Rus. arkhiv*, 1879, no. 2, inst. 6, p. 241).

Aleksandr Turgenev writes to Nikolay Turgenev in Paris: "I was at the opening of the theater yesterday evening. They presented a new Russian opera called "*Semeystvo Susaninykh*" [The family of Susanins] by the composer Glinka, which was outstanding in every respect: production, costumes, audience, music, and the ballet numbers. Nearly the entire court attended. The boxes were full of elegant ladies" (P. Shchegolev, *Duel' i smert' Pushkina* [The duel and death of Pushkin], M., 1928, p. 275; Fr. original).

M. Serdobin informs Boris Vrevsky that it was impossible to get tickets for the premiere of Glinka's opera (*Pushkin i ego sovremenniki* [Pushkin and his contemporaries], inst. 21–22, P., 1915, p. 396).

Mikhail Vielgorsky's opinion of *A Life for the Tsar:* "Glinka has mastered perfectly the spirit of Russian harmony. Everything you might find in his melodies is Russian, but there is not a single Russian song which you ever chanced to hear. . . . There is nothing I can say about the quality and appropriateness of the Polish choruses. The mazurka-like cadence of these choruses is a most felicitous inspiration, which a lesser composer would have certainly trivialized" (according to A. Komovsky, in *Istoricheskii vestnik,* 1885, v. 19, p. 369).

"An amateur of that time, famous in the drawing rooms for his performances of current romances accompanied on the piano with an affected strumming, said of this great work that it was the song 'If I distressed you' with drums." One heard such trivial remarks in the parterre during the performance" (Odoevsky, *Vosp.,* p. 103).

"I can recall the vacillation and dissension which [the opera's] appearance . . . caused among the Petersburg aristocracy and audiences of the time. The musical pedants, who commanded great authority then, shrugged their shoulders contemptuously whenever they spoke about the opera, and only a few impartial music-lovers and connoisseurs affirmed that Glinka was a great native talent. The public, *le gros du public,* did not know whom to believe. For want of custom and routine, much of Glinka's opera did seem strange to them. Hardly anyone among them dared to say aloud and without hesitation that this opera was no worse, for example, than *I Capuletti ed i Montecchi,* or that Glinka's musical gift was no less than that of the talented melodist Bellini, who was . . . in such fashion that Prince V. F. Odoevsky said audiences had not only become *'obellinilas' '* [Bellinized] but *'vzbelenilas' '* [mad]. However, instinct led them to the theater whenever *A Life for the Tsar* was being performed" (Loginov, *Vosp.,* p. 101).

"In speaking about my opera, several members of the aristocracy said with scorn *'C'est la musique des cochers.'* This is good and even true, for in my opinion coachmen are sensible fellows!"

"Many people criticized M. I. Glinka because the soprano part (in the trio *Akh, ne mne bednomu*) was too high. . . . M. I. Glinka responded to us by saying, 'You are judging on the basis of voices which you have heard, while in my head I hear the ideal voice, quiet and tender, whose high notes are silvery and not strident'" (Rostislav, "Musical Conversations," in *Sev. pchela,* 4 May 1853).

29 November

Performance of *A Life for the Tsar* in the Bolshoi Theater (*SPb. ved.*, 29 November 1836).

Serov and his father were at the second performance of *A Life for the Tsar*. "I felt the music's stylistic resemblance to our folk songs from its very first sounds, but at the same time I somehow was perplexed. The music was both folklike and not folklike. One could discern very learned and complex forms. . . . Its general character was not in the least like Mozart, or Weber, or Meyerbeer. . . . There was a certain unique seriousness of style (because of the predominance of counterpoint) and austere orchestral coloration (from the frequent combination of strings and brass) which I could not help being struck by, but I will not say that . . . these things particularly pleased me. The overall impression which this opera had on me . . . was confusing the first time" (Serov, *Vosp.*, p. 68).

Entry in Aleksandr Khrapovitsky's scrapbook: "I will swear that as I understand it, the opera is nonsense and rubbish. Glinka has lost touch with what is Russian but not yet adopted foreign ways, and garbage is the result" (*L.*, p. 119).

Vigel writes to Odoevsky about *A Life for the Tsar:* "To me it seems the libretto is worthless. . . . The opera might be more appropriately considered an oratorio with scenery and costumes. But what music! One must know the Russian spirit very well in order to speak so powerfully to it with sounds alone." Vigel advises Odoevsky to write an article about the opera for Pushkin's journal *Sovremennik* (*Sev. pchela*, 16 December 1836).

30 November

Performance of *A Life for the Tsar* in the Bolshoi Theater (*Sev. pchela*, 30 November 1836).

1 December

Memorandum from the Ministry of the Imperial Court to His Majesty's private chancellery "regarding the delivery of things" worth 3000 rubles "as a gift to the composer of the music of the opera *A Life for the Tsar*, Titular Councillor Glinka" (TsGIA, coll. 468, Second Section of His Imperial Majesty's Chancellery).

Performance of *A Life for the Tsar* at the Bolshoi Theater (*Sev. pchela*, 1 December 1836). "They presented *Ivan Susanin*. Several times the music and

Petrov's and Vorobieva's singing moved me to tears, though the rest was weak and rather ridiculous. . . . In the last act I was quite interested in the mobile crowd painted in the distant background, and I laughed heartily, but to make up for it I did not spare my hands in applause, and I shouted 'Brava!' . . . for Vorobieva" (Mokritsky, p. 95).

Konstantin Bulgakov writes to his father: "I was at the opening of the Bolshoi Theater, where they presented a remarkable opera by Glinka. High society was not satisfied with it and said it was boring, but as one who lives exclusively for music, I say to you that it is very beautiful and above all marvelously orchestrated, similar to *Robert le Diable*. Every instrument has its triumph. The vocal ensembles, bass arias, the tenor and particularly contralto, especially the last, were so touching that one could not listen to them without tears. . . . I was ecstatic that our own music had finally appeared" (G 2-A, p. 68; Fr. original).

3 December

"His Majesty has decreed that the duties of Director of the Court Chapel Choirs are to be performed by Aide-de-camp Colonel Lvov because of his father's illness." At that time Fedor Lvov "relinquished responsibilities to his son Aleksey Fedorovich Lvov with the consent of His Imperial Majesty" (*L.*, p. 119).

4 December

In *SPb. ved.*, no. 277, in the section "Internal News," there is a description of the premiere of *A Life for the Tsar* (signed by "S. P."). In *Rus. invalid*, no. 307, "Internal News," there is an article with the same signature and the same text describing the premiere of Glinka's opera.

A dinner at Glinka's celebrating the premiere. Gedeonov announced the office of Imperial Theaters' order raising Petrov's pay for each performance because of his continuing pursuit of perfection. Glinka warmly congratulated the artist (unpublished Autobiography of O. Petrov in M. Ivanov's article "25th Anniversary of the Death of Petrov," in *Novoe vremia*, 24 February 1903).

Performance of *A Life for the Tsar* in the Bolshoi Theater (*Sev. pchela*, 4 December 1836).

5 December

In *Journal de St.-Pétersbourg,* no. 146, *"Nouvelles d'interieur,"* there is a report about the opening of the Bolshoi Theater and the performance of *A Life for the Tsar.*

6 December

Performance of *A Life for the Tsar* in the Bolshoi Theater (*SPb. ved.,* 6 December 1836).

7 December

An article by Odoevsky (unsigned) appears in *Sev. pchela,* no. 280, "Letters to music-lovers about Glinka's opera *A Life for the Tsar,*" letter I: "You had asked that I report to you my first impressions of Glinka's new opera. I shall do exactly as I promised. I am writing to you immediately after the first performance, so do not look for strict clarity in my words. . . . Quite simply Glinka's opera appeared unexpectedly, as it were. Journalistic acclaim did not alert us to it in advance. . . . It had been said in passing in *Severnaia pchela* that there was a new opera, and there was a rumor circulating that there was Russian music in it. Many listeners expected to hear various arrangements of familiar folk tunes in the opera and only that. But how is one to express the surprise of true music-lovers when from the first act they realized that this opera had answered a question so important to art in general and Russian art in particular, a question, that is, about the existence of Russian opera, *Russian* music, and finally, about the existence overall of *folk* music. . . . The composer, educated in the secrets of Italian singing and German harmony, penetrated deeply into the character of Russian melody. With his abundant talent he demonstrated in this brilliant experiment, that Russian melody, by nature doleful, cheerful, or bold, could be elevated to a tragic style. . . . Glinka's opera represents what they have searched for for a long time and not found in Europe—*a new element in art.* With its history, a new period begins, *the period of Russian music.* We say that such an accomplishment, placing our hand over our heart, is an affair not just of talent but of genius."

8 December

In the "Miscellany" section of *SPb. ved.,* no. 280, there is a notice about the activities of the firm of Snegirev and its publication of the libretto as well as separate numbers from *A Life for the Tsar.*

After 4 and Before 10 December

Glinka received a gift for the opera, "a ring worth 4000 rubles," from Nicholas I. "It was made of a topaz surrounded by three rows of the most exquisite diamonds; I immediately gave it to my wife as a gift" (ltr. to his mother, 11 December 1836; *Zap.*).

From 27 November through 11 December

Six performances of *A Life for the Tsar* took place. ". . . the success far exceeded my expectations, and more and more my opera began to please audiences."

Beginning of December

Glinka made the acquaintance of Mikhail Volkonsky "and agreed to teach the singer Ostroumov, who was under his patronage and whom he [Volkonsky] referred to by his own name, Mikhaylov" (*Zap.*).
[Porfiry Mikhaylov-Ostroumov was a chorus member with the Russian Opera Troupe from April of 1836. Glinka worked with him before his trip to the Ukraine in 1838. After Glinka's return on 10 September 1838, Mikhaylov went abroad.]

11 December

Glinka writes to his mother about the opera's success, but he does not write about the details of the first performance, since "it is quite accurately described in the *Sev. pchela*." "I am now fully rewarded for all my work and effort, and if I have not yet succeeded in all my intentions, I hope that I will not be long in attaining my remaining goals." He enumerates "the gains received" from the opera: a ring, "from which I will have a beautiful necklace made for Masha. . . . Fame. I am universally recognized by everyone as the best composer in Russia, and in the opinion of connoisseurs, therefore no worse than the best composers," and finally, notification that E. A.'s case, under consideration in St. Petersburg, "will be decided in our favor *without fail*." He writes that he is trying to obtain a position in the civil service, but that "there are many difficulties, since what I want does not exist, and it will be necessary to create such a position again." He writes that the issue of his brother Andrey's appointment in school has still not been decided, but beforehand "he must be sent to an officer" to prepare him for the examination. For the time being his brother is living with him [Glinka] and is working with him on geography and Russian history. Glinka promises to send several printed numbers from his opera "next week."

Neverov relates in a letter to Shevyrev: "For two weeks now Petersburg has lived in the theater. We can not get enough of hearing Glinka's charming opera." He says that on Odoevsky's request he has written an article for *Nabliudatel'*, which he encloses with the letter asking that it be printed "if you have not already received something more interesting about Glinka's opera" (coll. *Glinka,* p. 133).

In *Mosk. ved.,* no. 100, among correspondence from St. Petersburg from 30 November, there is a detailed description of the remodelled Bolshoi Theater, which opened "with a work by an original Russian talent. . . . Everyone was fascinated by the sounds of native Russian national music and unanimous in sharing in the enthusiasm awakened by the opera's patriotic content."

13 December

Breakfast at Aleksandr Vsevolozhsky's in honor of the success of *A Life for the Tsar.* Present were Pushkin, Odoevsky, Vyazemsky, Zhukovsky, Mikhail and Matvey Vielgorsky, Petrov, Vorobieva, Stepanova, Leonov, Caterino and Ivan Cavos, Roller, Titus, members of the Bolshoi Theater orchestra, Snegirev, Laskovsky, Norov, Rezvoy, Struysky, and others. Odoevsky offered the first toast: "In honor of Mikhail Ivanovich Glinka—creator of Russian opera, opening a new period in our native musical art." Then Mikhail Vielgorsky, Vyazemsky, Zhukovsky, and Pushkin performed a canon they had written in Glinka's honor (with music by Odoevsky).

Vielgorsky:

Sing in ecstasy, Russian choir,
A novelty has appeared,
Make merry, Rus'! Our Glinka
Is no longer clay but china.

Vyazemsky:

The voice of rumor will praise
This beautiful novelty,
Our Orpheus, Glinka,
From the Neglinnaya to the Neva.

Zhukovsky:

In honor of such glorious novelties,
Let horns and drums sound forth.
Let us drink to Glinka's health
A glass of mulled wine.

Pushkin:

Hearing this novelty,
Envy, darkened with malice,
Let them grit their teeth, but Glinka
Will not be trampled in the dirt.

(*Pushkin in the Romances and Songs of His Contemporaries, L.,* 1936; GPB, coll. 539, no. 45.)

Rozen sends Pushkin the published libretto to *A Life for the Tsar* and in an accompanying letter attributes the opera's success exclusively to the merits of his libretto (Pushkin, *Soch.,* v. 16, p. 197).

14 December

Performance of *A Life for the Tsar* in the Bolshoi Theater "for Petrov's benefit" (*SPb. ved.,* 13 December 1836).

Death of the director of the Court Chapel, Fedor Lvov (*L.,* p. 122).

15 December

Odoevsky's "Second letter to a music-lover about Glinka's opera *A Life for the Tsar*" appears in *Sev. pchela,* no. 287: "My letters cannot keep up with the performances of this opera. It has already been presented five times, and five times the composer has been called out, not by the applause of friends but by the audience's unanimous voice. From this it does not follow that Glinka's opera has no enemies, even vehement ones. It could hardly be otherwise. Music is an unfortunate art in that everyone feels he has a right to judge it. . . . But we hasten to add, in the composer's and the listeners' honor, that the number of such enemies decreases with each performance, and the applause intensifies. Whoever has heard the opera twice no longer talks the same of it as he did after the first performance. This is a sign of long and certain success. . . . Neither time nor space allow me to tell you its content or the content's connection with the music. . . . The subject of the opera was born in the composer's head together with the music itself, and he had already established the entire course of the piece before he turned to the author of the words with the request to give them appropriate form for the stage." There follows a short analysis of the opera act by act.

Censor's authorization for the Canon in Honor of Glinka, music by Odoevsky, and words by Vielgorsky, Vyazemsky, Zhukovsky, and Pushkin.

16 December

Conclusion of "Odoevsky's second letter" (signed "K. V. O.") in *Sev. pchela*, no. 288, in which the analysis of the opera continues. He writes as follows concerning the music of the forest scene with the Poles: "Susanin's melody attains the highest tragic style, while—something hitherto unheard of—preserving its Russian character in all its purity." In the conclusion he introduces Vigel's letter from 29 November (q.v.). Odoevsky's article concludes with this issue (reprinted according to the autograph, in *Vosp.*, p. 327).

19 December

The beginning of Bulgarin's article, "A Review of the New Russian Opera *A Life for the Tsar*, with music by Glinka and text by Baron Rozen," is printed with an epigraph from Griboedov in *Sev. pchela*, no. 291: "'Why are only foreign opinions sacred!'—an answer to Odoevsky's article. The entire world knows Mozart and Rossini, and no one says of them that they discovered *a new element in art* which people *had searched for but not found* for a long time. No one said this of them, nor will they say it, because this *new element* in art is like the philosopher's stone, which exists only in the heads of music theorists and not in nature. . . . We believe that there can be no such *new element* in music and that in music *it is impossible to discover anything new*. Everything is there. Take it and make use of it."

20 December

Performance *A Life for the Tsar* in the Bolshoi Theater (*SPb. ved.*, 20 December 1836).

21 December

The conclusion of Bulgarin's article on *A Life for the Tsar* appears in *Sev. pchela*, no. 292: "On the whole, the music of his opera is excellent, charming, and delightful, but . . . the opera has lost touch with *music*, that is, its composition and arrangement do not correspond to the *harmony and melody* poured out in it. . . . There are too many choruses, and the choruses are too prolonged. . . . There are too few separate arias, too few duets, trios, etc., and consequently there is too little action, too little life. . . . The music for the orchestra is written too *low*. . . . There is too little variety in the music. . . . However delightful the music is, however charming the individual parts, the entire opera . . . pardon me . . . is boring. There is no opera without effect."

[With respect to the appearance of Bulgarin's article, Glinka wrote in his *Zapiski:* "These are curious articles which clearly confirm the degree of musical ignorance of their author."]

"When Glinka's opera *A Life for the Tsar* was first being presented, one well-known artist made the remark that in some places the orchestration did not have the proper effect because some of the woodwind instruments were scored too low. Somehow this opinion reached the journalist 'X,' who in his review thought he would show off with somebody else's opinion, and here is how he expressed himself: 'The orchestra in the opera is tuned to low notes and therefore is ineffective . . .'" (F. Koni, *Shmeli* [Bumblebees], in *Lit. gaz.*, 24 May 1842).
[The journalist "X" is Bulgarin.]

Petersburg "was gladdened by a Russian talent who, though still inexperienced in the world of drama, possessed warmth and love for his art. The reviewers . . . were as far apart as the four corners of the earth. Some detected *new elements in art* in Mr. Glinka's opera and a new epoch in music. Others inopportunely probed his learning, though they did not even possess an elementary knowledge of music, and therefore, in their opinion, *the orchestra was tuned to low notes"* (lit. supplement to *Rus. invalid,* 30 October 1837).

Performance of *A Life for the Tsar* in the Bolshoi Theater (*Sev. pchela,* 21 December 1836).

When he met Glinka backstage, Nicholas I said to him: "Glinka, I have a request to make of you, and I hope that you will not turn me down. My singers are well known throughout Europe, and, consequently, it would be worthwhile for you to work with them. I only ask that they do not become Italians under you."

"The minister of the court directed me to declare . . . my interest and respond." Reference is to Glinka's appointment to the Court Chapel. Assuming that either Matvey Vielgorsky or Count Volkonsky would be appointed director of the Chapel, and that the director would be occupied with administrative matters while Glinka would "only be involved in artistic affairs," he responded that he "agreed to accept the title of Kapellmeister of the Court Chapel."

22 December

Glinka visited Matvey Vielgorsky: "He received me more cordially than usual. We were both glad to serve together and looked forward to the possibilities of improving the Court Chapel."

27 December

"Memorandum" from the Minister of the Imperial Court concerning Glinka, who "with sincere gratitude accepts the offer made to him of the position of Kapellmeister of the Court Chapel, with a salary of 1500 rubles and board of 1000 rubles, in all 2500 rubles per year." On one side of the resolution is this annotation: "It has been directed by His Majesty to appoint Aide-de-Camp Lvov to carry out the duties of Director and Titular Councillor Glinka as Kapellmeister with a salary of 1500 rubles and board of 1000, which amount is also designated to Inspector Belikov, if he now receives less" (*L.*, p. 124).

29 December

Performance of *A Life for the Tsar* in the Bolshoi Theater (*Sev. pchela*, 29 December 1836).

End of December

Aleksey Verstovsky writes to Odoevsky: "With the opera *A Life for the Tsar* the sunrise of Russian opera has appeared on the horizon, and Alyabiev and I are in the garrison (Carlini's article), and Glinka's opera is an important epoch on the Russian stage . . . in a word, the entire twenty-year-long labor of a man whose entire effort was to wrap the character of Russian national music in European form is no longer worth a penny! . . . We have not yet seen the sun, nor will it ever appear until they stop turning their faces from everything with Russian folk character. . . . I was one of the earliest admirers of Glinka's beautiful talent, but I do not wish to, nor am I able to yield the right of first place. . . . I see no ability in Rozen: the time of Italian librettos has passed" (*Biryuch petrogr. gos. teatrov* [Herald of the Petrograd State Theaters], ed. A. Polyakov, P., 1920, p. 229).
[Yury Arnold's story (under the pseudonym Carlo Carlini), *Liubov' muzykal'nogo uchitelia* [A music teacher's love], was published in the *Biblioteka dlia chteniia* [Library for reading] (1836). In it Alyabiev and Verstovsky are introduced as privates in a musical garrison. Verstovsky thought that the author of the story was Odoevsky.]

Melgunov writes to Shevyrev from Frankfurt: "Apropos Neverov: why does he not write me even a word, if only about Glinka's opera?" (undated ltr., GPB, coll. 850).
[Tentatively dated the end of December 1836 by virtue of its contents.]

"The opera went better and better, and people attended the theater enthusiastically. Wherever there was singing at all, one would be certain to find printed pieces from my opera. By the way, it was more accurately transcribed for piano by Karl Meier and myself than it was printed by Snegirev. The paper was exceptionally bad, and the printing of some pieces could not keep up with the public's demand."

A poem by an unknown author dates from this period:

> There are Auber and Meyerbeer,
> Who have been strewn with flowers:
> But Glinka, for example,
> Is also with us.
> He was born in Russia,
> And for this reason,
> If he were an angel in heaven,
> He could not compare to Rossini.
> But speaking sincerely,
> If our Rus' does not vanish,
> Glinka, because of *Life for the Tsar*,
> Will not grow cold in his grave.
> (*L.*, p. 125)

"The initial idea for *Ruslan and Lyudmila* was given to me by our famous comic Prince Shakhovskoy. In his opinion, the role of Chernomor should be written for Vorobieva. At one of Zhukovsky's parties, Pushkin, in speaking of his poem 'Ruslan and Lyudmila,' said that he would have changed a number of things. I wanted to find out from him specifically what kind of changes he had in mind, but his premature death prevented me from carrying out my desire. . . . I expected to put the plan together according to Pushkin's instructions, but his premature death prevented me from realizing my intentions."

In "A Brief Overview of the Activities of the Imperial St. Petersburg Theaters," compiled by the Directorate of Theaters, it says that "the year 1836 was remarkable not for the great number of new dramatic works which appeared, but for the successful performance . . . and splendid production . . . of several important and difficult works. . . . The most important success of the opera troupe was the Russian opera *A Life for the Tsar*. This phenomenon had a twofold significance. *A Life for the Tsar* is the musical creation of a Russian composer. With this work, Mr. Glinka, the composer of the music, has placed himself alongside other famous composers. His work had a brilliant success. If the quality of the libretto had measured up to the quality of the music, its success would have been even more significant. But unfortunately, despite the richness and national interest of the plot, the author of the words did not work it out altogether satisfactorily. His style was too irregular and frequently absurd. The Russian Opera troupe's performance of this important and difficult work earned them audiences' attention and approbation. Because of his fine acting, excellent voice, and expert singing, Mr. Petrov proved himself to be a valuable asset to the opera. In a role which corresponded so completely to her musical and even physical capabilites, Mme Vorobieva could not have been anything but success-ful. Her success was incredible, however. Mme Stepanova was no less deserv-ing of the audience's approval, but her role, the hardest of all in the opera, does not possess the brilliant effects which one encounters in the roles of Petrov and Vorovbieva. She was graciously received, but audiences did not fully appreciate the difficulty of her role or her precise and gratifying performance. She deserved success at least equal to that of Vorobieva. . . . Ballet now plays a part in almost all large-scale operas. In *A Life for the Tsar,* Mr. Glinka himself inserted the dances. . . . Works performed in 1836, which were noteworthy for their cos-tumes included the operas *A Life for the Tsar, I Montecchi ed i Capuletti,* and *Le cheval de bronze*; and for scenery . . . Andrey Roller's . . . view of Moscow's Red Square crowded with people, for the opera *A Life for the Tsar"* (Livanova and Protopopov, *Glinka 2,* p. 198).

1837

New Year's Eve

Glinka brought in the New Year at Odoevsky's. "We drank to Glinka's health" (ltr. from V. Odoevsky to S. Sobolevsky, 10 January 1837, in *L.,* p. 126).

1 January

Glinka was appointed Kapellmeister of the Court Chapel Choir . "His Imperial Majesty the Emperor has the pleasure of directing the appointment of Titular Councillor Glinka to the post of Kapellmeister . . . his salary to be fixed from the first of January according to a schedule determined by His Majesty. Having announced His Majesty's will to Chief Marshal of the Court Naryshkin for appropriate implementation and having informed Your Honor of the same, I ask you, with your consent, to allocate a state furnished apartment in the singing building for Kapellmeister Glinka" (order of the Minister of the Court to A. Lvov, 1 January 1837, in *L.,* p. 126).

Performance of *A Life for the Tsar* in the Bolshoi Theater. "The success of my opera grows every day . . . the theater was full for the eleventh performance and the receipts were nearly 6300 rubles" (ltr. to his mother, 2 January 1837).

2 January

Order of the Senate confirming Aleksey Lvov as Director of the Court Chapel (*L.,* p. 126).

Glinka tells his mother of his appointment to the Court Chapel and writes: "But fate, which will not abide the complete happiness of mortals, has played a trick on me. On the death of the elder Lvov, his son, with whom I am not in complete harmony, has been appointed to his place. . . ." In the same letter: "I have become such good friends with Gedeonov and the Cavoses that I also hope to have a position in the theater, at first without salary, but later there will be no question about it."

A Life for the Tsar is mentioned in *Sev. pchela,* no. 1, in an article by "P. M." [Medvedovsky] entitled "The Alexandrinsky Theater": "Music-lovers here are rushing to the Bolshoi Theater and cannot hear enough of Glinka's charming opera. . . . at any gathering in the capital city, large or small, rich or modest, one hears conversations and opinions about our young composer's masterpiece. They even dance quadrilles based upon the opera's delightful tunes."

3 January

Memorandum from the Minister of the Imperial Court to Chief Marshal of the Court Naryshkin and to Aleksey Lvov concerning Lvov's and Glinka's appointments to the Chapel Choir (*L.,* p. 126). Glinka took up his duties with the Chapel Choir (Report No. 50 to the Office of the Court and an order addressed to Glinka dated 4 January 1837 about his appointment, in ITMK, coll. 6). Lvov received Glinka "with sincere cordiality, and we decided to proceed hand in hand in our new endeavor."

Beginning of January (?)

Lvov "gave an examination. Many of the older singers, that is the tenors and basses, turned out to be quite bad." Lvov wanted to separate them, but Glinka "undertook to teach them music, i.e., how to read music, and corrected their intonation, or, in Russian, adjusted their voices [*vyverit' golosa*]. . . . When I appeared for the first time for their instruction with chalk in hand, there were few volunteers to be found. The majority of the older singers stood off at some distance with a look of disbelief, and some of them even smiled. Without paying any attention to this, I got down to business so diligently, even cunningly, I might say, that after several lessons almost all the older singers . . . came to my lectures. . . . My method of teaching consisted of the analysis of scales, the meaning of semitones, and therefore an understanding of the basis for the use of sharps and flats. I then wrote short two-voiced exercises (*Sätze*) on the blackboard, had them first analyze the exercise, then sing one part, then analyze and sing the other part, and finally sing it all together, as I tried to improve their ability to listen and correct their intonation."

In *Bib-ka dlia chteniia,* v. 21, in the section headed "Literary Chronicle," there is a report of the unabated success of *A Life for the Tsar,* "whose subject will always be a patriotic one for Russians and its music highly national. Artistically the music is quite remarkable. There are ravishing places in it, which one already hears in all the drawing rooms."

Nikolay Milyutin writes to his parents in Moscow: "On the evening of 1 January I went to the theater, where Glinka's opera was being performed. I had already seen it, but because of the insistence of several young people who are enthusiasts of the opera, I wanted to hear it again in order to convince myself of its beauties. Unfortunately for me, I again was unable to grasp its beauties, and I nearly went to sleep imagining myself at some station among Russian coachmen who, chins resting on their hands, break into an interminable and monotonous song like a little Valday bell" (coll. *Glinka* 1958, p. 22).

6 January

In *Mosk. nabliudatel'* [Moscow Observer], no. 15 (Oct., part 1, 1836), there is an article signed "Y. N." [Yanuary Neverov] entitled "Glinka's New Opera *A Life for the Tsar.* Letter to the *Observer* from St. Petersburg, 10 December 1836." "Knowing what a mighty labor it is to fit an opera's poem to music, we will not reproach Baron Rozen for his verses. Everything depends upon the composer, who must create and sustain our interest throughout the entire work by himself. Our maestro has met his obligation. He has given the opera life and movement and has developed what the librettist only alluded to. With all this, many people remained dissatisfied after a first hearing of *A Life for the Tsar* and did not go into it carefully until they had heard it a second time. Then their attention was concentrated only on the composer, who fascinated his listeners. Mr. Glinka did everything which could have been done. Read through the poem and try to tell what kind of person Vanya is. You will be unable to get a satisfactorily clear idea. But listen to the music written for him, and a beautiful, clear image of the orphan will take shape in your mind, doleful even in happiness, brave, courageous. . . . In Vanya's last aria his sadness even appears elevated and solemn. Indeed for this aria alone we would not be bored to come to the theater twenty times. But this still does not describe everything worthwhile in Mr. Glinka's music. What is important is that his opera is a purely Russian, folklike, and native work. How can one convey the excitement with which the master has filled the hearts of music-lovers who understood the importance of his accomplishment. Never before has a work for the stage stimulated such lively enthusiasm among us as has *A Life for the Tsar.* Audiences understood the composer, or rather, were drawn instinctively to his lofty talent. . . . Each time enthusiastic listeners showered the celebrated master with applause. Mr. Glinka fully deserved the attention, for to create a folk opera is a feat which will cause his name to be engraved forever in our country's annals of art. The urge toward nationalism in music appeared some time ago. We were fully convinced that our folk songs concealed a rich source of totally original melody. There were even experiments in nationalistic opera. Without mentioning others, we may note that Mr. Verstovsky was an intelligent composer with genuine talent, though, incidentally, not dramatic talent, who tried to transfer Russian singing to the stage. However, he was unsuccessful because he thought he could create an opera by borrowing folk melodies, sometimes in their entirety, or by imitating them. . . . This was not nationalism, and moreover things lost all proportion, since opera came to appear like an arbitrary miscellany of arias, duets, and trios in every style. . . . Mr. Glinka behaved otherwise: he penetrated deeply into the character of our folk music, took note of all its peculiarities, which he studied and assimilated, and then he gave his imagination complete freedom, which it expressed in indigenous Russian form. When they heard the opera, many people thought they recognized something familiar and tried to recall what Russian song one or another melody might have come from, though they could not find the original. This is flattering praise for our master. In fact there is not one borrowed tune in the opera, but they all appear clear, understandable, and familiar to us because we hear native sounds in them. The main character of the music of *A Life for the Tsar* is beauty [*gratsiia*]. Its nationality is more easily understood because Russian music is inherently very melodious and lovely. However, Susanin's entire part and several of Vanya's arias are written in an elevated, pathetic style, and for all that they are completely Russian, which is a matter of some importance! Until now we had never heard Russian music in an elevated style. Mr. Glinka has created it. He also has created a totally distinctive type of recitative and thereby enriched art with new ideas. His recitatives are not like either the German or Italian styles. They combine the expressiveness and dramatic flexibility of the former and the melodicism of the latter, while one also seems to hear the intonations of Russian speech. To all of the merits of this important work which we have mentioned, add also the rich instrumentation, which adorns the beauty of the composer's musical ideas. . . . Three weeks have not yet passed since *A Life for the Tsar* first appeared on the stage, and one already hears tunes from it not just in the drawing rooms, where it now dominates conversation, but even on the street, which is new evidence of the opera's folk spirit. . . . A new era is beginning for Russia's artistic genius. For a long time it wavered in its flight, but now, it seems, it has embarked on a direct path, which the people pointed out to it" (dated according to the announcement of publication).

8 January

Letter from the office of the Ministry of the Imperial Court to Glinka about his appointment as Kapellmeister "effective the first of January . . . concerning which appropriate proposals have already been given to Chief Marshal of the Court Naryshkin and Aide-de-Camp Lvov, who occupies the post of Director of the Court Chapel" (*L.*, p. 127).

10 January

Odoevsky informs Sobolevsky that Glinka's opera "has had a marvelous success (they called him back five times). I have written a very long article about it which I must give to the *Sev. pchela*" (*L.*, p. 131).

14 January

Performance of *A Life for the Tsar* in the Bolshoi Theater (*Sev. pchela*, 14 January 1837).

15 January

Glinka accompanied Vorobieva at a musical evening, "and she sang marvelously. I [Bryullov] was ecstatic, but when she had sung Romeo's aria from *I Montecchi ed i Capuletti* and then Vanya's aria from *A Life for the Tsar*, 'Akh, ne mne, bednomu sirotinushke,' I could not restrain my tears and promised myself to do her portrait" (according to *Vosp. A. Mokritskogo o Bryullove* [A. Mokritsky's reminiscences of Bryullov], in *Otech. zap.*, 1855, no. 12).

15/27 January

Melgunov (from Frankfurt) writes to Shevyrev: "You write to me about his [Neverov's] adventures but not a word about whether or not you gave him my letter, where, by the way, I ask for news about Glinka's opera" (*L.*, p. 131).

Before 16 January

Artôt's concert, in which "Vorobieva was received with the incomparable enthusiasm which had become customary. However, several listeners, who were still under the influence of the marvelous effect this actress had had in the music of Glinka, remarked how Mme Vorobieva excelled even herself in music which demanded sincerity and fervor and how constrained her artistic spirit was in the pleasant but lifeless phrases of Italian music" (lit. supp. to *Rus. invalid*, 16 January 1837).

16 January

In a lit. supp. to *Rus. invalid*, no. 3, there is this unsigned notice in the "Miscellany" section: "Foreign newspapers are always unmercifully disfiguring our proper names. Not long ago a new example appeared when a certain German newspaper, reporting on the opening of the Bolshoi Theater in St. Petersburg and the new Russian opera *A Life for the Tsar*, called its respected composer M. I. Glinka by the name Glinat."

Aleksandr Karamzin writes to Andrey Karamzin: "Ball after ball St. Petersburg is in a sweat. . . . I cannot help becoming intoxicated with the intoxication of balls, even infatuated. I am not bored where for music they play dances and mazurkas from Glinka's opera" (*Karamziny*, p. 153).

23 January

In *SPb. ved.*, no. 18, there is an announcement that the music store in Chaplin's house has available a French quadrille from *A Life for the Tsar*, composed by the director "of court ball music," Aleksandr Lyadov.

29 January

Death of A. S. Pushkin. "Our Poetry's sun has set! Pushkin has died in the flower of his youth, in the midst of his great career! . . . We do not have the strength to say more, nor do we need to. Every Russian heart knows the full value of this irreparable loss, and every Russian heart will be distressed. Pushkin! Our Poet! Our joy, our people's glory! . . . Can it be true that Pushkin is no longer with us? . . . It is impossible to adjust to the thought. 29 January, 2:45 in the afternoon" (lit. supp. to *Rus. invalid*, 30 January 1837).
[This unsigned death notice was written by Odoevsky. His authorship is attested to by Sofia Karamzina (*Karamziny*, p. 176).]

30 January

In a lit. supp. to *Rus. invalid*, no. 5, there is an article by Odoevsky (signed "V. Nevsky") entitled "The New Russian Opera, *A Life for the Tsar*. Music composed by Mr. Glinka, libretto by Baron Rozen," and dedicated to "M. P. M." Odoevsky discusses the various opinions of the new opera in "society." "Many have said '*C'est mauvais*, one can hear it on any street, *dans tous les*

cabarets.' Others have been more favorable and said that the opera is respectable, but how can it be compared to our dear Bellini or Rossini? After their
effusions they sing some tune, you think by Rossini or Bellini, but not at all.
As evidence for what they say, our music-lovers cannot sing you anything
except the solemn march from *Fenella*! . . . There are still others, the most
pitiable remains of the upper class, who, though they feel the full charm of Mr.
Glinka's music, do not have the courage to utter their opinions aloud for fear
of compromising themselves. . . . For a long time now people have talked about
Russicism, Russianness, and nationality, but now it is clear that the upper circles
still remain piteous, characterless, and unconscionable imitators besides. . . .
They are pathetic, very pathetic. It is not worthwhile to get angry with them,
though it seems it is impossible to find their likes anywhere but in St. Petersburg. However, there are connoisseurs, and their opinions, unfortunately, are
printed. . . . Every poison has its antidote. . . . At each performance one may
count with considerable satisfaction several tens of true connoisseurs . . . but
their judgments, unfortunately, you rarely hear. . . . These are the real music-
lovers, who moreover have Russian souls. Glinka wrote for them. He sees and
understands them. . . . It is indisputable that Italian, French, and later German
music, which were worked over almost totally, received universal prominence,
and from them European music evolved. It became so firmly rooted everywhere
and people became so accustomed to hearing it, that the ordinary, ingenuous
sounds of native music could hardly make much of an impression on a large
number of people. This gave Mr. Glinka considerable difficulty. Following the
music of common practice, he had to transmit native sounds with complete
fidelity in order to place Russian music on the same level with the national
melodies of Western Europe. The extreme difficulty of this will be understandable to anyone who has gotten even slightly accustomed to hearing our melodies. There is nothing more stubborn or irregular and at the same time more
harmonious than Russian melodies. Glinka was fully aware of this fact. He
understood these melodies and transmitted them with a well-balanced unity,
adding to this his amazing orchestration, which would do honor to any opera
of Auber, Halévy, Bellini, or Donizetti. In his work he demonstrated something
else: he demonstrated how firmly he wielded his musical pen and how it never
betrayed him. . . . Everyone wished and still wishes Mr. Glinka success, except
high society. There has hardly been an opera here which was performed better,
either overall or in all its aspects. One might only wish that Mme Stepanova's
and Mr. Leonov's acting had been more lively. . . . For Mr. Leonov the best
example would be Petrov's outstanding acting. What can one say then about
Mme Vorobieva's acting? It's hard to know where to stop! Since the appearance
of *A Life for the Tsar* she has risen above judgment, both in her acting and in

her singing. She may be assured that the entire audience without distinction adores its darling little fledgling."

[Odoevsky's announcement of Pushkin's death was published in this same issue.]

24, 29, 31 January

In a letter to Timofey Granovsky in Berlin, Neverov writes: "This winter Petersburg rejoices in a remarkable phenomenon, Glinka's opera *A Life for the Tsar*. This lovely and even profound work has been beautifully produced, and Vorobieva and Petrov have simply charmed everybody. I have heard it eight times and am ready to hear it that many times again!" (coll. *Glinka*, p. 137).

January (?)

An article on *A Life for the Tsar* by Elim Meshchersky dates from this period. It was written for a French publication (but apparently remained unpublished?): "The composer has solved once and for all a problem which had been posed but not yet solved. He has enriched us with national music which has passed through the crucible of science. He has opened the musical world to a new era and led art to a land no one had discovered before." After a favorable assessment of the majority of scenes and individual numbers, the author sums up: "Thus it has been most pleasant for us to welcome the appearance of a national opera. . . . One of the primary manifestations of genuinely Russian civilization is its song. . . . Ancient traditions have not been forgotten. As before, Russians charge to victory singing their songs. Mikhail Glinka has created something more and better than an opera. He has fulfilled his obligation as a citizen. . . . He knows that the aim of art is not only the creation of beauty, but more than that, to do good, to influence the feelings, aspirations, and customs of the people. . . . We hope that Mikhail Glinka will not settle in the realm of beauty he has opened up to music, but that he will remain as now at the summit of the vocation he foresaw and pursue it with diligence and courage! Let not the icy breath of malevolence or stupid indifference extinguish the divine and patriotic flame in him which illumines his meditations and expresses itself in passionate harmonies! If envy should pursue him with its jabs or ignorance cast thistle on his path, may he still go forward, may he go forward. If, like a snake, slander should entwine his legs and strike at the artist's heart with its forked and poisonous sting, may he nonetheless move ahead. If the correctness of his thoughts should not be recognized or his merits not be understood, may he always go ahead! . . ." (*Sov. muzyka*, 1954, no. 6, p. 88).

2 February

In *Khudozhestvennaia gazeta* [Newspaper for the Arts], no. 1 (January), Kukolnik writes in an article "From the Publisher" that because of evolving musical tastes and the appearance of "an original Russian opera, *A Life for the Tsar,*" musical subjects also will be discussed beginning with the first issue of 1837. "In so far as the opera *A Life for the Tsar* is concerned . . . I cannot avoid sharing my thoughts and feelings with the readers of *Khudozh. gaz.,* when a work of such importance appears on the uninhabited steppe of music, Russian as well as European. . . ." In the same issue, in an article called "Scenery of the St. Petersburg Theaters," there appears an expression of appreciation for Roller's sets for the finale of *A Life for the Tsar:* "We feel that Red Square is Andrey Roller's finest accomplishment for the Russian stage. The locality is quite accurately preserved. Lighting has been thought out intelligently, and the scenic arrangement of the stationary groups of people has been figured out superbly. Even the procession of the popular masses in the distance, despite the fact that it does not agree with the course of the play and is dangerous to the performance in its daring, is so successful that it vindicates the artist completely. We are unable to cast even the first word of reproach. The fascination continues now for the fifteenth time. Audiences cannot get used to the deception and are captivated the same each time" (d.c.a.).

9 February

Report No. 50 to the office of the court about changes among the officials and employees of the Court Chapel. In the column headed "Who has been newly appointed, whence, and when," there is the following entry: "Retired Titular Councillor Glinka has been appointed Kapellmeister of the Court Chapel Choir as of the third of January" (ITMK, coll. 6).

12 February

I. Kalashnikov writes to P. Slovtsov in Podolsk: "The thing occupying the attention of the public is the appearance of a new Russian opera called *Susanin* by Glinka" (*Pushkin and His Contemporaries,* inst. 6, SPb., 1908, p. 107).

13 February

In *Rus. invalid,* supp. no. 7, there is a notice about Vorobieva, in which the author, speaking about the audience's enthusiastic reception of the artist's acting and singing, writes: "If during her final aria (in the opera *A Life for the Tsar*) Meyerbeer or Rossini themselves should stand up in the middle of the audience and say that Mme Vorobieva's singing was bad or cold, no one would believe them."

I. Maltsev writes to Sobolevsky: "Odoevsky has taken it upon himself to approach the Orpheus Glinka, who is extolled from the Neglinnaya to the Neva, concerning your legal action *en si-bemoll mineur"* (*L.,* p. 133).
[Apparently this concerns a debt Glinka owed to Sobolevsky. Maltsev was Sobolevsky's partner in the establishment of the Samson Textile Mill.]

January–February

Glinka often met with Lvov, who invited Glinka, Kukolnik, and Bryullov to his home. Lvov "played Mozart and Haydn excellently. At his house I heard Bach's trio for three violins. . . . Desirous of attracting artists to himself, [Lvov] did not begrudge even a cherished bottle of some rare wine" (*Zap.*).

27 February

In lit. supp. no. 9 to *Rus. invalid,* in the section headed "Criticism and Bibliography," there is a review (unsigned) of the libretto to *A Life for the Tsar.* "Baron Rozen, the author of the poem, is already known to the reading public as an intelligent and hard-working writer. The majority of readers . . . have long since been well-disposed toward his work, which is why, when we heard that he had written the libretto for M. I. Glinka's opera, we could be glad and assume that at least it would be well done. We were not deceived in our expectations. Not everyone realizes how hard it is to write an opera libretto, so not everyone is in a position to judge the strengths and weaknesses of one. While he is free to create characters, the poet must at the same time completely subordinate himself to the composer. He is only permitted to write what corresponds to the music and translate this to words. In his lines he must even use the vowels the composer needs. . . . The opening to *A Life for the Tsar* is weak, almost insignificant. The opera itself is not a poem but simply a historical picture, though a well-proportioned picture. It is true that the artist-poet held strictly to events and did not let his imagination go, but on the other hand the picture is not crowded with extraneous or unnecessary things. The overall effect is concentrated in Susanin, as it should be. With respect to the language in which *A Life for the Tsar* is written, we encounter many beautiful lines in this piece which would be entitled to a place of honor anywhere. For example, *"Vysok i sviat nash tsarskii dom"* [Sacred and sublime our royal home] . . . or the peasants' song in Act II, scene 8, which begins *Razgulialasia, razleleialas' voda veshniaia po lugam* [Vernal waters spread over the meadows and embrace them], which contain so much feeling and nationality. Further on there are these lines in

Susanin's aria before his death: *'Tebe, dobromu molodtsu, poruchaiu ia detishche'*
[To you, good fellow, I entrust the child] . . . and the orphan Vanya's well-
known romance, etc., etc. Among the beautiful lines, on occasion one meets
some which are inept, as, for example . . . in Antonida's aria *'V pole chistoe
gliazhu, v dal' po reke rodnoi ochi derzhu'* [I gaze on the open field and hold
my eyes in the distance along the native river], etc. Or *'Ne rozan v sadu, v
ogorode—tsvetet Antonida v narode'* [Not a rose in the garden, Antonida blos-
soms among the people] (!!). Or *'Tak ty dlia zemnogo zhit'ia, griadushchaia
zhenka moia'*! [As you for earthly life, my future wife] . . . etc." As examples
of unsuccessful librettos the critic names the operas *Les Huguenots, Robert le
diable, Zampa,* and *Le cheval de bronze,* where there is "not one line which
could be considered poetry. This is why we have concentrated such attention
on the brochure published by Baron Rozen as a unique occurrence in the genre
of librettos."

3 March

In *Bib-ka dlia chteniia,* no. 21, in the section called "Literary Chronicle," there
is this notice: "*A Life for the Tsar* is having the sort of success in Petersburg
that something patriotic and native and with such national music will always
have among Russians. Artistically this music is altogether remarkable. There
are lovely places in it which one hears already in all the drawing rooms. It is
said that M. I. Glinka intends to take advantage of Lent to make important
changes which are actually needed in the score. But is it true, as they say, that
the music was composed first and the words chosen later? Judging from the
words, they really seem to be music translated into poetry" (d.c.a.).

In no. 18 of "Special Announcements," *Mosk. ved.,* there is an announcement
about a concert on 11 March in which Leonov "will sing from the new opera *A
Life for the Tsar.*"

6 March

In testimony before the Senate, the Minister of Finance gave his assent to
compensate Evgenia Glinka 49,732 rubles, 29 1/4 kopecks, for her husband's
tax revenues, but he remarked that in the State Council's opinion, nothing was
said about payment of interest with this sum or why 21,581 rubles, 46 kopecks
were recovered from Ivan Glinka (G 2-A, p. 59).

9 March

In a Ministry of the Imperial Court memorandum (office of the court, No. 1221) concerning dispatch of the court singers to participate in a concert for the benefit of invalids, Lvov made this annotation: "I request that Mikhail Ivanovich discuss this with me" (*L.*, p. 133).

11 March

In a large vocal and instrumental concert in the Hall of Nobility in Moscow, the overture and Sobinin's aria with chorus (Leonov) from *A Life for the Tsar* were performed (*Mosk. ved.*, 24 March 1837).

13 March

In the lit. supp. to *Rus. invalid*, no. 11, it says the following in an article about a performance in the Bolshoi Theater of Bellini's opera *I Capuleti ed i Montecchi:* "With Glinka's opera *A Life for the Tsar,* which initiated a new epoch in our music for the stage, a new epoch in singing itself has begun. People who have not been in Petersburg for more than a few months are unfamiliar with our artists: the same people, the same voices, at that! Every day accuracy of intonation and trueness of expression improve. Still sometimes there will be a faintly perceptible inclination toward howling . . . but this shortcoming is disappearing by the hour. Glinka's efforts have not been wasted." In a note, this is added, "We saw Glinka's solfeggio excercises in manuscript. By printing them the author would render a great service to all music lovers."

In *Sev. pchela*, no. 57, there is an announcement about the publication of individual numbers from *A Life for the Tsar:* the orphan's song and a transcription for guitar by Morkov of the duet (published by Snegirev).

14 March

In *Syn otechestva* [Son of the fatherland], part 184, no. 8, in the section headed "Bibliography," mention is made of a forthcoming performance in Moscow of *A Life for the Tsar* (d.c.a.).

17 March

In *Sev. pchela*, no. 60, there is a report that the cellist Max Borer will perform the quartet from *A Life for the Tsar* in a concert on 18 March.

18 March

In *Sev. pchela,* no. 61, in an article by "P. M." entitled "The Bolshoi Theater," it speaks of Vorobieva, "whose captivating voice and inspired acting capture with equal effect the feelings of proud Arzas, Romeo's ardent soul, and the wails of the kind child Vanya's broken heart."

Stepanova, Vorobieva, Petrov, and Shemaev participated in a concert given by the cellist Max Borer, performing the quartet from *A Life for the Tsar* (*Sev. pchela,* 17 March 1837).

24 March

In *Mosk. ved.,* no. 24, there is a review of the concert on 11 March, which attracted "a fine, large audience who finally had the pleasure of hearing the beautiful, excellently performed overture and an aria with chorus [sung by Leonov] from the renowned national opera *A Life for the Tsar.*"

March

Glinka and his family moved into a state apartment in the building of the Court Chapel (*Zap.*).
[According to tradition Glinka's apartment was located in the right wing of the building on the Moyka Embankment, no. 20.]

9 April

In *Sev. pchela,* no. 79, there is a review of the book *A Conversation with Children about Home Economics, Farming, Manufacturing, and Commerce* by Viktor Buryanov. The author of the review (signed "N.") writes: "In reference to objects of technology . . . do not give these things special importance in a higher intellectual sense. A *practical* age is approaching in the arts, that is, some people would like to *bury* music, painting, poetry, and sculpture. No! As you wish, but Glinka, Bryullov, Pushkin, Baron Klodt, and Orlovsky are greater than Zelenkov, Butu, Tricheaut, Pel, and even Glazunov, Smirdin, and company. If you want absolutely and unconditionally to place the useful above the noble and beautiful, then you must first demonstrate that a turnip is more valuable than a rose or a scarecrow more important than a monument to a great military leader."

Between 1 March and 11 April

"Lent is the hardest time for our brother the musician" (ltr. to his mother, 13 April 1837).
[In 1837, Lent fell between 1 March and 17 April. No concerts could take place during Holy Week (the last before Easter).]

A note from Glinka to Odoevsky dates from this period (?): "Other than the published pieces, there is no piano score of my opera. Today I will have the score removed from the theater, and it will be at your disposal. Volkov and I agreed to go through Petrov's scene together; your presence would not hurt. However, you are well enough acquainted with the opera and with Volkov's singing to accompany well without it."
[Originally the letter was dated in connection with preparation for the rehearsals of *Ivan Susanin* in Yusupov's home in 1836, but the fact that the score of the opera was in the theater and separate numbers were already published indicates that the original dating was in error. Most likely the letter dates to Lent 1837, when excerpts from Glinka's opera were frequently performed in charitable and other fashionable concerts.]

Between 5 and 11 April

The trio *"Ne tomi, rodimyi"* was performed "with exceptional success" in a Patriotic Concert. The performers were Lobanova, Andreev ("who was outstanding"), and Andrey Pashkov. Nicholas I, who was present at the concert, said to Aleksey Stuneev, "Glinka is a great master. It would be a pity if we were to stop with this one opera" (*Zap.*).

"By the sixth week [of Lent] I was worn out with concerts. At the last of them, an amateur concert for the benefit of the Patriotic Society, I at least received some reward for my labors. At the conclusion of the trio from my opera I was called out to thunderous applause and had to exchange bows with the audience."

Before 13 April

Glinka received a text and letter from the Governor of Smolensk, Khmelnitsky, requesting him to compose a polonaise with chorus for the ball which "our gentry intends to give for the heir when he travels through Smolensk. However difficult for me, there is nothing I can do but compose one."

13 April

Glinka writes to his mother about his plans for the summer: "I only intend to come to the country if I am given a mission in Little Russia, otherwise I plan to spend the summer in Tsarskoe Selo."

After 13 April

Glinka wrote the polonaise with chorus *"Velik nash Bog, velik i slaven pervo-derzhavnyi nash narod"* [Great is our God, great and glorious our sovereign people] on a text by Sologub (instead of the text sent by Khmelnitsky, *"Kakoi vostorg, kakaia radost' se tsarskii pervenits griadet"* [What rapture, what joy, the first-born of the Tsar approaches]) (ltr. to his mother, 13 April 1837; *Sollogub*, p. 623).
[Initially the text sent by Khmelnitsky was written in the score; afterwards Glinka crossed it out in exchange for Sollogub's words.]

17 April

In *Sev. pchela*, no. 86, in an article by Koni (signed "K.") entitled "Melodies by D. Struysky for tenor and viola with piano accompaniment," there is a comparison of Glinka and Verstovsky: "In his opera *A Life for the Tsar*, Glinka became the first to give melody the rights of citizenship in Russian opera, and having demonstrated that recitative is just as adaptable to the sounds of the Russian language as it is to Italian, he dropped his beautiful melodies in the soul of each and made them folklike. Verstovsky, a composer not without talent, does not produce the same magical effect with his operas as does Glinka, for in his case there is an appreciable absence of melodiousness, and his arias are therefore similar to couplets and his operas to vaudevilles. . . . Verstovsky often took folk songs and turned them into operatic motifs, and they got lost. Glinka composed Russian melodies which then became folk songs. Thus it was necessary in the case of the former to coerce the folk song to conceal it in measured rhythm, while [Glinka] gave the melody complete freedom, as if it had just sprung from the breast of a peasant improvisor."

19 April

The overture to *A Life for the Tsar* was performed in a concert given by Crescini in the Bolshoi Theater (*Sev. pchela*, 17 April 1837).

30 April

In *Bib-ka dlia chteniia,* no. 22, in the section headed "Various News Items," there is an announcement stating that Snegirev has acquired the rights to publish *A Life for the Tsar* (d.c.a.).

2 May

In *Sovremennik* [Contemporary], vol. 6 (no. 2), under "St. Petersburg Notes for 1836," Gogol makes reference to *A Life for the Tsar:* "There is nothing more I can say about the enthusiasm generated by the opera *A Life for the Tsar:* it is understood and known throughout Russia. One must either say a lot or nothing about this opera. I do not like to talk about music or about singing . . . in music the biggest part of it is inexpressible and inexplicable. . . . What an opera can be composed using our national melodies! Show me a people who might have more songs. Our Ukraine rings with songs. On the Volga, from its upper reaches to the sea, the songs of the barge-haulers break out along the rows of barges. Throughout all Russia song accompanies the hewing of pine logs for peasant huts. People sing as they throw bricks from hand to hand, as cities spring up like mushrooms. Russian women sing as they swaddle, wed, and bury our Russian men. All travellers, gentry and nongentry alike, travel to the accompaniment of the drivers' song. On the Black Sea, the dark beardless Kazak with his resinous moustache, sings an ancient song as he loads his harquebus. And on the ice floes on the other side of the world, the Russian industrialist strikes up a song as he pierces a whale with his harpoon. Could one possibly claim that there is nothing here from which to compose an opera? Glinka's opera is only a beautiful beginning. In his work he successfully fused two Slavonic musics, and you may hear where the Russian speaks and where the Pole: in one there breathes the free melody of Russian song, and in the other the rash tune of a Polish mazurka" (Gogol, *Soch.,* v. 6, M., 1953, p. 113).

[This fragment about Glinka's opera was printed in the second part of an article which Gogol had intended earlier as an independent piece entitled "The Petersburg Stage, 1835/36." Gogol wrote this article during the period of *The Inspector General's* preparation for performance during March and April, 1836. At that time he had the opportunity to become acquainted with Glinka's opera (at Yusupov's, Vielgorsky's, and at rehearsals in the Aleksandrinsky Theater).]

4 May

In *Sev. pchela,* no. 97, in an article by "P. M." entitled "The Petersburg Theater: Short Chronicle of the Russian Theater for the 1836 Season," it states that *A Life for the Tsar* has been performed 18 times and *The Moldavian Girl and the Gypsy Girl* twice.

19 May

In a supplement to *Mosk. ved.*, no. 40, there is a notice that Lengold's music store has received copies of the Orphan's song and duet from *A Life for the Tsar*, transcribed for two guitars by Vladimir Morkov.

27 May

Glinka writes to Odoevsky that he will not be moving to the dacha before 29 May, because he is busy with examinations at the Chapel.

There is a note from this period (?) from Glinka to Odoevsky which states that it is impossible "for me to avail myself of A. V. Vsevolozhsky's invitation—I am busy all day and into the evening."

29 May

In the lit. supp. to *Rus. invalid*, no. 22, there is an unsigned article entitled "The St. Petersburg Theaters During the 1836/37 Season." "*A Life for the Tsar* is an original work belonging to no school. The composer has not imitated either Mozart, or Rossini, or Meyerbeer. The beauties and shortcomings of his work belong to him alone. Although the libretto offers few dramatic opportunities, this one must attribute, as we've said, more to the general lack of dramatic movement in Russian history than to any absence of artistry on the part of the writer. . . . In this opera . . . the talent of Mr. Petrov in the role of Susanin was apparent in all its brilliance. He has shown us what nationality in art means. He was truly outstanding. Mme Stepanova (Antonida) played her part beautifully, but the audience was unable to fully appreciate all the difficulties she had to overcome. Her role has neither musically nor dramatically brilliant effects. It demands an accurate, precise performance, and in this respect Stepanova deserved only praise." Concerning Vorobieva: "Her singing, which is always dramatic and moving, was even more powerful this time. The orphan's song ['*Kak mat' ubili*'], the duet with Susanin ['*Ty menia na Rusi*'], the trio after it ['*Vremia k devichniku*'], and the heart-rending aria '*Ne k moei-to grudi*,' during which, as one listener expressed it, 'I threatened to cry' with every sound, she performed to perfection." The critic also expressed a high estimation for the opera's sets, particularly "the view of Moscow's Red Square crowded with people. It was ravishing, both artistically and historically."

29 or 30 May

Glinka and his family moved to the Lanskoys' dacha "between the Black River and the Vyborg highway. The Odoevskys also lived there" (*Zap.*).
[The dacha of Odoevsky's wife (née Lanskaya) was located near the Lanskaya station on the Lanskoe highway (today Smirnov Prospect).]

1 June

Performance of *A Life for the Tsar* in the Bolshoi Theater (*Sev. pchela,* 1 June 1837).

5 June

In the lit. supp. to *Rus. invalid,* no. 23, there is this unsigned notice: "The 1836/37 theatrical season was noteworthy for the splendid performance of several important and difficult works. . . . Most of all our famous set designer Andrey Roller deserves the public's gratitude . . . for the opera *A Life for the Tsar.*"

Beginning of June

Glinka composed the Cherubims' Song in C major for six-part unaccompanied chorus "and began a fugue with text, though unsuccessfully."
[The "fugue with text" is apparently the unfinished liturgical work *Khvalia, prizovu Gospoda* [With praise I call upon God.]]

Glinka became friends with a professor of singing in the Theatrical School named Soliva: "I prepared Sarti's fugue for double chorus for him, which [the chapel singers] performed successfully" (*Zap.*).
[The fugue by Sarti is from his oratorio *Da voskresnet Bog* [May God Arise]. The third movement, "*I rastochatsia vrazi ego*" [And His enemies scatter], is written in the form of a fugue (Findeyzen, "Guiseppe Sarti," in the collection *Muzykal'naia starina* [Ancient Music], inst. 1, SPb., 1903, p. 17).]

26 June

Glinka was at the Bolshoi Theater with Pavel Kamensky for a performance of *Don Giovanni,* performed by artists of the German Opera (for the benefit of Ferzing). Glinka "defended" Ferzing, whom Kamensky had abused (ltr. from

P. Kamensky to Ya. Neverov, 1 July 1837, coll. *Glinka*, p. 147; *SPb. ved.*, 17 June 1837).

June–July

"Distress over domestic scenes led me to upsetting thoughts. Not only my wife's character but also her lack of education were positive obtacles to domestic happiness." Glinka "often visited" the Odoevskys, "for the most part alone . . . The countess guessed everything, even though I carefully kept secret our marital discord, and everyone else envied me my feigned happiness."

1 July

In a letter to Neverov, Kamensky reports: "Not long ago good fortune led me to become friends with Mikhail Glinka. Even though I am not a musician, our modern native talent does not disdain to converse with me. This Glinka is such an enthusiastic person." Further on he writes, "Glinka has been quiet for a long time now, though maybe Sokolovsky's libretto, which he is writing for him, will awaken his musical activity. It's not really a libretto but something like your opera-drama or tragedy with an overture and closure."

11/23 July

Melgunov (from Kreuznach) writes to Neverov: "Tell me about Glinka's opera, I know nothing about it except a few commonplaces" (coll. *Glinka*, pp. 147, 150, 137).

15 July

At a ceremonial ball in Smolensk, given by the gentry of Smolensk in honor of the arrival of the heir, he was received "with a beautiful new Polonaise composed for this occasion by the Smolensk landholder M. I. Glinka, already well known for his outstanding opera *A Life for the Tsar*" (*Sev. pchela*, 11 August 1837).

26 July

Lvov's instructions to Glinka to attend to the activities of the chapel during Lvov's absence (*L.*, p. 136).

Vladimir Sokolovsky informs A. N. Krenitsyn: "Today I finished writing the finale for Glinka's oratorio" (coll. *Glinka*, p. 150).

July–August

Glinka's work with the singers "went very well."

Beginning of August

In *Khudozh. gaz.*, no. 15, in an article entitled "The Roman Pictures of F. A. Bruni," Kukolnik censures the unscrupulousness and rashness on the part of Russian critics for their attitude toward *A Life for the Tsar*.

9 August

During a ball at the "Synthetic Mineral Waters" a quadrille on melodies from *A Life for the Tsar* was performed (*Sev. pchela*, 16 August 1837).

11 August

In *Sev. pchela*, no. 178, there is a "Letter from Smolensk," which refers to a performance of the Polonaise on 15 July.

16 August

In *Sev. pchela*, no. 182, there is a note signed "E." about the "Ball at the Synthetic Mineral Waters" on 9 August: "At the words '*Ty menia na Rusi vozleleial*' a group of gas sylphs broke off first to the left and then to the right. . . . These words and this music possess an ineffable charm; it fascinates you, and you cannot tear yourself from your place."

Performance of *A Life for the Tsar* in the Bolshoi Theater (*Sev. pchela*, 16 August and 2 September 1837).

After 16 August

Petrov requested Glinka to write an additional scene for the opera *A Life for the Tsar* for his benefit performance (*Zap.*).

17 August

In *Rus. invalid*, no. 204, there is a "Letter from Smolensk" (signed "S. P.") containing news of the heir's arrival in the city and of the ball in his honor given by the Assembly of Nobility on 15 July, at which the Polonaise was performed. The text of the Polonaise is attached.

18 August

The following notice (signed "E."), entitled "The Bolshoi Theater," appears in *Sev. pchela,* no. 184: "Since the month of June, the Russian Opera has not presented either *A Life for the Tsar, Semiramide,* or *Capuletti,* in all of which large audiences applauded Vorobieva. . . ."

23 and 24 August

Upon Glinka's request, Nestor Kukolnik wrote the text for a new scene for *A Life for the Tsar* (author's date on the manuscript of the libretto, in *L.,* p. 137).

After 24 August

Glinka completed Vanya's scene at the gates of the monastery. "In one place, adagio, I took advantage of Soliva's apt observation concerning the movement of the basses. . . . Petrov assures me that I composed this scene in the course of a day and that the next morning I visited him with the part for his wife."

At nine o'clock in the morning Glinka arrived at Petrova-Vorobieva's with the new scene so that she could see "if it was comfortably written for [my] voice. I sang it through and found that it was comfortably written for [my] voice" (Petrova-Vorobieva, *Vosp.,* p. 173).

25 August

In *Sev. pchela,* no. 190, over the signature "K." [Koni], there is an article entitled "Survey of the Theaters Since Their Opening on 25 April Through 1 August": "First among the operas was *A Life for the Tsar,* which inspired us the first time with its native Russian sounds. As a musical creation we are proud of it. We believe that after the clarity and profound musicianship of Glinka's opera it would be difficult to do anything of this sort better. . . ."

28 August

In *Khudozh. gaz.,* no. 16, in the section "Art Chronicle," Kukolnik writes: "Our music, like all Russian art, is adorned with an innocent charm which typically illumines the art of a young people capable of all things. M. I. Glinka's opera brilliantly demonstrates this thought of ours several times over. We have spoken of the trend which the appearance of Glinka's opera has initiated on the Russian stage. . . . Meanwhile Glinka has made preparations for the production of a new opera, whose plot is taken from Pushkin's poem *Ruslan and Lyudmila.*

According to his plan he must add a new character to the work, though it will be a contralto part, and the audience probably will not take him to task for that" (d.c.a.).

August (?)

Zhukovsky brought Maria Petrovna a ring from the tsesarevich for the Polonaise (*Zap.*).

Summer

Glinka "became close friends" with the oldest son of Aleksandr Gedeonov, Mikhail, "who occupied the post of censor for the theaters and had a great influence on his father." Glinka's relationship with Mikhail Gedeonov "was simply one of friendship with no other motivations" (ltr. to V. Shirkov, 20 December 1841).

"During the summer I was often in the city, mainly at the Kukolniks," where "many artists gathered, and I was completely in my element there. . . . Ayvazovsky, who often visited Kukolnik, gave me three Tatar melodies. Later I used two of them for the lezghinka and the third for Ratmir's andante scene in Act III of the opera *Ruslan and Lyudmila*."

End of the Summer

Aleksandr Gedeonov asked Glinka to give singing lessons to four pupils of the Theater School. "All of them were pretty. One of them was [Anna] Stepanova, a well-known beauty at the time. . . . However, it was not she, but another not quite so beautiful student, who little by little awakened my poetic feelings."
[This student was Karolina Iosifovna Kolkovskaya (determined from the archives of the Theater School and the Directorate of Imperial Theaters, TsGIA, coll. 498 and 497).]

Glinka's acquaintance with Andrey Lodi, whom Glinka, together with Kukolnik and the "fraternity," prepared for stage performances (*Zap.*).

1 September

Announcement in a supp. to *Mosk. ved.*, no. 70, of the availability of Variations on a theme from *A Life for the Tsar* by Cherlitsky at Müller and Grotrian's.

2 September

In *Sev. pchela,* no. 196, there is an article signed "P. M." entitled "The Bolshoi Theater": "Performances began with Glinka's opera *A Life for the Tsar*. This was the 23rd performance of the opera, and the hall was still full from top to bottom. The audience listened with new enthusiasm to the native melodies, which speak to the Russian heart so eloquently about Russia."

Ca. 14 September

Melgunov arrived in St. Petersburg for five days. Glinka made the acquaintance of Fedor Krasheninnikov through him.

The new scene to *A Life for the Tsar* is performed at Glinka's home. At the same time Glinka performed "glorious excerpts from his new opera *Ruslan and Lyudmila,* which, incidentally, will include many of Pushkin's lines in their entirety."

14 September

Krasheninnikov informs Neverov that he has heard the new scene "added to the opera *A Life for the Tsar* which will be given for the first time at Petrova's benefit performance, née Vorobieva," as well as excerpts from *Ruslan and Lyudmila* (coll. *Glinka,* pp. 150, 154, 152).

17 September

The additional scene for *A Life for the Tsar* is sent to the censor.

21 September

Censor's authorization granted for the additional scene to *A Life for the Tsar* (TsGIA, coll. 497, no. 7647).

September

Glinka "sometimes dropped by Soliva's and intended to work with him in the *strict style,* but this did not work out, and as the result of some stupid gossip" Glinka and Soliva "had a serious falling out."

3 October

Lodi-Nestorov's debut in the role of the Roman consul Pollonius in Bellini's opera *Norma* (from a poster).

During this period Glinka worked with the singer Solovieva to prepare her for performance of the part of Antonida. This displeased the Gedeonovs, since Stepan, son of the Director of Imperial Theaters, was courting Stepanova. The Gedeonovs were annoyed by Glinka's painstaking efforts with Solovieva (a rival of Stepanova), "who sang some parts, although not altogether accurately, with effect and great enthusiasm" (*Zap.*).

8 October

Verstovsky writes to Nikita Vsevolozhsky: "Another new scene has been added to your *Susanin*. That is better. Fuller and more original" (Livanova, Protopopov, *Glinka 1*, p. 182).

9 October

In the lit. supp. to *Rus. invalid*, no. 41, there is an unsigned article by Odoevsky entitled "Concerning the New Scene for the Opera *A Life for the Tsar*, Composed by M. I. Glinka": "This scene is simple but full of dramatic action. Insofar as we may judge from the score, it is one of the best parts of the entire opera, independently rich in beauty. We do not wish to prejudice the audience's judgment by a more detailed musical analysis of this scene. We will hear it at Mr. Petrov's benefit performance at the end of this month."

14 October

The following notice appears in *Sev. pchela*, no. 232, in the section headed "Miscellany": "A quite curious spectacle is in preparation for Petrov's benefit concert this coming Monday. They will be doing *A Life for the Tsar* with a new scene at the beginning of the fourth act, written by M. I. Glinka for Mme Petrova-Vorobieva. The words, they say, were written by N. V. Kukolnik. Above all, at this performance the audience will hear Mme Solovieva (Antonida) and Mr. Nestorov [Lodi] (Sobinin), about whose debut we hope to speak soon."

An evening at Kukolnik's: "there were musicians and poets, singers, orators, surgeons and painters, civilians and military. Lodi, Glinka, Aledinsky, Pelikan, Petrov, Basin, Chernyshev. The singing and playing were marvelous. . . . Petrov sang the robber's song *"Ne slykhal ia"* [I did not hear]. We spent the evening very pleasantly and did not break up until nearly 12 o'clock" (Mokritsky, p. 130).

17 October

In *SPb. ved.*, no. 235, there is the following announcement: "Tomorrow, 18 October. At the Bolshoi Theater, for the benefit of the performer Mr. Petrov, *A Life for the Tsar*, original grand opera in three acts. At the beginning of the fourth act, for the first time, a new scene."

18 October

Petrov's benefit performance in the Bolshoi Theater performing *A Life for the Tsar* with the added scene for Vanya. The part of Antonida was performed by Solovieva for the first time and Sobinin's part by Nestorov [Lodi] (Lit. supp. to *Rus. invalid,* 30 October 1837). The new scene "had a huge success. Both composer and performer were called out many times" (Petrova-Vorobieva, *Vosp.,* p. 173).

22 October

M. Kovalensky writes in a letter to Neverov: "There is a lot of theater news here now: first of all, Petrov's benefit performance was on Monday. He and Vorobieva have been married. . . . They did *A Life for the Tsar* with the new scene which has been added to it for the first time. . . . There are hardly any melodies in this scene. There is an andante, but it is in the German manner. Still the scene is receiving lots of praise. I did not see it. . . . Kukolnik wrote the words, the music was by the same M. Glinka. . . . It is said that Glinka is writing another new opera on a libretto by Kukolnik, *Ruslan and Lyudmila,* and that the scenery, that is sketches for the scenery, will be done by Bryullov. So they say" (coll. *Glinka,* pp. 152, 154).

In *Sev. pchela,* no. 239, in the section headed "Miscellany": "We have heard that our favorite and, moreover, nationalist composer Mr. Glinka is writing music for a new opera called *Ruslan and Lyudmila.* The subject is taken from A. S. Pushkin's poem. Mr. Glinka's talent guarantees that the music will be outstanding, and the subject is so poetic that it should be easy to make a brilliant opera from it. We impatiently await the moment when a poster will announce to us that the work is finished. It will be a real national musical feast!"

24 October

Announcement in *Rus. invalid,* no. 266, of the performance on 24 October of *A Life for the Tsar* "with a new scene added at the beginning of Act IV."

26 October

In an article entitled "Spectacles and Spectators" in *Sev. pchela,* no. 242, Bulgarin writes: "The talented artists of the Russian stage await popular tragedies, dramas, comedies, and vaudevilles while Mmes. Petrova and Stepanova await operas. They were luckier than the others because they got *A Life for the Tsar,* and they can be hopeful that our nationalist composer will give them new opportunities to demonstrate their abilities." *A Life for the Tsar* is mentioned along with operas for which "crowds" besiege the theater box office.

30 October

The following appears in an unsigned article by Dmitry Struysky(?) in a lit. supp. to *Rus. invalid,* no. 44. It is entitled *"A Life for the Tsar,* original opera in four acts; music by M. I. Glinka, words by Baron E. F. Rozen, with a new scene added at the beginning of Act IV (text by N. V. Kukolnik), presented on 18 October, at a benefit concert for Mr. Petrov." "We have noticed in the orchestration a *pianistic* handling of syncopated figures which is noisier than it is musical. Even with imagination, however, successful orchestration comes only with great experience and is never completely successful on the first attempt. In our opinion, in order to appreciate Mr. Glinka's opera without any kind of preconceptions pro or contra, one first must consider the elements which comprise nationalism in the fine arts." Later on Struysky argues that folk song per se "cannot be protracted throughout the entire drama. The simple folksong is fine in opera as a song. However, if the entire finale is developed according to the shape of a song, and if we hear one and the same song everywhere with minor variations, insignificant in themselves, aren't we then justified in repudiating this kind of nationalism in art, since it restricts imagination with no benefit for art? . . . But let us return to Glinka's opera. We must look at his work from two different aspects: 1) in relation to *Russian music,* and 2) to *European music.* In the first instance he is a talent of the first magnitude who merits the full attention of his contemporaries. There are melody and feeling in many of the numbers of his opera. Admirers of Russian song will take a twofold pleasure in the resemblance of all the melodies to Russian songs and in the simplicity of song unencumbered by the complexities of form. In the case of the latter, he follows Bellini, whose long, andante-like melodies provide the singer opportunity to demonstrate the loveliness of his voice. What place this opera will occupy in the European repertoire, however, only time will tell. We feel that the foreign listener will judge it according to its *musical* impression, irrespective of its so-called nationalism. . . . No doubt he will be pleased with several places because of their *elegance,* for example, the orphan Vanya's final song *'Ne ko mne na grud' '* [Not to my breast], the trio in the first act, and several choruses. However his impression of the entire work will be unsatisfactory. It will seem monotonous and constrained to him. For example, can a listener who has savored all the variety, splendor, and grandeur of Mozart's, Weber's, and Meyerbeer's finales be satisfied with a mazurka for a finale, one, in fact, which was even written for dancing in the character of an ordinary mazurka? If the triple meter only served to remind one of a mazurka, while the ominous theme of the conspiracy on the life of the tsar were developed in a gradual and contrasting manner gaining strength like a storm (as was masterfully done in *Fenella*), then this mazurka might have satisfied even the most exacting listener. But as it is this finale is somewhat unsatisfactory. An inaccurate view of his purpose always leads an author into error, which is then impossible to correct because it is reflected throughout the work. In a word, nationalism has been understood in a material sense and has constrained the composer's talent, and we may only observe that, despite the abundance of his imagination, he was able to write an opera which would provide real enjoyment only for those of the audience more apt to understand the indigenous tunes of national songs than Mozart's *Requiem* or a Beethoven symphony. However, we expect more of him. . . . To us the new scene is not extraneous: it is one of the most effective numbers, even though the final chorus is not quite as successful as the opening adagio song. But Vanya's character is completely changed in this scene. In the earlier version of the opera his naive character was portrayed very convincingly, and for the sake of unity his basic character should have been maintained in the new addition as well. Now, however, the 'little fledgling' boasts that he is a *heavenly ambassador!* This idea is not in the spirit of the age and is too contradictory to the foregoing scenes."

[In his book *Russkaia mysl' o muzyke* [Russian musical thought], Yuly Kremlev writes: "There is reason to suppose that this article was written by Trilunny [pseudonym of D. Struysky]" (v. 1, L., 1954, p. 82). There is no basis for refuting Struysky's authorship, as several scholars have tried to do.]

3 November

In *Sovremennik,* no. 4 (vol. 8), in the section headed "New Compositions," there is an announcement of the publication of an "Additional scene to the opera *A Life for the Tsar.* Music by M. I. Glinka. Text by N. K. [Kukolnik]. Dedicated to A. Y. Petrova. SPb., printed by Pluchard" (d.c.a.).

Performance of *A Life for the Tsar* in the Bolshoi Theater (*Sev. pchela,* 3 November 1837).

6 November

Kukolnik presents Glinka with a blank notebook with the inscription: "To M. I. Glinka, with best wishes for the composition of *Ruslan and Lyudmila,* from N. K." Below Glinka entered, "6 November." The general plan of the opera as well as musical sketches are written in this notebook.

16 November

Composer's dating on the rough draft manuscript of the romance *"Vot mesto tainogo svidan'ia"* [Here is the place of secret meeting]: "Stanzas written by Kukolnik since evening; music written in the morning in half an hour by Glinka, 16 November 1837."

18 November

Article by "P. M." entitled "The Bolshoi Theater" in *Sev. pchela,* no. 262: "This opera, which in one year has become a national work, was presented at Petrov's benefit performance with *a new scene* for Mme Petrova-Vorobieva. Many had felt that there was a small gap in the interval between the third and fourth acts of the opera when the Polish warriors are distracting Susanin, and the fate of Vanya, who had been sent to inform the tsar about the enemy's plans, was inconclusive for the viewer. . . . Dramatically there is no apparent necessity for this scene, the more so as Vanya's character changes in it. Instead of a mild youth he appears here as some kind of champion or hero. . . . Musically, however, the new scene is as good as the best places in Glinka's opera, especially given Mme Petrova's masterful performance. The andante maestoso, *'Ty ne plach', ne plach', sirotinushka!'* [Don't cry, little orphan], is permeated with profound and heartfelt grief. The allegro, *'Zazhigaite ogni!'* [Light the fires!], is an outstanding expression of impatience and dread mixed with decisiveness. But what scene does not make a strong impression on us if it is performed by Petrova! In this performance of *A Life for the Tsar* Mr. Nestorov played the role of Sobinin and Mme Solovieva the role of Antonida. Mr. Nestorov did his small part well. On the other hand, Antonida was not in voice, but she still sang the romance *'Ne o tom skorbliu, podruzhen'ki'* [It is not that which I lament] with expression and feeling."

20 November

Performance of A *Life for the Tsar* in the Bolshoi Theater (*Sev. pchela,* 20 November 1837).

21 November

Glinka inscribed the trio *"Ne tomi, rodimyi"* [Do not despair, dear one] in M. Sumarokova's album (GBL, no. 193/1).

Before 30 November

Retired Second Lieutenant of the Artillery V. Chernikov made application to the Chief Administration of the Censorship for permission to publish a music newspaper beginning in 1838. In the "program" for the publication it says that "M. I. Glinka, Prince V. F. Odoevsky, Mr. Shrentser, I. F. Laskovsky, Mr. Hunke, K. P. Masalsky, G. Lomakin, Mr. Struysky, and others will participate directly in the activities of the paper on a regular basis" (*Sov. muzyka,* 1954, no. 6, p. 104).

30 November

In the literary chronicle section of *Bib-ka dlia chteniia,* vol. 25, there is a notice of the publication, printed by Pluchard, of the text for the "additional scene to the opera A *Life for the Tsar*. Music by M. I. Glinka. Words by N. K., dedicated to A. Y. Petrova": "Something was lacking in Mr. Glinka's composition, some words, or music, to explain the connection between the rescue of the tsar and Susanin's death. It was necessary to add one scene. The audience's general approval of this additional scene has demonstrated that the composer guessed right. One of our best known poets composed the text for this scene. Of course, he had to heed the composer's demands and not his own inspiration. Nonetheless he was able to impart power and Russian expression to his lines. Probably in this instance the words were written first and then the music" (d.c.a.).

The censor granted V. Chernikov permission to publish a music periodical (*Sov. muzyka,* 1954, no. 6, p. 104).

Beginning of Winter

Glinka was introduced to Valerian Shirkov, "as a man fully capable of writing the libretto for my new opera. He was in fact a very well-educated and talented man, who drew beautifully and wrote poetry very fluently. On my request he wrote *as a sample* Gorislava's cavatina *'Liubvi roskoshnaia zvesda'* [Splendid star of love] and part of act one. His efforts turned out very satisfactorily."

December (Beginning?)

Glinka composed a handwritten addendum to the report of the Senate's general meeting asking that it give its attention to the following: 1) as a result of the Smolensk commission of inquiry it was apparent that wine had been emptied out by order of the civil authorities (in an amount worth a total of 64,000 rubles); 2) a sum amounting to 21,581 rubles, 40 1/2 kopecks, calculated for wine supplied in 1814 which had been paid; 3) interest on the amount returned to the treasury, which had been paid to other tax farmers, should also be paid to E. A. Glinka (G 2-A, p. 59).

6 December

Performance of *A Life for the Tsar* in the Bolshoi Theater (*Sev. pchela*, 6 December 1837).

8 December

Glinka asks his mother to provide him 10,000 rubles of the money obtained through their legal proceedings for payment of his debts (3,000 to Sobolevsky, 3,000 to Stuneev, 2,000 to Kukolnik, and 2,000 "to various people for trifles"). "Since everyone knows the fortunate outcome of our case, it is impossible for me to put off paying them—and if you should deny me now the means to do this, I would then be placed in the most dire circumstances, for until the new opera is finished (which will be at least a year or even longer), I have no other prospects for payment." In addition, he asks permission to retain an additional 10,000 rubles for his own personal use. "I feel that I have a right to such compensation because twice, by my own petitioning, I saved the case from ruin and also because people on whom our case depended participated specifically because of me (as the composer of a national opera), and for the fact that the case was decided *unanimously* we are obliged solely to the diligence of people who are genuinely devoted to me *because of my talent.*"

13 December

In the Bolshoi Theater at the ballet *Insurrection in the Seraglio,* with Maria Talioni, Glinka met Nicholas I ("in the theater on the stage"): ". . . having noticed me, His Majesty approached me, and putting one arm around me he led me away from the crowd in which I stood and then for a very long time deigned to talk with me about the chapel choir and the singers and promised to attend the theater when they present my opera in order to hear the new scene. He asked as well about the opera I have recently begun " (ltr. to his mother, 14 December 1837; poster).

14 December

In a letter to his mother, Glinka discusses his brother Andrey, who "is behaving himself and studying well. I am completely satisfied with him. If I do not write about him in every letter, it is because of my own absent-mindedness, which is magnified by the fact that all my attention is directed toward the new opera I am writing."

In a letter to Evgenia Andreevna Glinka, Maria Petrovna conveys her best wishes for the approaching Christmas holidays and her name-day and writes that "with the onset of winter" she is beginning "to get sick again, as before. My Misha, thank Heaven, is healthy and cheerful."

17 December

From the windows of his apartment Glinka witnessed the burning of the Winter Palace (*Zap.*).

30 December

In *Syn otechestva*, vol. 1 (Jan. 1838), in the section headed "Russian Literature," there is an article by Nikolay Grech entitled "Foreign Theaters" (letter to A. Gedeonov), in which it is stated that the author has not been in St. Petersburg "since the first performance of *A Life for the Tsar*." Later on he compares Meyerbeer's *Les Huguenots* to Glinka's opera: "Why, after the very first performance of *A Life for the Tsar*, could I remember melodies which still echo in my ear and heart?" Grech does not find this to be true with Meyerbeer's operas (d.c.a.). In the fourth section of the same issue there is a "Sketch of Russian Literature for the Year 1837" by Nikolay Polevoy which mentions the libretto to *A Life for the Tsar*.

31 December

Performance of *A Life for the Tsar* in the Bolshoi Theater "for the benefit of Mme Solovieva. Prior to this the first act of the opera *Jean de Paris* [Boieldieu] will be given" (*SPb. ved.*, 31 December 1837).

Nikolay Volkov's second portrait of Glinka was done during this year (Tretiakov Gallery).

1837/1838

Winter

Receptions at Kukolnik's, at which "there were frequently . . . people completely unknown to me. . . . Only our closest friends stayed for dinner."

"Things were not going well for me at home. My wife was one of those women for whom clothes, balls, carriages, horses, livery, etc., were everything . . . everything noble and poetic . . . was incomprehensible to her. . . . I unburdened my heart at school and on the stage. Sometimes I sang and played. On those occasions the face of a dear pupil of mine showed genuine delight."

Glinka and his wife were at the home of the counts Saltykov. There he met Leonty Dubelt (*Zap.*).

1838

4 January

Entry in Nikolay Polevoy's diary: "In the evening Chernikov sat down and talked about the music supplements [to *Sev. pchela*]. Idle talk."

5 January

Entry in the diary of Iosif Mikhaylovich Vielgorsky: "Glinka talked about the unfortunate situation of the Russian theater. All the attention is given to costumes and sets, while music and singing are considered secondary. Operas are only given to get them off their hands and to make money. How they go makes no difference to the Directorate" (coll. *Glinka*, pp. 165, 153).

6 January

The performance of *A Life for the Tsar* in the Bolshoi Theater "went very badly" (I. Vielgorsky's diary, 6 January 1838, in *L.*, p. 141; *Sev. pchela*, 6 January 1838).

10 January

Nikolay Polevoy writes to Verstovsky: "I have met Glinka, and, I admit, I don't like him. Now he is occupied with *Ruslan and Lyudmila*. The opera is almost finished, and there is still no text. A strange way to write! I have heard many excerpts. It was strange, good, but I was not touched by one of them. . . . It is amusing to see this little figure whose pride knows no limits walking *avec un air préoccupé* and just smiling whenever someone expresses an opinion contrary to his own. He does not deign to respond!" In the same letter: "Glinka and others had intended to publish a special musical supplement in the 'Bee,' but they missed their opportunity" (coll. *Glinka,* pp. 152, 154, 165).

13 January

In a letter to Neverov and Granovsky in Berlin, Vasily Grigoriev expresses surprise that Neverov "wants to sing bass in Glinka's opera at a concert at the Mendelssohns. . . . I have long since felt that music would lead him to no good, and so it has happened" (coll. *Glinka,* p. 137).

14 January

Performance in the Bolshoi Theater of *A Life for the Tsar* (*Sev. pchela,* 14 January 1838).

15 January

In *Khudozh. gaz.,* no. 1, in the section "Art Chronicle," under the heading "Music and Scenery," there is a reference to Solovieva's performance of the part of Antonida: "The romance *'Ne o tom skorbliu, podruzhen'ki'* took on a new physiognomy in Mme Solovieva's performance, more in accord with the composer's intentions." In the same issue there is an announcement of the publication of a "Musical Album of Vaudeville Couplets, assembled by N. Dyur, with a supplement including Stanzas set to music by M. I. Glinka."

18 January

At a concert of amateurs in Simferopol, K. Shashina performed "a charming aria by M. I. Glinka from *A Life for the Tsar* (*Sev. pchela,* 26 February 1838).

19 January

In an article "About Russian Books" in *Mosk. ved.*, no. 6, there is an announcement that the "Second Musical Album of Vaudeville Couplets," compiled by Nikolay Dyur, with a supplement including Glinka's Stanzas has been received from St. Petersburg.

20 January

Censor's authorization for a book by Cook Stafford, *History of Music, with Notes, Corrections, and Additions by G. Fétis, translated from the French by K. Voronov*, SPb. Everything pertaining to Russian music was written by Odoevsky. In the book it says that December (N.S.) 1836 "will remain forever memorable in the chronicles of music in Russia. The remarkable work by M. I. Glinka, *A Life for the Tsar*, made its appearance on our stage at that time" (p. 59). In another place it says: "We have an abundance of minor musical pieces, romances, and songs. The best known writers of romances are M. I. Vielgorsky, M. I. Glinka, Verstovsky, Titov, Varlamov, Lvov, Rupini [Rupin], Norov, Esaulov, Makarov, and others" (p. 397).

23 January

In *Rus. invalid*, no. 19, there is an announcement of the publication of the "Second Music Album of Vaudeville Couplets" for the year 1838, arranged for piano, "compiled by Dyur, with a supplement including Stanzas by Kukolnik set to music by M. I. Glinka."

Performance of *A Life for the Tsar* in the Bolshoi Theater (*Sev. pchela*, 22 January 1838).

25 January

Entry in N. Polevoy's diary: "Chernikov received permission for his musical supplement" (coll. *Glinka*, p. 165).

26 January

In an article in *Rus. invalid*, no. 22, occasioned by the transfer from Rome of pictures by F. Bruni, Kukolnik writes that hasty and premature judgment of great works of art is intolerable: "such haste has its exponents everywhere . . . especially . . . in music. . . . It is impossible to forget the music article that began with the following words: 'This music, or song, or anything else, was for the most part written in a major and minor tone.' The opera *A Life for the Tsar* was repeatedly analyzed in such fashion, even though it especially is one of the works whose value may be determined only if one observes the rule we have laid down."

31 January

In *Sev. pchela*, no. 25, there is an announcement about the proposed publication of the "Musical Supplements": "The growing enthusiasm for music in Petersburg and the public's regular and excellent attendance at the opera are the principal reasons for the publication of these Supplements. Not everyone interested in music has the means or the time to study it, i.e., to read through the huge number of theories, disputatious treatises, dissertations, etc., though still a basic, even if incomplete, understanding of the rules of art is necessary for any serious discussion of music or discernment of real musical beauty. . . . Every effort will be made to assure that the more learned articles in the journal will be accessible to everyone's understanding. Since this field is quite new in Russia, beginning with the first issue the basic fundamentals of music will be explained in order to make the theory to follow comprehensible. The organization of the publication will be as follows: 1. *Music Literature.* Biographies of famous musicians, general characteristics of musicality, musical stories and anecdotes, etc.; 2. *Theory of Art.* The rules of music. Different schools of music. Instrumentation, etc.; 3. *Criticism* of scholarly works and teaching methods of music; 4. *Dramatic Criticism.* Critique of operas, oratorios, etc., which have appeared in Europe; 5. *Petersburg Opera;* 6. *New Music;* 7. *Miscellany.* The editorship has been entrusted completely to V. V. Chernikov. In general, however, the opinions of the journal will be based upon a consensus of the best artists in Petersburg and Moscow. Music of various types by the best composers will be included with each issue . . . in the course of a year the reader will acquire from these Supplements *a music library of selected works. . . . The first issue will appear on Wednesday, 2 February.*"

1 February

V. V. Chernikov's application was rejected by the Directorate of Censorship: "Since we do not deem it for the good to increase the number of periodicals, and since we do not perceive the necessary certification either of the applicant's ability to perform the responsibilities taken upon himself as editor of the paper or of his reliability, the Directorate of Censorship has not found it possible to concur with Mr. Chernikov's request" (*Sov. muzyka*, 1954, no. 6, p. 105).

2 February

At an assembly of nobility in Engelgardt Hall, a gala dinner was held in honor of I. Krylov's 50 years of activity. The Polonaise from *A Life for the Tsar* was among the music performed (*ZhMNP*, 1838, part 17, no. 1; *Rus. invalid*, 5 February 1838).

3 February

The opinion of a contemporary French composer about the music of *A Life for the Tsar* is introduced in an article on "Georg Friedrich Handel" in *Khudozh. gaz.*, no. 2: "We have been told that when one of the most famous contemporary composers in France was shown several numbers from the opera *A Life for the Tsar*, he praised them as being extremely original: '*C'est du Handel! C'est du Bach!*' "

5 February

In *Rus. invalid*, no. 32, there is a detailed description of the gala dinner in honor of Krylov in Engelgardt Hall on 2 February; the performance of the Polonaise from *A Life for the Tsar* is mentioned.

6 February

Performance in the Bolshoi Theater of *A Life for the Tsar* (*SPb. ved.*, 6 February 1838).

8 February

In an article by Bulgarin entitled "Russian Periodicals" in *Sev. pchela*, no. 32, it states that in Russia, as in Europe, there is talent in every sphere of artistic activity. "We possess not only talents of the first order, but geniuses in every area. Even music, in the person of M. I. Glinka, possesses such a talent of genius, which Europe's best composers have recognized. We admit that this is our weakest area! Besides Bortnyansky and Glinka, who are first class, only Verstovsky and Alyabiev have a right to European fame."

9 February

Performance in the Bolshoi Theater of *A Life for the Tsar* (*Sev. pchela*, 9 February 1838).

10/22 February

Melgunov informs Neverov of his intention of publishing in Germany "a collection of the best works in the Russian language" in German translation and under his own editorship. Besides various literary works and articles about history and art, he intends to print "News about Glinka's opera and Bryullov's picture" (*L.,* p. 145).

11 February

Performance of *A Life for the Tsar* in the Bolshoi Theater. Koltsov was at a performance either on 6, 9, or 11 February (*SPb. ved.,* 11 February 1838; ltr. from A. Koltsov to V. Belinsky, 14 February 1838, in A. Koltsov, *Soch.,* M., 1955, p. 248).

Between 6 and 13 February

Glinka "because of a misunderstanding quarrelled with Gedeonov and ceased lessons at the school. At the same time I wrote the romance *'Somnenie'* [Doubt] for contralto, harp, and violin, for one of my dear pupils; the words were by N. Kukolnik" (*Zap.*).
[The romance for Karolina Kolkovskaya exists in two versions: for voice and piano, and for voice, violin, and piano.]

14 February

Koltsov writes to Belinsky that he has heard *A Life for the Tsar* and shares M. Bakunin's opinion: "he looks at it [the opera] from a present-day point of view" (A. Koltsov, *Soch.,* p. 248).

15 February

After a worship service in the Annichkov Palace, Lvov wrote to Glinka: "His Majesty the Emperor was very dissatisfied with the singing today . . . at the morning service His Majesty ordered that the person responsible be given a strict reprimand. . . . I ask your Honour to summon the one in charge and to give him a strict reprimand from me and explain that should anything similar happen in the future, I will find it necessary to take the strictest measures. As I understand, the main error consisted of the matter of an appropriate tone. I ask you therefore to issue instruction that in the future the assistant to the singing teacher Palagin always accompany the right choir and the singer Malyshev the left" (*L.,* p. 145).

20 February

Glinka is at a concert of the Directorate of Imperial Theaters where Ole Bull appears for the first time performing his fantasy, "Military Polonaise."

23 February

In *Khudozh. gaz.*, no. 3, it says, "The publication of musical supplements which we wrote about in the previous issue, have, because of circumstances, been postponed for a time" (d.c.a.).

25 February

Glinka is at a concert given by Ole Bull, who performed his own compositions.

26 February

In *Sev. pchela,* no. 46, in an article entitled "Concert in Simferopol" and signed "K. N. G." [Golitsyn], the performance of an aria from *A Life for the Tsar* on 18 January is mentioned.

February

In ZhMNP, part 17, no. 1, there is an article by Bulgarin (signed "B. F.") entitled "Dinner, given for Ivan Andreevich Krylov in the Hall of Nobility on 2 February 1838," which contains a detailed description of the program and mention of the performance of music by Glinka.

4 or 5 March

Glinka was present at Ole Bull's last concert, at which he performed his own compositions.

6 March

Glinka attends a concert by Vieuxtemps.

11 March

Glinka was present at Karol Lipiński's first concert, at which he performed his own works (*Zap.;* poster).

12 March

In *Khudozh. gaz.*, nos. 19–24, in the section "Art Chronicle," under the heading "Music," there is a discussion of Glinka's preparation for publication of a collection of music by Russian composers: "As many Russian composers as there are in the two capitals, at least the best known, provided M. I. Glinka with their music for the compilation of an album, or collection. A moving picture of concord among artists! . . ." The collection "consists of five small volumes. In each there will be six to seven pieces. Participants in the publication include Alyabiev, Count M. Y. Vielgorsky . . . Verstovsky, Haberbier, Genishta, Glinka (five romances and songs by Glinka, which have not been sung anywhere yet, and five piano pieces). . . . The edition will be completed in March" (d.c.a., 12 March 1839?).

In a supp. to *Mosk. ved.*, no. 21, there is an announcement of a forthcoming concert on 16 March by the singer A. Bote, who will perform a scene and aria from *A Life for the Tsar*.

15 March

Glinka is at a concert given by Vieuxtemps (*Zap.*; poster).

16 March

At a concert in the Bolshoi Theater in Moscow, prima donna of the German opera A. Bote performed Vanya's "scene and aria" from *A Life for the Tsar* (*Mosk. ved.*, 12 March 1838).

18 March

Glinka attended the second concert given by Karol Lipiński, who performed his own compositions as well as those of other composers. "I did not care for his playing in the concertos, but I was ecstatic over his strong performance in the Beethoven quartets. At Kukolnik's he played Beethoven's last quartets amazingly well. The cellist Knecht played masterfully; one would have thought that they had played together all their lives."

19 March

In a literary supp. to *Rus. invalid*, no. 12, in the "Miscellany" section, there is an announcement of the upcoming concert in the Hall of Nobility at Kazan Bridge on 23 March, given for the benefit of the Women's Patriotic Society schools. "At this concert, which is so remarkable for its genuinely charitable aim, we will hear, incidentally . . . an aria from Glinka's new opera *Ruslan and Lyudmila*."

22 March

Glinka is at Vieuxtemp's last concert (*Zap.*; poster).

23 March

The following is printed in the "Miscellany" section of *Sev. pchela,* no. 67: "Meanwhile, as Petersburg awaits Glinka's new opera *Ruslan and Lyudmila,* it is said that in Moscow two remarkable musical works are in preparation: an opera by A. N. Verstovsky, whose title we do not know. . . . Another opera is being written in Moscow by A. A. Alyabiev."

In an amateur concert in the Hall of Nobility for the benefit of the private schools of the Women's Patriotic Society, the polonaise *"Velik nash bog"* [Great is our God] for chorus and orchestra was performed, and Barteneva sang the aria *"Grustno mne, roditel' dorogoi"* [My father, I am sad] "from the opera *Ruslan and Lyudmila*." "I expected a great success. They applauded, but not as receptively as I am used to" (*Sev. pchela,* 30 March 1838; *Zap.*).

"Concert in the evening at 8 o'clock. A swarm of people, as usual" (I. Vielgorsky's diary, 23 March 1838, in Livanova, Protopopov, *Glinka 1,* p. 279). After Barteneva's performance of Lyudmila's cavatina, "the famous violinist Lipiński, who stood next to me and had listened to the cavatina with unfeigned interest, pressed my hand as a friend when it was over and said, *'que c'est bien russe, cette musique-là.'*"

26 March

Account of the concert on 23 March in literary supp. to *Rus. invalid,* no. 13.

30 March

In *Sev. pchela,* no. 72, in the "Miscellany" section, there is a review of the concert for the benefit of the private schools of the Women's Patriotic Society on 23 March.

31 March

Report from Lvov to the Ministry of the Imperial Court regarding his decision to send Glinka and the assistant singing teacher of the Chapel, D. Palagin, to the Ukraine to recruit twenty boys for the Chapel choirs. "If it please your Excellency to approve these plans, then I most humbly request that orders be given to provide these officials . . . with a carriage and travelling allowance for their expenses" (*L.*, p. 147).

March (?)

A concert of Italian music took place in Moscow. "[The voice teacher] Mr. Fest's special effort to please the rather large audience (as many as 150 people) was demonstrated by the fact that in an Italian concert he considered it absolutely necessary to include one of our beautiful Russian arias [Glinka's], which was sung . . . by Mmc Makovskaya with great enthusiasm" (*Mosk. nabliudatel'*, 1838, part 18, p. 348; d.c.a., 7 July 1839 [*sic!*]).

4 April

Nicholas I's order to send Glinka to the Ukraine to recruit choristers. Memoranda from the Ministry of the Imperial Court to Lvov of the decision to send Glinka to the Ukraine and to the chief equerry Dolgorukov to provide Glinka with a carriage for the trip. Glinka's receipt for 500 rubles.

5 April

Memorandum from the Minister of the Imperial Court to the Governor General of Little Russia, A. Stroganov, asking that Glinka and Palagin be shown "assistance in the fulfillment of the commission given to them." Lvov's instructions following a directive by the Minister of the Imperial Court that the chapel choir participate in a concert to be presented by Kapellmeister Hase of the guards corps: "I request that Mikhail Ivanovich be present at this concert and that it be assured *without fail* that the choir is comfortably situated and that the soloists in the finale of the Haydn are separate from and in front of the chorus so that their voices are heard, especially the young ones" (*L.*, p. 147).

9 April

Glinka and his wife participated (in a chorus of amateurs) in a charity concert in Engelgardt Hall for the benefit of the Children's Hospital (from a poster).

13 April

Glinka acquires "a bound book for notating expenses . . . for the trip to Little Russia for the recruitment of twenty youths for the court chapel choir in 1838." On the last page is a wax seal and inscription: "In this book there are 43 numbered pages. April 19, 1838." The book is signed by Lvov, and each page is certified by Inspector Belikov (*L.*, p. 148).

19 April

Lvov's instructions to Glinka about the trip (G 2-B, p. 233).

Mid-April (Before the 28th)

Glinka visited Konstantin Bulgakov, who had been taken ill: "Glinka acquainted me with his new opera *Ruslan and Lyudmila,* which was exquisite. It contained many beautiful things" (ltr. from K. Bulgakov to A. Bulgakov, undated, but before the beginning of May 1838, in G 2-A, p. 77).

28 April

Glinka's departure, accompanied by the assistant teacher of singing Dmitry Palagin, the chorister Nafanail Sheinov, the tutor Saranchin, and valet Yakov Netoev (Lvov's report to the Minister of the Imperial Court, 29 April 1838, no. 94, in *L.*, p. 148; *Zap.; SPb. ved.*, 1 May 1838).

Gatchina. Arrival and departure.

Luga. Arrival and overnight stay.

Lvov's report (Petersburg) to the Minister of the Imperial Court of Glinka's departure on 28 April, "having received from me appropriate instructions regarding the selection of young choristers."

30 April

Departure from Luga with stops in Gorodets, Plyusse, Novoselie, Zalazy (for dinner and repair of the carriage).

Borovichi. Overnight stop.

1 May

Ashevo. They pass through Porkhov, Dubrovka, Ashevo, Bazhanitsy, and Mikhaylovsky Pogost (*L.*, p. 148).

In *SPb. ved.*, no. 95, on the list "of those leaving the capital city of St. Petersburg on 28 and 29 April 1838" appears the following: "To Poltava: Court Chapel Kapellmeister Titular Councillor Glinka and assistant teacher of singing, 10th class, Palagin."

2 May

Usvyaty. Glinka and his companions travel through Pryskukha, Nedomerki, Velikie Luki (where they had breakfast, drank tea, ate dinner, and repaired the springs of the carriage), Senkovo, Setuty, Churilovo, and Usvyaty (where they ate supper and spent the night).

3 May

They departed from Usvyaty and travelled through Yurova Niva, Velizh, Koryaki, Porechie, Peregudy (where they ate lunch), Kiselevo, and Terikhi.

4 May

Smolensk. Arrival in Smolensk, where they ate supper and spent the night (*L.*, p. 148).

Glinka met with Aleksandr Rimsky-Korsak, who, at Glinka's request, wrote the words for the romance *"Vsegda, vezde so mnoiu ty soputnitsei moei nezrimoi"* [Always, everywhere you are with me] (*Zap.*).

5 May

Departure for Novospasskoe (*L.*, p. 149).

6–13 May

Novospasskoe. "These eight days flew by, unfortunately, too quickly" (ltr. to N. Kukolnik, 26 May 1838; *L.*, p. 149).

13 May

Departure from Novospasskoe.

14 May

Rukhani. Glinka and his companions travelled through Drozzhino, Lobkovo, Khmora, Voroshilovo (where they had dinner), Krapivka, Roslavl, and Rukhani (where they ate supper and spent the night).

15 May

Starodub. They left Rukhani and travelled through Svarskaya, Lukovitsa, Mglin (where they ate dinner), Belogoshchi, Ryukhov, and Starodub (where they had supper and spent the night).

16 May

Novgorod-Seversky. They left Starodub and stopped in Puporovka, Chaykin Village; on the same day they arrived in Novgorod-Seversky (*L.*, p. 149).

16–21 May

Stay in Novgorod-Seversky, where Glinka "did not find a single voice" (ltr. to N. Kukolnik, 26 May 1838; *L.*, p. 149).

20 May

Glinka composed the romance *"Vsegda, vezde so mnoiu ty"* and sent it to Kukolnik "to give to my former pupil, of whom I still preserve a vivid memory." Later Pushkin's words *"V krovi gorit ogon' zhelaniia"* [The fire of longing burns in my blood] were set to this music.
[The first version of this romance has not been preserved.]

21 May

Nezhin. They travelled through Voronezh, Krolevets, Altynovka (where they ate dinner), Baturino, Borzna, Komarovka, and arrived in Nezhin (where they ate supper and spent the night).

22 May

Departure from Nezhin with stops in Kushelev, Zhukov, and Gorbov.

Individual pieces from *A Life for the Tsar* were performed in an arrangement for wind orchestra in the train station in Pavlovsk (*Sev. pchela*, 26 May 1838).

23 May

Chernigov. Arrival in Chernigov (*L.*, p. 149).

23–26 May

During this time Glinka "found several rather good" voices, but "for the present nothing distinctive or of great moment."

26 May

Glinka writes to Kukolnik: "I was cruelly in error to think that this trip would dispel my depression. I have never been so melancholy and bored as I am now. Perhaps Little Russia is nice (particularly for those who have not been to Italy), but I have felt unwell from the day we left for this *blessed land*. My nerves suffer cruelly. . . . Here I am alone in the strictest sense of the word." He reports that in his free time he is studying "the whole range of church singing," and health permitting, will return to Petersburg "*as an expert* in this domain." He writes that he has sent Kukolnik a romance on Rimsky-Korsak's words: "They are not beautiful, but they express the matter well and clearly." He asks [Kukolnik] to deliver the romance "to the proper quarters," i.e., to K. Kolkovskaya, and to report "that I am *still in the same place*."

Glinka's report to Lvov about the recruitment of choristers in Chernigov: "I have found five boys. . . . All the necessary certifications concerning them have been obtained. . . . Above all, I have found an excellent bass here."
[Glinka's receipt (a note?) of certification for the five boys dates from this period.]

On the same day Glinka wrote a petition to Lvov about "returning in a legal manner" the chorister Nafanail Sheinov, who had been released for a reunion with relatives but was needed in transporting the young choristers "during the trip with me."

Kukolnik's article entitled "The Pavlovsk Station (letter to M. I. Glinka)" about the opening of the concert season in Pavlovsk is published in *Sev. pchela*, no.

116. Also mentioned is Glinka's work on the opera *Ruslan and Lyudmila* along with the assurance of its speedy completion.

28 May

Nezhin. Departure from Chernigov. Stops in Gorbolov, Zhukov, Kushelev, and Nezhin (where they ate supper and spent the night).

In St. Petersburg the Imperial Chapel administration issued Maria Petrovna Glinka a certificate for a trip to Revel for the summer.

29 May

Ichnya. Departure of Glinka and his companions from Nezhin with stops in Pochekin Village, Monastyrishche, Daudovka, and Ichnya (where they ate supper and spent the night).

30 May

Departure for Kachanovka.

31 May

Kachanovka. Arrival at the estate of Grigory Tarnovsky (*L.*, p. 150).
[In Glinka's notes the day of 31 May is omitted and dated 1 June, causing inaccuracy for the next three days, which has been corrected below.]

31 May–3 June

Stay at Kachanovka.

3 June

Kiselevka. They travelled through Makhnovka, Piryatino (where they had dinner), Smotriki, Yagotin, and Kiselevka (where they ate supper and spent the night) (*L.*, p. 150).

4 June

Pereyaslavl. Departure from Kiselevka and arrival in Pereyaslavl in the evening (*Zap.; L.*, p. 150).

5 or 6 June

The town governor mistook Glinka for an inspector, and this gave him the opportunity "to ruthlessly clean out the episcopal choir" (*Zap.*).

5–9 June

Stay in Pereyaslavl. Twice Glinka went to Andryushi.

9 June

Kiev. Departure from Pereyaslavl. Stops in Selimov, Borispol, Brovary (where they had dinner), and arrival in Kiev (*L.*, p. 150).

10 June

In *Kievskie gubernskie vedomosti* [Kiev Provincial News], no. 23, "ninth class civil servant Glinka, tenth class Palagin, and fourteenth class Sheinov" are named on a list of those arriving during the period 3 to 10 June.

14 June

In a certificate issued by the Kievan ecclesiastical consistory to S. Gulak-Artemovsky, it says that the bearer of this document, "an intermediate level pupil of the Kievan ecclesiastical seminary, a chorister in the choir of His Grace the Vicar of the Metropolitan See of Kiev . . . has been selected by the Kapell-meister of the Court Chapel and is now to be sent to the court of His Imperial Majesty (Artemovsky's personal file, in *L.*, p. 150).

16 June

In a report to Lvov, Glinka gives an account of his recruitment of choristers in Pereyaslavl and other cities: "All fifteen boys have been recruited already—10 discants and 15 altos. Among the former group, four can reach a high 'D.' All their voices are unstrained, and their hearing is excellent."

18 June

Tarnovsky (from Kachanovka) informs Markevich in Turovka of Glinka's arrival in the Ukraine (*L.*, p. 151).

Between 11 and 19 June

Glinka heard the singing of the episcopal singers "and was so fascinated with their voices that he said, 'If ever there is a conservatory founded in Russia, it could be in Kiev'" (N. Chernyshev, "Kievan Correspondence," in *Teatral'nyi i muzykal'nyi vestnik* [Bulletin of music and the theater], 1859, no. 47).

20 June

Departure from Kiev. Stop in Brovary, Borispole (where they ate dinner), and Selimova. Arrival in Pereyaslavl.

20–22 June

Pereyaslavl. Stay in Pereyaslavl.

22 June

Departure for Kachanovka with stops in Kiselev, Yagotin (where they ate dinner), Smotrinki, Piryatino, Makhnovka, and Priluki.

Markevich, who was in Kachanovka, invited "the priest from Olshansk, Ioann Persidsky," to come "with his gusli; Glinka wants to hear him."

23 June

Kachanovka. Arrival of Glinka and his companions (*L.*, p. 151).

24 June

Glinka inscribed the romance *"Gde nasha roza"* [Where is our rose] in Markevich's album. The composer's date: "Kachanovka, 24 June 1838, your old friend M. Glinka."
[Nikolay Findeyzen bought this page out of Markevich's album from N. Penchkovsky on 5 April 1927. The location of Glinka's autograph is not known (G 2-A, p. 14).]

25 June

Glinka's date on the title page of the rough draft of the score of Finn's Ballad, "Kachanovka, 25 June."

[In this manuscript the introductory recitative and duet are missing. There is another manuscript of the orchestral score of the entire scene with Finn (undated)—a different variant, including vocal parts, belonging to a later time, possibly 1842 (TsGALI, coll. 992).]

25–28 June

Markevich "helped me in Finn's Ballad: he shortened it and fabricated as many lines as were necessary to round out the piece. . . . While I was fitting in the lines that had been written, Markevich nibbled on his pen. It was not easy for him in the added lines to imitate those of Pushkin" (*Zap.*).

23–28 June

Glinka's stay in Kachanovka. In the orangerie, where Glinka stayed, "we played Russian and Little Russian songs, performed plays, and talked sometimes until three and four o'clock in the morning, to the considerable vexation of the punctilious proprietor. These scenes were repeated often, and Shternberg portrayed them well" (*Zap.*).
[Vasily Shternberg's drawing "Musical Gathering in Kachanovka" is in the Leningrad Public Library. His picture "Glinka in Kachanovka, Composing Finn's Ballad" is in the Russian Museum in Leningrad.]

28 June

Glinka's departure, together with Markevich and G. Tarnovsky (Markevich, *Zap.*, in *L.*, p. 151).

Romny. Stops in Ershovka and Bubny. Arrival in Romny.

29–30 June

Stay in Romny.

30 June

Departure from Romny with stops in Lipov, Gadyach, Zenkov (where they ate dinner), Pochiny, Dikanka, and departure for Poltava.

Poltava. Arrival in the evening (*L.*, p. 151).

June

In an article by Vissarion Belinsky entitled "The Petrovsk Theater" in the journal *Mosk. nabliudatel'*, part 17, it says: "The appearance of the large number of novels, dramas, and stories with material from Russian life; the opera *A Life for the Tsar,* which expresses the effort to make use of the elements of folk music in learned music; all these things are good and beneficial. This is all a guarantee and pledge of a beautiful future."

30 June–5 July

Glinka's stay in Poltava.

5 July

Departure for Kharkov by way of Dudnikovo, Voynovka, Kolomaki (where they ate dinner), Valki, and Lyubytin.

6 July

Kharkov. Arrival.

8 July

Composer's dating on the manuscript of the romance *"Gde nasha roza"* : "Kachanovka, 8 July 1838, Mikhail Glinka."
[The reference to Kachanovka is obviously because the romance was written on Tarnovsky's estate (cf. 24 June).]

6–10 July

Stay in Kharkov.

10 July

Glinka requests Archbishop Melety of Kharkov and Akhtyrka to provide the necessary documents for the young choristers whom he had selected.

Departure for Akhtyrka with stops in Olshan, Bogodukhovo (where they ate dinner), and Kupievakh.

Report from Governor-General Stroganov of Chernigov, Poltava, and Kharkov to the Minister of the Imperial Court P. Volkonsky concerning receipt of instructions to render assistance to Glinka and Palagin and payment to them of a sum for expenses "charged to the office of His Imperial Majesty."

11–13 July

Akhtyrka. Stay in Akhtyrka.

13 July

Departure for Kharkov with stops in Kupievakh, Bogodukhov, and Olshan (for dinner).

14 July

Kharkov. Glinka received an appropriation from the Kharkov office for public charity, issued to him by special order (memorandum from the Governor-General of Kharkov, Poltava, and Chernigov to the Minister of the Imperial Court, 29 July 1838, in *L.,* p. 152).

Not Earlier than 14 July

Glinka reports to Lvov concerning the recruitment of choristers: "After recruitment in the city of Pereyaslavl, I visited the cities of Romny, Poltava, Akhtyrka, and Kharkov, and in the latter I found only three boys. . . . In all I have so far selected 20 singers, 5 in Chernigov, 11 in Pereyaslavl, 1 has been delivered to the home of Tarnovsky, and 3 here in Kharkov. One must be excluded, however . . . because of illness. Thus in all I have selected 19. Of them 12 are sopranos and 7 are altos; for the most part they are from 11 to 12 years of age, a few are between 9 and 10." Glinka reports that the children have been taken to Tarnovsky's estate, "from whence I intend to prepare for the return trip." Glinka left instructions to deliver other children, if they were found to be "of the required age," "beginning 15 July and before 1 August."
[Glinka's indication that the report was written on 12 July in Kharkov conflicts with information in the book of expenses. According to an entry in the book, Glinka was in Akhtyrka on 12 July (most likely an error in the date, and the letter was written in Kharkov). At the same time Glinka signed an account of his expenses.]

14–18 July

Stay in Kharkov.

18 July

Departure for Poltava with stops in Lyubytino, Valki, Kolomaki, Voynovka (where they repaired the carriage), and Dudinkov (where they ate supper).

Poltava. Arrival late in the evening.

18–23 July

Stay in Poltava for "four and one-half days."

23 July

Departure for Kachanovka.

Reshetilovka. Stops in Kurilovka and Reshetilovka (where they ate dinner and spent the night).

24 July

Lubny. Stops in Belotserkovka, Brigadirovka, Khotel (where they ate dinner), Sotnitskaya, Lubny (where they ate supper and spent the night and repaired the carriage).

25 July

Stops in Ivanovka, Piryatino, Makhnovka, and Priluki (for dinner).

Kachanovka. Arrival in the evening.

29 July

Memorandum from the Governor-General of Poltava, Chernigov, and Kharkov to the Minister of the Imperial Court concerning Glinka's difficulties in obtaining the necessary funds, since there were no proper orders. Memorandum from the Department of the Treasury to the Ministry of the Imperial Court regarding difficulties in issuing Glinka the necessary allotment during his trip because there were no instructions from Nicholas I to His Majesty's Chancellery.

Entry in Markevich's diary: "Korba asks me to let him know when Glinka will be seeing me and when he will be coming to him" (*L.,* p. 152).

31 July

The following report appears in *Khudozh. gaz.*, no. 14, in the section "Art Chronicle": "The painter Roller, free during the summer months from his activities as a set designer, has done oil sketches for the setting of M. I. Glinka's future opera, *Ruslan and Lyudmila*, on which our composer is now actively working. In these exceptional sets, Roller has outdone many well-known artists in this type of work, including himself."

25 July–1 August

Glinka's stay in Kachanovka (*L.*, p. 152).

Glinka sang Finn's ballad "repeatedly with orchestra" (*Zap.*). He wrote a cantata in honor of Tarnovsky called *"Gimn khoziainu"* [Hymn to the host] (for solo, chorus, and orchestra) to words by Markevich. On the title page of the cantata this inscription appears in Markevich's handwriting: "Score written in rough draft by Mikhail Ivanovich Glinka to my words and sung by himself in Kachanovka in the year 1838 in honor of Grigory Stepanovich Tarnovsky, who was our host for a period of two months. But who rubbed out the words? The host, for something which wounded his pride, or Glinka, out of remorse?" (*Novoe vremia*, 12 February 1903, article by "G-ko" [V. P. Gorlenko], "Glinka in Kachanovka," where an arrangement for piano by A. Glazunov is also published; *Sov. muzyka*, 1939, no. 3, and 1986, no. 2; the text of the cantata was published in the periodical *Stolitsa i usad'ba* [Capital and country-seat], 1915, no. 41/42).

In performance of the "Hymn to the Host" Glinka sang the solo part (*Novoe vremia*, 12 February 1903; reprint in *RMG*, 1903, no. 3, "Glinkiana").
[In the manuscript of the cantata in honor of Tarnovsky no name is provided. The title "Hymn to the Host" was given by V. Gorlenko and has since been accepted in common usage (cf. *Sov. muzyka*, 1986, no. 2). The score is preserved in TsGALI (coll. 736, inventory 2, no. 1).]

1 August

Glinka departs for Romny "to purchase things to outfit the older and younger choristers." Stops in Ershovka and Bubny.

2–4 August

Romny. Glinka was at the fair and "nearly drowned in mud" (*Zap.; L.*, p. 154).

4 August

Turovka. Glinka and Tarnovsky arrive at Markevich's (Markevich, *Zap.*, *L.*, p. 154).

4–7 August

Glinka and Tarnovsky are guests in Markevich's home (*Zap.; L.*, p. 154).

7 August

Veysbakhovka. Glinka and Markevich visit the land owner I. Korba.
[The trips to Markevich and Korba are not mentioned in the expense account book.]

8 August.

Kachanovka. Return to Kachanovka (Markevich, *Zap.*, *L.*, p. 154).

9 August

Composer's dating on a piano arrangement of the Persian chorus: "Kachanovka, 9 August 1838, Mikhail Glinka."

8–13 August

Stay in Kachanovka (*L.*, p. 154). Glinka wrote music for two Little Russian songs by the poet Viktor Zabella (also visiting in Kachanovka), *"Gude viter"* [The wind blows] and *"Ne shchebechi, soloveiko"* [Sing not, nightingale]. For Gulak-Artemovsky, Glinka "orchestrated the elegy *'Shumi, shumi'* [Blow, blow], by Genishta. Gulak sang it well, but his accent was unspeakably harsh" (*Zap.*).

Glinka wrote Chernomor's March (ltr. from N. Markevich to S. Sobolevsky, 31 August 1838, in *L.*, p. 154). "Two numbers prepared (I do not know when) for *Ruslan* were found in my portfolio: the Persian chorus, *'Lozhitsia v pole mrak nochnoi'* [The gloom of night lies over the field], and Chernomor's March."
[Most likely the Persian chorus was also written during the trip to the Ukraine—otherwise why were there just two numbers in Glinka's portfolio? As has been rightly pointed out in G 2-A, p. 77, before the trip to the Ukraine, Glinka had been in such a mood in Petersburg that he "had dropped work on the opera," and "this mood radically changed when Glinka arrived in Kachanovka" (also see 1 October). The fact that the "Initial Plan" contains no musical material for the Persian chorus but only an indication of its tonality, is not evidence that the chorus was already written (of this nothing is said in the "plan"), but that it was clear to Glinka. Moreover, there would have been no point in the "Plan," written, most likely, for the librettist, in providing a detailed "working out" of a number to

be written on a text by Pushkin. Likewise in the "Plan" there is no "working out" for either Ratmir's romance or Chernomor's March or the dances in Act IV, although not one of these numbers existed at the time.]

Two excerpts from *Ruslan and Lyudmila*, the Persian chorus and Chernomor's March, were performed for the first time at Tarnovsky's. "They were well performed. In Chernomor's March we substituted wine glasses for bells, and Dmitry Nikitich Palagin played them very proficiently. Beethoven's music to Egmont was performed quite well, and the piece *Clärchens Tod* had a very profound effect on me. At the end of the piece I grasped my own hand, for I thought from the horns' vibrations that my pulse had stopped."

[In Markevich's notes to his unpreserved Memoirs, there is a synopsis of the entries for 1838, pertaining to Glinka's stay in Kachanovka: "Shein, Palagin, double-bass, and the tutor Mikhail; little Smolensk horns; Petr Petrovich [Skoropadsky], Viktor Nikolaevich Zabella, Maria Stepanovna [Zadorozhnaya]. Gusli and the priest Persidsky. Acquaintance with Chizhov. Korobka [Korba?]. Glinka. His music. Glinka's crane. Glinka admires the turkeys. Espenberg, Makhmud [a dog] and Glinka. *Ruslan and Lyudmila*. Chernomor's March, Finn's ballad. '*Ona nebesnykh snovidenii*' [*Ne nazyvai ee nebesnoi*]. Kachucha. Overture to *A Life for the Tsar*. Bathing. Palagin, Shein; double-bass. Kalinych and the clarinetist. Maria Stepanovna's love. Improvisations. Shternberg or Shterenbenko; our portraits; bacchanalia in the right wing; dinners, suppers, and tea in the garden. Couplets to the host and choruses. Homeopathy of medicine and the allopathy of wine. Holiday at Korba's. Gulak, bass and baritone. To sing in a deep voice and to sing bass; the letter 'O.' Boy choristers" (*L.*, p. 153).]

13 August

Departure. "Tarnovsky and his nieces, whom I had taken leave of in Kachanovka, comfortably overtook me, but after a few versts I found him again with his nieces in a grove of huge century-old oaks, where they were drinking a parting glass of champagne."

Grigorovka. They stayed at Skoropadsky's, "where varied entertainment was provided for me." Departure that same day (*Zap.; L.*, p. 154).

Baturin. Stop on the the way and overnight stay.

14 August

Glukhov. Stops in Altynovka, Krolevets, Tuligolov, and Glukhov (where they ate supper and spent the night).

15 August

Sevsk. Stops in Esman, Tolstodubov (where they ate dinner), Poznyakov, and Sevsk (where they ate supper and spent the night).

16 August

Chuvardin. Stops in Soshanska, Uporon (where they ate dinner), Dmitrovsk, and Chuvardin (where they ate supper and spent the night).

17 August

Orel. Stops in Kromy, Knupr and arrival in Orel (*L.,* p. 154).

17–19 August

In Orel, Glinka found a cordial reception at the Vice-Governor Semyonov's. "The well-known general Krasovsky was also there; he took a liking to me and provided me with an exceptional wine from his cellar, which lasted all the way to Moscow" (*Zap.*).

19 August

Bolshoe Skuratovo. Departure from Orel with stops in Otrad, Mtsensk (where they ate dinner), and Bolshoe Skuratovo (where they ate supper and spent the night).

20 August

Tula. Stops in Little Skuratovo, Sergievsky (where they ate dinner), Salova, Yasnaya Polyana, and Tula (where they ate supper and spent the night).

21 August

Serpukhov. Stops in Volota, Vashano (dinner), Somennye Zavodi, and Serpukhov (for supper and the night).

22 August

Moscow. Stops in Lopatinskaya, Podolsk (where they ate dinner), and arrival in Moscow (*L.,* p. 155).

Performance of *A Life for the Tsar* in the Bolshoi Theater in St. Petersburg (*Sev. pchela*, 22 August 1838).

23 August

Dmitry Stuneev (from Petersburg) writes to Maria Stuneeva: "Yesterday was a triumphal day for Russia and a memorable day in particular for us, for we were all together at the theater for the opera *A Life for the Tsar*. Only you were missing from the family's excitement! After 43 performances, the audience still listens to Michel's music enthusiastically. We hear here that he is fascinating everyone in the Ukraine with his playing and singing. Unfortunately, for her part his wife is trying to charm each and all! How will it all end? Between us it can be said that a good end can hardly be expected."

24 August

In *Mosk. ved.*, no. 68, there is an announcement that four mazurkas and three waltzes for piano, including Glinka's, are on sale at Müller and Grotrian's.

Memorandum from the Minister of the Imperial Court to His Majesty's Chancellery about reimbursement of the money given to Glinka in Kharkov and Chernigov. A notice concerning the memorandum was also sent to Stroganov in Poltava (*L.*, p. 155).

22–26 August

Glinka's stay in Moscow.

26 August

Departure for St. Petersburg.

Podsolnechnaya. Stops in Chernaya Gryaz and Podsolnechnaya (supper and overnight).

27 August

Tver. Stops in Klin, Davydov (dinner), Gorodnya, Tver (supper and overnight).

28 August

Vyshny Volochok. Stops in Medny, Torzhok (dinner), Vydropusk, and Vyshny Volochok (supper and overnight).

Aleksey Zhemchuzhnikov writes (from Petersburg) in a letter to his father: "Last Sunday I was at the theater. They played *A Life for the Tsar.* I wanted to see this opera again to listen to the music, which I had heard so often everywhere and which I very much liked."

29 August

Rakino. Stops in Khotilovo, Markovo, Edrovo (dinner), Zimogorie, Yazhelbitsy, and Rakino (supper and overnight).

30 August

Novgorod. Stops in Kresttsy, Moshnya, Zaytsevo (dinner), Bronnitsy, and Novgorod (supper and overnight) (*L.,* p. 155).

Performance in Petersburg in the Bolshoi Theater of *A Life for the Tsar* (*Sev. pchela,* 29 August 1838).

31 August

Ryabovo. Stops in Podberezie, Spasskoe, Polesie (dinner), Chudovo, Pomeranie, and Ryabovo (supper and overnight) (*L.,* p. 156).

Markevich (from Turovka) writes to Sobolevsky about his meeting with Glinka in the Ukraine: "I was again able to see my former schoolmate and to hear about you." He writes that in December he wants to come visit with them all: "I will come to you, but I have already transferred my Krokos-mastership to my candidate Zabella. You may not know what an important rank to us here in Little Russia that of Krokos-master is. If you are unable to find out about this in Poltava or Chernigov provinces, then ask Glinka. He grasped it all and knows all about it. He even composed a Krokos-master March, which you will all hear during performance of the opera *Ruslan and Lyudmila.* . . . Be like a nurse to Glinka, my friend, and get him to finish his opera faster. Don't let him play the hypochondriac. These fits of melancholy are unbecoming to a man who understands the value of music and champagne. I have told him already that a musician who has given birth to the idea for an opera is like a pregnant woman: if the opera is not full term, that's bad, but if he thinks he will leave it in place for a long time, that's murderous to the health of the mother. One must call for the help of a midwife immediately, that is, you or me, so that, like a healthy fat old woman, we can pull the opera out" (*L.*, p. 156).

31 August

In the "Miscellany" section of *Bib-ka dlia chteniia,* vol. 30, there is an announcement of the publication of music for piano including *Quatres mazurques et trois valses* by Glinka, Dubuque, Esaulov, and Rudolph (d.c.a.).

1 September

Tosno, Izhora. Stops on the Srednaya Rogatka in Tosno and Izhora (for dinner).

Petersburg. Arrival (*L.*, p. 156; *SPb. ved.*, 4 September 1838). "Mother," who had arrived not long before from Novospasskoe, "was there when I arrived" (ltr. to N. Markevich, 20 September 1838). E. A. Glinka left shortly thereafter (*Zap.*).

2 September

Glinka submitted his report to Lvov.
[Nineteen youths and two adult singers had been recruited. A list, signed by Glinka, is attached to the report. The report is in a clerk's handwriting; the signature is Glinka's.]

3 September

There is a notice about Petrova's appearance in *A Life for the Tsar* in a literary supp. to *Rus. invalid,* no. 36. The notice is entitled "The Bolshoi Theater."

4 September

The following entry is included in a list in *SPb. ved.*, no. 199, "of those arriving in the capital city of St. Petersburg on the first and second days of September, 1838": "From Kharkov, Kapellmeister of the Court Chapel Choir, Titular Councillor Glinka."

12 September

Lvov's report to the Minister of the Imperial Court about Glinka's return from the Ukraine and his selection of nineteen youths and two adult singers (*L.*, p. 156).

1–17 September

Glinka was sick (ltr. to N. Markevich, 20 September 1838).

After 17 September

Glinka took Artemovsky to Petr Stepanov and "had him sing. Artemovsky began with his warhorse at that time, Genishta's *'Pogaslo dnevnoe svetilo'* [The light of day has faded]" (P. Stepanov, *Vosp.,* p. 56).

Glinka came to the Petrovs "to escape" from family adversities. "He brought us numbers from 'Ruslan' which he had written in bits and pieces at odd moments, and either I or my husband sang them at once. The first thing he brought was Finn's ballad" (P. Veymarn, *Pamiati Mikhaila Ivanovicha Glinki* [To the Memory of Mikhail Ivanovich Glinka]. Anna Yakovlevna Petrova-Vorobieva, "Page from a Music Notebook," in *Nashe vremia,* 1892, no. 8, p. 142).

After 1 and Before 20 September

Glinka wrote "a new romance . . . in a somewhat Spanish manner," to words by Pushkin, *"Nochnoi zefir, struit efir"* [The night breeze], which "has turned out well."

Before 20 September

"My poet has finished the first act and has made a good beginning on the second. The scene-painter has done models of the sets, and some are outstanding."
[The poet was Valerian Shirkov, the painter Andrey Roller. In speaking of the second act, Glinka most likely is implying Ruslan's scene on the field of death (the original variant, which represents the definitive program Glinka put together, belongs to 1840).]

20 September

Glinka writes to Markevich: "I am now at work on the album about which I spoke to you in Little Russia. There will be twelve pieces by me in it, ten of which are already prepared. I hope that things will not come to a standstill over the last ones. . . . These minor and seemingly harmless pieces, however, keep me from continuing with *Ruslan,* and I will not hide from you the fact that I often grow depressed thinking that I have to employ my poor muse for a livelihood."

[Glinka undertook the publication of the "Collection of Musical Pieces" because he was forced to find a way to pay for his wife's extravagances. "Collecting these pieces was not only difficult for me but extremely annoying: for a finished apartment with firewood and my own horses, I received 7,000 rubles in cash from Mother, besides 2,500 rubles for service. In addition to what I receive from my compositions it should be possible to live well, if one lives prudently."]

25 September

There is an announcement in *SPb. ved.*, no. 216, of the performance of *A Life for the Tsar* in a benefit performance for Samoylov on 26 September.

26 September

Performance in the Bolshoi Theater, "For the benefit of the performer Mr. Samoylov I ["the first"], of the first act of the opera *Otets i doch'* [Father and daughter] and *A Life for the Tsar,* grand opera in four acts" (*SPb. ved.,* 25 September 1838).

30 September

In a report to Lvov, Glinka brings to his attention that he is enclosing "the bound book . . . for recording the receipt and expenditure of money" and 887 rubles, 89 kopecks remaining after his expenses.

September (End of the Month?)

In the "Music" section of *Khudozh. gaz.*, nos. 19–24, there is a notice that Glinka is preparing music by Russian composers for publication in five small volumes (d.c.a., 12 March 1839).

From the End of September

Artemovsky lived with Glinka. He was "a bass who in his own way was superior to Ivanov both vocally and in talent. . . . I am preparing him for theatrical roles." "It was not easy" for Glinka "to cope with his stern temper" (ltr. to his mother, 29 November 1838; *Zap.*).

1 October

In *Sev. pchela,* no. 221, it says: "M. I. Glinka, the composer of the opera *A Life for the Tsar,* has returned from Little Russia, where he had gone to select choristers for the Court Chapel. Under the semi-Italian skies of Little Russia,

Mr. Glinka captured a number of beautiful musical ideas, which he has already shackled in notes. His immense labor, the composition of the opera *Ruslan and Lyudmila,* is moving ahead swiftly. Everything which we have so far heard from this opera convinces us that it will hold a respected position among the best European works. We do not know if the voices of our Russian Opera troupe will be found sufficient for the performance of this opera or for producing the musical effect which the composer has so skilfully contrived in the disposition of sounds! . . . In addition, Mr. Glinka has written several individual romances, which music-lovers are eager to see in print and are requesting the author to get to the typesetter as quickly as possible. These romances are so good that there are few any better in recent times."

2 October

Performance in the Bolshoi Theater of *A Life for the Tsar* (*Sev. pchela,* 1 October 1838).

9 October

Performance in the Bolshoi Theater of *A Life for the Tsar* (*Sev. pchela,* 8 October 1838).

12 October

Lvov issued Artemovsky a certificate, "The bearer of which . . . was selected by the Kapellmeister of the Court Chapel, Mr. Glinka, for placement in the Chapel, but who for lack of a vacant position remains available for some other form of service here in St. Petersburg" (Artemovsky's personal case, in *L.,* p. 157).
[Glinka's acknowledgment of receipt on a copy of the certificate: "Original received by Kapellmeister of the Court Chapel Choir, Glinka."]

16 October

Performance of *A Life for the Tsar* in the Bolshoi Theater (*Sev. pchela,* 15 October 1838).

28 October

The State Council ratifies the decision of a temporary general assembly of the Senate to deal with Ivan Glinka's liquor revenue lease: 1) to pay for the wine poured out by order of civil and military authorities, 2) to return to E. A. Glinka the sum of 21,581 rubles, 40 1/2 kopecks unrightfully withheld, and 3) to pay her interest on 49,732 rubles, 28 1/2 kopecks (G 2-A, p. 59).

30 October

Performance of *A Life for the Tsar* in the Bolshoi Theater (*Sev. pchela*, 20 October 1838).

4 November

In a letter to N. Vsevolozhsky, Glinka reports that he has received two pieces by Verstovsky, which he "was in extreme need of for the completion of the musical album," which Glinka was preparing for publication.
[Only one piece by Verstovsky is included in the *Collection of Musical Pieces*, Torop's ballad (*"Uzh solntse pozdnimi luchami"* [The sun's late rays]) from the opera *Askold's Tomb*.]

6 November

Glinka was in the chapel of the Annichkov Palace for the first time to attend Lvov's wedding.

After 6 November

Glinka "was almost always present at the liturgy" in the Annichkov Palace chapel "and later in the Winter Palace for both great and little entrances" (*Zap.*).

7 November

Memorandum to Lvov from the Minister of the Imperial Court, "By His Majesty's order: 1) Resolved that the Court Choir shall each year prepare itself for three concerts, which normally will be given during Lent, for the benefit of invalids, the Women's Patriotic Society, and musicians' widows and orphans. 2) The first concert with participation of the Court Choir for the benefit of musicians' widows and orphans may be only a repetition of one of the aforesaid concerts. 3) In order that the prescribed pieces for the three concerts referred to above be performed by the court singers with the perfection which may be expected of them, you absolutely must be involved in the selection of the pieces." On the memorandum is a note by Lvov: "Bring to the attention of M. I. Glinka and I. Rupini" (*L.*, p. 158).

9 November

Performance of *A Life for the Tsar* in the Bolshoi Theater (*Sev. pchela,* 9 November 1838).

20 November

A Life for the Tsar in the Bolshoi Theater (*Sev. pchela,* 19 November 1838). Mokritsky and Ayvazovsky were present at the performance. "We listened to the music and singing with pleasure; there was applause, and the singers were called back" (Mokritsky, p. 135).

21 November

Presentation of the choristers selected in the Ukraine to Nicholas I. The Tsar, "in a show of his satisfaction bowed . . . in jest from the waist as he released" Glinka (ltr. to his mother, 29 November 1838).

24 November

Lvov forwarded to the Minister of the Imperial Court the bound book for receipts and expenditures which had been issued to Glinka for the trip to the Ukraine. In the accompanying report he remarks of Glinka's economy and modest expenditures, and, ascribing the successful selection of voices "to the diligence and efforts of Kapellmeister Glinka and Palagin," he requests that "the first receive an annual salary in recognition and the second 800 rubles in banknotes" (*L.,* p. 158).

28 November

Glinka received "written notification from Baron Korf himself" that on the 27th of November, Nicholas I confirmed "the decision of the State Council by which the Senate's report on our case is confirmed in full and that by his direction it will be referred immediately to the Minister of Justice" (ltr. to his mother, 29 November 1838; G 2-A, p. 59).

29 November

In a letter to his mother Glinka complains of his difficult material circumstances and his wife's illness. "If I were not extremely busy, this distress would lead me to despair. But service [with the Court Chapel], our case, and my efforts on the album take up so much time that I do not have a free minute left."

Fall

Glinka's brother-in-law (husband of Glinka's sister Maria Ivanovna), D. Stuneev, who had been appointed director of the administrative section of the Smolny Institute, moved with his family into a state apartment (*Zap.;* N. Cherepnin, *Imp. vospitatel'noe obshchestvo blagorodnykh devits* [Imperial educational society for girls of the nobility], vol. 3, P., 1915).

Beginning of Winter

P. Kukolnik helped Glinka sell his *Collection of Musical Pieces for 1839* to P. Gurskalin, "who operated a store named the 'Odéon,' . . . for 1000 rubles in cash" (*Zap.*).

6 December

Performance of *A Life for the Tsar* in the Bolshoi Theater (*SPb. ved.*, 6 December 1838).

12 December

The following appears under "Music News Items" in *Sev. pchela*, no. 282: "M. I. Glinka, composer of the opera *A Life for the Tsar*, has undertaken publication of a very wide-ranging collection of music exclusively by Russian composers or composers permanently residing in Russia. The collection is comprised of thirteen pieces of various types. . . . M. I. Glinka includes in this edition more than 10 pieces of various sorts of his own composition. . . . This collection will be printed in an edition of only 300 copies. . . ."

15 December

In the periodical *Syn otechestva*, section 6, vol. 4, it is reported that Glinka has written the opera *Ruslan and Lyudmila* (d.c.a.).

18 December

Performance of *A Life for the Tsar* in the Bolshoi Theater (*Sev. pchela*, 17 December 1838).

20 December

In an article entitled "Mr. Snegirev's Establishment" in *SPb. ved.*, no. 287, individual numbers from *A Life for the Tsar* are named in an enumeration of his publications.

29 December

Censor's release for publication of Glinka's romances *"Gde nasha roza," "Nochnoi zefir," "Somnenie,"* and the first installment of the "Collection of Musical Pieces," Compiled by Glinka (published by "Odeum").

[The contents include: the elegy *"Gde ty, prelestnyi krai?"* [Where are you, lovely land?] by Alyabiev; Torop's ballad from the opera *Askold's Tomb* by Verstovsky; *"O! giovanette inamorate,"* an Italian cavatina by Norov; a Lezghin song (*"Milyi Bek, vyezzhai poskorei na voinu"* [Dear Bek, make haste for the war]) by Dargomyzhsky; *"Ne govori ni da, ni net"* [Say neither yes nor no], a romance by Kopiev; and *"Somnenie"* and *"Gde nasha roza"* by Glinka.]

In the periodical *Bib-ka dlia chteniia*, vol. 32, there is a review of the second volume of the "Collection of Musical Pieces" collected by Glinka: "Almost every Russian composer has participated in this excellent publication. The music public will find in the two published volumes the names of many already favorite Russian composers, and they will come to like them even more for the beautiful pieces included in this edition. In all there will be five volumes. The engraving is proceeding quickly, and it probably will be completed in its entirety by the first of March." In the section "New Music," there is an announcement of the publication of the romances *"Akh ty, dushechka, krasna devitsa"* [O my beautiful maid], *"Zabudu l' ia"* [Shall I forget], *"Nochnoi zefir," "Ne poi, krasavitsa pri mne"* [Sing not, beauty, in my presence], and *"Ne iskushai menia bez nuzhdy"* [Do not tempt me needlessly] (d.c.a.).

In ZhMNP, no. 12, under "News Items and Miscellany," there appears a "Survey of books published in Russia in 1836" with a note on *A Life for the Tsar* as an opera "of the new Russian school." It mentions the opera's success in Russia and refers to the attention it has attracted abroad.

End of the Year

Glinka received an award of 1,500 rubles for the recruitment of singers and 1,000 rubles from Gurskalin's firm, "Odéon," for the "Collection of Musical Pieces for the Year 1839." "This income reassured my family for a while, but instead of using the money for domestic matters, they arranged dinner parties and *réceptions.*"

1838/1839

Winter

Weekly receptions at Glinka's: "In the evenings, besides friends and acquaintances of my wife and relatives, there were artists and writers, chief among whom were Bryullov and N. Kukolnik. Mikhaylov and Artemovsky, as students of mine, were always present at our parties. . . . Refreshments consisted of tea and small biscuits, pretzels, etc., and dessert. We did not play cards, nor did we dance. Conversation and music, often ensemble singing (*morceaux d'ensemble*), were the primary amusement at our receptions." Among the women there were Countess E. M. Saltykova ("our neighbor in property"), E. A. Glinkina "with her friend Krekshina," N. A. Sodolskaya (later the wife of Lomakin), Shterich's nieces—"the younger of them, Poliksena, was studying singing with me, and the older one, Princess Maria Alekseevna Shcherbatova, a young widow, was charming. Although she was no beauty, she was a distinguished looking, stately, and extremely fascinating woman" (*Zap.*). The receptions at Glinka's took place on Thursdays. "The Stuneevs, Petrov, Vorobieva, M. L. Yakovlev, Bryullov, Kukolnik, Lomakin . . . were always present. Our rooms were always full, and people from higher social circles intermingled with artists and other guests there. There was no dancing or card playing, just conversation and music. We sang songs and *morceaux d'ensemble*. Often the latter occurred spontaneously and without preparation. Glinka would choose some song or currently popular romance and divide up the voices: for himself, tenor; Petrov, bass; soprano, his wife; or, if there was a better soprano, Vorobieva or Stuneeva took the contralto parts; and at once the singing went excellently. Thus we heard the romance '*Prosti menia, prosti*' [Forgive me] without rehearsal for two voices. I think Stuneeva sang it by herself first, and then Glinka, *à la prima*, sang it with her taking the second voice. He subsequently wrote their duet down. . . . At these parties M. L. Yakovlev sang beautifully for the first time his romance '*Kogda, dusha, prosilas*' *ty*' [When, my soul, you asked], to which Glinka likewise fitted a second part. The pieces were exclusively Russian. . . . There was a gypsy song . . . '*Akh, kogda b ia prezhde zhala*' [Oh, if I had known before], which Stuneeva sang very well. Only three Italian songs were sung: Petrov sang '*Virraviso*' [an aria from Bellini's *La sonnambula*], and Glinka sang '*Raggio l'amore*' [romance from Donizetti's *Il furioso all'isola di San-Domingo*] and '*Una furtiva lagrima*' [an aria from Donizetti's opera *L'Elisir d'amore*]. French and German works were never sung. It was fascinating to listen when Petrov and Vorobieva sang some of Glinka's romances in their beautifully clear voices. One could never forget '*Tol'ka uznal ia tebia*' [I had but recognized you] and '*Sto krasavits svetlookikh*' [One hundred bright-eyed beauties] as Vorobieva sang them" (P. Stepanov, *Vosp.*, p. 56).

Glinka frequently visited Maria Shcherbatova, who lived with her grandmother, Serafima Shterich. "I was like one of the family there. . . . Sometimes the conversation, sometimes pleasant unaccountable daydreaming afforded me pleasant moments. The memory of a friend who had died was sufficient to keep my heart within the bounds of poetic friendship."
[Serafima Shterich's house was located on the Fontanka Embankment, today no. 101.]

Glinka visited his sister, Maria Stuneeva, at the Smolny Institute, where her husband served as director of the administrative section. "Their life was very cheerful. Sometimes in the evenings the inspectresses brought several pupils with them, and several classmates came. The Stuneevs, I, Stepanov and several other friends always enjoyed dancing a little with these sweet and pretty young girls. The orchestra, though not excellent, was always at D. Stuneev's disposal. . . . I sang enthusiastically at these parties . . . and distinguished myself in contredanses and waltzes. . . . I enjoyed myself thoroughly."

1839

1 January

Performance in the Bolshoi Theater of *A Life for the Tsar* (*SPb. ved.*, 1 January 1839).

3 January

Melgunov (from Moscow) asks Shevyrev if in 1835 he had received money from Glinka which Glinka owed Melgunov (*L.*, p. 161).

7 January

In in an article entitled "The Moscow Theater" in *Galatea*, no. 1, it says that "Moscow is awaiting" a performance of *A Life for the Tsar* "with such impatience" that "many purposely have travelled and still travel to Petersburg" to become acquainted with Glinka's opera.

10/22 January

P. Mikhaylov-Ostroumov writes to M. Volkonsky (from Paris): "Pay my respects to Mikhail Ivanovich and thank [him] for the directions" (*Muz. starina*, 1903, inst. 2, p. 143).

11 January

Receipt of the overture to *A Life for the Tsar,* arranged for piano four-hands, as well as the French quadrille "from the same work" in the Moscow store of Müller and Grotrian (*Mosk. ved.,* 11 January 1839).

12 January

Petrov's benefit performance in the Bolshoi Theater. "The nicest adornment to this divertissement was Mme Petrova, who sang Pushkin's well-known gypsy song *'Staryi muzh'* [The old husband] and a new romance by Kukolnik for which Glinka had written the music. The audience received its favorite with great enthusiasm. Mme Petrova had to repeat both the romance and the song twice" (Literary supp. to *Rus. invalid,* 21 January 1839).
[Reference is to the romance *"Somnenie."*]

14 January

Publication of the first part of the "Collection of Musical Pieces" compiled by Glinka is announced in *Sev. pchela,* no. 11. "We must thank our gifted composer for the superb idea of compiling a sort of musical almanac bringing together all the public's favorite names in music. The first volume includes pieces by Alyabiev, Verstovsky, Dargomyzhsky, Norov, Kopiev, and Glinka. All these pieces are distinctive for the freshness of their ideas and for the imagination and taste of the composers demonstrating their talent and knowledge. Until now there has not been such a music publication in Russia, so we can confidently predict that it will be a great success."

21 January

There is a review of Petrov's benefit concert on 12 January in an article entitled "The Moscow Theater" in the literary supp. to *Rus. invalid,* no. 3.

25 January

In Moscow "the Polonaise and romances *'Zabudu l' ia,' 'Akh ty, dushechka,' 'Akh ty, noch' li, nochen'ka'* [Oh, night, dark night], *'Golos s togo sveta',* [A voice from the other world] *'Ne poi, krasavitsa,' 'Ne iskushai,'* as well as arias, romances, songs, duets, trios, etc., from the opera *A Life for the Tsar* are offered for sale at Müller and Grotrian's."

26 January

Censor's approval for the second part of the "Collection of Musical Pieces, compiled by M. Glinka."
[Contents: Waltz by Haberbier; Waltz by Laskovsky; *Le rêve de l'Esmeralda, fantaisie pour le pianoforte* by Dargomyzhsky; Waltz, Contredanse, and Variations by Glinka on a theme from the opera *Faniska* by Cherubini (all are for piano).]

31 January

In *SPb. ved.*, no. 25, there is an article by Odoevsky (signed "W. W.") entitled "Letter to Moscow Concerning Concerts in Petersburg" about a concert by Camille Pleyel in the hall of Prince V. Golitsyn, in which A. and O. Petrov participated. In it the author expresses regret that the Petrovs performed Italian opera arias in chamber music concerts and not romances by Russian composers. "The works of Alyabiev, Verstovsky, Count Vielgorsky, Glinka, Norov, and Count Tolstoy might have provided them a rich store of such pieces appropriate for a quartet evening."

Performance in the Bolshoi Theater of *A Life for the Tsar* (*Sev. pchela*, 31 January 1839).

Beginning of the Year

Glinka and his wife attended a musical evening at A. Kireev's, "who at the time was serving as a member of the Theater Directorate." A. Serov "saw and heard" them there for the first time. "I scrutinized this couple with the utmost curiosity. Both were miniature in stature. She was a rather young woman of captivating beauty. He was somewhat over thirty . . . a dark-haired man with a pale-dark complexion, a very serious, thoughtful face, and narrowly trimmed jet-black sideburns. His black tailcoat was buttoned to the top. White gloves. His bearing was decorous, proud. Then the crowd drew apart. Quietly and in complete seriousness, without the slightest smile, Glinka approached the piano leading A. Y. Petrova by the hand. She sang something Italian. A true artist is always apparent in the simplest accompaniments. Glinka accompanied masterfully. Petrova, as always, sang ravishingly. . . . After an Italian cavatina (I believe, Arsace from *Semiramide*), this incomparable voice, which it was impossible to listen to without deep emotion (whatever A. Y. Petrova sang, the timbre of her voice alone imprinted itself on one's memory!), sang incomparable, moving music which was unknown to me. In this smooth, leisurely, expressive melody there was some kind of blending of Italian languor with a dolefulness and melancholy which were purely Slavic. It was Glinka's romance '*Somnenie,*' wonderfully sung by the voice for which it was created and wonderfully accompanied by the composer himself! I began to suspect that in Glinka's romances there was a whole world of poetic impressions which were still entirely new to me. . . . I believe that Glinka was very satisfied that evening both with his music and its outstanding performance. . . . After dancing to the accompaniment of the brilliant sounds of his polonaise from the opera *A Life for the Tsar,* in which he participated, Glinka became a little more cordial and talkative. He smiled and joked in different corners of the room with the ladies who surrounded him and importunately asked him to sing something. Finally he agreed. . . . He sang '*Ne nazyvai ee nebesnoi*' . . . of course, without music (he almost always performed his own music from memory). . . . Mightily great as a musical creator, he was just as brilliant in vocal performance. The ability to mysteriously transport the listener into a particular atmosphere from the first sounds, which is the aim of performance, into the particular mood expressed by the poetic idea of the piece, and to hold the listener under his magnetic charm from the first sound to the last—Glinka had mastered this magic with consummate skill. . . . The poetry of his performance . . . was indescribable. Like all first-class performers, he possessed a high degree of 'objectivity' and ability to immerse himself in the depths of what he was performing, causing the listener to live the life and breathe the breath present in the *ideal* of the piece he performed. There were, therefore, *character* and life in every word and phrase, and every word and phrase was fascinating" (Serov, *Vosp.,* p. 69).

[Serov mistakenly dates his first meeting with Glinka to the winter of 1840/41. If Glinka was at the party with his wife, then it could not have been later than 1839. However, among Glinka's works performed by Petrova, Serov mentions *"Kolybel'naia"* [Lullaby], composed in 1840. Therefore it is most likely to suppose that Serov, who met Glinka and Petrova repeatedly, combined two meetings in one in his memory.]

1 February

Divertissement in the Bolshoi Theater, in which Petrova performed *"Somnenie."*

6 February

Glinka writes to his mother: "'Now with the approach of Lent, I once again am abandoning the world to work on the opera, and if there are no unforseen hindrances my work will progress well."

From 24 December 1838 to 7 February 1839

"From Christmas to the first week of Lent my life has been like that of a post-horse driven at high speed: work at the school and at court, balls, dinners, lunches, and concerts have not only taken all my free time but also have deprived me of the possibility of getting the necessary rest at nights. However, even though this way of life is not to my liking and robs me of the opportunity of continuing on the opera I have begun, I have still been rewarded in that this year my dear Masha participated in a number of entertainments . . . and above all acquired several new friends and helpful acquaintances" (ltr. to his mother, 6 February 1839).

9 February

In *Sev. pchela,* no. 30, in an article by F. Koni entitled "The Bolshoi Theater," mention is made of Petrova's "beautiful" performance of the romance *"Somnenie"* in the divertissement in the Bolshoi Theater on 1 February.

10 February

The following concerning the music album appears in the "Miscellany" section of *Sev. pchela,* no. 31: "The second volume of the 'Collection of Musical Pieces' compiled by Glinka is now available. This part is even more extensive than the first. It includes three pieces: Waltz, French Quadrille, and Variations on a Theme from the Opera *Faniska* by Cherubini, composed by Glinka himself; a waltz by Haberbier; a waltz by Laskovsky; and *'Le rêve de l'Esmeralda'* [Esmeralda's dream], a fantasy by Dargomyzhsky. All these pieces are written for piano solo."

Between 14 and 22 February

In her own concert Petrova performed the romance *"Pobeditel'"* [The victor] (*Repertuar rus. teatra* [Repertory of the Russian Theater], 1839, vol. 1, bk. 4, p. 4).

14 March

Glinka and his wife sang in the chorus in a concert given for the benefit of schools of the Women's Patriotic Society (a poster).

19 March

Censor's approval for the third part of the "Collection of Musical Pieces, compiled by Glinka."
[Contents: *"Je t'aimais,"* romance for voice, piano, and cello by M. Vielgorsky; *"La sincère,"* waltz for voice and piano by Dargomyzhsky; *Duettino,* by M. Rezvoy; *"Vchera vakkhicheskikh druzei"*

[Yesterday I called upon a circle of Bacchic friends], by M. Yakovlev; *"Nochnoi zefir"* and the Little Russian song *"Ne shchebechi, soloveiko,"* by Glinka.]

28 March

Glinka visited Odoevsky. From there he went to his sister's at the Smolny. "As I approached her place, I all of a sudden felt a strong nervous irritation, such that I was unable to remain still, and when I arrived at my sister's I walked back and forth across the room. There for the first time I saw E. K. She was not pretty, and there was even an expression of suffering on her face. As I walked back and forth, my gaze involuntarily dwelled on her. Her clear, expressive eyes; her unusually graceful figure (*élancé*); and a special kind of charm and dignity which suffused her entire being attracted me more and more."
[E. K. is Ekaterina Ermolaevna Kern.]

30 March

In *SPb. ved.*, no. 69, in an article by Odoevsky (signed "W. W.") entitled "Letters to Moscow about Petersburg Concerts," it says the following regarding a *"Voennaia pesnia"* [Military song] by an unknown composer (performed in a concert for the benefit of invalids): "I sincerely hope that this unknown composer will not stop after such an auspicious beginning ... so that he may persuade the disbelievers that Russian music can exist distinctive in character from any other music, and that a new world lies ahead for music generally, one which Mr. Glinka began to cultivate so brilliantly in his opera *A Life for the Tsar.*"

2 April

Performance of *A Life for the Tsar* in the Bolshoi Theater (*SPb. ved.*, 2 April 1839).

Beginning of April

In *Repertuar rus. teatra*, part 4, there is an article by P. Medvedovsky entitled "Survey of Concerts Given During the Course of Lent, 1839," which contains a review of Petrova's performance of the romance *"Pobeditel' "* in her concert: "This new [?] work by the composer of *A Life for the Tsar*, as well as a large number of smaller pieces, demonstrate that his talent continues to grow in maturity and power."

From 29 March to Mid-April

Glinka is sick. "I had been deprived of sleep, had no appetite, and groaned from tormenting sensations." He was treated by the homeopath Dr. Schering, who was brought in by M. Volkonsky. "During my illness Lvov came to see me and read me an admonition saying that I was not attending to my duties, which he expressed very politely and even cordially. I was silent, but when I got better I began to see the choristers *less than before*."

Not Later than 9 April

Glinka gives Dargomyzhsky a series of errands related to rehearsals of a concert undertaken by himself and Mikhail Volkonsky for the benefit of Artemovsky and sends his instrumentation of an aria by Halévy from the opera *Guido e Ginevra*.

[Judging from its contents, the letter was written before 10 April, since the program is only outlined here. As is evident from a letter dated 10 April, which also discusses organizational questions decided by Glinka and Yusupov by 10 April, the program was by then fixed.]

9 or 10 April

Glinka was at Yusupov's and spoke about the organization of the concert for Artemovsky's benefit. He met with Kapellmeister Wenzel [i.e., Wenzel Kozel] "and arranged everything" (ltr. to A. Dargomyzhsky, 10 April 1839).

10 April

Glinka asks Dargomyzhsky to begin rehearsals with Yusupov's orchestra (who had placed the orchestra at their full disposal for the concert) and reminds Dargomyzhsky not to forget to take "Andreev's aria" (i.e., the Halévy aria). He also writes that the concert has been postponed until 17 April.

In *Syn otechestva*, vol. 8, in the section headed "News and Miscellaneous," there is a notice about the publication of the "Collection of Musical Pieces," compiled by Glinka (d.c.a.).

21 April

Performance of *A Life for the Tsar* in the Bolshoi Theater (*Sev. pchela*, 21 April 1839).

It is possible that at this time, on Odoevsky's request, Glinka wrote the romances *"Severnaia zvezda"* [The north star] and *"Zatsvetaet cheremukha"* [The bird-cherry tree is blossoming] to words of Rostopchina for a proposed concert for the benefit of orphanages (ltr. from V. Odoevsky to N. Kukolnik, without date, 1858, in *L.*, p. 169).

Before 29 April

Glinka asks Odoevsky to distribute ten tickets. "I cannot appear myself, I am worn out, and I have become irritable." In the same letter he writes: "Concerning the matter known to you, I most earnestly ask that nothing decisive be undertaken before Zhukovsky and Vielgorsky arrive. You may provide the song, since this will not interfere with anything."
[Dated in G 2-A, p. 84. To which matter Glinka is referring is not clear. The song which Odoevsky is to supply, apparently, to someone of the royal family, may be one of the romances *"Severnaia zvezda"* or *"Zatsvetaet cheremukha."*]

29 April

Concert for the benefit of Artemovsky in Boris Yusupov's hall. "The participants were Bilibina, the two princesses Lobanova, and Andreev, for whom I orchestrated the aria from Halévy's *Guido e Ginevra*. My wife also sang a duet from *A Life for the Tsar* with Artemovsky. Bakhmetiev played pieces of his own composition on the violin."
[The conductor, Yusupov's Kapellmeister, was Wenzel Kozel. "With the money collected from the concert, Artemovsky went abroad during the summer of 1839" (*Zap.*).]

2 May

"In the Bolshoi Theater for the benefit of the stage manager Mr. Lebedev, *Kliatva, ili Delateli fal'shivoi monety* [The oath, or counterfeiter], a grand opera; *A Life for the Tsar,* opera (Act III); *Maskarad,* a grand divertissement" (*Sev. pchela,* 2 May 1839).

9 May

Performance of *A Life for the Tsar* in the Bolshoi Theater (*Sev. pchela,* 9 May 1839).

16 May

In *Sev. pchela,* no. 106, there is an account by "F. K." [Koni] of Lebedev's benefit on 2 May, at which the third act of *A Life for the Tsar* was performed, [a work] "which we can never hear often enough."

19/31 May

Mikhaylov-Ostroumov writes (from London) to M. Volkonsky: "Gedeonov is completely wrong to say that Mikhail Ivanovich was corrupting me; on the contrary, he did me much good, and I will never forget it" (*Muz. starina,* 1903, inst. 2, p. 158).

20 May

The third act of *A Life for the Tsar* is mentioned in the literary supp. to *Rus. invalid,* no. 20, in a review of the performance in the Bolshoi Theater for the benefit of the stage manager Lebedev (2 May).

Before 23 May

At Stuneeva's in the Smolny, Maria Petrovna once said "contemptuously" to Glinka in the presence of Ekaterina Kern: "All poets and artists come to a bad end, like, for example, Pushkin, who was killed in a duel." Glinka "answered her directly and decisively: 'Although I do not pretend to be smarter than Pushkin, I will not expose my head to a bullet for the sake of my wife.'"

Glinka's family moved "to a dacha of the Forestry Institute. I was seldom there on pretext of activities connected with my work. In the city I found refuge at the Kukolniks' in Merts's house on Fonarny Lane."

23 May

Glinka spent the night at Kukolnik's.

24 May

Glinka and Kukolnik "took a carriage after dinner . . . and set out by way of Kamenny Ostrov Highway to Krestovsky, where we dropped in on Count Tolstoy, stayed for a minute," and went on to Petrovsky Island to the new Petrovsky Park and Yanenko's (Diary of N. Kukolnik, in *L.,* p. 164).

Spring

"Soon my feelings were fully shared by E. K., and meetings with her became more pleasant. On the other hand, relations with my wife got worse and worse. . . . I did not visit Maria Petrovna much at the dacha."

At the Kukolniks' apartment in Merts's house, Glinka wrote the *Valse-fantaisie* for piano for Ekaterina Kern, "although the printed copies were dedicated to D. Stuneev" (*Zap.;* ltr. to N. Kukolnik, 18 March 1856).

"E. K. selected a romance (*'Esli vstrechus' s toboi'* [If I should meet you]) from Koltsov's works and re-copied it for me. I then set it to music. . . . For my sister Elizaveta Ivanovna, who at that time was in Petersburg with our deaf-mute nephew Sobolevsky, I wrote the nocturne *'La séparation'* (F minor) for piano."

Beginning of June

Evgenia Glinka (from Novospasskoe) writes to Maria Stuneeva: "I feel bad for my Michel that he is always in need, and for the other [Andrey] I always fear that he won't study" (*L.,* p. 167).

5 June

The availability of Glinka's Polka and Waltz is announced in *Syn otechestva,* no. 5, vol. 9, in the section "News and Miscellany" (d.c.a.).

7 June

Censor's approval for *Mosk. nabliudatel',* part 18, 1838, in which "Letters to K***" is printed (p. 348) over the signature "N. N." It concerns a concert of Italian music in Moscow during Lent.

9 June

Evgenia Glinka (from Novospasskoe) writes to Maria Stuneeva: "I realize that I worry about arranging our affairs and having sufficient income, and hoping is no help in waiting for my children, even though Misha writes that one day it will be impossible to live in Petersburg and that he will settle in the country, which I would like very much, so that he can acquaint himself with my rural life here as well as our earnings. It is impossible to judge without experiencing it" (*L.,* p. 167).

First Half of June

Glinka wrote the Polonaise in E Major and *"La couventine," nouvelle contredanse* (*Sev. pchela*, 26 July 1839).

25 June

Performance in the Bolshoi Theater of *A Life for the Tsar* (*Sev. pchela*, 24 June 1839).

Before 30 June

Publication of the *Valse-fantaisie* for piano under the title *"Valse-fantaisie, exécutée par l'orchestre de M. Hermann. Composée par M. Glinka et dédiée a son parent et ami Dimitri Stounéeff."* *S.-Pétersbourg. Litographie de D'Avignon.*

30 June

In the "Miscellany" section of *"Bib-ka dlia chteniia*, vol. 35, there is an announcement of the availability of the *Valse-fantaisie*, the contredanse *"La couventine,"* and the Polonaise in E with dates of their first performances (d.c.a.).

June

Glinka "often visited [my] sister at the Smolny. In order to conceal the real reason for my frequent visits, I used my activities with the Institute's orchestra as a pretext. . . . Although the orchestra was very bad, I brought a certain order to it. First I arranged Labitzky's Waltz in G Major for it and, taking the abilities of the musicians into consideration, wrote another waltz in G major."

2 July

In the performance of his duties Glinka attended the wedding of the grand princess Maria Nikolaevna. "During dinner there was music, the tenor Poggi (husband of Frezzolini) sang as well as the court singers. I was with the choirs, and the clatter of knives, forks, and plates gave me the thought of imitating the sound in the introduction to 'Ruslan,' which I did subsequently, insofar as was possible." At the ball in the Winter Palace occasioned by the wedding of the grand princess Maria Nikolaevna, the Polonaise in E major, the Waltz in G major, and *"La couventine, nouvelle contredanse"* were performed (inscription on the first edition; *Sev. pchela*, 26 July 1839).

Pavlovsk. First performance of the *Valse-fantaisie* and Polonaise in E under the direction of Joseph Hermann in a concert at the Pavlovsk train station.

4 July

Second performance of the *Valse-fantaisie* and Polonaise in E under the direction of Hermann in the Pavlovsk train station (*Sev. pchela*, 26 July 1839).

Performance of the *Grande valse* in G at a ball in the Winter Palace (*Bib-ka dlia chteniia*, 1839, vol. 36).

14 July

Note from Glinka to N. Stepanov: "The unexpected arrival of my wife is upsetting all my plans. I will not be at your place tomorrow."

June, July

"Everything in life is *counterpoint,* i.e., contrast. . . . I loathed being at home, but there was so much life and pleasure to make up for this—my ardent poetic feelings for E. K., which she fully understood and shared. The expansive freedom of being with my dear and talented *fraternity.*" Glinka spent almost all his time with the "fraternity," which consisted of Nestor and Platon Kukolnik, Bryullov, Yanenko, Dr. Heydenreich, the singer Lodi, N. Nemirovich-Danchenko ("Knight Koko"), V. Bogaev ("Knight Bobo"), and others. "In the evenings we got together, and the stories flew. Sometimes we had supper, though it was never a feast of food and wine (for we had nothing to treat ourselves with) but of lively and interesting conversation. Most of the members of the fraternity were specialized people. There were outsiders who also came, but they were always practical people, either Petrov with his powerful bass, or Petr Karatygin with his own inexhaustible supply of puns, or some writer or another. Our conversations were lively and moved from subject to subject, and the time flew by quickly and pleasantly." The "fraternity's" evenings were repeatedly attended by Belinsky, Shevchenko, Krylov, and others. "Sometimes we sang, in which case those who took part less than the others in conversation did take part in the singing, namely Yanenko and Danchenko ('Koko'). . . . We sang the song '*Charochki po stoliku pokhazhivayut*' [They pass the goblet round the table], etc., best of all. . . . Sometimes Nestor Kukolnik wrote verses for us . . . either we found appropriate music or I composed it and then coached and directed the choir."

26 July

In *Sev. pchela,* no. 165, there is an article by Nestor Kukolnik entitled "The Fine Arts," which is about new works by Glinka: the Polonaise in E, *Grande valse* in G (performed in the Winter Palace), and the *Valse-fantaisie* (performed in Pavlovsk). "The Polonaise is distinctive for its solemnity and delicacy and, we might add, its excellent orchestration. This latter quality is very strongly developed in our composer. . . . The *Grande valse* . . . can stand alongside the best compositions in this genre. . . . We will not forget the audience's enthusiasm. The expansive and difficult *Valse-fantaisie* was repeated because of the audience's demand. Likewise we shall not forget the performance itself, which was a masterful combination of tenderness and surges of powerful and stormy feelings. It is always a pleasure to hear how listeners throng to Mr. Hermann's tent and ask to hear Glinka's waltz."

3 August

Evgenia Glinka (from Novospasskoe) asks in a letter to Maria and Dmitry Stuneev that Glinka clarify the status of her case before the State Council. "I am glad that my elder master intends to spend the summer in the country. Let him observe our life in the country and acquaint himself so far as he can, if even partially, with the estate, which has been completely alien to him lately" (*L.,* p. 167).

22 August

In *SPb. ved.,* no. 191, there is a notice that A. Heyde's music store in Engelgardt's house has romances by Glinka, Dargomyzhsky, and Rupin for sale. In no. 193 (24 August) of the same paper the notice is reprinted.

Glinka was at his sister's at the Smolny, where he saw his brother Andrey for the last time (*Zap.*).

June–before 25 August

Glinka was in Lesnoe, "or rather, suffered mentally throughout the greater part of the summer" (ltr. to L. Shestakova, 17/29 October 1853).

25 August

Within three days Andrey Glinka died "from enteritis, which developed into gangrene. The death of my brother disturbed and grieved me unspeakably" (*Zap.;* Petersburg Necropolis).

26 August

Glinka requested Lvov to grant him 28 days of leave "because of the death of my brother . . . in order to be with my mother."

27 August

Performance in the Bolshoi Theater of *A Life for the Tsar* (*Sev. pchela*, 27 August 1839).

30 August

Nikolay Pavlov in a letter (from Moscow) to Andrey Kraevsky asks that he print in the almanac *Utrenniaia zaria* [Dawn] the words of the romance *"Ne nazyvai ee nebesnoi"* and says that "until now it has only been published along with Glinka's music" (*Rus. arkhiv*, 1897, part 2, inst. 7, p. 455).

31 August

In the "Miscellany" section of *Bib-ka dlia chteniia,* vol. 36, there is an announcement of the publication of the nocturne for piano *"La séparation"* (d.c.a.).

1 September

Glinka received a certificate of leave for 28 days from the Chapel for a trip to "Smolensk and Moscow provinces in order to be with his relatives" (*L.*, p. 170).

After 1 September

Glinka's departure for Novospasskoe with M. Stuneeva and I. A. Glinka (*Zap.*).

10 September

Novospasskoe. Arrival from Petersburg.

11 September

Glinka writes to N. Stepanov: "I am sure that you will keep your word and do my wife's portrait, and if you accidentally or on purpose drop by the Smolny, then look carefully once more at the features ***."

17 September

Performance in Petersburg in the Bolshoi Theater of *A Life for the Tsar*. "Attendance was 536, 36 large carriages, and 14 other carriages" (*Ved. SPb. gor. politsii* [News of the St. Petersburg Municipal Police], 27 September 1839).

Mid-September

In a letter to Dmitry Stuneev, Glinka thanks him for giving his sister Maria permission to accompany him on the trip to their mother's and congratulates him on his upcoming nameday (21 September).
[In a note to Glinka's letter, their sister Elizaveta also thanks Stuneev for giving his wife permission to travel together with Glinka (*L.*, p. 171).]

20 September

Receipt in Lengold's music store in Moscow of the Polonaise in E, *Grande valse,* and contredanse *"La couventine"* by Glinka (*Mosk. ved.,* 20 September 1839).

27 September

There is an announcement in *Sev. pchela,* no. 217, that the publication "Russian Method for the Piano, Comprised of Russian Tunes by Messrs. Drobish and Hunke" is in stock in Richter's store. "The theoretical basis of these industrious musicians' method is fashioned after the best foreign schools of piano playing. The practical part of the work is comprised of favorite melodies from the opera *A Life for the Tsar* and from folk songs."

In *Ved. SPb. gor. politsii,* no. 26, there is an account of the performance of *A Life for the Tsar* on 17 September.

28 September

The following notice appears in *Sev. pchela,* no. 218: "Messrs. Hunke and Drobish have published a school of piano playing. The melodic themes of the exercises are drawn from Russian songs and the opera *A Life for the Tsar.*"

Beginning of October

"On the eve of my departure from Novospasskoe my brother-in-law Yakov Mikhaylovich Sobolevsky expressed himself so emphatically about my wife's infidelity, occasioned by what I do not remember, that it angered me, and I said to him then that if it were so I would leave my wife, which he doubted."

The road to Petersburg. "For the entire trip back I was in a feverish state. Outraged self-esteem, disappointment, and anger tormented me in turn."

Before 13 October

Petersburg. "On arrival . . . I got out of the coach and went home by cab, thinking that I would take my wife unawares, but they expected me, and my ladies had taken precautionary measures" (*Zap.;* ltr. to his mother, 13 October 1839).

13 October

Informing his mother of his arrival, Glinka writes: "A. F. Lvov has asked that I return to Little Russia again in March in order to recruit choristers."

October

Glinka attempted to verify his wife's infidelity. "I tormented myself; I hastened for advice to my experienced and highly respected distant relative Aleksandr Vasilievich Kazadaev. . . . It was all in vain."

1 November

The Moscow music store of Yuly Gresser receives the Polonaise from the opera *A Life for the Tsar* arranged for piano by Aleksandr Dubuque.

1/13 November

The composer Adolphe Adam, who was then in St. Petersburg, writes to his brother in Paris: "So far as Russian opera is concerned, with the exception of Glinka's work, everything performed is unimportant—translations of our French operas" (*RMG*, 1899, no. 42).

4 November

Glinka participated in judging a competition held by the Philharmonic Society for music to Zhukovsky's ballad "Svetlana." Besides Glinka, members of the jury were Matvey Vielgorsky, Odoevsky, Lvov, and Leopold Fuchs (Y. Arnold, "Bare Facts Without Comment from Our Artistic Life," in *L.*, p. 171).

5 November

Glinka accidentally overheard his mother-in-law and a servant arranging a meeting between Maria Petrovna and her lover. "For me this was sufficient."

6 November

In the morning Glinka moved in with Nikolay and Petr Stepanov, who lived in Garnovsky's house at the Izmaylovsky Bridge (ltr. to his mother, 8 November 1839).
[Garnovsky's house is on the corner of Izmaylovsky Prospect and the Fontanka Embankment, no. 2/120.]

In the evening Glinka sent a letter to Maria Petrovna in which he explained his decision to be permanently separated from her: "The suspicion which has crept into my heart and its causes, for which I cannot be blamed, prevent me from living with you any longer. Mutual trust, which is the basis of marital happiness, has not existed between us for a long time. We must be separated, but separated as befits honorable people, without quarrels, sensation, or mutual reproach" (a copy of the letter to Maria Petrovna is attached to a letter of 8 November 1839 to his mother).
[A similar copy is attached to a letter of 7 November 1839 to Kazadaev.]

7 November

Caricature by Nikolay Stepanov, done "7 November 1839, before dinner" (inscribed in Glinka's hand) in Album No. 1.

Glinka writes to Kazadaev about his separation from his wife: "This important event has caused me to postpone for several days my request for dismissal, the more so, since now she is preoccupied with her desire to be exonerated in the eyes of the emperor, and I do not want any additional favors."

After 7 November

Glinka was summoned by Senator Sumarokov. Sumarokov and the Archpriest Malov, who had married Glinka, tried to persuade him "to be reconciled with [my] wife, or at least to live under the same roof with her, if not conjugally. . . . For an entire hour I defended myself capably and stubbornly. I finally destroyed all their arguments so completely that they had to be silent."

7 or 8 November

Glinka went to Lvov and "explained to him that I no longer had the strength to continue my duties. Lvov convinced me to remain for another month and a half, in order to serve sufficiently long for the next grade."

8 November

Glinka tells his mother of his separation from his wife: "The venturesome behavior of my mother-in-law and . . . Maria Petrovna's perfidy serve . . . as evidence that my actions were well-founded and that I shall have nothing for which to reproach myself."

First Half of November

"All the Petersburg womenfolk, under the leadership of E. M. Saltykova and E. A. Glinkina, have risen up against me, and their slander knows no bounds. In order to avoid unpleasant visits, I have allowed no one in to see me except a few of my truest friends. I have been sick and during my illness have been closed up in Stepanov's apartment."

15 November

Glinka calms his mother over his separation from his wife: "I have behaved nobly and . . . my conscience is clear. You can easily imagine, dear Mom, that in the city, where gossip is a favorite pastime, this event has been an object of general conversation and that many people take the side of my former wife. But is that any wonder? The guilty ones themselves have spread the rumor that I allegedly robbed them, when . . . in fact I left Maria Petrovna in full possession of everything in the house, with the exception of the servants, horses, things purchased by Daddy, my own clothes and linens, and the piano, books, and music."

23 November

Evgenia Glinka, in a letter to Maria and Dmitry Stuneev, asks them, after "what has happened . . . to take care of Misha. I know his kind soul, and this has truly not been an easy time for him . . . I did not expect a good end, but just not so quickly" (*L.*, p. 172).

24 November

In a letter to his mother, Glinka expresses his certainty of being able to retire, because Lvov is trying "to get rid" of him. "I am not saying a word now about my ultimate plans. As soon as we see each other . . . I will open my heart to you, and from that minute I will keep no secrets from you. . . . This year has been the saddest and most difficult of my life for me. Up to now fate has not ceased to inflict heavy blows on my heart. . . . In this short period I have come to know more of life than ever before, and if most of the people who bear the name of relatives or friends abandon me, I have at the same time acquired a few friends who are genuinely devoted to me and wish me well."

25 November

In *SPb. ved.*, no. 207, there is a report that the jury of the St. Petersburg Philharmonic Society has announced the result of the competition for music to Zhukovsky's "Svetlana." Glinka is named as a member of the jury.
[A similar notice appears in *Sev. pchela* the same day.]

29 November

Evgenia Glinka thanks Maria Stuneeva "for taking care . . . of [her] brother" and says that she is sending him money "for redemption of silver and other necessities, which I did not foresee. . . . In January I will send 1000 rubles or bring them myself when I come for a better and quicker conclusion with Maria Petrovna. . . . I somehow do not understand Michel. I wrote to him that he should let me know without ceremony whenever he needed me, and that he should write to me candidly. I will not try to come and calm dear Michel." In a postscript to Dmitry Stuneev she asks: "Do not abandon my Michel. Apparently he made the best of a bad situation, but I myself do not understand. Something seems terribly sad. When the roads are clear, I will probably come myself, but I must wait out the snow and an answer from Mishenka" (*L.*, p. 173).

30 November

Glinka asks Sergey Sobolevsky for a loan of 500 rubles. "Except for you, I have no hopes. My relatives and most of my friends have abandoned me after my domestic problems."

Fall, Beginning of Winter

Evgenia Glinka writes to Maria Stuneeva: "I am sad about Misha, I'm awaiting his answer, if he needs my presence, I am ready. Kiss him for me, and see that he attends to our case and writes Ivanovsky" (*L.*, p. 173).

5 December

In a letter to his mother, Glinka complains that it is "very difficult" for him in Petersburg and asks her to come there, since he will not be able to come [to the country] before summer because of the condition of his health and also because he still has not submitted his request to resign from the Chapel—"I will submit it this week." "My pitiable domestic circumstances still are not over completely. We have separated honestly and nobly, it appears. But there are people in the world who do not understand nobility. On the contrary, it provides them with grounds for new claims. I could have disgraced my wife and her monstrous mother in the eyes of society and other people. I did not do this. Now they are accusing me and reviling me for a depraved life which ostensibly made our separation necessary."

7 December

Glinka wrote a petition to the Emperor requesting his release "because of ill health . . . and domestic disorders" and enclosed an official letter to Lvov in which he provides the principal reason for resigning: "Because of my weak physical condition and exhaustion from my prolonged suffering this past year . . . I do not have the strength to perform the duties required of me in my present position. . . . To these circumstances have been added my obligation to my family: my mother in her declining years has been deprived of two sons in the flower of their youth. . . . She is calling to me frequently, as her only son, to come to her for help and comfort."

9 December

Lvov's report to the Minister of the Court regarding Glinka's resignation: "Having taken notice during the course of three years that Glinka's undeniably poor health prevents him from carrying out in proper fashion the duties required of him, I have accepted . . . his petition and present it together with a letter for your Honor's consideration. I most humbly request that upon his retirement he gain promotion to the next rank" (*L.*, p. 173).

10 December

In the "Miscellany" section (under "Musical News") of *SPb. ved.*, no. 282, there is an article (unsigned) entitled "The newest piano method, compiled by F. Drobish and O. Hunke (on melodies from *A Life for the Tsar* and Russian folk songs)." The article begins: "For some time now there has appeared in our literature a striving toward nationality. From time to time the stage has been enlivened by pieces from Russian history and Russian life. During this period when the originality of Russian literature has been revived, could its devoted friend music remain behind? Certainly not. Verstovsky in Moscow and Glinka in Petersburg have filled all of Russia with their captivating sounds, and our country was delighted to hear folk songs for the first time instead of German and Italian operas. Now we can say that we have our own music."

13 December

Glinka writes to his mother that to live "inseparably" with her is his "abiding desire, and if my official duties and other no less important circumstances did not keep me here, I would fly to you." He asks his mother to come to Petersburg. "Without your parental blessing and prudent advice, from now on I will undertake nothing important. However, my affairs are such that it is impossible to leave them as they are now, and it is also impossible to conclude or take action toward any conclusion anywhere except here in St. Petersburg."

14 December

Proposal from the Minister of Justice to the Senate concerning Glinka's promotion "to Collegiate Assessor." On the same day the Minister of the Imperial Court submitted a report to Nicholas I "On the dismissal from service of Kapellmeister Glinka" (*L.*, p. 174).

In a review of the book "The Newest Piano Method . . ." (compiled by Drobish and Hunke), it makes mention of the fact that the examples in the book were taken from the opera *A Life for the Tsar*. The review appears in *Otech. zap.*, no. 12, in the section "Contemporary Bibliographical Chronicle" (d.c.a.).

15 December

In the Minister of the Imperial Court's report to Nicholas I regarding Glinka's request for resignation, a decision is stated: "His Highness is pleased to grant the request" (*L.*, p. 174).

18 December

Order by the Minister of the Imperial Court, no. 4190, to Lvov about Glinka's release from the Chapel "on account of illness" (*L.*, p. 174; "Mikhail Ivanovich Glinka at the Court Chapel," SPb., 1892).

19 December

Glinka received notification from Lvov about his retirement (G 2-B).
[Regarding Glinka's service with the Court Chapel, Konstantin Bulgakov recalls the following: "This was the unhappiest period of Glinka's life. He wanted fervently to work with the singers and undertook his work with sincere earnestness. . . . I enjoyed hearing the fruits of his efforts. He always said that it gave him great pleasure to be engaged with such a purpose, for he believed in that which rendered a service to the country . . . However, the ungifted and envious musician (although he was an excellent violinist) A. F. Lvov, tormented by his own insignificance compared to Glinka's genius, could not swallow his own gall and, like a boss, began to practice various deceptions on Mikhail Ivanovich, whose nature was too noble to tolerate all this. For this reason he withdrew from his . . . duties in the Chapel, leaving it to Lvov to spoil, which is what happened, for later it was impossible to recognize the singers" (*Vosp.*, p. 231).]

"At this time E. K. became dangerously ill. My sister Maria Ivanovna, who often visited me at Garnovsky's house, hid this matter from me for fear that it would distress me."

21 December

Decision of the Senate to promote Glinka to Collegiate Assessor (TsGIA, coll. 1341).

25 December/7 January 1840

In a letter (from Hanau) to Shevyrev, Melgunov, while discussing Italian composers, refers to Glinka's unfavorable reference to Bellini (*L.*, p. 175).

26 December

Performance of *A Life for the Tsar* in the Bolshoi Theater. Petrova-Vorobieva appeared "after a rather prolonged illness" (*Repertuar,* 1840, part 2).

31 December

The following is asked in *Syn otechestva,* no. 1, 1840, under "News and Miscellany": "Might we hear an opera by our favorite, M. I. Glinka, this year? His *Ruslan and Lyudmila?*" (d.c.a.).

December

Upon returning after a long absence, Petr Stepanov found Glinka in his apartment. "I see that Glinka, having drunk his morning tea . . . has gone to the clavichord and begun to play something from the score. I listen: some very unusual harmonies. 'What were you playing?' I asked Glinka when he had finished. 'The fugues of Bach.' 'Ah!!' The next day the same thing. I listen with great attention. The third and fourth and every day, always the same. I hated it terribly. 'Your Bach is an extremely boring gentleman,' I said to Glinka. *'Mon cher, c'est par ce que vous êtes ignorant dans l'art musical.'* 'I agree, but you must agree that the beauties of Bach's fugues are not natural but purely theoretical and artificial. Natural music pleases everyone, but theoretical music only those initiated into its secrets.' 'What is naturalness in music? Sounds are natural when they truly reflect the ideas or feelings of the composer. Bach's noble ideas are expressed in the clearest fashion in the simple sonorities of his fugues. These ideas are not accessible to you, but that is not my fault'" (P. Stepanov, *Vosp.,* p. 58).

"I got on with Stepanov not at all badly. With his younger brother Vladislav I drew pictures, particularly trees. Besides these two, there were always guests: Captain in the Regiment of Chasseurs Tilicheev, a very bright and well-educated man; the regimental doctor Sadovsky; Sergey Nikolaevich Muraviev (Timey), an ardent student of philosophy; and finally, Yanenko. . . . Also from time to time there were well-known writers there, such as Filimonov, Benediktov, and Bernet."

During the year Glinka began writing the nocturne *Le regret,* which, however, he did not finish. The melody was used for the romance *"Ne trebui pesen ot pevtsa"* [Do not demand songs from the singer] ("To Molly") in the cycle *Proshchanie s Peterburgom* [Farewell to Petersburg] (1840) (*Zap.*).

[On the fifth part of the "Collection of Musical Pieces Compiled by Glinka" there is no date of the censor's authorization. This part was not engraved by D'Avignon, as were the previous four parts, but by *"W. Mittelhaus grave et imprimé."* It includes: *"Obet zhenshchiny"* [A woman's promise], romance by Feofil Tolstoy; *"K prekrasnym glazam"* [To beautiful eyes], romance by Nikolay Norov; the romance *"Ty zaria moia"* [You are my dawn], by Dmitry Struysky; *"Les cloches du soir,"* romance by Genishta; *"Gusli,"* a Russian song by Nikolay Titov; *"V krovi gorit ogon' zhelaniia"* and the Little Russian song *"Gude viter"* by Glinka.]

"I did not work on the opera during the entire year of 1839."

End of the 1830s

Glinka visited the Aleksandrov family and gave singing assistance to the younger daughter of Vera Timofeevna (V. Stasov, "Memoirs of My Sister," in *Knizhki nedeli,* 1896, January, p. 211).

"I [Glinka] was often with Bryullov, and in his presence at Kukolnik's I said that it was impossible to do a caricature of me. Bryullov took careful note of my words and did a series of caricatures on my gestures which stung me to the quick. When he noticed this, Bryullov began to stalk me so viciously with his caricatures, that I completely cooled toward him. But then, when his niece got married, he came to me and asked me to accompany him to Wirt's to choose a piano for him. He took such pains to consider everything so that his gift would please his niece that I unconsciously began to question the coldness of his heart" (recorded by M. Zheleznov, in "Observations About K. P. Bryullov," *Zhivopisnoe obozrenie* [Painting survey], 1898, no. 33, p. 665).

1839/1840

Winter

"Every Wednesday at Kukolnik's there was a gathering. Sometimes there were as many as fifty people, all people of importance. The old Krylov often came. The samovar never left the table. Commotion, stories, drawing, a little music, all continued until around two o'clock. People left, and about ten close friends remained for dinner. . . . Then there were exuberant speeches, but more importantly, music and champagne. Glinka shed his coat, sat at the piano, and sang as enthusiastically as a god. I recall that his favorite pieces were '*V krovi gorit ogon' zhelaniia*' and '*Voglio il ciel*' from *Sonnambula*" (Bulgakov, *Vosp.,* p. 231).

In the company of friends—the Kukolnik brothers, Bryullov, the Stepanovs, Yanenko and others—Glinka "liked to entertain them" by acting out the Christmas choral song *"Zainka"* [The hare]. "Sitting in a circle, his friends sang the chorus 'Walk, little hare . . . walk, little grey one' (etc.) . . . and during the refrain Glinka acted out the part of the hare, dancing around the circle, tapping his feet, bowing, and kissing whomever he picked out" (V. Stasov's inscription, written in April, 1900, on a photocopy of N. Stepanov's caricature of Glinka as *"Zainka,"* in *L.,* p. 177).

1840

End of December 1839 or Beginning of January

Arrival of Evgenia Glinka, who stayed with her daughter at the Smolny. Glinka "then moved there [himself]" (*Zap.*). "Soon Glinka's mother arrived, and he moved in with her, leaving me at our parting the first ideas for 'Ruslan' written in a small notebook" (P. Stepanov, *Vosp.,* p. 59).
[The notebook is the "Initial Plan" for *Ruslan and Lyudmila.*]

Beginning of January (?)

In *Repertuar,* part 2 (January), there is a notice about Petrova's appearance on 26 December in *A Life for the Tsar* after her illness.

5 January

In *Sev. pchela,* no. 4, in the section "Miscellany," there is an announcement about the publication of the "Odessa Almanac for the Year 1840," with a supplement including Glinka's romance *"Esli vstrechus' s toboi"* to words by Koltsov.

11 January

In *SPb. ved.,* no. 7, there is an announcement about the publication of the "Odessa Almanac for the Year 1840."

14 January

Performance of *A Life for the Tsar* in the Bolshoi Theater (*Sev. pchela,* 13 January 1840).

Glinka in 1840
Watercolor by Yakov Yanenko.

15 January

Memorandum from the Ministry of Justice to the Minister of the Imperial Court about the Senate's decision "to promote Kapellmeister of the Imperial Chapel Choir Titular Councillor Mikhail Glinka to Collegiate Assessor" (*L.*, p. 176).

18 January

In a divertissement in the Bolshoi Theater after a performance of *I Puritani*, Petrova-Vorobieva performed the romances *"Somnenie"* and *"Pobeditel' "* (called "Spanish Song") (*Sev. pchela*, 27 January 1840).

25 January

Mokritsky (in Borzno) writes in his diary: "Toward evening Viktor [Zabella] arrived. By dinner time we had already talked ourselves to satiety. Shternberg's trip to Orenburg and stories about Bryullov, Glinka, and Pushkin were the subjects of our conversation" (Mokritsky, p. 166).

27 January

In an article entitled "The Bolshoi Theater" in *Sev. pchela*, no. 22, mention is made of the concert on 18 January.

30 January

Performance in the Bolshoi Theater of *A Life for the Tsar* (*Sev. pchela*, 30 January 1840).

31 January

In *Mosk. ved.*, no. 9, there is an announcement that Gresser has received romances and songs by Glinka.

January

Convalescence of Ekaterina Kern.
[By this time she had given up her duties at the Smolny and lived with her mother. Glinka often visited them.]

For Ekaterina Kern Glinka wrote a waltz for orchestra and the romance *"Ia pomniu chudnoe mgnoven'e"* [I recall the wonderful moment]—"I do not remember for what occasion" (*Zap.*).

["M. I., being engaged [?], dedicated" to Ekaterina Kern "the romance *'Ia pomniu chudnoe mgnoven'e'*. . . . The poem was written by Pushkin . . . for Anna Petrovna Kern. . . . Glinka's care to select this particular poem clearly demonstrates his feelings" (ltr. from Y. Shokalsky to A. Rimsky-Korsakov, 24 December 1929, in *L.*, p. 177). Anna Kern recalls that she gave Glinka Pushkin's autograph: "He wanted to write music which would fully correspond to the content, and for this it was necessary to write special music for each verse. He labored long over this" (Kern, *Vosp.*, p. 148).]

Arrival in Petersburg of Glinka's cousin, Sofia Nolde with her children (*Zap.*).

[Nolde moved in with the family of Pavel and Sofia Engelgardt.]

5 or 6 February

Glinka and his mother depart for the country (*SPb. ved.*, 8 February 1840).

[In his *Zapiski* Glinka mistakenly dates his departure from Petersburg with his mother to the end of February.]

7 February

In *Sev. pchela,* no. 30, there is a notice that the nocturne *"La séparation"* and the anthology *"Novosel'e"* [House-warming] with a mazurka by Glinka are available at the "Odeum."

8 February

In *SPb. ved.,* no. 31, in a list of those leaving Petersburg on 5 and 6 February, Glinka's departure for Smolensk is reported.

10 February

In *Mosk. ved.,* no. 12, in a review of Donizetti's opera *Belisario* by N. Lyzlov, it says that Verstovsky is the only representative on the stage of national opera, but in a footnote it makes the reservation: "As a Muscovite, I name Mr. Verstovsky as the only composer of national opera because here we have not heard Glinka's *A Life for the Tsar*."

10 or 11 February

Logachevo. Before Novospasskoe Glinka stops by the estate of his sister Lyudmila Shestakova (*Zap.*).

10 or 11 February

Novospasskoe. Glinka and his mother arrive in the country (ltr. from E. Glinka to M. Stuneeva, 6 March 1840, in *L.*, p. 178).

11 February

Performance in St. Petersburg in the Bolshoi Theater of *A Life for the Tsar* (*Sev. pchela*, 11 February 1840).

Not Later than 16 February

Meeting of Lermontov and Strugovshchikov in Petersburg: "To his [Lermontov's] question whether I had translated Goethe's 'Wayfarer's Prayer' . . . I answered that I had managed the first part, but in the second half I missed its lyricism and elusive rhythm and did not bother to show the thing to Glinka. 'And I, on the contrary,' Lermontov said, was only able to translate the second half,' and then and there . . . he jotted down . . . on a scrap of paper his '*Gornye vershiny*' [Mountain summits]" (Strugovshchikov, *Vosp.*, p. 196).
[Strugovshchikov dates this meeting to a later time. The dating here is based on the fact that Lermontov's clash with de Barant occurred on 16 February 1840. On 18 February their duel took place, and afterwards followed the poet's arrest and expulsion from Petersburg. The poem "From Goethe" (*Gornye vershiny*) was printed in July (*Otech. zap.*, no. 7). It follows that the poet could only have copied and shown his translation *before his exile* from Petersburg. Strugovshchikov's claim that he met with Glinka the following day is also inaccurate. At that time Glinka was in Novospasskoe. Various events have become transposed and combined in the writer's memory.]

29 February

In *SPb. ved.*, no. 47, there is a notice of a forthcoming concert on 7 March by Andrey Zusman, who is to perform a new potpourri for flute "of his own composition on a favorite theme from the opera *A Life for the Tsar*."
[Analogous announcements appeared on 3, 5, and 7 March.]

6 March

Elizaveta Glinka writes to Maria Stuneeva: "It is impossible to tell you how happy we are for Mama and Michel, who, however, is so sad and melancholy. He still has not recovered from the trip, and, perhaps, he is just depressed. If he were always like this, I would feel very sorry for him." Evgenia Glinka writes to Maria Stuneeva: "I acknowledge that I have had my share of torment, first from the bad weather, and then from Michel's restlessness. . . . My master has grown thin from the trip, and when I look at him I so yearn that he does not get the idea of going someplace and that he look at the farm." In a note: "I ask you to tell Ekaterina Ermolaevna of my attentiveness (*L.*, p. 178).

In *SPb. ved.*, no. 52, there is a review (by an unidentified author) of the "Odessa Almanac for the Year 1840." A supplement includes the romance *"Esli vstrechus' s toboi."*

7 March

Zusman's concert in Engelgardt Hall in Petersburg. He performed his Potpourri for Flute on a Theme from *A Life for the Tsar* (*SPb. ved.*, 3, 5–7 March 1840).

In *Otech. zap.*, vol. 9, nos. 3/4, there is a review [by Belinsky] of the "Odessa Almanac for the Year 1840," mentioning the romance "on Koltsov's song '*Esli vstrechus' s toboi*' with music by Glinka" (d.c.a.).

14 March

Upon arriving in Petersburg, Markevich notes in his diary: "Glinochka has left for the country, has separated from his wife, and has retired" (IRLI, coll. 488, no. 39).

Middle of March

Evgenia Glinka writes to Maria Stuneeva: "Michel and I often recall all the time and pleasant moments we spent with you, the dear children and grandchildren. . . . Console yourself, dear Mashenka, God has blessed you with everything. . . . What do you lack? Your husband . . . loves you with all his heart. . . . And to comfort you, your good friend Katerina Ermolaevna can take the place of all of us who are far away. I am grateful to her, because she loves you. Tell her of my efforts and wish her my best, but most of all good health. . . . My Michel and I are not anticipating either spring or the thaw. Because of the cold, all the rooms are heated like a greenhouse, and everything is dull and gloomy, and the sun does not cheer us up. Your letters are a big comfort to him, but never for long, two days or so, and that is all. Your brother stays upstairs in the big room. Every evening we recall the past and play whist. Sometimes I play, but Irina Fedorovna Meshkova plays every day. So we exist. Sometimes we cheer up, but not for long. He is so depressed there's no way you can comfort the child, if only a little bit. However you try, he gives no reasons and will not talk about it. Instead of tranquility, he gets sadder and more melancholy. We eat dinner and supper separately. Our Lenten food is bad for him. He does nothing but read. Soon he will have read everything he is most interested in.

Perhaps then it will get warm, and maybe he can busy himself more with the garden."

16 March

Markevich (in Petersburg) renews his earlier acquaintance with N. Kukolnik: "He told me everything pertaining to Glinka." Kukolnik passed on to Markevich the current gossip in "society" about Glinka.

March

In *Repertuar*, part 3, there is an article entitled "Panoramic View of the Current State of the Theaters in St. Petersburg, or Characteristic Sketches of the Theater Audience, Dramatic Artists, and Writers": "We only have three nationalist composers: M. I. Glinka in Petersburg, and Messrs. Verstovsky and Alyabiev in Moscow. The first has written music for *A Life for the Tsar*, where he displayed his great gifts and deep understanding of theory. This opera will remain in the repertoire. Now he is writing music for a new opera called *Ruslan and Lyudmila*. We have heard several numbers and admit that this opera is comparable to Mozart's best works. Glinka has been chosen to make the name of Russia famous in the musical world! . . . At the Petrovs' benefit performances . . . the front seats in the stalls and the boxes of the first two circles were occupied by the cultured members of the audience, i.e., the service aristocracy, wealthy merchants, writers, and officials. . . . Whenever the court attends Russian performances, the theater takes on a different appearance, with different customs and habits. By virtue of his talent N. A. Polevoy earned the enviable right to attract high society to the performances of his plays; N. V. Kukolnik likewise enjoyed this pleasure several times; and M. I. Glinka, with his opera, caused the whole city of Petersburg to begin attending Russian performances. The higher social strata attend translated operas at premieres or on unusual occasions. The Russian opera is attended by families of the lesser nobility (whose daughters are musicians and singers), by serious amateurs, and by people seeking whatever diversion is available. The entire city flocks to the ballet."

In *ZhMNP*, part 25, there is a notice by Mentsov entitled "New Books," in which it says that the "Odessa Almanac for the Year 1840," published in 1839, includes a supplement containing "music to Koltsov's song '*Esli vstrechus' s toboi*' by the well-known composer of *A Life for the Tsar*, M. I. Glinka."

3 April

In Petersburg, in the hall of Count Kushelev-Bezborodko (near Gagarin Pier) there was a musical event "completely different from other concerts this year: first of all, singing prevailed, secondly, Russian singing, and third, the Russian composer M. I. Glinka (the trio '*Ne tomi rodimyi*' was performed by Solovieva, Petrov, and Bantyshev; '*Ne nazyvai ee nebesnoi*' and '*Somnenie*' were performed by Petrova; '*Nochnoi smotr*' was performed by Petrov)" (*Sev. pchela*, 3 April 1840).

4 April

Evgenia Glinka writes to Dmitry Stuneev: "Irina Meshkova is here. She jokes with Michel. I celebrated the first of April according to the old customs, everything the same, without variations. . . . My Michel is looking forward to an early spring and is glad. I think that my guest and master will not be with me much longer. God be with him, if only he could be happy and tranquil" (*L.*, p. 187).

Notice in *Sev. pchela*, no. 76: "It is already known that M. I. Glinka is writing a new opera called *Ruslan and Lyudmila* and that he has finished the introduction and many numbers. True connoisseurs of music are elated over these excerpts. They say that the character of this new music by M. I. Glinka represents a completely new kind of music, totally different from the works of other composers and even approaches the greatness of Mozart's and Beethoven's profound works, that it simultaneously exhibits the lyricism and grace of Rossini and remains completely original. The character of the music of M. I. Glinka's new opera is not so entirely Russian as in *A Life for the Tsar*, but Russian-European. We do not pose as *learned* connoisseurs of music, but we were amazed when we heard the introduction to the opera *Ruslan and Lyudmila*, Bayan's song with chorus, Ruslan's aria under the appellation *sword*, Finn's aria, and the aria of the *Head*! Here is genuine dramatic music! Without words it has an effect on the soul and at will moves one to emotion and shuddering! . . . We heard this music only with piano accompaniment, though for all its other beauties, its instrumentation is also amazing. Will we hear this incomparable music on the stage? And will it be soon? . . ."

10 April

Entry in Ksenofont Polevoy's diary: "Glinka has been granted permission to publish a periodical, and apparently a new company is to be formed, headed by 'Knyazko' [Odoevsky], for they have all fallen out with *Istorichestkii vestnik* (1887, vol. 30, p. 328).

11 April

Glinka submitted an application to the governor of Smolensk, Trubetskoy, for a foreign passport to travel "for treatment . . . to Germany, France, and Italy."

Beginning of March–End of April

To this period dates "the evolution of *Kamarinskaya*" (pencil note by Glinka in his *Zap.*).

21 April

In the Bolshoi Theater in Petersburg, for the opening "of Russian productions after Lent," a performance of *A Life for the Tsar*, "which Petersburg audiences always listen to with fresh enjoyment" (*Sev. pchela*, 20 April 1841; *SPb. ved.*, 21 April 1840; *Repertuar*, 1840, bk. 5). Markevich was present at this performance. "Because of a public walk, it was almost empty. Antonina [Antonida] sang tolerably; the actors worse; but the contralto Petrova was fascinating. '*Akh, ne mne bednomu*' was charming; finally, the sets were very good" (N. Markevich's Diary, in *L.*, p. 180).

21 April (?)

Maria Petrovna writes to Glinka (from Kronstadt) of her decision to enter a convent and requests money for this (*L.*, p. 181).

End of April

Evgenia Glinka writes to Maria Stuneeva: "So my Misha is coming to be with you. For how long, why, and what for, I do not know. Take care of him if he needs you. He is a good person, but a victim of misfortune. I do not know what will become of him, and my heart grieves for him" (*L.*, p. 181).

Glinka's departure for Petersburg. Because of ill health, he "decided not to travel alone, but asked K. F. Gempel to go along" (*Zap.*).

Evgenia Glinka (from Novospasskoe) asks Maria Stuneeva not to let Glinka "out of your care. . . . He did not stay here long, he tormented himself and was upset, and many times I regretted that he had come with me" (*L.*, p. 181).

In his article entitled "And My Memories of the Theater" in *Repertuar*, no. 4, Rafail Zotov expresses indignation that the French and Italians have crowded

"Russian melody from Russian ears" and displaced native composers. "We shall wait. There will be a celebration on our street. Glinka's genius has not been exhausted with one opera. Either he or others will certainly continue the process which has begun so nobly. . . . "

2 May

Aleksandr Markov-Vinogradsky (in Lubny) writes in his diary about Glinka: "His wonderful sounds are enough to convince even the most desperate sceptic of the existence of happiness on earth" (*L.*, p. 181).

Between 3 and 5 May

Petersburg. Glinka's and Gempel's arrival. "We took one small room in a monastery guest house on New Lane" (*Zap.; SPb. ved.*, 7 May 1840).
[The building has not been preserved, and a school has been built on the site (today Antonenko Lane, part of bldg. no. 8).]

7 May

In *SPb. ved.*, no. 100, in a list of those arriving "in the capital city of St. Petersburg" during the period 3–5 May, Glinka's arrival from Smolensk is noted.

Evening at Strugovshchikov's. "After dinner Glinka sang excerpts from his new opera *Ruslan and Lyudmila*. How fascinating! Glinka is a true poet and artist!" (Nikitenko, *Diary*, p. 406).

Strugovshchikov showed Glinka the autograph of Lermontov's *"Gornye vershiny"* and read "both halves. The entire work pleased him. Glinka immediately noticed the alternation of the rhythm and the musical effect it might have and what reading the original sounded like. He then asked that the entire thing with Lermontov's variation be written down for him, but I somehow procrastinated in doing this and then forgot to do what he wished" (Strugovshchikov, *Vosp.*, p. 196).

8 May

Glinka and Markevich had dinner at Korba's. Prume and Vieuxtemps were present. "The former played his grand fantasy for violin. What fire, what feeling, what eyes!" Entry in Markevich's diary: "Had dinner with Glinka at Korba's" (*L.*, p. 181).

9 May

Evening at Markevich's: "There were many people of all sorts there. Senkovsky ... Grech, Bulgarin ... Polevoy.... Dreyschock played, and Glinka sang. Servais was also there, though he did not play" (Nikitenko, *Diary,* p. 406). Glinka attended a dinner at Markevich's in honor of his name day "with his two companions." Present besides him were F. P. Tolstoy, Tarnovsky, Shternberg, Nikitenko, Polevoy, Bulgarin, Grech, Strugovshchikov, Guber, Senkovsky, Kamensky, Shevchenko, N. and P. Kukolnik, Yanenko, Prume, Stör, Dreyschock, K. Meier, Servais, Lodi, Nemirovich-Danchenko, Korba, Sobolevsky "and others: in all, 53 people."

18 May

Markevich received a note from Sobolevsky—"an invitation for Glinka and me to have lunch with the Ibis."
["Ibis" was Sobolevsky's nickname at the boarding school.]

20 May

Entry in Markevich's diary: "Spent the night at Kukolnik's. The tragedy *Kholmsky*.... At Glinka's. Not at home" (*L.,* p. 182).

21 May

On the way from the monastery guest house to Stepanov's, "the melody of the Bolero occurred" to Glinka.... "I asked Kukolnik to write lines for the new melody. He agreed and at the same time offered me several romances he had written. Apparently this gave Platon the idea for 12 romances."

24 May

Entry in Markevich's diary: "At Glinka's. At Kukolnik's, at his dear Amalia Ivanovna's ... on this score there is little poetry in him.... From there with Glinka to the steamer. To Pavlovsk ... a harp quartet! Hermann's orchestra."

29 May

Dinner at Glinka's, at which Markevich was present (*L.,* p. 182).

May

Caterino Cavos's obituary appears in the "Miscellany" section of *Panteon*, part 5: "He left a beautiful memorial to himself: the first large Russian opera, *Ivan Susanin*. Perhaps now, for the time being, M. I. Glinka's *A Life for the Tsar* has crowded the beautiful score of *Ivan Susanin* from the public's memory, though genuine admirers of art will always render what is due to the lucid, graceful, and purely Russian music of Cavos's opera." In the same issue there is a notice of the performance of *A Life for the Tsar* on 21 April.

5 June

From morning on, Glinka is at Markevich's: "The poor fellow is depressed, first he thinks of going to Italy, then Paris, and then of coming to see me in Turovka. This is what the beauty Maria Petrovna brought upon him" (Markevich's diary, IRLI, coll. 488, no. 39).

Beginning of June (?)

After Gempel's departure Glinka moved to his sister's, Maria Stuneeva's, in Troitsky Lane (*Zap.*).

Ekaterina Kern's health worsens: ". . . the doctor announced to her that she was threatened with consumption."

Glinka "often visited Shirkov and painted in watercolors with him, but without much success. On his request I began to write 'Kamarinskaya' for piano three-hands, but the result was such rubbish that I destroyed what I had written on the spot. . . . "

15 June

Meeting of Bryullov, Kukolnik, and Glinka at Strugovshchikov's: "Several sketches in pencil and ink, among them a sketch by Bryullov, a study of the twelve-domed St. Isaac's Cathedral, and scraps of music from Glinka's improvisations remained with me from the evening. . . . The weather was splendid; the windows were opened, and we feasted until five o'clock in the morning."

16 June

"Toward the end of our conversation Glinka vigorously proposed putting a stop to the disintegration of the circle which gathered at Kukolnik's. . . . 'And how are we to do this?' asked Kukolnik. . . . 'Very simple,' answered Glinka. 'Find a small apartment, and don't tell a soul about it before fall. . . .' 'So be it!' answered Kukolnik. . . . Bryullov ended the conversation with a decisive '*Basta!*' and proposed a toast to a bright new life!" (Strugovshchikov, *Vosp.*, p. 192).

June

Kukolnik wrote the texts for Glinka's Barcarolle, *"Virtus antiqua,"* Cavatina, *"Stoi, moi burnyi vernyi kon'"* [Stand, my true, tempestuous steed], and Rakhil and Ilyinishna's songs (N. Kukolnik's diary, in *L.*, p. 185).

First Half of the Year

The "program" for the third act of *Ruslan and Lyudmila* dates from this period.

June–July (?)

"Gossip about Glinka's and Bryullov's recent tiffs with their wives still circulated in the city, embellished, of course, by the Petersburg gossips. What was strange about this was that Petersburg society, especially the ladies, attacked their favorites at a time when they had set them up as examples of disinterested independence and creativity. It was as if it was plain to all Petersburg that this remarkable activity did not entitle them to a more cautious judgment in matters which were obscure to outsiders" (Strugovshchikov, *Vosp.*, p. 194).

10 July

In a note to Anna Kern, Glinka asks her to give Ekaterina Kern the enclosed book, *"comme un faible souvenir de ma part."*

11 July

Glinka visited Anna Kern (ltr. to A. Kern, 10 July 1840).

Kukolnik wrote texts for Glinka's romances *"Kolybel'naia pesnia"* [Lullaby] and *"Zhavoronok"* [The lark].

12 July

Kukolnik writes in his diary: "Since the 15th, working out *Kholmsky* in the mornings, getting up diligently about 6, and working until 11 . . . after sleeping, music until 9 . . . 25 days in all for *Kholmsky*, and no more" (*L.*, p. 185).

15 July

There is an announcement in *Khudozh. gaz.*, no. 14, of the publication of the nocturne for piano *"La séparation."*

18 July

Evgenia Glinka (from Novospasskoe) writes to Maria and Dmitry Stuneev: "Whenever will my Misha arrive? I will wait until 25 August, and if he comes earlier, then I'll be all the happier. My master is not a country dweller. It will be sad for me to see him go abroad. Can I expect him to return? Spasskoe is so pretty and nice that it's a shame to be away from it, but Michel does not like it at all" (*L.*, p. 185).

Middle of July

Summing up his work "through July" of 1840, Kukolnik includes in his list of completed works the tragedy *Prince Kholmsky* (N. Kukolnik's diary, in *L.*, p. 187).

Second Half of July

Glinka persuaded Ekaterina and Anna Kern to travel to the Ukraine and provided them means to do so, after requesting 7000 rubles from his mother (*Zap.*).

"From the Bolero I made an entire piece for piano. Hermann transcribed it very well for his orchestra."
[The Bolero for piano was published later; Hermann's score is not extant.]

Pavlovsk. The Bolero and *Valse-fantaisie* in Hermann's orchestration were successfully performed in Pavlovsk. "Hermann's orchestra performed it [the Bolero] with several additional turns and performed it beautifully, led in expression by the composer himself. The square in front of the Pavlovsk train station resounded repeatedly with requests for the Bolero" (*Khudozh. gaz.*, 1 Sept. 1840). "Both of the these pieces were extremely popular with the public. For this occasion our fraternity stayed several days in Pavlovsk, where we spent the time very cheerfully" (*Zap.*).

Before 29 July

Ekaterina Kern "in a fit of jealousy distressed me cruelly with undeserved and prolonged reproaches. . . . It was not that I was sick or well: I bore a heavy residue of distress, and vague, gloomy thoughts oppressed my mind" (*Zap.*). "Luckily at the time my muse cheered up from a prolonged slumber and sustained me in this new disappointment. My ideal had been destroyed. Traits I had been unable to even suspect for such a long time repeatedly revealed themselves and so harshly that I thank Providence for their opportune disclosure" (ltr. to V. Shirkov, 22 August 1840).

29 July

In the evening Glinka, in the company of Yanenko, visited Petr Stepanov, who had just returned from maneuvers. The conversation touched upon Ekaterina Kern and Glinka's temporary disagreement with her (ltr. from P. Stepanov to N. Stepanov, 3 August 1840, in *L.*, p. 186).

31 July

In *Panteon,* no. 7, under "This and That," there is an announcement of the publication of Heyde's musical periodical *Drug vesel'ia* [Friend of merriment], from which the following had already been published: "six pieces of vocal music and seven for piano. And what pieces! Here is everything we love, which caresses our hearing in the drawing rooms, in the city, and in the country! . . . There are romances by Glinka, Rupin, and Arnold; couplets by Moore and Beauplan; arias by Donizetti and Morlacchi; fantasies by Auber; and waltzes by Strauss and Karl Meier." In the same issue Kukolnik's completion of *Prince Kholmsky* is reported along with notice of a reading of the new tragedy "among a close circle of friends who are writers and artists." In the same issue, in an article entitled "My Memories of the Theater," Rafail Zotov writes: "Russian national songs are no longer sung on the stage, and if it were sometimes not for the sounds of Glinka's excellent work *A Life for the Tsar,* we probably would completely forget about folk melodies" (d.c.a.).

End of July

Glinka received money from his mother for Ekaterina Kern with a letter in which [his mother] spoke out "so strongly that it was clear to me that her consent to my plans was mandatory" (ltr. to V. Shirkov, 22 August 1840). Once he received the money, Glinka bought a carriage for Anna and Ekaterina Kern and ordered a barouche for himself. "I wanted to leave Petersburg (which is why the collection of romances is called *Farewell to St. Petersburg*)."

June or July (?)

For Pavel Kukolnik, who was arriving from Vilnius, Glinka wrote the *Chorus to Pavel Vasilievich* to words by Nestor Kukolnik. "I do not recall the music. It seems there was a solo for Lodi."

Having written "his famous series of 12 romances, *Farewell to St. Petersburg,*" Glinka "declared upon request of his friends that he would not publish them until I [Anna Petrova] had sung all twelve in succession at an evening at my place attended by a large number of people." "As is known A. Y. complied with Glinka's request and performed all twelve romances alternating with her husband" (P. Veymarn, "To the Memory of Mikhail Ivanovich Glinka," Anna Yakovlevna Petrova-Vorobieva, "Pages from a Musical Notebook," in *Nasha vremia,* 1892, no. 8, p. 142).

Before 3 August

At Kukolnik's "a large number of people were rehearsing. They were singing Glinka's 'Farewell Song' with chorus, which was to be sung at a farewell dinner prior to his departure. The song is fine, but they were at sixes and sevens singing it" (ltr. from P. Stepanov to N. Stepanov, 3 August 1840).

3 August

Petr Stepanov informs Nikolay Stepanov that Glinka is planning to go to Paris. In a week he is going to see his mother, from there to Shirkov's, and then to France. He asks: "Glinka's album is missing, do you maybe have it, or do you know where it's gotten to. I have rummaged everywhere and can't find it" (*L.,* p. 187).

Summer, Before 9 August

While visiting Anna and Ekaterina Kern in their apartment on the Petersburg side, Glinka performed his own music in the presence of Aleksandr Markov-Vinogradsky: "I listened to the music he had written for Kukolnik's 12 romances. How lovely! How deeply he had understood the poem's meaning and how appropriately he had set the music to the words. His music is intelligent, it breathes feeling, and inspires pleasure in the listener! He . . . caressed our ears with musical excerpts [from *Ruslan*] . . . skillfully setting the scene when Ruslan searches for his sword and then forgets himself in reminiscing over his mournful Lyudmila. In this excerpt one is first struck by loud heroic sounds— one shudders! Then tenderer feelings gradually take over, your heart is touched by the sweet sounds of love. . . . Under the melody's spell you begin to dream, like Ruslan. . . . You are passionately in love and forget that a minute before, inspired by heroic lyrics, you were ready to enter the heat of the battle! Effortlessly you feel what the gifted composer wished to express! But the music for his romance called *"Parokhod"* [The locomotive], is surprisingly realistic. You hear the noise and movement of the engine, and a smile flashes across your face because of the composer's skillful imitation. The steamer sails, but then you hear the melancholy sounds of the poet dreaming! How excellent the imitation is in '*Zhavoronok*', and how charming! The music reminds you so vividly of the trill of the herald of spring that you begin to daydream and feel the spring breeze, and you imagine yourself in a grove listening to the lark's early song. He ceases his singing when he hears Glinka's lovely sounds! Then his '*Guadalquivir*'! How wonderful it sounds! But then I cannot re-tell them all" (A. Markov-Vinogradsky's diary, after August 1840, in *Muz. letop.*, 1923, coll. 2, p. 53).

Before 9 August

Glinka "was in good form and was writing. The romances which were ordered are ready, and the opera also is moving along" (ltr. to N. Stepanov, 9 August 1840). Glinka assembled the "program" for Act IV of *Ruslan and Lyudmila* (ltr. to V. Shirkov, 9 August 1840).

Glinka writes to Maria Vever that he cannot meet her "demands," since he is getting ready to leave and does "not have enough money." He asks her to give him her new address.
[In LNG II, the letter is dated 1840–44, and in G 2-A, March-April, 1852. Since the contents concerns repayment of a debt (Vever's "demands"), it is difficult to suppose that Glinka is preparing to travel abroad. More likely he is writing about a trip to the country to his mother's. Glinka's last departure from Petersburg for Novospasskoe occurred on 10 August 1840. In the spring of 1841, Glinka made a brief unanticipated trip to the country. Therefore the most probable date is the beginning of August, before the 9th, 1840. M. Vever, apparently, is a civil servant paid on a percentage basis (the tone of Glinka's letter rules out the possibility of its being directed to a person of the same social position).]

9 August

Glinka sent Shirkov the "program" for the fourth act of *Ruslan and Lyudmila*. He tells him about his departure for the country the following day: "My fate has in many ways changed, but I am not complaining or grumbling—my muse sustains me. Never have I written so much, nor have I ever felt such inspiration. I implore you, write the fourth act for the program I have sent. When I arrive in the country I will provide you all of it and in greater detail."

In a letter to Nikolay Stepanov in the country, Glinka invites him to come to Novospasskoe: "I will tell you about myself and my situation when we see each other."

Farewell party at the Kukolniks. "I sang the 'Farewell Song' with unaccustomed enthusiasm, our fraternity sang the chorus, and, in addition to the piano, there was a quartet with bass" (*Zap.;* N. Kukolnik, "Ceremonial Send-off for Glinka," in RMG, 1894, no. 5).
[In his *Zapiski* Glinka erroneously dates the party 10 August and his departure 11 August.]

10 August

Glinka departs from St. Petersburg. In Gatchina he separates from Ekaterina and Anna Kern (ltrs. to N. Stepanov and V. Shirkov, 9 August 1840; papers of A. Kern, in *L.,* p. 188; *SPb. ved.,* 13 August 1840).

10 and 11 August

"At the stations I would pay for the horses and order dinner or lunch and so forth. When he had gotten out of the carriage, he would immediately sit down in the corner of the station's sofa and not involve himself in anything. While we travelled from one station to the next, he conversed and sang from . . . the opera *Ruslan and Lyudmila,* delighting us especially with the tender melody from the aria 'O Lyudmila, Lel promised me happiness, my heart believes that the foul weather will pass'" (A. Kern, *Vosp.,* p. 157).

11 August

Kukolnik wrote in his diary: "Announcement in the *Sev. pchela* about Glinka's collection" (*L.,* p. 188).

12 (?) August

Katezhna. Glinka "accompanied the ladies as far as Katezhna . . . they were going to Vitebsk and I to Smolensk." "You can imagine how distressing it was for me to continue my journey after parting from you."

Porkhov. Toward evening of the same day Glinka arrived in Porkhov, since "the horses were dragging their feet on the scorching sand, and at every station . . . we had to take three or four hours" (ltr. to A. Kern, 17 August 1840).

13 August

In *SPb. ved.*, no. 181, in the list of those leaving Petersburg on 9, 10, and 11 August, Glinka is named with a destination of Smolensk.

"From Porkhov . . . we decided to travel day and night" (ltr. to A. Kern, 17 August 1840).

14 August

Kukolnik notes in his diary that he sent a letter to Glinka (*L.*, p. 188).

Evgenia Glinka (from Novospasskoe), in a letter to Maria Stuneeva, expresses alarm over the fact that "I have not received a letter from Misha in two deliveries. Before I thought that he had left, but now I know that he is still in Piter" (*L.*, p. 188).

16 (?) August

Smolensk. Glinka arrived "a day earlier than planned."

17 August

In a letter to Anna Kern, Glinka asks: "Give me a detailed description of your stay there [Trigorskoe], especially of the spot where Pushkin lies buried." In the morning, after writing to Anna Kern, Glinka set out for Novospasskoe (ltr. to A. Kern, 17 August 1840).

18 August

Novospasskoe. Glinka "arrived in the country." In a letter to Nikolay Stepanov he says that he will be staying in Novospasskoe until 6 September and asks him to come visit. He asks about his album, "which I have not been able to find after I was at your apartment . . . ask that it be looked for, and if it is found, bring it with you. I will be desperate if your *chef-d'oeuvre* is missing."
[The "Album" is Album No. 1 in the Glinka collections (GPB).]

By 22 August

Glinka assembled the programs for the fourth act ("in addition to what I had written") and fifth act of *Ruslan and Lyudmila*.

22 August

Glinka writes to Shirkov that his nerves in the country "are already wrecked" and that he does not feel "the salutary effect of the pure country air. . . . Such is my entire fate, that there is joy nowhere and in nothing. . . . All my plans have been ruined. . . . You know that I asked for a considerable sum to liberate ***. In spite of need, Mother sent me the sum, but in her letter I could read her heart so clearly (against her will, which I could see in her style), that it became evident to me that I would have to get her permission for my plans. Fortunately at that time my muse awoke from a deep slumber and saved me from another disappointment. My ideal had been destroyed. Traits which I for so long had been unable to suspect were repeatedly evident and were so sharp that I thank Providence for disclosing them to me so opportunely. I have decided, after spending several weeks here, to return again to the capital . . . with the firm intention of finishing our *Ruslan* as quickly as possible. Circumstances have never been more favorable—the entire theater is at my disposal, and I may test what I have written as I wish, or, rather, with confidence find earnest assistance. The Petrovs (both of them) sing extremely well. I am sending the program with this and ask you first of all to look at the fifth act, especially the duet and finale. By my calculations copying what is already composed will require about two months work. If you send the fifth act by that time, then things will be in full swing."

Second Half of August

Novospasskoe/Bezzabotie. "I got to work and in three weeks wrote the intro-duction to *Ruslan*. What I had begun in Novospasskoe I finished at the estate of my brother-in-law Nikolay Dmitrievich Gedeonov."

29 August

Novospasskoe. Glinka wrote again to the Governor of Smolensk, Trubetskoy, saying that "now because of domestic circumstances" he is unable to travel abroad.

1 September

On the title page of the manuscript of the score of Ruslan's aria is the com-poser's date, "1 September 1840. Novospasskoe."

10 September

Departure for Petersburg.

Night of 13/14 September

Glinka "caught a chill."

14 September

Gorodets. On arrival at the station, Glinka "asked for tea, and having warmed myself, continued the trip" (*Zap.*).

In *Khudozh. gaz.*, no. 17, there is an article by N. Kukolnik about the [song cycle] *Farewell to St. Petersburg,* in which Kukolnik tells the story in chronological order of the romances' composition "in the course of some six weeks" and enumerates their contents. He points out, moreover, that "the simple folklike song of Ilyinishna was not included by the publishers among the songs of this elegant collection." Of the Bolero he says: "I fitted words to this already written Spanish melody. . . . We concur that *Farewell to St. Petersburg* is worth many operas, especially contemporary ones." In a remark "from the editors" the statement is made that the collection is available in the "Odéon" music store, each romance individually (d.c.a.).

The road from Gorodets to Petersburg, from 14 to 15 September. "All night I was feverish, my imagination was astir, and that night the finale of the opera came to me, which subsequently served as the basis for the overture to the opera *Ruslan and Lyudmila*."

15 September

Petersburg. Glinka's arrival. Address: "Fonarny Lane, Merts house (formerly Schlothauer), Kukolniks' apartment" (ltr. to V. Shirkov, 22 August 1840; *SPb. ved.*, 17 September 1840).

17 September

In *SPb. ved.*, no. 209, in a list of those arriving during the period 12–15 September, "retired Collegiate Assessor Glinka—from Smolensk" is named.

18 September

In an "Obituary for Cavos" in *Sev. pchela,* no. 210, Guillou expresses a preference for Cavos's *Ivan Susanin* over *A Life for the Tsar.*

19 September

Composer's dating on the title page of the manuscript of the score of the "Overture to the Tragedy *Prince Kholmsky,* written by N. V. Kukolnik. Music by M. Glinka, dedicated to the author of the tragedy. 19 September 1840, St. Petersburg, at Kukolniks' apartment."

20 September

In *Sev. pchela,* no. 212, in the section "Miscellany," there is a review (unsigned) of *"Farewell to St. Petersburg.* Romances and songs. Words by N. V. Kukolnik. Music by M. I. Glinka. . . . We have heard all the romances sung by Glinka himself, but we did not know which we preferred. . . . The 12 romances together comprise the most diverse gallery. All are rich in harmonic interest. All the melodies are new, full of life, truth, and charm. Hearing them all you would think that it must have taken not one but 12 months to find so many melodies, to finish with such precision so many musical pieces, and furthermore not to repeat oneself once, not only in these 12 pieces but also in reference to M. I. Glinka's earlier compositions. We will sing through these romances, dear artist, sing them through completely, but on condition that next summer in their place, for variety, there will be not a 'Farewell' but 'Greetings to Petersburg.' . . . One must certainly be grateful to the publisher for this beautifully elegant edition. . . . Its outer appearance corresponds to its inner worth, and in this respect *Farewell to St. Petersburg* may contend with any foreign publications."

26 September

Composer's dating on the last page of the manuscript of the score of the overture to *Prince Kholmsky:* "Completed 26 September."

In *SPb. ved.,* no. 217, Kukolnik's article about *Farewell to St. Petersburg* from *Khudozh. gaz.* is reprinted under the general heading "Music" and is signed "Kuk-k."

28 September

Composer's dating on the title page of the manuscript of the score of Rakhil's dream: "Begun 28 September 1840."

29 September

Composer's dating at the end of the manuscript of the score of Rakhil's dream: "Completed 29 September."

30 September

In *Syn otechestva,* vol. 4, in the section "News and Miscellany . . . Petersburg Music," the composer Adam's opinion concerning Russian music after his visit to Petersburg is expressed: "He also had great praise for our national opera *A Life for the Tsar* and admired Mr. Glinka's art for his extraordinary orchestration" (d.c.a.).

In the "Miscellany" section of *Bib-ka dlia chteniia,* vol. 42, there is an unsigned article entitled "Musical News. Twelve new romances with words by Kukolnik and music by Glinka called *Farewell to St. Petersburg."* "But why is Glinka saying farewell to Petersburg? Where in heaven is he being taken? To Paris! Why? To compose, or better, to finish his new opera. . . . Oh! Oh! . . . Just return to us quickly, great tone poet. And return just as nice and generous in cheerful inspirations as you are leaving. It is said, however, that Glinka is spending the entire winter in Petersburg." Later on the article says that in Russia there is little opera, since for opera's creation "an intolerable condition is demanded, behind which I stand solidly, that is, so-called musical learning, musical theory. . . . Only one opera, *A Life for the Tsar,* has been a brilliant exception. With it we have entered a new period in Russian music, an authentic period, the first period. It was Russia's first musical manifesto. Envy drew the line with her own hand: new periods always begin from such a line. . . . Meanwhile, what will there be? Perhaps, besides 'Ruslan,' nothing, just as there was nothing before the opera *A Life for the Tsar.* Therefore we give our attention to what there is, namely romances. In this arena . . . we have many worthwhile names. . . . With respect to the romance, both in number and quality, first place belongs to Glinka." Later there follows an analysis of the 12 romances of the cycle, which the critic evaluates highly, especially sorting out the following: "'Hebrew Song'. . . . This excellent romance deserves particular attention. . . . Harmonic intricacies receive double value if they are used . . . consistently with the aim and character of the piece, which is the case in this romance. They give the piece the coloration of Hebraism, though not the kind in which musical literature abounds, but something elevated and mystic. . . . Lullaby—this is a difficult and trite assignment which, apparently, provides no opportunity to do anything new. However, besides the exceptionally pure and naive melody, like a mother's love, Glinka, in the accompaniment, has strewn a great number of very ingenious harmonic turns. . . . Despite the great value of the Lullaby in this respect, it is very easy for the performer, and because of its elegance, it will probably remain a favorite of all mothers, both those who sing and those who do not, as well as connoisseurs." Regarding the Fantasy: "It offers few difficulties in performance, and like a beautiful outline of the introductory romance, it portrays envy in true recitative and by means of an excellent story. The Fantasy will remain on most pianos, and, no doubt, as a semidramatic work, it will receive its share of theatrical fame in the inspired performances of Mme Petrova. 'The Lark'. . . . should not seek to translate the singing of a bird sound for sound, but should only express its general character, or still better, as Glinka did, limit itself to only an allusion, with echos. In the very melody of the romance you feel the impression of harvest and listlessness from the intense heat. . . . A continuous poetic comparison with the lark is outlined by the imitative accompaniment. You have often heard the Bolero in Pavlovsk. No one among composers imitates the nationality of various peoples with such artistry as Glinka. . . . Listen and tell me. Where are they singing? . . . In Spain. I have already spoken of the 'Hebrew Song.' The music to the two songs by Zabella are Little Russian to the point of deception. The Polonaise and Krakowiak in the opera *A Life for the Tsar* are straight from Cracow and Warsaw. The entire opera is a triumph of folk-art music. Finn's ballad is genuinely charming Finnish music. . . . The Barcarolle in *Farewell to St. Petersburg* is straight from the grand canal of Venice in the local color of its melody. Its artistic finish comes from the school of Monsieur van Beethoven. . . . In this romance Glinka preserved . . . the movement of the accompaniment . . . in the passionate contrast of the storm of life with the nocturnal quiet of the waves. . . . Movement itself in music is often the form. . . . Sometimes movement alone lends a piece of music truth of character, and, in *'Poputnaia pesnia'* [Travelling song] movement itself expressly determines the peculiar life, the restless quality, the haste, and the essential qualities of a trip on the Tsarskoe Selo railroad. . . . The outward feeling of the journey and passionate inner agitation filled with hopes and expectation are told with definitive elegance. . . . 'Farewell Song' is a noble expression of lofty feeling, wounded from various sides by the events of life. This is the sad story of every artist" (d.c.a.).

[Judging from the style and character of the article, the author appears to be Senkovsky.]

September

In the conclusion to his article "And My Memories of the Theater" in *Repertuar*, part 9, Rafail Zotov writes: "The revival of Russian opera began with *Robert*. . . . Soon thereafter a gratifying event completely restored the fallen spirit of Russian opera. With the restoration of the Bolshoi Theater Russians saw something long unprecedented: a national opera! *A Life for the Tsar*, composed by Mr. Glinka, laid a firm foundation for musical nationalism, and its brilliant success demonstrated that the demands of our audience since time immemorial have been the same, namely, the demand for nationality. . . . God grant that Glinka's talent allows him to create new works like his first opera. . . . After *A Life for the Tsar* audiences returned in droves under the banner of Russian opera, which they had long abandoned. . . . A little time passed, and everything changed again. . . . Operas were deserted again. Again nobody listened to them. . . . This is almost incomprehensible. However, the answer to the riddle lies before our eyes. . . . Everything now is concentrated on the person of Talioni." In the same issue, in an article entitled "Some words about the Nizhegorod Theater" mention is made of the poor performance by the chorus in a Petersburg performance of *A Life for the Tsar*.

In the same issue the publication of *Farewell to St. Petersburg* is announced.

1 October

Composer's dating on the manuscript of the score of the entr'acte to the second act of *Prince Kholmsky*: "Begun 1 October 1840 in Kukolnik's apartment."

2 October

Composer's dating at the end of the manuscript of the entr'acte to the second act of *Prince Kholmsky*: "Completed on 2 October." Composer's dating on the title page of the manuscript of the score of the entr'acte to the third act of *Prince Kholmsky*: "2 October 1840."

4 October

Composer's dating at the end of the manuscript of the score of the entr'acte to the third act of *Prince Kholmsky*: "Completed on 4 October."

7 October

Composer's dating on the title page of the manuscript of the entr'acte to the fourth act of *Prince Kholmsky:* "Begun on 7 October (St. Petersburg, at Kukolnik's apartment)."

8 October

Glinka writes to his mother: "Despite my ailments, I am leading a quiet and restful life, and what is even better, without worries. Even if my heart is perhaps empty, music consoles me unspeakably. I work nearly the entire morning, and in the evening I am distracted by the conversation of good friends. If things go like this next year, the opera will almost be finished by spring."

11 October

Composer's dating at the end of the manuscript of the entr'acte to Act IV of *Prince Kholmsky:* "Completed on 11 October."

12 October

Composer's dating on the title page of the manuscript of the entr'acte to Act V of *Prince Kholmsky:* "Begun 12 October 1840."

15 October

Composer's dating at the end of the manuscript of the entr'acte to Act V of *Prince Kholmsky:* "Completed 15 October."

19 September–15 October

The overture and entr'actes to Kukolnik's tragedy *Prince Daniil Dmitrievich Kholmsky* were composed. "I was able to write them as I wished, and I feel right in considering them among my best works" (ltr. to V. Shirkov, 18 December 1840).

Before 19 October

A new edition ("Odéon") of the "Collection of Musical Pieces, compiled by M. I. Glinka, in five parts" is published (*Sev. pchela,* 19 October 1840).

19 October

In the "Miscellany" section of *Sev. pchela,* no. 237, there is a review of the second edition of the "Collection of Musical Pieces": "Hardly ever are we given such a musical gift as this, inexpensive and elegant both with respect to its inner content and exterior appearance. It is . . . a musical almanac. In it are 34 pieces, either for voice or piano. The names are all . . . those of our best composers. . . . Of the vocal pieces the ones that pleased us most were '*V krovi gorit ogon' zhelaniia,*' a romance by M. I. Glinka to Pushkin's words and '*Somnenie,*' a romance accompanied by harp and violin. Audiences have heard this romance sung by the incomparable Mme Petrova and had her repeat it, despite its length and difficulty. . . . Of the piano pieces we particularly liked M. I. Glinka's Waltz in E-flat as well as his Variations on a Theme by Cherubini and the Contredanse." Later on all of Glinka's pieces included in all the parts are enumerated. "Hardly ever in Russia has there been such a publication. . . . We might add, by the way, that M. I. Glinka's well-known *Valse-fantaisie,* which was so successfully performed by Hermann's orchestra, has not been available for some time. Other copies of this remarkable piece were tracked down and found to be available at the 'Odeum.' "

After 19 October

On a published copy of the *Valse-fantaisie* for piano there appears the dedicatory inscription, "To P. P. Sokolov from the composer" (*L.,* p. 194).

29 October

Glinka writes to his mother that he has not gotten back to work on *Ruslan,* since he was writing music for *Prince Kholmsky,* and after he had recovered, he "had to finish the chorus for the graduation ceremonies at the girls' institute." He writes that his album has "turned up. The romances caused a lot of sensation and are being written about constantly." In the same letter he asks that his mother send "more provisions, especially ham, butter, and other things helpful to our housekeeping, particularly birds," since he "would like, so far as possible, to help our artel with resources."

In *Repertuar,* part 10, in an article entitled "Biography of Kapellmeister Cavos," Rafail Zotov writes about the opera *Ivan Susanin:* "The creation of Vanya belongs among the composer's most beautiful inspirations. Rural simplicity, youthful cheerfulness, and the sly keenness of Russian youth are very successfully combined in his character and beautifully expressed in the music. We recently saw this same Vanya in Glinka's opera, and for all the beauties of his work, we regret that Vanya has changed so much, especially in the added aria, where he appears not as a Russian country boy but as some kind of ancient hero, Arsace, or bogatyr" (d.c.a.).

8 November

In *SPb. ved.*, no. 254, there is a report about the well-known water-colorist Petr Sokolov's intentions of publishing a "Portrait and Biographical Gallery" of writers and artists with biographical sketches by Kukolnik. Among those who have established Russian art's reputation, Glinka is named.
[The publication of this project never occurred.]

9 November

In the "Musical News" section of *Sev. pchela,* no. 255, the success of Glinka's compositions with the public is reported: the romances and *Valse-fantaisie* have been sold out.

Between 16 October and Mid-November

Glinka "fell ill with a nervous fever. . . . My illness stole . . . the entire month" (ltr. to V. Shirkov, 18 December 1840). The Kukolniks "during my dangerous illness looked after me more sincerely than my nearest relatives. . . . I was not ashamed to live with him in this condition, because I did not bring any new expenses on them and also because he owed me money" (ltr. to his mother, 1 April 1841).

From the Second Half of November

"Having once again gotten back to work, I was only able to write Ruslan's aria [the jealousy scene in Act IV] and the 'chorus of flowers' (from . . . Lyudmila's scene *'Ne setui, iunaia kniazhna'* [Do not mourn, young princess], etc.)" (ltr. to V. Shirkov, 18 December 1840).

16 November

In a "Biographical Report of Leopold Meier" in *Galatea,* no. 17, Glinka's opinion is cited: "Speaking of Thalberg, Dreyschock, and Henselt, our famous composer M. I. Glinka once said to Mr. Markevich that Thalberg was all grace, Dreyschock, all power, and Henselt, all feeling" (d.c.a.).

21 November

Performance in the Bolshoi Theater "for the benefit of the performer Leonov" of *A Life for the Tsar* (*Sev. pchela*, 20 November 1840). Giuditta Pasta, who had arrived in Petersburg, was with Glinka at the performance. "When Petrova began to sing '*Akh, ne mne, bednomu,*' accompanied, as is known, by four cellos and bass, Pasta, turning toward me, said, 'How beautifully these cellos cry.'"

25 November

In *Bib-ka dlia chteniia*, vol. 43, in "Miscellany," there is an announcement of the publication of the bolero *"O deva chudnaia moia"* [O my beautiful maid], *"éxecuté á Pavlowsk par l'orchestre de M. Hermann; arrangé pour le piano par l'auteur"* (d.c.a.).

26 November

Concert by Pasta in the Hall of Nobility (a poster).

After 26 November

Party at Pasta's at which Glinka, Bryullov, Kukolnik, P. Stepanov, and others were present. "She [Pasta] and Glinka sang by turns and together" (P. Stepanov, *Vosp.*, p. 59).

30 November

Directive from Aleksandr Gedeonov to the office of the Imperial theaters concerning acceptance of the tragedy *Prince Kholmsky* by Kukolnik (*L.*, p. 195).

2 December

Glinka was present at a dinner in honor of Pasta at Myatlev's. After dinner Pasta sang. "We also persuaded Mikhail Glinka . . . to sing something for Pasta. He not only afforded her pleasure as a musical maestro, but even enticed her to sing something big. She sang an aria from *Otello* accompanied by Glinka" (ltr. from P. Pletnev to Y. Grot, 3 December 1840, *Perepiska Ya. Grota s P. Pletnevym* [Correspondence of Y. Grot with P. Pletnev], vol. 1, SPb., 1896, p. 157).

Beginning of December

Glinka orchestrated his Lullaby (for string orchestra) for a concert by Petrova-Vorobieva (inscription by L. Shestakova on the manuscript copy of the score, *L.*, p. 195).

8 December

Performance in the Bolshoi Theater of *A Life for the Tsar* (*Sev. pchela*, 7 December 1840).

14 December

In the hall of the Commercial Society on the English Quay "a musical evening with Mme Petrova, arranged by M. I. Glinka" took place. On the first half of the program were an overture; Italian aria (sung by Petrova); Glinka's Barcarolle, premiere (Petrova); Genishta's "Elegy" [The light of day has faded] (Petrov); Lomakin's *"Chernyi tsvet"* [The color black] and Glinka's Bolero, premiere (Petrova). On the second half were an overture; Rossini duet (Petrova and Stepanova); Glinka's Lullaby (Petrova); Prume's Variations for Violin (Latyshev); *"Somnenie"* by Glinka (Petrova, accompanied by harp, played by Schultz, and violin, played by Latyshev); *"Poputnaia pesnia"* by Glinka (Petrov); and an aria from *Ruslan and Lyudmila*, premiere (Petrova) (program in Vielgorsky's album, in *L.*, p. 195; *Sev. pchela*, 19 December 1840).

Before 18 December

Glinka conferred with Kukolnik, Bryullov, and Roller about Act IV of *Ruslan*. "Result of scenic as well as musical considerations" is the remark which is recorded.

By 18 December

Glinka compiled a "program" for the fourth act (variants) of *Ruslan and Lyudmila*.

18 December

Glinka writes to Shirkov that the composition of *Ruslan* "has stopped again because of commissions. I must prepare in a very short time a *graduation chorus* (Obodovsky's words) for the girls of the Ekaterininsky Institute, and then by mid-January, music for a tarantella (words by Myatlev)." He sends the program for the fourth act, reworked after his meeting with Kukolnik, Bryullov, and Roller. Of himself he writes: "Do not demand of me detailed news either of my earlier or my present circumstances. Of the former I will say: my conviction that my mother's consent was compulsory, as well as the certainty that happiness is not possible on such fragile foundations as I had intended to establish it, compelled me to decide once again to return to the capital, *voluntarily* denying myself my dearest hopes. Now my life is colorless, despite the caresses, entertainment, friendship, and distractions of life in the capital. Only my muse and work afford me true and genuine pleasure." He asks that Aleksandra Shirkova be told that he preserves in his memory "all the smallest details of the pleasant minutes spent with you, and that the pieces I heard her perform, such as the Chopin mazurkas, induce a sweet reverie in me."

19 December

In *Sev. pchela,* no. 287, in "Musical News," there is a comment on *Farewell to St. Petersburg:* "The demand for these beautiful pieces is unprecedented in Russia. . . . One of these romances, entitled 'Bolero', has been arranged by the author himself into a rather large orchestral piece and was played superbly by Hermann's orchestra in Pavlovsk throughout the summer, sometimes, by public demand, several times a day. Now this popular Bolero has appeared in a piano arrangement in the music stores of the 'Odeum' firm, and one must admit that it would be difficult to imagine anything more original and nicer than this elegant piece. We are sure that the piano version of the Bolero will have the same good fortune as the vocal version. . . . Moreover, in the same stores new pieces for voice . . . have appeared: the Russian song *'Khodit veter u vorot'* [The wind is at the gates] and Rakhil's romance from Kukolnik's tragedy *Prince Kholmsky* with music by M. I. Glinka. These two romances are in no way inferior to this composer's best works in the same form, and in a certain respect they represent a supplement to his *Farewell to St. Petersburg* in character and time of composition. . . ." In the same issue mention is made of Petrova's performance of new romances by Glinka in her concert on 14 December.

20 December

In the first issue of *Rus. vestnik* for 1841, in an article entitled "Notes on Works of Art," Kukolnik writes: "Our other arts have left music far behind . . . at this time the only brilliant exception is M. I. Glinka. After the opera *A Life for the Tsar* he wrote a large number of charming small pieces and completed in main almost the entire opera *Ruslan and Lyudmila,* which he is now quickly committing to paper. . . . Musically there are not many novelties, though several of the pieces have received special attention. *Farewell to St. Petersburg* by M. I. Glinka, consisting of 12 romances, rapidly spread throughout Russia. It is now almost out of print for the third time. Every drawing room resonates with these lovely pieces. His anthology, comprised of pieces by all Russian composers, had an extraordinary success. And add to this M. I. Glinka's recently published works: the *Valse-fantaisie* and Bolero for piano, and Ilyinishna's song and Rakhil's dream from the drama *Prince Kholmsky*" (d.c.a.).

26 December

Petrova-Vorobieva again appears in *A Life for the Tsar* after an illness (*Repertuar,* 1840, vol. 1, no. 2).

29 December

Composer's dating on the title page of the manuscript of *Tarantella* to words by Myatlev: "Begun 29 December 1840."

Performance of *A Life for the Tsar* in the Bolshoi Theater (*SPb. ved.,* 29 December 1840).

End of December

Glinka visited Strugovshchikov and took him a copy of *"Zhavoronok"* with a dedication. After dinner he performed the romance: "He varied it with such artistry that one could imagine the same song as two separate compositions." Then Glinka spoke of contemporary literature and complained of the absence of life in it. The verses of our poets he found "after Pushkin ponderous, with an absence of lyricism." That same day he "was sad . . . and it was like he was looking for someone to whom he might confess his sadness. At that time it did not occur to me to draw him out" (Strugovshchikov, *Vosp.,* p. 196).

31 December

In *Bib-ka dlia chteniia,* vol. 44, in the section "New Musical Compositions," there is an announcement of the publication of Ilyinishna's song and Rakhil's dream from *Prince Kholmsky* (d.c.a.).

End of the Year

At the Karamzins' "every evening a circle gathered made up of the pick of the literary and artistic world of the time: Glinka, Bryullov, Dargomyzhsky" (Sollogub, p. 302).

To this year belongs the composition of the romance *"Priznanie (Ia vas liubliu, khot' ia beshus')"* [Confession (I love you, though I am furious)] (*Teatr. i muz. vestnik,* 1858, no. 12, p. 144).

During this year Bayan's second song, *"Est' pustynnyi krai"* [There is a deserted place] (words by Shirkov), from *Ruslan and Lyudmila* was published with piano accompaniment and dedicated to the memory of Pushkin.

1840–1841

Shirkov's draft of the libretto for *Ruslan and Lyudmila* dates from this period. It includes completed scenes mentioned by Glinka in the "Initial Plan" (1837) and worked out in letters to Shirkov which did not become a part of the final version.

[By comparison of the "Initial Plan," Shirkov's drafts, and Glinka's letters with the final version of the text, it may be established that the principal librettist for *Ruslan and Lyudmila* was Shirkov, who wrote most of the numbers of the libretto and participated in working out the scenario. Glinka's other assistants fulfilled separate tasks: Markevich polished up Finn's ballad; Kukolnik and Mikhail Gedeonov wrote "transitions" between the principal numbers, that is, they accomplished work which Glinka was unable to get done by means of correspondence with Shirkov who had left for the country. So far as Konstantin Bakhturin is concerned, who allegedly whipped out the plan in a quarter of an hour while drunk, this story (*Zap.*) is an anecdote invented by Glinka. He may be eliminated from consideration regarding the composition of *Ruslan and Lyudmila*.]

Winter

Glinka frequented the home of "the widows, that is, the kind, gentle Mollerius family." He also visited the Aleksandrovs and his cousin Sofia Nolde, who, with her daughters, lived with Pavel and Sofia Engelgardt: "I liked it there very much." At that time Glinka wrote the romance *"Kak sladko s toboiu mne byt'"* [How sweet for me to be with you] for Sofia Engelgardt to words by Petr Ryndin, "who was a relative of the Engelgardts and also visited them." "Sofia Grigorievna loved music," and Glinka "often played excerpts for her from *Ruslan and Lyudmila,* in particular Lyudmila's scene in Chernomor's castle."

After Platon Kukolnik's marriage to Aleksandra Timofeevna, the oldest daughter of the Aleksandrovs, he moved in with them, "and the entire well-known Bryullov-Glinka-Kukolnik group began to gather there frequently. Sometimes Glinka sang excerpts from 'Ruslan' there, which he was composing at the time, most often Finn's ballad and Gorislava's cavatina. Sometimes he even danced, if there was time before dinner. He very much liked to dance" (V. Stasov, "Remembrances of My Sister," in *Knizhki nedeli,* 1896, January, p. 212).

Ivan Panaev met Glinka at a party at the Kukolniks. "After dinner he ... gradually began to let himself go. He told me about his musical plans, about *Ruslan,* which he was working on at the time, about Russia's future (this was one of his favorite topics of conversation), and about the Russian people, since he felt that he knew the people well and could talk with them. During conversations of this type he usually became very animated, and his eyes sparkled. ..." (Panaev, *Vosp.,* p. 182).

Glinka frequently heard Henriette Rossi (Sonntag) perform Tyrolian songs, Schubert ballads, Preziosa's song by Weber, and others (A. Smirnova, *Zapiski,* part 2, SPb., 1897, p. 39).
[Even though Aleksandra Smirnova's "Memoirs" are a fabrication of her daughter Olga Smirnova and only partially based upon the elder Smirnova's actual recollections, the information concerning Glinka's hearing Henriette Rossi and his opinion of her does not contradict known facts.]

1841

1 January

Composer's dating at the end of the score of the "Farewell Song" for the students of the Ekaterininsky Institute: "Finished by the 1st of January, 1841."

4 January

Of his intended trip abroad Glinka writes to his mother: "My heart wishes to stay, but reason certainly compels me to go. ... Stubborn fate has not met one of my heart's desires, but I obey her without complaining. Considering my present circumstances, I find that there is nothing for me to do here in Petersburg and that a trip abroad would be beneficial not just for my health but for my frame of mind as well. My opera is moving very slowly, since ceaseless commissions steal my best hours, and I see no possibility of getting rid of them."

In an article entitled *"Parasha Sibiriachka"* [Parasha the Siberian woman] in *Khudozh. gaz.,* no. 1, it says: "Four years have passed since Russian opera was born unexpectedly on the Petersburg stage, like golden-haired Cythera from the ocean foam. The opera *A Life for the Tsar,* which astonished foreigners, caused rejoicing among native music lovers. They saw that, in this area as well, Russia possessed hidden, undeveloped powers. On the other hand we were saddened by the thought that such a brilliant beginning should remain for so long without heirs, as we would have expected. ... Here now is Struysky's opera."

Glinka attended a concert given by Giuditta Pasta (a poster).

Beginning of January

The romance *"Kak sladko s toboiu mne byt' "* is published in the first issue of *Le Nouvelliste*.

5 January

Composer's dating on the last page of the manuscript of the score of the *Tarantella* to words by Myatlev: "Completed 5 January 1841."

8 January

Death of Ekaterina Kern's father, General E. F. Kern (*Ved. SPb. gor. politsii*, January 1841). "Something important has happened; her father has died, and he . . . was our fiercest enemy" (ltr. to V. Shirkov, 18 February 1841).

9 January

In *Lit. gaz.*, no. 4, there is an article by Fedor Koni called "A Russian Opera. *Parasha Sibiriachka*," in which it is said that the first composer to provide us an opera in European form "was M. I. Glinka. The laurels for first place go to him. *A Life for the Tsar* is still the best Russian opera, although, the merits of the music aside, we might criticize his incorrect view of musical nationalism. Even he was carried away by an error made by others. What kind of thinking is it, for example, that requires Poles to speak, think, and act to the accompaniment of the mazurka? Is it really possible that all the passions of this nation are confined to three-quarter time and cannot be expressed in any other meter? In *A Life for the Tsar*, however, this error is a detail redeemed by a hundred other good qualities. The step taken by M. I. Glinka is a service to Russian art. Now a new composer has stepped onto the Russian operatic stage, and we should be pleased by this, the more so as in his first easy attempt we see development of the idea which we stated above."

12 January

Performance of *A Life for the Tsar* in the Bolshoi Theater (*Sev. pchela*, 11 January 1841).

13 January

First performance of the *Tarantella* at a benefit performance for Vasily Karatygin under the direction of Karl Albrecht in the Aleksandrinsky Theater. It was marred by "a bad performance" (*Sev. pchela,* 13 January 1841; ltr. to V. Shirkov, 18 February 1841).

14 January

Composer's dating on the title page of the manuscript of the adagio from Lyudmila's scene in Act IV of *Ruslan and Lyudmila:* "Begun 14 January 1841."

15 January

Performance of the *Tarantella* in the Aleksandrinsky Theater (*Sev. pchela,* 15 January 1841).

16 January

In the "Musical News" section of the periodical *Mayak* [The lighthouse], part 13, there is an announcement that works by Glinka, including the Bolero, arranged for piano, and *Farewell to St. Petersburg,* are available at the "Odeum" (d.c.a.).

17 January

Performance of the *Tarantella* in the Aleksandrinsky Theater (*Sev. pchela,* 17 January 1841).

19 January

Composer's dating on the last page of the manuscript of the Adagio of Lyudmila's scene in Act IV of *Ruslan and Lyudmila:* "19 January 1841."

21 January

Performance of the *Tarantella* in the Aleksandrinsky Theater (*Sev. pchela,* 21 January 1841).

29 January

In *Sev. pchela,* no. 23, there is an article by "F. B." [Bulgarin] entitled "Impressions of the performance of the Shakespearean tragedy *Coriolanus* and a scene called *Tarantella* by I. P. Myatlev at a benefit performance for V. A. Karatygin": "I. P. Myatlev's talent is better known in society than to the general public. . . . The name of M. I. Glinka attracted those interested in music. The idea for this scene is beautiful. . . . However, the whole thing was spoiled by the music, which is monotonous and tiring in the extreme. The action continues for nearly three-quarters of an hour (perhaps because of the music, the time seemed even longer). The poet recites everything to the accompaniment of the same melody, the choruses repeat the same thing, and the *khorovod* is danced to the same music, which is so pallid that the dancers and singers, as well as spectators, all doze off until Mr. Karatygin wakes them up with his silvery voice. . . . We spoke so enthusiastically last spring about excerpts from the new opera *Ruslan and Lyudmila* composed by the very same composer, although we did not presume to predict what the entire opera might be like (but that's just the point). With all due respect to his talent, we must now tell the truth (following public opinion) and say that the music to the *Tarantella* is not good. This fact is not intended as a criticism of the young man! Who hasn't slipped up? Even the greatest performers, artists, and writers have their 'tarantella'! . . . However, our humble remarks should not offend the gifted composer. He has his own trombones to shout even the *Tarantella*'s praise and to demonstrate how in its learned way it is playful, cheerful, and distinctive and that we do not understand the matter. So much the better! We will not attempt to respond. We must remark, incidentally, that we had never seen the dancers who performed the *Tarantella*. They were new faces to us. They expressed sleep and boredom exceptionally well in their dancing. . . . The choruses bore out the Russian saying of being at sixes and sevens. . . ."

Performance of the *Tarantella* in the Aleksandrinsky Theater (*Sev. pchela,* 29 January 1841).

30 January

In a letter to Anna Kern, Glinka excuses himself for his long silence because of illness, which changed his plans and interfered with his thinking about the future. Regarding the death of Ermolay Kern he writes: "The news of M. Kern's death caused me even keener grief, because I can imagine the sorrow your daughter has felt as a result. It is very fortunate that you were there to dry her tears and share her grief. Those who are not present cannot provide that sweet solace. They are missing at the time that their presence might be of some use, and written condolences usually arrive too late" (Fr. original).

January (?)

The Moldavian Girl and the Gypsy Girl is presented in Saratov (*Repertuar,* 1841, no. 1, p. 78).

Glinka was present at a musical evening at Dargomyzhsky's (Arnold, pp. 501, 503).

January–February

In *Rus. vest.,* vol. 1, part 2, there is an article by Nestor Kukolnik called *"Parasha Sibiriachka,* opera . . . by Struysky," in which *A Life for the Tsar* and its success are mentioned. In the same issue there is an article by N. K. [Kukolnik] entitled "Theater, the Arts, Music," which includes mention of the performance of the *Tarantella* in the Aleksandrinsky Theater.

2 February

In *SPb. ved.,* no. 27, there is a notice that Glinka's Variations on Alyabiev's Romance "The Nightingale" is on sale at Bernard's.
[This is the first edition of the piano piece written in Berlin in 1833/34.]

Performance of *A Life for the Tsar* in the Bolshoi Theater (*Sev. pchela,* 1 February 1841).

In *Repertuar,* part 2, the following report appears: "N. V. Kukolnik's new drama . . . *Prince Kholmsky* awaits us. . . . M. I. Glinka has written special music for the entr'actes of the drama." In the section "Chronicle of the Petersburg Theaters" there is a review of the *Tarantella.* The following is written about the music: "The orchestra played rather pallid music to which several *girls from the other world* danced, as it is said, grandaughters of Countess Khryumina in *Woe from Wit.* As F. V. Bulgarin remarked, 'they expressed sleep and boredom exceptionally well in their dancing,' and the choruses sung in the *tarantella* bore out the Russian saying of being at sixes and sevens."

3 February

There is a review of the *Tarantella* in an article entitled "The Aleksandrinsky Theater" in *Sev. pchela,* no. 27. "On one side of the stage stand the men, on the other the women, all probably Italians. The music begins—everyone sings. Mr. Karatygin stands on the proscenium. . . . At the rear of the stage the girls stomp around to the accompaniment of the music. They . . . are to be perceived as Italian girls and their clumsy jostling as a tarantella. . . . The music is monotonous, flaccid, and lifeless. . . . There is singing, dancing, recitation, and yawning. . . . Here's a tarantella for you!"

11 February

The following excerpt (signed "M. F. St.") on the text of the new scene for Vanya in *A Life for the Tsar* appears in a survey of "Music in the Journals" in *Lit. gaz.,* no. 7: "Generally, in all . . . Kukolnik's dramatic works we see the same attitude toward drama—declamation takes precedence over the simple and direct expression of feeling. Let us take for example the libretto to the opera *A Life for the Tsar,* in which Vanya's naive character is outlined with the hand of a poet-artist. Throughout the role one hardly finds a word that does not correspond to the overall conception. Now Mr. Kukolnik has enlarged upon this, and look what has happened. Vanya has barely gotten on stage when he exclaims, 'I am a heavenly ambassador.' Now tell me, to what Russian Vanya does it occur to call himself *a heavenly ambassador*? Is this the way he appears in reality? People might later recognize the great feat a boy has accomplished, but he does not declaim such things about himself. Mr. Kukolnik, however, does not need to know this, provided there is a long aria where Vanya can exclaim, 'I am a heavenly ambassador, saddle the horses, light the fires,' and the appointment, the tremendous recitative, the storms of the heart, and Vanya's solemn march still remain. . . . What else is needed? Such is the view of this dramatist."

Ivan Panaev writes to Verstovsky that he has heard about Glinka from Anna and Osip Petrov, through whom the letter is forwarded (coll. *Glinka,* p. 153).

15 February

Glinka thanks his mother for promising to give him money for his trip abroad: "I will repeat again that although I am not drawn as before to better parts, common sense still tells me that a trip is the only thing that will blot out the traces of the storms I have endured. The memory of what has happened is still too much alive, and a thousand things, which have renewed my suffering and spoiled my happiness, prevent me from being at peace. . . . Finally art—the joy given to me by heaven—perishes here because of deadly indifference to everything beautiful. . . . Compared to earlier years, I accomplished a considerable amount of work last winter."

In *Syn otechestva,* vol. 1, no. 7, there is an announcement of a proposed performance of the entr'actes from the music to *Prince Kholmsky* in a concert by the pianist Haberbier, "but it is not yet known when" (d.c.a.).

From Mid-January to 18 February

"Already a month has passed since I have written anything. My muse is sad and will not obey . . . and ceaseless rehearsals have prevented me from working even if I were able."

End of January to the First Half of February

"Recently I have been busy with rehearsals at the Institute, which reminds me so vividly of the Smolny. The chorus which I wrote for the girls' graduation went well and was performed excellently."

By 18 February

Glinka assembled the "program" for Act V of *Ruslan and Lyudmila* and a variant ("a note") to the "program" for Act II.

18 February

Glinka writes to Shirkov: "Believe me, . . . my feelings have not changed. No one here can replace you. My sad heart searches vainly for a comforting corner of tranquility. Happy times have whirled away. My hopes have collapsed. Days of quiet and poetic felicity have been replaced by the colorless and hollow activity of a scattered life. I have become another person. I do not know myself what I am doing. I am bored everywhere. There is no joy anywhere. There is no corner where I may unburden my heart and find relief. . . . What does the future hold for me? I will go to Paris, and if you believe it, more under duress than because of my own desire. Despite the difficult year, money for the trip has been found, meaning Mother *wants* me to go, and she is right. If it were not for this, nothing could prevent me from coming to Little Russia. Everything to which my troubled heart had grown accustomed is there. You see, I may speak frankly with you. My feelings have not changed, but my common sense is not so clouded as before, and it clearly sees all the difficulties and absurdities of my earlier plan. What's to be done? One thing remains: to put myself in the hands of fate, to wait, and hope." He sends Shirkov the "program" for the fifth act, comments on the second act, and requests that Aleksandra Shirkova be thanked "for her kind and touching lines. If words would obey me as music does, it would be easy for me to convey to her my gratitude and feeling of deep and lasting friendship. . . . Whenever I play Chopin mazurkas, or someone plays in my presence those which Aleksandra Grigorievna played for me, my heart is transported back in time, and hearing those sounds I see you standing in front of me."

By this time Glinka had written the introduction and Lyudmila's aria for the first act; Finn's ballad and Ruslan's aria for the second act; the Persian chorus and Gorislava's cavatina for the third act; excerpts from Lyudmila's scene (the chorus of flowers "Do not mourn, young princess" and "O fate, my fate") and Chernomor's march for the fourth act; and Ratmir's romance "She is my life" from the fifth act. He is thinking about ("beginning to prepare"): 1) the finale to the first act, 2) the Head's scene from the second act, 3) the dances for the third act, 4) Lyudmila's scene and the dances for the fourth act, and 5) the final chorus of the fifth act. "I have not gotten into the other numbers of the opera: . . . in the fifth act there is still much that is not clear to me. . . . The overture and entr'actes will come last" (ltr. to V. Shirkov, 18 February 1841).

After 18 February

"During Lent Glinka moved from the Kukolniks' to Petr Stepanov's in Garnovsky's house at the Izmaylovsky Bridge. Stepanov "let me a room in which caricatures and other devilry were drawn all over the walls. During the night, as often happened, when carriage lanterns would illuminate my room with their light, strange figures would dance one after another before my eyes, and it seemed like the head over the stove smiled at me mockingly. It often seemed to me that it was laughing at my suffering; I slept badly then and succumbed to gloomy thoughts about my fate."
[In 1841, Lent began on 9 February, but in letters to Shirkov (18 February) and to his mother (15 February) there is no mention of a change of address. Consequently, one may reckon that Glinka moved from Kukolnik's to Stepanov's after 18 February. Cf. ltr. to V. Shirkov of 29 March.]

Immediately after moving to Stepanov's, Glinka "worked productively on 'Ruslan.' Concentrating on his creative work, he would walk about the room . . . then go to the piano and play a few chords, hurry to his own room, and write rapidly on large sheets of music paper which were spread out on his table. Then he would walk and write again, often without the assistance of the piano. Thus things went until it got completely dark. Then, completely fatigued, he would lie down and complain of illness and exhaustion. Supper revitalized him, and occasionally he would become cheerful and talkative in the evening. The very same friends as before visited us, especially Bryullov and Yanenko" (P. Stepanov, *Vosp.*, p. 60).

20 February

In *Sev. pchela*, no. 40, there is an announcement about Osip and Anna Petrov's concerts in Moscow, which included performances of "authentic Russian tunes" and "numerous romances" by Glinka. It also announces a new edition of *Farewell to St. Petersburg*.

21 February

In the "Musical News" section of *SPb. ved.*, no. 41, there is a notice that *Farewell to St. Petersburg*, Ilyinishna's song and Rakhil's dream from *Prince Kholmsky*, the *Valse-fantaisie*, and the Bolero are on sale. In the same issue the Petrovs's forthcoming performance of works by Glinka in Moscow is reported.

22 February

In *Syn otechestva*, vol. 1, no. 8, there is a report of a forthcoming concert by the singer Alexandrine Damier, who is to perform "an andante with violin obbligato accompaniment from Glinka's new opera *Ruslan and Lyudmila*" (d.c.a.). In a supplement to *Mosk. ved.*, no. 16, there is an announcement of a concert in the Maly Theater on 28 February, in which Petrova will perform works by Glinka.

25 February

Glinka writes to his mother: "The trip does not excite my imagination as it did before . . . I consider a trip abroad more a necessity than a pleasure. . . . After all the unexpected blows of fate which have befallen me, I do not dare to make plans for the future. . . . If I could follow the promptings of my heart, I would remain in Russia for the summer and spend part of it with you . . . and share the rest with my *friends* in Little Russia, with whom I correspond regularly. This must not distress you, dear Mother, the more so as I myself am now convinced of the absurdity of my earlier plans and am not hiding them from others." He reports that work on "Ruslan" "has made some progress—and I can say that most of the opera is ready in my head, though to copy out what is ready, I need a quiet, pleasant retreat for the summer and a less severe climate for the winter. If it pleases fate to send me such a year, the opera will be ready, but to finish it in less than a year is impossible. There are so many letters to write, and my strength does not allow me to work long or continuously. Nor am I writing now, since concerts and the winter prevent me from working."

28 February

In the journal *Mayak*, part 14, there is a report of Haberbier's performance in concert of the overture to *Prince Kholmsky* and of the availability of Ilyinishna's song and Rakhila's dream at the "Odeum" (d.c.a.).

Alexandrine Damier performed Lyudmila's adagio *"Akh, ty, dolia, doliushka"* in the hall of Kushelev-Bezborodko (ltr. to V. Shirkov, 18 February 1841; *Syn otechestva,* 1841, no. 8, p. 20).

First of the Petrovs' concerts in the Maly Theater in Moscow, at which they performed "the beautiful duet from the opera *A Life for the Tsar,* both the music and performance of which were new to Moscow. When Petrova performed the Orphan's song, at the words 'Neither the cries of children, nor the moans of relations, but the enemy's howling echoed over him,' there were no *ordinary* spectators or listeners in the theater. There was only personified elation, ready, apparently, to forget the world, the eruption of a single spirit. . . . Finally the cries and applause merged in a unanimous, concordant hurrah, and the Orphan's song once again transported everyone to a world of feeling and harmony. Five curtain calls in a row concluded the concert." Additionally, Petrov performed *"Nochnoi smotr"* (supp. to *Mosk. ved.,* 22 February 1841; *Repertuar,* 1841, part 3, p. 5).

February

In the second issue of "Current Repertoire of the Russian Stage" (supp. to *Panteon*), there is an article by Rafail Zotov entitled "On the Current Condition of the St. Petersburg Theaters," where Glinka and both of his operas are mentioned.

1 March

Glinka writes to Anna Kern of the uncertainty of his position, of his mother's desire that he travel abroad, and of his discouragement and lack of inspiration. "If fate would take pity on me and grant me just a few days of happiness, I am sure that my poor *Ruslan* would quickly come to completion. In my present condition I am not about to work at it."

3 March

The Petrovs' second concert in Moscow. "The Maly Theater seethed with people. By common request the concert was changed. Again everyone demanded the Orphan's song. . . . They did not know, nor did they expect, that an even greater pleasure awaited them that evening. . . . The Orphan's song was Petrova's farewell song . . . and the public demanded that it be repeated. . . . Petrova granted their request" (*Repertuar,* 1841, part 3, p. 6).

After 3 March

In their third concert in Moscow, Petrova performed *"Akh, ne mne, bednomu"* as an encore demanded by the audience (*Repertuar*, 1841, part 3, p. 5).

6 March

In an article by "F-ni" [Koni] entitled "Past Concerts" in *Lit.gaz.*, no. 28, the public is rebuked for "preferring to comfort itself with Glinka's romances rather than a symphony by Beethoven."

The overture and entr'actes from *Prince Kholmsky* were performed in a concert given by Haberbier. "My ears suffered considerably . . . from this performance. My poor offspring were tortured so badly that, despite my forbearance, I was unable to contain my indignation" (ltr. to V. Shirkov, 29 March 1841; *SPb. ved.*, 6 March 1841).

7 March

Glinka inscribed Ilyinishna's song in Dargomyshzky's album. Composer's dating: "St. Petersburg, 7 March 1841, M. Glinka" (*L.*, p. 203). Evening at Dargomyzhsky's, at which Glinka performed Ilyinishna's song (Arnold, p. 506; Glinka's entry in Dargomyzhsky's album, in *L.*, p. 204).

15 March

Maria Petrovna Glinka is secretly married to Nikolay Nikolaevich Vasilchikov, cornet of the Horse Guards (ltr. to V. Shirkov, 24 May 1841).

21 March

Glinka writes to his mother about his final decision to travel abroad with his sister Elizaveta, his brother-in-law Yakov Sobolevsky, and the latter's deaf-mute son. He writes of Giuditta Pasta's forthcoming tours and advises his travelling companions to hurry in coming to Petersburg in order to hear this famous singer.

22 March

Under "The Musical Season in Petersburg" in *Khudozh. gaz.*, no. 7, there is a notice by Kukolnik about Haberbier's concert. "M. I. Glinka's participation was indirect and Mme Bishop's direct in Haberbier's concert. Mr. Glinka allowed the overture and four entr'actes written for the tragedy *Prince Kholmsky* to be performed in this concert. Is it not astonishing that previous concerts have not convinced Mikhail Ivanovich of the impossibility of performing polyphonic works in our concerts? . . . Nothing really new, but still complicated and difficult. What a misfortune! One instrument doesn't finish before another begins. Nowadays to prevent these inevitable occurrences they have devised an entertaining way of taking odd tempos, which is what happened when the allegro agitato of Glinka's overture was played andante sostenuto. This must certainly mean, Mikhail Ivanovich, that you do not love your children, if you allow them to be introduced to the world in such a manner. The entr'actes, which are small, not very difficult pieces, shared the fate of the overture, though not so badly. We did not hear in performance what we saw in the score" (d.c.a.).

28 March

Glinka writes to his mother: "Your will has been and always will be my command. However agonizing for me the many true statements in your letter were, they were sincere, and I thank you. My fate is decided, I will travel abroad. If it were not for my heart's deep, newly opened wounds, I would hurry to you. . . . But do not demand, do not require me to come to you now. I am spiritually sick, deeply sick. In my letters to you I hid my suffering, even though it persisted." Glinka explained his refusal to travel to the country by the fact that several relatives had become his enemies and that he "did not wish to meet" with them. "The tone of your letter reveals to me that besides my own words, much has been communicated to you by others. . . . Fate has taught me a lesson which has changed my character. I have become suspicious and distrustful of people." Abroad Glinka hopes to live quietly. "There neighbors do not know their neighbor's business, and everyone lives to himself. Here, however, friends, relatives, gossips, and commentators exist in large numbers." He writes of his former wife: "With my hand over my heart, I tell you that it holds neither enmity, nor anger, nor even bad memories, but only deep pity and a sincere desire for her happiness. All the infamy, for which I was the plaything, has only left in my mind an overpowering aversion to her, and even if I wished, my pride would never permit me, now that we have parted, to return to her again." Glinka writes to his sister Elizaveta: "Mother's letter has persuaded me to leave, the more so since, according to the latest news I have received from Little Russia, I see that if I were to go there I would put myself in a compromising position. . . . K.'s mother is here, but alone. I have not seen her yet. . . . You must imagine how much suffering this visit causes me, for my heart is unchanged, and from some of my friend's comments I can guess that she is far from happy. Thus I suffer beyond telling. . . . If I must relinquish happiness, at least may I be permitted to show myself worthy of our dear mother's love and kindness.

Tell her that my grief is subdued, that I will never allow myself, despite the passionate nature of my feelings, to succumb to despair, and that, on the contrary, I will try to allay my suffering by thought, study, and work." He writes that he would like to spend the winter in Paris to avoid the cold winter of St. Petersburg, which is "detestable to me since *she* is not here. . . . If my friend were *alone,* everything would be fine, for I know society sufficiently well to find a way of managing better than it may seem, but she has countless relatives . . . relatives, relatives—the scourge of all sensitive people" (Fr. original). In a letter to Anna Kern, Glinka promises to help her obtain a pension after the death of her first husband and tells her what kind of documents are required for this.

Adeliada Solovieva's and Petrova-Vorobieva's appearance in *A Life for the Tsar* is mentioned in an article entitled "On the Present-day Condition of the St. Petersburg Theaters" by Rafail Zotov in *Panteon,* no. 2 (d.c.a.).

In *Repertuar,* part 3, in an article by N. Korovkin entitled "The Petrovs' Concerts in Moscow," the writer reports the performers' success, especially in their performances of Glinka's music and above all in the duet from *A Life for the Tsar.* For Muscovites "both the music and performance" were a novelty, which "introduced new pleasures to them." Petrova drew particular acclaim for her performance of the Orphan's song (*"Akh, ne mne, bednomu"*) (d.c.a.).

Before 29 March

Glinka "wrote the finale to Act IV (the jealousy scene); Ruslan's singing is very simple, but expressive. The piece ends with a *march* (accompanied by all the characters). Kukolnik is ecstatic about this piece and considers it one of the best of the opera. In this scene your words remain without alteration, with the exception of the omission of a few lines with no loss of meaning. After this I worked on the Head's scene and wrote half of it, but various activities and bad news from a *friend* stopped the surge of my muse" (ltr. to V. Shirkov, 29 March 1841).

During Lent in Nizhny Novgorod an aria from *A Life for the Tsar* was performed "as battalion music." "It always went quite well before, but this time somehow it did not" (*Moskvityanin,* 1841, part 4, no. 8, p. 561).

29 March

Glinka writes to Shirkov: "My feelings have not changed, but a sad experience and cold intellect have killed my hopes. I myself now see the absurdity of my intentions. We are too bound by circumstances, she in particular. She has relatives beyond counting. I am extremely sad and have no one with whom to share my grief. I have many acquaintances, but they are more inclined to scoff at my sufferings than to understand or console me. You alone fully understand me, but you are not here, and our vast capital is now a wasteland for me, like the endless Ukrainian steppe. You are right. I am going reluctantly and not almost, but *definitely by force.* I have done everything I could to visit Little Russia instead of Paris. But *her relatives* and my mother's wishes (she is well-meaning, but perhaps too careful) have destroyed my hopes. I must go. I must sacrifice myself for my dear mother, perhaps for her true happiness. I will obey my unhappy fate without complaining. I will not give in to senseless despair, but my heart aches. God willing, my psychological ailment will be changed by this trip, and my music will once again be resurrected. . . . For just over a month I have lived with the Stepanovs in the fantastic room you are acquainted with. These devils, skeletons, and skulls harmonize with my present mental state. My album has been enriched with a large number of new portraits *en caricature,* each better than the last. I am unable to look at your drawings with indifference." Glinka writes to Aleksandra Shirkova: "One could say that you have taken away my happiness. Soon after your departure everything changed for me. Return to the capital, and we will be together again. We will play Chopin and perhaps even Thalberg."

In a supp. to *Mosk. ved.,* no. 26, there is a notice of Varlamov's forthcoming benefit concert on 4 April in the Hall of Nobility. The program includes the Orphan's song from *A Life for the Tsar* (to be sung by S. Evreinova) and the aria *"V pole chistoe gliazhu"* [I gaze upon the open field] (sung by Z. Yakovleva) from the same opera.

1 April

Because of his earlier letter (28 March), Glinka writes to his mother: "I am rash and impulsive and for that reason answered you too hurriedly and perhaps reacted too sharply to your letter." He writes once again about the compulsory trip abroad, to which he consents. "But if something interferes, I hasten to assure you . . . wherever I may be and whatever might happen to me, I will not undertake anything which might lead to an extended separation from you or to your distress. . . . If I am in Little Russia, I will be very careful, not for the sake of the gossips and those who wish me ill, but only so as not to distress you." He writes that his sister Maria and her husband Dmitry Stuneev are spreading rumours about him and Ekaterina and Anna Kern. He continues: "Now a few words in self justification: in this last difficult year you gave me 7,000 rubles for a given purpose. If you had not done this and *she* had perished, I would not have outlived her. Consequently you gave this sum to save your son. . . . My heart has not changed. Your letter of last year poisoned my bliss (I am not grumbling about that). Remorse over the thought of forsaking you tormented me to such an extent that I was unable to sort out my own feelings. This is why I seemed indifferent when I came to see you and searched for and magnified K.'s shortcomings. But my secret sorrow was hidden inside my heart. I felt ill, and when I returned to Petersburg I nearly died. Her letters resurrected me. Despite assurances, I am now unable to give in to hopes of happiness as before. I mourn and am depressed. Now that I have grown accustomed to a hostile fate, I am ready for anything. If it becomes possible, I will go to Paris. If I stay, I give you my word not *to hurry*. It is impossible to ask any more of me. Despite suspicion, I have no cause to think that things have changed toward me, but if they have, *pride* will save me from despair. I do not fear children but desire them. I cannot look at others' without tears of emotion. To you I must say that children love and pity their parents, but relatives are calculating." He writes that he frequently has thoughts about death. He gives instructions in the event of an untimely death to give all his inherited property to Sofia Nolde, "who has been deprived of her husband," and her children, since Glinka's sisters "are settled," and his cousin is "in a very pitiable situation."

Report from the secretary of the second department of the ecclesiastical consistory to the Chief Procurator of the Synod, Count Nikolay Protasov, of an illegal marriage performed on 15 March by the priest Fedor Opolsky in the village of Opolie in Yambursk province (*L.*, p. 208).

To this period belongs Glinka's letter to his sister Elizaveta: "Mama writes that I must control my passions. Surely you know that my attraction to her [Ekaterina Kern] is my *heart's need* and that when the heart is satisfied the passions need not be feared. . . . Near someone who *understands* him, *the artist* draws new strength, whereas debauchery weakens the spirit and exhausts the body" (Fr. original).

4 April

At Varlamov's benefit concert in the Hall of Nobility in Moscow, S. Evreinova performs the Orphan's song and Z. Yakovleva the aria "I gaze upon the open field." Varlamov conducted the orchestra (*Mosk. ved.,* 29 March 1841).

10 April

In the "Miscellany" section of *Sev. pchela,* no. 78, there is a review entitled "Moscow Concerts During the Period of Lent in the Maly Theater": "The selection of pieces was satisfactory; those selected from the works of Glinka were especially well received." The concerts took place under the direction of Iogannis.

First Half of April

Glinka's servant, Yakov Ulyanych, told Glinka about Maria Petrovna's marriage to Vasilchikov. "These rumors are not only confirmed, but there is also the case before the Synod about the priest who performed a marriage during Lent, though he is responding that he does not know whom he married. Apparently they are trying to hush up the affair, since according to a newly published statute, it is criminal and those found guilty go to Siberia."

18 April

Glinka tells his mother about Maria Petrovna's secret marriage and writes: "I cannot even think about travelling abroad. I necessarily must remain in Petersburg to observe. Maria Petrovna's new husband is a none too clever man, though he is rich. So far as I can make out, the affair was inevitable. . . . There is no necessity to explain to you how I am. And although right is on my side, I have grown out of the habit of hoping. My own fate has taught me that." He asks that what he says be kept secret, "especially" from the Stuneevs.

21 April

Glinka sends a ticket for *A Life for the Tsar* to Anna Kern: "Be so kind as not to miss using it, since I am eager to know what impression this work will have on you." He asks that she respond, "if just a brief word." "Do you have any news from home? Is everyone well?" He writes that Maria Petrovna's case is now before the Synod, and perhaps "everything will be taken care of without any steps on my part, inasmuch as an officer is involved" (Fr. original).

Performance of *A Life for the Tsar* in the Bolshoi Theater (*Sev. pchela,* 21 April 1841).

24 April

Glinka writes to his mother: "You accuse me of being mistrustful of you, and you say that I was dissembling when I was in the country, that I was deceiving myself and thought that my feelings had been completely silenced when they were suppressed by the belief that what I intended to do was incompatible with my obligations as a son and that, as an honorable man, I should not repay the person ready to sacrifice everything for me with infamy and the scorn of society. . . . The first letter I received after a three-month break revitalized me. As I was without hope, I behaved crossly. I did not write to you, not because I feared your opposition, but only so as not to alarm you. When the matter came to the trip, the thought of going so far from everything dear to my heart caused me to speak out." He writes that Maria Petrovna's case is with the consistory and "is even going to the Defense Ministry."

28 April

In Saratov, the amateur singer "O. N. K-va" performs Antonida's aria "I gaze upon the open field" in a concert for the benefit of the violinist Malkov (*Sev. pchela*, 16 May 1841).

Between 25 April and the Beginning of May

Arrival from the country of Glinka's sister Elizaveta with her brother-in-law Yakov Sobolevsky and his deaf-mute son Nikolay (ltrs. to his mother on 24 April and 7 May 1841).

7 May

Glinka informs his mother that the case concerning Maria Petrovna's second marriage "has taken a completely unexpected turn," and that now *"it is impossible not to receive the divorce. . . ."* He thanks her "for the sad lines last year, inspired by your maternal heart, which saved me just in time from unhappiness and crime."

In a note from Elizaveta Ivanovna to her mother, she writes, "Michel's destiny has been broken most fortuitously. What would probably have been impossible to achieve without expense and effort has happened, or will happen, without the slightest participation, even on his part."

11 May

In a letter to Boris Glinka, Glinka asks him to assist his sister and brother-in-law in Paris.

14 May

Glinka gave power of attorney to the lawyer I. Stepanov to conduct his divorce proceedings. That same day the document was registered in the consistory.

Before 15 May

"Dubelt said personally that *my wife is married and that it is impossible to deny me a divorce.*"

15 May

Glinka submitted "a formal petition" for divorce to the consistory (ltr. to V. Shirkov, 24 May 1841; *L.*, p. 209).
[In his letter to Shirkov, Glinka inaccurately indicates the date of the petition (16 May), which was registered in the consistory on the 15th (LGIA, coll. 19, inventory 33, no. 153). The document was removed from the dossier, apparently at the same time as the originals of Vasilchikov's letters.]

16 May

Glinka's departure for Novospasskoe (ltr. to V. Shirkov, 24 May 1841; *SPb. ved.*, 18 May 1841). In *Sev. pchela*, no. 106, in correspondence from Saratov on 28 April, there is a report of a concert for the benefit of the young violinist Malkov, in which the amateur singer "O. N. K-va" gave an "excellent" performance of the aria "I gaze upon the open field" from *A Life for the Tsar*.

18 May

In *SPb. ved*, no. 109, "Retired Collegiate Assessor Glinka, for Smolensk" appears on the list of those departing "from the capital city of St. Petersburg on 15–16 May."

20 May

Novospasskoe. Glinka's arrival at his mother's, "in order to reassure her and to explain the case to her" (ltr. to V. Shirkov, 24 May 1841).

21 May

Glinka is named in a list in *SPb. ved.* of those leaving St. Petersburg by 16 May.

Between August 1840 and 24 May 1841

In Lubny, Anna Kern's second husband, Aleksandr Markov-Vinogradsky, makes this extended entry about Glinka in his diary: "I so love to tell about this tone poet! In recollecting the happy times when I heard him, I recall my past life . . . and past pleasures. . . . I am deeply grateful to Glinka for the poetic moments he gave us, filling our hearts with the piano's melodic sounds. His marvelous music inspires love in the soul, it delights the most unmusical, and it elicits rapture from the breast of the most indifferent. Under his hands, the keyboard produces a thousand different sounds. And how soft, how sweet those sounds . . . Glinka is like an orator with his eloquent music! His marvelous music can persuade the most desperate sceptic of the existence of happiness on earth, if only it reaches the unfortunate person's ears! His music stuns one to the depths of one's being, and its well-considered purpose gives sustenance to the mind. Its melodic charm delights the feelings, and with modulations full of feeling and wonderful harmony it can soften an iron will. Tracing wonderful visions for the imagination, it charms the heart and remains in one's memory forever, so that, if ever you hear a poor imitation, you sink into reverie with pleasant recollections and mentally fly back to the place where they echoed so magically. . . . Glinka does not need words. Everything he wishes to say he says by means of music! His mastery is so free and so artistic, like an orator gifted in words. His music murmurs in words of love, it cries, or marvelously reminds one of waves breaking on a craggy shore. Then suddenly one hears a lark's trill, and again the sounds flow smoothly, gracefully, like quiet, serene love! You hear the wonderful rumbling of loud, stormy chords, which then flow suddenly and smoothly into a sweet song of love, into the tender sounds of pleasant feelings . . . Tears of pleasure well up in one's eyes. You gasp from happiness and are unable to breathe for fear of stopping the harmonic flood of sounds!" (*Muz. let.*, 1923, coll. 2, p. 52).

24 May

Glinka writes to Shirkov that he intends to settle temporarily in Kiev after the conclusion of the divorce proceedings "and not appear in Petersburg until the new opera is completed, so as to stop all the malicious and spiteful talk." He writes that although he "has forgotten about music" for the present, "if you have the time and inclination, at your leisure begin to work on" the libretto.

27 May

Departure for Petersburg (ltr. to his mother, 2 June 1841).

28 May

Smolensk. Glinka met with Aleksandr Rimsky-Korsak, who had arrived from Warsaw. He performed "many Polish couplets with piano accompaniment," and together they "danced the quadrille" (ltr. to A. Kern, 2 June 1841).

1 June

Petersburg. Arrival at 5 o'clock. Glinka settled into furnished rooms (ltr. to his mother, 2 June 1841; *SPb. ved.,* 4 June 1841). Address: Bolshaya Meshchanskaya, house of Schuppe, formerly of Varvarin, no. 24 (today, Plekhanov Street, no. 16).

2 June

Glinka writes to his mother that the divorce proceedings "are not expected to be completed by fall" and that he wishes to travel to Kiev at the end of the summer.

In a letter to Anna Kern he asks her "to take care of *la chère enfant*" and promises to send her books.

4 June

"From Smolensk, retired Collegiate Assessor Glinka" is the entry appearing in the list of those arriving in Petersburg on 1 and 2 June, in *SPb. ved.,* no. 122.

7 June

In *Rus. vestnik,* part 6, in the section "Art and Music News," Kukolnik reports: "Russian music, thanks to the judiciously strict attitude of a few of our composers, has been enriched with some very remarkable works. Glinka's genuinely enchanting opera *Ruslan and Lyudmila,* one may say, is almost finished" (d.c.a.).

9 June

Glinka's divorce proceedings begin (Protocol of the consistory, in *L.,* p. 210).

First Ten Days of June

Glinka received Dubelt's notice that the serf Ekaterina Shulevina, former housemaid to Maria Petrovna, who had turned over to Glinka Vasilchikov's letters to

Maria Petrovna, was, as a result of Glinka's petition, "granted her freedom. Thank God that at least one person has gained something from this" (ltr. to his mother, 11 June 1841).

11 June

Glinka writes to his mother that his case is "in progress" and that in a few days he and Maria Petrovna will be called to the consistory "to hear their admonition," after which "the trial begins properly, conducted by the attorneys." He also writes that Vasilchikov "has been held for about four days now . . . in the guard house and has been turned over to the military court . . . because of the local command's censure."

16 June

Glinka tells his mother about the course of his divorce case: "The slow progress of the case and not knowing what to expect, despite the Metropolitan's gracious response and the justness of the case itself, frequently cause me to become absorbed in sad thoughts." He complains of his solitude. "There is no one to unburden myself on. Sophie and Eugénie [Sofia Nolde and her daughter Evgenia] love me deeply, but then I am imposed on by Sofia Grigorievna Engelgardt to sing. It is impossible to get away, so I see my cousin less than I should."

23 June

Glinka gave a signed statement to the Directorate of the First Section's second ward to the effect that it "had been explained" to him "by a summons to appear this date at 12 o'clock." Glinka and Maria Petrovna appeared at the consistory. She was given a copy of Glinka's petition. Signed statements were taken from Glinka and Maria Petrovna that, "until the case has been decided," they were "to appear upon request at the consistory and to give notice to the consistory of any change of address." Glinka's address is indicated as Fonarny Lane, house of Merts. "Having been admonished to renounce their disagreement and return to married life . . . he did not consent to marital cohabitation with his wife but desired that according to his petition legal proceedings be initiated." At the ecclesiastical consistory Glinka received "a card . . . instructing him to appear on the 30th of June at the consistory for a formal hearing, resulting from the petition submitted on 15 May 1841 for the dissolution of his marriage, . . . with all documentation or evidence pertinent to the suit." The notice of receipt on the document states, "Caution money received. Collegiate Assessor Mikhail, son of Ivan Glinka" (LGIA, coll. 19, inventory 33, no. 153).

On returning from the consistory, Glinka in a letter told his mother of the "admonishment," which "was very short," and of his meeting with Maria Petrovna.

24 June

Glinka writes to his mother that the attorney Aleksandrov does not advise him "to present the case myself, since if I get worked up I may spoil the entire case." He reports that he is soon leaving for Kiev.

25 June

Tsarskoe Selo. Meeting of Glinka and Maria Petrovna in the Ekaterininsky Park in the presence of P. Kukolnik, at which time "she acknowledged everything to me, including her main thought that it was not the monastery but *eternal celibacy which she feared*" (ltr. to V. Shirkov, 22 July 1841).

After 24 and Before 30 June

Petersburg. Glinka submitted a request to the consistory that in his place the attorney Stepanov be admitted to the divorce proceedings and that he be permitted to absent himself from Petersburg to another province for the management of his hereditary estates (*L.*, p. 211).

June

A Life for the Tsar is mentioned in *Tekushchii repertuar russkoi stseny* [Current repertory of the Russian stage], no. 6, in a review by Fedor Koni of Polevoy's *Kostromskie lesa* [The forests of Kostroma] and Verstovsky's *Askold's Tomb*.

1 July

In a letter to his mother Glinka discusses the course of the proceedings, his meetings with Maria Petrovna, and Aleksandrov's promise to help him compose the "pleading."

In a letter to Anna Kern, Glinka expresses concern over the health of Ekaterina Kern and the manner of her treatment. He writes of his longing for her. "Only with you and your charming family do I hope to find comfort and to forget my sorrows" (Fr. original).

8 July

Glinka tells his mother of his intentions of travelling to Kiev on the 20th of July. "My case is certain, though it has been put off."

9 July

Glinka informs his mother that "the consistory is discharging" him and "is allowing . . . an attorney at the pleading," although officially this has still not been announced. He asks his mother to come to Kiev at the end of August.

The consistory concluded that "attorneys are to be admitted in divorce cases in event of illness . . . and other circumstances when warranted," but since "his suit, based on his wife's desertion for someone else, is of such a nature, the formal proceedings should be cleared of personal explanations on the part of both parties . . . thus satisfying Mr. Glinka's request to be dismissed" (LGIA, coll. 19, inventory 33, no. 153).

15 July

Glinka writes to his mother that "so far there has been no final answer from the consistory" to his request to travel to Kiev.

22 July

Glinka informs his mother: "Finally I have received permission from the consistory" to depart for Kiev, and "an attorney . . . will be allowed to present my case. To personally be the accuser would have been too difficult for me. I am amazed now how I was able to withstand the court appearance and the meeting with Maria Petrovna." He asks his mother to come to Kiev by 20 August.

After relating in a letter to the Shirkovs the slow pace of the divorce proceedings, because Maria Petrovna "reports sick" and does not appear at the consistory, Glinka adds: "My case is in sure and experienced hands. Aleksandrov, who is a member of the governing authority of the church . . . has taken my case in his own hands. Before this I was already on close terms with him. For a year now I have taught his youngest daughter singing!" He asks that letters to him be addressed to Lubny. "My muse is completely silent." He sends Aleksandra Shirkova the *Valse-fantaisie* and Bolero for piano: "Play them and think of me."

25 July

It is explained to Glinka that he has been denied transfer of the power of attorney on the basis of section 224 of the rules of the ecclesiastical consistory (*L.*, p. 211).

26 July

Glinka "gave this written statement to the officer of administrative affairs of the second Admiralty unit saying that the content of the letter of 25 July from the St. Petersburg ecclesiastical consistory . . . had been explained" to him, that he would appear on 30 July, and that he would not leave "the capital without the permission of the consistory."

Glinka informs his mother that he "had no sooner begun to prepare for the trip . . . when I quite unexpectedly received a notice to appear personally in the consistory for the pleadings." Maria Petrovna "arrived with a request" asking that, because of illness, her attorney be admitted in her place, and she presented a certificate of illness (LGIA, coll. 19).

Between 27 and 29 July

Glinka wrote a draft of the pleading in which he portrayed his relations with his wife and presented evidence of her immoral way of life along with Vasilchikov's letters to her.

30 July

Glinka appeared at the consistory "for the pleading," which did not take place because of "the defendant's, his wife's" failure to appear (ltr. to his mother, 1 August 1841; Glinka's acknowledgement, in LGIA, coll. 19).

In the "Bibliographical Chronicle" section of *Otech. zap.*, vol. 17, no. 17/18, there is an article entitled "Russian Literature: The Works of Aleksandr Pushkin, Volumes IX, X, and XI," in which Belinsky indicates that when Pushkin's works were published, both of Laura's songs were omitted from *The Stone Guest.* "The second of these songs, '*Nochnoi zefir struit efir,*' has long been known to the public, as has the first, even though it has never been printed. Our well-known composer, M. I. Glinka, set it to music, and the words of the song have become even better known than the music itself. The song is '*Ia zdes', Inezilya*' [I am here, Inezilla]" (d.c.a.).

31 July

In Glinka's album there is a pencil drawing by Nikolay Stepanov, which is inscribed "Yakov [Yanenko] makes a speech in a German dialect" (Album No. 1).

1 August

Glinka writes to his mother that [my] "request to absent myself has been flatly denied, and they are demanding my personal presence at the pleadings. . . . Indirectly I have found out that the Vasilchikovs are standing up staunchly for my rival and do not wish to give him up for anything." The secretary of the Synod assures Glinka that his case is "certain."

7 August

Glinka gives a written statement that he will appear at the consistory on 8 August by 12 o'clock. (LGIA, coll. 19).

8 August

Glinka "once again was called to the consistory and appeared, but, just as on the previous occasion, to no purpose, for Maria Petrovna was not there. She had reported sick and meanwhile was conducting still another new intrigue in Tsarskoe Selo" (ltr. to his mother, 9 August 1841).
[In the dossier for Glinka's divorce proceedings is his acknowledgment that he "appeared for the pleading," but "the above-mentioned did not occur because of the defendant's, his wife's, failure to appear."]

9 August

In a letter to his mother Glinka writes about how the divorce proceedings are being prolonged.

12 August

At the interrogation before the consistory, Vasilchikov confesses that he married Maria Petrovna before her divorce from Glinka, thinking that she would receive the divorce later. The priest Opolsky confessed that he had married "the maiden Maria Petrovna and cornet Nikolay Vasilchikov" (LGIA, coll. 19).

15 August

Glinka writes to his mother: "My nervous state has made me indifferent to everything. I am prepared for anything to happen, either success or failure."

22 August

Elizaveta Ivanovna Glinka's and Yakov and Nikolay Sobolevsky's return from Paris (ltr. to his mother, 23 August 1841).

Performance of *A Life for the Tsar* "for the benefit of invalids injured on the field of battle" in the Bolshoi Theater (*SPb. ved.*, 22 August 1841).

The first act of *A Life for the Tsar* was presented in Kharkov on the occasion of the opening of a new theater (*Khar'k. gub. ved.*, 1841, no. 34).

23 August

Glinka writes to his mother: "Everything is going as it has been, that is, the important matter is not progressing."

In *Moskvityanin,* no. 8, section 4, there is an article entitled "Musical Evenings in Nizhny," which is signed ". . . v" [P. I. Melnikov]. It refers to the performance of an aria from *A Life for the Tsar* during Lent as part of "divisional music."

End of Summer

Glinka "felt an unusual inclination to compose" (*Zap.*).

4 September

In a personnal letter to Benkendorf, the priest Opolsky denied his confession that he had performed Maria Petrovna's and Vasilchikov's wedding ceremony. He explained his previous confession by the fact that he was "impaired in his reason because of an illness caused by tapeworm" (LGIA, coll. 19).

Beginning of September

Glinka and his sister and nephew settle permanently in Schuppe's house "across from the Council of Guardians." Elizaveta moved into an apartment on the same floor with Glinka, while he settled in "two small, though very bright rooms. . . .

My inclination to compose did not change. Moreover, I began to study drawing, landscape in particular, from an academy student named Solntsev and progressed to the point that I was able to copy several landscapes in pencil for my acquaintances."

8 September

A. Afanasiev (from Kharkov) in a letter to Aleksandr Veltman tells him of a performance of the first act of a *Life for the Tsar* in Kharkov (*Sov. muzyka,* 1955, no. 9, p. 79).

11 September

Glinka presented a memorandum "to the administration of the third ward, Second Section" that in accordance with the consistory's order on 1 September, he would appear "tomorrow without fail" before the consistory.

12 September

Glinka appeared for the pleading, but Maria Petrovna did not appear and once again presented a certificate of illness (*L.*, p. 19).
[During the course of September and October, Maria Petrovna refused demands to appear before the consistory (since she had presented a certificate of illness) (LGIA, coll. 19).]

16 September

In *Lit. gaz.,* no. 104, there is an article by Fedor Koni entitled *"Askold's Tomb* at the Bolshoi Theater": "Verstovsky's opera did not satisfy even patriotic loyalty in St. Petersburg. Here they are familiar with *A Life for the Tsar,* which is a truly exemplary Russian opera, written in European form according to all the requirements of art."

27 September

The priest Opolsky registered a complaint against Glinka with the Metropolitan and Chief Procurator, saying that Glinka "is talking everywhere contrary to his conscience about his lawful wife's behavior as a married woman . . . and that I allegedly confessed of participating in her misdemeanor . . . and broadcast everywhere that he gave [me] ten thousand rubles. Such unscrupulousness on the part of Mr. Glinka has compelled me to fall at the feet of Your Grace." Opolsky writes that he is inclined to have "obscured judgment" and that in this condition Glinka caused him to confess (LGIA, coll. 19).

29 September

Glinka writes to his mother: "Since my little sister arrived I have completely changed my way of life and have become a stay-at-home. . . . It seems my case is to be decided independently of me, and, whatever might happen, I have decided not to worry about the future but to take advantage of the present and continue the opera. Moreover . . . I have started to draw." He asks his mother to send from Novospasskoe all the drawings he bought in Petersburg, "except those which are framed and behind glass." He states that Kukolnik's tragedy *Prince Kholmsky* "is playing tomorrow in the Aleksandrinsky Theater," and "judging from the rehearsals one may hope that my music will be successful."

30 September

First performance of *Prince Kholmsky* in the Aleksandrinsky Theater (*Sev. pchela,* 1 September 1841). Glinka, "as the composer's privilege took a box" and invited his sister Elizaveta and his cousin Sofia Nolde and her daughter Evgenia (ltr. to his mother, 29 September 1841). "From the very start Mr. Kukolnik's incredibly long work fell with a terrible racket on the ears of the poor listeners, who could scarcely sit out the five long acts of this composite divertissement with singing, dancing, Bengal lights, and splendid spectacle" (*Lit. gaz.,* 26 April 1842).
[Kukolnik's drama failed and was quickly withdrawn from the stage, a fate which the music undeservedly shared.]

Beginning of September, October, and Later

Glinka accompanied his sister Elizaveta Ivanovna "on the violin, incidentally, in the Beethoven F-major sonata."

"There was a serf girl in the service of my sister Elizaveta who was learning to sew from a milliner. Mother had designated her as housemaid to my younger sister Olga. She was 18 years old, had a very nice figure, and was a rather attractive young girl. She . . . often entertained me with her amusing and unexpected antics. For example, she referred to my opera *Ruslan and Lyudmila* as *her own. . . .* In a word . . . I got very accustomed to her in a short time:

> Habit turns to feeling,
> And feeling to many days' happiness, etc.

In fact, I am obliged to her for many, many pleasant minutes. I enjoyed myself so much at home that I very rarely went out, and sitting at home, I worked so industriously that in a short time the better part of the opera was ready (*Zap.*).

2 October

Performance of *Prince Kholmsky* in the Aleksandrinsky Theater (*Sev. pchela,* 2 October 1841).

6 October

Performance of *Prince Kholmsky* in the Aleksandrinsky Theater (*Sev. pchela,* 6 October 1841).

8 October

In an article entitled "The Bolshoi Theater," signed "M-ch" [Mezhevich], in a supp. to *Ved. SPb. gor. politsii,* no. 29, there is a comparison of *A Life for the Tsar* with *Askold's Tomb:* "Whenever they talk about *Askold's Tomb,* enthusiasts for comparison and argument cannot avoid talking about *A Life for the Tsar,* the only opera by our Petersburg composer, M. I. Glinka. Truth to tell, there are very few points of comparison to be found between these two operas. One may allow the comparison . . . only because in all there are only *two* Russian operas . . . which . . . have earned the designation *opera.* Consequently, speaking of one of them, you involuntarily think of the other. But the points of comparison end here. There are no others, nor can there be . . . the first belongs to the highest order of musical composition. To compare it to Verstovsky's opera . . . is like judging a small, light drama by Polevoy by the gigantic standards of Shakespearean drama. . . . You say that there is a point of comparison between Glinka and Verstovsky in the sense that both are Russian composers, so consequently you ask yourself, which of them better divined the secret of folk melody? Which more accurately captured the sound of Russian music? In this respect you would also be incorrect, because, if you were to take one feature, and perhaps the weakest, from Glinka's opera, you would be taking the position of comparing it with Verstovsky's entire opera, and on the basis of one feature . . . pronouncing your verdict on the whole. . . . No . . . there is no comparing our two Russian operas, nor should there be, because both composers wrote under different conditions, with different resources, and in different genres."
[The article was written on 7 October, after the fifteenth performance of *Askold's Tomb* in Petersburg.]

11 October

In *Sev. pchela,* no. 227, Bulgarin polemicizes with the journal *Magazin für Literatur des Auslandes,* which refers to *Lit. gaz.* as the basis for its evaluation of Verstovsky's and Glinka's operas. ("We have gotten these remarks from the *Literary Gazette* published in St. Petersburg by Mr. F. Koni, whose ideas are expounded there with an understanding of the matter [sic!] and with impartiality . . ."). Bulgarin writes about *A Life for the Tsar:* "This opera has held its place on the stage for a long time, and it even pleases foreign musicians. Consequently it must have musical merit." Further on he brings up the opinion of the German magazine that "the content contributed largely to the success of this opera." The journal "is kind to M. I. Glinka, but in return it is terribly unkind to Verstovsky!" He also introduces the German magazine's claim that Verstovsky, as head of the Moscow theaters, "would not allow a single Russian opera to be performed on the Moscow stage, denying the Moscow audience the pleasure of hearing the best Russian opera, namely *A Life for the Tsar,* composed by Glinka."

13 October

Glinka writes to Sergey Sobolevsky about his material affairs. He promises to repay a debt after the conclusion of the divorce proceedings, which he feels will be soon, and he asks to borrow more money.

14 October

At the second hearing in the consistory, Vasilchikov denied his initial testimony and declared that he had not married Maria Petrovna (LGIA, coll. 19).

22 October

Performance of *A Life for the Tsar* in the Bolshoi Theater (*Sev. pchela,* 25 and 27 October 1841). Karl Albrecht conducted the opera for the first time. Anfisa Petrova played the role of Vanya. "The opera did not go very smoothly. His honor, Mr. Director, said to me, 'The orchestra is not flexible enough.'"

23 October

Glinka visited Albrecht (K. Albrecht's diary, in *Muz. letop.,* 1923, coll. 2, p. 72).

24 October

Glinka did a pencil drawing of a tree. Author's date: "24 October" (*L.*, p. 214).

25 October

In the "Bibliographical and Other News" section of *Sev. pchela*, no. 239, there is an announcement that Glinka's Variations on Alyabiev's Romance "The Nightingale" is in stock at Bernard's. In the same issue there is a report of Anfisa Petrova's debut in the role of Vanya on 22 October: "Her voice is exceptionally fine, especially in the lower register."

28 October

Performance of *A Life for the Tsar* in the Bolshoi Theater (*SPb. ved.*, 28 October 1841).

29 October

In *Sev. pchela*, no. 242, there is a review over the signature "L. L." of Kukolnik's drama *Prince Daniil Dmitrievich Kholmsky* (which says nothing about the music).

Performance in the Bolshoi Theater of *A Life for the Tsar* (*SPb. ved.*, 29 October 1841).

31 October

In the "Literary Chronicle" section of *Bib-ka dlia chteniia*, vol. 49, the writer points out that Laura's song *"Nochnoi zefir struit efir"* is omitted from Pushkin's tragedy *The Stone Guest* (in the recently published *Collected Works*), even though it is already well-known to the public because of Glinka's setting of it (d.c.a.).

October

In the section "Contemporary Chronicle of the Russian Theater, the Petersburg Theaters" of *Repertuar*, part 10, there is a review of *Prince Kholmsky*. It says of the music that "Rakhila's song, sung by Mme Samoylova II, was well received. The music of this song is nice."

Arnold visited Glinka and "found him in exceptionally good spirits. He had just finished the large scene for Ratmir ('*I zhar i znoi*' [Oppressive heat] and '*Chu-*

dnyi son zhivoi liubvi' [Marvelous dream of living love])." Glinka performed excerpts from *Ruslan* (the Persian chorus and Ratmir's scene) and expressed his view of Ratmir's aria: "This piece has too much of an Italian flavor, and the waltz rhythm is shocking. . . . In a strictly musical aesthetic sense, you perhaps are right, but you see that this is the one number out of my entire opera which audiences like best" (Arnold, p. 509).

7 November

Glinka writes to his mother about the slow course of the divorce proceedings because of Maria Petrovna's failure to appear at the consistory. Concerning what he had been charged with, that he had allegedly bribed Opolsky for 10,000 rubles so that the priest would testify falsely that he had married Maria Petrovna, Glinka answered that he did not have "enough income to spend such a sum." He expressed the hope that the proceedings will soon end, since the military administration is demanding a decision of Vasilchikov's fate, as he is under arrest. Of himself he says, "I am a stay-at-home now, I am writing the opera."

In a letter to Shirkov, Glinka discusses his divorce case and life with his sister Elizaveta Ivanovna "in the same house . . . My newly returned muse brightens my life with fruitful work. I have never appreciated art more than now, and even though my heart has been exhausted by prolonged suffering and no longer believes in earthly happiness, it is still possible for me to live for the sake of art. In the accompanying aria from the third act you will find a detailed account of my activities and information necessary to continue work. . . . Since the moment I ceased to live on fragile dreams of the future, I have completely changed the way I live and try to fill each hour of the present. Besides the opera, I am busy with the violin and pencil. . . . In the spring I want to take up watercolors." He asks Shirkov to send him the drawing "left" with him. "In particular I need the study from which you drew the tree in my album. I do not dare ask for another of your drawings, though the peasant hut with the pear tree would make me happy for a while."

8 November

Glinka did a drawing on which Karl Bryullov wrote across the top, "Not copied badly at all." Author's dating on the drawing: "M. Glinka, 8 November 1841" (*L.*, p. 215).

In *Sev. pchela,* no. 251, in the section "Journalistic Odds and Ends," Bulgarin remarks while enumerating the best (and not many) exponents of literature and drama that "There are two folk composers, A. N. Verstovsky and M. I. Glinka, and that is not a long list!"

First Half of November

Glinka hosted a dinner to which he invited Nestor Kukolnik and Mikhail Gedeonov. "Because of Shirkov's departure for the Ukraine, Kukolnik and Gedeonov undertook to help "finish writing the missing parts of the libretto for *Ruslan and Lyudmila.*"
[Apparently, soon after this Kukolnik wrote the text for the finale of the opera.]

20 November

Performance in the Bolshoi Theater of *A Life for the Tsar* (*Sev. pchela,* 20 November 1841).

Between 20 and 25 November

Glinka writes "the most difficult number of the opera" (ltr. to his mother, 25 November 1841).
[He is probably speaking about the finale (see *Lit. gaz.,* 13 December 1841 and 11 January 1842).]

24 November

Because of Maria Petrovna's refusal to appear before the consistory, members of the consistory came to her and "recorded her responses in the presence of a police official." Maria Petrovna denied her marriage with Vasilchikov (LGIA, coll. 19).

25 November

Glinka writes to his mother that he and his sister are impatiently awaiting her arrival in Petersburg. About himself he writes: "I am working quite diligently and because of the bad weather staying at home. If nothing unforseen happens, by about March I hope to have finished my work and begun dealings with the Directorate, so that the opera can be given next fall while you are here. I am also drawing and playing the violin a lot, so that when I have to leave the house it not only bores me but I actually get irritated for having to abandon what I am doing. . . . I know nothing about the case." He also writes that his sister Elizaveta "has arranged things for little Nikolay very appropriately," that is, she placed their nephew in a school for deaf-mutes.
[The director of the school was Viktor Fleury, to whom Elizaveta Ivanovna was later married.]

28 November

The consistory ordered Maria Petrovna to present a medical certificate of her illness, without which they would not allow an attorney to represent her. A similar "notice" was sent to her on 12 December (LGIA, coll. 19).

2 December

Maria Petrovna's confrontation with Vasilchikov: she denied that she entered into marriage with him. He admitted it, though he said that he did not know if the wedding ceremony had in fact been completed (LGIA, coll. 19).

8 December

On orders of Aleksandr Gedeonov, Albrecht held a quartet rehearsal of *A Life for the Tsar* (K. Albrecht's diary, in *Muz. letop.*, 1923, coll. 2, p. 42).

13 December

In *Lit. gaz.*, no. 141, in the section headed "What's New in St. Petersburg?" Fedor Koni writes: "M. I. Glinka, they say, has finished his new opera *Ruslan and Lyudmila*. Those who have heard significant parts of it confirm that it will be the best Russian musical work of its kind. They particularly praise Finn's ballad, which has a beautifully distinctive melody and also demonstrates the solution of a very difficult musical problem."

17 December

The Chief Procurator of the Synod sent to the consistory "a copy of the document concerning Mme Glinka's testimony furnished to him by the military governor-general." It says in the document that members of the medical corps found "a weak, delicately built and undersized young woman of pale complexion with a face expressing suffering." They expressed the opinion that she "is prone to heart palpitations" indicative of "nervous suffering" and that in their estimation calling her to the consistory "may have a harmful effect on her health" (LGIA, coll. 19).

Before 18 December

Before sending Shirkov the changes in the fourth act, Glinka "prepared a number of things, namely the chorus of flowers and adagio 'O fate, my fate' and the chorus of flowers to the words 'Do not mourn, young princess,' etc." (ltr. to V. Shirkov, 20 December 1841).

18 December

Composer's dating on the title page of the manuscript: "Act IV. Lyudmila's scene in Chernomor's castle. Begun 18 December 1841."

Before 20 December

On the advice of Mikhail Gedeonov, Glinka "drafted a detailed program of the entire opera in order to dispose the Director in my favor well in advance. As it turned out, a number of concessions will be necessiated for scenic considerations, and consequently a meeting on the subject with the Director will be needed before the work is completely finished, because undoubtedly there will be changes." Mikhail Gedeonov "undertook to rework my program for his father so that it would match his taste and to prepare a letter for the Director such that he would accept my work with enthusiasm (it was well known that *art* did not exist for the old man Gedeonov). In a moment of candor he (the son) expressed the desire that I dedicate my work to him. I naturally agreed, especially since he had already shown Kukolnik his enthusiasm for staging the tragedy *Prince Kholmsky*. Consequently this diplomatic measure agreed with my feelings" (ltr. to V. Shirkov, 20 December 1841).

[The manuscripts of individual scenes from *Ruslan and Lyudmila* which have been preserved (the complete score burned in the fire of the Theater-Circus in 1859) as well as the published editions do not include the dedication to Mikhail Gedeonov.]

20 December

Glinka thanks Shirkov for sending the text to the fourth act of *Ruslan and Lyudmila*. "The words for Lyudmila's scene have been reworked perfectly according to what my music requires, and they seem very apropos. Before you sent them I was unable to continue writing for several days. I have now returned to work, and Lyudmila's scene is already half done. . . . The words of the lilies, roses, violets, and forget-me-nots I am unable to place, because I cannot guarantee a decent performance of them. . . . Similarly, Lyudmila's dressing scene will only be effective if we have attractive prima donnas, which my Lyudmilas are not. I certainly understand that Kukolnik's participation is unpleasant for you, but the capriciousness of my muse and your remoteness force me to run to him. I think my excuses are completely natural. However, everything is being done as you wish. Kukolnik throws out words hastily without paying attention to the beauty of a line, and everything that he has written for *Ruslan* up to now has been so sloppy that it has had to be redone. Furthermore, however I may value Kukolnik's gift, I remain of the same opinion as before: he is a writer, not a poet, and his poetry, after Pushkin, Batyushkov, and others, is generally too ponderous and graceless. No doubt the meters are giving you trouble, but Bayan's songs, Gorislava's aria, and other places in your libretto vouch for your talent. Do not hurry your rewriting, for there is still time. The main thing is to send me Naina's scene with Farlaf in the fifth act, that is when Naina disposes Farlaf to kill Ruslan. . . . This scene—*recitative*—must be short but extremely clear. . . . The following duet for Ratmir and Finn . . . is impossible to write in your absence. . . . A detailed program for *the finale of the fifth act,* written with Kukolnik's assistance, I will send to you shortly. . . . The opera is so near to completion that one of these days I will have to begin my dealings with the Director of Theaters." Regarding the divorce proceedings Glinka writes that he has little hope "of success, since it seems that the consistory has been bribed, and to contend with Vasilchikov, who has an income of 60,000, is impossible for me, the more so since the people to whom I entrusted the case have deceived me unconscionably. . . . *In my native land* I have encountered only grief and disappointment in my actual life. Most of my friends have become bitter enemies . . . and from Little Russia, her mother has caused me to have a falling out. Do not ask for details. I have calmed down now and am living in seclusion with my sister . . . The opera, violin, and pencil are my companions. In a month I expect Mother. I will spend a year with her, present the opera, and then travel to the West without goals or purpose, except nature and art."

[Glinka's quarrel with Ekaterina Kern occurred, apparently, because of Anna Kern. Yuly Shokalsky claims that the fault lay with Lyudmila Shestakova, based on a letter to him from Yulia Ber, daughter of Stuneeva, but the Stuneev family had long been on the outs with Shestakova. During the time of Glinka's love affair with Kern, Shestakova lived in the country and at that time was unable to exercise any influence on her brother.]

At their second hearing Maria Petrovna and Vasilchikov testified that "the priest did not complete the marriage ceremony" (LGIA, coll. 19).

Second Half of December (after the 20th)

Mikhail Gedeonov "wrote a little duet following Finn's ballad" in the second act "('I thank you, extraordinary patron'), Finn's recitative in Act III, 'Knights! perfidious Naina,' etc., and the prayer in four parts which closes the third act. I myself wrote Farlaf's scene with Naina and Farlaf's rondo and also the beginning of the finale of the third act."

28 December

"Finished on 28 December 1841" appears in the composer's hand on the final page of the score for "Lyudmila's scene in Chernomor's castle."

Vasilchikov's official letter to Maria Petrovna, in which he disclaims any relation between them.

29 December

Glinka and Maria Petrovna are sent notices from the consistory stating that on 12 January he is to appear in person and she is to send an attorney (LGIA, coll. 19).
[A second notice was sent on 2 January 1842.]

30 December

Decision by the Second Section of the ecclesiastical consistory that the validity of Maria Petrovna's marriage with Nikolay Vasilchikov had not been demonstrated (*L.*, p. 219).

31 December

In the section "Miscellany, Musical News," in *Bib-ka dlia chteniia,* vol. 50, mention is made of a fantasy for violin entitled *"La Nationale"* on themes from *A Life for the Tsar* by Nikolay Bakhmetiev (d.c.a.).

December

The following comments appear under "Book Reviews" in ZhMPN, part 32, section 6: "Mr. Glinka has given us the best work in this branch of knowledge with his *Farewell to St. Petersburg.* In this collection there are 12 charming romances and songs which demonstrate the high caliber of the composer's poetic sensibilities."

During the course of the year and after the beginning of the divorce proceedings, Glinka, who often attended the musical evenings given by the secretary of the St. Petersburg ecclesiastical consistory N. A. Lisenko, met Aleksandr Nikolaevich Serov (Serov, *Vosp.*, p. 72).

Sketches of a plan for the fifth act (choruses, scene of Lyudmila's awakening, and the libretto for the finale) come from this year. This material is associated with Glinka's work with Kukolnik on the libretto for the finale of the fifth act.

During this same year arrangements of arias from *A Life for the Tsar* were repeatedly performed by a military orchestra in Nizhny Novgorod (*Moskvityanin,* 1841, vol. 3, p. 561).

Beginning of the 1840s

Glinka, in the company of the Kukolnik "fraternity," often visited Dargomyzhsky at his home on the Fontanka at Obukhovsky Bridge.

1842

1 January

In the magazine *Repertuar i Panteon,* no. 1, under "Survey of Activities of the Russian Theaters for the Year 1841," Petrova II's performance of the part of Vanya is mentioned (d.c.a.).

1 January (?)

The first of the "Astrakhan Letters" written by "C." appears in part one of the magazine *Dagerrotip:* "They say that a new opera by M. I. Glinka, *Ruslan and Lyudmila,* will be performed at the Bolshoi Theater. You nearly know the entire opera already because of its main numbers. However, I saw sketches of the scenery done for the opera by our gifted Roller. It can truly be said that in these magical and fascinating drawings Roller has even outdone himself."

Beginning of January

The following words appear in the "News and Miscellany" section of *Rus. vestnik,* no. 1: "I do not know if we can expect to hear M. I. Glinka's opera *Ruslan and Lyudmila* this winter. We are waiting for you, esteemed artist!"

4 January

In the preface to *Theater Album,* Aleksandr Bashutsky writes that in this edition "amateurs will find everything which captivates them in the works of Meyerbeer, Auber, Adam, Maurer, Glinka, Verstovsky, Keller, et al." (d.c.a.).

Glinka Composing *Ruslan and Lyudmila* in 1842
As imagined by the artist, Ilya Repin, in 1887.

6 January

In Glinka's Album No. 1, Nestor Kukolnik wrote a "Caricature in Verse" of Dargomyzhsky entitled "An Official and His Muse."

11 January

Under "Various News Items" in *Lit. gaz.*, no. 2, there is a remark about Glinka's work on the opera *Ruslan and Lyudmila*.

13 January

Directive from Aleksandr Gedeonov to Fedor Ral charging him "with full management of military music employed in performances, with all preparation of the same for performances and arrangements for the stage, with the obligation to arrange and compose the above-mentioned as required, and to correct proofs" (*L.*, p. 219).

14 January

The ecclesiastical consistory agreed to find Vasilchikov not guilty of being illegally married to Maria Petrovna Glinka and to transfer his case from the ecclesiastical to the civil authorities to adjudicate the issue that by courting Glinka's wife, he "provoked discord between the Glinkas, diverted the wife from obedience to and respect for her husband . . . and finally caused Mr. Glinka to seek a divorce" (*L.*, p. 219).

25 January

Announcement of the consistory's decision on Glinka's divorce case, stating that there was no wedding ceremony, since Opolsky deceived Vasilchikov. However, insofar as Vasilchikov, "by his own admission," actually wanted to get married to Maria Petrovna and had thereby "diverted the wife from obedience to and respect for her husband . . . such of his actions are to be transferred to his superiors for consideration," since he committed no crime against the church and in actual fact had not gotten married.

28 January

Glinka gave a signed statement to appear in the consistory "in the near future" (LGIA, coll. 19).

In *Sev. pchela,* no. 22, in the section "Musical News," there is an announcement of the performance in a concert on 4 February of Bakhmetiev's fantasy *"La Nationale"* on themes from *A Life for the Tsar*.

30 January

Glinka appeared in the consistory for the pleading. Maria Petrovna's attorney (A. Fedorov) announced that she "had indeed lived apart from her husband for about two years, because her husband had expelled her from her own house while she was ill without the slightest cause on her part for his action. . . . She had not gotten married . . . to the cornet Vasilchikov. . . . Whether she wished . . . to continue to live conjugally with her husband, Mr. Fedorov was not prepared to answer." A continuation of the hearing was scheduled for 6 February (LGIA, coll. 19).

3 February

Under "Concerts," (signed "O."), in *SPb. ved.,* no. 27, there is an announcement of the performance of the fantasy *"La Nationale"* by Bakhmetiev on themes from *A Life for the Tsar* in a concert on 4 February.

4 February

In the hall of Mme Mamonova at the Horse-Guards riding school, there was "a musical evening for the benefit of the well-known guitarist Sikhra," who performed "Mr. Bakhmetiev's beautiful fantasy on our favorite opera *A Life for the Tsar* (*Sev. pchela,* 28 January 1842).

6 February

Glinka did not appear before the consistory but sent "a statement that yesterday he fell ill with a cold accompanied by serious swelling of the face and gums" (LGIA, coll. 19).

7 February

In *Mosk. ved.,* no. 11, there is an announcement that V. Frakman's piano arrangement of the Orphan's song from *A Life for the Tsar* is available at Gresser's.

20 February

Glinka received a summons to the consistory for 23 February (LGIA, coll. 19).

21 February

At the graduation ceremonies of the Educational Society for Young Ladies of the Nobility, Aledinskaya and Perkhurova performed a duet from *A Life for the Tsar* (*Zvezdochka*, 1842, no. 4, p. 54).

22 February

In *Rus. invalid*, no. 44/45, there is an enthusiastic review by "K." of a new volume, "Theatrical Album," consisting of portraits of artists, scenes from performances, and music. In the album "amateurs will find everything which captivates them in the works of Meyerbeer, Auber, Adam, Maurer, Glinka, and Verstovsky."

23 February

Glinka appeared at the pleading and "as evidence in his defense wrote . . . that he did not expel his wife, the defendant, but left her in their apartment . . . that he designated for her upkeep about three thousand rubles a year . . . and that he himself moved to the apartment of Aide-de-Camp Stepanov of the regiment of chasseurs Life-Guards." Glinka again referred to the 13 letters Vasilchikov had written to Maria Petrovna and introduced excerpts from them into the record. Glinka emphatically declined to continue "conjugal life" with Maria Petrovna (LGIA, coll. 19).

24 February

Performance of *A Life for the Tsar* in the Bolshoi Theater (*Sev. pchela*, 24 February 1842).

25 February

In a supp. to *Panteon*, no. 6, under "Current Repertoire of the Russian Stage," there is a review of Kukolnik's drama *Prince Kholmsky*: "What an amazing drama! Amazing in every respect. In its mixed character, length, obscure meaning, and number of characters, it must certainly be related to the kind of stage works called composite divertissements. It is neither drama, nor comedy, nor opera, nor is it a vaudeville or ballet, though there is a little bit of everything here except drama. . . . Mr. Kukolnik's drama . . . despite the striking, splendid decor and costumes, will not remain long in the Russian stage's repertoire." There is not a word about the music. In the same issue, on the occasion of a performance in Petersburg of Verstovsky's *Askold's Tomb,* Koni expresses the hope that Moscow will follow the example of Petersburg and present *A Life for the Tsar* there (d.c.a.).

28 February

In a review by Belinsky in *Otech. zap.,* vol. 21, no. 3/4, of Vladimir Stroev's book *Paris in the Years 1838 and 1839* (parts 1 and 2), it says: "In Italy . . . you become a music lover, even though your ears are incapable of distinguishing a romance by Glinka from a song by Schubert . . ." (d.c.a.).

End of Winter (Lent)

Glinka met the Tabarovsky and Serov families. Aleksandr Serov "was at the time a very young man, well educated (he was a student at the School of Jurisprudence), and a very fine musician" (*Zap.*).
[Glinka had actually met Serov before this.]

Serov and his sister Sofia Dyutur repeatedly heard Glinka perform his romances within an intimate circle. "Mikhail Ivanovich's listeners at those evenings were almost all young people, poetically as youthful as he. There were young men who had barely left their school benches and young women just beginning to blossom. The sounds of Glinka's music, which he performed himself, struck these youthful souls profoundly . . . and it was gratifying to the artist to catch in more than one pair of eyes the fire of excitement which his music ignited. But then how he performed in such a circle! . . . Nature's gifts were combined in the most felicitous way in Glinka, gifts which in aggregate are *essential* for genuinely elegant singing but which usually are distributed singly among totally different people and which therefore makes the ideal of a true singer an extreme rarity. These include the gifts of a good voice (at least sufficiently attractive, strong, and flexible); the talent to control the voice and ability to technically manage it, which is an ability developed by deliberateness and study; and finally, thirdly, a profound, aesthetic understanding of music's spirit and purpose to an extent inaccessible to those less artistic, and a high order of perfection in declamation and musical performance in general" (Serov, *Vosp.,* p. 72).

"During . . . my visits [to Nestor Kukolnik] I often found Mikhail Ivanovich Glinka there. In my presence he would seat himself at the piano and sing his exquisite romances. And how he sang them! He possessed a very weak voice, but he sang these wonderful pieces with such feeling and such expression" (P. Sokolov, *Vosp.; L.*, 1930, p. 115).

"Since he knew through others and from conversations with me that I spent a great deal of time with music and that I viewed art seriously, Mikhail Ivanovich gladly allowed me to ask him about his opinions of various composers. . . . Glinka's answers were unexpected for me. He responded laconically about *Freischütz:* 'It is a fine opera and contains excellent moments, especially the trio in the first act. . . .' Glinka's general reaction to Meyerbeer was even more concise: 'I do not respect charlatans. . . .' He often chuckled over Rossini, Bellini, and Donizetti and referred to their lyricism as 'flowery. . . .' When the conversation touched Mozart, Glinka always added: 'Fine, but what is he compared to Beethoven!' In bewilderment I once asked him: 'And in opera?' 'Yes,' Glinka answered, 'in opera also. I would not exchange *Fidelio* for all of Mozart's operas together.'"

Once when Serov had been struck by the expressiveness of Glinka's declamation, he asked how he achieved such an effect (in a performance of the romance *"V krovi gorit"*). Glinka answered: "It's a very simple matter, sir, in itself. Particularly in vocal music, the expressive resources are limitless. The same word may be pronounced in a thousand different ways without even changing the intonation or pitch but only changing the accent, or by shaping the lips in a smile or serious, stern expression. Normally voice teachers give no attention to this, though true singers, which are quite rare, always know these resources well." In one of their conversations Serov "expressed amazement . . . at the perfection of the performance and the degree of inspiration, which almost always approached the level of ecstasy. Glinka . . . commented: 'It's not as difficult as you imagine. Once in a while in a particularly inspired moment it happens that I am able to sing a piece completely in accord with my ideal. I try to capture all the nuances of that fortunate instant, fortunate "impressions" or "performance models," if you will, and I stereotype all the details once and for all. After that I just let the piece flow in its prepared form. Because of this, I can appear to be in a state of ecstasy when inside I am in no way inspired but am only quietly obeying the will of my listeners. To be inspired every time! . . . That would be impossible.'" (Serov, *Vosp.*, p. 73).

Evgenia Andreevna and her daughter Olga arrived and stayed with Glinka in Davydov's house on Gorokhovaya Street. "Mother and my sisters and nephew occupied the first floor, and I had two rooms on the courtyard with the kitchen." [The house no longer stands. Today this is part of no. 5, Dzerzhinskaya Street.]

"Our gatherings in Merts's house ceased, and the fraternity disbanded. First Nestor Kukolnik moved into his own apartment. Still he was as fond of me as before, and whenever I asked him he wrote verses for my new opera and corrected those which I had composed. Whenever I let him know that I had finished a scene or number for the opera, he was extremely pleased and became *agitated* in his eagerness to hear the new composition. . . . V. I. Bogaev had gotten married. Platon Kukolnik moved into the Aleksandrovs' house. . . . Most of the fraternity gathered there. . . . We sang, played the piano, and danced. From time to time Nestor read new things he had written. Conversations were cordial. Finally, an appetizing and substantial dinner further disposed everyone to merriment. Less frequent, but also pleasant, were our evenings at Vladislavlev's, where Russian and foreign artists met. Here too there were singing, dancing, and considerable merriment. Late in the evening I often visited Misha Gedeonov, who at that time started having gatherings after the theaters closed. He and his brother Stepan Aleksandrovich won their father over to me to such an extent that when he left for Moscow, he gave me free rein over the production of my new opera."

February

"The opera had gotten to a point where it was impossible to write the little bit that remained without thinking of matters of production and without the cooperation of the set designer and ballet master."

End of Winter, Beginning of Spring

Glinka met "frequently and on friendly terms" with Ekaterina Kern, who had returned from the Ukraine, "but the former poetry and passion were gone. She had become acquainted with Maria Stepanovna [Krzhisevich]. . . . Through her . . . I became quite close with her relatives, the Tarnovskys. Anna Nikolaevna Tarnovskaya . . . a young, attractive, and extremely cordial woman . . . had become friends with E. K."

3 March

Under "Musical News" in *SPb. ved.,* no. 49, there is an announcement of the publication of "Music Theater Album of Vaudeville Couplets for the Year 1842," which contained 10 romances "from favorite vaudevilles with music by P. S. Fedorov, M. I. Glinka, K. N. Lyadov," and other composers.

4 March

Glinka's application to "His Excellency, Director of the Imperial Theaters of St. Petersburg, Privy Councillor and Knight Aleksandr Mikhaylovich Gedeonov": "In presenting to you the music for an opera which I have written called *Ruslan and Lyudmila,* the libretto for which I will have the honor of presenting in the near future, I most humbly request of Your Excellency that it be accepted under current regulations. Collegiate Assessor Glinka."

Glinka "appeared with the score before the Director, Gedeonov, who without discussion accepted . . . the opera and ordered that its production be undertaken immediately. According . . . to [Glinka's] request, instead of a one-time payment of 4,000 rubles, he agreed that . . . for this time only [Glinka] receive one-tenth of one percent of two-thirds of a full house for each performance."

Beginning of March, After the 4th

The score of *Ruslan* was submitted to the "music office of the Directorate of Theaters" to copy the parts (*Zap.*).

Beginning of Spring

Pieces from the opera *Ruslan and Lyudmila,* which Glinka was completing then, began to appear more and more frequently in the repertoire of songs which he performed. Gorislava's aria represented "the first captivating sounds we heard of the opera *Ruslan,* the grand preparations for which many were already speaking about. After singing several romances at a party at Lisenko's, Glinka said: 'Now I shall sing "ennui" for you.' 'What "ennui"? Whose "ennui"?' we asked in chorus with eager impatience. 'From my *Ruslan,* Gorislava's romance.' 'Who then is Gorislava? There is no such name in Pushkin's poem.' 'On the poster it will say "Gorislava, captive of Ratmir." Listen, I don't think it turned out badly.' And he sang, and we melted with pleasure."

Serov came to see Glinka, who was not at home. "He lived alone in a small, poorly furnished apartment facing the courtyard with a servant . . . 'from a musical family' . . . who sometimes copied music for Mikhail Ivanovich." Yakov Ulyanych told Serov that Glinka "just left to take a walk." To Serov's question, "Is he not awfully busy with his opera?" Yakov Ulyanych answered: "No, sir, not really. We just about have everything ready. We're just writing the dances now" (Serov, *Vosp.,* pp. 80, 86).

12 March

Glinka provided an affidavit that he had been "notified . . . concerning [his] appearance" before the consistory on 16 March.

15 March

In a letter to Vladimir Stasov, Serov discusses how "genuine folk poetry can only be adequately expressed in *music*" and states that attempts in music "have been incomparably more important than in poetry. Specifically there are two [such] Russian operas, *A Life for the Tsar* and *Askold's Tomb*. To my genuine regret, I have had to compare, for the sake of greater clarity, two compositions which are not at all of comparable *tendency* or *value*. In both cases the tendency approaches what is genuinely Russian, but the real path has not yet been discovered. In the first case the following conditions prevented this from happening: 1) the jingoistic and unoperatic, undramatic plot (even the composer admits this with regret); 2) the composer's inexperience in opera. For these reasons, unity is completely lost, despite many outstanding sections, and the goal is not attained, despite inspired and attractive means." Serov continues: "In my opinion, Russian opera requires a magical plot in order to display all the riches of our mythology and to express a true Russian attitude toward nature. . . . Glinka has almost finished his second opera, *Ruslan and Lyudmila*. I do not know the work, but, judging from the plot and what the composer has told me, I can be optimistic. Ever since I had the opportunity to become personally acquainted with M. I. Glinka, I have believed in him like a deity! There is still much I must talk to you about concerning this man, and, of course, we will not be able to avoid new and heated arguments!" (MN 1, p. 161).
[At the point where Serov writes about magical opera, Stasov adds the comment: "This is not A. N. Serov's own idea. It is undoubtedly influenced by Glinka's convictions at the time" (MN 1, p. 293).]

16 March

Maria Petrovna's attorney's (Fedorov's) "Declaration" denying her infidelity and affirming her hope that Glinka "repent of his errors," because "being guiltless she feared the thought of living apart from him." She denies her marriage with Vasilchikov or that she had received any letters from him, claiming that Glinka bribed "the serf girl" to give false testimony. "The defendant is not in agreement with the plaintiff regarding annulment of the marriage." Glinka signed an affidavit stating that he would inform the consistory "within seven days" of the place of residence "of the housemaid Ekaterina."

23 March

Maria Petrovna was summoned to the consistory "to hear the court's decisions," and if she could not appear, that "she authorize somebody to present her petition to the consistory" (LGIA, coll. 19).

27 March

Glinka's "summons" to the consistory "regarding the place of residence of the girl Ekaterina Shulevina, called in the case as a witness." (Her address is given as "Peterhof highway, at the 7th *versta,* in a house of the Hospital of All Mourners, as a maid to the clerk Shidlovsky.")

28 March

In a letter to Maria Stuneeva, Evgenia Andreevna Glinka writes that she is attending concerts. She conveys Glinka's respects and states that "he is busy with his opera and the case" (*L.,* p. 224).

4 April

"An aria composed by Glinka" was performed by Aleksandra Bilibina at one of the University Concerts. The orchestra was directed by Karl Shubert (*Sev. pchela,* 3 April 1842).

Franz Liszt's arrival (*Ved. SPb. politsii,* 7 April 1842).

Beginning 4 April

On the occasion of Liszt's arrival, Glinka, who "had renounced society from the time of separation . . . from my wife . . . was once again dragged out among people. The Russian composer who had been forgotten by almost everybody once again had to appear in the salons of the capital on account of the famous foreign artist's recommendation" (*Zap.*).

5 April

In *Lit. gaz.,* no. 14, in the section "Miscellany—New Items in the Repertoire," there appears an announcement of Petrova's forthcoming concert on 10 April, in which she is to perform works by Glinka.

8 April

Glinka attended "the famous Liszt's" first musical matinee (*Sev. pchela*, 7 April 1842). Vladimir Stasov saw Glinka for the first time at Liszt's concert. During the intermission Glinka talked with the amateur pianist Elizaveta Palibina about *Ruslan* and about Liszt. Glinka told Palibina that at the moment he was finishing the dances for the third act, and he complained that "these cursed dances" were giving him a lot of trouble. When Palibina asked him what his opinion of Liszt was, Glinka "without the slightest difficulty answered that Liszt played some things exceptionally well, like no one else in the world, but other things he played unbearably, with totally inappropriate expression, dragging tempos, and embellishing others' works—even those of Chopin, Beethoven, Weber and Bach—with often tasteless, worthless, vacuous ornamentation of his own" (V. Stasov, "Liszt, Schumann, and Berlioz in Russia," SPb., 1896, p. 9; "The School of Jurisprudence Forty Years Ago," in Stasov, *Izbr.*, v. 3, p. 412 and v. 2, p. 378).

9 April

Glinka attended Liszt's first musical matinee in the Vielgorskys' salon (*Sov. muzyka*, 1937, no. 8). That day after the concert, Glinka had dinner with the Serovs. "Of course there was much talk about Liszt. While granting the strength and facility of his fingers, Glinka did not approve of his idea of playing orchestral works on the piano, for example the overture to *Guillaume Tell* and Beethoven's symphonies. 'These are pieces which demand orchestral sonority. The piano does not bear comparison to the orchestra in this respect.'" Serov asked Glinka's opinion about the overture to *Guillaume Tell* itself, to which Glinka answered: "It is one of Rossini's unimportant fabrications, a saccharine copy of Beethoven's Pastoral symphony. I don't even like the opera. It is too obvious that it was written for Paris." "After dinner Glinka spoke with Aleksandr Kireev about the approaching production of *Ruslan*. He asked him to expedite arrangements for the small bells tuned 'in a scale.' 'In the fourth act they serve to entertain Miss Lyudmila [Glinka said], while the silver and gold trees "chime." It is already written, but I must have bells of the right tone. . . .' Kireev promised to try and praised Roller's scenery." Glinka "did not remain long" that evening at the Serovs, but rushed off to hear Liszt's performance of *Ruslan*, which he "was to play . . . *à livre ouvert*" (Serov, *Vosp.*, p. 86).

Glinka provided the consistory with Shulevina's new address: "In Mr. Semyon Mikhaylov Khromov's apartment, which is located in the third Admiralty section of the fourth ward, Shterich's house, no. 84."

In the "Musical News" section of *Rus. invalid,* no. 81, there is an announcement of Osip and Anna Petrov's forthcoming concert on 10 April, when they are to perform works by Glinka.

Glinka attended a party at Odoevsky's, at which Liszt, "to everyone's amazement, played *à livre ouvert* several numbers from *Ruslan* from the handwritten score . . . which no one knew as yet, without missing a note" (*Zap.;* Serov, *Vosp.,* p. 86).
[According to Serov, Liszt's performance of *Ruslan* occurred at Vielgorsky's.]

10 April

The Petrovs' concert in the Hall of the Commercial Society. Petrova performed Glinka's *"Zhavoronok," "Kolybel'naia pesnia,"* and Barcarolle (*Lit. gaz.,* 5 April 1842; *Rus. invalid,* 9 April 1842).

In *Journal d'Odessa,* no. 29, under *Odessa, 9 avril,* there is an announcement of a performance of an aria from *A Life for the Tsar* on 12 April (which aria is not indicated).

Between 5 and 11 April

"Liszt had dinner at my house with Vielgorsky, Odoevsky, and Glinka. He played *à livre ouvert* . . . from *Ruslan and Lyudmila,* after which Glinka sang for him . . . [*'V krovi gorit'*]. I translated Pushkin's poem. Liszt closed the piano and said, 'After this we should hear no more. It is a pearl of poetry and music.'" (A. Smirnova, *Zapiski,* part 2, SPb. 1879, p. 36).

11 April

Liszt's second concert in the Hall of Nobility (*Sov. muzyka,* 1937, no. 8).

12 April

An aria from *A Life for the Tsar* is performed in a concert in Odessa (*Journal d'Odessa,* 10 April 1842).

Middle of April (?)

"When the individual roles and choral parts were ready, I set to work learning my music."

After 19 (?) April

Serov visited Glinka, who "was at home, asleep in his dressing gown on the sofa." Glinka began to complain about his health. "Soon, however, the conversation turned from the realm of physiology and hygiene to music and the opera in preparation." Glinka complained: "I am tired, sir, from all the activity, and take note that there still has not been one orchestral rehearsal. However, our orchestra has spirit. My hope rests on the orchestra." Serov then said: "Besides the things you have already shown us in the opera, I have overheard that there are a great number of 'harmonic' novelties, things completely out of the ordinary." Glinka responded: "There are a few. For example, there is a scale made up of six whole tones. Its effect is very strange, and I have used it wherever Chernomor appears. In general I have tried to use even familiar effects differently from others. I have a storm, though it's not at all like in *Barbière*, or 'Tell,' or other operas. My wind will howl like it does in a Russian chimney." After this conversation Glinka and Serov took a walk on the Admiralty Boulevard. "Among the crowd, naturally, there were many who were acquaintances of Mikhail Ivanovich. He would bow to them very politely, but seriously. He even met the singer Leonov. After talking to him for about five minutes about the upcoming rehearsals, when Leonov had left, Glinka remarked . . . , 'You see, sir, Finn's part doesn't come easily to him. I have gone through the ballad with him nearly a hundred times, and he still does not remember the words'" (Serov, *Vosp.*, p. 86).

20 April

Serov writes to Vladimir Stasov: "Russian history does not include anything fit for the operatic stage, which is the source of Glinka's error. Why did he elect to take *Ivan Susanin* as the theme for his first opera, or rather, why did he agree to write music for this unproductive theme. . . . All the shortcomings of *A Life for the Tsar* are related to the subject" (MN 1, p. 173).

22 April

Liszt's third concert in Engelgardt Hall (V. Stasov, "Liszt, Schumann, and Berlioz in Russia," in Stasov, *Izbr.*, v. 3, p. 414).

25 April

Liszt participates in a charity concert in the Hall of Nobility for the benefit of the private schools of the Women's Patriotic Society (*Sov. muzyka*, 1937, no. 8).

26 April

In *Lit. gaz.,* no. 16, under "Overview of theatrical events of the past year and of new items in the coming year," it speaks of the failure of *Prince Kholmsky*.

A request by Glinka to the consistory: "It has come to my attention that my wife Maria Petrova, who is living in the Liteiny section of Furshtadskaya Street in a house belonging to the Annensky Lutheran Church, despite the . . . statement given to her, intends in the very near future to leave St. Petersburg, to where, I do not know. Since I consider that I am entirely correct in our divorce case and envision that my wife's intended absence will only delay the settlement of the case, I most humbly ask . . . that my wife's departure from Petersburg before the decision of our case be prevented."

27 April

"Glinka entered a petition to have his wife's departure from St. Petersburg prohibited before the conclusion of their case." Glinka's request was granted (LGIA, coll. 19).

28 April

Liszt's fourth concert in Engelgardt Hall (*Sov. muzyka,* 1937, no. 8).

30 April

Liszt participated in a concert in the Hall of Nobility for the benefit of the St. Petersburg Children's Hospital (*Rus. invalid,* 28 April 1842).

April

Glinka was present at a dinner in Liszt's honor at Senkovsky's. Also present were Karl Bryullov, Nestor Kukolnik, the painter Moller, Servais, and "all the musical celebrities then residing in St. Petersburg" (Osip Ivanovich Senkovsky, "Biographical Notes of His Wife," SPb., 1858, p. 142).
[Senkovsky's wife was Adel Senkovskaya, sister of Fedor Ral.].

1 May

Maria Petrovna protested Glinka's charge (LGIA, coll. 19).

2 May

Glinka applied to the committee of the Association for Charity to Poor Children of the Imperial Philanthropic Society for acceptance "as an active member of the association."

3 May

Glinka facsimile (album annotation?) with the date: "M. Glinka, 3 May 1842, SPb." (*Gazeta Gattsuka,* 1885, no. 21).

4 May

Maria Petrovna, because of illness, requests permission "to spend the summer in the cities of Odessa and Kharkov, following her doctors' advice" and to entrust the reading of pleadings to her attorney, V. Pogrebov (LGIA, coll. 19). [She was granted permission on 22 May.]

5 May

Glinka sold the romances *"Ia pomniu chudnoe mgnoven'e"* and *"Kak sladko s toboiu mne byt' "* to the publisher Bernard for 300 rubles (Glinka's receipt).

Liszt's fifth concert in Engelgardt Hall (*Sev. pchela,* 4 May 1842).

10 May

Morning concert by Liszt in the Hall of Nobility (*Sev. pchela,* 10 May 1842).

11 May

In a humorous letter to Ludwig Heydenreich, Glinka asks that the pharmacy be removed from the hall of the Bolshoi Theater, where, on the 14th of May, rehearsals for *Ruslan and Lyudmila* are to begin. He writes that smells and even the sight of medicine "excite sensitive nerves" and "inspire fear and panic in anxious imaginations."

14 May

First rehearsal of *Ruslan and Lyudmila* in the Bolshoi Theater (ltr. to L. Heydenreich, 11 May 1842).

15 May

Liszt's last concert in the Hall of Nobility (*Sev. pchela,* 15 May 1842).

Between 4 April and 16 May

Besides the Vielgorskys and Odoevsky, Glinka was also with Liszt at Evdokia Rostopchina's and Elizaveta Palibina's. "Whenever we met socially . . . Liszt always asked me to sing one or two of my romances for him. He liked '*V krovi gorit*' best of all. In turn he would play something by Chopin or a fashionable piece by Beethoven for me."

Glinka's opinion of Liszt's concerts: "Despite my general and partially warranted enthusiasm, I can still . . . fully account for the impression which *Liszt's playing* made on me. On the whole he played Chopin mazurkas, nocturnes, etudes, and anything that was brilliant and fashionable very nicely, though with highly mannered nuances. . . . However, his performances of Bach and the Beethoven symphony which he had transcribed (*transcrité*) for piano were (in my opinion) less satisfactory. In Beethoven sonatas, and generally in classical music, his playing lacked the appropriate character, and there was a hacking quality in the way he struck the keyboard. His performance of Hummel's Septet showed a certain contempt, and, in my opinion, Hummel played it incomparably better and *more simply*. The Beethoven E-flat concerto he performed much more satisfactorily. In general, I could not compare Liszt's playing in terms of polish with that of Field, Karl Meier, or even Thalberg, especially *in scales*."

16 May

Liszt's second concert in the Vielgorskys' salon. After the concert, at 5:30, there was dinner, at which Glinka, Liszt, Henselt, Lenz, Lichtenthal, Bulgakov, Lvov, Meier, Herke, Arkady Kutuzov, Gedeonov, Matvey Vielgorsky, Ferzing, Etter, Sollogub, Wylde, Romberg, V. Kutuzov, Vyazemsky, Mikhail Vielgorsky, Odoevsky, and M. Rheinhardt were present. "Ferzing performed the father's [Mikhail Vielgorsky's] couplets to words by Apollinaria Mikhaylovna [Vielgorsky's daughter, whose married name was Venevitinova] accompanied by the orchestra of the cavalier guards and a chorus of all those present. It was repeated three times and was a resounding success. A speech by Liszt. Departure by steamer at 7:30 in the evening" (Annotations by M. M. Vielgorsky in the margins of the program, in *Sov. muzyka,* 1937, no. 8). Liszt's departure from Petersburg (*Sev. pchela,* 16 May 1842).

24 May

Serov writes to V. Stasov that he has many subjects to write about, among them *"Russian* music and Glinka" (MN 1, p. 186).

25 May

The score of *A Life for the Tsar* is sent from the Bolshoi Theater in St. Petersburg to Moscow to be copied for Moscow performance (TsGIA, coll. 497, no. 9002).

Spring

Together with the chief costumier Gaydukov, Glinka "surveyed the immense wardrobe which belonged to the Theater Directorate. Together we established which costumes had to made new and which could be restored and altered. The costumes for the principals were made according to Karl Bryullov's directions. Bryullov also passed on his ideas about sets to Roller, who had already done oil sketches of the scenery for *Ruslan and Lyudmila"* (*Zap.*). "These sketches were so good, especially the scene of Chernomor's enchanted castle, that the rank of Academician was conferred on Roller for this" (N. Kukolnik's annotation, *ibid.*). [The sets were not done from these drawings (ltr. from V. Engelgardt to N. Findeyzen, 31 December 1909/13 January 1910, in *Sov. muzyka*, 1953, no. 9, p. 48). Roller's drawings are in the All-Union Pushkin Museum.]

End of Spring, Beginning of Summer

"Rumors about the production at the Bolshoi Theater of M. I. Glinka's opera *Ruslan and Lyudmila* gathered force. At the same time the expectant public's impatience increased, since they had already gotten rather bored with *Askold's Tomb"* (P. Sokolov, *Vosp.*, p. 213).

5 June

Sofia Aledinskaya performed Vanya's scene from *A Life for the Tsar* with orchestra under Glinka's direction. Glinka inscribed the romance *"Pour un moment"* in her album. It is signed and dated, *"M. Glinka le 5 juin 1842"* (S. Zybina-Aledinskaya's annotation indicates that Glinka copied the romance in the album after her performance of *"Ty ne plach', sirotinushka"* [Do not cry, little orphan] with orchestra under the direction of "our own great Glinka. Sofia Zybina, née Aledinskaya, St. Petersburg, 1896," in *L.*, p. 230).

Beginning of Summer

Glinka had dinner for the balletmaster Titus, in order to "come to an agreement" with him about the dances in *Ruslan*. Also present at the dinner were Mikhail and Stepan Gedeonov, Bulgakov, and Pavel Kamensky. The latter, "in our opinion . . . danced the lezghinka excellently. Since I had used eastern melodies in composing the dance music for the fourth act, I wanted Titus, insofar as possible, to fashion the dances in an eastern style. . . . The dinner was a success, and the wine had its effect. After dinner Kamensky danced the lezghinka, which the Frenchman Titus did not especially like, though he agreed to set the dance according to my wishes." Soon after this Titus invited Glinka to dinner at his dacha on Krestovsky Island. "After that he began composing the dances, and I was glad to go to the school to understand his requirements and to rework what might require change."

"Glinka was preoccupied with the decoration of Chernomor's garden. 'I'm afraid,' he said to me, 'that they'll draw me pretty little balconies with little roses, when I would rather have *strange* trees and flowers.' . . . Before me lay a book by the famous Ehrenberg with drawings of microscopic plants and animals. 'What's that?' Glinka asked. 'Your Chernomor's garden,' I answered jokingly. After sorting through the drawings, we chose a number of them, and . . . the scenery for Chernomor's garden . . . was made up entirely of microscopic plants we had gotten from the famous entomologist's book, magnified, of course, to monstrous proportions" (Odoevsky, *Vosp.*, p. 104).

"I led a very pleasant life then. In the morning I reworked the dances and a few other unfinished places in the opera. At noon I went to rehearsals in the theater hall or to the school. . . . I had dinner with Mother and spent the time after dinner with our family. In the evening I usually went to the theater, where for the most part I remained backstage."

9 June

Glinka acknowledged that he had been told of the consistory's decision to allow Maria Petrovna to leave Petersburg (LGIA, coll. 19).

25 June

Performance of *A Life for the Tsar* in the Bolshoi Theater (*Sev. pchela*, 25 June 1842).

27 June

Remarks in the "Astrakhan Letters" (signed "S.") in *Dagerrotip,* parts 9–11, about preparations in Petersburg for the production of *Ruslan and Lyudmila* in the Bolshoi Theater (d.c.a.).

29 June

"During the holidays my mother and sister took me to Elagin" (ltr. to N. Stepanov, 2 July 1842).

2 July

Glinka writes to Nikolay Stepanov: "I cannot brag about my life. Besides heat and dust, no one is in the city. Everyone has left . . . for the present (i.e., for the holidays). Rehearsals have stopped, but to make up for it I will return to them with even greater frenzy."
[The year has been established according to the calendar and content. This is Glinka's postscript to a letter dictated to him by an unknown woman (the signature is struck out).]

3 July

Glinka attends the debuts of Mikhaylov-Ostroumov and Gulak-Artemovsky in the Bolshoi Theater (ltr. to N. Stepanov, 2 July 1842).
[Both artists, who had just returned from Italy, "made their successful debuts on the Russian stage in Donizetti's *Lucia di Lammermoor*" (Serov, *Vosp.*, p. 93).]

4 July

Glinka makes a trip to Rybatskoe to see Vladislavlev.

6 July

Return from Vladislavlev's (ltr. to N. Stepanov, 2 July 1842).

8 July

Glinka is at the Bolshoi Theater, where Mikhaylov-Ostroumov and Gulak-Artemovsky appear for the second time in Donizetti's opera *Belisario* (*Sev. pchela,* 8 July 1842).

21 July

Glinka received a summons to the consistory "regarding his divorce case" for 24 July, for which he acknowledged receipt.

24 July

Glinka appeared in the consistory, where, together with Maria Petrovna's attorney, "they promised to appear" on 29 June.

29 July

Glinka and Fedorov appeared in the consistory, which was acknowledged.

Beginning of August

In the section "Literary Chronicle" in *Bib-ka dlia chteniia*, v. 53, it says: "Glinka's new opera *Ruslan and Lyudmila* has been accepted by the theater and is being studied diligently. The artists and connoisseurs participating in the rehearsals are responding with uniform enthusiasm to the music. In all likelihood the first performance will not be soon, but sometime in the month of November."

13 August

The first quartet rehearsal of *Ruslan and Lyudmila* took place in Evgenia Andreevna Glinka's apartment. The participants included first violinists, Mes and Albrecht (conductor); second violin, Weitzmann; cello, Shubert; and bass, Memel. Glinka forgot the name of the violist. Also present were the theorist Hunke and the conductor Ral (who had done the orchestration for the military stage orchestra). "During the rehearsal I played the woodwind parts at the piano. There were no voices. The rehearsal was very successful, and when we had finished, Mother treated my coworkers splendidly" (*Zap.;* Albrecht's diary, in *Muz. letop.,* coll. 2, p. 73). "The first orchestral rehearsal of the entire opera with the composer was the 'proof rehearsal.' The orchestra consisted of a small number of our finest artists, who were both outstanding performers and critics. The composer had the voice parts at the piano. This was the first time they had the opportunity to hear the music in its entirety themselves and to evaluate it properly. One must understand what 'proof rehearsals' are. Ordinarily at these preliminary examinations the most remarkable operas seem . . . so complicated and obscure that initially even the performers do not fully understand the composer's intention and have to strain to see the beauty of the piece. In this case things went just the opposite. . . . From the outset the unusual beauty of this unusual work so struck the performers, its effect was so unanticipated, and their amazement so great, that in their enthusiasm they threw their instruments aside to indulge their spontaneous excitement. It is impossible to describe the impression that this first acquaintance with *Ruslan and Lyudmila* made on them. They could find nothing in musical literature to compare with this marvelous, original, powerful music. Naturally their exclamations were such as would have satisfied the most exacting self esteem" (O. Senkovsky, "Musical Novelties," in *Bib-ka dlia chteniia,* 1842, v. 54, p. 45).

19 August

Report from the stage manager for the opera troupe, Lebedev, to the office of the Theater Directorate: "I have the honor of presenting . . . an opera entitled *Ruslan and Lyudmila,* which I most humbly request you to send to the censorship committee" (*L.,* p. 231).

Second Half of August

"The rehearsals began, at first in halls and then on the stage. At that time it became apparent that many of the opera's numbers needed to be shortened. For example, Bayan's second song, *'Est' pustynnyi krai'* [There is a deserted place], had to be cut from the introduction, and likewise the entire *final development (développement et péroraison)* of the main theme

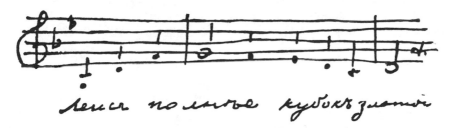

subsequently had to be eliminated. In the finale to the first act, the chorus to Lel in B-flat major and $\frac{5}{4}$ meter had to be shortened. In the second act, Finn's ballad seemed too long, but I did not shorten it, and audiences subsequently got used to hearing it as I had originally written it. The Head's chorus, that is, the finale to the second act, which I had so counted on . . . they sang . . . so inaccurately that I could not bear to listen to it myself. In the third act, in place of . . . an entr'acte, it was essential to begin directly with the chorus *'Lozhitsia v pole mrak nochnoi'* [The gloom of night lay over the field]. . . . In the finale, the trio *'Zachem liubit', zachem stradat''* [Why love, why suffer] had to be

excluded, because it slowed down the progress of the drama. . . . In the finale
. . . to [the fourth] and last acts, many things likewise had to be abbreviated.
Despite these circumstances, the stage manager M. S. Lebedev guaranteed that
the opera would go well. I wrote the overture directly in score, quite often
during rehearsals in the producer's studio."

["Glinka always composed directly for orchestra, but in his head, and he did not write anything
down until it was all ready in his head. Only then did he proceed to write the final draft, without
corrections or erasures. He loved the 'transparency of the full score' (his words), that is, no extraneous notes" (ltr. from V. Engelgardt to V. Stasov, 22 February/7 March 1906, in *Sbornik pamiati
Glinki* [Glinka Memorial Collection], p. 553).]

20 August

The office of the Imperial Theaters forwarded the libretto of *Ruslan and Lyudmila*
to the censorship committee (*L.*, p. 231). That same day authorization was
granted "for the St. Petersburg theaters" by the censor Mikhail Gedeonov (Lu-
nacharsky Library of the Theater, published in A. Gosenpud, *Russkii opernyi
teatr XIX veka* [Russian 19th-century opera theater] (1836–56), *L.*, 1969, p.
140).

[Lebedev's production notes appear on the censorship's copy of the libretto.]

22 August

Production of *A Life for the Tsar* in the Bolshoi Theater (*Sev. pchela,* 22 August
1842).

Report from the wardrobe master Zakaspysky to the office of Imperial Theaters
concerning shipment to Moscow of costumes for the opera *A Life for the Tsar*.

25 August

Order from the chief of the office of the Imperial Theaters Kireev to the wardrobe master Zakaspysky to exclude from the inventory of costumes being sent
to Moscow those for *A Life for the Tsar* (*L.*, p. 231).

End of August

Glinka encountered Serov "in Lisenko's home again." Glinka "spoke about the
work with which he was occupied at the time. 'Last week, sir, I finished the
overture to *Ruslan.* I've taken such a tempo that it flies full sail, a cheerful
presto, like Mozart's overture to *Figaro,* and also in D major. Of course the
character is different, it's Russian. It begins and ends with clapping. In the
middle there are "troubles" for the cellos, a cantabile passage in the upper

register. There are also some "nasty" places in the development. You'll like it!'" (Serov, *Vosp.,* p. 87).

31 August

Glinka acknowledged a summons to the consistory "at 10 o'clock in the morning" on 4 September. Maria Petrovna's former housemaid, Ekaterina Shulevina, testified under oath that she had taken Vasilchikov's letters from Maria Petrovna's chest of drawers. "These letters were brought from Mr. Vasilchikov to Mrs. Glinka and her answers . . . delivered by Mr. Vasilchikov's house serfs" (LGIA, coll. 19).

[The originals of Vasilchikov's letters were taken from the divorce case file, but excerpts from them are preserved in the "abstract" of the case. In them Vasilchikov refers to Maria Petrovna as his wife and signs his name "your husband Kolya."]

Summer

Glinka "spent the time very pleasantly" with Anna Tarnovskaya, Maria Krzhisevich, and Ekaterina Kern (*Zap.*).

Beginning of Autumn

Pavlovsk. Glinka quarrelled with Bulgarin "over nonsense . . . Bulgarin was whispering something in Hermann's ear while the audience was waiting for one of its favorite pieces. I half audibly said to Hermann jokingly: 'Don't listen to him. He doesn't understand anything about music.' Bulgarin got furious over my joke. . . . A quarrel ensued, and since it was about music, then naturally it was easy for me to show that he did not understand our art. The argument dragged on, and in the presence of a large crowd."

2 September

Memorandum signed by the Director of the Third Section, Dubelt, to the Directorate of Imperial Theaters: "The Third Section of His Majesty's chancellery has the honor herewith to return the piece entitled *Ruslan and Lyudmila* approved for performance." Beneath is a note from Gedeonov: "Piece forwarded to Mr. Lebedev, stage manager for the opera troupe, on 5 September" (*L.,* p. 232).

Announcement in *Mosk. ved.,* no. 70: "In the near future . . . *A Life for the Tsar,* an original opera in 4 acts with epilog, choruses, and dances," will be given for the first time in the Bolshoi Theater. "The music is by M. I. Glinka, the words by Baron E. F. Rozen."

Beginning of September

Senkovsky's account of the quartet rehearsal of *Ruslan and Lyudmila* appears in *Bib-ka dlia chteniia,* vol. 54, in the section headed "Miscellany, Musical News." "At the moment the primary object of curiosity and conversation in the musical world is Glinka's new opera. Everyone is asking: 'Whatever is *Ruslan and Lyudmila*? When will it come out? . . . and what will it be like?' Everyone hopes to hear an opinion corresponding to general expectations or to their own preferences. . . . A great musical and poetic festival is being prepared for us. A native composer of genius and a native poet of genius appear together. This . . . has not yet happened in recent music." In the same notice there is the comment that "the active and diligent publisher 'Odeum' is issuing the opera in piano transcriptions for two- and four-hands, with voice and without. . . . These editions, prepared under the supervision of the composer, will appear shortly."

4 September

Glinka appeared in the consistory (receipt of summons from 31 August 1842).

5 September

First orchestral rehearsal of *Ruslan and Lyudmila* in the theater. Mes conducted. The first seven numbers were played through (Albrecht's diary, in *Muz. letop.,* coll. 2, p. 73).

In *Mosk. ved.,* no. 71, there is a notice of the first "subscription" performance on 7 September of *A Life for the Tsar* and of a second "non-subscription" performance on 8 September. A list of the principal performers is attached.

6 September

Rehearsal of *Ruslan* (Albrecht's diary, in *Muz. letop.,* 1923, coll. 2, p. 73).

7 September

First performance of *A Life for the Tsar* in the Moscow Bolshoi Theater. The performers were Kurov (Susanin), Petrova II (Vanya), Leonova (Antonida), and Bantyshev (Sobinin). "Scenery representing the village of Domnino on the river Shacha and a wild forest covered in snow done by Shenyan. Red Square with a view of the Kremlin, by Serkov. Dances composed by Peshkov."

8 September

Performance of *A Life for the Tsar* in the Moscow Bolshoi Theater (*Mosk. ved.*, 5 September 1842).

10 September

Memorandum from the Director of Imperial Theaters Gedeonov to the Minister of the Imperial Court about obtaining gifts of value for Serkov and Shenyan for their scenery for the Bolshoi Theater. Gedeonov mentions in particular the sets for *A Life for the Tsar* (*L.*, p. 233).

Performance of *A Life for the Tsar* in the Bolshoi Theater in Moscow (*Mosk. ved.*, 9 September 1842).

12 September

Notice in *Mosk. ved.*, no. 73, that the libretto for *A Life for the Tsar* is available in F. Pavlov's bookstore.

13 September

In *Lit. gaz.*, no. 36, under "Miscellany, Various News Items," daily rehearsals of *Ruslan and Lyudmila* are reported. "By the end of October or beginning of November we shall finally hear the new work by our leading composer. As connoisseurs of the matter and musicians affirm, this new opera is much superior to *A Life for the Tsar*. This demonstrates that our esteemed composer neither imitates others nor rests on his laurels, but continues to strive for perfection. Thus can one recognize the true artist."

Performance of *A Life for the Tsar* in the Bolshoi Theater in Moscow (*Mosk. ved.*, 12 September 1842).

14 and 15 September

Rehearsals of *Ruslan* (Albrecht's diary, in *Muz. letop.*, 1923, coll. 2, p. 73).

16 September

Memorandum to the Director of Theaters, Gedeonov, from His Majesty's chancellery presenting diamond rings to the set designers Serkov and Shenyan for the sets to *A Life for the Tsar* in the Bolshoi Theater (*L.*, p. 233).

18 September

The Synod's decree confirming the decision by the consistory not to annul Glinka's marriage. Attached are Glinka's refutation as well as the attorney Fedorov's accusation of Glinka's "adultery" with Shulevina and "indecorous behavior." Vasilchikov was transferred to the Vyatsk home garrison as an ensign and required to do confession for his attempts to "persuade" Maria Petrovna to marry him (LGIA, coll. 19).

19 September

In *Mosk. ved.*, no. 75, there is an announcement stating that Gresser's music store has the following piano arrangements from the opera *A Life for the Tsar* for sale: *Variations sur un air favori de l'opéra "Zhizn' za tsaria,"* by I. Duvernois; transcription for piano of the Orphan's song by V. Frakman; and the Polonaise by Aleksandr Dubuque.

20 September

In *Lit. gaz.*, no. 37, under "Miscellany, Moscow News Items," there is a report of the Moscow premiere of *A Life for the Tsar*. "It was unusually successful and is being given every other day. Mme Petrova, a young alumna of our theater school who performed the part of Vanya, was received with particular enthusiasm. . . . Among many beautiful sets, those of Serkov depicting Red Square with a view of the Kremlin were especially well received. A long time ago we predicted such a success for Glinka's opera, but, regrettably, until now Verstovsky's operas did not allow room for it on the Moscow stage. We are pleased that our prediction has finally come true."
[The Petrova referred to here is Anfisa Petrova ("the second").]

21 and 22 September

Rehearsals of *Ruslan*. "Solovieva tried her numbers on the 22nd and announced after the rehearsal that she was in no condition to sing. Thus Stepanova will be singing" (K. Albrecht's diary, in *Muz. letop.*, 1923, coll. 2, p. 73).

25 September

In the section headed "Moscow Chronicle" in *Moskvityanin,* part 5, no. 9, there are two articles under the common title "The Opera *A Life for the Tsar* in Moscow," the first by Nikolay Kashevsky and the second, by an unidentified author. The first analyzes the opera in detail and says in conclusion: "Both as a man and as a Slav the composer of *A Life for the Tsar*, more than anything else, has brought *profound sentiment* to our dramatic music. The *doleful melodies* of his opera, accompanied by endless, prolonged orchestral sonorities, are especially beautiful. As an artist he is better known for melodic development, unique transitions, and the sequence of sections than he is for motivic wealth and variety. It was sweet indeed for us to hear this opera and with every sound to feel in our hearts that it was created by a profound Russian soul and worked out by a genuine artist whose talent had been developed in the best tradition provided by modern Europe." In the second article it says: "The richness and musical mastery, which the beauty of the work made accessible to everyone, created a natural attraction to this truly beautiful and worthy work of art" (d.c.a.).

26 September

Rehearsal of *Ruslan* (K. Albrecht's diary, in *Muz. letop.*, 1923, coll. 2, p. 73).

There is a report in *Sev. pchela*, no. 215, "Miscellany: Journalistic Odds and Ends," saying that Moscow, which "until now had not heard the opera *A Life for the Tsar* . . . is now enjoying the production. . . . The opera has had a huge success in Moscow."

Performance of *A Life for the Tsar* in the Bolshoi Theater in Moscow (*Mosk. ved.*, 26 September 1842).

30 September

Under the heading "Drama Telegraph" in the journal *Repertuar i Panteon*, part 19, there is a statement from Moscow (signed "C.") about the reception of *A Life for the Tsar*. "C." complains of the many cuts made by the Moscow conductor Iogannis. Nonetheless, he concludes, "I had heard *A Life for the Tsar* in Petersburg, but I must confess that even here the opera has gone very successfully and smoothly. It was produced like no other opera in Moscow ever has been" (d.c.a.).

6 October

Evgenia Glinka writes to Maria Stuneeva: "Michel is very anxious about his opera, whether it will be given at the end of this month or the beginning of next month" (*L.*, p. 235).

7 October

Orchestral rehearsal of *Ruslan and Lyudmila*.

8 October

Quartet rehearsal of *Ruslan and Lyudmila*.

10 October

Orchestral rehearsal of *Ruslan and Lyudmila*.

11 October

Quartet rehearsal of *Ruslan* (V. Latyshev's diary, in *Muz. starina,* 1903, inst. 2, p. 173).

12 October

Performance of *A Life for the Tsar* in the Bolshoi Theater in Moscow (*Mosk. ved.,* 10 October 1842).

13 October

Glinka wrote the romance *"Liubliu tebia, milaia roza"* [I love you, dear rose]. On the manuscript is the inscription, "To my friend K. Bulgakov, for various illusory things and other such expressions of feeling. 1842, the 14th of October" (*L.,* p. 235).
[In the *Zapiski,* Glinka names his boarding school companion Samarin as the author of the text, without indicating either first name or initials. Petr Kvashnin-Samarin, who entered the boarding school in 1817 but did not graduate, went to school with Glinka. Konstantin Bulgakov asserts that the text was written by Mikhail Gedeonov. In the published version of the romance in *Le Nouvelliste* (June, 1843), the author of the text is not indicated at all.]

15 October

Rehearsal of *Ruslan* (K. Albrecht's diary, in *Muz. letop.,* 1923, coll. 2, p. 73).

16 October

Quartet rehearsal of *Ruslan* (V. Latyshev's diary, in *Muz. starina,* 1903, inst. 2, p. 173).

E. A. Elagina writes from Moscow to A. A. Elagin: "We attended the theater on Monday and saw Glinka's opera *A Life for the Tsar*. Petrova ["the second"] sang and thrilled me immensely. She both sings and acts well" (Livanova, Protopopov, *Glinka 1*, p. 192).

17 October

Orchestral rehearsal of *Ruslan* (V. Latyshev's diary, in *Muz. starina*, 1903, inst. 2, p. 173).

18 October

In the section headed "Various News Items" in *Lit. gaz.*, no. 4, there is a report about the rehearsals of *Ruslan and Lyudmila* and Roller's sets. "There is an exceptionally large number of effective places in the music of the opera *Ruslan and Lyudmila*. Finn's ballad, which bears the clear imprint of Finnish folk melodies, is especially fine. The head of the bogatyr Polkan [*sic!*], which likewise plays a not unimportant role in the opera, is very cleverly and effectively characterized by the author. . . . The splendor of the costumes and staging exceeds in sumptuousness anything we have ever seen in the theater. After all this, could one possibly doubt that the opera will have a huge success? Perhaps M. I. Glinka, with his successes, will awaken Russian music from its slumber so that it can go hand-in-hand with the rest of Russian art, which advances daily like the magic boots in the fairy tales." There is also a report of the success of *A Life for the Tsar* in Moscow, "where until now they had not even suspected that Russian music superior to *Askold's Tomb* or a composer equal in genius to Verstovsky might even exist. After the *vaudeville* operas of Moscow arrangement, *A Life for the Tsar* probably seems a little too serious and even boring to Muscovites. However, it is becoming apparent that with each performance they finally are beginning to understand the music and take pleasure in it."

21 October

In *Mosk. ved.*, no. 84, in a notice entitled "At the Bolshoi Theater," there is an announcement about Anfisa Petrova's final performance in the role of Vanya on 25 October.

23 October

Orchestral rehearsal of *Ruslan* (V. Latyshev's diary, in *Muz. starina*, 1903, inst. 2, p. 173).

Odoevsky's arrival from abroad (ltr. from P. Pletnev to Yakov Grot, 24 October 1842, in the book *Perepiska Ya. Grota s P. Pletnevym* [Correspondence of Ya. Grot and P. Pletnev], vol. 1, SPb., 1846, p. 625).

25 October

Orchestral rehearsal of *Ruslan* (V. Latyshev's diary, in *Muz. starina,* 1903, inst. 2, p. 173).

Odoevsky heard *Ruslan and Lyudmila* for the first time at rehearsal. "I was surprised and enchanted by the freshness of the melodic writing and the originality and novelty of the vocal and instrumental constructions. . . . I sensed that he had matured, that his genius had gained power, and that the musical issues themselves and their solution were of a higher order than in his first opera, despite all its great artistry" (V. Odoevsky, "Two Letters to V. Stasov," in EIT, 1892/93).

Performance of *A Life for the Tsar* in the Bolshoi Theater in Moscow. For the final time before her departure "the role of Vanya in the opera . . ." was performed by "Mme Petrova ["the second"], actress of the Imperial St. Petersburg Theater" (*Mosk. ved.,* 21 October 1842).

October

Because of Leonova's illness, Glinka performed Finn's ballad on stage at one of the rehearsals of "Ruslan," "so that the orchestra could rehearse."

End of October

Serov was with Glinka at a rehearsal of *Ruslan and Lyudmila.* The first three acts were being rehearsed. "They began immediately with the introduction, without the overture. I [Serov] was struck by the impression that the choruses, Bayan's song (that is, the first couplets) . . . Lyudmila's and Ruslan's replies, and Farlaf and Ratmir made on me. . . . The nurses' chorus and the chorus to Lel opened up horizons for Russian music broader even than all the music of *A Life for the Tsar.* A thunderclap opens the incomparably mysterious adagio in canon *'Kakoe chudnoe mgnoven'e'* [What a marvelous moment]. It was all a marvel of musical beauty . . . and there were new marvels in the second act! The symphonic interlude, in which some hostile sounds flash by, is a virtual phantasmagoria of monsters and apparitions. Immediately then comes Finn's ballad, which I already knew from Glinka's performances at parties. . . . My enthusiasm was immeasurable. . . . The composer himself sat in an armchair beside me and, as usual whenever he was not playing or singing himself, prevented me from listening by talking to me all the time. . . . The old man Tosi, in Farlaf and Naina's scene, was quite amusing because of his mangled Italian pronunciation of Russian. . . . This distracted one's attention somewhat. . . . In Farlaf's rondo Tosi's voice was not audible at all, but again the orchestra was like an entire symphony! . . . O. A. Petrov was not totally satisfied with Ruslan's aria, and in my presence he discussed it with Glinka. Afterwards he sang it lethargically and unwillingly. . . . Ruslan's scene with the giant's head was incomprehensible without the sets. I did not understand anything. The chorus members bunched up in the middle of the stage singing *in unison* and completely out of tune. Again, marvels in the orchestra. This was the place with the howling wind of a Russian storm, which the composer had told me about. . . . By the third act Glinka got on stage, and during the Persian chorus he walked around among the singers and tried to explain to them the subtlety and delicacy of sound necessary for the performance of this piece. . . . At this rehearsal the first verses of the chorus were sung by three selected soloists, rather than the entire chorus. Their beautiful voices had a marvelous effect. . . . Mme Lileeva, who was making her debut, sang Gorislava. Of course, so far as the meaning was concerned, the impression she made was little like the enchanting effect that this aria had when Glinka sang it himself. Anna Petrova . . . who was suffering from a cold . . . only gave cues to the orchestra, but that allowed me to listen to the orchestra all I wanted to. . . . On this occasion they still were not rehearsing the dances. The third act finale was still quite unsteady and did not go without interruption. It was impossible to grasp the general flow of thought and the beauty of the music's development" (Serov, *Vosp.*, p. 88).

31 October

Orchestral rehearsal of *Ruslan* (V. Latyshev's diary, in *Muz. starina*, 1903, inst. 2, p. 173).

Senkovsky's response to *Ruslan and Lyudmila* appears in *Bib-ka dlia chteniia*, vol. 55, in the section headed "Musical News." "First several initial impressions. . . . What is the nature of this new music by Glinka? . . . We would recommend calling the genre *Russian Fairytale* [*russko-skazochnyi*]. All the exotic, original, utterly eastern fantasy of the Russian tale [*skazka*] is here in the story and sets as well as in the music. This is not a so-called *magic opera* [*volshebnaia opera*]. Glinka, who from the beginning has followed a distinct and unique path, had no intention of writing a *magic opera* following the examples of [the operas of Mozart and Weber]. This genre had already been exhausted. He very aptly selected a Russian tale. In Germany, 'the magical' takes the form of vagueness and mystery, of gloom, of clouds of superstition, and lofty inspiration. In the Russian fairytale, on the other hand, everything is bright, cheerful, playful, sharp, varied, unusual, and unexpected. For such a subject to be successful, the music must also include these qualities, and it is these very qualities which you will find here, developed to the highest degree and with great mastery. . . . It combines almost all types of music: eastern and western, Russian, Italian, German, Finnish, Tatar, Caucasian, Persian, Arabic, all of which come together in a most artistic and picturesque whole. . . . Nowhere else has Glinka shown such musical imagination, such mastery of technique, and such jubilant creative audacity in harmony and counterpoint as in the terrifying difficulties of this fairytale subject. . . . Here . . . everything is new: the use of instruments . . . their combination . . . even the entire musical framework is new. From the first numbers, one is immediately struck by the absence here of traditional operatic forms. . . . The composer . . . has lavishly scattered throughout the score special competitions among masses of sound. . . . He has rejected traditional, hackneyed transitions from one number to the next as well as routine openings and conventional endings." The article mentions Ral's great service in orchestrating the military music. "This opera opens such a wide spectrum and variety of artistic delights . . . that *Ruslan and Lyudmila* alone would suffice in itself to fill the winter, even if all our other musical pleasures let us down" (d.c.a.).

There is an announcement in *Mosk. ved.*, no. 87, that the tercet *"Ne tomi, rodimyi"* from *A Life for the Tsar* in a transcription for piano with variations by Gurilev as well as Vanya's song in a transcription for 7-stringed guitar are on sale in Müller and Grotrian's music store.

1 November

Performance of *A Life for the Tsar* in the Bolshoi Theater in Moscow. "In the opera the role of Susanin will be played by Mr. Lazarev and that of Vanya by Mme Mikhaylova" (*Mosk. ved.*, 31 October 1842).

3 November

Orchestral rehearsal of *Ruslan* (V. Latyshev's diary, in *Muz. starina*, 1903, inst. 2, p. 173).

Censor's authorization for publication of the libretto to *"Ruslan and Lyudmila. Grand magical opera in the manner of the Russian fairytale, in five acts. Music by M. I. Glinka. The plot from Pushkin's poem. St. Petersburg, typography by Eduard Prats, 1842."*

4 November

In *Mosk. ved.*, no. 88, there is an announcement that the soprano and contralto duet *"Somnenie"* as well as three mazurkas from *Kachucha, Les Sylphides,* and *A Life for the Tsar* in piano transcription by Dewitte are available in Yuly Gresser's music store.

5 November

Glinka provided an affidavit stating that his summons from the consistory of 2 November had been explained to him.

Beginning of November

"Out of desire to deflect any new unpleasantnesses from me, Senkovsky, with whom I was on friendly terms at the time, tried to reconcile me with Bulgarin. He invited the Belgian singer Merti and her mother for dinner at the Coulon in Pavlovsk . . . as well as myself and Bulgarin. We offered each other our hands as a sign of reconciliation, though I did not wish to ask for his patronage. When the conversation turned to my opera, Bulgarin said with a feigned look of pity, 'It is irritating that such an excellent work must be entrusted to artists who are not capable of performing it appropriately.' My response to this was that I had written my opera knowing already who the artists to perform it were, that I had adjusted to their capabilities, and that I was perfectly satisfied with them."

6 November

Quartet rehearsal of *Ruslan* (V. Latyshev's diary, in *Muz. starina*, 1903, inst. 2, p. 173).

7 November

In the section "Journalistic Odds and Ends" in *Sev. pchela*, no. 250, there is an [unsigned] article by Bulgarin about the performers in *Ruslan and Lyudmila.* He writes, "All composers write for the well-known talents, but who will Glinka write for? We do not think that our singers will be angered if we say that our opera troupe, though of course better than any vaudeville troupe, does not have the capacity to perform operas of large dimensions. Now we ask, what could Glinka do? Obviously, he could either adjust to the capabilities of his singers or not write a Russian opera at all. . . . So Glinka stooped and allowed himself to be limited by the strengths of the performers."

Orchestral rehearsal of *Ruslan* (V. Latyshev's diary, in *Muz. starina,* 1903, inst. 2, p. 173). When Glinka arrived at the rehearsal he learned that the singers and orchestral players were offended, because they suspected that he had written the article in *Sev. pchela* (*Zap.*).

8 November

In *Lit. gaz.,* no. 44, "Journalistic Amalgam," Petrova II's successful tour in Moscow is mentioned. The article says that she "charmed everyone with her performance of Vanya in the opera *A Life for the Tsar.*" At a farewell benefit concert on 25 October, "the public bade her farewell with thunderous applause."

9 November

Glinka appeared in the consistory "for the reading and verification of an abstract compiled of the suit at his request concerning his divorce from his wife Maria Petrovna and signed a document confirming his appearance."

11 November

In *Mosk. ved.,* no. 90, there is an announcement that Gresser's has received three mazurkas from *Kachucha, Les Sylphides,* and *A Life for the Tsar,* arranged for piano by Dewitte.

12 November

Orchestral rehearsal of *Ruslan* (V. Latyshev's diary, in *Muz. starina,* 1903, inst. 2, p. 173).

14 November

Sofia Dyutur does Glinka's silhouette. Glinka's inscription on the silhouette reads "1842, 14 November, M. Glinka" (*L.,* p. 241).

Under the heading "St. Petersburg Drama Telegraph, assorted news items, talk, and rumor," in *Repertuar i panteon,* no. 22, there is a notice about the rehearsals of *Ruslan and Lyudmila,* which "continue tirelessly. The splendor of the performance, they say, will be most unusual" (d.c.a.).

15 November

In *SPb. ved.*, no. 260, there is an article by Odoevsky (signed "A lover of Glinka's music, of truth and moderation") about the forthcoming production of *Ruslan and Lyudmila* which includes an assessment of the opera and the performers. "All the papers and everyone who likes music are preoccupied with this great opera's future. And justifiably so. That's the way it should be. We are obliged to feel appreciation for the value of national beauty. We should be concerned with such a significant artistic event. There are not many musical talents of the order of Glinka's in Europe, nor are there many subjects like Pushkin's 'Ruslan and Lyudmila' in Russian literature. . . . Those who already have an idea as to how this important musical-poetic work will be performed are enthusiastic. Those who still do not have any notion are afraid that their enjoyment may not be complete. They have every right to be concerned about their enjoyment, but so far as its completeness is concerned, they can probably be at ease. . . . The brilliance and splendor of this performance exceeds everything we have seen in Russian theaters up till now, and in our time the theaters of other capital cities do not even bear comparison in this respect. . . . Never has the orchestra had to contend with a more difficult score—a completely new use of military music, new and extremely learned orchestration, and new harmonic progressions all present difficulties for the performers which would make the academies of music hesitate for a moment. But all this has been successfully overcome by their concerted efforts."

20 November

There is a new attack by Bulgarin against the performers of the Russian Opera and "Ruslan" in *Sev. pchela*, no. 261, under "Miscellany."

Orchestral rehearsal of *Ruslan* (V. Latyshev's diary, in *Muz. starina*, 1903, inst. 2, p. 174).

The first act of *A Life for the Tsar* is performed in a mixed concert in the Bolshoi Theater (*Sev. pchela*, 20 November 1842).

Performance of *A Life for the Tsar* in the Bolshoi Theater in Moscow (*Mosk. ved.*, 18 November 1842).

24 November

Quartet and orchestral rehearsals of *Ruslan* (V. Latyshev's diary, in *Muz. starina*, 1903, inst. 2, p. 174).

In the consistory, Glinka acquainted himself with an "abstract" of his divorce case and certified each page of it. Further on he provides a point by point denial of things stated in the abstract (which almost corresponds verbatim with his appeal to the Synod [cf. 30 July 1843]). Each page is certified, "Collegiate Assessor, Mikhail Glinka" and signed likewise (*L.*, p. 243).

25 November

Orchestral rehearsal of *Ruslan* (V. Latyshev's diary, in *Muz. starina,* 1903, inst. 2, p. 174).

Before 26 November

"At one of the last rehearsals, Count Mikhail Yurievich Vielgorsky, who had just heard the first half of the fifth act, turned to me and said: '*Mon cher, c'est mauvais.*' '*Retirez vos paroles, m-r le compte,*' I answered him, '*il est possible, que cela ne fasse pas de l'effet, mais pour mauvaise, certes, que ma musique ne l'est pas.*' This entire section of the fifth act was subsequently omitted. I left the cuts (*coupures*) to Count Vielgorsky, who cut things mercilessly, and often the best parts, while he said with a look of self satisfaction: 'Isn't it true that I'm a master at making cuts?'"

[Mikhail Vielgorsky "loved Glinka . . . and had an intense appreciation for him, though he sometimes took him to task for his, in [Vielgorsky's] opinion, improper innovations. For example, he did not like it that Glinka had written the finale of the first act of *Ruslan* for three basses and contralto, that is, for a fourth bass, while the tenors and sopranos appeared only in the chorus. 'It is indistinct,' he said, 'and contrary to acoustical demands; it spoils a splendid finale, which under ordinary circumstances could produce a tremendous effect.' Furthermore it angered him that the only tenor part in the opera was given to a one-hundred-year-old man. '*C'est absurde,*' he exclaimed excitedly, 'the tenor voice is distinguished by gentleness, sonority, and tenderness. It's the voice of love, and the voice, consequently, of youth. To use it in life's declining years is unnatural and completely unnecessary. . . .' Nor could he excuse five arias in succession in *Ruslan*. '*C'est absurde,*' he said, '*c'est un opera manqué.*' His words stung Glinka sharply" (Sollogub, p. 601).]

26 November

Dress rehearsal of *Ruslan* (K. Albrecht's Diary, in *Muz. letop.,* 1923, coll. 2, p. 73). "Those who were present, and there were many, were perplexed to find so much that was strange, unusual, incomprehensible, long, and consequently, boring" (Longinov, *Vosp.,* p. 102).

27 November

"Today, Friday, November 27, in the Bolshoi Theater, *Ruslan and Lyudmila,*
a fairytale opera. First performance" (*Sev. pchela,* 27 November 1842).
[Comparable announcements appeared in *Rus. invalid, SPb. ved.,* and *Ved. SPb. gor. politsii.*]

Premiere of *Ruslan and Lyudmila* in the Bolshoi Theater. A poster advertising
the performance lists the participants as follows: Sets after drawings by A.
Roller. Conductor, K. Albrecht. Dances by Titus. Costumes by Mathieu. Military orchestra, F. Ral. The performers include Baykov (Svetozar); Stepanova
(Lyudmila); Petrova II (Ratmir); Likhansky (Bayan); Tosi (Farlaf); Lileeva [a
student] (Gorislava); Leonov (Finn); Marcel (Naina); and Isakov [a student]
(Chernomor). Dances in the fourth act by Andreyanova II and the students
Prikhunova, Gorina, and Kostina. Also on the poster is a notice that "The music
for the opera *Ruslan and Lyudmila* is available at the 'Odeum.'"

"Despite the tormenting doubt that overcame me every time one of my dramatic
works was premiered, I nonetheless hoped for success. The first act went quite
well. The second act was likewise not bad, with the exception of the chorus in
the Head. In the scene [*I zhar i znoi*] in the third act, the student Petrova was
quite weak, and the audience became noticeably cooler. The fourth act did not
have the effect they expected. At the end of the fifth act the Imperial family left
the theater. When the final curtain fell, they began to call for me, but the
applause was not friendly. Meanwhile there were intermittent hisses, primarily
from the stage and orchestra."
[At the first performance of *Ruslan* the hissing was not directed toward Glinka but toward Bulgarin
(Vladimir Zotov, "The First Performance of *Ruslan and Lyudmila,*" *Vosp.,* p. 227; Arnold, inst. 2).]

"After this pure and absolute pleasure . . . it was something to hear Bulgarin say
during the intermission that *Ruslan* was an *undistinguished* work. . . . But N.
V. Kukolnik was right there . . . and in quite a loud voice he dramatically said
to those standing around him, 'Perhaps *Ruslan* is bad, but Bulgarin is a scoundrel.' The latter gulped and without batting an eye withdrew" (Bulgakov, *Vosp.,*
p. 233).

"Allegedly they bargained with Glinka over the performance of *Ruslan* and
made things unpleasant for him, as if the opera would not be a success, etc.
Certainly Glinka was distressed over the cuts which were demanded and over
Petrova's illness (for which no one could be blamed), because of which Ratmir's
part had to be performed in the premiere by her namesake, Anfisa Petrova,
who, however, was in no way her rival. The Directorate, however, almost
attempted the impossible. The costumes, all brand new, were beyond luxury

and elegance. In the fourth act, Chernomor, the womenfolk, sorcerers, Arabs, fairies, and Lezghins were like extraordinary inhabitants of some magic kingdom. The sets (nine in number) were all new. In the fourth act Roller even outdid himself in his representation of Chernomor's castle and gardens. At the end of the third act, the scene of a northern forest and the very first *lever du rideau* representing a banquet in Svetozar's tower were so dazzlingly splendid that even the oldest and most demanding theater goers were astounded. . . . We have not seen anything even remotely similar in *Fenella*, or *Robert*, or *La Juive*, or in Talioni's ballets" (Longinov, *Vosp.*, p. 102). "With the exception of Ruslan (Petrov) and Finn (Leonov), the performance was so ill prepared, so uncertain and unsteady (in tempo), that an exceptional piece was quite undeservedly a near fiasco" (Yury Arnold, "Is the establishment . . . of a Russian national school possible in music, . . ." *Bayan*, 1888, no. 22).

"The public had already issued its judgment, honoring him [Glinka] with three curtain calls at the first performance. Consequently, any other assessment became an individual one, and perhaps mistaken" (R. Z. [Zotov], *"Ruslan and Lyudmila,"* Sev. pchela, 10 December 1842).

"After returning from the theater, Mother and I hid our annoyance and cordially invited my friends to come have dinner with us" (*Zap.*). "After dinner that evening someone jokingly said that Bulgarin had written an article in which he claimed that Glinka had been given considerable help in his work by his servant Yakov Ulyanov, a man of tremendous talent. He claimed that this was confirmed, furthermore, by Ulyanov's conversations in which he called the opera, said to be Glinka's, 'our opera.' You should have seen Yakov's fury. He announced that tomorrow he would go to Bulgarin and to his face call him 'a rogue and a scoundrel. . . .' He could hardly be persuaded to do otherwise" (P. Stepanov, *Vosp.*, p. 63).

Late in the evening Voin Rimsky-Korsakov writes to his parents: "In the evening, my uncle [Nikolay Petrovich Rimsky-Korsakov], as a service obligation, went to the theater with the sovereign for the first performance of *Ruslan and Lyudmila*. . . . At twelve o'clock he arrived home completely dissatisfied with the way the opera had gone. The music was beautiful, and the sets were splendid, but the performers were not good at all. Petrov was a real peasant in the role of Ruslan. Stepanova sang the role of Lyudmila like a strangled cat. Glinka himself was upset as never before. When he was called out, he appeared looking exceedingly glum. The sets for the opera were very expensive and certainly magnificient. The huge head, with which Ruslan does battle in Pushkin's poem, was represented on the stage. An entire chorus sat inside and roared out like a herd of bulls" (*Muz. letop.*, 1922, coll. 1, p. 42).

A note by Vladimir Zotov: "This is strange music. Everything about it is splendid, grandiose, and fascinating, but at the same time it seems incomplete and unfinished. Music for the stage must be in clear, defined forms, even if it is not original. Genius does not always take the form of originality, nor is originality always genius. Music cannot be mathematics set to notes. First of all it must speak to one's feeling. There is feeling in the music of *Ruslan,* but not in its libretto, which is why the audience remains indifferent to what happens on the stage" (*Vosp.,* p. 227).

"At the first performance [the public] seemed indifferent. There was no clapping for the composer, and the curtain calls were chilly. Still there was no one daring enough to express an unfavorable opinion. The audience left the theater somewhat dissatisfied, but, under the influence of Glinka's music, they already felt that there were pearls of beauty hidden in the depths of these great waves of harmony which mere hearing could not discern after only one performance" (*Mayak,* 1843, vol. IX, book 17).

"All the same, the general impression made by the opera was favorable to Glinka. Important personages did not speak of it as they had about *A Life for the Tsar,* saying '*c'est joli, mais trivial,*' or that it was music for peasants. Instead they said, '*c'est sérieux, mais ennuyeux,*' it is music for contrapuntists" (Zotov, *Vosp.,* p. 227).

After 27 November

Serov writes to Stasov: "Whoever does not remember the poem will fail to understand much about the opera. . . . One *should not* look at the music of an opera independent from its text, and with Glinka's operas (as well as Meyerbeer's and others') to do so is simply *impossible.* Thus we will conclude with the libretto. To study it means to expound upon its absurdities, and to do that, to *systematically* demonstrate its absurdity one would have to say much more about the nature of musical drama in general and about *magic opera* in particular. . . . In order for me to fully express my opinion to you of 'R. and L.,' it will suffice to show what, as I understand it, *could have been done* with Pushkin's poem in a magic opera and what *was done,* and then proceed to an analysis of the music. Pushkin's poem 'R. and L.' is one of his youthful works and is a pure imitation of Ariosto. If not *altogether,* then in sections, it is rich in poetic beauty (though I am not speaking here of the poetry itself). As a whole it exudes *a single mood,* which, as everyone knows . . . is highly *national.* Pushkin did not search out nationalism, but, as a Russian, he wrote a light-hearted Russian poem. . . . The problem that confronts anyone who aspires to make an opera of 'R. and L.' is to capture the *spirit* of the poem and to transfer it to the stage.

Otherwise it would not have been necessary to touch Pushkin's work. But will 'R. and L.' work on the stage? Is there a *ready-made* plot in the poem for an opera? In its present form, decidedly *not*. A dramatic plot is made up of *characters* and *situations*. In the poem the characters are sharply outlined and sparkle with life, meaning they would work superbly on the lyric stage, but the *situation,* the *course of events,* is not at all theatrical. A drama it most certainly is not. The action is too *split up*. Don't think, though, that I would want at all to destroy the *possibility of transforming* Pushkin's 'R. and L.' into a magic opera. That would mean destroying one of my most cherished dreams. The ancient Russia of fables, the fascinating atmosphere, light and dark, of enchantment (as in Ariosto), a beautiful princess abducted from her handsome bridegroom and languishing under the spell of a frightful dwarf, various other suitors, the intrigues of Chernomor and Naina, Finn's secret powers, the radiant dénouement— good heavens! Wouldn't it be cruel to forfeit such possibilities? No, it proves to be unnecessary, but . . . for these potentialities to be realized on stage . . . the entire opera would have to be redone. Apparently not a single scene of the poem remained without changes, but extremely *significant* changes should have been made in the overall course of action. This would require a labor of no small significance and demand a special dramatic gift, but it is *possible*. . . . Such an opera, with the supernatural effect of outstanding music, would be a genuinely fascinating work. Pushkin's 'R. and L.' breathes *comedy,* which permeates almost all its characters. To preserve the general character of the poem, the opera would of necessity then become *magic-comic,* which would fit the music perfectly. Isn't it a pity then, since Glinka himself would have been totally within his element. . . . Cheerfulness, good humor, and playfulness alternating with the energetic expression of the opera's serious elements would hold the spectator permanently in an atmosphere of wonder. Vigorous development of Pushkin's flexible characters would lend 'a breath of life' to each moment of the opera, and under music's magic influence three good acts would slip past the enchanted spectator like one *marvelous moment*! Thus, in my opinion, the plot of 'R. and L.,' suitably transformed, could become the most entertaining and luxuriant of magic operas. We may see what we [with this the letter breaks off] (Leningrad Theater Museum, no. KP 6320/1).

[The letter has no beginning or end. Apparently it was not sent and therefore did not appear in the collection of Serov's letters to Stasov in GPB. Judging from its content, it most likely was written soon after the first performance of *Ruslan,* which corresponds to the acknowledgment in the letter of 17 January 1843 (q.v.).]

28 November

Letter from Bulgarin to Kukolnik concerning the incident in the theater the evening before: "I was the only one who spoke on Glinka's behalf, and I did

so when they were persecuting me. Glinka has *powerful* enemies . . . but because of your uncalled-for behavior, you have pushed me to the point where I
can no longer defend Glinka as I wanted to previously. I hand him over to the
judgment of informed and popular opinion and wash my hands of him like
Pontius Pilate" (*Otchet publichnoi bib-ki za 1884 g.* [Account of the public
library for the year 1884], SPb., 1887, p. 143).

In *Ved. SPb. gor. politsii*, no. 43, mention is made of the performance in the
Bolshoi Theater on 27 November of *Ruslan and Lyudmila,* "which has been so
eagerly awaited by theater lovers and admirers of native talent."

Orchestral rehearsal of *Ruslan* (V. Latyshev's diary, in *Muz. starina,* 1903, inst.
2, p. 174).

29 November

In *Lit. gaz.,* no. 47, there is an unsigned notice by Koni about the first performance of *Ruslan and Lyudmila* which expresses an enthusiastic opinion of the
performance and makes the promise to submit a detailed assessment of the opera
after hearing several more performances: "Perhaps in many respects we are not
of one mind with the honored composer, but this does not prevent us from
according his talent and conscientious labor its full due."

Performance in the Bolshoi Theater of *Ruslan and Lyudmila.* "The second
performance went no better than the first" (*Zap.; Sev. pchela,* 28 November
1842). At the second performance the part of Ruslan was performed by Gulak-
Artemovsky, who "also possessed a beautiful, clear, and powerful voice, so
that one could listen with pleasure to Ruslan. Of course he was not Ruslan-
Petrov" (V. Panaev, *Vosp.,* in *Rus. starina,* 1901, vol. 108, part 10, p. 126).

"After brilliant debuts . . . [Artemovsky] has now appeared in the second performance of the opera *Ruslan and Lyudmila.* He was faced with comparison with
Mr. Petrov, but the young singer emerged from the battle with honor" (*Repertuar i Panteon,* 1843, part 1, p. 233).

30 November

In the theater chronicle of *Repertuar i panteon,* no. 23, there is a short review
of the first two performances of *Ruslan and Lyudmila.* "It is not possible to, nor
should one, judge music, especially learned music, after one hearing. . . . After
hearing the new piece . . . several times, we can say what kind of verdict of the
music the public handed down. A composer like M. I. Glinka may be on the

wrong course, but he is incapable of writing a bad opera. At this point we can only say that at the first performance of *Ruslan and Lyudmila* the length of the piece and the unentertaining opening tired everyone . . . and that the performance of the opera in general left much to be desired." At the conclusion of the review: "We have heard the second performance of the opera and will take the time to share the pleasant news with the reader that the audience found the new performance more attractive than the first," referring to Artemovsky's performance of the role of Ruslan. In the same issue there is information about the audience and carriages at the first three performances (d.c.a.).

Performance in the Bolshoi Theater of *Ruslan and Lyudmila.* "The older Petrova, who appeared in the third performance, sang her scene in the third act with such passion that the audience was beside itself. There was loud and prolonged applause, and I first and then Petrova were ceremoniously called out. These curtain calls continued throughout the course of 17 performances" (*Zap.; Sev. pchela,* 28 November 1842).

"From the very first performances of *Ruslan and Lyudmila* the opera made a strong impression on me, thanks, of course, to those two outstanding artists, Petrov and his wife Vorobieva-Petrova. Petrov was a true bogatyr in the role of Ruslan, both vocally and dramatically. . . . No offense intended, but the Ruslans who followed Petrov all seemed to me weak compared to him. . . . Fairness requires me to say that . . . Artemovsky . . . also possessed a beautiful, clear, strong voice. . . . Naturally he was not Ruslan-Petrov, but . . . he was much better than all the other Ruslans. . . . In writing for the part of Ratmir, one can say that Glinka's genius attained the expressive apotheosis of langour and voluptuousness. Vorobieva-Petrova made a miracle of this part. . . . Of the others . . . I cannot say anything in particular" (V. Panaev, *Vosp.,* in *Rus. starina,* 1901, vol. 108, part 10, p. 126).

"The later performances went better and better, especially when Petrova I . . . appeared in the part of Ratmir" (Arnold, "Is the establishment of a Russian school in music possible. . . ." in *Bayan,* 1888, no. 22).

1 December

N. I. Zagryazhsky writes to Mikhail Pogodin: "No good news, but you can let the bad news pass. Just for example, I lacked the patience to hear the new opera *Ruslan and Lyudmila* through. It was just pure boredom. They say they don't understand it, that the music is too learned and inaccessible. Good luck, but how can they play it if they don't understand it? It seems like a simple matter that wanted to emerge but couldn't, and it came to nothing. To me it's all for effect, I can't stand it" (coll. *Glinka*, 1958, p. 56).

The following comments appear in an article by Bulgarin entitled "First Impression of the Opera *Ruslan and Lyudmila*" in *Sev. pchela*, no. 269: "The sets were outstanding . . . I won't say a word about the music! What, for heaven's sake, does it mean? The audience was quiet, cool, and speechless during the first performance, though occasionally here and there one could hear the sound of solitary applause. Not once was there any widespread enthusiasm . . . not once was there any collective excitement . . . which usually happens at performances of great or even graceful music. The audience waited in silence for something to happen, but they waited in vain and then dispersed in silence in a sort of dejection permeated with sadness! . . . everyone left the theater as they would have a funeral! The first word that escaped everyone's lips was '*boring*'!" ["Bulgarin's review here was intended to echo the opinion of the public, in whose silence he perceived a death sentence for the opera. He himself desired to assess its musical shortcomings, but all he found was a similarity with the operas of Mr. Cavos and muted (?!) instrumentation" (*Mayak*, 1843, vol. 9, part 17).]

In *Bib-ka dlia chteniia*, vol. 55, in the section "Miscellany" (December), there is an article by Senkovsky (unsigned) entitled "Opera in Petersburg. *Ruslan and Lyudmila*. Music by M. I. Glinka." "With this opera Glinka has placed himself in the front row of the world's composers along with the best of them. *Ruslan and Lyudmila* is one of those great musical creations which will be immortal and to which one can point with pride as the art of a great people. From the first to the last note, *Ruslan and Lyudmila* is a *chef d'oeuvre* in the full sense of the word. It is beautiful, majestic, and inimitable . . . such a wealth of beautiful things emerging one after another in endless succession, without musical commonplaces or conventional embellishments is not to be found in another single opera. All this does not mean, however, that we were completely satisfied with M. I. Glinka's new opera. In fact, we were dissatisfied because it was too beautiful and too wonderful. . . . The first time we heard *Ruslan and Lyudmila* in its entirety, it had the same tiring effect on us that reading a very learned book has, when every word reflects cleverness, intricacy, and originality. . . . Similar specific examples in music are Beethoven's *Fidelio* and Weber's *Oberon*. . . . One notices this especially in well-known magical operas, which are always based on great originality of form and detail, since they express not feelings but ideas. This describes Glinka's *Ruslan and Lyudmila*." After further categorizing music into two types, the popular, which is immediately understood, and the difficult, which has to be listened to several times, Senkovsky states: "M. I. Glinka has beautifully accomplished what he did not concede to us earlier. The better we now get to know his new opera, the more beautiful things we discover in it." An enthusiastic analysis of the opera number by number follows. However, Senkovsky indicates that the opera should be shortened: the "numbness" scene in the first act; Finn's ballad, Ruslan's aria, and the Head's scene in the second act; Ratmir's aria up to the allegro in the third act; the beginning and end of the ballet in the fourth act; and the scene in the valley in the fifth. "In evaluating *Ruslan and Lyudmila,* even as a musical poem . . . we would place it alongside *Oberon,* although the new Russian opera, in our opinion, is in many respects better than it. . . . Our overall conclusion is that . . . *Ruslan and Lyudmila* should be cut, but liberally, like Beethoven, if it is to be intended for performance. Then its success would be complete." The complete libretto of the opera is appended to the article.

"The second opinion [Senkovsky's], with greater pretensions to musical learning [than Bulgarin] and excessive words of praise, is attributable to the opponent of *Sev. pchela.* However, everyone was so accustomed to seeing the sophistry and paradox hidden behind the facade of his dialectic that even in his perhaps unhypocritical praise of the new opera they saw a new joke on the public's credulity . . . and they [the public] were correct to suspect this, because they had paid several times before for their trustfulness" (*Mayak,* 1843, vol. 9, part 17).

1 December

Performance of *Ruslan and Lyudmila* in the Bolshoi Theater (*SPb. ved.,* 1 December 1842).

3 December

In in a letter to Zhukovsky, Fedor Litke writes: "Several days ago we heard a new Russian opera, Glinka's *Ruslan and Lyudmila.* I suppose Count Mikhail Yurievich will write you about the incomparable erudition of this music. But the public, and we sinners among them, have not read the score. We just heard it, and we found it incomparably boring. In comparison to it, *A Life for the Tsar* is like *The Barber of Seville*" (*Rus. arkhiv,* 1897, part 2, inst. 5, p. 166).

In a letter to Elizaveta Akhmatova, Senkovsky thanks her for her letter and says that it contains "such thought, such subtlety, such subtle and noble sentiments that it seemed like Naina's second enchantment to me, or Chernomor's second castle, covered with roses and emerging from the water, fire, gold, and ether. This is what I saw, or rather, heard yesterday in the picturesque sounds of Glinka's music" (*Rus. starina,* May, 1889).

Orchestral rehearsal of *Ruslan* (V. Latyshev's diary, *Muz. starina,* 1903, inst. 2, p. 174).

An announcement on a poster states that "Since seats for the first four perform-ances of the opera *Ruslan and Lyudmila* have been sold, the sale of tickets for the next four performances has begun."

4 December

Performance of *Ruslan and Lyudmila* in the Bolshoi Theater. "Lyudmila will be sung for the first time by Semyonova. There will be big cuts and therefore a great success" (K. Albrecht's diary, in *Muz. letop.,* coll. 2, p. 73). "They were enthusiastic. After the opera there was howling and foot-stamping . . . and they cried for Misha" (ltr. from O. Senkovsky to N. Kukolnik, 5 December 1842, in *Muz. sezon,* 1870/71; reprint in *L.,* p. 251).

In a letter to Elizaveta Akhmatova, Senkovsky writes: "Because of the intrigues of ill-wishers, at the head of which stood *Sev. pchela,* the most beautiful music written in our time was badly received at its first performance, and *Sev. pchela* maligned a man of genius of whom Russia can be justifiably proud. I was deeply distressed. Kind-hearted Glinka was in despair. I considered it my responsibility to apply all my means toward turning his misfortune around and see that he be justly recognized. It had to be explained to the uninitiated public what Glinka's opera was like, what was beautiful in this splendid work, what the characteris-tics of magical music were, and how to compose and listen to such an opera. I worked four days and four nights without ceasing, and I had to read through the huge score and several older works of the same type with Kukolnik, who volunteered to help me in this good work. I added a large article and the libretto of the opera to the paper. For his part Glinka made cuts and shortened things, which we had insisted on, and everything is *corrected.* The audience understood his splendid work. I have just come home from the theater. After a complete failure, a total, frenzied success! Glinka was applauded more than necessary. He must be happy now. I confess that, for my part, I am beside myself with joy. I am completely happy and in this blissful state I am writing to you" (*Rus. starina,* 1889, vol. 62, part 5, p. 289; Fr. original).

[In connection with the cuts in *Ruslan,* Bulgakov recalls: "Although it makes me sick, and I regret to say so, Count Mikhaylo Yurievich Vielgorsky, who was a fine, intelligent, and learned man, was only envious of Glinka. He said to me several times that Glinka often got carried away with his own genius and wrote absurd things. I saw this with my very eyes" (Bulgakov, *Vosp.,* p. 233).]

"Glinka's new opera *Ruslan and Lyudmila* was given with great success, despite the doubts expressed . . . by Mikhail Yurievich Vielgorsky" (Sokolov, *Vosp.*, p. 248).

5 December

Some of Bulgarin's arguments concerning *Ruslan and Lyudmila* appear in the "Miscellany" section of *Sev. pchela,* no. 275: "If someone says, I want to write an *original* work which is unusual and will create a revolution in art, then he may well write something unusual, but it's more apt to be strange than original. Instead of a revolution, maybe things have been turned wrong side out."

The following appears in the "Musical News" section of *SPb. ved.,* no. 276: "The first performance of M. I. Glinka's new opera did not make the impression on listeners which those who already knew it expected it to. . . . For that reason, the celebrated composer rushed to make significant cuts in it, to change many things, and to completely rework many other things. This gave it a quicker pace, removed the tediousness of several places, and, as they say, set many of the beautiful places in greater relief. In the fifth performance on Friday, it appeared in its new form and was crowned with a total, brilliant success. Lyudmila's cavatina in the first act, Finn's ballad and Ruslan's aria in the second, Gorislava's aria in the third and Lyudmila's [in the fourth], and the entire fourth act including the grotesque ballet with Chernomor were received with loud, prolonged applause. The audience demanded a repeat of the lezghinka, and when the opera was over their warranted shouts of enthusiasm could not be silenced."

Senkovsky writes to Kukolnik asking him to persuade Glinka "to shut the Head up *immediately*. . . . He's going out of his mind. He's willingly destroying the whole opera's success by allowing this barrel to hold forth. . . . I'll choke Glinka if he doesn't shut this awful Head's trap!" (*L.*, p. 251).

Performance of *Ruslan and Lyudmila* in the Bolshoi Theater. "Artemovsky was timid. Stepanova was boring." (K. Albrecht's diary, in *Muz. letop.*, 1923, coll. 2, p. 73; *Sev. pchela*, 5 December 1842).

From 27 November through 6 December

Ruslan and Lyudmila was performed six times. The performers of the principal roles, in order, were Petrov and Artemovsky (Ruslan), Semyonova and Stepanova (Lyudmila), Petrova I and Petrova II (Ratmir), Leonov (Finn), and Lileeva (Gorislava).

6 December

In *Lit. gaz.*, no. 48, in the section "Miscellany," there is an unsigned article (by Koni) about the growing success of *Ruslan and Lyudmila*. The opera "to which the audience gave a chilly reception at its first performance is now holding its own on the stage and acquires new supporters with each performance. Those who were dissatisfied at first have migrated over because of the opera's impressive qualities and musical beauty. For this to happen is quite natural. The opera is written in a strict and, moreover, fantastic style, and one must first listen attentively to the music in order to understand the composer's thoughts! Furthermore, this is a serious work, laid out on a broad scale, and not just another ordinary opera in the French manner with their silly themes. . . . We are ready to predict that *Ruslan and Lyudmila* will soon be the favorite opera of Russian audiences, despite its initial failure. Good things have their way, whatever might be said about them."

Performance of the first act of *A Life for the Tsar* and the ballet *Don Juan* in the Bolshoi Theater (*Sev. pchela,* 5 December 1842).

Performance in the Moscow Bolshoi Theater of *A Life for the Tsar* (*Mosk. ved.*, 5 December 1842).

8 December

In the beginning of an article about *Ruslan and Lyudmila* in *Sev. pchela*, no. 275, R. Zotov writes as follows about the libretto: "What marvelous scenes Pushkin left us in his poem! But what has happened? What we see on the stage is a very involved opera with cold and vacuous scenes which are in no way warranted."

9 December

Performance of *Ruslan and Lyudmila* in the Bolshoi Theater (*Sev. pchela,* 9 December 1842).

10 December

In *Sev. pchela*, no. 277, Rafail Zotov's article about *Ruslan and Lyudmila* is continued: "The composer has given the orchestra too important a role in the opera. Perhaps, because he could not count on our singers, he wished to preserve his harmonic ideas by entrusting them to the orchesra. We will not blame him for being mistrustful. We only wish to say that the orchestra's role is to *accompany,* and that if the orchestra is given such importance in performance, then viewers are automatically distracted from the stage, and their attention is drawn more to the beautiful instrumentation. . . . The overture had no effect on us at all. The three shifts from tone to tone at the very beginning reflected a musical refinement which the audience was not able to grasp. Further on the composer gave a lot of mechanical work to the instruments, but we did not hear the main idea." Each section is evaluated in similar fashion. "The crown of the opera is the dance music. Harmonically the opera . . . has great value, but melodically it is not as good as *A Life for the Tsar.*"

11 December

Performance of *Ruslan and Lyudmila* in the Bolshoi Theater (*Sev. pchela,* 11 December 1842). An entry in K. Albrecht's diary after the performance reads, "So far the receipts from nine performances come to 45,000 rubles" (*Muz. letop.,* 1923, coll. 2, p. 74).

12 December

The following article entitled "The Bolshoi Theater: *Ruslan and Lyudmila,*" by V. Mezhevich, appears in *Ved. SPb. gor. politsii,* no. 47: "So far there have been eight performances of *Ruslan and Lyudmila,* the first of which made a very unfavorable impression on the audience. After assembling in the theater with the best of intentions, *avec toute sa bonne volonté,* and prepared to applaud and be transported on the slightest pretext, the audience listened to the beginning of the opera in disbelief. They waited and waited, and when they had finally gotten bored, they began to yawn. The opera bored and exhausted them. Calls for the composer were far from unanimous, and it was apparent that the audience wished more to console him than to hail his success. After the first performance the opera was almost uniformly put down as the unsuccessful work of a man of great talent. Subsequent performances of the opera, each time subjected to rewriting, changes, and abbreviation, produced a much more favorable impression of the composer on the audience, though, nonetheless, they did not stir the enthusiasm which the composer's friends and passionate supporters thought the opera deserved. Yes, the audience received M. I. Glinka's new work coldly. . . . Pushkin's poem 'Ruslan and Lyudmila' presents a broad spectrum for an operatic libretto, and it does not require a particularly fervid imagination to see the charm, variety, and fantasy which music might evoke from it. In fact, it is the very dryness and lifelessness of the libretto, in a word, its unsatisfactory quality, that is the primary cause of the opera's failure. The audience was surprised by the poverty and absence of dramatic action in the opera. . . . Subsequent performances, which were cut, shortened, and changed, were more successful and more effective. . . . Now the audience knew what to expect, and they matched their expectations to it. They no longer focused on the libretto, nor did they demand dramatic action from the opera. Instead they sought visual pleasure in the sets and aural pleasure in the music, and they made peace with the composer. Certainly there are many beautiful places in M. I. Glinka's opera, without reference to the libretto. We make no effort to speak of the composer's erudition or the complexities of the opera. That may be left for cognoscenti to admire. However, every amateur will be able to listen with instinctive musical pleasure to Lyudmila's cavatina in the first act (*'Grustno mne, roditel' dorogoi'* [I am sad, dear father]) and the following women's chorus on ancient wedding motives. Lyudmila's lines in the first act, *'Ne gnevis', znatnyi gost''* [Do not be angry, noble guest] and *'Pod roskoshnym nebom iuga'* [Under the luxuriant southern sky], are beautiful. . . . The same may be said of Ratmir's lines, *'Krai zhelannyi, krai dalekii'* [Beloved land, distant land], which breathe tenderness. Finally, Ratmir's solo in the finale of the first act, *'O vitiazi, skoree v chisto pole'* [O knights, soon to the open field], is outstanding. In the second act, Ruslan's aria . . . is about the best piece in the opera. But on the other hand, Finn's celebrated ballad, *a model of epic music,* is, in our opinion, the most unsuccessful thing in the opera. It is true that its theme lingers long in one's memory, but it remains, first of all, because one hears it over and over again for nearly a quarter of an hour, and secondly, because it conflicts with the content of the ballad. Finn's powerful and passionate story is set to dance music. They say that this tune was taken from Finnish songs, which may well be, but perhaps Finnish music does not charm us. In the third act, Ratmir's aria (*'Chudnyi son zhivoi liubvi'* [Marvelous dream of living love]) is charming! The aria was performed with emotion and tenderness. It is also one of the best places in the opera. This act also contains the wonderfully beautiful dance music. In the fourth act we are struck by the novelty and strangeness of the combination of three different orchestras playing simultaneously for Chernomor's magical holiday. It is deafening music; there's simply nothing else to say. Lyudmila's aria in this act (*'Akh! Ty dolia, doliushka, dolia moia gor'kaia'* [O, my fate, my sad fate]) was performed with grace and feeling. In the same act is the famous lezghinka accompanied by music based on Lezghin themes. They say that this dance and music are suitable for the *kachucha.* . . . Ratmir's aria in the fifth act (*'Ona mne zhizn', ona mne radost''* [She is my life, my joy]) was unsuccessful in the first two performances. In subsequent performances, thanks to Petrova I, the full brilliance of the aria was displayed. Lyudmila's last tune (*'Kak tuman rassypletsia razluki zloi bezvremen'e'* [Like a cloud, evil times spread separation]) is beautiful. The theme of the chorus, *'Radost' schast'e iasnoe'* [Joy, pure happiness] and then in particular, *'Slava velikim bogam'* [Praise to the great gods], and the entire finale in Russian style, were thought out and performed extremely well. . . ." Regarding the Head's chorus: "This is one of the least successful choruses in the entire opera. . . . Connoisseurs say that in *Ruslan and Lyudmila* Mr. Glinka demonstrated an amazing knowledge of music, extreme originality, nearly supernatural musical reason, etc., etc. . . . Furthermore, they say that Glinka was a century ahead of his audiences, which may not be in a position to understand him. . . . We are pleased for Mr. Glinka and our successors a hundred years from now who will enjoy this opera more than we have enjoyed it. So far as we, Glinka's contemporaries, are concerned, we have listened with pleasure, and more than once, to several of the arias and choruses and have taken pleasure with others that after waiting so long, Glinka has finally presented his new work to us."

13 December

In the "Criticism and Bibliography" section of *Lit. gaz.*, no. 49, there is an article by Koni entitled *"Ruslan and Lyudmila,* grand magical opera in the Russian fairytale manner, in five acts. The text from Pushkin's poem. SPb., 1842 (libretto)." The article contains a harsh evaluation of the text and makes the assertion that a number of places are not in verse. Consequently, "we must allow that M. I. Glinka wrote his beautiful music to prose . . . and that the opera's libretto is in prose, which by the laws of opera and man cannot be accepted. . . . It is a shame that this fine Russian composer, M. I. Glinka, embroidered his musical flowers on such terrible cloth, because they warranted much better." Koni's article entitled *"Ruslan and Lyudmila,* a magical opera in five acts, music by M. I. Glinka. Dances by the ballet master Titus. Sets by Jourdeuil, Fedorov, and Roller. Costumes by Mathieu." appears in the "Theater" section of the same issue. "One can look at it in two ways: first, as an opera in the strict sense, that is, as a work where all the arts are combined to produce a complete dramatic effect on the feelings and imagination of the viewer and listener; or secondly, as a purely musical work, where music plays the leading role, and everything else is conceived and adjusted in order to give a logical meaning to the music. . . . To which of these . . . types of music then does *Ruslan and Lyudmila,* our composer's *creation* [*sozdanie*], belong? A possible answer is to neither and to both. One must note, however, that this is not a *creation,* but simply a musical composition. By *creation* is meant a large musical work permeated by one general idea expressed in numerous particular thoughts. M. I. Glinka's opera does not have an overall idea but rather many particular ones, which comprise *not a large, but a long* composition, for the parts have no positive connection and make up a musical chain whose meaning is not destroyed if a link or two or more are removed. Accordingly, it is impossible to consider *Ruslan and Lyudmila* an *opera* in the contemporary sense of its meaning. First of all, the composer selected a fantastic fairytale genre. Secondly, he chose a libretto devoid of any shadow of thought. . . . One cannot speak at all of an idea. He has taken a simple tale such as the painters of Suzdal portray and like nurses tell children at bedtime with all their absurd and miraculous, disconnected events and absence of poetic ornament. . . . M. I. Glinka's work *Ruslan and Lyudmila* cannot be viewed as an opera but as a large musical composition in lyrical style, because it lacks the necessary verse and fails to meet the demands of true opera. Much is gained by looking at M. I. Glinka's work from this point of view. It is impossible not to recognize his remarkable talent, melodic mastery, and warmth of coloration and taste which permeate the slightest details of his music. One must be amazed at the abundance of musical ideas scattered throughout *Ruslan and Lyudmila*. Glinka never repeats himself, nor does he foist off on you some inane tune like Italian and French composers do. He gives us what suffices for an evening, and he plays with ideas and illuminates them like an Indian juggler with his daggers and golden apples. He moves from one modulation to another with the ease of a chamois jumping from cliff to cliff, and each new musical phrase eclipses the previous one with its grace and animation. This causes many, who are accustomed to repetition of the same thing, to think that his pieces are too long and exhausting for both singer and listener. . . . Glinka's entire opera is written in a strict, serious style. This is the most difficult type of music. . . . But it is not double Dutch, which only connoisseurs can understand. The composer's learning leads to one result: to make an impression on both connoisseurs and laymen. . . . Analyzing Glinka's musical composition in detail, you encounter everywhere intentions which clearly attest to the fact that he has taken the matter of being an artist as a serious calling." A detailed and enthusiastic analysis of the opera piece by piece follows, singling out especially Finn's ballad as "the pearl of the whole opera" and also noting the shortcomings connected, in the critic's opinion, with the libretto, namely the absence of dramatic movement and the drawn-out quality of several places. Speaking of the opera's success, Koni remarks that, as a consequence of perceptual difficulties (primarily because of the absence of dramatic development and the striking beauty of the music and staging), its success grew gradually, "not by the day, but hourly. . . . The best proof of this is that it is being given daily, and the theater is always packed. Now the audience's attention is focused only on the music. . . . There was a time when everyone was crying that *Ruslan and Lyudmila* was boring and exhausting. Now almost everyone has reconciled himself to it, and the time will come when they all will admire it. Many have complained that there are no melodies in it and nothing imprints itself on one's memory. Just wait, not a month will pass before they will be dancing quadrilles, mazurkas, galops, and waltzes to this music. And in a year every Russian will be singing these marvelous tunes, because street organs will carry them throughout Russia."

14 December

Performance of *Ruslan and Lyudmila* in the Bolshoi Theater (Albrecht's diary, in *Muz. letop.*, 1923, coll. 2, p. 74).

15 December

Directive from the Director of Imperial Theaters, Aleksandr Gedeonov, "to grant the composer payment per performance of two-thirds of a tenth part [6.67%] of the proceeds on the basis of the resolution of 13 November 1827, approved by His Imperial Majesty" (*RMG*, 1901, no. 47).

16 December

Performance in the Bolshoi Theater of *Ruslan and Lyudmila* (*Sev. pchela*, 16 December 1842).

17 December

For performances of *Ruslan and Lyudmila* on 27, 29, 30 November and 11 and 14 December, Glinka received 947 rubles 48 kopecks. The proceeds for these performances amounted to 14, 212 rubles 12 kopecks (records of the accounting office of the Imperial Theaters, 15 December 1842, in *L.*, p. 255).

In the journal *Repertuar i panteon*, vol. 24, in the section "Theatrical Chronicle," there is this review of the opera *Ruslan and Lyudmila* (without signature): "In the last issue . . . we rushed to share our first impressions with our readers . . . and promised to speak further about the opera after we had heard it several times. . . . We . . . did not know what it meant *to listen to Ruslan and Lyudmila several times*! We candidly confess that we did not have the strength to sit through the entire opera from beginning to end a second time and that we listened to it in excerpts, in order to come to some understanding of the performances of the same roles by various singers." Criticism of the libretto follows: "The author of the libretto had the widest latitude for a grand magic opera in Russian fairytale style . . . and what has he made of this rich, national theme? Scenes which are pointless and inconsistent, senseless verses alongside Pushkin's resonant lines, absence of dramatic action, disregard for all dramatic and operatic effects, and all this has been called opera in the Russian fairytale style!" The author mentions the splendid staging and evaluates the performers, placing Artemovsky over Petrov, Semyonova over Stepanova, and Petrova I over Petrova II. There is no evaluation of the music. "In one Petersburg paper they have written that Glinka's opera should not be viewed as an *opera* but simply as a *musical composition*. After this there is nothing left to say!" (d.c.a.).

19 December

Aleksandr Gedeonov writes to Glinka of the necessity of reworking parts of *Ruslan and Lyudmila* "so that they will not be difficult for our singers," since Chekka, teacher of singing at the Theater School, complains that her students' voices are being ruined. "I have already received one aria from you. I am waiting for another one" (*RMG*, 1846, no. 12).
[Apparently Glinka also reworked Finn's scene at this time (B. Dobrokhotov, "M. I. Glinka's autographs in Moscow archives," coll. *Glinka*, 1958, p. 337).]

"Gedeonov made fun of me to my face, saying that I am ruining our musicians, since some of them do not perform at times, and that I should not write in such a learned manner, etc. In my absence, however, he always defends me fervently."

20 December

In the section "Journalistic Amalgam" of *Lit. gaz.*, no. 50, it is noted that "in the musical world M. I. Glinka still holds sway despotically with his opera on the stage and with quadrilles and waltzes in the salons made from it by the dexterous Lyadov." It also refers to the publication "of the piano score" of *Ruslan* with Russian and German texts by the publisher "Odeum."

22 December

Performance in the Bolshoi Theater of *Ruslan and Lyudmila* (K. Albrecht's diary, in *Muz. letop.*, 1923, coll. 2, p. 74). At this performance "genuine enthusiasm prevailed among the audience. The composer was called out four times to deafening applause" (*Bib-ka dlia chteniia*, 1843, v. 56, p. 78).

23 December

Sergey Krasheninnikov writes to Yanuary Neverov: "Yesterday I heard and saw Glinka's new opera *Ruslan and Lyudmila*. The music moved me a couple of times, the sets are really marvelous, the costumes are sumptuous, and on the whole it is a beautiful work, though others find it boring. You can't please everyone" (coll. *Glinka*, p. 157).

28 December

Performance in the Bolshoi Theater of *Ruslan and Lyudmila* (*Sev. pchela*, 28 December 1842).

The musical materials for *A Life for the Tsar* are returned from Moscow to Petersburg (TsGIA, coll. 497, no. 9087).

30 December

Performance in the Bolshoi Theater of *Ruslan and Lyudmila* (*Sev. pchela*, 30 December 1842).

31 December

Performance of *Ruslan and Lyudmila* in the Bolshoi Theater (*Sev. pchela*, 31 December 1842).

27 November through 31 December

There were fifteen performances of *Ruslan and Lyudmila* attended by approximately 15,000 people (*Repertuar i Panteon*, 1843, part 1).

31 December

In the section "Miscellany" of *Otech. zap.*, no. 1/2, there is an article by Odoevsky (signed Plakun Goryunov, retired Titular Councillor) entitled "Notes for my great-great-grandson about the literature of our time and other things (*Ruslan and Lyudmila*, an opera by the Russian composer Glinka, excerpts from letters to the journalist Mr. Bichev)." "The other day I read somewhere, I don't remember where, the statement of a gentleman that the public was cold at performances of *Ruslan and Lyudmila* and that neither this gentleman nor the public understood the opera. There is an obvious gap here: doubtless this doesn't refer at all to the Petersburg audience but rather to the audience at Ekaterinhof, that is, to those who received their musical education on Sunday holidays at Ekaterinhof or on Krestovsky Island amid the sounds of Tyrolian guitar music and street organs. Probably such an audience did not understand the new opera. But I can assure you that I have not missed a single performance, and I heard and saw how the real Petersburg audience called the composer out four times in succession. How else could they have received a new opera which, along with with *A Life for the Tsar*, has placed Russian music for the first time on the same level as the best new music. On the contrary, according to my observations, at each performance the audience discovered new beauties in the opera which they had not noticed initially, and they gained a better grasp of the charm and melodic freshness which imbues the opera. What was not noticed in the first performances was in subsequent ones received with genuine, sincere enthusiasm. Such a gradual, solid, effect is produced by the unique and original music which has poured from the soul of a man of genius. We are not talking here about the outburst of friends who have gathered for a first performance and which then fades with that performance. . . . Everything false wanes; the success of the truly beautiful grows with every day. This is not news, and it is very natural: it has been this way with all works of genius from Mozart's *Don Giovanni* through and including *Ruslan and Lyudmila*. The great beauty of original music of genius does not come with the first hearing like a vaudeville couplet. It has to be listened to attentively. . . . All of this is very natural, but . . . isn't it strange? . . . The public thinks one thing, feels one thing, quietly goes to sleep, and wakes up the next morning to hear the announcement that it has thought and felt something else. . . . The virtuous gentleman had the innocent intention of pleasing the dilettantes of the barrel organ by presenting their opinion in print. . . . The development of [Glinka's] talent is a very remarkable event, since he began with what others conclude. Already in his first opera, *A Life for the Tsar*, you don't encounter a shadow of imitation. After serious study of the works of Western music, he listened to the melodies of his native land and tried to discover the secret of their origin, their fundamental elements, and on their basis to establish a new type of melody, harmony, and operatic music of an unprecedented character. . . . Glinka noticed the musical character of Russian melody. He was not afraid to base an entire opera on it, which led him to a tragic style, something which had not entered anyone's mind. With this feat he initiated a new epoch in music. *A Life for the Tsar*, as was formerly the case with *Don Giovanni*, is the seed from which an entire musical period must evolve. *Ruslan and Lyudmila* is the second branch of the same tendency; in it a Slavic character prevails, a *fantastic* character. It is our tale, our legend, but in the world of music. Its Russian character has come into contact with the limitless world of fantasy and is generalized without losing its distinctive qualities. To look for ordinary drama here is fruitless. Drama in the world of fantasy and folktales has its own peculiar conditions and belongs exclusively to that world. Struggles among people, which comprise one of the elements of earthly drama, do not exist here, but there remains another element, namely the struggle with one's self and with superhuman powers. This struggle is so powerful that any other struggle lacks interest altogether. . . . If I had the voice, and if I thought that my ignorant cries might have the slightest influence on the opinions of others . . . I would make the following simple speech: 'Dear Sirs! There are 21 numbers in *Ruslan and Lyudmila*. Among them are the following: Bayan's song, Lyudmila's cavatina 'Do not be angry, noble guest,' Finn's ballad, Ruslan's

aria 'O field,' the chorus 'The darkness of night lay over the field,' Gorislava's aria 'Splendid star of love,' Ratmir's 'Oppressive heat' and 'She is my life,' Lyudmila's aria 'Far from my beloved,' the march and dances in Chernomor's castle. These pieces are so fresh that if it were said to the people whom you are afraid not to admire, like Meyerbeer, Halevy, Auber, that if they were to walk one hundred versts and this music would be their own, they would come running, so that each might have the entire opera. . . . O, believe me! A splendid flower has sprung up on Russian musical soil, our joy and glory. Let worms attempt to crawl up its stalk and stain it. They will fall to the ground, and the flower will remain. Preserve it. It is a tender flower which only blooms once in a century'" (d.c.a.).
[The article appeared in February. It is reconstructed in part from the manuscript *Vosp.*, p. 342.]

In the "Musical News" section of *Bib-ka dlia chteniia,* vol. 56, there is a notice about the twelfth performance and the growing success of *Ruslan and Lyudmila.* "This is an unusual musical poem in which everything is new, from melody to instrumentation. . . . Whoever has once studied its beauties sufficiently will never part from them. . . . *Ruslan and Lyudmila* is the Russian *Oberon.* The composer was called out four times to deafening applause." There is an announcement in the same issue of the publication of dances from *Ruslan* in a transcription for piano of a French contredanse, a galop, and a mazurka on themes from *Ruslan* in an arrangement by Aleksandr Lyadov. In a review of literary novelties presented in the form of dramatized parody, a ballet performed to music from *Ruslan and Lyudmila* is depicted.

"Another critic [?], turning to the Director, Gedeonov, once said, 'How bad that you spent so much on the performance of Glinka's opera. You know it won't work.' 'Not at all,' Gedeonov answered, 'I am not sorry, and I'm convinced that it will go beautifully, and that you will write more favorably.'" (*Zap.*).

"Count . . . Vielgorsky, whenever conversation turned to my opera, always said: '*c'est un opéra manqué.*'"

Aleksandr Serov's self-caricature, "The Theorist at Work," which he gave to Glinka, dates from this year. At the top is the inscription, "Happy is he who can laugh at himself and justly reject the evil ridicule of others." At the bottom, "To my dear maestro and precursor, in recognition and memory of our friendship" (*Sov. muzyka,* 1957, no. 2, p. 81).

"I clearly, vividly, and indelibly remember him [Glinka] as young, attractive, gracious, and witty during the *Ruslan* period, when he sang so inimitably in my presence at my parents home. I can hear his phrasing, pronunciation, and wonderful voice in my memory to this day!" (ltr. from Engelgardt to N. Findeyzen, 9 April 1913, in *Sov. muzyka,* 1953, no. 9, p. 49).

During the year [?] Glinka "said to him [Dal] several times that after *Ruslan and Lyudmila* he definitely intended to set to work on *'Noch' na rasput'e'* [Night at the crossroads]" (Bozheryanov, "To the Memory of V. I. Dal," in *Rus. starina,* 1907, vol. 132, part 11, p. 280).

[An analogous piece of information, in virtually the same words, appears in P. Melnikov-Pechersky's critical-biographical study "V. I. Dal," in V. Dal, *Poln. sobr. soch* [Complete works], vol. 1, SPb., 1897.]

1842/1843

Winter

Serov "on several occasions . . . spent entire evenings with Glinka in the homes of Lisenko and the Tabarovskys. . . . Quite often Glinka's most favored singers, the tenor Mikhaylov and the baritone Artemovsky, were present. The outstanding musician V. M. Kazhinsky, who had just arrived from Warsaw, was among the guests. He played many Chopin mazurkas from memory, which Glinka always listened to with special satisfaction, and he conversed a great deal with Kazhinsky about composers of various schools, about his *Ruslan,* and about plans for another opera in a completely 'different taste.' Glinka once again sang many things from his usual repertoire. He also frequently accompanied Artemovsky (always from memory) in Ruslan's arias and in the drinking song (Brindisi) 'Lucretia Borgia'" (Serov, *Vosp.,* p. 93). Longinov saw Glinka frequently "and our circle of friends spent many nights in lively conversation, enlivened by Glinka's improvisation and singing" (M. Longinov, *Vosp.,* p. 101).

1843

2 January

Performance of *Ruslan and Lyudmila* in the Bolshoi Theater (*Sev. pchela,* 2 January 1843).

3 January

Theatrical events are summed up in "Journalistic Amalgam (Send-off for the Year 1842)," in *Lit. gaz.*, no. 1. "It seems that the Roman rule *Finis coronat opus!* prevailed in our theaters during 1842. It brought us Glinka's *Ruslan and Lyudmila*, the charming ballet *Giselle*, and Gogol's folk caricature *Zhenit'ba* [Marriage]."

4 January

Performance of *Ruslan and Lyudmila* in the Bolshoi Theater (*Sev. pchela*, 4 January 1843).

5 January

SPb. ved., no. 3, contains an announcement of the publication of the first issue of *Le Nouvelliste*, which includes the romance *"Kak sladko s toboiu mne byt'."*

7 January

Quartet rehearsal of *Ruslan* (V. Latyshev's diary, in *Muz. starina*, 1903, v. 2, p. 174).

Performance of *Ruslan and Lyudmila* in the Bolshoi Theater (*Sev. pchela*, 7 January 1843).

Serov wrote in his diary: "I attended *Ruslan and Lyudmila* (for the fifth time) and was convinced that undistinguished performances of works studied at home cannot leave a comforting impression. Everything is cold, lifeless, and incomplete. It gives the overall impression of something sick" (excerpt from A. Serov's diary in a letter to V. Stasov dated 28 February 1843, in MN 1, p. 208). [In published sources Serov's entry is dated "before 5 March." However, the date can be correctly ascertained from his letter to Stasov on 17 January and the dates of the opera's performances before the letter, which was written after the sixth performance of *Ruslan and Lyudmila*.]

8 January

Orchestral rehearsal of *Ruslan and Lyudmila* (V. Latyshev's diary, in *Muz. starina*, 1903, v. 2, p. 174).

9 January

"Audiences are now captivated by M. I. Glinka's opera *Ruslan and Lyudmila* in the Bolshoi Theater. . . . One group finds many places in Glinka's opera which will give the composer immortality in a hundred years. Others, not wishing to put things off, would give the composer of *Ruslan and Lyudmila* the crown of immortality now. A third group finds the opera an unconditional failure and is unable to see anything noteworthy in it. A fourth, more restrained, holds the opinion that the opera has many fine qualities but that it also has its faults and that the abundance of lyricism in the music and the total absence of dramatic action in the libretto have hurt its success and made it boring for the majority of listeners. This, by the way, is completely unjustified. In a word, opinions of *Ruslan and Lyudmila* are quite varied. However, all who have seen the opera agree that M. I. Glinka is a man with a great gift for composition" (*Rus. invalid,* no. 5, "Journalistic Notes").

10 January

Quartet rehearsal of *Ruslan* (V. Latyshev's diary, in *Muz. starina,* 1903, v. 2, p. 174).

In a letter to V. Stasov, Serov complains that because of illness he has been unable "to listen as [he] wished to *Ruslan and Lyudmila,* an opera, which, despite its great shortcomings in respect to my first and third points, I cannot help but like because of the second and fourth, which are certainly beautiful and fascinating" (MN I, p. 200).
[According to Serov's and Stasov's terminology at the time, the first point was general poetic conception; the second, choice of characters; the third, layout and scenario; and the fourth, composition and instrumentation.]

11 January

Performance in the Bolshoi Theater of *Ruslan and Lyudmila.* On the occasion of this performance (the nineteenth), K. Albrecht made this extensive entry in his diary: "The music is testimony to the composer's talent. Nonetheless, the all too obvious pursuit of originality very often hinders the free display of emotion, and there is hardly a single number in the opera which is free from oddity. Of the three primary qualities of a piece—truthfulness, beauty, and originality— only the last is present, sometimes at the expense of the first two. In the end this tendency leads to unacceptability, and only total caricatures are possible if one follows such a course. Searching at the piano for strange-sounding chords is also an obstacle which often makes the melody unrecognizable, although one can't deny that some of these harmonic turns produce a marvelous effect. It seems the composer was least able to deal with musical form, especially the form of finales. The first finale is the only exception. For the most part the arias are in sonata form, as is the overture. This is a great error. The cast of performers is bad. The orchestra played well until the fourth performance, but from that point on it played more and more lethargically. Frequently the singers had to change parts. Today a role might be sung by one person, but tomorrow another appears and drives him off. Under such conditions how is a good ensemble possible?" (*Muz. letop.*, 1923, coll. 2, p. 74).

["In 1840, the indefatigable conductor, Cavos, a true friend of Russian talent, was no longer around . . . and his place was taken by the German conductor Karl Albrecht. He was a learned, thorough musician, who, however, did not like Russians" (Yury Arnold, "Is it possible in music, . . ." *Bayan*, 1888, no. 22).]

In a letter to his parents, Voin Rimsky-Korsakov shares his impressions of *Ruslan and Lyudmila:* "I am not a part of the musical world and consequently can be neither an advocate nor an opponent of Glinka. Therefore I am judging the opera solely according to the impression it made on me. Likewise, I can only evaluate the music, because the opera's libretto has no dramatic value at all. It has no continuity, and the individual parts stir no interest whatever. Consequently, there is no need to evaluate the music as a whole, but only in parts. . . . So I will pass over the overture, which I did not understand. To keep things in order, I will begin with Bayan's song . . . the last two couplets of which, '*Odenetsia s zareiu*' [He dressed with the sunrise] are beautiful. The music of the last four lines, '*A rok emu navstrechu*' [He met his fate], is particularly expressive . . . Lyudmila's cavatina follows after this . . . a pretty Russian tune. . . . This is followed by the chorus of nurses . . . a true Christmas Eve [*podbliudnaia*] song. . . . Then Lyudmila's cavatina '*Ne gnevis*', *znatnyi gost'*' [Do not be angry, noble guest]. The first part, in which she turns to Farlaf, is a light, playful melody without any kind of character. Then, when she turns to Ratmir with '*Pod roskoshnym nebom iuga*' [Under the splendid southern sky], the melody changes, and here it is beautiful. . . . After this, when she turns to Ruslan, the music returns to the earlier playful melody, which does not correspond at all to the words. . . . The quartet for Ruslan, Lyudmila, Ratmir, and Farlaf is beautiful. Ratmir's part is especially beautiful ('*Krai dalekii, krai zhelannyi*' [Distant land, longed-for land]), in particular the beautiful solo . . . which Petrova performs masterfully. A second quartet at the point of Lyudmila's abduction is also beautiful. The music expresses fear and bewilderment beautifully. Still another quartet ('*O vitiazi, skorei vo chisto pole*' [O knights, soon to the open field]) is also very good. The feelings of decisiveness and hope on the part of the three knights is very aptly represented in the music. Even though it's long, Finn's ballad in the second act is beautiful. . . . Then Farlaf's fine rondo . . . *'O pole, pole'* [Oh, field, field] . . . a beautiful aria, almost the best place in the entire opera. . . . Then the mist clears, and the Head is presented to our view, inside of which a chorus so awful sang that there was no possibility of making out anything. In the third act is Ratmir's recitative *'Net, son bezhit'* [No, sleep flees]. How beautiful it is! Until now I could never find anything beautiful in recitative. They all seemed dry and vacuous to me, they had no meaning for me. But this one is somehow alive, fiery, and passionate. Words, though, are useless to describe this music. You must hear it, and hear Petrova. . . . I have been to the opera four times. From the first, this recitative made a strong impression on me, and then each time it seemed like the best thing in the opera. Audiences are enthusiastic about it. Every time Glinka has been called out after it. . . . In the fourth act Lyudmila's adagio on a Russian folk melody is very nice. Then there is the excellent little recitative *'Bezumnyi volshebnik'* [Dreadful sorcerer]. . . . In the ballet Andreyanova dances the lezghinka. . . . The music is very simple and monotonous, but it is attractive because of the transitions from a lazy, languorous rhythm to a stormy, fiery, and lively one. In the fifth act, first of all, the entr'acte is excellent. Then Ruslan and Lyudmila's duet is rather good. . . . The melody in minor mode of the chorus *'Ne prosnetsia ptichka utrom'* [The little bird will not awake in the morning] is also rather nice. So here . . . is a short sketch of the opera based upon my own opinions" (*Muz. letop.*, 1922, coll. 1, p. 40).

13 January

Quartet rehearsal of *Ruslan*.

14 January

Orchestral rehearsal of *Ruslan* (V. Latyshev's diary, in *Muz. starina*, 1903, no. 2, p. 174).

An announcement in *Mosk. ved.*, no. 6, advertises the sale of individual numbers from *Ruslan and Lyudmila* (nos. 1, 2, 4, 6, 8, 9, 10, 11, 13, 14, 15, 18, 19, and the overture).

15 January

In an account of the activities of the St. Petersburg theaters during the year 1842, in *Repertuar i panteon*, no. 1, it says that during the year "they presented a new national opera called *Ruslan and Lyudmila,* which, according to general opinion, was inferior to M. I. Glinka's first opera, *A Life for the Tsar.*" In an article entitled "Dramatic Letters, Letter One (to Count A. A. Shakhovskoy)," Bulgarin writes, in admiration of the "operettas" of Cavos: "Our only composers, Messrs. Glinka and Verstovsky, would do much better if they were to write small folk operettas within the limits and capabilities of our performers and more in line with audiences' patience. . . . It has been said that M. I. Glinka wrote *Ruslan and Lyudmila* for future centuries! Why, then, did they invite us, his contemporaries to the theater?" (d.c.a.).

Performance of *Ruslan and Lyudmila* in the Bolshoi Theater (*Sev. pchela*, 15 January 1843).

17 January

In *SPb. ved.*, no. 13, there is a notice stating that Bernard's has for sale Glinka's new romances *"Ne govori, liubov' proidet"* [Do not say that love passes], *"Ia pomniu chudnoe mgnoven'e"* [I recall the wonderful moment], and *"Kak sladko s toboiu mne byt' "* [How sweet for me to be with you].

Serov shares his impressions of *Ruslan and Lyudmila* in a letter to V. Stasov: "If from the time of the first performance of *Ruslan and Lyudmila* someone had carefully observed me, he would have been struck by the strange and sharp contrasts occasioned in my behavior by this opera. When I returned home after the first performance, I was in extremely low spirits, and in the days following I rather savagely abused the opera (which meanwhile I *came to admire . . . at rehearsal*). Then I saw it again, and I attended the opera six times, finally, with growing pleasure, and I will go again and again. . . . I sang and played it at home. . . . Its melodies simply began to pursue me. Meanwhile, however, and frequently, . . . I continued to speak frankly and even with indignation of the shortcomings of Glinka's work. . . . I could not help but enjoy what was actually *beautiful* in the opera . . . but at the same time I could not avoid subjecting the entire work, in whole and part, to the anatomical knife of *our* criticism. . . . In a word, my opinion of *Ruslan and Lyudmila* is just the same as yours. . . . We differ only in particulars" (MN 1, p. 202).

A. Raev writes to Nikolay Chernyshevsky: "In the Bolshoi Theater they presented *Ruslan and Lyudmila*. Almost everything was there, even the Head itself with which Ruslan contends, and the castle to which Lyudmila was abducted. Pushkin's intentions were fully realized. They called the re-creator Glinka to the stage and received the one who did the sets as if he were an academician" (N. Chernyshevsky's *Diary*, part 2, M., 1932, p. 260).

19 January

For performances of *Ruslan and Lyudmila* on 16, 22, 28, 30, and 31 December 1842, and for 2, 4, 7, 11, and 15 January 1843, Glinka received 741 rubles, 68 kopecks from the overall receipts of 11,125 rubles 30 kopecks (*L.*, p. 263).

Performance of *Ruslan and Lyudmila* in the Bolshoi Theater (*Sev. pchela*, 19 January 1843).

"Over the course of 20 performances . . . the opera's success has been a continuous crescendo" (*Mayak*, 1843, vol. 9, no. 17).

23 January

In *Sev. pchela*, no. 18, there is a concluding article by Kliment Kanevsky entitled "Monuments of Patriarchal Times in Georgia," containing a comparison of the Lezghinka from *Ruslan* with folk dances of Georgia.

24 January

Performance of *A Life for the Tsar* in the Bolshoi Theater in Moscow (*Mosk. ved.*, 23 January 1843).

25 January

Performance of *Ruslan and Lyudmila* in the Bolshoi Theater (*Sev. pchela*, 25 January 1843). "For more than two months Petersburg has not stopped talking about Glinka's new opera. More than 20 performances of the work have been crowned with fully warranted success. Never before has the opera of a Russian composer had such an effect on audiences or excited such talk and opposing opinions. One critic heaps lavish praise on *Ruslan and Lyudmila* and even favors it over Beethoven's wonderful symphonies, while others can scarcely bear to compare it with the operettas of the venerable Cavos. . . . Notice that there is no middle ground in all the praise and criticism of the new opera. What you hear is either unreasoning praise or unsubstantiated censure" (*Mayak*, 1843, vol. 9, no. 17, "Miscellany," p. 28).

29 January

Quartet rehearsal of *Ruslan and Lyudmila* (V. Latyshev's diary, in *Muz. starina*, 1903, inst. 2, p. 174).

Performance of *Ruslan and Lyudmila* in the Bolshoi Theater (*Sev. pchela*, 28 January 1843).

In a letter to Aleksandr Gedeonov, Verstovsky writes about the debut of the singer Konyaeva in *A Life for the Tsar* (in the part of Vanya) and gives her an unfavorable recommendation (*L.*, p. 264).

30 January

Pletnev writes to Grot: "I went to Odoevsky's for dinner. From proof-sheets he read me his article about Glinka printed in *Fatherland Notes* under the strange title, 'A Great-Great-Grandfather's Letter to His Great-Great-Grandson'" (*Perepiska Ya. Grota s P. Pletnevym*, v. 2, p. 4).

31 January

In a feuilleton called "Journalistic Amalgam" in *Lit. gaz.*, no. 5, Koni criticizes Bulgarin's article in *Repertuar i Panteon* ("Bulgarin's Dramatic Letters to Prince Shakhovskoy"): "This article is quite remarkable and fully deserving of the appellation *dramatic* because of its *comic* content." As for Bulgarin's recommendation that "Glinka and Verstovsky write small folk operettas," Koni asks: "What else has Mr. Verstovsky written so far but *folk operettas*?"

In *SPb. ved.*, no. 25, there is announcement that the following excerpts from *A Life for the Tsar* are on sale at Bernard's: *"V pole chistoe gliazhu," "Kak mat' ubili"* and Vanya's duet with Susanin, the trio with chorus *"Akh, ne mne bednomu," "Ne o tom skorbliu,"* and the mazurka, ballet, overture, and polonaise.

January

Ulybyshev sent Glinka "his work about Mozart": *Nouvelle biographie de Mozart, suivie d'un aperçu sur l'histoire générale de la musique et de l'analyse des principales oeuvres de Mozart* (in three volumes, SPb., 1843). "I read part of the work and once again studied all of Mozart's operas in orchestral score. Count M. Yu. Vielgorsky's comments and criticism and these exercises awakened a critical spirit in me which subsequently continued to develop."

2 February

Performance of *Ruslan and Lyudmila* in the Bolshoi Theater (*Sev. pchela*, 2 February 1843).

4 February

In *Mosk. ved.*, no. 15, there is an announcement that the romance *"Ne govori, liubov' proidet"* is available in music stores.

5 February

Performance of *A Life for the Tsar* in the Bolshoi Theater (*SPb. ved.*, 5 February 1843).

12 February

Performance in the Bolshoi Theater of *Ruslan and Lyudmila*. Glinka was with the Serovs at this performance (ltr. from A. Serov to V. Stasov, 14 February 1843, in MN 1, p. 203; *SPb. ved.*, 12 February 1843).

13 February

Serov, his sister, and Artemovsky spent the evening at Glinka's. Dyutur and Artemovsky performed a duet from Donizetti's *Belisario*. Glinka "spoke with regret of Italian composers invariably getting stuck in the same well-worn rut, when the same melodies could take on new charm with differently thought-out trimming. They depended upon their audiences' pedestrian tastes and, without any qualms of conscience, they put what really belongs in only one opera into 10 different ones and repeat themselves forever. As I see it, Glinka continued, the two roles in a duet should be discrete. Melody or idea A, followed by idea B, and finally A + B combined, which itself should be different from A or B. Everything should be based on contrasts. However, in standard Italian operas one character sings A, then another sings A, and then both sing the same A together in thirds or sixths. According to this theory, a quartet should be A + B + C + D, etc." In conversation with Serov, Glinka recommended to him that he read Ulybyshev's book about Mozart, which he spoke of "with highest praise, as being the most complete account of Mozart and all his works." "In the matter of *criticism* I depended completely upon Glinka." Glinka expressed satisfaction with Odoevsky's article about *Ruslan and Lyudmila* in the *Fatherland Notes*. "He was extremely pleased with this little article by Count Odoevsky . . . which precisely expressed *his aim in writing Ruslan and Lyudmila*." When Serov expressed regret that the article was so short and that its main theme was insufficiently developed, Glinka answered: "Further development would have required a broader, even *learned* exposition, which does not belong in a periodical which people read *pour passer le temps*." In conversation with Serov, Glinka expressed the opinion "that the latest works for individual instruments, the so-called *pièces de concert* or *de salon* were unbearable for him. An instrument can only imitate the human voice in caricature, which is why one should not expect an instrument to sing the same thing as the voice sings (for example, romances, operatic melodies, these even less, since they can only work in their proper place in relation to the entire work). In general extended pieces for one *instrument* are nonsense. They are talk without meaning or words and phrases without significance. . . . Each instrument possesses its own inimitable charm, but only when it is used appropriately, as in a phrase, in two or three bars, or sometimes even one unadorned note (especially the woodwinds)" (ltr. from A. Serov to V. Stasov, 14 February 1843, in MN 1, p. 203; *SPb. ved.*, 12 February 1843).

14 February

Performance of *A Life for the Tsar* in the Bolshoi Theater (*SPb. ved.*, 14 February 1843).

Senkovsky writes to Elizaveta Akhmatova: "How dear you are! And how kind! You took my side so enthusiastically in the Glinka matter that you even wanted to hate Bulgarin. . . . But Bulgarin is not worth hating or loving. He is a man without character or principles. . . . You can easily imagine that his ignobly motivated persecution of Glinka filled me with indignation. I do not know whether Glinka's character is the most pleasant or not, nor do I know if his friends are the most charming people. This, however, does not justify these gentlemen's vile effort because of some personal remarks to try to berate a talent Russia may be proud of or to destroy at its outset the labor of six years and ruin the fame of a Russian composer, to whom all of us should show respect as a man of true genius. Fortunately the article which you read . . . [Senkovsky's, in *Bib-ka dlia chteniia*] saved Glinka's opera, which, even if it was performed with serious shortcomings, nonetheless deserves to stand alongside the best magical operas. Even now the theater is full, and the piece has successfully reached its twenty-fifth performance. The number of admirers of this original and clever music is already huge. Furthermore, thanks to the exercise of my personal influence on my dear enemies, whom I hastened to console, they also have calmed down and stopped abusing *Ruslan and Lyudmila*. Now it's up to Glinka to maintain his reputation himself with a new work which will take full acount of theatrical effects. . . . I will send you a copy of the piano-vocal score of *Ruslan and Lyudmila*" (*Rus. starina*, 1889, vol. 62, no. 5, p. 296; Fr. original).

15 February

Performance of *Ruslan and Lyudmila* in the Bolshoi Theater (*Sev. pchela*, 15 February 1843).

17 February

Morning performance in the Bolshoi Theater of *Ruslan and Lyudmila* (*Sev. pchela*, 17 February 1843).

18 February

Morning performance in the Bolshoi Theater of *Ruslan and Lyudmila* (*Sev. pchela*, 18 February 1843).

19 February

Ruslan and Lyudmila in the Bolshoi Theater (*SPb. ved.*, 19 February 1843).

Nikolay Polevoy writes to Verstovsky: *"Ruslan and Lyudmila* has now so gotten on the nerves of everyone that no one goes to see it, despite the fact that it's Shrovetide. By chance I happened to be at the twenty-ninth performance [18 February] and was surprised at the emptiness of the theater. I cannot grasp why good people have to be fooled by giving at any time a work which no one comes to see. Meanwhile Glinka's friends cry out shamelessly in the press. . . . He is working on a new opera, and what do you think he has selected for his libretto? *Hamlet!* I think this is foolishness of the first order and a misunderstanding of the basis of his art. It would be interesting to hear just how Hamlet might sing 'To be or not to be.' . . . Have you heard about the new drama, music, and art journal which Glinka, Odoevsky, and Vyazemsky wish to publish? Its prospectus has already been given to the censor" (coll. *Glinka*, pp. 154, 161, 164).
[Polevoy attended a performance of *Ruslan and Lyudmila* which, like the previous one, occurred during the days of the traditional Shrovetide festivities.]

20 February

Performance of *Ruslan and Lyudmila* in the Bolshoi Theater (*SPb. ved.*, 19 February 1843).

There is an announcement in *Mosk. ved.*, no. 22, that the romance *"Kak sladko s toboiu mne byt' "* is on sale in music stores.

21 February

Performance of *Ruslan and Lyudmila* in the Bolshoi Theater (*Sev. pchela,* 21 February 1843).

In *Lit. gaz.,* no. 8, in the section "Petersburg Theaters," there is a review of Aksel's vaudeville *"Eshche Ruslan i Lyudmila, ili Novyi dom sumasshedshikh"* [Ruslan and Lyudmila once again, or the new madhouse]. It refers to the fact that one of the participants in the vaudeville sings lines based on the Head's theme in *Ruslan and Lyudmila.*

From 27 November 1842 through 21 February 1843

"*Ruslan and Lyudmila* has been given 32 times. Audiences developed a taste for the music as performances continued, and many places in the opera soon became popular. Ratmir's scene in the third act, which Petrova I performed wonderfully, made the greatest impression, as well as the passionate '*Chudnyi son zhivoi liubvi*' at the end. Although not every performance brought huge returns, the opera was successful enough that the Directorate found it profitable to give *Ruslan and Lyudmila* . . . 35 [32] times in three months" (M. Longinov, Preface to Glinka's letters to K. Bulgakov, in *Rus. arkhiv,* 1869, book 1, inst. 2, p. 345).

After 21 February (?)

The Chief of Repertoire for the Moscow Theaters, A. E. Mukhin, writes to Verstovsky: "I saw *Ruslan* and found it better than I expected. The orchestration was very good, as it seemed to me, although perhaps I should not assert this in a letter from a nonmusician to a musician. Petrova's aria in the third act fascinated me, and in general this act was the most effective, especially the best parts of the music and ballet. The sets were exceptionally effective. Insofar as the bride's first cavatina in the first act goes, it was burdened to the point of excess with embellishment. Just one more observation, and that is that there is no dramatic point to the opera, and there are neither duets nor trios, just one quartet, and that's the finale. The characters enter, sing, and exit without meeting anyone or without arguments or making up. There is no dramatic element. Earlier I attributed the guilt to the librettist, though I later found out that the music was written as the Italians do, not to a libretto, but prior to it. The words were added out of generosity . . ." (coll. *Glinka,* p. 158).
[When it was first published, the letter was dated in March, since it contains a reference to Polevoy's play *Lomonosov,* whose premiere occurred on 2 February. Most likely the letter was written in February while the impressions of what he had seen were still fresh, though not later than 21

February, which was the date of the last performance of *Ruslan and Lyudmila* before the interruption for Lent.]

23 February

The production of *Ruslan and Lyudmila* is mentioned in *Sev. pchela,* no. 41, in the section "Miscellany."

24 February

For performances of *Ruslan and Lyudmila* on 19, 25, and 29 January, and for 2, 8, 12, 15, 17, 18, 19, 20, and 21 February, Glinka received royalties amounting to 592 rubles 74 kopecks from the overall receipts of 8,891 rubles 20 kopecks (*L.,* p. 268). "By Lent I had received nearly 3,000 rubles in separate amounts from the theater accounting office which I gave to Mother to keep."

27 February

Serov writes to Stasov: "I find in your letter the exposition of a sad reaction to our orchestra's performance of *Ruslan and Lyudmila,* and in general your thoughts are very close to those which I had all that time. . . . As you are quite correctly finding out, Glinka is an excellent conductor. However, if fate were to put him in the place of Cavos, I do not think that he would be very close to our ideal. A number of things prevent this . . . e.g., his unfortunate egoism. He has too little regard for anything contemporary. . . . Furthermore, I feel I know that Glinka's views on art are incomplete. Consequently, he could not give outstanding performances of operas without the help of another person to oversee everything, including production" (MN 1, p. 205).

There is an announcement in *Mosk. ved.,* no. 25, that Lengold's music store has individual numbers from *A Life for the Tsar,* including a French quadrille and the Polonaise transcribed for flute and piano. In the "Miscellany" section of the same issue, there is an announcement of Bantyshev's concert in the Maly Theater on 3 March, when he is to perform selections from *Ruslan and Lyudmila.*

28 February

In an article by Vasily Mezhevich in *Repertuar i panteon,* no. 3, *A Life for the Tsar* is referred to as an example of the embodiment of the patriotic ideal in art. The article also criticizes Aksel's vaudeville *Eshche Ruslan i Lyudmila.* In "Musical Observations. First Article" (signed "S. K.") in the same issue, a separate section is devoted to *Ruslan and Lyudmila.* The reviewer subjects many of the opera's numbers to criticism, beginning with the overture. However, he speaks favorably of the nurses' chorus and that of the maids, of Finn's ballad, Farlaf's rondo, Gorislava's cavatina, Ratmirs's aria, the ballet music, Lyudmila's adagio, Ruslan's aria "*O, pole, pole,*" etc., using epithets of enthusiasm. He remarks about the length of individual pieces and the insufficient justification for this. In conclusion he writes: "Several people have asserted that one should not look at *Ruslan and Lyudmila* as an opera, but as an oratorio, performed on the stage in costume and with sets. In this respect, perhaps, Glinka's work might be really novel and original!!! Though we must confess to not understanding oratorio like this but rather tend to feel that if music is written in the form of an opera, then it must be an opera and not an oratorio, which has its own special significance and conditions" (d.c.a.).

[Boris Shteynpress suggests that "S. K." is Sergey Petrovich Krasheninnikov (coll. *Glinka*, p. 156). While not disputing this, Kremlev shows that there are frequent borrowings in "S. K.'s" piece from articles by Guillou and Rezvoy (Yuly Kremlev, *Russkaia mysl' o muzyke* [Russian musical thought], L., 1954, p. 106). Shteynpress names other sources for "S. K.'s" article (coll. *Glinka*).]

Serov characterizes Glinka's creative work in a letter to V. Stasov: "He is a *phenomenon,* actually quite *remarkable,* because one can study his individuality in the *beauties* of his work. . . . With *Ruslan and Lyudmila* he has demonstrated what one should not do, that is, he has provided an example to show the errors of contemporary Western European opera composers. With what he has given us . . . he has shown what should not be done as he did it. In any event, his works deserve profound study, which is what I am doing" (*MN* 1, p. 209).

In the section headed "Miscellany" in *Otech. zap.*, vol. 27, no. 3/4, there is a review by Belinsky of Aksel's vaudeville-farce *Eshche Ruslan i Lyudmila*. In the review he describes a character who, with his head in a bucket, "sings the Head's aria from the opera *Ruslan and Lyudmila.*" In the same issue *Ruslan and Lyudmila* is referred to in a poem by Nekrasov entitled *Govorun. Zapiski peter-burgskogo zhitelia A. F. Belopyatkina* [The talker. Notes of the Petersburg inhabitant A. F. Belopyatkin] (d.c.a.).

In the "Miscellany" section of *Bib-ka dlia chteniia*, vol. 57, there is notice of the publication of several new romances and songs by Glinka: *"Pamiat' serdtsa"* [Heart's memory], *"Dedushka, devitsy raz mne govorili"* [Grandfather, maids once told me], *"Skazhi, zachem"* [Tell me, why], *"Akh ty, noch' li, nochen'ka"* [O night, dark night], *"Noch' osenniaia, liubeznaia"* [Gentle autumnal night], and *"Akh, ty, dushechka, krasna devitsa"* [You darling, beautiful maid]. There is also a notice that the romances *"Ne govori, liubov' proidet"* [Do not say that love passes], *"Ia pomniu chudnoe mgnoven'e"* [I recall the wonderful moment], and *"Kak sladko s toboiu mne byt' "* [How sweet for me to be with you] are on sale at Bernard's (d.c.a.).

3 March

In a large instrumental and vocal concert in Moscow, Bantyshev and Bobovsky performed the "grand ballad-scene and duet." Bantyshev also performed a "recitative and cavatina from the opera *Ruslan and Lyudmila,* and, in addition, a grand aria with chorus by Glinka" (*Mosk. ved.,* 27 February 1843).

4 March

In a concert in the Moscow Maly Theater, Mikhaylov performed a "grand aria with chorus" from *A Life for the Tsar* (*Mosk. ved.,* 4 March 1843).

9 March

In *Sev. pchela,* no. 53, there is an article by R. Zotov entitled "Overview of the Petersburg Theaters for the Past Theater Season. Second Article: Russian Opera." It says with respect to *Ruslan and Lyudmila* that it "represents an epoch in theater annals. . . . All the pros and cons with which everyone is deafened every day are probably hated by one and all. Glinka is a man with tremendous talent. Audiences find his opera a pleasant and gratifying experience. Its shortcomings? Where aren't they? Nonetheless, we should be proud of it as the work of a Russian composer. One thing about it saddens us, and that is the length of time from one opera to the next. Now the entire wealth of our theater consists of his two operas."

13 March

There an announcement in *Mosk ved.,* no. 31, that a French quadrille on themes from *Ruslan and Lyudmila* is on sale at Müller and Grotrian's.

27 March

In *Mosk. ved.,* no. 37, there is an announcement of a concert in the Maly Theater in which the trio from *A Life for the Tsar* is to be performed.

28 March

Koni writes about *Ruslan and Lyudmila* in an article entitled "Overview of the Dramatic Activities of the Petersburg Theaters During the Second Half of the

1842/43 Theater Season" in *Lit. gaz.,* no. 13: "Grand lyric opera in five acts. Clumsy libretto by an unknown author. Excellent music by M. I. Glinka. In battle this opera has won audiences' attention and admiration and has clearly proven that the theater can manage without pandering . . . to poor taste, but, on the contrary, it can cultivate taste and give art a proper direction and acquaint people with true aesthetic enjoyment. *Terrific success.* It has been performed 32 times in the course of two months. Mme Petrova I stood out in particular." In the same issue there is a notice of the publication of two of Glinka's romances (among the "best of new publications"), transcribed by Henselt for piano ("although somewhat difficult, it is an outstanding piece of 17 pages"). The immediate publication (by May 1) by "Odeum" of still unpublished parts of "Ruslan" is also reported here. Cited are the introduction and two finales and two choruses, with a portrait of Glinka ("a remarkable likeness") accompanying the publication. "It is not insignificant that the price is quite moderate . . . the more so as the edition is sumptuous and fully worthy of this beautiful, nationalist work."

In a mixed vocal and instrumental concert with tableaux vivants in the Moscow Maly Theater, Leonova, Leonov, and Bobovsky performed the trio with chorus from *A Life for the Tsar* (*Mosk. ved.,* 27 March 1843).

30 March

The consistory's decision concerning Glinka's denial in his divorce suit was rendered (*L.,* p. 271).

In a vocal and instrumental concert in the Moscow Maly Theater, Mikhaylova performed an aria with chorus from *A Life for the Tsar* (*Mosk. ved.,* 30 March 1843).

Beginning of Spring

"Evenings at Misha Gedeonov's got more and more lively and entertaining. Besides the Gedeonovs, regular guests included Count Kutuzov, Varlamov, K. Bulgakov, P. P. Kamensky, Goronovich (Alisa), the secretary to the Director Aleksandr Lvovich Nevakhovich, Heydenreich, Dr. Bers, and my old school companion Samarin. We got along in perfect harmony and often had supper on the leftovers from the Director's dinner, and if this was not enough, then we pooled our resources, and everyone contributed whatever he happened to have. We parted very late, so that I rarely got home from Gedeonov's before 5 o'clock in the morning."

["At about this same time" Glinka wrote the Tarantella in A Minor for piano on the theme of the Russian folk song *"Vo pole berezon'ka stoiala"* [In the field there stood a little birch tree] (ITMK, coll. 6).]

14 April

"Liszt, who dropped in on us completely unexpectedly, like snow falling on your head, gave a concert in Engelgardt Hall immediately on his arrival" *(Rus. invalid,* 16 April 1843).

16 April

Glinka was at the Karamzins' and, together with Evdokia Rostopchina, Vladimir Odoevsky, and others, made a humorous annotation in Sofia Karamzina's album: "Retired Collegiate Assessor Mikhail Ivanov, son of Glinka, was a witness and does affix his signature, 16 April 1843" (facsimile in *Rus. bibliofil,* 1916, no. 6).

17 April

The sculptor A. Gavrilov applied to the office of the Imperial Theaters to be released from his obligation to repair the mechanism of the Head in the opera *Ruslan and Lyudmila (L.,* p. 271).

18 April

Liszt's concert with Rubini took place at 2 p.m. "For Mikhail Ivanovich this was all quite amusing, especially considering his ironical and embittered mood at the time" (Serov, *Vosp.,* p. 94; *Sev. pchela,* 17 April 1843).

Performance of *Ruslan and Lyudmila* in the Bolshoi Theater *(Sev. pchela,* 17 April 1843). At the performance "in a box with a small group of literary and musical celebrities one could see a thin, young man with an enthusiastic look . . . who followed the course of the opera with rapt attention. . . . It was easy to recognize who the lofty connoisseur of this piece of Russian music was. One can imagine what kind of impression his approving applause had on the audience. Both the Petrovs, Leonov, Semyonova, and Tosi were called out, and the composer of *Ruslan and Lyudmila* was honored with two curtain calls. Liszt did not utter a sound and . . . left the theater with an expression of amazement and complete satisfaction. How strange that the opera did not seem long and boring to Europe's premier musician. Now judge the criticisms of *Ruslan and Lyudmila* for yourselves" *(Lit. gaz.,* 25 April 1843). "Liszt listened to my opera and correctly appreciated all the noteworthy places. . . . He made me feel better about the work's success. In his words, not just in Petersburg, but also in Paris, my opera could be considered a success for having lasted for 32 performances in the course of one winter."

19 April

Directive from the office of the Imperial Theaters to the scenery director about transferring responsibility for looking after the mechanism of the Head in *Ruslan and Lyudmila* to Roller. Roller wrote in response: "Because of its size, the Head requires repair before every performance. It must not be seen in a marred and dirty condition, which would diminish its entire effect. *Ruslan and Lyudmila* is not being performed as often now as it was before . . . so I certainly think that Mr. Gavrilov's own interests will not suffer. I hope that these remarks of mine will not be taken to mean that I wish to avoid my responsibilities. The matter is too insignificant to be worth this, the more so as I am present at every performance" (*L.*, p. 273).

Performance in the Moscow Bolshoi Theater of *A Life for the Tsar* (*Mosk. ved.*, 19 April 1843).

22 April

Instructions from the Directorate of Theaters to Roller: "When it is necessary to repair [the Head], Gavrilov will come, but the maintenance and functioning of the Head must be the mechanic's responsibility" (*L.*, p. 237).

25 April

There is a comment in *Lit. gaz.*, no. 16, about Liszt's attendance at *Ruslan and Lyudmila* on 18 April.

26 April

Karl Bryullov, in a humorous letter with a drawing, invites Glinka to come to Yanenko's.
[There are similar letters in Stepanov's and others' archives. In *RMG*, no. 12, 1896, Yanenko is identified as the author of the letter, but Bryullov's handwriting and drawing refute this assertion.]

Ruslan and Lyudmila is referred to in a notice by R. Zotov in "Journalistic Odds and Ends" in *Sev. pchela*, no. 90.

28 April

Glinka attends a party arranged by pooling everyone's resources at Yanenko's (ltr. from K. Bryullov to Glinka, 26 April 1845, in *RMG*, no. 12, 1896).

29 April

In a letter to Gedeonov, Verstovsky reports that the season in Moscow opened with the opera *A Life for the Tsar* (*L.*, p. 274).

1 May

In the "Miscellany" section of *Mayak,* vol. 9, part 17, there is an article signed "O***" [Odoevsky] entitled *"Ruslan and Lyudmila,* Opera by M. I. Glinka." "Someone a long time ago made a very justified observation, which fully applies to Glinka's new opera. If a composition stirs strong enthusiasm in one quarter of society and equally strong enmity in another, you may be assured that it is no ordinary composition. . . . Our audiences have not received a musical education. . . . but the verdict of society, the final code of all opinions, is nonetheless almost always reliable. . . . Audiences have now heard more than 20 performances of *Ruslan and Lyudmila.* The opera's success is not to be doubted. Judgment has been made. . . . Everyone knows Pushkin's 'Ruslan and Lyudmila' . . . but the opera has a completely different character than the poem. The poem is one of the immature works of a young poet, who did not take advantage of the full wealth of his subject but simply told a legend of magic from olden times using melodious verses set in contemporary form. His is a magical opera *buffa* of the Italian school—light, playful, melodic, but not striking either to the mind or the heart. A more mature artist grasped what it was in this fantasy and these characters that might be musically sublime. . . . To arrange the outlines of the opera more expertly would have been impossible. The action begins in Russia with Slavic music. Later we hear the tunes of the Chuds and Tatars with whom Russia consorted. We hear the melodies of the West from the mouth of Farlaf and the sensuous South from the lips of Ratmir. And once again, in the person of Ruslan, we celebrate Russia's victory in sight of grand-ducal Kiev. To catch the distinctive character of various primitive musics which have not yet attained the level of art; to make something elegant from them; and to create out of their confusion a beautiful whole was a gigantic undertaking. Failure would have been nothing to be ashamed of. Glinka, however, did not lose the battle with this difficult subject. The basic idea—Finnish and Tatar closed in the magic ring of Slavism—is clearly developed on the involved canvas of a magic tale. Individual musical elements are vividly distinguished from one another on the opera's prime coat, and the distinctive character of each is maintained throughout the entire work. The ear immediately distinguishes the composed Finn's gloomy singing from the passion of the South, or the wild fantasy of the East from the light melodies of the West. It is strange to hear the libretto chastised for lack of action and distinctive characters when the opera's real drama consists in the conflict of musical elements and not of characters. Drama occurs in the contrast between the rich musical lives of peoples, not between individual characters. To criticize such an opera because of insufficient dramatic action and inconsistency of characters amounts to the same as criticizing an epic because it is not a drama or a novel. It is above them all! . . ." (d.c.a.).

[A controversy arose between Abram Gozenpud (*Sov. muzyka*, 1957, no. 5) and Tamara Livanova and Vladimir Protopopov (*Russkaia kritika*, vol. 1, part 2, p. 278) over the authorship of this article. However, the character and similarity of many ideas with others of Odoevsky's articles do not call Odoevsky's authorship into question. (Incidentally, Odoevsky on several occasions signed his name simply "O" with one or more asterisks.)]

In an article on Italian opera by "A. E." [Aleksandr Elkan] in *SPb. ved.*, no. 95, Petrova-Vorobieva's best roles are mentioned, among which the author includes the part of Vanyusha in *A Life for the Tsar.*

2 May

Performance of *Ruslan and Lyudmila* in the Bolshoi Theater (*Sev. pchela*, 1 May 1843).

3 May

The ecclesiastical consistory announces to Glinka the dismissal of his divorce suit (*L.*, p. 274).

Serov writes to V. Stasov: "Your idea that I already possess the means for us to get closer to Bryullov, i.e., through Glinka, does not seem entirely feasible to me. The main and only obstacle . . . is the difference between the way they live and the way I live. This difference prevents me from getting as close to Glinka as I need to be (though I'm already on quite close terms with him)" (*MN* 1, p. 219).

Beginning of May

Elkan's transcription for piano of Glinka's romance *"Ne govori, liubov' proidet"* is printed in *Le Nouvelliste*, no. 5.

8 May

In a performance in Moscow of *Russkaia boiarynia XVII stoletiia* [A noble Russian lady of the seventeenth century], Saburova performed Ilyinishna's song from *Prince Kholmsky* (*Mosk. ved.*, 8 May 1843).

16 May

There is an announcement in *SPb. ved.*, no. 108, that Elkan's transcription for piano of Glinka's romance *"Ne govori, liubov' proidet"* is available at Bernard's.

20 May

In *Mosk. ved.*, no. 60, there is an announcement that Leopold Langer's Fantasy for Piano on the Cavatina *"Grustno mne"* from the Opera *Ruslan and Lyudmila* is available at Gresser's music store.

29 May

In *Sev. pchela,* no. 118, "Journalistic Odds and Ends," Bulgarin takes exception with Rubini's critical comments about the singing of the Court Chapel Choir. "Rubini is just a famous performer, that is, a performer of other people's works, and not a creative artist. We have musical artists: A. F. Lvov, M. I. Glinka, and Count M. Yu. Vielgorsky."

April–May

Glinka was present at a dinner at Senkovsky's in honor of Liszt (*Osip Ivanovich Senkovsky. Biograficheskie zapiski ego zheny* [Biographical notes of his wife], p. 142).

It was announced that at his fifth concert Liszt would also do "free improvisations on themes provided by the audience. . . . In a basket in which the themes had been collected there were not more than 15–16 tunes . . . from the works of Haydn, Mozart, Beethoven, and Mendelssohn, and only two or three themes belonging to other non-German composers. . . . After the first seven or eight themes . . . only sparse applause could be heard here and there. Suddenly Liszt pulled out a sheet of music paper of somewhat larger format. '*A la bonne heure! Voilà deux thèmes à la fois!*' he said, and played them. The first theme was from *A Life for the Tsar,* namely Vanya's song ('*Kak mat' ubili*'), and the second was Chernomor's march from *Ruslan and Lyudmila*. When Liszt played the first theme it was met with unanimous, deafening applause throughout the hall, and after the theme from the march there was even more enthusiastic clapping from all quarters." Mikhail Vielgorsky provided these themes (Arnold, p. 218).

While walking with Mikhail Vielgorsky in Pavlovsk Park, Liszt met Grand Prince Mikhail Pavlovich. Taking Liszt aside, the Grand Prince asked, "Does Liszt really seriously believe that Glinka is a genius? Liszt answered him, saying that it was his profoundest conviction" (M. Sabinina, *Vosp.*, in *Rus. arkhiv*, 1901, bk. 2, inst. 7, p. 439). "I remember a startling comment that Grand Prince Mikhail Pavlovich made to me. He said, 'Whenever I have to put one of my officers under arrest, I send him to performances of Glinka's operas'" (ltr. from F. Liszt to Countess Mercy d'Argenteau, 24 October 1884, in Stasov, *Izbr. 3*, p. 432).

"Liszt . . . often drank with us in the company of the Gedeonovs . . . and Count Arkady Pavlovich Kutuzov. . . . I candidly expressed my views to him [Liszt] on art and composers. I said that in my opinion I found Karl Maria Weber quite unsatisfactory (even in *Freischütz*) because of his excessive use of dominant seventh chords in first position. Liszt's response to me was, '*Vous êtes avec Weber comme deux rivaux, qui courtisez la même femme.*'"

"In the spring my mother and sister Olga Ivanovna went to the country, while my sister Elizaveta Ivanovna went with my nephew to a dacha belonging to the Forestry Institute." Glinka stayed in Davydov's house.

Bachelors' party at Glinka's in honor of Liszt. Present were Mikhail Vielgorsky, Sollogub, Dargomyzhsky, Petrov, the pianist Karl Vollweiler, the Kukolnik brothers, Arnold, Bulgakov, Lodi, and Yanenko. The following works were performed: Ruslan's aria (Petrov), Finn's tale (Lodi), Ratmir's aria (Glinka). Liszt played the overture, Persian chorus, and Chernomor's march from score. During dinner Glinka "gave a speech, in which he announced that all the intelligentsia of the world comprise one common family, *le bohème*, and that at the present time the king of the bohemians was none other than Liszt, who should be honored with swinging [*kachanie*]. Liszt attempted to hold off those who were trying to get to him and thanked us sincerely for the honor accorded him, but he remarked that our dress did not befit true bohemians. Coats and ties were thrown off, Liszt was swung, they drank hot punch and sang gypsy songs. Liszt was ecstatic with our gypsy singing" (Arnold, 220).

"Trouble and unpleasantness in the theater, just like in the divorce, became loathsome to me, and I grew indifferent to everyone. Although I had found out that Maria Petrovna had borne a daughter of her second husband, I in no way wanted to prosecute her for this, rightly fearing new trouble and unpleasantness."

1 June

Glinka's romance *"Liubliu tebia, milaia roza"* [I love you, dear rose] is printed in *Le Nouvelliste*, no. 6 (d.c.a.).

2 June

In a concert (with the assistance of Rubini, Blaes, and Mme Merti) Liszt performed Vollweiler's Capriccio on Dances from the Opera *Ruslan and Lyudmila* and Chernomor's march on Lichtenthal's new piano (*Lit. gaz.*, 6 June 1843). "Glinka's self-esteem was quite flattered when Liszt played his masterful transcription of Chernomor's march and Vollweiler's fantasy on the lezghinka at one of his concerts" (Serov, *Vosp.*, p. 95). "In his last concert . . . in the Bolshoi Theater, he [Liszt] was the object of enthusiastic ovations, especially after his performance of the march from *Ruslan and Lyudmila*" (V. Zotov, *Vosp.*, in *Istoricheskii vestnik*, 1890, vol. 39, p. 47).

6 June

Koni's review of Vollweiler's dances from *Ruslan and Lyudmila* as performed by Liszt appears in *Lit. gaz.*, no. 22, "Journalistic Amalgam": "In the Capriccio, variations on themes from Arabic and Lezghin dances are arranged . . . with great artistry and effect. The embellishments are tasteful, and transitions are original without being abrupt, all of which adds up to considerable musical value. The piece is rather long, but it is so well arranged and has such variety that one can hear it through to the end with great satisfaction. One can imagine how much it profited from Liszt's performance."

In *SPb. ved.*, no. 124, there is a notice that Glinka's unpublished romance *"Liubliu tebia, milaia roza"* [I love you, dear rose] has been printed in *Le Nouvelliste*, no. 6.

In *Rus. invalid*, no. 123, "Journalistic Notices," there is an announcement of a concert on 2 July, in which Liszt is to perform Chernomor's march and Vollweiler's capriccio from *Ruslan and Lyudmila*.

Farewell dinner in honor of Liszt at Count Arkady Golenishchev-Kutuzov's. Present were the host, Natalia Andreevna, "known for her beauty," Bryullov, Glinka, Henselt, Norov, Mikhail and Stepan Gedeonov, Nestor Kukolnik, Mikhail

Vielgorsky, Heydenreich, Etter, I. K. Varlam, Nashchokin, Liszt, Count Teleki, and Yanenko. "There was much singing and talking, but mostly music making. We parted in the morning" (Bulgakov, *Vosp.*, p. 234). During dinner "conversation turned to my opera, and Count Mikhail Yurievich Vielgorsky said again, *'C'est un opéra manqué.'* Since I was tired of hearing the same thing again and again, I asked for the attention of everyone at dinner. 'Gentlemen!,' I said, turning to him, 'I consider the Count to be one of the best musicians whom I have ever met.' Everyone unanimously agreed with my proposal. 'Now, with your hand over your heart, tell me, Count, would you sign your name to this opera if you had written it?' 'Of course, gladly,' he answered. 'Then permit me too to be satisfied with my work.'"

7 June

In an article entitled "Rubini and the Opera" by R. [Zotov] in *Sev. pchela,* no. 124, Glinka is mentioned as Cavos's successor in the creation of Russian opera.

26 June

In *Sev. pchela,* no. 140, there is an announcement that Glinka's new romance *"Liubliu tebia, milaia roza"* [I love you, dear rose] is available at Bernard's.

Before 29 June

Glinka gave Serov, who was leaving for Nizhny Novgorod, a copy of the full score of *A Life for the Tsar* for Ulybyshev. "By giving Ulybyshev the score, Glinka had in mind (which his letter to him mentions) that the Russian critic, who had written a book about the life and works of Mozart, might also favor an opera by a Russian musician with a long, detailed analysis." Serov fulfilled Glinka's request, although later Glinka was amused by his gullibility. "Sir, you might just as well have kept the score for yourself as to give it to Ulybyshev. I would have never known the difference" (Serov, *Vosp.*, p. 95).

29 June

Serov informs V. Stasov that "I already have a letter of recommendation from Glinka" to Ulybyshev, and that "in my suitcase . . . I have the score (in manuscript) of Glinka's *A Life for the Tsar* to deliver *to him"* (MN 1, p. 222).

30 June

Glinka wrote a petition to the Synod requesting reconsideration of his divorce case. "Since I take the fairness of my case for granted and am convinced of the correctness of my evidence, I . . . cannot accept . . . the consistory's decision as satisfactory. Without really indicting me, it still does not vindicate me, and it lays such a heavy burden on me that my physical and moral strength cannot bear it. My wife's illegal and completely immoral behavior, which have made me the object of perverse gossip and deprived me of domestic and spiritual peace, have slandered my good and till now untarnished name. In the eyes of society I am the object of unwarrented disgrace, which I must bear, knowing the full measure of my innocence. I see no possibility of being reconciled at some time with a person I formerly loved, but who now, along with womanly shame has lost any claim to people's respect and has voluntarily estranged herself from me." There follows a detailed account of the separation.

In *Bib-ka dlia chteniia,* vol. 59, "Musical News," there is a report about the "piano-orchestra" invented by Lichtenthal. "In order to gain a genuine appreciation for the variety of colors of which this instrument is capable, one should hear Glinka improvise on the piano-orchestra. He was fascinated with it and in just a few evenings acquired a knack for playing it with the quickness of a brilliant composer used to orchestrating his thoughts." In the same article it also mentions Liszt's performance of Vollweiler's Fantasy on Themes from *Ruslan and Lyudmila* (d.c.a.).

1 July

In an article entitled "Slavonic Literary News" in *Mayak,* vol. 10, parts 19/20, texts are introduced from songs of the Luzhitsky Serbs from the collection *Wendische Volkslieder.* "What a treasure these original tunes are for Slavic composers . . . M. I. Glinka! Here is a vital source for a new opera with pan-Slavic music!" (d.c.a.).

2 July

"Case concerning Collegiate Assessor Mikhail Glinka's request in his divorce suit" is opened in the Synod (TsGIA, coll. 796, no. 1018, in *L.,* p. 276).

Glinka's Mazurka for Piano is printed in *Le Nouvelliste,* no. 7 (d.c.a.). Glinka is mentioned among composers of published works in an article entitled "The Journal *Le Nouvelliste*" in *SPb. ved.,* no. 146.

5 July

The pianist Nikolay Kashevsky publishes his Grand Fantasy for Piano on Themes from *A Life for the Tsar* in Odessa (*Odessk. vestn.*, 14 July 1843).

6 July

In *SPb. ved.*, no. 149, there is an announcement of the first publication of Glinka's Mazurka in *Le Nouvelliste*, no. 7.

13 July

In *Mosk. ved.*, no. 83, there is an announcement of a performance on 15 July, in which Saburova will perform Ilyinishna's song "The wind is at the gates" from *Prince Kholmsky*.

14 July

Performance of *Ruslan and Lyudmila* in the Bolshoi Theater. "Mikhaylov's debut" in the role of Finn (*SPb. ved.*, 14 July 1843; *Sev. pchela*, 15 July 1843).

15 and 16 July

At mixed concerts in the Maly Theater in Moscow, Saburova performs Ilyinishna's song (*Mosk. ved.*, 13 and 15 July 1843).

27 July

In a note to Maria Krzhisevich, Glinka asks that some books be given to Ekaterina Kern, and adds *"Adieu, à ce soir au théâtre."*
[The letter is dated "Tuesday." In the summer of 1843, there was a performance of *Ruslan and Lyudmila* in the Bolshoi Theater on Tuesday, July 27, which provides the basis for dating Glinka's note.]

Performance of *Ruslan and Lyudmila* in the Bolshoi Theater. "Mikhaylov was bad and Semyonova fatigued. There was no military orchestra. During the first act there were only two cellists in the orchestra. By the third act, Romberg arrived and played first chair. Härtel had a day off in Pavlovsk, and Rubets had no trumpet. By the third act one arrived, since it had to be gotten from the Mikhaylovsky Theater (K. Albrecht's diary, in *Muz. letop.*, 1923, coll. 2, p. 75).

30 July

Serov (from Nizhny Novgorod) writes to V. Stasov that his meeting with Uly-byshev was disappointing to him. "He praises Glinka too unreasonably" and in general creates the impression of a "chatterer." Serov felt that Ulybyshev did not understand the sense and meaning of *A Life for the Tsar* when he compared it to performances from 1812 and 1813. "As if that were *all!* Those performances were *pièces d'occasion* . . . Glinka hoped for a *permanent* impression. In analyzing his opera, one must not omit consideration of the patriotic mood of the people, since then it came from *outside,* and now it must be *from within.* First of all one would have to understand what the *idea* of this music drama is, i.e., love for the Tsar and fatherland may be the *only* motive force of a lyric poem, taken *independently* of the people." Serov writes that he has studied the score of *A Life for the Tsar* and was particularly struck by the "Polish scene . . . here the drama is better than nearly anything else Glinka has written" (MN 1, p. 230).

July

"The famous harpist Dewitte" arrived from Moscow. "He played very precisely, and his own compositions were not bad. I met him repeatedly, either at his home, or at the Vladislavlevs, and finally, he spent an evening at the Tar-novskys."

Beginning of August

Soon after Dewitte's departure, Glinka was taken ill. "I suffered for several months and finally entrusted myself to the care of Heydenreich, who cured me" (*Zap.*).

7/19 August

The romance *"Il desiderio,"* transposed for mezzo-soprano or baritone, was given to the publisher Ricordi for engraving (coll. *Glinka 1958,* p. 393).

10 August

Dargomyzhsky writes to Vladimir Kastrioto-Skanderbek about *Ruslan and Lyudmila:* "Here is a splendid thing, which didn't quite make it! But the talent and work it took to write it! There are many numbers I am genuinely enthusiastic about" (coll. *Dargomyzhsky,* p. 14).

11 August

Glinka's divorce petition was heard in the Synod and an order issued to transfer the case from the consistory (TsGIA, coll. 796). The order was sent on 14 September. (The journal of the session was signed on 10 September).

18 August

Serov (from Nizhny Novgorod) writes to Stasov that assigning the part of Ruslan to a bass, "which, in my opinion, really should have been a tenor," as Finn is a tenor, is "Glinka's effort to be original" (MN 1, p. 237).

20 August

Glinka asks Krzhisevich to forward a letter and some books to Ekaterina Kern, since he is sick. He writes that on Sunday he is going to *A Life for the Tsar*.
[The letter is dated "Friday." Dating is based on comparison with the foregoing letter to Krzhisevich, the performance of *A Life for the Tsar* on Sunday, August 22, and Glinka's illness in August 1843.]

22 August

Mikhaylov performs the part of Sobinin for the first time in a performance of *A Life for the Tsar* in the Bolshoi Theater (*SPb. ved.*, 22 August 1843).

26 August

Performance of *Ruslan and Lyudmila* in the Bolshoi Theater "for the benefit of the singer Mme Petrova I." "It went very badly. Big mistakes in the orchestra" (K. Albrecht's diary, in *Muz. letop.*, 1923, coll. 2, p. 75; *Sev. pchela*, 26 August 1843; *Rus. invalid*, 29 August 1843).

28 August

Memorandum from the office of the Imperial Theaters to the accounting section: "For yesterday's performance of *Ruslan and Lyudmila*, given for the benefit of Mme Petrova, her husband, Mr. Petrov, assures us that the composer, Mr. Glinka, has agreed to receive no payment, but if the contrary is true, Mr. Petrov will assume obligation" (i.e., pay Glinka from his own honorarium) (*L.*, p. 277).

29 August

Glinka thanks Krzhisevich for forwarding Ekaterina Kern's letters to the country. He asks that books be sent to her in the city, where Kern is returning on Wednesday morning, rather than to the country. He writes that the doctor is not allowing him out of the house, that he has a great deal of time for reading, and therefore asks that books be sent to him.

[The letter is dated "Sunday." Judging from its content it was written at the end of the month.]

31 August

In *Bib-ka dlia chteniia,* vol. 60, no. 9, "Miscellany," an announcement states that the following pieces are available at Bernard's music store: Variations on Alyabiev's Romance "The Nightingale" and the romances *"Liubliu tebia, milaia roza"* and *"Kak sladko s toboiu mne byt'"* (d.c.a.).

Summer

Kukolnik's letter to Verstovsky dates from this period: "The Italians have driven us mad. . . . Given a good, Italian libretto . . . in my opinion, both you and Glinka might have filled us with the honeyed sounds of Italians songsters. I am always chiding Glinka, though I rarely see him, and one has to be inseparable from him to subdue him into such an undertaking" (coll. *Glinka,* p. 163).

[Dating of first publication.]

4 September

In a notice entitled "Hermann's Concert in Pavlovsk" in *SPb. ved.,* no. 207, Glinka is mentioned among the composers Hermann's orchestra has introduced to the public.

5 September

In *Lit. gaz.,* no. 35, in a review of the third and fourth parts of "Theatrical Album," desire is expressed for early publication of Glinka's portrait.

7 September

Mikhaylov's appearance in *Ruslan and Lyudmila* is mentioned in *Sev. pchela,* no. 199.

8 September

Performance of *Ruslan and Lyudmila* in the Bolshoi Theater, "without rehearsal. Very bad. Artemovsky and Mikhaylov were bad, as was the chorus" (K. Albrecht's diary, in *Muz. letop.*, 1923, coll. 2, p. 75).

9 September

In Moscow, "Today, Thursday, 9 September (for the opening of the Bolshoi Theater after its restoration) there will be a subscription performance of *A Life for the Tsar*" (*Mosk. ved.*, 9 September 1843). At this performance the overture to the opera was replaced by an overture by Iogannis for the opening of the theater (on the theme of "God, Save the Tsar"), and a number of cuts were made in the opera (*Lit. gaz.*, 24 October 1843). On his return from Nizhny Novgorod via Moscow, Serov heard *A Life for the Tsar* in the Bolshoi Theater "in a really pitiful performance for an audience completely lacking any semblance of understanding or sympathy" (Serov, *Vosp.*, p. 95).

15 September

Works by Glinka are performed in one of Hermann's concerts in Pavlovsk (*SPb. ved.*, 4 September 1843).

First Half of September

Glinka paid a visit to Serov upon his return, who told "about . . . the unfavorable *status quo* of his first opera in the capital of white stone [i.e., Moscow]. 'What's to be done!' remarked Glinka. 'In musical matters they lag behind us by 50 years, if not more. It's impossible to expect anything of them.'" Glinka sang his new romance *"Liubliu tebia, milaia roza"* for Serov: "I was enchanted by the grace of this simple melody. 'But there is also *anger* here, sir. I wanted to illustrate the possibility of a *free* use of the chord of the augmented fifth. To me it is desirable that every little thing, however small, serve somehow in its way toward new changes in the art and science of music'" (Serov, *Vosp.*, p. 95).

17 September

Listok dlia svetskikh liudei [Fashionable people's leaflet], no. 35, is devoted to a parody of *Ruslan and Lyudmila* (d.c.a.).

26 September

Performance of *Ruslan and Lyudmila* in the Bolshoi Theater (*Sev. pchela*, 25 September 1843).

3 October

Performance of *A Life for the Tsar* in the Bolshoi Theater (*SPb. ved.*, 3 October 1843).

Beginning of October

In *Bib-ka dlia chteniia*, vol. 60, no. 10, "Miscellany," there is an announcement that Glinka's *Nouvelle mazurka*, published separately from the journal *Le Nouvelliste*, is on sale at Bernard's music store.

In *Repertuar i panteon*, no. 10, "Feuilleton for 30 September," reference is made to the opening of the Bolshoi Theater in Moscow with the opera *A Life for the Tsar*, preceded by Iogannis's overture on a hymn tune.

7 October

In *Moskvitianin*, part 5, no. 10, there is a notice entitled "Opening of the Restored Bolshoi Theater" (signed "X"): "The Bolshoi Theater, beautifully restored, was opened again on the 9th of September. . . . *A Life for the Tsar* was given. We do not understand why Iogannis's overture had to displace Glinka's own, since he looked upon it as a necessary introduction to the opera, corresponding to it in character. Perhaps after a brief interval, after Iogannis's solemn overture written for the opening of the restored building, it might have been possible to play Glinka's overture, since it prepares the way for the opera so beautifully. . . . Besides the overture, we do not understand why the peasant chorus (A major) in the third act was omitted, or Susanin's marvelous prayer in the fourth act, or especially the second half of the famous trio in the epilog. We won't even mention other less important cuts and omissions. Whatever you might say, Glinka is our musical glory, and performing his works carelessly, with cuts and modifications, means that one has no respect for Russian art or for oneself" (d.c.a.).

9 October

In *Sev. pchela*, no. 226, "Journalistic Odds and Ends," one of Bulgarin's recurrent attacks on Glinka is printed.

21 October

Glinka's divorce case, with the record of proceedings for the entire case, is transferred from the St. Petersburg consistory to the Synod (*L.*, p. 279). Receipt of the record is registered 27 October (TsGIA, coll. 796).

24 October

In *Lit. gaz.*, "Journalistic Amalgam," there is a report of the opening of the season of the Bolshoi Theater in Moscow with *A Life for the Tsar* preceded by Iogannis's overture. It includes quotations from *Moskvitianin*, no. 10.

31 October

In a notice entitled "Musical News" in *SPb. ved.*, no. 247, it says that the romance *"Liubliu tebia, milaia roza"* is on sale in Bernard's store.

1 November

Composer's dating on an autograph fragment of the romance *"Dubrava shumit"* [The leafy grove howls]: "Night of 1 November 1843. Michel Glinka."
[The romance was composed in 1834. This autograph does not correspond to the first edition of 1856.]

5 November

In *Sev. pchela*, no. 249, there is an article by "R. Z" [Zotov] entitled "The Aleksandrinsky Theater," which reviews the vaudeville *"Demokrit i Geraklit, ili Filosof na Peskakh"* [Democritus and Heraclitus, or the philosopher on the sands]. It mentions that the lezghinka from *Ruslan and Lyudmila* was performed in the final act.

14 November

Performance of *Ruslan and Lyudmila* in the Bolshoi Theater (K. Albrecht's diary, in *Muz. letop.*, 1923, coll. 2, p. 75; *Sev. pchela*, 14 November 1843).

25 November

In a benefit performance in the Bolshoi Theater in Moscow for the dancer Andreyanova, she performed the "Lezghinka from *Ruslan*" (*Mosk. ved.*, 23 and 25 November 1843).

Fall

"Rubini, Tamburini, and Viardot-Garcia arrived in St. Petersburg. An Italian theater was established. Viardot was outstanding, and Tamburini was still relatively good. Rubini sometimes sang so-so, but sometimes his voice betrayed him to the point that he even cried" (*Zap.*).

5 December

Performance in the Bolshoi Theater of *Ruslan and Lyudmila* (*SPb. ved.*, 5 December 1843).

8 December

In an article entitled "The Journal *Le Nouvelliste*" in *SPb. ved.*, no. 278, compositions by Glinka are mentioned in a list of piano works published in the journal.

9 December

Glinka's date and signature on his portrait (drawing by Tikhobrazov): *"M. Glinka le 9 decembre 1843"* (*Gazeta Gattsuka*, 1 June 1885).

13 December

Glinka attends a performance of Mozart's *Don Giovanni* (Tamburini's benefit performance) in the Bolshoi Theater: "All the important roles were murdered. Only Zerlina (Viardot) and Masetto (Artemovsky) went excellently. . . . I cried from irritation and at that moment conceived a hatred for Italian songsters and fashionable Italian music" (*Zap.;* poster).

20 December

Performance of *Ruslan and Lyudmila* in the Bolshoi Theater (*Sev. pchela*, 20 December 1843).

28 December

In *Mosk. ved.*, no. 155, there is an announcement that the Orphan's song, transcribed for guitar, from *A Life for the Tsar*, is on sale in Müller's music store.

During the course of the year Glinka visited Arnold, to whom Glinka gave "invaluable advice regarding Russian peasant style" (Yury Arnold, *Golye fakty bez rassuzhdenii iz khudozhnicheskoi zhizni* [Bare facts without argument from an artist's life], in *L.*, p. 280).

"In the same year, 1843 . . . [Glinka] wrote the romance *"K nei"* [To her], translated from Mickiewicz by Prince S. Golitsyn."

1838–1844

"Once in Sergey Lvovich Pushkin's presence . . ." Glinka "sang Finn's aria. At the line 'A heavy tear rolls down my grey beard,' the old man broke into tears and threw his arms around Glinka. There were tears in the eyes of everyone there" (A. Kern, *Vosp.*, 153).

1840s, Before 1844

Glinka, either by himself or with his mother, often visited the Engelgardts on Mokhovaya. "He was attractive and refined in his manners and conversation. . . . There was something fascinating about his pronunciation, and I cannot explain what it consisted of, something like a slight lisp. . . . His conversations were always intelligent. He possessed a very attractive tenor voice. He never sang anything but his own romances. I had always heard everyone's opinion that his singing was fascinating and incomparably better than the best opera singer. I greatly admired his singing, and I looked upon him then as a genius, as a superman. At the time he sang romances from *Farewell to St. Petersburg* and, besides these, '*V krovi gorit,*' '*Nochnoi smotr,*' '*Kak sladko s toboiu mne byt',*' and '*Somnenie*'. . . . His '*Poputnaia pesnia*' he sang very effectively. His patter was like that of a fine Italian singer. He often sang his Bolero. Best of all, however, without exception, was his 'Farewell Song.' He only sang this at partings. . . . The last couplet, 'There is one true family. . . . To it my final song . . .' was striking. He made a fermata here and then, picking up the tempo, began to sing impetuously and emotionally and toward the end, at the words, 'And I break the lyre's strings' . . . on a high *la fermata longissima*. The way he sang this note in chest voice was beautiful, and I will never forget it! When he sang, he sat straight with his head up, as though striving upward. . . . He only played excerpts from his music on the piano. . . . He played clearly and distinctly, like he expressed himself. . . . He always improvised between the verses of his romances when he sang them. These *Zwischenspiele* of his were excellent and sometimes lengthy" (ltr. from V. Engelgardt to V. Stasov, 11/24 February 1906, in coll. *Pamiati Glinki,* p. 549).

1843–1844

Winter

"Karl Bryullov joined Misha Gedeonov's parties, and then also Yanenko. . . . Our gatherings were made considerably more lively by his [Bryullov's] presence. He spoke with intelligence and originality. Nestor [Kukolnik] also frequented Misha's. At the Gedeonovs' then, at Stepan's in particular, a passion for imitating Rubini developed, and Bulgakov and I kept pace. Samarin and I, in turn, acquainted our audience with the pranks of Kolmakov and Oginsky. It could be said that we had our own theater. One time even Bulgakov and Nevakhovich did *tableaux vivants* for us and were very entertaining."
[Glinka's and Mikhail and Stepan Gedeonov's message in humorous verse to Nestor Kukolnik to the melody "I have fallen in love with Taras," "Dear Nestor, we are waiting for you at your place," etc., dates from this period.]

Evgenia Andreevna's arrival from the country with her daughter Olga for the forthcoming wedding of Elizaveta Ivanovna and Viktor Ivanovich Fleury, director of the school for deafmutes (*Zap.*).

During the winter "the remarkable singer Solovieva appeared" in the roles of Antonida and Lyudmila. "(She was French by birth, and her actual name was Verteuil.) Glinka was totally satisfied with her singing, especially her Antonida, where she set off many details which till then had passed by unnoticed."

When he met with Serov, Glinka often talked with him about the new performers in *A Life for the Tsar* and in *Ruslan* as well as about the Italian performances. "It was impossible for me to accustom myself to Glinka's paradoxical opinions. He was always catching one off guard with the unexpectedness of his views." During their meetings "he again sang many of his romances with great enthusiasm and added a new gem to his repertoire, the mazurka on Mickiewicz's words '*K nei*' [To her]. . . . His animation and ardent declamation at the words 'And her eyes flashed more brightly than crystal' and the artistic finish of the entire romance . . . were impressive, although the composer considered this mazurka a trifle, a bagatelle written in half an hour. Sometimes Glinka allowed us to see the treasure of his improvisational talent. Once when he had agreed to play 'a little quadrille' to dance to, he got carried away with his imagination and improvised an entire ballet for us, during which, of course, everyone stopped dancing . . . fearing to utter a sound that would interrupt the chain of beautiful ballet music of the freest, most artistic sort" (Serov, *Vosp.*, p. 96).

On Glinka's request, the ballet-master Nikolay Golts included the mazurka in *A Life for the Tsar* again. "The Mazurka had become recognized as an outstanding choreographic composition, and Titus's dances, included earlier, had been cancelled" (*Materialy po istorii russkogo baleta* [Material for the history of the Russian ballet], vol. I, L., 1938, p. 107).

Beginning of the 1840s

Glinka regularly attended Bryullov's parties and "brought tears to the eyes of those present" when he performed his music (Samoylov, *Vosp.*, p. 185).

End of the 1830s and Before 1844

"Your [Odoevsky's] Sundays, my [Rostopchina's] dinners, first with Glinka, then with Liszt" (ltr. from E. Rostopchina to V. Odoevsky, 4 February 1858, in *Rus. arkhiv*, 1864, no. 7/8, p. 848).

1844

4 January

Performance of *A Life for the Tsar* in the Bolshoi Theater (*SPb. ved.*, 4 January 1844). This was the eighty-seventh performance of the opera; there were 265 people in the audience (*Ved. SPb. gor. politsii*, 5 January 1844).

In *Repertuar i panteon*, vol. 5, no. 1, "Theater Chronicle," Andreyanova's performance of the Lezghinka from *Ruslan and Lyudmila* in a divertissement in the Moscow Bolshoi Theater is mentioned (d.c.a.).

8 January

In *Sev. pchela*, no. 5, in reference to Aleksandra Bilibina's outstanding ability, Bulgarin writes: "We must ask M. I. Glinka's pardon, for we confess that, even after hearing *A Life for the Tsar* more than 20 times, we have not understood his music. We only grasped its charm fully when we heard the music sung by A. Ya. Bilibina."

12 January

In a conversation with Tarnovsky (in the Ukraine) Seletsky, "granting Glinka's talent . . . found numerous faults with *A Life for the Tsar* and had the impru-dence to say that overall the opera was inconsistent, incoherent, and incomplete, and that it was a boring, monotonous opera devoid of drama, notwithstanding the fact that it abounded in outstanding places, profound learning, and some singable melodies. Grigory Stepanovich was indignant, but he was extremely offended when I took exception to his description of how Glinka would compose several numbers and then send them to Rozen to supply a text. I said that here in part lay Glinka's error, that no one wrote operas like that by setting text to music, but that normally music was written to the libretto, and that the very manner of composing Glinka had chosen only confirmed what I had said about the shortcomings of *A Life for the Tsar*" (P. D. Seletsky's Memoirs, in *Kievskaia starina*, 1884, vol. 9, p. 625).

20 January

In Part I of Odoevsky's *Russian Nights* (SPb., 1844) Mendelssohn, Berlioz, and Glinka are mentioned. "You will be surprised to learn that not all the roads of melody have been trodden and that an artist begotten of the Slavic spirit is the only one of this triumvirate who has preserved the sacred things of the corrupted, humiliated, and defamed art of the West and found a fresh, uncharted path" (d.c.a.).

23 January

Performance of *Ruslan and Lyudmila* in the Bolshoi Theater. The performance went badly. "The chorus, particularly the women's, forgot their entrances and could barely refrain from laughing when they entered a bar or two later. . . . The orchestra of the Russian Opera will soon be so bad that a player, however ambitious, will have to be ashamed to participate in it" (K. Albrecht's diary, in *Muz. letop.*, coll. 2, SPb., 1923, p. 75; *SPb. ved.*, 23 January 1844).
[This was the forty-third performance. There were 455 in attendance (*Ved. SPb. gor. politsii*, 25 January 1844).]

26 January

A Life for the Tsar is mentioned in an article entitled "The Bolshoi Theater—Italian Performances" by "R. Z." [Zotov] in *Sev. pchela*, no. 20.

27 January

In a supp. to *Mosk. ved.*, no. 12, there is an announcement that Leopold Langer's Fantasy for Piano on Themes from *Ruslan and Lyudmila* is available at Gresser's store. In an advertisement of the music store "Odeum," arias and romances by Glinka are cited among works in their stock.

Repeat of the advertisements in no. 13, 29 January.

Between 6 and 28 January

Marriage of Elizaveta Glinka and Viktor Fleury.
[Dated according to when in 1844, by church law marriage ceremonies could take place. Weddings were prohibited during the Christmas fast, i.e. between 14 November 1843 and Christmas [5 January], and again beginning with the week of Shrovetide.]

28 January

Performance of *A Life for the Tsar* in the Bolshoi Theater in Moscow. Ivanova performed the role of Vanya for the first time (*Mosk. ved.*, 12 January 1844).

31 January

In *Repertuar i panteon,* vol. 5, no. 2, "Theater Chronicle," in a notice by "N. S." entitled "The Kharkov Theater," a performance in the Kharkov Theater of the trio from *A Life for the Tsar* by artists Bezmatny, Dushina, and Sklyarov is mentioned.

January to Beginning of February

After the marriage of her daughter Elizaveta, Glinka's mother became seriously ill. Glinka remained with her constantly and "occupied her with conversation and questions about her youth, especially about how she got married" (*Zap.*).

2 February

Matinée performance of *Ruslan and Lyudmila* in the Bolshoi Theater (*SPb. ved.*, 2 February 1844).

4 February

Performance of *Ruslan and Lyudmila* in the Bolshoi Theater (*Ved. SPb. gor. politsii,* 3 February 1844).

5 February

Performance in an amateur concert in Kiev of the Fantasia-concertante on Themes from *A Life for the Tsar* for violin and piano by the music teacher G. Vitvitsky (*Sev. pchela,* 26 February 1844).

6 February

Performance of *A Life for the Tsar* in the Bolshoi Theater in Moscow (*Mosk. ved.*, 5 February 1844).

Sergey Aksakov writes to Ivan Aksakov: "We have just returned . . . from the theater. For the first time I saw the opera *A Life for the Tsar*. I want to write . . . a few lines while the impression of this lovely music is still fresh on my mind. . . . It is just what I have dreamed of and everything that Verstovsky's operas lack. It is neither Russian songs nor even purely Russian melodies. It is Russian music. . . . It is music whose every sound is native to me, my own. I have heard it and sung it, or certainly I will hear it and sing it. . . . I heard the opera cut by a full third. . . . The performance was less than mediocre. . . . That we should appreciate such a rare talent as Glinka so little! In Petersburg they have received the opera with loud, though official, applause. Everyone says that it is outstanding, but boring and long. They immediately began to cut it, and here Verstovsky sacrilegiously spoiled the creation of an artist. To cut the development of a musical thought . . . is the same as cutting a picture, knocking an arm or leg off a statue, rejecting several scenes from a Gogol comedy, or tearing several pages out of *Dead Souls*! . . . It is simply barbarism. The epilog itself pleased me considerably . . . the libretto is worthless" (*Ogonek*, 1951, no. 37, p. 19).

15 February

In a supp. to *Mosk. ved.*, no. 20, there is an announcement that Aubel's *Contredanse de Ruslan e Lyudmila* for piano is on sale at Lengold's music store.

16 February

In her concert in the Bolshoi Theater in Moscow, Sofia Dall'Occa-Schoberlechner performed an aria from *A Life for the Tsar* (*Mosk. ved.*, 12 February 1844).

Before 21 February

Evgenia Andreevna Glinka "decided to let [Glinka] go" to Paris (*Zap.*).

21 February

Glinka made application to the Synod for permission to leave Petersburg, since "present circumstances confronting me absolutely require my absence from here," and the conduct of the divorce case does not require his personal presence.

24 February

Glinka's request "for removal of the prohibition to his unimpeded travel from St. Petersburg" was heard in the Synod and granted in his favor (*L.*, p. 286).

26 February

"Letter from Kiev" of 5 February (q.v.) is printed in *Sev. pchela,* no. 45.

27 February

Ivan Aksakov (from Astrakhan) writes to Sergey Aksakov: "So you liked *A Life for the Tsar* . . . but one must say that, with respect to the opera, Moscow audiences apparently share the opinion of Petersburg. I am not talking about the opinion of two or three of our acquaintances but of the official status given to the opera, which vulgarizes the way people think about it. This is a shame and obstructs understanding of this beautiful, wholly Russian opera" (*I. S. Akaskov v ego pis'makh* [I. S. Aksakov in his letters], part I, vol. 1, Moscow, 1888).

29 February

In *Repertuar i panteon,* vol. 5, part 3, "Theatrical Chronicle," there is an article by "M. K." entitled "Moscow's Theaters," which refers to Ivanova's debut at the Bolshoi Theater in the role of Vanya as well as to Mikhaylova's performance of the same role (d.c.a.).

Beginning of March

Evgenia Andreevna's departure for the country. Glinka saw his mother off and caught a cold in the freezing weather. "After Mother left I played the violin until dinner to occupy my thoughts and to excite my birds. There were about sixteen of them. . . . After dinner I frequently visited at Fleury's."

6 March

In *Sev. pchela,* no. 52, in an article entitled "Statistical overview of the past theatrical season," R. Zotov writes: "Our opera . . . which not all that long ago reigned supreme with splendid performances of *Robert, A Life for the Tsar,* and the entire Italian repertoire . . . alas, hardly exists now."

18 March

Glinka was present at a musical evening at the Vielgorskys. A Mendelssohn symphony and Beethoven's Overture, "Leonore" No. 3, were performed. Robert and Clara Schumann were also present at the gathering. ("From C. Schumann's Travel Diary," in D. Zhitomirsky, *Robert i Klara Shuman v Rossii* [Robert and Clara Schumann in Russia], Moscow, 1962, p. 144).

["Three overtures" to Leonore are indicated in Clara Schumann's diary, though the Overture No. 2 was not published until 1854. Probably reference is to the third overture (misread as "three.")]

29 March

In *Le Nouvelliste*, literary supp. no. 4, there is an announcement that Glinka's romance *"Ne govori, liubov' proidet"* is available at Bernard's (d.c.a.).

March

In an article in *Revue de Paris*, *"Une année en Russie, lettres à M. Girardin écrites de Moscou en 1840,"* Henry Mérimée writes: "M. Glinka's *A Life for the Tsar* is distinctive for its exceptional originality. It may be the first [Russian] work of art in which there is nothing imitative. Its erudition assumes simple and accessible form. It is an accurate poetic and musical summation of everything that Russia has suffered and poured out in song. Russia recognizes in it a faithful depiction of her love and hate, grief and joy, utter darkness and radiant dawn. In the first place, it is a sorrowful lament, and then a hymn of atonement so proud and triumphant that even the humblest peasant would be touched to the depths of his heart if he could be transported from his cottage to the theater to hear it. It is more than opera, it is a national epic, a lyric drama restored to the nobility of its original sources, when art was not just frivolous entertainment but a patriotic and religious rite. Even though I am a foreigner, I never attended a performance when I was not gripped by deep emotion" (*Memoirs*, Fr. original, p. 350).

Glinka "begged" Fedor Gedeonov, brother of his brother-in-law Nikolay Gedeonov, to travel with him to Paris (*Zap.*).

9 April

The forty-fifth performance of *Ruslan and Lyudmila* in the Bolshoi Theater. "Petrova's singing [i.e., Petrova-Vorobieva's] was terribly strained, and Lileeva sang out of tune" (K. Albrecht's diary, in *Muz. letop.*, coll. 2, p. 76; *SPb. ved.*, 9 April 1844; *Ved. SPb. gor. politsii*, 11 April 1844).

21 April

The eighty-eighth performance of *A Life for the Tsar* in the Bolshoi Theater (*SPb. ved.*, 21 April 1844; *Ved. SPb. gor. politsii*, 24 April 1844).

Performance of *A Life for the Tsar* at the Bolshoi Theater in Moscow (*Mosk. ved.*, 20 April 1844).

25 April

In supps. to *Mosk. ved.*, no. 50, an announcement entitled "Musical News" mentions a fugue by Glinka as being among piano pieces available for purchase.

27 April

Performance of *Ruslan and Lyudmila Once Again* [*Eshche Ruslan i Lyudmila*], a vaudeville comedy in one act, at the Aleksandrinsky Theater (*SPb. ved.*, 27 April 1844).

30 April

In *Bib-ka dlia chteniia*, vol. 64, under "Miscellany. Musical News," there is a report of a concert given by Liszt in Paris at which he played "Chernomor's March." "The audience demanded that it be repeated" (d.c.a.).

In *Repertuar i panteon*, vol. 6, part 5, "Theatrical Chronicle," there is an article by P. Tolobugin entitled "The Ostashkovsky Theater," which mentions a performance of Vanya's song *"Kak mat' ubili"* from *A Life for the Tsar* (d.c.a.).

6 May

In *SPb. ved.*, no. 100, Glinka is listed among those travelling abroad.

9 May

In *SPb. ved.*, no. 102, Glinka is listed for the second time among those travelling abroad.

13 May

In *SPb. ved.*, no. 106, there is a notice by A. Elkan about the publication of a "Collection of New Compositions" entitled "The Northern Lyre," "the names in which alone guarantee the music's worth." The composers include Viardot-Garcia, Vielgorsky, Glinka, Dargomyzhsky, Arnold, Lvov, Derfeldt, Romanus, and Pascua.

18 May

In *Moskvityanin,* part 3, no. 5, under "Criticism," there is an article called "Glinka's Opera *A Life for the Tsar*" by Aleksey Khomyakov: "Glinka's opera is not yet properly appreciated. It has been spoken of as music based on Russian themes, written in Russian style, as folk music or an imitation of nationality [*narodnost'*], and still they have not understood it as a totally Russian phenomenon created from end to end in the spirit of Russian life and history. It has to be considered from this point of view without analyzing separately either the libretto or the music, for in any genuine work of art thought and value are of a whole. . . . Susanin is not a hero. He is a simple peasant, the head of a family, and member of a community [*obshchina*] of brothers. But a great deed's destiny has fallen upon him, and he fulfills this great deed. It is not personal strength which he embodies but the profound, indestructible strength of a healthy society, a strength which expresses itself not in momentary outbursts or the impulses of individuals and their individual feats, but which motivates and animates the entire great social body, transforming each separate member and making him capable of any feat of suffering or struggle. . . . A feat of endurance is accomplished in the person of Susanin. . . . But with Susanin the enemy also perished, for never has anyone encroached, nor will anyone ever encroach upon Russia's inner life without paying for it. . . . Perhaps something better will be written in the world of Russian music, maybe even by the same composer to whom we are indebted for *A Life for the Tsar*. Whatever may lie ahead, however, this work will remain immortal, not only as the first Russian opera, but as an entirely Russian creation. . . . There is nothing humanly true without the truly popular" (d.c.a.; reprinted from A. S. Khomyakov, *Poln. sobr. soch.,* vol. 1, Moscow, 1961, p. 413).

21 May

Lidia Bludova, daughter of the minister Dmitry Nikolaevich Bludov, sent Glinka Henry Mérimée's article printed in March in the *Revue de Paris.* "This article cheered me. Not a one of my countrymen has referred to me so far in such flattering terms."
[Henry Mérimée copied the text of his article in Glinka's Spanish Album (in Paris, 21 February/5 March 1845).]

Before 28 May

Glinka visited Yanenko's dacha daily; Bryullov and other friends also came there. "We all pitched in for dinner and supper. That was when the mask of me was made" (*Zap.*). "His face and hair were smeared with oil, tubes were placed in his nose, and plaster of Paris was applied. After several minutes the gypsum dried, and the mask was imprinted perfectly" (P. Stepanov, *Vosp.*, p. 63). "My brother told me that it was unendurable torture" (ltr. from L. Shestakova to E. Nápravnik, without date, 1876, in *L.*, p. 289).

[In his memoirs, Petr Stepanov says that he modelled the mask. In a letter to Vasily Afanasiev, V. P. Engelgardt says that the bust was modelled by Yanenko and then "passed" to Bryullov (ltr. of 30 May 1908, in *L.*, p. 289), and in a letter to Findeyzen, Engelgardt names Stepanov, Yanenko, and Bryullov as the creators of the bust (*L.*, p. 289).]

28 May

In Nadezhda Barteneva's album Glinka inscribed a single line of music from the romance *"Kak sladko s toboiu mne byt'"* and dated it *"Le 28 mai avant le départ pour l'etranger M. Glinka"* (*L.*, p. 289).

[To this period belongs Konstantin Bulgakov's presentation of a portrait to Glinka with the inscription "To my musical friend Mikhail Ivanovich Glinka from K. A. Bulgakov" (*L.*, p. 289).]

31 May

In the sixth literary supp. to *Le Nouvelliste* it says: "Our famous composer M. I. Glinka is travelling abroad. We shall hope that he returns inspired by the bright Italian sky with a rich store of lovely themes for a new opera" (d.c.a.).

1 June

Performance of *A Life for the Tsar* in the Bolshoi Theater (*SPb. ved.*, 1 June 1844).

Before his departure Glinka was at the Engelgardts' and sang. "Late in the evening, for a conclusion, he sang his 'Farewell Song' and made a long fermata at 'and I break the lyre's strings,' sang a beautiful high 'A' in chest voice, and actually broke the strings" (ltr. from V. Engelgardt to V. Stasov, 5/18 February 1906, in coll. *Pamiati Glinki*, p. 548).

Beginning of June

Glinka's departure, accompanied by Fedor Gedeonov and [Gedeonov's] friend Adèle Rossignol. "I was at the Tarnovskys, where E. K. and Maria Stepanovna also were. My carriage came for me, I took my final leave of the ladies, picked up Gedeonov and Adèle, and we set out on our journey."

8 June

In *Lit. gaz.*, no. 22, under "Miscellany," the following notice appears: "Of the truths expressed in the fifth issue of *Moskvityanin,* Mr. Khomyakov's article had a lot to say about Glinka's opera *A Life for the Tsar.* . . . If anyone should wish to know what Moscow, 'Moskvityanin,' or Muscovite really means, we advise him to read this article without fail. You will not learn a hundredth as much from Zagoskin's two volumes."

First Half of June

Novospasskoe. "We rode into the country for a short time. I spent several days with mother."

Second Half of June Until the 18th or 19th

Bezzabotie. From Novospasskoe Glinka stopped by his brother-in-law's, Nikolay Gedeonov's.

19 or 20 June

Smolensk. Glinka departed from Bezzabotie and travelled through Smolensk to Warsaw. "We travelled by post-chaise in the carriage which I had bought in 1840."

23 June

Performance of *A Life for the Tsar* in the Bolshoi Theater in Moscow (*Mosk. ved.,* 20 June 1844).

24 or 25 June

Warsaw. Arrival "after a six-day journey . . . I hoped to enjoy myself in Warsaw, but things went otherwise. It was pouring rain, and we were exhausted. Finally, the fact that I did not find what I was most counting on depressed me."

25 June

Glinka writes to his mother that "today I have definitely decided to continue my trip. . . . I do not know what to say about Warsaw. I am here for the second time, and it's like I have never been here. . . . The city is fine, though somewhat crowded. Everything is cheaper, but the water is foul. This is all that I have been able to observe."

Departure in the evening for Paris via Poznan and Berlin (ltr. to his mother, 25 June 1844).

Performance of *A Life for the Tsar* at the Bolshoi Theater in Moscow (*Mosk. ved.*, 20 June 1844).

End of June (O.S.)

Berlin. Glinka spent several days with Dehn. "I had the scores of my operas with me. Dehn was extremely satisfied with my tercet from *A Life for the Tsar*, '*Ne tomi, rodimyi.*'"

1 July

Performance of *A Life for the Tsar* in the Aleksandrinsky Theater in Petersburg (*Sev. pchela*, 1 July 1844).

Beginning of July (O.S.)

Berlin–Cologne. "From Berlin we travelled by post-chaise to Cologne, where we left the carriage."

Cologne–Aachen. "We quickly reached Aachen by railroad."

Aachen. Here they spent several days and then set out for Brussels.

Brussels. "In Brussels it was the time of the Kermèsse holidays. Blaes (the clarinettist) was frequently with me, and in the gardens I heard an exceptionally well-balanced orchestra of wind instruments made up of artisans."

From Brussels they travelled by railroad to Mons.

First Ten Days of July (O.S.)

Mons. From Mons they travelled by stagecoach to Paris.

12/24 July

Paris. Glinka's arrival in Paris. "We entered the city via the streets of Faubourg Montmartre, rue Montmartre. The immensity of the seven-story houses and the unusual activity on the streets struck me very pleasantly." Gedeonov immediately found an apartment "in the *Passage de l'Opera (de l'Hôrloge)*" on the sixth floor, "small, but tidy" (*Zap.*; ltr. to his mother, 9/21 August 1844).
[Glinka's arrival in Paris is dated according to his letter to his mother: "It has been four weeks now since I arrived."]

End of July (O.S.)

Glinka watched the fireworks on the Seine celebrating the July holidays ("in memory of the July days") and was nearly crushed: "A Frenchman by the name of M. Edouard from Petersburg saved us. He carried me on his shoulders along the large avenue of the Champs Elysées so that I could see the fireworks better."

29 July

In Petersburg the Over-Procurator of the Synod, Protasov, who was "related to the Vasilchikov family," declined to conduct Glinka's divorce case. As a result, Nicholas I "entrusted" the case to the director of the office of religious education of the Synod, Karasevsky.

31 July

The Synod acted in accordance with His Majesty's "order" (G 1-B, p. 278).

July

Glinka met Aleksandr Nevakhovich (future publisher of the paper *Eralash*) and Ilya Norov. "The former entertained me with his jokes and caricatures, while the second demanded that I always participate in all the *parties de plaisir* which he organized."

Between the End of July and the Beginning of August (O. S.)

Versailles. Together with Mikhail Vielgorsky and Elim Meshchersky, Glinka saw the sights at Versailles (ltr. to his mother, 9/21 August 1844; *Zap.*).

Beginning of August

In *Repertuar i panteon,* vol. 7, part 8, in the section "New Musical Works," sale of the *Etude fugué* for piano is announced (d.c.a.).

Before 9/21 August

Paris. Glinka and Gedeonov moved into "a nice little apartment: two bedrooms, a hall, and kitchen—tight by our standards, but spacious by standards here." The address was "Paris, 5 rue de Provence."

9/21 August

Glinka writes to his mother: "Every day I thank you for the fact that I am now in Paris. In all my life I have not found a place to live which satisfies so completely all my needs. For me the climate here is outstanding. . . . Life is quiet despite distractions. They do not drink here or play cards, and by eleven o'clock in the evening everyone is accustomed to going home. There is so much variety in Paris that when you go out into the streets it is impossible to be depressed. . . . I still have not been able to see all the sights. . . . My favorite place in Paris is the Jardin des plantes, where there is a menagerie, many birds, and extraordinary plants." Of how he is spending his time, he writes: "I am not doing anything and am still busy the entire day. . . . I was prevented from continuing my letter. An Italian I know stopped by wanting to go visit another common friend of ours . . . little by little through him I have come to know other musicians. In a word, it is beginning to appear that people already know me by name here."

10/22 August

In addition to the set amount, Glinka asks his mother to send him an additional "600 or 700 rubles on loan strictly for shopping," since "However indifferent I am to stores, things tempting even to me do turn up."

13/25 August

In the *Revue et gazette musicale,* no. 34, in the section *Nouvelles,* it says that Glinka, Russia's best-known composer, who has written numerous operas which have been staged with great success in Petersburg, has arrived in Paris, where he intends to spend the winter. The hope is expressed that Glinka will write a work for the Opéra-Comique.

23 August

In Petersburg, Serov writes to V. Stasov: "What about *Ruslan* interests you? Perhaps the counterpoint. There is a lot of it, but like everything of Glinka's, it's not good, because it's out of place" (*MN* I, p. 258).

31 August

In the ninth literary supp. to *Le Nouvelliste,* under "Foreign News," it is reported that "The well-known Russian composer M. Glinka has arrived in Paris and will stay here the entire winter. It is hoped that he will write a new work for the Opéra-Comique" (d.c.a.).

In *Moskvityanin,* part 5, no. 10, "Various News Items," there is an article by Melgunov (signed "N. L-sky") entitled "Russian Musical News from Abroad": "It is not only in a political sense that Russia has attracted attention to itself in the eyes of Europe. No, our literature and art are likewise beginning to arouse the interest of foreigners. This is particularly true with respect to our emerging musical school. . . . A beginning has been made." It goes on to report the news printed in the *Revue et gazette musicale,* no. 34, of 13/25 August (d.c.a.).

Summer

Glinka surveyed "the monuments and environs of the city" (ltr. to E. Fleury, 29 September/11 October 1844).

12 September

In an article called "Musical News" by "A. E." [Elkan], in *SPb. ved.,* no. 208, there is mention of Glinka, whose operas "have proven that in this arena Russians are making gigantic strides."

Before 16/28 September

Elim Meshchersky, Glinka's "friend . . . of long standing," "has undertaken to translate [Glinka's] best romances" into French "and is working at it very diligently."

16/28 September

In a letter to his mother Glinka writes: "We often walk in the environs of Paris, which are outstanding and remind me of the environs of Milan. Generally Paris's appearance and manner of life are similar to Italy, and I have so gotten used to life here now that it seems I have always lived like this."

17 September

Performance of *Ruslan and Lyudmila* in the Bolshoi Theater in Petersburg: "24 good chorus members had been sent to Moscow . . . but the choruses went excellently nonetheless. Artemovsky stood out for his conspicuous mistakes" (K. Albrecht's diary, in *Muz. letop.*, coll. 2, p. 76; *SPb. ved.*, 17 September 1844). This was the forty-sixth performance of the opera (*Ved. SPb. gor. politsii*, 19 September 1844).

24 September

Performance of *Ruslan and Lyudmila* in the Bolshoi Theater in Petersburg (*SPb. ved.*, 24 September 1844).

28 September/10 October

Glinka tells his mother that during the summer he has seen Paris and is now attending the theaters. "Of the 23 theaters in Paris I have now been to seven. . . . The Italian theater here is a delight. Not just the singers and orchestra but also the hall . . . are splendid and nice. If I were still to write for the theater (this winter I intend to study the city and the taste of audiences here, which is overall very unmusical), I would not wish to write for any other than the Italian opera here." He asks that his mother come to Paris in the summer with his sisters Olga and Natalia.

29 September/11 October

In a letter to Elizaveta Fleury, Glinka shares his impressions of the Italian opera in Paris: "The Italian theater here, in my opinion, is the best opera theater in the world. The ensemble is marvelous; the orchestra and chorus, to say nothing of the principal singers, are outstanding; and even the hall is a lovely sight. I will not attempt to compare the singers here with those in St. Petersburg. In my opinion comparisons do not prove anything, because every great talent has his own peculiarities. I have not yet heard Grisi, but I have heard Persiani. She sings distinctly, with feeling and rare grace, and reminds me of Rossi, though, in my opinion, her voice is stronger, and she sings with greater passion than Rossi. I will not attempt to compare her with Viardot. You know that I am her zealous admirer, which, however, does not prevent me from being fair to Persiani. Brambilla, the contralto, or rather alto, brought tears to my eyes with the unusual delicacy and charm of her voice, and she also sings very well. Mario, the tenor, is in my opinion simply bad and extremely ignoble. Despite this, the ensemble is so good that I definitely favor the opera here to ours [Italian]." He characterizes the other theaters. "In the Funambules [I saw] an excellent *Pierrot;* in the Gymnase dramatique, the comedian Achard; in the Variétés, which is everyone's favorite here, *Bouffé*. Over the coming winter I hope to attend all the theaters. In a word, I'm studying Paris in all its aspects." Of his life he writes: "I am getting used to Paris more and more, although my manner of life has not changed still, and I live like a bird of passage, without acquaintances except for a few compatriots. But there is something pleasant and carefree about this kind of life. Walks, the theater, and sometimes friendly conversations provide variety. . . . I attend the theaters and public balls and observe the ways and customs of different classes of Parisian residents. . . . [Meshchersky's] translation of my romances is nearing completion; some of them translated very well."

Glinka met Emile Deschamps and Victor Hugo at a party at Meshchersky's (ltr. to E. Fleury, 29 September/11 October 1844).

September

Glinka found out that "Liszt is going to Spain. This awakened my long-standing desire to go to Spain."
[Liszt spent the winter of 1844/45 in Spain and Portugal.]

In *Zhivopisnoe obozrenie* [Painting Review], vol. 9, in an article by "V. P." entitled "Letters from St. Petersburg," it says that "The success of the Italian Opera in St. Petersburg has eclipsed all other shows and performances. *Ruslan and Lyudmila* was performed two or three times to an empty hall."

5 October

In *Lit. gaz.*, no. 39, in an article called "Some Things about the Bolshoi Theater and Its Public," *A Life for the Tsar* is cited as one of the favorite operas.

Beginning of October (O.S.)

Glinka was introduced to Auber and to "Banderali, the top voice teacher" (ltr. to E. Fleury, 29 September/11 October 1844).

14 October

In a supp. to *Mosk. ved.*, no. 124, Glinka's *"Zhavoronok,"* in a transcription for piano by A. Gudkov, is mentioned along with other music then available.

27 October

In the Bolshoi Theater in Moscow, performance of *A Life for the Tsar* (*Mosk. ved.*, 26 October 1844).

October

Through Meshchersky, Glinka is introduced to the Spanish Marqués de Souza. "He was attached to the Spanish Embassy and had been in Petersburg before this. He knew music well, since he had studied with the famous composer Schubert, and overall he was a well-educated and socially agreeable man."

October–Beginning of November

"There are many Russians here: among others, the Kraevskys, mother and daughter; Countess Vielgorsky with her youngest daughter; and my boarding school colleague Melgunov. Despite the large number of my compatriots, I am living quietly and modestly and always have dinner at home" (ltr. to his mother, 4/16 November 1844).

October–November

Souza recommended to Glinka "a Spaniard by the name of Biesma Guerrero as a Spanish teacher," and Glinka began studying with him. "In the very first lesson he explained to me the characteristic traits of the Spanish language. I immediately translated *Gil Blas* from French to Spanish. For the second lesson I wrote out a translation, which he then corrected, and I rewrote it, read it aloud several times to practice my pronunciation and get used to Spanish turns of speech and almost memorized the entire piece in doing so. At that time I also read the Spanish comedy *El si de las niñas* and several literary excerpts from a collection which included selections from Cervantes's *Don Quixote*. Following this excellent system, in a short time I began to understand Spanish and even to speak it a little."

Before 4/16 November

Glinka learned of the death of his brother-in-law Yakov Sobolevsky.

4/16 November

Glinka explains to his mother what ends he intended to pursue by his trip abroad: "First, to improve my health by being in a better climate and to calm my heart by being a long way from the places and especially the people who remind me of my mental anguish. Second, to satisfy my curiosity about places and cities to which my imagination has long attracted me and, as an artist, to acquire a store of new ideas and impressions. Finally, to acquire a certain fame and to establish relations with the well-known names of Europe. In the first respect my trip has not been altogether successful. . . . During the entire summer there have been scarcely five weeks of clear, warm weather. . . . Despite all the distractions, I am often overcome with depression because of all my bitter memories. As an artist, I have studied the city and the theaters, and as strength permits I will attend social functions. I am waiting for Liszt to return from Spain, and I hope that through him I will get closer to the important artists of Paris. I do not want to leave here without becoming known (not so much for myself as for my detractors)." He writes that he will try to travel to Spain: "It is an old dream, a dream of my youth. . . . Besides satisfying my ardent imagination, I will be looking for new things to study from a musical standpoint." He writes that he is continuing to study Spanish.

4 November

Performance of *Ruslan and Lyudmila* in the Bolshoi Theater in Petersburg (K. Albrecht's diary, in *Muz. letop.,* coll. 2, p. 76).

Beginning of November, After 4/16

Elim Meshchersky dies (ltr. to his mother, 22 November/4 December 1844).

7 November

In *Sev. pchela,* no. 254, there is an excerpt of an article by Louis Viardot called "On Music in Russia" (which was printed in the *Gazette musicale*). "There are no artist-composers here who make a profession of their talent. . . . A composer who writes music like a writer writes books is unknown here. . . . In a word, they are all amateurs. M. Glinka is the composer of several well-loved Russian operas, incidentally of *Ruslan and Lyudmila* (a fantastic subject from a poem by Pushkin), where without overstatement he proves himself a worthy associate of Weber for his originality and musical intelligence."

22 November/4 December

In a letter to his mother Glinka complains about the cold and the expensiveness of Paris: "Paris is a city of calculation and egotism. Money is everything here." He writes of studying Spanish, "which by spring I hope to know very well (I am now beginning to read books and to understand when people speak)," and he says that he is giving singing lessons "to Adèle and two other nice French girls. . . . I am so busy here that I do not have a free minute, so it follows that it is impossible to be bored or burdened by life." He writes of Meshchersky's death and of his intention of publishing his romances in Meshchersky's translation. "Generally, though, my music loses something when translated into French. . . . I see no possibility of acquainting the public here with my operas. The effort and expense required would be so great that I cannot even think of it any more. . . . People attend the opera frequently here, and consequently they have time to listen properly and understand the music. However, at concerts one can't expect them (particularly the French) to completely comprehend things from the first." He writes that he intends to travel to Spain with his good friend the Marqués de Souza.

November

Glinka and Fedor Gedeonov held parties to which they invited "several young actresses as well as some compatriots and foreigners. The company was pleasant . . . all enjoyed themselves. . . . Everything had to be over at 11 o'clock" (*Zap.*).

15/27 December

Glinka writes to his mother: "Paris has revived me in every respect. Musically, however, I do not foresee any success or prospects here."

Second Half of December

Glinka wrote to Nikolay Norov requesting that he "find out about . . . the case, and notify [me] . . . of how things stand" (ltr. to his mother, 15/27 December 1844).
[Glinka's letter to Norov is unknown; the "case" is his divorce suit.]

19/31 December

Glinka writes to Elizaveta Fleury: "During December my life has become more pleasant and interesting, even though the climate here is abominable. . . . I have managed to make a few close friends, and when the chaos of Parisian life in the winter gets on my nerves or my health suffers from the dampness and chill . . . I unburden myself in the quiet conversation of friends. I find no sincerity among musicians, just dry civility. . . . As a composer I forsee no possibility of the slightest success in Paris, since there is no way to establish any relation with the public. In theaters, in concert halls, everywhere, performers are on their guard, each commanding his own theater, his own hall. . . . I am waiting for Liszt from Spain, for I know that he is sincerely well disposed toward me. We will see what will happen for me. . . . I am sick with a cold now, as are almost all Parisians."
[Liszt travelled from Spain to Germany, and Glinka did not see him.]

24 December/5 January 1845

In a letter to Anna Gidella, [Glinka] says that it will be impossible for him to be at Countess [L. K. Vielgorsky's?] ball on 12 January [N.S.], since he must be at Félicien David's concert.

29 December

In *Moskvityanin,* part 6, no. 12, under "Miscellany," there is an article by Nikolay Sushkov entitled "Some Things about the Cantata." In it Glinka is mentioned as the creator of a truly Russian opera, *A Life for the Tsar* (d.c.a.).

30 December/11 January 1845

Glinka writes to his mother that even abroad he is "not relieved . . . of the thoughts of my affairs. I am beginning to forget my grief here and hope that with time all these sad memories will be completely effaced." He thanks her for permission to travel to Spain: "I already wrote to you that I have an artistic objective for travelling to Spain."

30 December

In the first issue of *Repertuar i panteon* for 1845, in the section called "Humor," the author ridicules the passion for Italian opera and mentions Glinka's operas, which have been forgotten because of this new fashion (d.c.a.).

31 December/12 January

Glinka attended Félicien David's concert (ltr. to A. Gidella, 24 December 1844/5 January 1845).
[Reference is apparently to a rehearsal, since the concert in which David's symphonic ode, *La désert,* was performed took place on 2/14 January.]

Glinka held a New Year's Eve party. "His students, along with members of the French demimonde who had returned from Petersburg, drank punch and champagne with us. The dancing was very animated. The men were for the most part middle-aged Russian gentlemen. . . . Among the ladies at Glinka's ball there was Désirée Mayer. . . . In admiration of Russia . . . she sings Russian songs. She and I made a great impression dancing a Russian dance. . . . They said that it was very moving. I returned home at two o'clock in the morning" (A. Dargomyshzky's ltr. to his father, 6/18 January 1845; coll. *Dargomyzhsky,* p. 22). "The last party (which occurred exactly on the Russian New Year's eve) in fact turned out delightfully" (ltr. to V. Fleury, 5/17 January 1845; Fr. original).

31 December

Performance of *Ruslan and Lyudmila* at the Bolshoi Theater in Petersburg (*SPb. ved.,* 31 December 1844).

1845

4 January

In *Lit. gaz.,* no. 1, in an article entitled "Italian Opera in Petersburg (*Roberto d'Evereux,* lyrical drama in three acts, music by Donizetti)," there is a remark about the similarity between the melody of an aria in Donizetti's opera and a melodic idea from Vanya's aria in *A Life for the Tsar.*

5/17 January

In a letter to Viktor Fleury Glinka writes that Adeliada Solovieva, former prima donna of the Petersburg opera, is in Paris and that she intends to sing excerpts from *A Life for the Tsar* in a concert at the Théâtre Italien. "I agreed . . . since Mme Solovieva performs them well, and although she is not a first-class singer, she does sing better than many other singers who enjoy great popularity here." Besides the Rondo from the first act and the Romance from the third, Glinka decided to include the Krakowiak in the program as well. He asks Fleury to send money quickly (Fr. original).

6 January

Performance of *Ruslan and Lyudmila* in the Bolshoi Theater in Petersburg (*Sev. pchela,* 6 January 1845).

7/19 January

Berlioz's first concert in Champs Elysées circus (*Revue et gazette musicale,* 1845, no. 2).
[Judging from Glinka's letter to Heydenreich on 16/28 February, where he only mentions Berlioz's second concert, Glinka was apparently not at this concert.]

11/23 January

Glinka tells his mother of Solovieva's proposed appearance in Russian costume singing arias from *A Life for the Tsar.* "If my debut here is successful, Melgunov and I, with the help of other Russians, intend to arrange a concert for the benefit of the poor. This will give me the possibility of creating greater interest with audiences here, of acquainting them with my musical name, and thereby disposing them in my favor for future times. I see no possibility of writing for the theaters here. There is more intrigue here than anywhere else, but above all, living abroad, I become more and more convinced that by nature I am Russian and that it would be difficult for me to imitate another style. I intend to visit Spain with the goal of studying the tunes of that place, since they are somewhat similar to Russian ones and will give me the possibility (I hope) of beginning a big, new work."
[The performance of excerpts from *A Life for the Tsar* in the Théâtre Italien did not take place.]

17 January

In *Sev. pchela,* no. 13, the program of a new weekly is published, *Illiustratsiia,* written by the chief editor, Nestor Kukolnik. It also says that in 1845, Glinka will participate in the journal.

19 January

In *Sev. pchela,* no. 15, Glinka is mentioned in an article by Kukolnik (signed "N. K-k") entitled "The Polkas of Mr. Kazhinsky."

20 January

In *SPb. ved.,* no. 15, in a notice by "A. E-n" [Elkan] about the forthcoming performance of Lvov's opera *Bianca e Gualtiero,* it says that both operas "of our native composer of genius, M. I. Glinka, have been given with supreme success."

21 January

In *SPb. ved.,* no. 16, while introducing comments from the foreign press about Dargomyzhsky, "A. E-n" [Elkan] mentions Glinka and observes that his operas "have become a part of our folk heritage."

End of January (?)

Glinka called upon Berlioz with a letter from Prince Grigory Volkonsky. At first Berlioz received Glinka "very coldly," but then his attitude changed, and in his third concert he included *"V pole chistoe gliazhu"* (performed by Solovieva) and the lezghinka from *Ruslan.* "He would not have tried to do me this good turn if at the time he had not had in mind a trip to Russia" (lr. to V. Fleury, 15/27 February 1845; Fr. original).
[In his *Zapiski* Glinka says that Souza introduced him to Berlioz.]

4/16 February

At Berlioz's second concert in the Champs Elysées circus, Glinka heard Berlioz's overture *Les francs-juges,* a chorus from David's *Janissaires,* Leopold Meier's *"Marche marocaine"* for piano (with the composer performing), the *Dies irae* and *Tuba mirum* from Berlioz's *Requiem,* and David's symphonic ode *Le désert.* "I have had no greater musical pleasure than this second concert of Berlioz's. In my opinion Berlioz is one of the most remarkable composers of our time. He is original and orchestrates like no one else" (ltr. to L. Heydenreich, 16/28 February 1845; *Revue et gazette musicale,* 1845, no. 6).

5/17 February

Glinka moved from his apartment with Gedeonov into another apartment (22 rue de Provence) with his Spanish servant Don Hernández Santiago (ltrs. to E. and V. Fleury, 15/27 February, and to his mother, 6/18 February 1845).

6/18 February

In response to his mother's request that he not travel to Spain, Glinka attempts to reassure her and demonstrate the necessity of prolonging his stay abroad. He writes, "I am preoccupied with concerts on which I am working."

8 February

In a review of Lvov's opera *Bianca e Gualtiero* in *Lit. gaz.,* no. 6, it talks about the monotonous orchestration: ". . . for the most part the instruments play *en masse*. However, the combination of individual instruments with the voices is also one of dramatic music's important effects. Glinka grasped this secret quite well and used it to great success in *Ruslan and Lyudmila*."

12 February

In *Teatral'naia letopis'* [Chronicle of the theater], no. 6/7, under "The Petersburg Theaters. First Performances," there is a review signed "S. K." of *"Bianca e Gualtiero . . .* with music by Mr. Lvov," which contains an appraisal of the Russian operatic school and the operas of Glinka (d.c.a.).

13/25 February

Glinka "spent the evening at the Polmartins' [acquaintances of V. Fleury]. . . . They were very cordial toward me, inviting me to attend a concert of Mme [Polmartin's] students on Sunday morning and even offering me a seat in their box in the conservatory."

15/27 February

From Heydenreich, Glinka received a detailed letter about the premiere in Petersburg of Lvov's opera *Bianca e Gualtiero*. "I know this studentlike work (I am in the habit of calling things by their names), and I know what to think about it. I do not intend to imitate Mr. Lvov at all in any way, and if he envies others, then I, for my part, do not envy either his talent as a composer or his social position, because my life, vagrant but independent, has its charms for me, and

I prefer it to the attentions of people highly placed in society. All this does not keep me, however, from being very sensitive to the interests expressed to me by my friends. But after my two operas, the originality of which is not disputed even by my enemies, can I degrade myself to the sorry role of an imitator of Donizetti as Mr. Lvov has done? It would be better to renounce art, which I have worked at now for 30 years, than to do something so absurd" (lr. to V. Fleury, 15/28 February 1845; Fr. original).

Glinka informs Viktor and Elizaveta Fleury that Berlioz has included two excerpts from his operas in the program of his third concert in the *cirque* of the Champs Elysées. "Having available such beautiful possibilities and artistic forces as does M. Berlioz, I will have less to fear from the malicious critics in the honorable matter of acquainting the public with my works, since M. Berlioz is one of the most influential rulers of the destinies of the Parisian musical world." He expresses the intention "of writing an opera to an Italian text, but as I understand it, and for that I need to see Spain." He also writes that he spends very little time "in society," since he considers that "it is unworthy of an artist to seek the successes of the salon," besides which he does not enjoy Parisian parties, "where the charm of naturalness is alien. Even more, the theaters, public balls, and most importantly the nearness of several male and female friends as well as constant activity leave me . . . little time. I sometimes suffer in Paris, but I am never bored." He sends the poster of Berlioz's forthcoming concert and asks that it be passed on to Nestor Kukolnik (Fr. original).

Toward the Middle of February

Glinka transcribed the lezghinka from *Ruslan and Lyudmila* for one orchestra (lr. to his mother, 18 February/2 March 1845).
[The autograph has not been preserved.]

16/28 February

In a letter to Heydenreich, Glinka writes of Berlioz's forthcoming concert, in which *"V pole chistoe gliazhu"* from *A Life for the Tsar* and the lezghinka from *Ruslan and Lyudmila* were planned for performance. He tells of his life in Paris: "You may be surprised that I am writing nothing for Paris. If you were here, it would be easy for you to understand the reason, my friends. The French language, which is charming in the mouths of attractive women, is disgusting in grand opera, so far as I am concerned. I have had to give up the idea of publishing several romances in French translation." He writes that he is preparing for his trip to Spain. He is studying the language and reading books "quite fluently already—Cervantes, with the help of my teacher. I am surrounded by extensive maps of Spain and Andalusia and have acquired a 700-page geography of Spain in Spanish. Not until I have seen Andalusia will I undertake new work." He writes about the impression Berlioz's second concert made on him and says that he has still not been to the concerts at the conservatory. He adds that he has "only attended" the Italian opera "twice (I am not a lover of sweets) and heard Grisi and Persiani. In my opinion, our dear Viardot is better. The others are so-so. I have still not heard Lablache, but he is already getting old." He asks Mikhail Gedeonov "to go to the trouble" of sending him "the money owed [me] for *Ruslan*. I know that the sum is not large, but it is important to me because I wish to obtain several scenes of Paris and Spain."

18 February/2 March

In the morning Glinka attended a concert by students of Mme Polmartin (lr. to V. and E. Fleury, 15/27 February 1845).

In a letter to his mother, Glinka describes his manner of life in Paris: "Paris has been beneficial to me in many respects, even though my heart's wounds have not yet healed. However, I have gotten out of the habit of idleness." He tells about preparations for Berlioz's concert on 16 March.

21 February/15 March

After including an excerpt from his article on *A Life for the Tsar* in Glinka's album, Henry Mérimée added the following in Russian: "Dearest Mikhail Ivanovich, when I wrote these lines five years ago I was not personally acquainted with you at all. I could only express my genuine, deep admiration for your work. Now it would be possible for me to add the degree to which your personal qualities go right along with your talent. For me to say this in Russian is very bold, but I hope that you will not be too strict with me for unbecomingly spoiling your noble language, which I love zealously. Even a passionate lover's unskillful admiration is not offensive. Your friend, Genrikh Aleksandrovich" (Glinka's Spanish Album, in *L.*, p. 301).
[Mérimée's article appears at the entry for 21 May 1844.]

24 February/8 March

Glinka's Spanish teacher, Guerrero Biesma, made an entry in Glinka's album which is a list of recommended Spanish writers (Glinka's Spanish Album, in *L.*, p. 302).

Glinka inscribes Alfred de Beauchamp's musical album with the theme of Finn's ballad, for piano, two-hands (16 bars in A major). *"Paris, le 8 mars (thème de la ballade de l'opéra Rousslan et Loudmila), M. Glinka"* (*Sov. muz.*, 1971, no. 10, p. 124).

25 February/9 March

Glinka attends a concert in the Conservatoire. "They played Beethoven's Sixth Symphony (*Symphonie pastorale*). The performance was so extremely affected that I did not recognize it as a Beethoven symphony and said, *'on m'a escamoté la symphonie.'* Besides this, the wind instruments sometimes cracked, especially the French horns and clarinets" (*Zap.*; ltr. from N. Melgunov to S. Shevyrev, 26 February/10 March 1845, *L.*, p. 302).

In *Revue et gazette musicale,* no. 10, in the section *Nouvelles,* there is a notice of Berlioz's forthcoming third concert on Sunday, 4/16 March.

Glinka was present at a party of Russians which ended with "Russian and gypsy songs" (lr. from N. Melgunov to S. Shevyrev, 26 February/10 March 1845, in *L.*, p. 302).

Performance of *Ruslan and Lyudmila* in the Bolshoi Theater in Petersburg (*SPb. ved.*, 25 February 1845).

26 February

In *Sev. pchela,* no. 45, "Journalistic Odds and Ends," Bulgarin mentions a concert fantasy for piano on themes from *A Life for the Tsar* by the Kiev composer Vitvitsky.

February

Glinka visited Berlioz "as often as three times a week and spoke with him openly about music and especially about his compositions which I liked, most particularly those of a fantastic sort, like the scherzo *'La reine Mab'* from *Roméo et Juliette,* *'La marche des pèlerins'* from *Harold,* and the *Dies irae* and *Tuba mirum* from his *Requiem*" (*Zap.*). "I strongly dislike . . . the French. I don't like the folds of their minds, but Berlioz's mind fascinates me. There is something Mephistophelian about it, *d'une causticité à toute épreuve,* and when he wants to be pleasant, then you listen to him with delight. What a fascinating fellow" (Glinka's account, in Serov's *Vosp.*, p. 97).

1 March

In *Moskvityanin,* part 2, no. 2, "Literature," there is an article by Aleksey Khomyakov entitled "Letter to Petersburg on the Occasion of the Railroad." The author says that in Russian music, "as in literature also, a spiritual emancipation has occurred, and a great artist has awakened the sleeping strength of our musical creativity" (d.c.a.; reprinted from A. Khomyakov, *Poln. sobr. soch.,* vol. 1, M., 1861, p. 419).

February (?) or Beginning of March (?)

Glinka visited Ippolit Shirkov. The composer expressed his great joy at being able to meet "the brother of his friend" ("Travel Notes" of I. F. Shirkov, GPB, coll. 608, no. 148).

4/16 March

"V pole chistoe gliazhu" (Solovieva) from *A Life for the Tsar* and the Lezghinka from *Ruslan and Lyudmila,* which was called *Grand air de danse sur des thèmes du Caucase et de la Crimée,* are performed at Berlioz's third concert in the Champs Elysées circus. In the same concert excerpts from Berlioz's *Roméo et Juliette,* Weber's *Invitation to the Dance* in Berlioz's orchestration, Rossini's *Prière de Moïse,* and Jean Madeleine Schneitzhoeffer's *Ouverture du Spectre* were also performed (ltr. to his mother, 6/18 March 1845; poster, in *L.,* p. 302).

"Finally I have made my debut in Paris, and, thank God, successfully.... But on this occasion also there were things which went contrary to my expectations. I had thought beforehand that, as in Russia, the Lezghinka would have a terrific effect here, and I held little hope for Solovieva. I was quite worried when at the beginning of her aria she got nervous and her voice cracked. But since I was next to her, as Berlioz had advised, despite my inner nervousness, I did not lose my composure and, losing no time, signaled to Berlioz to begin the aria over again. In the treacherous place I prompted Solovieva, and she corrected herself and sang the aria so well that they interrupted her several times with applause, and at the end we were deafened with applause. The Lezghinka, as much from the disadvantageous arrangement of the orchestra as from the difficulty and novelty of the composition, did not make the wished-for impression, although the musicians liked it very well.... The audience was not large—several of my compatriots, however, kept their promise and were there" (ltr. to his mother, 6/18 March 1845). "My Lezghinka did not have the success I had wished for in Berlioz's concert in the circus, since for the greater part of its effectiveness I had calculated on the play between two orchestras, one on the stage made up of wind instruments, and another beneath the stage (in the pit), where the strings were predominant. Berlioz had nearly 150 musicians, who, consequently were spread out, and this kept the listener from grasping the whole, since the only sounds which reached him were of those instruments which were located closest to him" (*Zap.*). The aria *"V pole chistoe gliazhu"* elicited the "general and loudly vocal enthusiasm of the listeners. The charm of the original and expressive melody fascinated the audience." The Lezghinka "had no less an effect, but in a different respect: the Caucasian melody, foreign to the European ear, though not barbaric, and capricious, though not contrary to musical sensibility, amazed the Parisians. '*C'est sauvage, mais c'est beau,*' they exclaimed while clapping with all their might. Because of terribly bad weather . . . the circus was not full . . . but true connoisseurs were satisfied to pay M. Glinka his due" (N. Grech, "Parisian Letters," in *Sev. pchela*, 27 March 1845).

6/18 March

After describing to his mother the concert of 4/16 March, Glinka writes of his intention ("on the advice of friends") to give "a concert in my own name for the benefit of the poor in Paris. . . . In a concert of my own I can arrange things as I like. Above all . . . I will be in the public eye, and . . . this, it is said, will put me in good standing in the eyes of Parisians. For this occasion I will select pleasant pieces, not complicated ones, so as to please everyone. . . . Prince Golitsyn . . . promises me every kind of assistance and is giving me in advance a sum for expenses." He writes about how he spends his time and expresses the satisfaction he feels since he has begun living alone. He asks that money for his trip to Spain be sent very soon. "Although I like Paris and have found more advantages here than I expected, I would like to leave at the end of April, as much because of the expense as because I foresee no prospects since the concert is over. . . . I am used to being busy, and once I have looked around in Spain, I will get to work, especially since, besides a third opera, I have other compositions in mind. . . . I must value my time. My summers are the best time for working, and I must take advantage of them. And if my intentions are favorably fulfilled, then your son, now known in Paris, will be at home throughout Europe, to say nothing of Russia, where I hope to establish myself on another footing."

Musical autograph by Auber in Glinka's album (Glinka's Spanish Album, in *L.*, p. 303).

8 March

"An Answer to the *Northern Bee* Concerning Its Assessment of *Bianca e Gualtiero* and *Literary Gazette's* Criticism of this Opera" appears in *Lit. Gaz.*, no. 9, in the "Journalism" section. Excerpts from *Sev. pchela* [Northern Bee], no. 39, where Glinka is mentioned, are quoted.

9 March

Rafail Zotov refers to *Ruslan and Lyudmila* in an article entitled "Review of the St. Petersburg Theaters During the Past Year" in *Sev. pchela*, no. 54.

11/23 March

There is an article by Maurice Bourges entitled "Berlioz's Third Concert" in *Revue et gazette musicale,* no. 12, which says of Glinka's music that the freshness and melodic tenderness of Antonida's pretty rondo are distinctive. In the allegro a coquettish and simple-minded naivety and touching manner prevail. In the slow part there is a deep melancholy feeling in the character of the melody which the composer sustains in the style of Russian national songs. The dances from *Ruslan and Lyudmila* are based upon Caucasian and Crimean themes and are in the form of euphonious variations full of movement, though the strangeness of some of the rhythms, the harmonic surprises, and the indefiniteness of the tonality render the work very difficult for performance.

In *Le Ménestrel,* no. 17, there is a notice entitled *Causeries musicales* (unsigned) about Berlioz's concert, in which it says of Antonida's aria that the first part has its own distinctive character and coloration, though the rondo as a whole would fit in Italian forms. It says of the Lezghinka that it is remarkably orginal, maybe even too much so, and that the triple meter, like a waltz, has a charming effect.

15/27 March

Glinka receives a letter from Berlioz requesting information about himself, his first studies, musical institutions in Russia, and about his own . . . works, in order to provide readers of the *Journal des débats* some understanding of the great value of Glinka's work, however approximate." "It's not enough, sir, to perform your music and to tell many people that it is fresh, lively, and charming, with verve and originality. I must have the pleasure of writing a few columns about it, especially since it's my duty." "This letter should serve as proof of the sincerity of his opinion of me" (ltr. to N. Kukolnik, 6/18 April 1845).

15 March

Glinka's music is mentioned in association with P. Viardot's repertoire in *Sev. pchela,* no. 59, "Miscellany, Concert Echo."

19 March

In a concert in the Bolshoi Theater in Moscow, Leonova performed the trio *"Ne tomi, rodimyi"* from *A Life for the Tsar (Mosk. ved.,* 17 March 1845).

23 March

There is mention of *Ruslan and Lyudmila* in a notice entitled "Music" by "D. S." in *Sev. pchela,* no. 66.

In St. Petersburg, the trio *"Ne tomi, rodimyi"* from *A Life for the Tsar* is performed in a concert given by Döhler, Viardot, Rubini, and Tamburini. "The audience listened to the trio three times, and there would have been no end to the piece if enthusiasm could be sustained like boredom. Marvelous sounds spread through that same theater in which the audience not so long ago had been bored listening to the same trio and was amazed how one could write Russian operas from Russian songs" (*Illiustratsiia,* 7 April 1845).

Before 25 March/6 April

Glinka prepared a new orchestration of the *Valse-fantaisie.*
[The autograph has not been preserved. There is a copy of the score in the Bibliothèque Nationale.]

25 March/6 April

In the section *Nouvelles* of *Revue et gazette musicale,* no. 14, it is reported that Glinka is giving a concert in Herz Hall on Thursday, 10 April (N.S.). "Many works for orchestra will be performed." Participants in the concert are to include Solovieva, Marras, Haumann, and Leopold Meier; the conductor is to be Til-mant (Fr. original).

Glinka attends Berlioz's fourth concert in the Champs Elysées circus, where the following works were performed: *Une cavatine russe de M. de Glinka; Dies irae* and *Tuba mirum* from the *Requiem;* the scherzo (Queen Mab) from *Roméo et Juliette;* March of the Pilgrims from *Harold en Italie* by Berlioz; *La Prière des âmes du Purgatoire et la Marche marocaine* by L. Meier; the overture to

Weber's *Freischütz;* Rossini's *Prière de Moïse;* David's *Nonetto;* and an aria with chorus from the opera *Esmeralda* by Mlle Bertin (poster).

27 March

Grech's article, "Parisian Letter," regarding performance of excerpts from *A Life for the Tsar* and *Ruslan and Lyudmila* in Berlioz's third concert on 4/16 March appears in *Sev. pchela,* no. 69: "Even at the rehearsals the musicians (who rarely yield the palm to a foreign rival) cheered him enthusiastically. Mr. Glinka has not written anything here. Perhaps the strings of his harp will respond to the winds of southern skies."

28 March/19 April

In a letter to Vasily Petrovich Golitsyn, Glinka asks for an appointment on the following day before the concert.

In *Rus. invalid,* no. 69, there is an article by Odoevsky (signed, "An Old Dilettante") about Viardot, Rubini, and Tamburini's performance of the trio *"Ne tomi, rodimyi"* from *A Life for the Tsar* in Döhler's concert on 23 March, and about the concert that day by Ludwig Maurer, at which the trio was to be repeated by the same performers.

In *Sev. pchela,* no. 70, "Miscellany," there is a notice of the performance on 3 April in Artemovsky's concert of the trio from *A Life for the Tsar* (Viardot, Rubini, Petrov).

In Ludwig Maurer's concert (in Petersburg), Viardot, Rubini, and Tamburini perform the trio *"Ne tomi, rodimyi"* from *A Life for the Tsar (Rus. invalid,* 28 March 1845). "The theater is always full when the poster mentions Glinka's trio" (ltr. to his mother, 22 April/4 May 1845).

29 March/10 April

Glinka's concert in Herz Hall. On the program were: overture to Rossini's *Semiramide;* Glinka's romance *"Il desiderio"* (performed by Marras); Berio's *Andante et rondo russe pour violin* (performed by Haumann); Glinka's *Scherzo (en forme de valse) à grand orchestre* [*Valse-fantaisie*]; a duet from Bellini's opera *I Puritani* (performed by Solovieva and Marras); *Airs russes* and *La marche triomphale par d'Isly* by L. Meier (performed by the composer); *La Cracovienne, grand air de danse* from *A Life for the Tsar* and *Romance dramatique pour soprano* (performed by Solovieva) *accomp. de Harpe* (Tarkot) *et de*

Violoncelle (Chevillard); and Lyudmila's cavatina and *Marche fantastique* [Chernomor's march] from Glinka's *Ruslan and Lyudmila*. Orchestra of the Italian Opera, conducted by Tilmant; Glinka accompanied on the piano (poster). This program was changed. Solovieva "got stage fright" during the duet from *I Puritani* and was unable to sing the remaining numbers. In addition to what was on the program, Marras performed the cavatina from Donizetti's *L'elisir d'amore*. "Fifty-two musicians of the Italian orchestra performed my pieces excellently, and they were very favorably received by the audience. They liked my scherzo (the Pavlovsk waltz) extremely well and are publishing it here as well as the romance '*Il desiderio*.' The translating effort has not succeeded, and I have been constrained to restrict my concert debuts to those insignificant pieces which can be understood with one hearing, since here one must only perform uncomplicated pieces. Most of all, I have not wanted to start out with anything other than pieces written in Russia for Russians" (ltr. to N. Kukolnik, 6/18 April 1845). "The hall was full. It was as if the Russian ladies had agreed to adorn their compatriot's concert. They were there in splendid attire, so that one of the journals wrote of my concert: *c'était un parterre de fleurs*" (*Zap.*). "The capacious Herz Hall was filled with people of all nations. It seemed to me that I was sitting in our own Philharmonic Hall. Everyone spoke French, and only rarely were Russian phrases by chance heard from a few people. . . . Compositions of Glinka's which were performed included the Krakowiak from *A Life for the Tsar*, Scherzo (Pavlovsk waltz), and the March from *Ruslan*, . . . Mr. Glinka was very limited in his selection of works. First of all, there were no singers to perform the best parts of his operas, and besides, it is impossible to offer the Parisian public anything difficult or serious. Here they like music which is light and easy to understand. Secondly, Mr. Glinka had decided to give audiences here only original Russian works, written and performed in Russia and not to write something new in accordance with Western tastes. These constraints, however, did not damage his success. The entire audience did our composer justice" (N. Grech, "Parisian Letters," in *Sev. pchela*, 24 April 1845).

29 March

Pauline Viardot performs in the home of Count Lavalle in St. Petersburg. It is possible that at this concert "in the presence of the Empress and the court" she [Viardot] "sang the aria 'Oh, My Ratmir' from *Ruslan* in Russian . . . and made such an effect that she had to repeat it" (ltr. to his mother, 22 April/4 May 1845, according to P. Barteneva; A. Rozanov, *Polina Viardo-Garsia, L.*, 1973, p. 52).

31 March/12 April

In a letter to his mother, Glinka tells her about his concert and asks that she repay the debt he owes V. Golitsyn, since the concert's expenses were not covered by receipts. He sums up his stay in Paris: "I have gotten to know many remarkable people, among them Berlioz, who, in my opinion, is the most remarkable composer of our time. He is also the most important critic in Paris and is now preparing a huge article about me. . . . Perhaps others will be luckier in their debuts, but I am the first Russian composer to acquaint the Parisian public with his name and his own works written in Russia and for Russia."

In *Le Ménestrel,* no. 20, it says in an article about Glinka's concert that the compositions of this artist afford satisfaction.

31 March

In the first issue of *Illiustratsiia* there is a report in an article by Kukolnik entitled "Music" of Glinka's concert in Paris on 4/16 March. "Thus Paris has heard the music of a composer whom Russia should be proud of. According to private letters from Paris there has been news that Mikhaylo Ivanovich might begin to write for the Opéra-Comique. He has gotten to be good friends with Auber and other celebrities. . . . Still the rumors of a new opera have gone unconfirmed. Our Glinka would surely not sing an entire opera in a foreign land. That would be hard to believe. Perhaps a few ephemeral romances, two or three ardent, impassioned waltzes, transient, as they say, things inspired by his travels might be heard by foreigners before we hear them . . . but hardly an opera. . . . We are waiting for an opera from Glinka in Petersburg, where they're beginning to refer to *Ruslan and Lyudmila* as a hackneyed opera . . . as music critics express themselves nowadays. . . . The French put their Halévys, Adams, and Berliozes on a pedestal, which is perhaps half-undeserved, and we get bored listening to Glinka. . . . Against their will Russian composers will begin to write polkas." In the same article, referring to the popular fascination with the polka, it says that "they're waiting for Glinka, Meyerbeer, and Donizetti to write an opera called *The Polka"* (d.c.a.).

1/13 April

Entry in Glinka's album by the prima donna of the St. Petersburg opera Adeliada Verteuil-Solovieva. Musical entry by Edward Wolff in Glinka's album (Glinka's Spanish Album, in *L.,* p. 307).

In *Revue et gazette musicale,* no. 15, in the section *Nouvelles,* the reader is informed that the next issue will include a detailed account of the concert of a charming Russian composer and his ravishing works.

2/14 April

Entry by V. Golitsyn in Glinka's album (Glinka's Spanish Album, in *L.,* p. 307).

3 April

Viardot, Rubini, and Petrov performed the trio *"Ne tomi, rodimyi"* from *A Life for the Tsar* in Artemovsky's concert (*Sev. pchela,* 28 March 1845). It is possible that at this concert Viardot sang Gorislava's cavatina and "had such an effect that she had to repeat it." "Two merchants offered to pay double for tickets and requested that they be allowed in the hall to hear the Italians sing their favorite song from *Ruslan*" (ltr. to his mother, 22 April/4 May 1845).

[Glinka is retelling here what he had heard from Barteneva and Stepan Gedeonov. It is not clear whether Glinka erred in naming *Ruslan and Lyudmila* instead of *A Life for the Tsar* or if he was repeating the merchants' error in the letter to his mother as an anecdote. As is known, entrance to the Hall of Nobility was closed to those who were not members of the nobility.]

4/16 April

Berlioz's article "Michel Glinka" appears in the *Journal des débats.* The article includes a short biographical sketch, information on the operas and his service in the Chapel, as well as a general description of his work. "Uncommon versatility and variety distinguish Glinka's talent. He has the rare ability to transform his style at will according to the demands and character of the subject with which he is working. It is simple and even naive, but never demeaned by clichés. Unexpected sounds appear in his melodies. His phrases are strangely charming. He is a great harmonist, and he writes the instrumental parts with such care and profound understanding of their hidden possibilities that his orchestra is one of the most novel and vital orchestras of our time." Concerning the performance, Berlioz writes: "His 'Scherzo' in the form of a waltz [*Valse-fantaisie*] and the Krakowiak received loud applause ... and if his fantastic march from *Ruslan and Lyudmila* did not make as strong an impression, it was because of the march's premature conclusion. The coda makes such an abrupt turn and ends so unexpectedly and laconically that one has to have seen that the orchestra has ceased playing to believe that the composer actually concluded the work this way. The Scherzo is fascinating, is executed with a most striking rhythmic coquetry, and is genuinely novel and excellently worked out. The Krakowiak and March are likewise especially distinctive for their original melodic style. This is an extremely rare virtue, and if a composer brings to this other qualities as well, such as elegant harmony and beautiful, clean, colorful orchestration, then he can legitimately claim a place among the outstanding composers of our time" (Fr. original). "My creative self-esteem was fully gratified" (ltr. to N. Kukolnik, 6/18 April 1845).

Aleksandr Ivanenko's entry about the trip to Spain in Glinka's album. A. Châteauneuf's entry in Glinka's album: "In token of my admiration and satisfaction for all the pleasure which his beautiful music has afforded me" (Glinka's Spanish Album, in *L.*, p. 307; Fr. original).

After 4/16 April

Glinka gave the issue of *Journal des débats* with Berlioz's article to Ippolit Shirkov for him to forward to Valerian Shirkov (I. Shirkov's "Travel Notes," GPB).

5/17 April

Berlioz inscribed Glinka's album with the *Thème du scherzo (La reine Mab) de "Romeo et Juliette."* Entries by Nikolay Grech and Melchior (Solovieva's husband) in Glinka's album.

[The entries dated on the same day provide evidence that Glinka apparently had a party attended by those who inscribed his Spanish Album. Probably on the same day (unspecified) Melgunov wrote his long entry about "Harmony," which concluded with the following words: "Let us not disturb the emerging harmony of the Future with our mercenary and petty little quarrels. May Love and Peace, Peace and Love be with us all" (Glinka's Spanish Album, in *L.*, p. 307).]

Glinka forwarded the issue of *Journal des débats* with Berlioz's article to his sister Elizaveta Fleury (ltr. to N. Kukolnik, 6/18 April 1845).

5 April

In *Lit. gaz.*, no. 13, "Petersburg Chronicle," it mentions Viardot, Rubini, and Tamburini's performance of the trio *"Ne tomi, rodimyi"* from *A Life for the Tsar* in Maurer's concert.

6/18 April

Glinka tells Nestor Kukolnik about life in Paris and draws several conclusions: "For me my most remarkable encounter, without question, was with Berlioz.

To study his works, which are so censured by some and so extolled by others, was one of my musical intentions in Paris, and good luck obliged me. I not only heard Berlioz's music at concerts and *rehearsals,* but I got to know, in my opinion, the *most important* composer of our century (of course, in his specialty). . . . And this is my opinion: in the realm of the fantastic in art no one has approached his colossal and original conceptions. The overall scope, development of details, continuity, *harmonic substance,* and finally, consistently powerful and original orchestration are the things which characterize Berlioz's music. In drama, since he is preoccupied with the fantastic aspect of situations, he is unnatural and consequently false. Of the works of his which I have heard, '*L'ouverture des Francs-juges,*' '*La marche de pèlerins*' *de la symphonie* '*Harold*' *et le scherzo* '*La reine Mab ou la Fée des songes*' as well as the *Dies irae* and the *Tuba mirum* from the *Requiem* made an indescribable impression on me. I now have several unpublished manuscripts of Berlioz which I am studying with inexpressible pleasure." Further on Glinka tells about the concerts at which his works were performed and about the opinions of the press and public. "In sum I am extremely pleased with my trip. Paris is a marvelous city, the variety of intellectual pleasures is inexhaustible. . . . In artistic respects the study of Berlioz's music and the public here has led me to extremely important results. I have decided to enrich my repertoire with several (and, if strength permits me, many) concert pieces for orchestra under the heading of *fantaisies pittoresques.* Until now instrumental music has fallen into two opposing divisions: quartets and symphonies, which are appreciated by a few but which frighten most listeners with their profound and complicated ideas; and the properly designated concertos, variations, etc., which tire the ear with their incoherence and difficulties. It seems to me that it should be possible to combine the requirements of art and the requirements of the age and, while profiting from the perfection of instruments and execution, to write pieces which are equally *accessible* to connoisseurs and the general public. . . . In Spain I will take up writing my proposed *fantaisies.* The uniqueness of the melodies there will be a significant help to me, the more so as until now this is an area which has not been traversed by anyone, and, besides their originality, for my unbridled fantasy a text or some positive reference is necessary."

7/19 April

Henri Herz inscribed Glinka's album with the Krakowiak from *A Life for the Tsar* (Glinka's Spanish Album, in *L.,* p. 309).

7 April

The "Music" section in *Illiustratsiia,* no. 2, says in connection with Viardot, Rubini, and Petrov's successful performance of the trio from *A Life for the Tsar:* "In order for Russians to like Russian songs they have to be sung by Italians. What a sad display of obstinacy!" In reference to a romance by Tal, "rewritten" by Henselt, it says: "Isn't this M. I. Glinka's romance 'To Molly' to the words 'Do not demand songs from the singer'? The outlines are the same exactly, note for note. Coincidence. . . . Chance. . . ."

8/20 April

In *Revue et gazette musicale,* no. 16, there is an article by Maurice Bourges entitled "M. de Glinka." The critic observes that he is acquainted with Glinka's operas and that Glinka obligingly agreed to supplement his practical familiarization by allowing him to leaf through both scores with him of the the works staged in St. Petersburg. Bourges provides a general evaluation of Glinka's work. In the critic's words, a nation's soul is most fully revealed in its folk songs, which have no source other than naive, native instinct. Here the secret spiritual life of a people is exposed. . . . In Bourges's opinion, Glinka's music at times has a sentimental, dreamy character, despite resoluteness and rhythmic freedom in some places where circumstances permit. Every melody of Glinka's is genuine; they disturb and touch one.

10 April

In his "Parisian Letters" in *Sev. pchela,* no. 81, Nikolay Grech makes reference to performances of Glinka's works in Paris.

12 April

In the "Petersburg Chronicle" section of *Lit. gaz.,* no. 14, Viardot's performance in her concert of Gorislava's cavatina from *Ruslan and Lyudmila* is mentioned.
[The date of the concert is not mentioned, but it could not have occurred later than the first week of April, after which Viardot departed for Moscow, where she arrived on 11 April (A. Rozanov, *Polina Viardo-Garsia,* L., 1973, p. 53).]

14/26 April

In *L'illustration,* no. 13, there is a short biography of Glinka and an appraisal of his work (the author is Benoit Jouvin). To the critic, Glinka's talent is especially charming and attractive. In Jouvin's opinion, Glinka's melodies are frequently intricate and refined, easy, at times unusual, but never trivial. Moreover Glinka's outstanding mastery of harmony and his excellent understanding of the orchestra, including the ability to combine instruments in a harmonic ensemble, have earned him a place of honor among composers of any nation. Jouvin considers Glinka to be Russia's leading composer. The critic also mentions Glinka's abilities as a performer who proved to be a remarkable pianist (Fr. original).

14 April

The following appears in a feuilleton entitled "February" in *Illiustratsiia*, no. 3: "We complained because we were not in Paris, not because 500 people were performing Berlioz's *Requiem,* but because we could not see with our own eyes what kind of effect M. I. Glinka's original music had on the Parisians, whose hearing has arbitrarily become quite cosmopolitan. . . . Nikolay Ivanovich Grech attests to their furious enthusiasm. Quite understandably . . . since facile music plagiarists have not yet appropriated the riches of . . . Weber and Glinka. The works of both of these nationalist composers appeared without precursors in Paris in their original and undistorted form, and the enthusiasm was genuine and unfeigned. . . . That one can guarantee. News of the success of M. I. Glinka's music is very gratifying and would be more so if in Russia, instead of mediocre Italian arias even more mediocrely performed, they would begin to sing Glinka's music, initially on Paris's recommendation and then in acknowledgment of its musical superiority." Concerning the lottery, in the same article: "At the time of the first lottery, all people talked about in society were the French theater, the return of Bryullov and Bruni, the opera *A Life for the Tsar,* and the artists' lottery." In a section headed "Dramaturgy," there is an article about Russian opera and its performers: "We will not argue with or contradict the fact that Russian composers themselves care little for Russian opera and do little to maintain it. Of course *A Life for the Tsar* and *Ruslan and Lyudmila,* for all their colossal status, cannot assure the independence of Russian opera. The very scope and attributes of these operas belong to a category with which great opera begins and ends. What then have other composers done? What subjects have they chosen for Russian operas, and what has been the style of their treatment of them?" In the section "Music": "Not long ago in a Parisian paper we saw a little article called 'Russian Music,' and we were delighted. We thought we would be reading about the music of Glinka and Dargomyzhsky." (It turned out that the article was about Maresh and horn music.) Further on the names of outstanding Russian composers are listed, among them Glinka.

15/27 April

The first day of the orthodox Easter Glinka "spent with . . . my dear countrymen. We went together to church, broke our fast together, and spent the rest of
the day together" (ltr. to his mother, 22 April/4 May 1845).

Before 19 April/1 May

In the chronicle of the journal *La revue britannique* there is a notice about
Glinka's concert. The critic is carried away by the style of Glinka's music, his
knowledge of harmony, and the originality and freshness of his ideas. Even
though Glinka is Russian, according to the critic, he is rather cosmopolitan and
even a bit Italian. The question is asked: "Have librettists really let him get
away? Why doesn't the Opéra or Opéra-Comique entrust him with a libretto?"
But then he adds that he hears a cry of alarm from all their laureates; still, that
is why "we shall not be enemies of an artist who possesses such a modest
character and ravishing talent" (Fr. original).

"They have written about me in many newspapers. The editor of the *La revue
britannique* wrote an extremely nice article about me; Maurice Bourges also
wrote about me; and finally, Berlioz has written a huge article with a short
biography of me. . . . Melgunov provided Berlioz with the necessary information for his article."

Glinka received "joyful news" from Stepan Gedeonov and Praskovya Barteneva
about the success of excerpts from his operas sung by the Italians. "This good
news delighted me" (ltr. to his mother, 22 April/4 May 1845).

To this period belongs Bernard Latt's publication of the romance *Il desiderio*
and the piano edition of the *Valse-fantaisie* under the title *Scherzo en forme de
valse composée pour orchestre par Glinka réduit pour piano par l'auteur* (Music Department of the Bibliothèque Nationale in Paris).

19 April/1 May

In a letter to Viktor Fleury, Glinka asks him to send money quickly, since he
does not wish to linger any longer in Paris. "I have gotten everything that I
wanted from Paris. . . . You know very well that saving has never been my
strong point, and especially not now when I have acquired a certain fame, for
it is absolutely impossible for me to change my way of living without losing
my social standing" (Fr. original).

Glinka saw the festivities celebrating the King's nameday. Following that, Russian students of the medical faculty "organized a celebration in my honor and brought me a *wreath* in recognition of my successes in Russia" (ltr. to V. Fleury, 20 April/2 May 1845; Fr. original).

Entry in Glinka's album by ten medical students: S. Alferiev, F. Hefner, D. Krüger, F. Zhurkovsky, Pavel Ilienko, A. Khodnev, N. Lyaskovsky, Aleksey Polunin, V. Basov, and K. Sokologorsky.
[Beneath there is this postscript: "Paris, 1 May 1845." I. Shirkov was also among the medical students. Glinka was a guest at Sokologorsky's several times.]

Souza's entry in Glinka's album (Glinka's Spanish Album, in ITMK, coll. 6, and *L.*, p. 311).

19 April

In *SPb. ved.*, no. 85, there is an article by Amply Ochkin entitled "Berlioz's Opinion of M. I. Glinka" (which is a translation of Berlioz's article).

20 April/2 May

Glinka writes to Viktor Fleury again about money. He also talks about the Russian students' celebration for him and the opinion of the Parisian press of his music. "I am filled with gratitude to the cultured and benevolent Parisian public, and I somehow feel myself obliged, while writing for my fatherland, to also write for Europe as well" (Fr. original).

20 April

The conclusion of the translation of Berlioz's article about Glinka is printed in *SPb. ved.*, no. 86.

22 April/4 May

In a letter to his mother, Glinka writes that he has gotten the money he needed for his trip from the Polmartins, acquaintances of Viktor Fleury.
[Mme Polmartin's piano concert took place the same day. It is possible that Glinka was present (*Revue et gazette musicale*, 1845, no. 19, 11 May).]

24 April

In *Sev. pchela,* no. 90, Grech's next "Parisian Letter" is published with a description of Glinka's concert in Henri Herz's concert hall and a supplement including Berlioz's letter to Glinka (cf. 15/27 March).

26 April

In the cellist Piatti's concert in the Bolshoi Theater in Moscow, Theodor Döhler played the trio from *A Life for the Tsar* in a piano transcription (*Mosk. ved.,* 24 April 1845).

The beginning of Berlioz's article about Glinka, under the title "Berlioz's Opinion of M. I. Glinka," is printed in *Mosk. ved.,* no. 50 (reprinted from *SPb. ved.,* 19 and 20 April 1845).

28 April

In the fifth literary supp. to *Le Nouvelliste,* under "Miscellaneous News Items," there is a report about Berlioz's third concert in Paris, at which "among many exemplary pieces, the Rondo from the opera *A Life for the Tsar* . . . and the March from *Ruslan and Lyudmila* were performed. These outstanding works by M. I. Glinka prove that there is great musical talent in Russia also" (d.c.a.).

Conclusion of the translation of Berlioz's article about Glinka in *Mosk. ved.,* no. 51.

In the fourth issue of *Illiustratsiia,* in an article entitled "April," there is reference to the performance by singers from the Italian Opera of the trio from *A Life for the Tsar* and to Viardot's performance of Gorislava's cavatina from *Ruslan and Lyudmila.* In the same issue, under "Miscellany, Various News Items," it says: "This week we have received letters from Paris from M. I. Glinka and about M. I. Glinka. Berlioz has written an article about our composer. . . . We will remain silent for the time being. However, we should present for the reader's judgment some explanation of this article." Later on it reports that Glinka is leaving for Spain. "There he intends to work on an opera, and if not an opera, then at least other compositions."

April

News of the performance of Glinka's music by Italian artists in Petersburg appears in the newspaper *Corsaire Satan.*

2 May

In the Aleksandrinsky Theater in Petersburg, "a benefit performance for Mme Petrova" of *A Life for the Tsar* (*Sev. pchela,* 2 May 1845).

5 May

In the fifth issue of *Illiustratsiia,* under "Music," it says: "Our composers likewise pay little attention to our musical interests. M. I. Glinka has left for Madrid. Sometime we shall see and hear him. . . . I do not know if we should consider the new edition of the trio from *A Life for the Tsar* news, even though it really has been revived by the outstanding singing of our Italian guests. Now even Russians are buying and singing this trio."

6 May

In a benefit concert for the stage manager of the opera troupe in Kharkov, the trio from *A Life for the Tsar* was performed (*Repertuar i panteon,* 1845, vol. 11, part 9, p. 64).

9/21 May

Glinka sends Barteneva the poster of his concert as well as copies of *L'illustration* with Jouvin's article and *Journal des débats* with Berlioz's article. "I am sure that you will read this article with concern, which is all the more important to me because Berlioz himself offered to write about me. He is the most important critic here, and it is said that he is incorruptible. I owe my acquaintance with him to Prince Grigory Volkonsky. This acquaintance is one of the most important for me in Paris, beneficial not only because of his influence on the musical world in his capacity as a critic, but, in my opinion, Berlioz is *the most remarkable composer of our era*. I am convinced of this since learning his music, which I have heard in concerts and at rehearsals. Finally, I have studied his unpublished manuscripts. The novelty of conception in his works is amazing!" He thanks her for the joyful "information that in my absence I have not been forgotten and that finally my humble sounds have been performed by Europe's most outstanding performers." He tells of the success of his concert in Paris and repeats again the thought that "I decided to appear before audiences here with pieces written *in Russia and for Russia*." He shares impressions of Paris and writes of his departure "in four days" for Spain. "I cannot think about Petersburg without horror . . . for when I do, all the tormenting things which have happened are vividly renewed in my memory."

10 May

Excerpts from Berlioz's article about Glinka are printed in the "Miscellany" section of *Lit. gaz.*, no. 17.

11/23 May

The Polmartins' entry (musical autograph and greeting) in Glinka's album (Glinka's Spanish Album, in *L.*, p. 314).

12/24 May

Informing his mother of his departure from Paris the following day, Glinka writes: "There is no necessity of telling you that I speak Spanish better than Italian."

12 May

In *Illiustratsiia,* no. 6, in an article entitled "Weekly" and dedicated to the conductor Hermann, it says: "Because he loved Russians from his heart, he also loved Russian music. Recall how he performed Glinka's Waltz, this amazing elegy full of love, languor, and melancholy, and the Bolero." In a note "From the editor" it mentions that there are compositions by Glinka in the newspaper's portfolio.

13/25 May

Glinka writes an inscription on the lithograph portrait of himself donc by Léon Couderc: *"A ma chère soeur Loudmila. Paris le 25/13 Mai 1845"* (*L.*, p. 314).

In the evening Glinka "set out in a rented carriage on the Orleans railroad" accompanied by Don Santiago and his nine-year-old daughter Rosario (*Zap.;* ltr. to his mother, 12/24 May 1845).

14/26 May

Orleans. They left "Orleans by post-chaise" for Pau.

16/28 May

Pau. Arrival at night. "The spectacular scene of the Pyrenees with snow-covered peaks struck me vividly."

17/29 May

Glinka tells his mother about his trip: "I have been revived by the sight of the charming natural world of the south. I have feasted my eyes for almost the entire trip on the charming and fascinating sights."

19/31 May

Departure at 5 a.m. by stagecoach (ltr. to his mother, 22 May/3 June 1845).

20 May/1 June

St.-Jean-pied-de-port. "From Pau by stagecoach to a little frontier city," and after that "we reached a small border village" (*Zap.*).

Val Carlos. By cart from the French customs house. It was "about two versts on foot to the Spanish border. That same day [we went] on horseback . . . across very high mountains to the first Spanish settlement. The places through which we travelled were extremely picturesque . . . valleys . . . ravines . . . waterfalls . . . bare, inaccessible cliffs" (ltr. to his mother, 22 May/3 June 1845). "I arrived in Spain on 20 May, my own birthday, and was in total ecstasy" (*Zap.*).

21 May/2 June

Ronces Valles. Through the Pyrenees "we travelled more than 30 versts by *mule* and, no doubt, would have reached *Pamplona,* if pouring rain had not first forced us to seek shelter and then spend the night in a village two-and-a-half hours" from Pamplona (ltr. to his mother, 22 May/3 June 1845).

21 May

In *Sev. pchela,* no. 113, in an article by "R. Z." [Zotov] entitled "The Aleksandrinsky Theater. Mr. Petrov's Benefit—*A Life for the Tsar* (2 May)," it says: "Russian audiences always take pleasure in listening to this beautiful work by our Russian composer, and now his melodies are even fascinating Paris."

22 May/3 June

Pamplona. Arrival. Glinka describes his trip in detail in a letter to his mother. In the evening he attended the theater. "The theater was satisfactory. They did a play in Spanish, and quite well. I was occupied not so much with the play as with the audience . . . their appearance and dress differ sharply from the French.

After the play they danced the national dance, the *jota*. Unfortunately, like in Russia, passion for Italian music has possessed musicians to such an extent that national music is completely distorted. In their dancing I also noticed a lot of imitation of the French ballet-masters. Despite this, in general, the dancing was lively and entertaining."

23 May/4 June

In a letter to his mother, Glinka describes the national cuisine, the theater (where he had been the day before), the Spanish character and the extreme courtesy with which he was received everywhere. "Because of a letter of recommendation from Pau, we were passed from hand to hand. . . . They fussed over us, got us horses, mules, guides, they fed us and feted us, and looked after us with uncommon cordiality, all for a very small sum."

25 May/6 June

Departure for Valladolid (ltr. to his mother, 23 May/4 June 1845).

26 May

In the "Miscellany" section of *Moskvityanin,* part 2, no. 4, there is a "Letter from Paris" by Aleksandr Turgenev containing news that a concert given by Berlioz in the *cirque* on the Champs Elysées included as a participant "the Petersburg singer Mlle Alexandrine Verteuil." [She received the sobriquet "Solovieva" because of Nicholas I's wish.] "Glinka has wanted for a long time to become known to the public here as he has in Milan and Russia. But here it is difficult to penetrate the throng of talented people who besiege the temples of fame, which are accessible only to a few" (d.c.a.).

Between 25 May/6 June and 27 May/8 June (?)

"From Pamplona we travelled by stagecoach to Vittoria, from which, after crossing the Ebro at Mirando de Ebro, we found ourselves in the ravine of Pancorvo."

28 May/9 June (?)

Burgos. "In Burgos we looked at the cathedral."

29 May

In his next "Parisian Letter" in *Sev. pchela,* no. 119, Grech tells of Glinka's departure from Paris.

Between 28 and 30 May/9 and 11 June

Valladolid. Arrival in Valladolid, "where we decided to spend the summer. . . . We took rooms with Don Santiago's sister. They rented me two neat rooms" (*Zap.*). "Our arrival roused everyone. They got a bad piano" (ltr. to his mother, 8/20 June 1845). "I resumed my study of Spanish, and in a short time I began to speak Spanish freely" (*Zap.*).

31 May

In the "Humor" section of *Repertuar i panteon,* vol. 9, part 5, there appear "Notes of a Petersburg Idler. Section 5. The Physiology of the Dilettante." After deriding the worship of Italian opera, the author writes: "Despite the fact that several remarkably talented people have appeared among our musicians and the melodies of Glinka and Varlamov have moved several hearts, their music has not had any apparent success in Petersburg," and "even the remarkable talent" of Glinka "has not had a more profound influence on the public" (d.c.a.).

June

In *Repertuar i panteon,* vol. 9, part 6, in the section "Theatrical Chronicle. May," in reference to Petrov's benefit on 2 May, it says: *"A Life for the Tsar* is the only opera which one can listen to after the Italians. The artist for whom the benefit performance was given was very good in it" (d.c.a.).

7/19 June

On the nameday of their host (Santiago's brother-in-law) "about 30 guests gathered. I was not in the mood to dance, and so I sat down at the piano, where two students accompanied me quite well on guitars. The dancing continued with tireless activity until 11 o'clock in the evening. The waltz and quadrille, called *rigadon* here, comprise the main dances. They also dance the Parisian *polka* and a national dance called the *jota.* The evening acquainted me with many of the inhabitants here. On the whole they are extremely affectionate and unpretentious, which is quite new after Paris, and in many ways it reminds me of our Russia, as do many things in Spain. In this province, called *Old Castille,* the inhabitants are not attractive and are of small stature, so that *Don Miguel,* as they honor me here, is included among those of medium height. The women here also cannot boast of their beauty."

8/20 June

In a letter to his mother, Glinka shares his impressions of the people and character of Valladolid. "Spain is not like any of the other parts of Europe, in that every province is clearly distinctive from the others. This is why most travellers describe her inaccurately, judging the whole from the parts. I, however, prepared for a long time for my trip and selected the most interesting provinces."

10/22 June

Glinka wrote down the Spanish folk song *"La colasa."* Unknown entry in verse in Glinka's album (Spanish Album, in *L.,* p. 316).

16/28 June

Glinka wrote down the Spanish folk song *"Las aves verdes"* (Ibid.).

22 June/4 July

Glinka describes his life in a letter to his mother. "Horseback riding is very good for me. . . . During walks in the city and while riding I constantly encounter interesting new things." He writes that he is keeping a diary, "a journal, in which I am writing what happens each day. . . . In the evening mostly I visit acquaintances. I play the piano with guitars and violins accompanying, and when I stay home, they gather here, and we sing Spanish national songs in chorus, and we dance, which I haven't done for a long time. . . . One of the students is an excellent guitarist. He and I distinguish ourselves almost every evening, as Uncle Ivan Andreevich and I did formerly in Petersburg, playing piano four-hands. Everywhere here I receive respect and an affectionate reception. . . . By living with the family I am learning about domestic life and customs and am beginning to speak tolerably in a language which is not at all easy."

"In the evenings neighbors and acquaintances gather here to sing, dance, and talk. Among our acquaintances, the son of a merchant here by the name of Felix Castilla plays the guitar very lively, especially the *jota aragonesa,* which I have committed to memory along with his variations."

25 June

Performance in the Bolshoi Theater in Moscow of *A Life for the Tsar* (*Mosk. ved.*, 21 and 23 June 1845).

28 June

In *Illiustratsiia,* no. 17, in a section headed "Wanderer among Alien Publications," it says that Glinka is in Madrid.

29 June

In the seventh literary supp. to *Le Nouvelliste* it reports Glinka's departure from Paris (d.c.a.).

2 July

Performance of *A Life for the Tsar* in the Bolshoi Theater in Moscow (*Mosk. ved.*, 30 June 1845).

3/15 July

Glinka notes down the theme of a Spanish folk dance, *"El Bail de Plaza (Catalon)."* The composer's dating is *"15 julio de la S. Dolores."*

3 July

In *SPb. ved.,* no. 147, in a review by "I. G." of Aleksandr Nikitenko's book, *Opyt istorii russkoi literatury* [Essay in the history of Russian literature], it says: "We already have a right to Europe's attention for our intellectual labors. . . . We are not saying this in a fit of patriotic self-love, but we present it as an historical fact. No, it is not a dream, because the works of Karamzin, Derzhavin, Krylov, Pushkin, the Pulkovsk Observatory, electroplating, the memoirs of Ostrogradsky, Pirogov's anatomy, *The Last Days of Pompeii,* and Glinka's music all represent our vital contributions and right to European attention."

6/18 July

Glinka writes to his mother: "If my successes in Paris satisfied the requirements of my self-esteem, only Spain can cure my heart's wounds. It seems to me that here, beyond the Pyrenees, no one will disturb me. . . . I did not expect such cordiality, hospitality, and *nobility.* Here *money* does not acquire you friendship and favor, but with kindness you get everything on earth. . . . Musically there are many interesting things, but searching out these folk songs is not easy. It is even more difficult to capture the national character of Spanish music. All this is food for my restless imagination, and, as always, the more persistently and continuously I strive after it, the more difficult is the attainment of my goal."

11/23 July

Glinka notes down the theme of a Spanish folk dance, *"El contrapas (Baile Catalon)."* The composer's dating is *"23 Julio, Valladolid (de Dolores)."*

20 July/1 August

Glinka writes to his mother: "Today it's exactly two months that I've been in Spain. I'm living quietly and peacefully, which hasn't happened to me for a long time."

Berlioz writes to Lvov (from Paris) that Glinka supports the idea of his trip to Russia (*Muz. starina,* part 4, 1907, p. 146).

3/15 August

Glinka writes to his mother that with the summer heat he does not go out during the day. "Studying Spanish and reading Spanish books fills up the day, which is very short here during the summer. . . . Nights, especially when it is moonlit, are enchanting. . . . Literature and the theater here are better than I would have supposed, and therefore, having looked around, I think I might undertake something for Spain."

10/22 August

Glinka travels with Don Santiago's family to Segovia and San Idelfonso (ltr. to his mother, 3/15 August 1845).

Between 10/22 and 19/31 August

Segovia. Journey to Segovia and stop there. "The city is remarkable for its ancient aquaduct and the palace of Alcazar, which, besides its exterior appearance, has noteworthy plafonds" (*Zap.;* ltrs. to his mother, 3/15 August and 25 August/6 September 1845).

San-Idelfonso. "We were also in *S.-Idelfonso,* or *La Granja,* and saw the gardens there, the orangerie, and, in particular, the fountains, which are outstanding. The water is crystal clear. In general appearance it is like Peterhof, no, for the fountains gush one after another."

Not Later than 20 August/1 September

Valladolid. Return from their trip.

20 August/1 September

Dolores Termenes's entry in Glinka's album: "I will never forget the talent of my friend Don Miguel Glinka nor the impression which his ardent feelings made on me when they were revealed during the time we spent outside the city [there follow several indecipherable words]. Accept my own admiration and that of everyone who has had the honor of associating with you. I do not know if these lines will reach his mother, but if I knew that they would, I send her a thousand best wishes, for she can be proud to have a son whose talent brings glory to himself from the distant North to the lands of the South. Such are the honest outpourings of the heart of one Spanish woman, who is unable to pretend and who will never forget this Russian (coll. *Glinka,* 215–16; Sp. original).

21 August/2 September

Jose Vitega's entry relating feelings of friendship in Glinka's album (Glinka's Spanish Album, in *L.,* p. 318).

22 August

Performance of *A Life for the Tsar* in the Aleksandrinsky Theater in Petersburg (*Sev. pchela,* 22 August 1845).

25 August/6 September

In a letter to his mother, Glinka tells about his trip to Segovia and San-Idelfonso. "As before my life goes on, quiet and carefree. I am beginning to get along well with the language, but with the music—I don't know. I will see if I might not begin something in Madrid."

26 August/7 September

Glinka wrote down the theme of the *"De Valladolid jota."* The composer's dating is *"(de Dolores) il 7 septiembre 1845."*

26 August

In the ninth literary supp. to *Le Nouvelliste,* it says in a review of Lvov's opera *Undine* that, besides Lvov, "two other Russian composers, Glinka and Bernard, tried to make use of Russian folk music for the stage. In his opera *A Life for the Tsar,* Glinka displayed many ancient folk melodies" (d.c.a.).

30 August/11 September

Glinka departs for Madrid with the Santiagos (ltrs. to his mother, 25 August/6 September and 10/22 September 1845).

31 August

In the "Theatrical Chronicle" section of *Repertuar i panteon,* vol. 2, part 9, there is an "Overview of the Activities on the Kharkov Stage during the Present Year" (signed by "An Old Kharkov Resident, Wolin Wold"), which mentions the benefit concert of the director of the Kharkov troupe on 6 May: "The Kharkov audience certainly has not forgotten its excitement over the trio from *A Life for the Tsar*" (d.c.a.).

1/13 September

Madrid. Arrival. Glinka and the Santiagos took a small apartment in the center of the city. The address was Puerta del Sol, Nos. 4 and 6 (*Zap.;* ltrs. to V. Fleury, 8/20 September, and to his mother, 10/22 September 1845).

6 September

In *Lit. gaz.,* no. 34, regarding Bernard's opera *Ol'ga sirota, ili Doch' izgnannika* [Olga the orphan, or the exile's daughter], it says: "If we had somewhat fewer musical geniuses, we most likely would have more good operas, though for now there are only two, and they belong to M. I. Glinka."

Before 8/20 September

Glinka witnessed the bull fights, "a barbaric and bloody spectacle, which, however, is interesting because of the people's excitement and the moments of danger for the contestants."

8/20 September

Glinka writes to Viktor Fleury: "The orchestra of the main theater of Madrid is excellent, which makes me think of doing something in a Spanish style, though I still have not come to know it thoroughly.... As in the rest of Europe, contemporary civilization has also struck a blow here to the ancient folk customs. It takes a lot of time and patience to become thoroughly familiar with the national melodies, since contemporary songs are composed more in an Italianate than Spanish style and have become completely naturalized" (Fr. original).

8 September

In the "Correspondence" section of *Illiustratsiia,* no. 22, there is an answer to someone unknown ("A. S. A-n"), to whom texts for Glinka had been sent. It reports that Glinka is in Spain.

8/20 or 9/21 September

Glinka sees the bullfights for a second time (ltr. to his mother, 10/22 Sept. 1845).

9/21 September

Glinka visits the Prado, in which "there are a large number of outstanding pictures, especially of Spanish painters" (ltrs. to his mother, 10/22 September, and to V. Fleury, 8/20 September 1845).

10/22 September

Glinka describes his life in Madrid to his mother. "There are so many noteworthy things here that I am forced to value every minute. I have a lot to see, my language studies to continue, and this week I intend to begin working." He writes that the climate of Spain "has a salutary effect" on his health. "If this trip entails significant expenses, to make up for it, it does me obvious good. I have completely forgotten my grief, I live in my own way, busy and hoping even here in a distant land to find a new arena for my musical efforts."

12/24 September

Inscription on the title page of the manuscript of the score of the *Jota aragonesa:* "*Capricho Brillante para gran orchestre sobre la Jota Aragonese compuesto par Miguel de Glinka. Madrid, año 1845.*" On the first page of the jota's theme: "Jota. Vivace," and the date, "Madrid, 24 *septiembre* 1845."

Between 1/13 September and 27 September/9 October

News of Glinka's arrival in Madrid "was published three times in the newspapers" (ltr. to his mother, 27 September/9 October 1845).

Between 10/22 September and 27 September/9 October

Glinka attended the ballet twice. "Guy-Stefani danced *Olé* and *Jaleo de Xeres* excellently (though mannered). I liked the music of the latter dance (although it was composed by the Czech director of the ballet orchestra, Skozdopole), and I have committed it to memory. Guy-Stefani also danced the *Seguedillas manchegas* excellently in the costume of a Spanish student" (*Zap.*). Several times Glinka attended the theater for a better assimilation of Spanish. "They performed tragedies and comedies with equal mastery. The Spanish language is strong, expressive, and has a rather pleasing sound" (ltr. to his mother, 27 September/9 October 1845).

Glinka met two compatriots in Madrid, the architect Karl Beine and the musician Wilhelm von Lenz.

"There is an amazing picture gallery here, in particular its collection of the works of Spanish painters, which can't be seen anywhere else. I visit this museum often. I have become captivated by several pictures and have looked at them so closely that it seems I see them in my mind's eye even now." He visited the Prado together with Beine. (ltr. to his mother, 27 September/9 October 1845; *Zap.*).

27 September/9 October

Glinka writes to his mother that in Madrid "I still have not found it possible to continue my study of Spanish national music. In the theaters and everywhere Italian music prevails." In the same letter: "To stay with you and be a comfort to you would be gratifying for me also. . . . What am I to do though, when my health cannot bear the dampness, the cold, and the eight-month confinement to one's rooms, when my irrepressible imagination demands new activities, and, especially, when my heart is so sensitive that the slightest reminder of the past reopens my spirit's deep wounds? Here I am not troubled, and this, probably, is the chief reason for my peace of mind."

28 September/10 October

Lenz's entry in Glinka's album recollecting the time when they heard Beethoven's Ninth Symphony together (Spanish Album, in *L.*, p. 321).

29 September

The following compositions are listed in an advertisement with the heading "The Odeum. New Musical Works," in *Illiustratsiia*, no. 25: *Deux nouvelles compositions sur l'opéra Rousslan et Loudmila: no. 1, Marche des Tcherkesses par Fr. Liszt; no. 2, Caprice* [Vollweiler].

30 September

In *Repertuar i panteon,* vol. 12, part 10, under "Theatrical Chronicle. September. The Petersburg Theaters," there appear a positive review of the libretto for *A Life for the Tsar* and a negative one of the libretto for *Ruslan and Lyudmila* (d.c.a.).

4/16 October

Aranjuez. Trip to Aranjuez, "The Tsarskoe Selo of the Spanish kings . . . we saw the palace there, which is incomparably poor in comparison to the Imperial palaces. I only liked the hall in Chinese style made entirely out of porcelain. . . . The garden is quite large but in poor taste and extremely neglected."

After 4/16 October

Toledo. From Aranjuez "we went to Toledo. I have not seen a more picturesque city in Spain. . . . Toledo is full of remarkable buildings and antiquities, and, above all, most of the streets and houses are in Arabian style. In my opinion, the cathedral is the best building in this style. . . . The weather has been excellent, clear, and warm. There have been parties every evening, and we have been received with unusual cordiality" (ltr. to his mother, 22 October/3 November 1845).

A partial translation of Berlioz's article about Glinka from the *SPb. ved.,* nos. 85 and 86, is reprinted in the October volume of *ZhMNP,* part 48, section 6,

"Survey of Russian Newspapers and Periodicals for the Second Quarter of 1845. The Fine Arts."

13 October

Ruslan and Lyudmila is referred to in an article entitled "Karl Maria Weber" in *Illiustratsiia*, no. 27.

16/28 October

Escorial. Trip to the Escorial. "Here they consider this building to be the eighth wonder of the world. I and the Russian architect here [Beine] did not like it: it's huge, but boring. What is remarkable about it is *el panteon de los reges* (pantheon of kings), a subterranean hall or chapel, where the coffins of many of the kings of Spain are laid out on shelves" (ltr. to his mother, 22 October/3 November 1845).

From the Second Half of October

Madrid. Glinka "attentively studied Spanish music, namely the songs of the common people. A certain *zagal* (muleteer on the stagecoach) would come to me and sing folk songs, which I then would try to capture and record. I especially liked two *Seguedillas manchegas (airs de la Mancha),* and later I used them in the second Spanish overture."

22 October/3 November

Glinka writes his mother: "I am living quietly and pleasantly in Madrid. I have searched out singers and guitarists who sing and play national Spanish songs well. They come in the evening to sing and play, and I copy out their songs and record them in a special notebook. I am keeping a journal. Above all, I have acquired quite a few acquaintances, and when the weather is bad and it's impossible to go out, there is always company and the possibility of spending the time pleasantly. More and more I like life in Spain. . . . In the next few days it will be decided, will I make my debut as a composer in Madrid or not?"
[The "Journal," i.e., Glinka's diary, has not been discovered.]

27 October

In *Illiustratsiia*, no. 29, under "Dramaturgy. The St. Petersburg Theaters," it says the following about Russian opera: "Furthermore, we enjoyed hearing Bernard's light opera [*Olga the Orphan, or the Exile's Daughter*]. The audience's old favorites are seldom given, but they are nonetheless satisfied. We admit to being a part of this audience. We always wait for Saturday's poster with impatience. What will Sunday's performance at the Bolshoi be? Shall it be *A Life for the Tsar* or *Ruslan and Lyudmila* or *Freischütz* or *Robert*? It is true that these operas have given us so much pleasure that we are ready to go hear our honored artists out of gratitude alone."

30 October

In *Rus. invalid,* no. 243, in an article "From Letters to the Editor" by Nayrelav, there is a laudatory review of the Kievan composer Vitvitsky's *Fantaisie-concertante* for violin and piano on themes from *A Life for the Tsar*.

End of October–Beginning of November

"For the latter part of the fall, I was a stay-at-home. An acquaintance of Don Santiago's niece, Ramona Gonzales, a quite attractive girl, often visited us. . . . She introduced me to a young man, Don José Álvarez, who played the flute well and was passionately interested in music."

7/19 November

Glinka writes to Viktor Fleury that because of the bad weather he rarely leaves the house, though he always has "a circle of acquaintances, work, and even amusements. People of ordinary occupations come to see me to sing, play the guitar, and dance. I am continuing to write down the melodies whose originality strikes me." He writes of the necessity of prolonging his stay in Spain. "The work which I plan to complete will require much more time than I had projected. So far I have only seen the two Castiles. I have yet to visit Granada, Seville, Cordova, Murcia, and part of the province of Alicante (the kingdom of Valencia), and after that Saragossa in Aragon. For the time when I must leave the city, I am making connections which will be beneficial for my work. Here I know many singers and guitarists from among the people, but I am only partly able to make use of their knowledge. I have to leave before the seasons change" (Fr. original).

Entry (signature) of Ramona Gonzales in Glinka's album (Glinka's Spanish Album, in *L.*, p. 322).

8/20 November

Karl Beine writes to Nikolay Ramazanov: "We are acquainted with all the outstanding artists here, who, however, are very few in number. Of our own countrymen, it appears there is only one who is really interesting, and that is Glinka. I have met him, we are neighbors and see each other every day. He lives quietly but very sensibly. He often has *Tertulias,* at which they play and dance the *jota.* In private he explains the black keys to me, the relations of sounds, instruments, drama in music, and talks about Bortnyansky. He also talks about Verdi, and so on without stopping with eloquence and *eruditione.* In several days his *morceau* on a very nice *jota* motif is going to be played by an orchestra in the Teatro del Circo. It will be a success for sure. He is leaving soon for Granada. We will spend about a month and a half there together, I'm sure, in the most pleasant way. He gives his regards to all our friends, particularly Ramazanov and Shternberg. . . . Glinka speaks Spanish like a Spaniard already (Livanova, Protopopov, *Glinka II,* p. 25).

13/25 November

In telling his mother about his departure the following day, Glinka writes that nothing came of plans to perform his music in Madrid, since he did not wish to present his music "any old way" and had "decided to postpone it to another, more favorable opportunity." He mentions once again that in Spain he has "finally found a pleasant and peaceful refuge."

14/26 November

Departure for Granada at 12 o'clock noon (ltr. to his mother, 13/25 November 1845).

17 November

In *Sev. pchela,* no. 261, "Journalistic Odds and Ends," Bulgarin makes a remark about Viardot's performance of Lyudmila's cavatina from *Ruslan and Lyudmila* as an "inserted aria accompanied by piano" in the opera *Il barbiere de Siviglia.*

14/26–20 November/2 December

The road from Madrid to Granada. "It was cold in Madrid, and it rained the whole way to Sierra Morena. We passed through the most picturesque part of the mountains, known as *Despena perros,* during the night. When we reached the crest of the ridge in Santa Elena, we were already in Andalusia. . . . The more we descended from Sierra Morena the perceptibly milder the climate became and the view of nature more pleasant. . . . In Carolina . . . we had an excellent lunch, and that night we arrived in Jaen, where they fed us badly. That night and the next day we travelled through picturesque, uninhabited mountains and then entered a narrow valley, which adjoined a large valley called Vega di Granada."

20 November/2 December

Granada. Arrival. They took rooms in a hotel. "Alhambra, the ancient fortress of the Moors . . . is supposed to be a magic castle" (*Zap.;* ltr. to his mother, 23 November/5 December 1845).

20 November

Performance of *A Life for the Tsar* in the Bolshoi Theater in Petersburg (*Sev. pchela,* 20 November 1845).

22 November/4 December

Glinka settled not far from Alhambra "on the mountain, in a valley with a garden. In all my life I have not encountered a place to live more to my liking—clean rooms, bright and facing the sun, so that during the day even now it is almost hot. The garden is not big . . . and is arranged in terraces. . . . From the garden side the view is marvelous—to the left, the Sierra Nevada; opposite the windows, the valley; and to the right, the panorama of the city. From the opposite side you can see the fortress of Alhambra." Address: Granada, *Carmen de San Miguel, torre Vermeja* (ltr. to his mother, 23 November/5 December 1845).

After 22 November/4 December

Glinka made the acquaintance "of the best guitarist in Granada, a man by the name of Murciano. Murciano was a simple, illiterate man who dealt in wine in his own tavern. He played with unusual dexterity and clarity. The variations he composed on the national dance there, the *fandango,* which his son wrote down, attest to his musical ability" (*Zap.*).

23 November/5 December

In a letter to his mother, Glinka shares his impressions of Granada.

29 November

In an article entitled "The Italian Opera" in *Sev. pchela*, no. 270, "R. Z." [Zotov] refers to Pauline Viardot's performance of Lyudmila's cavatina as an inserted number in Rossini's *Il barbiere de Siviglia*.

1/13 December

Glinka writes to his mother: "If you could see the lovely countryside here, the dark blue sky, and the bright sunshine, then you would be convinced that it is not for nothing that I am attracted to Spain. . . . Little by little I am beginning to make acquaintances." He relates that everyone is preparing for the Christmas holidays, and since "everything happens on the street . . . it is possible, more than before, to study the customs, songs, and dances of the people who live here." In a letter to Viktor Fleury, he tells about Granada and the guitarist Murciano, and he asks that he prepare his mother for the prolongation of his stay in Spain. "If our dear mother could be witness to my quiet and peaceful life in Spain, I am convinced that she would not have the heart to tear me away from here. Perhaps this is the last oasis of repose in my life" (Fr. original).

1 December

In an article about the Italian Opera in the "Dramaturgy" section of *Illiustratsiia*, no. 34, Petrova-Vorobieva is mentioned. It says that her "deserved fame . . . was established by the opera *A Life for the Tsar*. She belongs to the Russian Opera."

13/25 December

Glinka wrote down the Spanish folk song with text, *"De bajo di nuestra cama."* The composer's dating is recorded as *"Granada, il 25 deciembre 1845."*

17 December

In *Kazansk. gub. ved.*, no. 51, under "Miscellany. Kazan Chronicle . . . The Winter Concert Season in Kazan," mention is made of a concert by the singer E. Konyaeva, who performed excerpts from *A Life for the Tsar*.

Second Half of December

Glinka "was a witness of everything that happened during the holidays as well as domestic parties and customs" (*Zap.*).

28 December/9 January 1846

Glinka writes to his mother: "Here, as in other Spanish cities, I am beginning to make acquaintances, and I am received affectionately and cordially. Besides studying folk songs, I am also studying the dancing here, because both are necessary for a perfect understanding of Spanish folk music. My study is attended by great difficulties, since everyone sings differently." He writes that he intends to remain until the middle of April, "in order to greet the spring, which is supposed to be enchanting here. Then I will go once again to Madrid to acquaint Spanish audiences with some of my works. Several pieces will be in a Spanish style." Later he introduces arguments in favor of extending his stay in Spain: "I am living quietly and *peacefully* here (as I have never lived), and it is entirely natural that I should want to prolong the time. In my circumstances it is impossible to expect anything good. . . . In Petersburg they will once again begin these ordeals which are so trying for me and probably again be issuing an order not to leave the capital. . . . Thus I cannot hope for even one short year to breathe freely." Additionally, "I foresee that my restless imagination will give me no peace. I need at least one more year to study what I had planned."

31 December

In the "Petersburg Chronicle" section of *Lit. gaz.,* no. 50, Koni refutes charges that the paper does not like Russian music. *"Literaturnaia gazeta* definitely only dislikes music composed *in Russia* which is bad, and it denounces pretense and lack of talent in a composer not worthy of the name of *Russian music.* Every other kind of music *Lit. gazeta* likes very much and always praises, not *a priori* because of the zealous and humble requests of composers, but on the basis of the evidence at hand. The operas of M. I. Glinka might serve as an example. He is a true composer of Russian operas."

Not Later than 1845

In a "Proposal on the Establishment of a Book Repository," A. P. Balasoglo characterizes the cultural life of Russia during the forties and refutes the opinion of those who consider that "in Russia . . . there is nothing to read and nothing to learn." "What about the music of Glinka, and if you believe European opinion, Dargomyzhsky's experiments?" (The Petrashevsky Case, vol. 2, M.-L., 1941, p. 19).

1845/1846

Winter

"Don Francisco [a glove maker and acquaintance of Glinka's] sought out at my request an attractive Andalusian girl [Dolores Garcia] who was famous for her singing of folk songs. She was about 20, of small stature, interesting physiognomy, and well-built. Her frame was that of a girl, and her voice was very pleasing. I got along with her not without some effort and taking a few chances." Winter "was so nice and warm that, with the exception of three weeks, we had dinner in the garden every day over the course of three months and often wore our summer coats. . . . In the evenings I went into the city, where I spent the time pleasantly with friends of Don Francisco. We sang, danced, and amused ourselves in different ways. Don Francisco introduced me to the ladies. . . ." Beine soon arrived with his colleague, the artist Robinson. "We spent the time cheerfully. . . . I walked to the Alhambra when they were painting, and they in turn visited me. . . . Once when I met a nice-looking gypsy girl (*gitana*), I asked her if she could sing and dance. I received an affirmative answer and as a consequence invited the gypsy girl and her colleagues to a party at my house. Murciano managed this and also played the guitar. . . . I tried to learn how to dance from a dancer there, Pello, and though my legs obeyed, I could not manage the castanets."

"We spent our first occasion in Granada marvelously. The winter was wonderful, Glinka was with us, and there were the Alhambra, the *fandango, serenat'y,* Andalusian wine, and women. Everything was on stage" (ltr. from K. Beine to N. Ramazanov, 10/22 April 1846, in G I, p. 411).

1846

3/15 January

Theodor Döhler's Variations for Piano on the Theme of the Trio from *A Life for the Tsar* is printed by the publisher Ricordi (coll. *Pamiati Glinki,* p. 398).

5 January

In the section "Weekly" of *Illiustratsiia,* no. 1, it reports that "M. I. Glinka is still abroad. He has visited the blessed land of southern Spain and has probably gathered in his genius's memory many motifs, themes, phrases, and musical turns. Mozart composed half of *Don Giovanni* on the road from Vienna to Prague. To compose music is difficult. It is composed in moments of solitude and tranquillity. The greater part of the ideas for *A Life for the Tsar* turned up and were hummed in a carriage. This is why we expect rich results from M. I. Glinka's journey. They say that he will be returning to Petersburg this spring. Probably by winter then we can expect another opera."

6/18 January

Announcement of Glinka's selection as a corresponding member of the Athenian Society of Fine Arts. To the announcement is attached a "document in lieu of a diploma," which "must be printed" (*Sov. muzyka,* 1960, no. 10, p. 85; original in Greek).

13 January

Performance of *Ruslan and Lyudmila* in the Bolshoi Theater in Petersburg (*SPb. ved.,* 13 January 1846).

17/29 January

Glinka writes to his mother: "I am working diligently at my study of Spanish music. . . . The prevailing song and dance type in Granada is the fandango. . . . The music and dancing are so original that I still have not been able to completely take in a melody, because everyone sings them differently. To fully understand this, I am studying three times a week . . . with the best dancing teacher here, and I am working with my arms and legs. . . . Music and dance here are inseparable. The study during my youth of Russian folk music led me to the composition of *A Life for the Tsar* and *Ruslan.* I hope that I am not exerting myself in vain now."

27 January

At a large charity concert in Petersburg, Bilibina performed Antonida's aria *"V pole chistoe gliazhu"* from *A Life for the Tsar* (*SPb. ved.,* 24 January 1846).

31 January

In the second literary supplement to *Le Nouvelliste,* under "What's New?" it states that "M. I. Glinka is still in Spain. He is expected back by next year. What probably is keeping him there is not just the fascinating melodies but also the warm climate, which is necessary for his ill health" (d.c.a.).

Not Later than the Second Half of January

Glinka shares his impressions of Spain in a letter to Nestor Kukolnik. "The national music of the Spanish provinces which were under Moorish domination is the primary object of my study. This study, however, is attended by great difficulties. Neither Spanish nor foreign *maestros* living in Spain know anything of this business, and if they sometimes perform national melodies, they immediately disfigure them and give them a European character, even when they are purely Arabian melodies. For me to attain my goal I have to run to coachmen (*arrieros*), workmen, and common people and listen very attentively to their singing. The melodic turns, placement of words, and ornamentation are so original that even now I have been unable to capture all the melodies I have heard. I am speaking here of purely Spanish folk music. They also have a lot of printed songs and romances, which have a somewhat folklike flavor, but they are mostly of the Italian school. Of the properly national melodies in Castille and Aragon, the most prevalent is the *jota*. Jotas come in many different types and subdivisions. In Madrid, and generally in New Castille, Arabian music is still very much alive. Here in Granada, the *fandango* is about the primary form of entertainment of the inhabitants. . . . Spanish dances are generally very noble, except for the *uncan,* a gypsy dance reminiscent of the Parisian cancan."
[Dated by Aleksandr Dolzhansky by comparison with [Glinka's] letter to his mother of 17/29 January 1846 (coll. *Glinka*, p. 200).]

1/13 February

Glinka writes to Viktor Fleury that since he has adequately studied Andalusia in the environs of Granada, he has decided to return to Madrid a month earlier than planned. He characterizes the customs and appearance of the inhabitants of Andalusia.

2 February

In *Illiustratsiia,* no. 5, in the section "Weekly," there is a notice about Léon Couderc's portrait of Glinka: "Portraits can be awful! Not long ago we received from Paris a new portrait of M. I. Glinka, and we could not refrain from laughing. It's surely someone else. He's even twice as tall."

4 February

Serov (from Simferopol) writes to V. Stasov: "The more I work with the orchestra . . . the more I am convinced that *to know the orchestra is a great science* (which, by the way, was not revealed to Glinka. His orchestra looks good on paper, but not in the theater, of which I am now convinced by the facts, recalling his score . . .).'' And further: "The *only operas possible* in our time are those where to Mozart's manner . . . are added everything Beethoven did outside the realm of theatrical music and, perhaps, much of what Meyerbeer, Berlioz, and, very likely, Glinka attempted" (*MN* II, 1, pp. 54 and 56).

10 February

In a University Concert in Petersburg, Aleksandra Bilibina performed the aria *"V pole chistoe gliazhu"* from *A Life for the Tsar* (literary supp. to *Le Nouvelliste*, no. 3, 1846).

17 February/1 March

Glinka writes to his mother: "I am hurrying . . . to Madrid to begin my musical ventures." He writes that he has fixed his departure "for [this] half of the month" (N.S.).

28 February

In the third literary supplement to *Le Nouvelliste,* in an article by "K***" entitled "What's New?" there is a review of the University Concert and Bilibina's performance of Antonida's aria from *A Life for the Tsar:* "We admit that native sounds have made a greater impression on us than the intricate roulades of Italian fantasy" (d.c.a.).

4 March

Serov (from Simferopol) writes to V. Stasov: "I strongly suspect that even Glinka is far from hearing in his head everything that he sketches out in his scores" (*MN* II, 1, p. 58).

Before 5/17 March

Departure for Madrid accompanied by Dolores Garcia (Lola). Glinka made part of the trip on foot and therefore was able "to carefully observe the way this part of Spain looks" (ltr. to his mother, 11/23 March 1846). "The trip from Granada to Madrid will always remain in my memory" (*Zap.*). "Glinka is a really fine fellow . . . especially as he has brought with him to Madrid a marvelous Granadian girl with a voice like your Ivanov" (ltr. from K. Beine to N. Ramazanov, 10/22 April 1846, in G 1, p. 411).

6 March

"R. Z." [Zotov] mentions Glinka's operas in "Survey of the Activities of the St. Petersburg Theaters for the Past Theatrical Season," in *Sev. pchela*, no. 52.

9 March

In *Illiustratsiia*, no. 9, under "Weekly," Nestor Kukolnik writes the following on the occasion of Nikolay Polevoy's death: "The loss of a gifted man lies heavily on a deeply wounded, unhealed heart, and an involuntary feeling of apprehension is awakened for others working in the world of art. You look around, you recount them all, and you rejoice if you find many on the path of useful activity. You mourn with poignant grief if you encounter one among them sick in bed or travelling in distant parts. These you love doubly. . . . M. I. Glinka was not present at the roll-call. He is far away; he is happier than us, for he still does not know of the loss of the man who so loved Glinka and so admired his talent. Glinka is still in Spain. His last letter destroyed our hopes of meeting soon." Kukolnik then introduces the text of a letter Glinka wrote him (in January) from Granada. "We have no doubt that Glinka will make good use of his time in Spain. No one has the ability as Glinka does to preserve the integrity of national melodies without disfiguring them by the addition of even one extraneous sound while at the same time clothing them in stylish harmony exuding national color and adorning them with the sparkles of exceptional instrumentation. We believe that Glinka's stay in Spain will provide the occasion for this poetic land to receive its own national opera from the hands of a Russian composer."

Before 11/23 March

Madrid. Glinka's arrival in Madrid. Glinka and Dolores Garcia together move into the same apartment where earlier Glinka had lived with Santiago (ltr. to his mother, 11/23 March 1846; *Zap.*).

11/23 March

Glinka writes to his mother: "I cannot say anything positive about my debut in the theater. Once I have gotten situated in the apartment, I will begin to make arrangements, especially as I hope, in the event of success, to be in a position to write, in addition to those pieces already done, several others in a totally new and Spanish national style." He writes that he has made the acquaintance of "the court pianist," Juan Guelbenzu, "who . . . may be extremely beneficial" in arranging a concert.

22 March

Serov (from Simferopol) writes to V. Stasov: "I remember very well how in 1842 in one of my first conversations with Glinka, *quels grands yeux j'ai fait,* he said to me that he did not like Meyerbeer!! I also remember that I was extremely surprised when Glinka said to me that he considered *William Tell* to be Rossini's *weakest* work and that everything respectable in the overture is just a feeble imitation of the Pastoral symphony. Isn't this the way we feel now? My guess is that Glinka (who even sometimes all but imitates the Meyerbeer manner) never disliked this as much as he claimed to."

23 March

Serov writes to V. Stasov: "Apropos *Ruslan and Lyudmila,* I once . . . joked with my sister Sophie that Glinka couldn't have written *two measures* of music to an operatic plot where the characters were in contemporary clothes and there was no escape in choruses or marches or strange dwarfs and lezghinkas" (*MN* II, 1, p. 68).

26 March/7 April

Glinka writes to his mother that he will not make a decision to return to Petersburg "before the favorable settlement of the case" concerning his divorce.

31 March

In *Repertuar i panteon,* vol. 14, part 5, "Theatrical Chronicle," there is an article called "The Petersburg Theaters in 1845," which lists the operas performed during the past year in the Aleksandrinsky Theater. Included are *A Life for the Tsar* (Petrov's benefit) and *Ruslan and Lyudmila* (d.c.a.).

10/22 April

Glinka writes to Viktor Fleury: "I do not know if I will be able to use my stay here to present myself as a composer. . . . My enemies are the Italians with their 'Lucias,' 'Sonnambulas,' etc., with their Bellini, Verdi, Donizetti, and with their success. . . . They have taken possession of the best theater in Madrid and the Spanish audience, which, like all audiences in the world, bows before fashionable idols." He writes that he still has not been to the Italian opera and does not know "if I have enough courage." He says that he prefers "the dramatic theater here, which is really outstanding" (Fr. original).

In a letter to his mother Glinka says that he has taken an apartment separate from Santiago. He shares his ultimate plans: "Until September I intend to stay in Madrid and its environs and then go to the southern provinces of Spain, probably alone, in part to cut down on expenses, but also because my colleague is now busy attending to his own affairs and family."

14 April

Performance of *Ruslan and Lyudmila* at the Bolshoi Theater in Petersburg (*SPb. ved.*, 14 April 1846).

19 April

In *Sev. pchela*, no. 86, "Theatrical Chronicle," "R. Z." [Zotov] refers to Glinka's romances, performed by Artemovsky in a concert given by Vieuxtemps.

21 April

Performance of *Ruslan and Lyudmila* at the Bolshoi Theater in Petersburg (*SPb. ved.*, 21 April 1846).

24 April/6 May

Glinka thanks his mother for sending money and asks her to send more, excusing himself for the request: "This is the last year of my trip." He reports about himself: "I am living a quiet and modest life. There is an outstanding Italian theater here, which I have not attended, since for a long time now Italian music has bored me. Also, because all the audience's attention is on the Italians, I will not be able to perform my pieces in the theater now."

30 April

In *Bib-ka dlia chteniia*, vol. 76, "Miscellany, New Musical Works," Döhler's Variations for Piano on the Trio *"Ne tomi, rodimyi"* from *A Life for the Tsar* is mentioned (d.c.a.).

14 May

The Synod issues its decision: "Having found the defendant Maria Petrova guilty of matrimonial breach of trust to her husband, her marriage with Collegiate Assessor Mikhail Glinka, in accordance with his request and on the basis of ecclesiastical laws . . . is dissolved, and subsequently, Glinka, as the innocent party, if he desires, is permitted to enter into another marriage, and Maria Petrova is to remain forever unmarried" (TsGIA, coll. 796, inventory 124, no. 1018).

17/29 May

Glinka writes to his mother, that he has not felt well recently, but "since it has gotten warmer in the last few days" he has begun "to come to life."

22 May/3 June

Glinka records a Spanish folk song. The composer's dating reads "(*estudiantina*) *Madrid, 3 de junio 1846 (de Lolita*)."

24 May/5 June

Glinka records the Spanish folk song *"Copla del fandango."* The composer's dating reads *"Madrid, el 5 junio (de Lola)."*

25 May

In an article entitled "Municipal Herald" (signed "X. Z.") in *Sev. pchela,* no. 116, there is a reference to Glinka's romance *"Ne iskushai menia"* [Do not tempt me] (printed as *"Ne ponimai menia"* [Do not understand me]).

Reproductions of caricature figurines by Nikolay Stepanov of Glinka, Bryullov, Koni, Lodi, Benediktov, and Kukolnik appear in *Illiustratsiia,* no. 19.

27 May/8 June

Glinka recorded the Spanish folk song *"El punt de la Habana."* The composer's dating: *"Madrid, el 8 junio 1846 (de Lolita)."*

28 May/9 June

Entry (signature) of Dolores Garcia (Lola, Lolita) in Glinka's album (Glinka's Spanish Album, in ITMK, coll. 6).

May

José Álvarez introduced Glinka to his fellow-countryman Pedro Fernández-Nelasco-Sandino, "who has come from Palencia to perfect himself in music." Don Pedro "from time to time visited" Glinka.

3 June

In *Repertuar i panteon,* vol. 14, part 5, "Theatrical Chronicle," there is an article entitled "The Petersburg Theaters in 1845" (unsigned), in which operas performed in the Aleksandrinsky Theater are enumerated, among them *A Life for the Tsar* (Petrov's benefit) and *Ruslan and Lyudmila* (d.c.a.).

Beginning (?) of June

Seeing that "she would never be an artist," Glinka sent Dolores Garcia back to Granada to her parents.

11/23 June

Glinka writes to his mother that the summer in Madrid is very hot and that in the shade "it is over 30 degrees Réaumur. Nights are enchanting. There is a splendid park here in Madrid, the so-called Prado. At night it's a fascinating spectacle." He writes that "in several days" he is going to Segovia to spend July there.

End of June

La Granja and Segovia. Glinka's trip with Don Santiago: "I wanted to stay there for the summer, but that turned out to be inconvenient."

Madrid. "On my return to Madrid I wrote to Don Pedro. He came to see me, and when he found out that I wanted to live with him and his comrades, he became embarrassed and said that they lived very poorly. But I insisted on having it my way."
[From that point on Pedro Fernández-Nelasco-Sandino ("Don Pedro," "Pedrusha") became Glinka's companion for many years, as well as his student, secretary, and servant (according to Don Pedro's later comments).]

"After fulfilling the lease on [his] apartment," Glinka moved in "with several acquaintances and educated young people. . . . We live happily and cheaply."

4/16 July

Glinka writes to his mother: "I like it so much in Spain that it seems like I was born here . . . here my spirit is able to rest from all its sad adventures."

11/23 July

Iradiere's musical entry in Glinka's album (Glinka's Spanish Album, in ITMK, coll. 6).

15/27 July

Verse inscription in Glinka's album by those with whom he lived: Mariano Casado-Diez, Castoma Álvarez, Pedro Fernández-Nelasco-Sandino, Emilio Gomez-Diez, Bautistio Santos-Diez, and José del Muso-Pastor (Glinka's Spanish Album, in ITMK, coll. 6).

15 July

The Marshal of Nobility of Elninsk province appealed to the Chief Procurator of the Synod, Protasov: "The widow of a Captain Evgenia Andreevna Glinka, after repeated and bitter ordeals in her life, and now deprived in her old age of the comforts of her family, has solicited my petitioning and patronage in the case of her son." The letter asks for information concerning "the status of [Glinka's] divorce case. . . . Undoubtedly, a favorable decision in this case would contribute to the serenity of a distressed mother, who has been tormented by the unworthy and criminal behavior of a woman who to the present time has restricted the freedom and social position of her son . . . who has likewise been put in the sad position of having to leave his homeland and family circle and everything which comprised his earthly happiness" (TsGIA, coll. 797, no. 200).

Between 1 and 16/28 July

"Don Pedro memorized Cramer's etudes under my tutelege. With our landlord, another Don Pedro, I read Calderón, but not with much success, since the writer's language was quite difficult for me. I knew the museum by memory. After dinner I would go with my colleagues to the Prado, and in the evenings acquaintances would gather at our place and stay until long past midnight. Toward dawn I often went walking outside the city. Returning around 8 a.m., I had tea and went to bed."

16/28 July

Glinka thanks his mother for her letter and the money. "I was terribly uneasy for nearly two months, because I had not heard from you."

After 16/28 July and Before the Beginning of August

Escorial. Glinka "spent nearly two weeks at the Escorial. . . . In the summer it is a fascinating residence, as much for the fresh air as for the many remarkable objects located there" (ltr. to his mother, 6/18 August 1846). "Trips on foot and on donkeys, the theater, but most of all the art treasures of the monastery occupied us all very pleasantly during our stay there" (*Zap.*).

6/18 August

Madrid. Glinka writes to his mother that in November it is "essential to visit Andalusia, Seville, Cordova, and Granada."

15/27 August

Glinka informs his mother that on 18/30 August he is leaving for Murcia with his student.

16 August

In his fourth "Livonian Letter" (conclusion), in *Sev. pchela,* no. 182, Bulgarin attacks Kukolnik: "The honorable publisher of *Illiustratsiia* loudly sounded the alarm when *Severnaia pchela* did not agree that Glinka's operas were equal to those of Mozart. Now the very same honorable publisher . . . prefers ballet to opera!"

18/30 August

Glinka and Don Pedro leave for Murcia (ltr. to his mother, 24 August/5 September 1846).

19/31 August

Albacete. Arrival and departure the same day.

Night of 19/31 August and 20 August/1 September

Nellin. They spent the night in the small city of Nellin.

Night of 20 August/1 September and 21 August/2 September

Cieza. They spent the night in Cieza. Glinka and Don Pedro were joined by a smuggler and a little girl about ten years old.

21 August/2 September

Between Cieza and Molina. "At one point . . . so much water had accumulated in a swampy place that the baggage wagons got stuck. Our smuggler . . . knew the area. After looking around for a better place to cross, he carried us over the water on his shoulders and then helped the driver pull the *tartana* across."

22 August/3 September

Molina. "After eating dinner in Molina, we continued our trip."

22 August/3 September

Murcia. Arrival that evening. Glinka and Don Pedro stayed with a certain official (*Zap.*).

24 August/5 September

Glinka writes to his mother: "Thanks to the travel and my stay in this blessed country, I have completely forgotten all my past anxieties."

30 August

Performance of *A Life for the Tsar* in the Bolshoi Theater in Moscow, with a divertissement after the opera (*Mosk. ved.*, 29 August 1846).

31 August/12 September

Entry in verse by Merced Julian in Glinka's album (Glinka's Spanish Album, in ITMK, coll. 6).

6/18 September

Glinka shares his impressions of Murcia in a letter to his mother.

9/21 September

José Álvarez-Gonzáles's musical entry *"Mis sentimentos intimos"* in Glinka's album (Glinka's Spanish Album, in ITMK, coll. 6).

22 August/3 September–19 September/1 October

"We had a huge hall and a bedroom each. We found a piano, and since the official with whom we were living was a family man, there were his daughters, relatives, and all their acquaintances who came to visit. Every evening we arranged gatherings in the hall, where we sang, played the guitar, and danced. . . . We spent the time no less pleasantly with the family of Don José Álvarez, with whom almost daily we travelled around the environs in a large *tartana*. The nearby mountains and *Monte agudo,* which are beautifully shaped and covered with cactuses, are extremely picturesque." Glinka heard a rehearsal of Bellini's *Norma* performed by children. "Actually the children did not sing badly. Norma was sung by an 11-year-old, and though it was not altogether satisfactory, she did sing with enthusiasm, and her acting was outstanding. During the fair, many ladies and gentlemen put on picturesque national costumes. The gypsies here are more attractive and richer than in Granada. They danced for us three times; a nine-year-old gypsy girl danced especially well."

19 September/1 October

Departure for Madrid.

19 September/1 October–25 September/7 October (?)

Road from Murcia to Madrid. They travelled through Orihuela, Elche, Aspe, Novelda, Elda, Villina, and Almansa. "These places belong to the kingdom of Valencia . . . and are very visually interesting and picturesque" (*Zap.*).

23 September

Aleksandr Gedeonov (from Petersburg) writes to Verstovsky: "In several days I am sending to you in Moscow the opera singers Petrov, Leonov, Strelsky, Stepanova, and Petrova II for performances before Lent. I have in mind using them to perform Glinka's opera *Ruslan and Lyudmila* in Moscow, if not for large receipts, then for the novelty. I am sending some of the costumes and several things for the opera that will facilitate its production in Moscow. I also considered sending some of the sets, but that turned out to be inconvenient. . . . Look around, and assemble what you can from old sets and make adjustments. I would not wish for the expenses for this opera to be large, since I am not counting on much from it" (Livanova, Protopopov, *Glinka I*, p. 320).

25 September/7 October (?)

Madrid. Glinka arrived in Madrid. "We took rooms with an Andalusian woman from Seville. She was a middle-aged woman, affectionate and cordial, with an attractive 19-year-old daughter and a 20-year-old son. Besides us there was one other lodger, a lawyer from Tarif."

5 October

Glinka is referred to in *Illiustratsiia*, no. 37, in the section "Weekly."

8 October

Production of *A Life for the Tsar*, performed by singers from the Petersburg opera (Petrov, Stepanova, Leonov, Petrova II), in the Bolshoi Theater in Moscow (*Sev. pchela*, 22 October 1846).

12 October

In the "Weekly" section of *Illiustratsiia*, no. 38, it says that the underestimation and misunderstanding of Glinka's operas serve as a barrier to other composers as well.

17 October

Serov (from Simferopol) asks V. Stasov to send him "from Glinka's *Ruslan and Lyudmila* what I had laid aside before my departure. . . . The things I had copied from the score are also there" (*MN* II, 1, p. 133).

22 October

In *Sev. pchela*, no. 238, in an article by "N. N." entitled "The Moscow Theater," there is a review of the performance of *A Life for the Tsar* on 8 October as performed by singers from the Petersburg opera troupe.

31 October

In the "Musical News" section of *Bib-ka dlia chteniia*, no. 79, it reports: "Three charming and tasteful compositions by Count Vielgorsky, Alyabiev, and Glinka . . . can expect a warm reception from admirers of Russian melodies." In the same place there is a review of Döhler's Variations for Piano on the Trio from *A Life for the Tsar*.

Beginning (?) of November

Glinka moved to the Parador de las diligencias in Alcala street.

Ca. 15/27 November

"We saw the celebrations occasioned by the wedding of the queen and her sister" (*Zap.*).

15/27 November

Glinka reports to his mother that several of his works have been translated into Spanish. "This evening '*Ne tomi, rodimyi*' is being sung in a concert at court."
[The French scholar A. Ya. Zvigilsky suggests that Glinka mistakenly dated the letter 15/27 November, since in the archives of the royal court in Madrid there is a note that on Thursday, 26 November (N.S.) 1846, the queen invited the court to a "small concert" (G 2-A, p. 281).]

17/29 November

Glinka and Don Pedro "set out to find warmth and sun in Andalusia" (ltr. to his mother, 15/27 November 1846).
[If the dating of Glinka's letter to his mother is in error, then his departure took place one day earlier, i.e., 16/28 November.]

After 17/29 November

Cordova. "We stayed in Cordova just over a day, looked at the Mesquite which had been turned into a *catedral,* and made several acquaintances."

18 November

The Synod's decision made on 14 May concerning Glinka's divorce is signed by the Synod members.

27 November

The Synod's decision concerning Glinka's divorce takes effect (TsGIA, coll. 796).

28 November

Under "The Imperial Moscow Theater" in *Mosk. ved.,* no. 143, there is an announcement of the forthcoming premiere in Moscow of *Ruslan and Lyudmila* with the participation of singers from Petersburg. Osip Petrov is to perform the role of Ruslan.

Ca. 30 November/12 December

Seville. Arrival. They stayed in the hotel Fonda de Europa. "Of all the cities in Spain which I have seen so far, there is no city more cheerful than Seville" (ltr. to his mother, 30 November/12 December 1846; *Zap.*).

On the day after their arrival "we saw dancing at the house of the principal dancing master. . . . Everything of this sort which I have seen so far is nothing in comparison to the women dancers here" (ltr. to his mother, 30 November/12 December 1846).

30 November/12 December

In a letter to his mother, Glinka shares his impressions of Seville and says that he is examining the city. He writes that he plans to leave in April.
[This is Glinka's last preserved letter from Spain to his mother.]

2 December

Verstovsky (from Moscow) writes to Aleksandr Gedeonov: *"Ruslan* has been announced for next Monday, the 9th of December, and since there have already been two full rehearsals, although without sets, the opera is beginning to go rather well. The regimental musicians, who've caused no little difficulty in moving forward with the piece, are starting to play decently from memory. The chorus, which has been distracted daily, is likewise beginning to sing without the music. The dances are coming along" (*L.,* p. 333).
[Verstovsky "never allowed an accurate, conscientious performance" of Glinka's operas in Moscow (Obituary for A. N. Verstovsky, in *Rus. listok,* 1862, nos. 47 and 48).]

3 December

In an announcement in *Mosk. ved.* of the forthcoming premiere of *Ruslan and Lyudmila,* the performers are indicated, among them, Artemovsky as Ruslan, and Petrov as Farlaf.

Beginning of December

"We tried to live in the Casa del huespedes (en pension), which, however, proved to be unsatisfactory, and for the time being took an entire little house for by ourselves in the Calle de la ravetta. Soon after our arrival, old acquaintances of Don Pedro turned up, and with a letter of recommendation and by happenstance we acquired several new and agreeable acquaintances. Now we were afforded the opportunity of seeing dancing by the very best female dancers. Among them, Anita was exceptionally fine and fascinating, particularly in gypsy dances and in the *Olé* as well" (*Zap.*).

4 December

Serov (from Simferopol) writes to V. Stasov: "Perhaps there is a possibility of using the sounds of the piano *en grand* in a full orchestra (. . . in special, rare cases). Berlioz and Glinka have already made attempts, but, I think, both were equally unsuccessful." And further: "In fact I expressed myself imprecisely concerning Meyerbeer and Mendelssohn [in a letter to Dmitry Stasov] . . . but regarding Glinka . . . I don't remember what I said and am sincerely sorry. He, of course, is in no way any less remarkable . . . it's just that it's impossible to *equate* the three. Mendelssohn is much closer to present-day norms of composition than either of the others, and he has written incomparably more music . . . which is proved by the fact that neither Meyerbeer nor Glinka, except for their operas and insignificant romances, have written anything else. . . . From another perspective, even Meyerbeer has a great advantage over Glinka (just take for example the French understanding of the stage, of which Glinka has no conception). In any case, it must be said of Glinka that the more the issue concerns instrumentation, of course, he's not inferior to the two of them by even a hair" (*MN* II, 1, p. 146).

6 December

In the Bolshoi Theater in Moscow, *A Life for the Tsar,* in a performance by artists from the Petersburg opera, Petrov, Stepanova, Leonov, and Petrova II (*Mosk. ved.,* 5 December 1846).

Verstovsky (from Moscow) writes to Aleksandr Gedeonov about the military band in *Ruslan,* which "in my opinion could be eliminated, but that would necessitate altering the score, and I would not dare abolish it without special permission of Your Honor." Having enumerated the numbers written specially for the "regimental band" and those in which the orchestra participates, Verstovsky writes: "Despite these necessary places, I have thought from the outset of laying a hand to eliminating the regimental orchestra."

9 December

Verstovsky writes to Aleksandr Gedeonov: "Today *Ruslan* will be performed for the first time, and judging from yesterday's dress rehearsal, it should go smoothly. The fact that all the boxes had been taken by the eve of the first performance impelled me to designate tomorrow for this opera as well, thereby adhering to the saying, 'Strike while the iron is hot!'" (Livanova, Protopov, *Glinka I,* p. 320).

First performance of *Ruslan and Lyudmila* in the Bolshoi Theater in Moscow with the assistance of artists from Petersburg (Artemovsky as Ruslan; Stepanova as Lyudmila; Petrova II as Ratmir; Lileeva as Gorislava; Leonov as Finn; and Petrov as Farlaf). Dances by the ballet-master, Richard. Sets for the first act by Jourdeuil; for the second act, third scene, Shenyan; for the third act, Fedorov; for the fourth act, Braun; and for the fifth act, Serkov. "Military music arranged by Baron Ral" (*Mosk. ved.,* 7 December 1846). "The first performance . . . could not have gone better in every respect. It is hard to say about the opera's success, whether everyone liked it or not. They clapped a lot for Stepanova's, Artemovsky's . . . Petrov's . . . Leonov's, Lileeva's, and especially Petrova's individual numbers, and after every act they had separate and collective curtain calls. Mme Petrova had the greatest success of them all, for every time after the general curtain call they called her out individually. The theater was completely full. Receipts were 1,575 rubles in silver. The dances were well done by Richard. Our trumpet players and regimental musicians played carefully and correctly. Such praise is not excessive in the case of this opera, because it is hard enough to play such difficult modulations with the music. From memory it's a great accomplishment. Despite the short time and proximity of other performances, the chorus likewise performed correctly, though I must candidly say that I don't think I have ever seen such obscure and difficult choral parts in any other opera I know. The general obscurity of ideas and melodic line are almost a hindrance to complete success. Not every listener knows counterpoint, and the listener who follows the basic idea of an entire composition is a rarity in our audiences! This is my [Verstovsky's] opinion of the opera, both before and after its many rehearsals" (Livanova, Protopopov, *Glinka I,* p. 321).

10 December

Performance of *Ruslan and Lyudmila* in the Bolshoi Theater in Moscow (*Mosk. ved.*, 10 December 1846). "The repeat performance of *Ruslan* was not quite as satisfactory as the first . . . receipts were 1,057 rubles, and the piece was given a much more chilly reception. Only Petrova's aria drew general applause and a curtain call. A full half of the audience began to leave by the beginning of the last act" (ltr. from A. Verstovsky to A. Gedeonov after 10 December 1846, in Livanova, Protopopov, *Glinka I*, p. 321).

13 December

Performance of *Ruslan and Lyudmila* at Moscow's Bolshoi Theater. "At the third performance . . . though the applause was not loud, the receipts were 1,032 silver rubles 70 kopecks. They say it is boring, but they go. This in all is better. It is really funny that Yusupov and others like him are saying that the music of *Ruslan* is dull because Verstovsky cut out the best numbers, and it is even funnier that, looking at the Petersburg sets and not knowing that they are the same, they say that they wanted to do something similar to what was done in St. Petersburg here but were not able to! In the last performance of *Ruslan* the military march music was actually reworked for trumpet players alone and orchestra, as were the dance numbers in the finale of the last act, which, with the accompaniment of the full orchestra, may have come out better and fuller; moreover, 125 rubles will remain in pocket from each performance" (ltr. from A. Verstovsky to A. Gedeonov, after 13 December 1846. Livanova, Protopopov, *Glinka I*, p. 321).

17 December

Performance of *Ruslan and Lyudmila* in the Bolshoi Theater in Moscow (*Mosk ved.*, 17 December 1846).

19 December

In a supplement to *Mosk. ved.*, no. 152, there is an advertisement for "musical novelties," including Langer's Fantasy on the Cavatina from *Ruslan and Lyudmila* and a quadrille from the same opera composed by Dubuque.

22 December

Performance of *Ruslan and Lyudmila* in the Bolshoi Theater in Moscow (*Mosk. ved.,* 21 December 1846).
[The receipts were 690 rubles 90 kopecks (ltr. from A. Verstovsky to A. Gedeonov, after 22 December 1846, in TsGIA, coll. 497).]

31 December

Performance of *Ruslan and Lyudmila* in the Bolshoi Theater in Moscow. Eight hundred and four people attended (*Mosk. gor. listok,* 2 January 1847).

1846/1847

Winter

Glinka found out about the annulment of his marriage.

"We spent the winter of 1846–47 pleasantly: we attended dancing parties at Felix's and Miguel's, where during the dances the best native singers there poured forth in an oriental style, while the dancers adroitly executed their steps; it seemed that one could hear three different rhythms. The singing flowed along all by itself. The guitar played alone, and the dancer clapped her hands and tapped her feet, seemingly completely independent of the music. The noted, but now aged, national singer Planeta was there and sang. His nephew Lazaro was often with us. Almost every evening our acquaintances and young ladies gathered with us" (*Zap.*).

1847

2 January

In *La Russie musicale,* no. 1, *Nouvelles diverses* (signed, "G."), there is a report of a performance of *Ruslan and Lyudmila* in Moscow.

7 January

In *Sev. pchela,* no. 4, "Moscow Municipal Herald," a piece of correspondence signed "A." [Pimen Arapov] mentions successful performances of *Ruslan and Lyudmila.*

"Glinka's Flight from Spain to Warsaw" in 1847
Part of an album of caricatures by Nikolay Stepanov presented to Glinka by the artist.

9 January

Performance of *A Life for the Tsar* in the Moscow Bolshoi Theater (*Mosk. ved.*, 9 January 1847). Six hundred and ten people attended (*Mosk. gor. listok*, 1847, no. 9).

14 January

Performance of *Ruslan and Lyudmila* in the Bolshoi Theater in Moscow. Four hundred and eighty-seven people attended (*Mosk. gor. listok*, 16 January 1847).

3 February

Serov (from Simferopol) writes to V. Stasov about his arrangement of Beethoven's Third Symphony and asserts that on the whole a better arrangement of this symphony is impossible. "The big obstacle is the *orchestral* quality of the thing itself. . . . As Glinka already observed, everything is in masses" (*MN* II, 1, p. 157).

8 February

In the "Announcements" section of *Illiustratsiia*, no. 5, there is information about the new periodical *La Russie musicale*, published by Bauman, with supplements including recent works by the "favorite composers Glinka, Varlamov," *et al*.

15 February

Serov writes to Vladimir Stasov: "Nowadays who isn't able to orchestrate more or less perfectly? Meyerbeer, Mendelssohn, Glinka, Berlioz, even Félicien David and Donizetti . . . and everyone who is of any importance in the musical world" (*MN* II, 1, p. 162).

22 February

In *Illiustratsiia*, no. 7, under "Weekly:" "We barely know what Glinka and Bryullov have actually done. The former is known to us as the composer of the operas *A Life for the Tsar* and *Ruslan and Lyudmila*. We recall how quite recently a so-to-speak respectable gentleman asked who had composed the opera *Ruslan and Lyudmila*. After that it's not surprising that many of our talented people are little known or not known at all. In order to attain any kind of lasting fame one must have a European recommendation, and even that sometimes does not spare a Russian from strange verdicts" (d.c.a.).

In *Odesskii vestnik* [Odessa Herald], no. 16, in an article signed "A." and entitled "A Concert in Nikolaev," there is mention of the performance of a chorus from *A Life for the Tsar*.

1 March

Under "Weekly" in *Illiustratsiia,* no. 8, there is the following unsigned report [by Kukolnik]: "There is a rumor about that our Glinka is returning from foreign parts. Of course, he will not be bringing with him either a dramatic symphony or a polyphonic drama, but he will arrive with a supply of those fresh, new, intoxicating melodies which the pen cannot trace but which are composed by the musical spirit of the composer in those sad or cheerful hours of poetic selflessness. These fresh, bright, and always novel melodies, which comprise true musical originality, abound in Glinka's works to such an extent that one could extract at least ten operas or ten dramatic symphonies, etc. from each of his operas. Glinka's music is not wanting in polyphonic embellishments. It is accessible and comprehensible to everyone who can hear. It is music which one does not forget, like the melodies of Mozart and Weber. Even the French, among whom glory is homemade and ascribed to ignoramuses . . . could not but recognize Glinka's talent in print. We could not refrain from laughter when we read that that blissful homemade mediocrity, elevated to the status of celebrity, had favored Glinka with such a flattering review. We . . . must reproach our composers for not breaking themselves of our Russian modesty."
[A lithograph portrait of Glinka by Volkov (1837) is attached to the article. Kukolnik is apparently thinking of Berlioz as a "mediocrity."]

In the section "Musical Chronicle" of *Repertuar i panteon,* vol. 3, no. 3, Koni ridicules the narrowness, self-assurance, and illiteracy of several critics, one of whom "called the music of *Ruslan and Lyudmila* boring and *intellectual* music which is impossible to listen to without yawning and is impossible to understand." Regarding Berlioz's concert, it says that, rather than create a new, independent school, Berlioz "should study, master, and reconstruct such works of his contemporaries" as the Night of St. Bartholomew from Meyerbeer's *Les Huguenots,* the introduction to Act I of Bellini's *Norma,* and "even the introduction to Ratmir's cavatina in *Ruslan and Lyudmila,* because this introduction has to be included with the exemplary instances of musical inspiration" (d.c.a., 20 January 1847).

2 March

In his article "Berlioz in Petersburg" in *SPb. ved.,* no. 49, Odoevsky says: "We must add as an item of exceptional interest that *Berlioz* was one of the few in western Europe who *learned* about *Glinka's* music. Berlioz wasted no time in performing several numbers from *A Life for the Tsar* in his famous Paris festival, and reviews of Glinka's music by the best Parisian critics all expressed their respect for his originality and unique melodic style, things our papers hadn't half thought of but which they'd do well to study."

5 March

In *SPb. ved.,* no. 51, there is an article by Odoevsky (signed "K.V.O.") entitled "Berlioz's Concert in Petersburg (ltr. to M. I. Glinka, 3 March 1847, 12 o'clock midnight)": "I have always believed in the deeper instincts of the public. I trusted it when semiliterate scribblers wrote nonsense about your operas and got confused in the distinction between melody and harmony and flats and sharps. Experience has not betrayed my conviction. Audiences become ecstatic when they hear your original melodies, not when they hear the cries of your uninvited judges. They sympathize with your music when it is half-way performed and are able to fill in what they do not hear."

In a concert by Iogannis at the Bolshoi Theater in Moscow, Petrova-Vorobieva performed an aria by Glinka. "Her amazing contralto voice reminded us of the time when her wonderful talent was still in full flower" (*Mosk. gor. listok,* 8 March 1847; *Mosk. ved.,* 4 March 1847).

8 March

In *Illiustratsiia,* no. 9, in the section "Weekly," dedicated to Berlioz's concert, an article begins with the following words: "Did you read it? Yes, in all likelihood you read the panegyric to M. Berlioz printed in the *S.-Peterburgskie akademicheskie vedomosti* [St. Petersburg Academic News] by 'K. V. O.' in the form of a letter to M. I. Glinka."

At a large vocal and instrumental concert given by amateur musicians in the Hall of Nobility in Moscow, N. Volkov performed Döhler's Variations for Piano on the Trio from *A Life for the Tsar* (*Mosk. ved.,* 6 March 1847).

9 March

In a letter to V. Stasov, Serov quotes Bryullov's words "regarding his [Glinka's] ballad for Finn: 'it's beer that hasn't yet fermented'" (*MN* II, 1, p. 165).

14 March

In a large vocal and instrumental concert for the benefit of invalids at the Bolshoi Theater in Moscow, Bantyshev, Kurov, and Semyonova performed the trio *"Ne tomi, rodimyi"* from *A Life for the Tsar* (*Mosk. ved.*, 13 March 1847).

20 March

Serov writes to V. Stasov concerning the difficulty of writing for a military orchestra: "I now understand why Glinka, when he introduced the orchestra on stage . . . only wrote the music in *piano* score himself and left the instrumentation to Baron Ral (which was even advertised on the poster)" (*MN* II, 1, p. 171).

Before 29 March/10 April

Ole Bull's arrival in Seville. "Actually his playing was powerful and distinct. But like most virtuosos, he was not very strong musically. He spent about six weeks in Seville. I got to know him to a certain extent, and he often visited me."

29 March/10 April

Ole Bull's musical inscription (a siciliana) in Glinka's album (Glinka's Spanish Album, in ITMK, coll. 6).

March–April

Glinka acquires birds. "There were as many as 14 of them, and they flew about in a room set aside for them" (*Zap.*).

1 April

Performance of *A Life for the Tsar* in the Bolshoi Theater in Moscow (*Mosk. gor. listok,* 4 April 1847).

Berlioz was present at this performance. "The huge theater was empty. . . . There are many charming and very individual melodies in this work, but one almost had to guess what they were, so imperfect was the performance" (Berlioz, *Memoirs*).

2/14 April

Drawing by Villamel entitled "Girl Playing the Guitar" in Glinka's album (Glinka's Spanish Album, in ITMK, coll. 6).

3 April

In *Mosk. ved.,* no. 40, in an article by Melgunov (signed "L.") called "Berlioz and His Musical Compositions," written in connection with Berlioz's arrival in Moscow, there is a reference to how "obliging and cordial [Berlioz] was to volunteer to perform several of Glinka's pieces in his concerts [in Paris] and then to place an article about him in *Débats,* where with the authority of his name he authenticates the fame which Glinka can profit from not just in Russia."

Glinka is referred to in the "Petersburg Chronicle" of *Rus. invalid,* no. 71.

12/24 April

Zabalburu's verse inscription in Glinka's album (Spanish Album, in ITMK, coll. 6).

14/26 April

Manuel Gerrino-Rincora's entry, "In memory of Guadalquivir," in Glinka's album (Glinka's Spanish Album, in ITMK, coll. 6).

17 April

Serov (from Simferopol) asks V. Stasov to tell him his opinion of Berlioz: "How is his music, his purely musical creation, for example, in comparison with Glinka's?" (*MN* II, 1, p. 180).

30 April/12 May

Musical entry in Glinka's album by the organist of the cathedral of Seville, Eugenio Gomez (Glinka's Spanish Album, in ITMK, coll. 6).

First Ten Days of May

Glinka left for Madrid "with regrets."

Madrid. Glinka spent three weeks in Madrid with Don Pedro. They lived in the Parador de las diligencias. "Among our acquaintances in Madrid, I will mention the pianist Maria-Christina Don Juan Guelbenzu, his friend Zabalburu, and his student, Sofia Vela, who had an excellent contralto voice and was an altogether excellent musician."

15/27 May

Guelbenzu's musical inscription (a mazurka) in Glinka's album (Glinka's Spanish Album, in ITMK, coll. 6).

15 May

Serov (from Simferopol) informs V. Stasov that he had played "many things from *Ruslan and Lyudmila*" for Maria Anastasieva. "'*Toute cette musique me déplait souverainement*,' she said. This in general. In particular, she said that the ballad was 'for laundresses' and that the E-flat major chorus ('*Lozhitsia v pole*' [He lies in the field]) was a *wild fantasy*. To tie such a beautiful accompaniment to a theme so *vile,* etc. Maria Pavlovna . . . took a dislike to Glinka. . . . Of course, she likes the music of *Robert* better than Glinka's. . . . Whenever I sit down to play *Robert* now, after not seeing this music for so long, I am surprised that this could have *excited* me and all of us 'in those days'! . . . There is, however, still a great deal of *mastery* in [Meyerbeer's] polish and instrumentation, but most of all in his knowledge of *theatrical objectivity* . . . which Glinka has no knowledge of at all. (Of course, he is always striving toward objectivity, but it's not *scenic,* because he doesn't know the stage at all)" (*MN* II, 1, p. 191).

16/28 May

Musical inscription (a mazurka) by Sofia Vela de A in Glinka's album (Glinka's Spanish Album, in ITMK, coll. 6).

End of May

The departure of Glinka and Don Pedro.

End of May and before the Beginning of June

Zaragoza. "We spent several days in Zaragoza, and from there we went by way of Tudela to Pamplona."

5/17 (?) June

"We had safely completed our travels in Spain, finally, and crossed the Pyrenees."

6/18 June

In a letter to his mother Glinka excuses himself for his slow journey: "We have had to travel across most of Europe."

7/19 June

Departure via Toulouse to Paris (ltr. to his mother, 6/18 June 1847).

12 June

Serov (from Simferopol) writes to V. Stasov about sonata form in the symphonies of Beethoven: "In my opinion, this form is more difficult than nearly any others, and that is why now no one can manage to deal with it. Meyerbeer has given it up completely; Glinka and Mendelssohn hold on, but their writing is dry and dull, in the overture to *Ruslan and Lyudmila*" (*MN* II, 1, p. 197).

June 1845 to June 1847

Glinka writes about Spain: "I spent two years there, and they were among the best in my life" (ltr. to M. Krzhisevich, 7 May 1849).

June (1847)

Paris. Glinka and Don Pedro spent about three weeks in Paris. "Several days before our departure, Colonel Komarov came to us as a messenger with greetings from Petr Stepanov, who was then in Kissingen and wanted to see me."

Ca. 1/13 July

Departure from Paris.

Through Cologne along the Rhine to Biberich, and via Frankfurt to Kissingen. The route from Paris. They travelled with Colonel Komarov (*Zap.*).

Beginning of July (O.S.)

Kissingen. Five-day stay in Kissingen. On the first day, Glinka and Don Pedro found an apartment with a piano. When Stepanov came to see Glinka, "Don Pedro got his guitar, and they began to recall Spain with their music. Here for the first time I heard the '*Jota.*' Glinka played the piano brilliantly, and Don Pedro deftly plucked the strings of the guitar and in other places danced. The music was fascinating" (P. Stepanov, *Vosp.,* p. 64). "Stepanov was very glad to see me, and he told me that my former wife received a rich inheritance upon the death of Vasilchikov, which news made me very happy. Although I admit I did not love Maria Petrovna, it would have been painful for me to see her in poverty."

"From Kissingen I travelled with Don Pedro to Regensburg."

Regensburg. "From here along the Danube to Vienna."

Middle of July (O.S.)

Vienna. Arrival in Vienna, where "an advisor at our embassy named Fonton and the secretary, Ubri, entertained us cordially. On the advice of Fonton we went to Warsaw."

Second Half of July (O.S.)

Warsaw. "We were in Warsaw about six days, which I spent very cheerfully, thanks to the obliging humor of N. A. Novoselsky" (*Zap.*).

Glinka attended a party at Novoselsky's. "Mikhail Ivanovich was unusually inspired at the time and played and sang many of his own compositions. . . . At this party he sang his 'Farewell Song,' which is so well known and cherished . . . by everyone who has had the great pleasure of hearing Mikhail Ivanovich sing this song himself." After many years of separation, Glinka met Pavel Dubrovsky again at this party (Dubrovsky, *Vosp.,* p. 259).

Beginning of the Third Week of July (O.S.)

Departure for Novospasskoe in a carriage which they were able to get "on directions from Fonton" (*Zap.*).

28 July

Novospasskoe. Glinka's and Don Pedro's arrival (Shestakova, *Vosp.*, p. 39). "My younger sister Olga Ivanovna was engaged to a young cavalry captain, Izmaylov, of the Ulan life-guard regiment. Mother was well, but she looked very bad" (*Zap.*).

After 28 July

"Every day we made music. Mostly my brother sang his own romances, but he also liked the romances of Yakovlev and Dargomyzhsky. Don Pedro often got out his guitar as well, would sit near the piano, and my brother accompanied him. Together they sang and played various Spanish songs and melodies . . . my brother gave me castanets and showed me where I had to use them in the songs" (Shestakova, *Vosp.*, p. 39).

3 August

An article entitled "Letter on Russian Folk Music" is reprinted in *Rus. invalid*, no. 172, from *Kazansk. gub. ved.* It mentions Glinka's operas and songs.

22 August

Performance of *A Life for the Tsar* in the Bolshoi Theater in Moscow (*Mosk. ved.*, 21 August 1847).

August

"Life was cheerful at first . . . we took rides on horseback and in carriages, walked, and amused ourselves . . . But I soon began to feel that I was beginning to lose my appetite and ability to sleep" (*Zap.*).

Khislavichi, Mogilevsk province. Glinka went with his mother, his sisters Olga and Lyudmila, and Don Pedro to purchase Olga's trousseau. The first day there Glinka arranged an improvised house party. He and Don Pedro performed Spanish songs together and then sang the Ukrainian song *"Pie Kuba do Yakuba, Yakub do Mikhata."* After the Ukrainian song "we heard from the street the applause and loud shouting of many voices crying 'bravo! bravo!' Only then did we look around and see the crowd standing at the open window." They closed the window and Glinka sang 'Mother's favorite thing,' the romance *"Spi, moi angel, pochivai"* [Sleep, my angel, go to sleep] (Shestakova, *Vosp.*, p. 40).

1 September

Novospasskoe. Glinka "had a serious nervous spell."

Beginning of September

Glinka decided not to wait for his sister's wedding but to set out for Petersburg, in order to "entrust myself to Dr. Heydenreich" (*Zap*.). Glinka left Novospasskoe and "never again returned there" (Shestakova, *Vosp*., p. 40).

Smolensk. On leaving Smolensk "I again had a nervous seizure, which was so strong" that Glinka "was compelled to return to and stay in Smolensk" (*Zap*.). "He was already on his way to Petersburg, when at the first station out of Smolensk an unexpectedly cold wind enveloped him, and a nervous disorder forced him immediately to return to the city to seek medical help" (*Finskii vestnik*, 1847, no. 10).

Glinka and Don Pedro stayed "in the home of a relative of Ushakov. Colonel Romanus of the gendarmerie gave me his piano for the time being."

Second Half of September

Glinka wrote the piano pieces *Souvenir d'une mazurka* and *La Barcarolle*, which were published later under the title *Privet otchizne* [A greeting to my native land], and dedicated them to Romanus "as a token of gratitude" for the piano (*Zap*.).

25 September

Composer's dating on the title page of the manuscript of the *La Barcarolle*: "Smolensk, 25 September 1847. *Barcarolle pour le pianoforte dédiée à M-r I. de Romanus par M. Glinka*" (ITMK, coll. 6).

28 September

"In Pedro's absence and alone at dusk, I felt such a profound melancholy that sobbing I prayed to myself and improvised in its entirety the '*Molitva*' [Prayer] for piano, without words, which I dedicated to Don Pedro. Lermontov's words, '*V minutu zhizni trudnuiu*' [In a difficult moment of life] were fit to the 'Prayer'" [in 1855] (*Zap*.). "The 'Prayer' was torn with a cry from my soul . . . at a time of cruellest nervous suffering" (ltr. to K. Bulgakov, 23 June 1855).

Composer's dating on the manuscript: "Prayer" for piano: "Smolensk, 28 September 1847." An epigraph in Ekaterina Kern's hand is appended:

> "My thoughts are sad,
> Prayer is sweet.
> Koltsov" (ITMK, coll. 6).

[Kern's inscription was apparently done in 1849 while Glinka was in Petersburg. On a copy of the "Prayer" there is the dedication: *"à Don Pedro Nolasco Fernandez Sendino par son ami M. Glinka"* (GPB, coll. V. D. Komarova-Stasova).]

Beginning of October

"Mother and the newlyweds moved for a time to Smolensk" (*Zap.*).

4 October

In the "News from the Interior" section of *Sev. pchela*, no. 224, Ivan Romanus reports from Smolensk of Glinka's return to Russia and his plans.

11 October

In *Illiustratsiia*, vol 5, no. 38, "Chronicle," there is a report of Glinka's return from abroad and of his composing three pieces upon his return.

13 October

Serov (from Simferopol) asks V. Stasov to send him several scores: "You see, except for excerpts from *Les Huguenots* and several numbers from *Ruslan*, I have *nothing* in the way of instrumentation *after Beethoven*" (*MN* II, 1, p. 233).

14 October

Under "Miscellany" in *Finskii vestnik*, no. 10, there is a report that Glinka intends to spend the winter in Smolensk because of illness. It also remarks that he has written three pieces for piano: *"Souvenir d'une mazurka"* [Caprice], *La Barcarolle*, and "Prayer" (d.c.a.).

19 October

Performance of *Ruslan and Lyudmila* at the Bolshoi Theater in Moscow (*Mosk. ved.*, 18 October 1847).

20 October

First performance at the Bolshoi Theater in Moscow of *Prince Kholmsky,* in a benefit performance for the actor Nemchinov. "In this drama Mme Kositskaya will sing two songs [Rakhil's] to new music composed by M. I. Glinka. Mme Saburova I will sing a Russian song [Ilyinishna's song] to music composed by M. I. Glinka" (*Mosk. ved.,* 18 October 1847).

Beginning of November

Glinka's mother left for Petersburg, while Shestakova, "out of genuine friendship" for Glinka, decided to spend part of the winter with her brother in Smolensk. Glinka, Don Pedro, and Shestakova "moved into Sokolov's house at the Nikolsky Gate" (*Zap.*).

17 November

Composer's dating on the title page of the manuscript of the romance *"Milochka"* [Darling]: "'Milochka,' romance for voice and piano, dedicated to his sister L.I. Shestakova by M. Glinka, composer of the music. Smolensk, 17 November 1847" (ITMK, coll. 6). "The melody I took from a *jota,* which I often heard in Valladolid" (*Zap.*).

Performance of *Prince Kholmsky* in the Bolshoi Theater in Moscow (*Mosk. ved.,* 4 November 1847).

End of the Year

"I lived agreeably with my sister, and despite my sufferings, we got along well together. I sat at home without leaving, in the mornings I composed. . . . Pedro played and memorized *Gradus ad Parnassum* [Clementi] under my instruction. My sister read to me in Russian and French, and Pedro in Spanish. In the evenings some acquaintances would visit, and a circle was formed of our close and very dear friends. I will mention Dr. Stroganov, who treated me, and an old friend, the apothecary Mego. They often played preference with my sister, which often amused me. . . . There were other visitors. I will name here the relatives of my sister Lyudmila's husband, the Shestakovs, whom we saw often. A young, attractive, and cheerful little lady, E. P. Zabela, a distant relative of ours, was always ready to visit us" (*Zap.*). "Since I was his constant companion over a lifetime, I understood my brother and his tender, kind, and angelic soul completely" (Shestakova, *Vosp.,* p. 40).

Glinka composed the romance *"Ty skoro menia pozabudesh' "* [Soon you will forget me] (to words by Zhadovskaya).

10 December

Performance of *Ruslan and Lyudmila* in the Bolshoi Theater in Moscow (*Mosk. ved.*, 10 December 1847).

17 December

Composer's dating on the title page of the manuscript of the Variations on a Scottish Theme: *"Smolensk, 17 decembre 1847. Thème ecossais varié pour le piano-forte et dédiée à Mademoiselle Elise d'Ouchakoff par son parent Michel Glinka, l'auteur."* [The title page was written by Glinka, the music copied by Don Pedro.] Lines by Batyushkov served as an epigraph:

> "O, heart's memory, you are stronger
> Than the sad remembrance of reason"
> (ITMK, coll. 6).

[The theme serving as the basis for the variations is an Irish folk song taken from the collection *Irish Melodies*, collected by Stevenson and Moore (*Sov. muzyka*, 1957, no. 2, p. 74).]

18/30 December

The Athenian Society of Fine Arts sends Glinka the "Transactions of the Society" (*Sov. muzyka*, 1960, no. 10, p. 87).

1848

11 January

Performance of *Ruslan and Lyudmila* in the Bolshoi Theater in Moscow (*Mosk. ved.*, 8 January 1848).

15 January

In the section "Kaleidoscope" of *Panteon i repertuar russkoi stseny* [Pantheon and repertoire of the Russian stage], vol. 1, no. 1, there is an article entitled "Theatrical News and Rumors," which reports the Moscow success of Dargomyzhsky's opera *Esmeralda*. "There are so few creative talents among us in the area of music that we must greet every new artist with a genuine calling with outstretched arms. Welcome, honored composer. Your place, next to Glinka, is unoccupied!" (d.c.a.).

23 January

In the Hall of Nobility there was a dinner "in honor of our well-known composer and countryman, M. I. Glinka. The Polonaise from *A Life for the Tsar* was played."

Entry in Glinka's album: "A remembrance of the dinner" (text of the welcoming speech, signed, "A.") (Glinka's Spanish Album, in ITMK, coll. 6).

30 January

There is a notice about Glinka in *Ved. Mosk. gor. politsii,* no. 24: "It is remarkable that a sort of unanimity prevails among the musicians of Moscow, a general attraction to our brilliant Glinka. We haven't yet heard anyone speak of him coldly or indifferently. However, this is entirely understandable and should not be otherwise. Glinka's passionate, energetic spirit is profoundly consistent with Russian nature. His melodies, like whole phrases from Griboedov's *Woe from Wit,* are objects of great value for us, our national pride. Could it be that his trip to the south, to luxurious, poetic Spain, inspired our maestro? Could it be that we shall hear something more significant than some barcarolle or romances? Even if we must be restricted to the latter, it will be comforting and gratifying. Perhaps our salon musicians will introduce us to Glinka's new, fresh, and intimate romances."

End of January to the Beginning of February

"In order to show my gratitude for the dinner in my honor, I had to give up my quiet domestic life. Every day I attended balls and parties and repeatedly had to entertain audiences with my singing and piano playing" (*Zap.*).

8 February

Having received Nikolay Stepanov's caricature-statuettes of Dargomyzhsky, Bryullov, Shchepkin, Karatygin, Odoevsky, Vyazemsky, Benediktov, and Bulgarin, Glinka wrote in a letter to both Stepanov and Dargomyzhsky that "I take no little comfort in them—some of the likenesses are amazing, and often when I look at them I mentally migrate toward you, my friends." He writes that he is sending his new romance, *"Ty skoro menia pozabudesh',"* "the melancholy article of a sick fantasy."

10 February

In a concert before the ballet *Satanilla* at the Bolshoi Theater in Petersburg, Tamburini, Giuli-Barsi, and Guasco performed the trio *"Ne tomi, rodimyi"* from *A Life for the Tsar* (*Sev. pchela,* 19 February; *SPb. ved.,* 18 February 1848).

12 February

On Aleksey Antipovich Shestakov's nameday, Glinka and his sister Lyudmila were the guests of Aleksey and Ivan Shestakov. Before their departure he performed his "Farewell Song" (Shestakova, *Vosp.,* p. 41).

In *Sev. pchela,* no. 34, there is an article by Romanus entitled "Greetings to M. I. Glinka in Smolensk" (signed "I. R., a music lover"), which describes the dinner given for Glinka in Smolensk (The text of the article was inscribed by the author in Glinka's Spanish Album, in ITMK, coll. 6).

14 February

In *Severnoe obozrenie* [The Northern Review], under "Miscellany. Odds and Ends," there is a report about the dinner in Smolensk in honor "of the gifted composer of *A Life for the Tsar* and *Ruslan and Lyudmila*" (d.c.a.).

Mid-February

"This fussy life has gotten on my nerves even more. I sank into a wild despair and asked my sister to send me packing to Warsaw. . . . When Mother returned, despite the events in Paris in February, I wanted to go abroad and made application for a passport" (*Zap.*).
[The events in Paris in February were the revolution of 1848.]

19 February

In the "Theatrical Chronicle" in *Sev. pchela,* no. 40, "R. Z." [Zotov] reports that on 10 February, the Italian singers Giuli-Barsi, Guasco, and Tamburini performed the trio from *A Life for the Tsar*.

29 February

In the section "Miscellany" of *Sovremmenik,* vol 8, no. 3, there is a report about the publication by Stepanov and Dargomyzhsky of a "Musical Album," which contains Glinka's romance *"Ty skoro menia pozabudesh'"* (d.c.a.).

Beginning of March

Glinka, Don Pedro, and Vasily Shestakov leave for Warsaw.

11 March

Brest-Litovsk. Entry in Glinka's album: "Irène Witkowski, Jules Witkowski, Lucien Witkowski, Jacque Tarnowski, Tabarovsky, V. Sterligov [?], I. Kolobov [?], Mikh. Somov, Prince Nikolay Khimsheev, Nikolay Ramzin." And below this: *"Je vous prie, mon cher Glinka, de vous rappeler de la casa mayor et de vos amis à Brest. Alexander Helmersen, An ein gleiches Billet. Antonin Helmersen"* (Glinka's Spanish Album, in ITMK, coll. 6).

12 March

In the hall of Kushelev-Bezborodko in Petersburg, E. Balasheva performed an aria from *A Life for the Tsar* in her concert (*SPb. ved.*, 12 March 1848).

After 12 March

Warsaw. Arrival.

16 March

In Petersburg, "in the hall of Mme Myatleva . . . a concert by Mr. Evseev," in which N. Levitskaya, P. Renenkampf, and Evseev performed the trio from *A Life for the Tsar* (*Illiustratsiia*, 1848, vol. 6, no. 10, p. 159; *Sev. pchela*, 15 March 1848).

17 March

In *SPb. ved.*, no. 62, in a note concerning Petr Gumbin's forthcoming concert, it says that in 1844 he "took lessons from A. Lodi, availing himself of the advice of M. I. Glinka."

Mid-March

Glinka was denied a foreign passport. "Once while looking for an apartment, Pedro and I met Prince Paskevich, who was riding accompanied by Cossacks. When I saw him, I took off my hat, but Pedro, who did not know the Prince, looked at him without removing his hat. When His Highness saw this, he rode into us with such fury that he nearly knocked me down. This infuriated me, and

I remember that I wanted to leave Warsaw, but somehow things turned out all right."

Glinka moved into an apartment on Rymarskaya Street and acquired "about 16" birds.

Glinka was taken ill. Through Vladimir Kastrioto-Skanderbek he met Dr. Moritz Wolf, with whom "I subsequently became quite close friends" and who continually attended to him in Warsaw.

19 March

In a vocal and instrumental concert in the Bolshoi Theater in Moscow, Semyonova, Bantyshev, and Kurov performed the trio *"Ne tomi, rodimyi"* from *A Life for the Tsar*.

21 March

In St. Petersburg, Arnold gave a lecture entitled "The History of Music," in which excerpts from Glinka's works were performed (*Sev. pchela,* 20 March 1848).

26 March/7 April

Pavel Dubrovsky writes to Stepan Shevyrev: "Our dear fellow-countryman, M. I. Glinka, who conveys his sincere regards to you, is now our guest. He intended to be in Spain, but with the situation now, he paused and quickly returned to his home in Smolensk province. In the fall he hopes to be in Moscow and to spend the winter there. It is impossible to express how much we here are enjoying his music, which he performs himself. You have heard him, consequently you know. Now he considering writing *Ilya Muromets"* (*L.,* p. 345).

27 March

In the "Chronicle" section of *Illiustratsiia,* no. 12, there is a notice about the forthcoming publication of a musical album which will include compositions "of our favorite composers," among them, Glinka.

28 March/9 April

Dubrovsky presents Glinka with a copy of the periodical *Dennits* from the year 1842 with the inscription, "To the creator of *Ruslan and Lyudmila* and *A Life for the Tsar*, Mikhail Ivanovich Glinka, as a token of respect from the publisher." There follows a poem beginning with the words, "Our Glinka, honor and fame," and ends with the lines:

> "Hurry to your homeland,
> And create your marvelous sounds there,
> For us, create your *Ilya Muromets*"
>   (ITMK, coll. 6).

March–April

Glinka becomes acquainted with the family of the wife of Kastrioto-Skanderbek, Konyar. "The girl Ekaterina M. Konyar sang with great enthusiasm, and in the early spring I often spent very pleasant evenings with them."

1 April

In the Bolshoi Theater in Moscow, Artemovsky performed "an aria composed by Glinka" in a concert with tableaux vivants (*Mosk. ved.*, 1 April 1848).

Beginning of April (?)

"Prince Paskevich, when he found out that he had ridden into me, wanted to make up for the incident and often invited me to his home for dinner and received me very affectionately. . . . At the Prince's request, I sometimes worked with his orchestra. Though it was not all that good, it was beneficial for me nonetheless. I gave the conductor Pohlens my *Jaleo de Xeres,* which His Highness liked very much, and he often requested that it be played in the presence of his guests. Later, on his orders, a dance was composed to my *Jaleo* music for the Warsaw Theater. Polens shortened the *Jota* for this orchestra and orchestrated the 'Prayer' under my direction with trombone obligato, which was not ineffective" (*Zap.*).

9 April

In *Sev. pchela,* no. 80, in an article (signed "F.F.") entitled "Contemporary Musical Tendencies in St. Petersburg and in Russia in General," *A Life for the Tsar* and *Ruslan and Lyudmila* are mentioned.

15 April

In *SPb. ved.*, no. 82, there is a review (signed "P. M-sky") of Dargomyzhsky's and Nikolay Stepanov's "Musical Album with Caricatures."

15 April

Under "Petersburg Telegraph" in *Panteon i repertuar,* vol. 2, part 4, it speaks of the publication of the "Musical-Caricature Album": "As a musical phenomenon this Album is remarkable for its content, which is varied and attractive. It is comprised almost entirely of lyrical pieces by M. I. Glinka, A. E. Varlamov, A. A. Alyabiev, A. S. Dargomyzhsky, F. M. Tolstoy, Prince V. F. Odoevsky, Prince V. Kastrioto, and A. F. Lvov . . . So far as the refinement of the publication and caricatures is concerned, they too are outstanding" (d.c.a.).

21 April

Performance of *A Life for the Tsar* in the Bolshoi Theater in Petersburg. The student Lileeva (contralto) made her debut in the role of Vanya (*SPb. ved.,* 2 May 1848).

25 April

Dargomyzhsky writes to Kastrioto-Skanderbek: "If Glinka is with you in the country, embrace him for me, and say that, despite the fact that he does not write me and that he shows a dislike for me, I still take part in his creative work and play his music with great pleasure for everyone who visits me. Of his pieces I particularly like the *'Souvenir d'une mazurque.'* Glinka is a man like all us sinners, but his talent, in my eyes, is very great. Incidentally, tell him that the 'Odeum' has announced to me that apparently all copies of *Ruslan and Lyudmila* have been withdrawn by the publisher, and I must therefore ask Glinka to tell me where I can get everything which has been printed of his opera" (coll. *Dargomyzhsky,* p. 30).
[In the published collections this letter is incorrectly dated 1849. I have corrected this based upon the publication of the *Musical Album with Caricatures,* which Dargomyzhsky sent to Kastrioto as a novelty. Moreover, in April 1849, Glinka lived in Petersburg.]

30 April

In *Sev. pchela,* no. 95, "Theatrical Chronicle," "R. Z." [Zotov] makes reference to Lileeva's successful debut in the role of Vanya.

In *Otech. zap.*, vol. 52, no. 5, "Domestic News," the *Musical Album with Caricatures* is mentioned (d.c.a.).

"My repeated attempts to make something of the Andalusian melodies came to nothing. The greater part of them are based on an eastern scale which is not at all like ours."

"They were learning the polonaise from *A Life for the Tsar* with chorus as well as the famous chorus from Gluck's *Iphigénie en Tauride*, '*Les fureures d'Oreste.*' (This is an exemplary work.) Thus I heard Gluck's music performed for the first time in Warsaw, and from that time I began to study his music" (*Zap.*).

"Once the conductor Pohlens surprised him. Knowing that M. I. liked Gluck's music, he prepared the chorus of the furies tormenting Orestes from the opera *Iphigénie en Tauride*. I vividly remember this chorus being performed in the huge hall of the ancient princely castle. Besides Glinka, . . . the Kapellmeister, Don Pedro, and myself, there were no outsiders present. The orchestra and singers began to perform this amazing chorus. Mikhail Ivanovich listened, and tears flowed from his eyes" (Dubrovsky, *Vosp.*, p. 261).

On Novoselsky's request, Glinka began to give singing lessons to P. Kanar-skaya. "She came to me three times a week and began to sing not too badly. Her voice (soprano) was pleasant though somewhat tired, and sometimes it broke."

2 May

In an article by "V. T." entitled "The French Theater" in *Sev. pchela*, no. 97, the debut of the student Lileeva in *A Life for the Tsar* is mentioned.

9 May

In the Bolshoi Theater in Petersburg there was a performance of *A Life for the Tsar*, "followed by a divertissement" (*Sev. pchela*, 8 May 1848). At this perfor-mance a number was inserted in the Polish act for the dancer Hüge.

14 May

In *Sev. pchela*, no. 107, in a feuilleton by "R. Z." [Zotov], entitled "Theatrical Chronicle," there is a notice about the dancer Hüge's debut in the Polish act of *A Life for the Tsar*.

22 May

In an article entitled "Music" in *Mosk. ved.*, no. 62, Glinka is named as one of the "Russian composers who most make use of nationalism," along with Varlamov, Verstovsky, Alyabiev, Dargomyzhsky, Lvov, and Kazhinsky. In the same article it says, "The great musicians are able to and do make use of national sounds, the best proof of which are, for example, Chopin's mazurkas, or, in a higher artistic realm, Weber's *Der Freischütz* and Glinka's *A Life for the Tsar*."

24 May

On the day after Whit Monday, Glinka, with Dubrovsky and several acquaintances, left for the country (to Belyany). When he returned home Glinka sat down at the piano and played the romance *"Slyshu li golos tvoi"* [When I hear your voice], which he had composed during the walk (Dubrovsky, *Vosp.*, p. 261).
[In 1848, Whit Monday occurred on 23 May.]

25 June

Performance of *A Life for the Tsar* in the Aleksandrinsky Theater in Petersburg (*Sev. pchela*, 24 June 1848).

19 July

Composer's dating on a copy of the score of "Recollections of Castille": *"Recuerdos de Castilla. Potpourri composé par M. I. de Glinka à Varsovie le 19 juillet 1848"* (GTsMMK, coll. 49).

After 19 July

Prince Paskevich's orchestra performed the *Recuerdos de Castilla* "not badly" (*Zap.*).

30 July

Under "Petersburg Telegraph" in *Panteon i repertuar*, vol. 3, part 6, Koni writes about the appearance of a new, talented composer named Lazarev, who promises much "for our meagre Russian opera, in which arena so far only Glinka has obtained a name, expertise, and success" (d.c.a.).

End of July–Beginning of August

"At that time, quite by accident, I discovered a similarity between the wedding song *"Iz-za gor, gor vysokikh, gor'* [From behind the mountains, the high mountains],

which I had heard in the country, and the dance tune *'Kamarinskaya,'* which everyone knows. My imagination was immediately ignited" (*Zap.*).

Paskevich, "because of his special liking for Mikhail Ivanovich, put his house orchestra and singers at his disposal. He was already planning to write the *Kamarinskaya* at the time. He threw several parts of it together on paper and tried them out with the prince's orchestra, which sometimes gathered at his house, as he wanted. Several times I was present at these rehearsals and witnessed the dirty work. . . . At last, the rehearsals were abandoned. For a long time M. I. made no effort to put the finishing touches on the piece, but he continued to think about it constantly. At that time he hardly played the piano at all" (Dubrovsky, *Vosp.*, p. 260).

6 August

Composer's dating on the first page of the manuscript of the score of *Kamarinskaya:* "6 August 1848, Warsaw."

6 August–19 September

Glinka "wrote the piece called 'Wedding Song and Dance Song' directly in full score rather than piano score. I can say with assurance that in the composition of this piece I was guided solely by internal musical feeling and never thought about what happens at weddings or how our Orthodox folk celebrate or about a drunken husband coming home late and knocking at the door for someone to let him in" (*Zap.*).
[Feofil Tolstoy (Rostislav), commenting on the last part of the "Kamarinskaya," asserted that the horn pedal on F# and then the trumpets on C "represented a drunken peasant knocking at the door of his hut." "This notion struck me as the sort of well-intentioned thing one is often entertained with in life" (*Zap.*).]

"Once I went to see him in the morning . . . and found him in a room where, behind a partition made of net, about 15 birds similar to nightingales were flying about. . . . He sat at a little table in the middle of the room in front of his birds and was writing something on a large sheet of paper. . . . It was the *Kamarinskaya*. It was finished in his mind. He wrote it out like an ordinary mortal making some hurried notes and talked and joked with me at the same time. Shortly two, three, friends arrived, and he continued to write amid loud laughter and talk, not in the least bothered by it all. Meanwhile, one of his most remarkable works was being transferred to musical notation!" (Dubrovsky, *Vosp.*, p. 260).

19 September/1 October

Composer's dating on the last page of the manuscript of the score of *Kamarinskaya:* "19 September/1 October 1848, Warsaw."

24 September

Performance of *A Life for the Tsar* in the Bolshoi Theater in Moscow (*Mosk. ved.*, 21 September 1848). There were 310 people in the audience, two large carriages, and 14 regular carriages (*Ved. Mosk. gor. politsii*, 27 September 1848).

30 September

Dargomyzhsky (from Petersburg) writes to Kastrioto-Skanderbek: "Do you have any news of Glinka? I know only that he is still living in Warsaw, but is he writing? This is the main point. I consider his music extremely important not only for Russian music but in general for all music. Everything that comes from his pen is new and interesting. But then, how much he has taken from us. Audiences want to measure everything by his standard, which is hard for the rest of us. Not long ago they performed Lvov's opera *Undina* here. It was a large work, and there were many good melodies in it, but the audience winced. If you investigate the cause, you see one thing: comparison spoils everything" (coll. *Dargomyzhsky*, p. 29).

August and September

Dubrovsky visited Glinka repeatedly, and together they read and took walks. "He and I read the greater part of Russian writers together as well as other authors, especially Shakespeare" (*Zap.*). "Then we reread the best poets. One could not but be amazed at his [Glinka's] broad knowledge of European literature and art. He fascinated me with his remarks on works of Spanish poetry and art. I am not talking about music. An extraordinary master of music himself, he would frequently become self-effacing when he was listening to a performance of the better works of Haydn, Gluck, et al., and once he said to me: 'I should chop off this hand for daring to write music after such great works!'" (Dubrovsky, *Vosp.*, p. 260).

September

Cholera broke out in Warsaw, and Glinka "did not leave [his] rooms. . . . Sitting at home, I got to work and wrote the romances '*Slyshu li golos tvoi*' to words by Lermontov; '*Zazdravnyi kubok*' [The toasting cup] by Pushkin, which I dedicated to the widow Kliko; and 'Marguerite' [Gretchen's song] from Goethe's *Faust*, translated by Guber. The texts for these romances were shown to me by P. P. Dubrovsky, who was then the censor in Warsaw" (*Zap.*).

15 October

Performance of *Ruslan and Lyudmila* in the Bolshoi Theater in Moscow (*Mosk. ved.*, 14 October 1848). There were 491 people in the audience, 12 large carriages, and 115 ordinary carriages (*Ved. Mosk. gor. politsii*, 18 October 1848).
[This was the last performance of the opera during Glinka's lifetime.]

31 October

In *Sovremennik*, vol. 12, no. 11, "Miscellany," Russian opera is mentioned in "A Letter on Italian Opera in Petersburg." "Recall Petrova. . . . Recall the excitement which *A Life for the Tsar* and *Ruslan and Lyudmila* caused and sustained for so long" (d.c.a.).

Fall, Before the End of October

"Acquaintances would arrive in the evening . . . dancing was arranged. . . . This pleasant living continued until the end of October."

From the End of October

"Novoselsky gained me several pleasant new acquaintances . . . [including] the family of Dr. Grünberg, whose daughters were very amiable and talented. The older one, named Yulia, played the piano very well. She had studied with Henselt. . . . The younger one, Izabella, sang with enthusiasm and meaning. . . . I spent pleasant evenings with them as well as with acquaintances of theirs, the Aleksandroviches" (*Zap.*).

Glinka "was continuously surrounded in Warsaw by a circle of friends who were well educated and gifted with outstanding abilities in every area of art. Among his associates was Mr. Palm, who drew Glinka's portrait" (A. Paprits, *Vosp.*, in *RMG*, 1898, No. 5/6).

1/12 November

Drawing by Palm in Glinka's album (Polish characters) with the artist's dating: "Warsaw, 1848, 12/1 [*sic!*] November, I. Palm" (Glinka's Spanish Album, in ITMK, coll. 6).

2/14 November

Composer's dating on an autograph excerpt from *Ruslan and Lyudmila* (an eight-bar solo for English horn from Ratmir's aria in Act III): "M. Glinka. Warsaw, 2/14 November 1848" (*Musiker Autographen aus der Sammlung Wilhelm Meyer in Köln*, Leo Lipmannssohn, Berlin, 1926).

Portrait of Novoselsky in Glinka's album (drawn by Palm?) with the signature: *"dnia 14 listopada,* 1848. Nikolay Aleksandrovich *w Warszawie"* (Glinka's Spanish Album, in ITMK, coll. 6).

3/15 November

An entry by Dubrovsky in Glinka's album ends with the following words: ". . . two of [Russia's] powerful strings have already been touched, poetry and music. The first was marvelously tuned by Pushkin . . . the other belongs to you. Together the two of you, more than any others, have penetrated the depths of the Russian spirit and elicited sounds from it unknown to the world" (Glinka's Spanish Album, in ITMK, coll. 6).

Beginning of November

Having found out that his mother was in Petersburg, Glinka "decided to travel there to meet her" (*Zap.*).

7/19 November

Glinka's inscription on a copy of the romance *"Slyshu li golos tvoi"* : "'*Slyshu li golos tvoi,*' romance to words by M. Lermontov, music dedicated by M. Glinka to Anna Adrianovna Volkhovskaya. Warsaw, 7/19 November 1848" (ITMK, coll. 6).

Glinka wrote the following inscription on his portrait (done by Palm) for Anna Vogak (married name, Paprits): *"7/19 novembre 1848—jour de départ de Varsovie à la personne qui veut se rappeler de moi."* Glinka did not leave that day (*RMG,* 1898, no. 5/6).

After 7/19 November

Departure for Petersburg.

Mid-November

Petersburg. Glinka and Don Pedro "arrived safely" from Warsaw (*Zap.*).

Glinka invited Petr Stepanov and sang his new romances *"Pesn' Margarity"* and *"Slyshu li golos tvoi"* for him. When he had finished singing the last romance, Stepanov asked him: "'Is that all?' That's all. 'It's like the romance is unfinished.' I wanted it that way, unfinished. It doesn't all end with throwing your arms around her neck."

24 November

Glinka attended Ekaterina Konyar's nameday party at Mme Palibina's, "who entertained her brother Prince Kastrioto, relatives of his wife, the Konyars, and other acquaintances. There was music all evening."

25 November

Glinka attended a party at Prince Kastrioto-Skanderbek's. This party initiated Kastrioto's musical evenings (P. Stepanov, *Vosp.*, p. 64).

28 November

SPb. ved., no. 269, contains a notice of the forthcoming publication of a musical album edited by Andrey Lodi: "Not long ago we learned that the famous Russian composer M. I. Glinka had returned to Petersburg from abroad. True friends of true music had not seen nor heard from him in nearly five years. He has returned with a rich store of the richest and most diverse melodies. The architect and the materials are here. Whether he will undertake the completion of the building soon, we do not know. We are sure, however, that Glinka will not tear down his secrets but will cast them in artistic form." Among the things included in "A. P. Lodi's Album," "Skozdopole's 'Passionate Dance, *Jaleo de Xeres,*' sent from Spain by M. I. Glinka," and the romance *"Milochka"* by Glinka are named.

Last Ten Days of November

Glinka was at Praskovya Barteneva's (ltr. to P. Barteneva, 8 January 1849).

End of November

Glinka became ill, and so as not to be apart from his mother, he moved in with his brother-in-law (Viktor Fleury) at the School for Deaf-Mutes, "which is at the Krasny Most. My sister Olga and her husband and Maria and her children were there. We were crowded, but it was pleasant for me despite my poor health" (*Zap.*).

In a letter to Adolph Henselt, Glinka tells him of his arrival, and that since he is "exhausted, he sees no possibility of coming to embrace his exceptional friend." He therefore invites Henselt to come visit him (Fr. original).

1 December

In lit. supp. no. 12 to *Le Nouvelliste,* in an article called "What's New Among Us," it reports: "M. I. Glinka, after spending two years in Spain, has returned to his native north and brought with him an entire portfolio of new compositions. Two new pieces of his for voice, beautiful ones, like all our leading composer's music, are being published by M. Bernard and fully compensate us for the long silence which the singer of *Ruslan* has finally broken. M. I. Glinka has promised to adorn the pages of *Nouvelliste* with his romances. This promise will probably suffice for the periodical's success" (d.c.a.).

6 December

Performance of *A Life for the Tsar* in the Bolshoi Theater in Moscow (*Mosk. ved.,* 4 December 1848).

19 December

The romance *"Ty skoro menia pozabudesh'"* is performed at one of the University Concerts (*Sev. pchela,* 18 December 1848; *Syn otech.,* 1849, no. 1, "Miscellany").

29 December

Sev. pchela, no. 292, announces the publication of an "Anthology of Musical Pieces, Collected by A. P. Lodi" and cites the contents of the anthology.

[A single (perhaps the only) copy is preserved in Vladimir Odoevsky's library with the inscription: "To His Highness Prince Vladimir Fedorovich Odoevsky, a fervently given gift from the publisher." The contents of the anthology are as follows: no. 1. *Barcarolle. Paroles de Victor Hugo, Musique de M. Th. Tolstoy;* no. 2. Mazurka, by I. F. Laskovsky, for piano; no. 3. a romance, *"Temnorusye kudri"* [Dark brown curls], music by Count M. Yu. Vielgorsky; no. 4. the romance *"Milochka"* [Darling], music by M. I. Glinka; no. 5. *Ballade du drame Catherine Howard, par A. Dumas. Musique d'A. Dargomijsky;* no. 6. Galop for piano by K. N. Lyadov; no. 7. *"Bog pomoch' vam"* [God help you], romance by A. Pushkin, music by G. Kuzminsky; no. 8. *"Ne vse beznadezhnost' "* [Not everything is hopelessness], romance, words by A. G. Kuzminsky, music by "G. K." [Kuzminsky]; no. 9. Polka-Mazurka for piano by A. Derfeldt; no. 10. *"Krasavitsa"* [Beauty], words by A. Andreev, music by A. Derfeldt; no. 11. *Der Savoyard. Gedicht von R. Spato,* translated from the German by Yu. Arnold, music by Yu. Arnold; no. 12. Spanish dance *Jaleo de Xeres,* composed by J. Skozdopole for piano; no. 13. *"Seren'kie glazki"* [Grey eyes], romance, words by A. Popov, music by A. Lodi; no. 14. Polonaise for piano *de S. Grabovsky;* no. 15. *Moja luba gdzie ty? gdzie?* romance by A. Mickiewicz, translation by V. Lyubich-Romanovich, music by Yu. Arnold; no. 16. *"Solntse skrylosia"* [The sun has hidden itself], romance by Prince Shakhovskoy, music by A. Lodi (G 1, p. 410).]

31 December

In lit. supp. no. 1 to *Le Nouvelliste* for 1849, there is a notice stating that Glinka's new romances *"Pesn' Margarity"* and *"Zazdravnyi kubok"* are available at M. Bernard's (d.c.a.).

In *SPb. ved.,* no. 293, "Petersburg Chronicle" (signed "K."), it says in reference to the forthcoming performance of Feofil Tolstoy's opera *Il Birichino di Parigi:* "We are glad in advance for the opportunity to add another name to the small number of native composers. That Russia is a musical nation, there should be no doubt. In our own time sufficient evidence of this is provided by the names of Glinka, Lvov, Count Vielgorsky, Dargomyzhsky, Alyabiev, et al. But in music, as in everything, our modest national character tells on us. If the French had equally remarkable musicians, they would already have been buzzing about them to the whole world. After even one campaign with them, they would be ready to welcome them to the ranks of genius along with many others."

Winter, 1848/49

Glinka "and Don Pedro . . . played an improvisation on *Kamarinskaya* for piano three-hands. Sometimes surprising variations occurred" (ltr. from V. Engelgardt to V. Stasov, 11/24 February 1906, coll. *Pamiati Glinki,* p. 551).

1849

1 January

In the section headed "Miscellany, Musical News," in *Syn otech.*, no. 1, there is a review of the University Concerts, which had begun on 5 December [1848]. The romance *"Ty skoro menia pozabudesh'"* [Soon you will forget me] was performed at one of these concerts on 19 December. "We must not omit thanking the artist for the pleasure she gave us in acquainting us with Glinka's new piece. It seems to us that, judging from the way in which she sings, our Russian composer assisted considerably with his advice in the education of such an outstanding singer" (d.c.a.).

[As in many other instances, the name of this fashionable amateur singer is not indicated. It cannot be excluded that it was Ekaterina Konyar, who had gained a reputation at the time for her performance of this romance by Glinka, but it is also possible that it was Aleksandra Girs or Vera Bunina.]

4 January

Verse entry by Lodi in Glinka's album (Glinka's Spanish Album, in ITMK, coll. 6).

8 January

In a letter to Praskovya Barteneva, Glinka asks her to assist Novoselsky in obtaining a position "with Count Protasov, with whom he has already served for seven years."

[At the time Protasov was Over-Procurator of the Synod.]

Vasily Botkin writes in the section "Miscellany, Theatrical Chronicle" of *Otech. zap.*, vol. 62, no. 3: "The existence of national opera depends strictly upon the presence of the dramatic element in national music. *If this element is missing, there can be no national opera.* If we proceed from this general proposition to Russian music, we see that currently it does not satisfy all the conditions which would make Russian opera possible. In it we notice a complete absence of the dramatic element. . . . M. I. Glinka is indisputably the creator of national Russian opera. He is a musical person . . . there is no doubt that his talent is greater than all other contemporary Russian composers. With *A Life for the Tsar*, M. I. Glinka made an attempt at the creation of Russian national opera. Why, then, despite the large number of beautiful individual places, despite the brilliant trio, which is a stylistic model of classical purity, is the music of this opera on the whole somewhat tiring? The cause is very simple. The fact of the matter is that *A Life for the Tsar* if a purely lyrical opera, lacking the element essential to the complete realization of opera's purpose, namely drama. Once he had restricted himself to the sphere of Russian national music, M. I. Glinka should have submitted to all its requirements. Lacking this, its sudden creation is not within the capabilities of any genius. Verstovsky also wrote an opera in Russian style, *Askold's Tomb*. . . . What is the difference between *Askold's Tomb* and *A Life for the Tsar*? It isn't that M. I. Glinka dared to confront difficulties and obstacles or that he struggled successfully or unsuccessfully with them, though Mr. Verstovsky prudently side-stepped these issues." He continues: "There are exceptional natures who are granted the ability to assimilate all the dialects of musical language . . . but they are rare. One must unquestionably include M. I. Glinka among them. If he writes music to Polish words, his music is completely steeped in Polish character. Take, for example, his Spanish bolero, and you would think that it is a Spanish national melody. If he intends to write a Little Russian song, his imagination expresses itself in purely national forms, preserving the originality of the melody" (d.c.a.).

29 January

Glinka attended a party given by Vyazemsky in his home in honor of the fiftieth anniversary of Zhukovsky's literary career. "Bludov read a poem by Prince Vyazemsky for the occasion, and we also sang a chorus in honor of Zhukovsky composed by Count Mikhail Yurievich Vielgorsky" (*Zap.*). "The Grand Prince left, and then Glinka, a musician, began to sing several of his romances . . . he sang Spanish melodies and his own compositions with unusual verve. This is indeed an artist of genius. I made his acquaintance, and tomorrow I am reading him *'Brodiaga'* [The vagrant]" (ltr. from I. Aksakov to his parents, 31 January 1849. *I. Aksakov v ego pis'makh* [I. Aksakov in his letters], vol. 2, M., 1888, p. 100).

January (?)

Erminia Frezzolini "wished to select . . . *A Life for the Tsar* for her benefit performance. She herself made the initial visit to me and brought me a ticket for the benefit. However, my opera was not produced by the Italians, because audiences were displeased with the unsuccessful efforts of Russian composers and were completely exasperated after the *fiasco* of F. M. Tolstoy's opera *Il Birichina di Parigi*. An order was issued by His Majesty not to accept works by Russian composers for the Italian theater" (*Zap.*).

"Glinka, Dargomyzhsky, and Moniuszko were always present at Kastrioto's evenings, as was Rubinstein, who was then just starting out and was, one might say, still a youth. . . . All kinds of amateurs attended, including Prince Odoevsky,

Count Vielgorsky, Damcke (the music critic), and others. Music was performed by the composers themselves, by singers, and by amateurs, among them, Bilibina. The best of all of them was E. M. Konyar. . . . No other singer I had heard understood so well what she performed or expressed so well what she understood. Her singing caused quivering, shivering in the veins, fever. Once, accompanied by Glinka, she sang his 'Soon you will forget me,' and one lady fainted. Damcke went into another room so no one would see his emotion and embarrassment. When she finished there was no applause or expression of approval, just profound, concentrated silence. Glinka stood up and said: '*Après vous je ne chanterai plus cette romance.*' Besides the works of composers who were present, they also sang Mendelssohn: excerpts from his *Paulus* went especially well" (P. Stepanov, *Vosp.*, p. 64).

[Glinka made the acquaintance of Stanislaw Moniuszko through Viktor Kazhinsky (G 1, p. 414).]

After a five-year separation, Serov visited Glinka, who received him "very cordially. He was noticeably pleased with the opportunity to chat . . . about this and that. He immediately introduced . . . his interlocutor and inseparable companion at the time, the Spaniard Don Pedro, who was just as short as Glinka himself was." "He talked a lot about his life in Paris and Spain. . . . He told me that he had written two large pieces: one Russian (*Kamarinskaya*), the other Spanish (*Jota*), and that he intended to rework another Spanish fantasy, the *Souvenir de Seville*. 'I am still quite dissatisfied with this piece.' He said that he needed to rewrite the entire score. It was particularly interesting . . . to learn about Glinka's opinion of Berlioz. . . . 'Berlioz is a musician of genius,' said Mikhail Ivanovich. 'The French do not understand him and never will understand him. He is too serious for Paris. So far as I am concerned, I see true originality in his music, true creativity. He writes *differently* from others and depends mostly on *chromaticism,* on the chromatic scale. Because of this his melodies do not project clearly at first and do not satisfy most people. But his melodicism is just as strong as the harmonic side. And what can one say about his orchestration! In this respect there is striking novelty at every turn.'"

Glinka attended the Symphonic Society and the University Concerts at which Beethoven's Sonata for Piano and Violin in C Minor, Op. 30, No. 2, orchestrated by Serov, was performed.

On his next visit, Serov found Glinka "at the piano, and he played . . . his three recently published piano pieces: 'Prayer,' '*La Barcarolle,*' and '*Souvenir d'une mazurque.*' In these pieces I saw a completely new side of Glinka's creativity. The Barcarolle was a very nice and graceful little thing without the slightest pretensions, though of course it far exceeded the worth of most so-called salon pieces. . . . Glinka performed the Barcarolle with a soft, delicate, velvety touch, which reminded me of Field's style, familiar to me only through descriptions. Of course, the '*Souvenir d'une mazurque*' was a pure imitation of Chopin. Glinka said to me that he had even wanted to inscribe the piece '*Hommage à Chopin,*' but that he had refrained because of the too frequent abuse of such 'homages.' Capriciousness, mischievousness, outbursts of passion, and little clouds of melancholy succeeded one another in this delightful piece. It goes without saying that it requires the same artistry of rendition as the composer himself possessed. The 'Prayer' is in a much more serious musical category. . . . Glinka said to me that the 'Prayer' came into being in 1848 in Smolensk, where he had been in a very dismal mood during the outbreak of cholera. . . . In the instrumental dissonances (introduzione, allegro moderato, like an orchestral tremolo) Glinka had imagined (according to his own interpretation) a noxious, fatal miasma in the air. In the cantilena itself (A major) there is little originality (which the composer himself pointed out to me). The melody is closely related to the major episode in the middle of the famous allegretto in A minor in Beethoven's Seventh Symphony. It is likewise related, it would seem, to Mendelssohn's cantilenas. Then a bold harmonic step leads to the key of C major, in which there is a majestic chorale in pure church style, which upon its fortissimo repetition certainly *demands* a full complement of vocal and orchestral forces. In the second half of the piece, after the reprise of the first cantilena (A major), the chorale appears in the principal key, after which a fascinating coda (a development of the first cantilena) leads the music in a superlative way out of the chorale to the concluding chords. It would be impossible not to be fascinated by this masterful and inspired music." Serov "was delighted" with the "Prayer" and said to Glinka that he regreted "that such austere beauty and profound thought perished in part because of the pale and characterless sound of the piano. 'And what if someone, sir, would impose on you to orchestrate the piece? I would be very happy to.' "

Serov and his sister Sofia Dyutur were at Glinka's, where Serov acquainted him with his friend Vladimir Stasov. "Before a small circle of listeners composed of the three of us, Don Pedro, and sometimes two or three of his relatives, Glinka sang his new vocal composition, Gretchen's song, from Goethe's *Faust*. . . . There was a purely Slavic character about this music . . . it was not Goethe's 'Gretchen' but rather Gorislava, a Russian woman. . . . Margaret's anguish was more finished, more mature, and more serious and profound than Gorislava's grief. In the very sounds of Glinka's music there were, if not more inspiration, then certainly greater freedom in his mastery of musical declamation and the greatest refinement of harmonic language. One modulation especially struck me every time because of its unexpectedly new and lovely effect. The principal key of the piece is B minor. By means of the parallel [*sic*] major key, D major, the music moves to the key of B-flat major.

> The smile of his mouth and his noble appearance,
> His tall stature, the power of his gaze,
> The magical fluency of his speech,
> The ecstacy of his embrace, and his kiss . . .

stopped on a high 'D' in the melody. After the brightly impassioned love episode, Margaret returns once again to her grieving, and at this point, with one chord, the music moves from the key of B-flat major back to the principal key, the melancholy tonality of B minor. Because I admired the marvelous quality and dramatic beauty of this enharmonic modulation (by means of the chord A#-D-F# or *la dièze-re-fa dièze*), I expressed my fascination to the composer. 'Such modulations are also common in Chopin. It is our native inclination,' Mikhail Ivanovich remarked. How he himself performed this marvelous romance, I suspect there is no point in enlarging upon. . . . Under Glinka's direction, and accompanied by him, my sister performed 'Margaret' quite successfully. The composer was completely satisfied with the expressiveness and dramatic truth of my sister's singing. He went through a lot of his own compositions with her, but he always had special praise for her 'Margaret' and for Ratmir's romance 'She is my life, my joy'" (Serov, *Vosp.*, p. 97).

Glinka "read through all his *most recent* romances," with Dyutur, "but most of all 'Margaret' and '*Ty skoro menia pozabudesh*'.' He admired her exceptional musical intelligence and her dramatic and passionate expressiveness. . . . I was always present at these 'lessons.' One could say that our conversations were endless" (ltr. from V. Stasov to N. Findeyzen, 20 March 1893, *L.*, p. 345).

1 February

In *Rus. invalid,* no. 25, in an article called "V. A. Zhukovsky's Birthday," Glinka's participation in the performance of songs in honor of Zhukovsky on 29 January is mentioned.

January–February

"Kastrioto's evenings generated other evenings at which the same artists gathered. Of the guests, some had been there before, and new ones appeared. Thus the same company met several times a week" (P. Stepanov, *Vosp.*, p. 65).

6 February

In the "Miscellany" section of *Bib-ka dlia chteniia,* no. 93, the publication of new romances is reported. Among these *"Pesn' Margarity"* and *"Zazdravnyi kubok"* are mentioned (d.c.a.).

15 February

At a public examination in the Ekaterininsky Institute in Moscow, the student Novitskaya performed an aria from *A Life for the Tsar,* transcribed for piano by Döhler, and the student Protasieva performed the aria *"Ne o tom skorbliu, podruzhen'ki"* with chorus, from the same opera.

19 February

In Moscow, for a celebration in the home of Count Zakrevsky, the "Russian March" from *A Life for the Tsar* was performed (*Mosk. ved.,* 19 February 1849).

23 February

At a party at Odoevsky's, Glinka, on Odoevsky's advice, renamed the *Jota* "Spanish Overture," and the "Wedding Tune and Dance Tune," *Kamarinskaya* (*Zap.*).

On the title page of the first issue of the "Collection of Musical Pieces, assembled by Glinka" (1839), there is this inscription: *"Ce cahier appartient à Michel de Glinka.* Given to me on the 23rd of February, 1849, by Mikhail Ivanovich Glinka, with the stipulation that I do not pass them on or give them to anyone. [Prince] V. Odoevsky." A note by Glinka reads, "precisely, M. Glinka" (*L.,* p. 355).

26 February

Serov (from Pskov) sent Glinka a letter with the request "to send your 'Prayer' quickly, from which you can see ... [Serov's] impatience to get to work immediately" (ltr. from A. Serov to V. Stasov, 1 March 1849; *MN* III, p. 62).

February (?)

"At one of the last of Kastrioto's evenings, attended by many people, certain women who were enthusiastic about Glinka tore off branches of laurels and myrtle standing in the rooms and wound a wreath. When Glinka sang his

'Farewell, Dear Friends' [Farewell song], they approached him as a group and placed the wreath upon him, which he wore throughout dinner" (P. Stepanov, *Vosp.*, p. 65).

When Odoevsky had completed work on the organ he had contrived, which he named "Sebastianon," he "got together several musical celebrities to examine it. . . . Playing on the *Oberwerk* requires particular skill. It was remarkable, incidentally, that M. I. Glinka solved the problems of playing on this instrument immediately" (*Otech. zap.*, 1849, vol. 66, no. 10, p. 341). "Odoevsky had built his famous organ, Sebastianon . . . and I happened to encounter Glinka there. He sat down at the organ and improvised thoughtfully, smoothly, splendidly. Two or three people listened reverentially to his intimate improvisation, which even Beethoven would have envied" (V. Sollogub, *Vosp.*, p. 626).

At V. Engelgardt's, Glinka "sometimes improvised . . . amazingly" on the organ (ltr. from V. Engelgardt to D. Stasov, 10 December 1908; IRLI, coll. 294). "I once remember when . . . [Glinka] sang a lot . . . how, though it was already late, he came to my rooms from his relatives' apartment and, after removing his coat, began to improvise on my little organ. With his left hand he struck tonic and dominant in imitation of bells, and with his right hand began to invent things, which, as he put it, would make the devil feel sick!" (ltr. from V. Engelgardt to V. Stasov, 26 June 1893; ITMK, coll. 6, no. 74). "[Glinka] improvised on my little organ by Wirt simply divinely!" (ltr. from V. Engelgardt to V. Stasov, 18 February 1906; coll. *Pamiati Glinki*, p. 548).

Beginning of the Year

Glinka's mother lost her sight at the time of her return from Petersburg to Novospasskoe (Shestakova, *Vosp.*, p. 41).

End of February–Beginning of March

"Heydenreich put me back on my feet, and in the early spring I began to go out, mostly with Novoselsky, who had returned from Warsaw during the winter. He acquainted me with young people and writers of the new generation, some of whom, unfortunately, came to misfortune during the course of 1849" (*Zap.*). [This reference is to the Petrashevtsy, who admired Glinka as a great Russian composer (Petrashevsky Case, vol. 2, M.-L., 1941, p. 18). Apparently Glinka attended evenings at Sergey Durov's.]

"At the time Glinka was on friendly terms with two cohorts and friends of mine who lived with him, Nikolay Aleksandrovich Novoselsky . . . and Vladimir Ippolitovich Dorogobuzhinov. . . . Both were great music lovers who surrounded

Glinka with affectionate attention. They lived in an apartment with him and always accompanied him to musical parties at the Bunins' and Girses'. The sisters of V. I. Bunin and A. I. Girs sang his romances beautifully. After they sang, Glinka himself would sit down at the piano and begin to sing his romances in a somewhat jaded voice, though with so much life and expression that everyone was deeply moved. In Glinka's opinion, no one at that time performed his romances as well as Aleksandra Ivanovna Girs and Vera Ivanovna Bunina, who had a very clear voice. They gave an expressiveness to each romance that he, one might say, created with them. When male voices were needed, the best performers of Glinka's and Dargomyzhsky's works were the outstanding baritone Opochinin (later an admiral) and the tenors Kharitonov and Mollerius. Glinka's simplicity and genuine goodness charmed us all" (Semyonov-Tyan-Shansky, *Memuary* [Memoirs], vol. 1, Petrograd, 1917, p. 215). At one of the evenings "Glinka let himself go and played and sang all his popular things, among them this romance" [*Kogda v chas veselyi*]. "He . . . no longer had much of a voice," though Dostoevsky "remembered the extraordinary impression which this particular romance made. Another expert or salon musician could never achieve such an effect. There is a tension in the romance which is elevated and increased with every verse, with every word. . . . To sing this little, though unusual piece, there had to be truth, genuine inspiration, real passion, and their complete poetic assimilation. Otherwise this romance . . . could seem almost shameless . . . but truth and ingenuousness saved everything" (F. Dostoevsky, "The Eternal Husband").

1 March

Serov (from Pskov) asks V. Stasov "to sincerely thank Mikhail Ivanovich" for sending his "Prayer" and "apologize for me for being so bold as to *remind* him of his promise. . . . I will orchestrate (putting the chorus aside) without hurrying (because I have to think about it), and immediately upon finishing it, I will send the score to you" (*MN* III, p. 62).

2 March

In the Maly Theater in Moscow, Petrova-Vorobieva performs Ratmir's aria from *Ruslan and Lyudmila* and the orphan's song from *A Life for the Tsar* (*Ved. Mosk. gor. politsii*, 28 February 1849).

3 March

Serov (from Pskov) writes to his sister: "I am especially interested in hearing about your visits to our *precious* M. I. I certainly understand why you do not wish to see him too often. You have a long way to go before your visits will become *burdensome* to him, but he is a person with whom it is impossible to be *too* delicate. . . . It's therefore good that you do not make too frequent visits to him, but on the other hand that's a *pity!* Soon he will be leaving Petersburg. And once again for heaven knows how many years, and the loss can never be repaid! I would just like to know one thing: does he fully understand how much we appreciate and admire him?" (*RMG,* 1895, no. 3).

5 March

At Rossi's concert in the Hall of Nobility in Moscow, Petrova-Vorobieva performs an aria from *A Life for the Tsar* (*Ved. Mosk. gor. politsii,* 5 March 1849).

Glinka played "his *Kamarinskaya*" for Vladimir Stasov and Sofia Dyutur, "with a million newer and newer variations. . . . I played the theme for him in the treble of the piano and frequently asked him to repeat this or that variation which he had just played or had played the time before. Often, however, he had already forgotten them, and instead he would continue to play new variations, endlessly. Our admiration knew no bounds!" (ltr. from V. Stasov to N. Findeyzen, 20 March 1893, in *L.,* p. 356).

12 March

In a University Concert organized by Dargomyzhsky for the benefit of Varlamov's family, Aleksandra Girs performed an aria from *Ruslan and Lyudmila;* Maria Shilovskaya, *"V pole chistoe gliazhu"* from *A Life for the Tsar;* and Princess Urusova, "Margaret's Song," "Glinka's latest work" (*SPb. ved.,* 19 March; *Sev. pchela,* 12 March 1849).

In *Odessk. vestnik,* no. 21, in a review entitled "Musical Evening for the Benefit of Two Philanthropic Establishments," performance of an aria from *A Life for the Tsar* is mentioned.

16 March

Artemovsky performs Ruslan's aria in a concert given by the St. Petersburg Italian Opera singer Frezzolini in the Bolshoi Theater in Moscow (*Mosk. ved.,* 15 March 1849).

26 March

Serov (from Pskov) writes to Dmitry Stasov: "Whenever I play *Così fan tutti,* I involuntarily think about Rossini, *qui à vendu son talent* (in Glinka's words)." He writes that the orchestration of the "Prayer" is completely ready in draft and is being rewritten at leisure. . . . It is too bad that I do not have M. I.'s permission to send you a copy of the piano original which he sent me of the 'Prayer.' . . . What a piece!!" (*MN* III, pp. 62–63).

28 March

In a survey of concerts by "R. Z." [Zotov] in *Sev. pchela,* no. 68, an excerpt from Berlioz's article in the *Journal des débuts* of 15/27 March is quoted: "Not counting the Counts Mikhail and Matvey Vielgorsky . . . or General Lvov . . . or even Glinka, who several years ago in Paris acquainted us with the captivating and noble grace of his melodies and resources of his occasionally fantastic but extremely original harmony, there are many amateurs genuinely worthy of being singled out in Russian society."

2 April

Serov (from Pskov) sends V. Stasov his orchestration of the "Prayer" and asks that his questions and thoughts about the work be conveyed to Glinka (*MN* III, p. 64).

12 April

Composer's dating on the manuscript of the *"Paz'ka"* [Polka]: "Written by M. Glinka on 12 April 1849 in the apartment of Vasily Pavlovich Engelgardt."

19 April

Glinka gave Engelgardt permission "to recopy all my compositions in the possession of His Highness Prince Odoevsky, providing that each work which Mr. Engelgardt wishes to have, he should sign for." The permit was written by Engelgardt and signed by Glinka: "Collegiate Assessor, Mikhail Glinka, 19 April 1849."

26 April

Glinka's signature on a lithograph portrait of himself (done by Volkov in 1837): "To my dear old chap Nikolay Aleksandrovich Izmaylov, in token of true friendship, M. Glinka. St. Petersburg, 26 April 1849."

28 April

In a concert in Moscow, the pianist Seymour-Schiff "improvised on Glinka's popular aria '*Akh, ne mne bednomu*'" (*Ved. Mosk. gor. politsii*, 30 April 1849).

April

When Serov returned from Pskov, Glinka "very attentively read through . . . all the details" of Serov's orchestration of the "Prayer" with him. "He praised many things and changed others according to his ideals. All the while he passed on to me . . . his invaluable observations about the nuances of orchestration and the character and color of individual instruments. This entire effort, however, came to nothing, because, according to Glinka, the concept of the work demanded not an *orchestra*, but a *solo voice* with chorus. It was essential to have a text corresponding to the idea. Here things stopped" (Serov, *Vosp.*, p. 99).

In V. Stasov's presence, Glinka "tried to compose music to Odoevsky's words, 'Palermo' (written to commemorate the visit of the Empress Aleksandra Fedorovna to Palermo), but [I] was unable to and took the words with me to Warsaw" (*Zap.*).

1 May

In *Syn otechestva*, no. 5, in the section "Miscellany," there is an announcement of the publication of the fifth issue of *Le Nouvelliste*, in which the romance "*Milochka*" was printed.

3 May

Musical annotation by Glinka with the composer's date: "M. Glinka, 3 May 1849, SPb." (*Gazeta Gattsuka*, 1 June 1885, p. 344).

6 May

Composer's dating on the autograph of an attached excerpt: *"Thème de la Ballade de 'Rousslan.'"*

In *SPb. ved.,* no. 99, there is a story by "A. N." entitled *"Sosedka"* [The neighbor woman], dedicated to Glinka, in which the heroine of the story performs the Barcarolle.

5 or 6 May

Glinka "paid a visit" to Yakov Dovgolevsky and at the same time was brought a letter from Maria Krzhisevich.

7 May

Glinka writes to Krzhisevich: "If I might see you again on the banks of the Vorskla or Seym, my muse, which has long been slumbering, might again be awakened. . . . Now I am limiting myself to individual little pieces."

Before 9 May

Glinka visited Bryullov, who was sick: " 'I will soon be leaving here to die, and probably I will not see you again,' Bryullov said to Glinka. 'I often annoyed you, but forget that. I understand very well that of all the people who surrounded me here, you alone were my brother in art' " (M.I. Zheleznov, "A Note about K. P. Bryullov," in *Zhivopisnoe obozrenie* [Survey of painting], 1898, no. 33, p. 665).

Ivan Cavos asked Glinka to write a graduation chorus for the students of the Smolny. "I agreed with reluctance to his request, because I did not want to be in competition with Duke Petr Oldenburgsky or with Lvov and Count M. Yu. Vielgorsky, who had written quite successful graduation choruses for the girls of the Smolny Monastery" (*Zap.*).

Glinka makes the acquaintance of Vladimir Kashperov.

Ekaterina Kern's inscription—an epigraph from Koltsov—on the manuscript of the "Prayer" for piano dates from the time of Glinka's stay in Petersburg (ITMK, coll. 6).

9 May

Glinka departs with Don Pedro for Warsaw. "We travelled by post-chaise in a carriage of the most comfortable sort. The weather was excellent—mild, spring verdure, the birds singing—everything disposed one's spirit toward happiness."

Toward the Middle of May

"As we went from Neman to Kovno, nature's appearance became absolutely holidaylike" (*Zap.*).

Middle of May

Warsaw. Arrival "in the happiest frame of mind." Address: Netsalaya Street (ltr. to V. Engelgardt, 5/17 October 1849; *Zap.*).

18 May

In *SPb. ved.*, no. 108, the hero of the story *"Sosedka"* performs the romance *"Ne poi, krasavitsa, pri mne."*

22 May

Conclusion of the story *"Sosedka,"* dedicated to Glinka, in *SPb. ved.*, no. 112.

27 May/8 June

Glinka made the acquaintance of Pavel Grabbe ("From the Diary and Notebooks of Count P. Kh. Grabbe," in *Rus. arkhiv*, 1888, book 3, part 11, p. 416).

By the End of May or Beginning of June

"Two weeks hadn't passed since our arrival before my nerves . . . got increasingly irritated, and I was possessed by such a strong and profound *depression* that I was ashamed of myself" (ltr. to V. Engelgardt, 5/17 October 1849).

For amusement Glinka drank with friends (at the time several of his schoolmates lived in Warsaw). "Most of the group gathered at my apartment or that of my boarding-school companion General A. N. Astafiev." Nonetheless, "this dissipated way of living did not really cheer me up or inspire me musically" (*Zap.*).

2 June

The 101st performance of *A Life for the Tsar* in the Bolshoi Theater in St. Petersburg. "The performance of the opera is well known: Petrov rendered the role of Susanin beautifully. . . . Mme Stepanova . . . [sang] conscientiously; Mme Lileeva has a voice which is too weak for the stage, but then most dilettantes are still constrained by the memory of how A. Y. Petrova sang the role of Vanya. . . . For a debut, Mr. Bulakhov came out of his difficult part quite successfully" (*Otech. zap.*, 1849, vol. 65, no. 7, p. 88).

9/21 June

A line of music from the romance *"Proshchaite, dobrye druz' ia"* and under it the inscription: "Warsaw, 21 June 1849, M. Glinka," written on a strip of paper attached to I. Palm's portrait of Glinka.

17 June

In *Sev. pchela,* no. 133, "Theatrical Chronicle," "R. Z." [Zotov] mentions P. Bulakhov's debut in *A Life for the Tsar.*

June

In the Tivoli gardens in St. Petersburg "Mr. Sachs and his orchestra revived one of M. I. Glinka's most remarkable works, his 'Fantastic Waltz'" (*Otech. zap.,* 1849, vol. 65, no. 8, p. 285).
[Contemporaries referred to the *Valse-fantaisie* in various ways, as the "Pavlovsk," "Melancholy," and "Fantastic Waltz."]

June–July

"Over the summer, my most profound musical pleasure . . . was occasioned by Freyer's organ playing in the Evangelical Church. He performed Bach's music extremely well. His pedalling was precise, and his registration was so good that in several pieces, especially the 'BACH' fugue and the F-major toccata . . . he brought tears to my eyes" (*Zap.*).

At one of Astafiev's evenings, Glinka made the acquaintance of Nikolaev, who had sung his romances (without knowing that the composer was present). Afterwards Glinka sang improvisations on the theme of a folk (robber's) song, *"Oi, spasibo tebe sinemu kuvshinu"* [Oh, thank you, blue jug] (Nikolaev, *Vosp.,* pp. 238–39).

3 July

In *Otech. zap.,* vol. 65, no. 7, "Musical Chronicle," there is a review [by Vasily Botkin] of the one hundred and first performance of *A Life for the Tsar.* This fact is "considerable evidence in the opera's behalf. . . . The vocal writing of all the opera's numbers illustrates a perfect knowledge of the capabilities of voices.

In the duets and *morceaux d'ensemble* the voice leading is exceptional; choruses are used without affectation or strained interpretation. The melodic style of the vocal parts is artfully set off by the symphonic effects of the orchestration. M.I. Glinka's harmony is always intelligent, well thought out, and original, and it bears the stamp of learning. Bold and unexpected modulations and chords are striking in their sonorousness, and there is richness of instrumentation. . . . So far little attention has been paid to the overture. It is an extremely remarkable symphonic composition both in conception and for the absence of a *dramatic program,* which is characteristic of all the newest overtures" (d.c.a.).

Beginning of August

In *Otech. zap.*, vol. 65, no. 8, there is a report "of agreeable events," namely the revival of the *Valse-fantaisie* by Sachs's orchestra: "What melody, what harmony, what orchestration! We invite all music lovers to listen to this waltz. It is music of the highest order, which . . . Mr. Sachs's orchestra performs very well."

End of August

"Depression . . . led me to the most extreme apathy, and the better part of the day I spent at home lying on the couch" (*Zap.*).

31 August

The following comments appear in *Otech. zap.*, vol. 65, no. 9, under "Musical Chronicle": "Just last month we praised" the performance of the *Valse-fantaisie* by Sachs's orchestra in the Tivoli gardens. In the same issue there is a report about Schindler's benefit concert, during which the orchestra and singers performed the barcarolle and chorus from Verstovsky's *Askold's Tomb* and the trio and chorus from *A Life for the Tsar*. "We will remain silent about the performance of the first two pieces. One must be very bold to profane Glinka's wonderful trio" (d.c.a.).

Beginning of September

Colonel Kubarovsky once took Glinka to his home in a suburb of Warsaw. For a time Glinka stayed with Kubarovsky. With him Glinka began to frequent Ohm's restaurant, where there was a nice garden and large hall, "a piano which was not all that bad, and outstanding acoustics." Glinka made friends with

Ohm's youngest daughter Emilia ("Mitsya") and "gave her some voice and piano lessons" (*Zap.*).

Beginning of October

Glinka "moved to a secluded part of the city, having decided to stay at home and to visit a very small number of only [my] closest acquaintances. This change in the way [I] lived was good for me. . . . My muse became more gracious" (ltr. to V. Engelgardt, 5/17 October 1849). Glinka continued to frequent Ohm's establishment until winter" (*Zap.*).

5/17 October

Glinka writes to Engelgardt: "Society in Warsaw is boring and uniform, though there are several remarkable musical talents here—the Grünberg girls, the older of which (a pupil of Henselt) plays the piano excellently, even classical music; and the younger, who sings well, particularly my romances. However, in my opinion, the most remarkable artist in Warsaw is the organist Freyer, whose hands and feet are equally agile. I cannot listen to him play the preludes and fugues of Bach without experiencing a terrible nervous excitement."

8/20 October

Glinka writes to Maria Krzhisevich: "I am afraid . . . that your visit with me might have disappointed you, for, though it is true that my hands and voice are still in good order, I generally look terribly older these last years. . . . I do not see well and already have had to resort to glasses."

18 October

In an article by "I. M." [Mann] entitled "Petersburg Chronicle" in *SPb. ved.*, no. 232, Glinka is mentioned as one who "immediately grasped the problems of performance" on the organ which Odoevsky had built.

23 October

In *SPb. ved.*, no. 237, in the section "Bibliographical News," there is an announcement of the publication, among works by various composers, of Glinka's romance *"Milochka."*
[An analogous announcement appears in the issue of 26 October, no. 239.]

27 October

Performance of *A Life for the Tsar* in the Bolshoi theater in Moscow (*Mosk. ved.*, 27 October 1849).

October–Beginning of November

"My poetic feelings toward dear Mitsya awakened my musical activity: during the course of the fall I wrote the romance *'Rozmowa'* [Conversation] by Mickiewicz in Polish and dedicated it to Emilia Ohm. I also wrote 'Adèle' and 'Mary' by Pushkin, the first of which I dedicated to her sister, Olga Izmaylova, and the second, to Maria Stepanovna [Krzhisevich]" (*Zap.; ltr. to V. Fleury, 11/23 November 1849).

To this period (?) belong the undated autograph of the romance *"Rozmowa"* (the title of which is written in an unidentified hand), as well as the undated manuscript of the romance "Mary." (G 2-A, p. 293).
[The autograph of "Adèle" is not extant.]

8 November

Censor's authorization for Adolph Harras's book, *Pocket Musical Dictionary, with Supplemental Biographical Information on Composers, Performers, and Dilettantes, with Portraits*. M., 1850. On p. 70 it says "Glinka M. von, born in Moscow [*sic*], in 1812 [*sic*], piano virtuoso and serious composer; known for his opera *A Life for the Tsar*."

11/23 November

Glinka asks Viktor Fleury to find out through Engelgardt what has happened to the publication of the romances which he left in Petersburg.

Fall

Glinka made the acquaintance of the "then well-known Polish composer" Karol Kurpiński. "He was a knowledgeable man, with whom I enjoyed talking about art" (*Zap.*).

6 December

Performance of *A Life for the Tsar* in the Bolshoi Theater in Moscow (*Mosk, ved.*, 3 December 1849).

20 December

In *Sev. pchela,* no. 283, in a feuilleton (signed "A.") entitled "Moscow Munici-pal Chronicle," it says that the operas *Robert, Norma,* and *A Life for the Tsar* "afford pleasure to true music lovers and connoisseurs in Moscow."

25 December/6 January 1850

Glinka sends Odoevsky his new romances to words by Pushkin and Mickiewicz for transmittal to Engelgardt. He writes: "I have taken advantage of the observa-tion which you made and have reworked 32 bars at the beginning of the allegro, or rather, vivace, of the 'Spanish Overture.' The passage which, in your opin-ion, should be divided between two harps, I arranged for two hands, but the *solo* violins, very spiccato, in unison with the harp, I believe will create a new effect. In the enclosed excerpt from the same overture, one must pay attention to the flutes from the crescendo at the main theme. They should play in the lower octave, which, by the way, is also apparent from the parts of the other wind instruments. In the excerpt from *Kamarinskaya, sons harmoniques,* one should hear the following sounds from the violins:

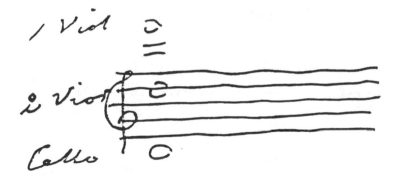

"If this overture and scherzo should be performed in concerts, I earnestly ask you to inform me of the effect." He writes that he intends to spend the winter in Warsaw, to go see his mother in the country in the spring or summer, and to arrive in Petersburg for the fall and winter.

31 December

In the first literary supplement to *Le Nouvelliste,* there is an announcement that Bernard has the romances *"Pesn' Margarity"* and *"Zazdravnyi kubok"* in stock (d.c.a.).

December

Pavel Kovalevsky makes Glinka's acquaintance at a party at Novoselsky's ("the fidgeter"). Glinka performed only Chopin, Gluck, and his own compositions, including "Bayan's verses, which had been supressed by the censor at the time because they were dedicated to Pushkin, who had taken the liberty of dying in a duel:

> There is a deserted spot, a cheerless shore,
> In the north, far away . . .

"This 'far away,' like the endless and uniform northern expanse, was prolonged by a uniform sound and then vanished somewhere, just like it, in endlessness.

> All are immortal in the heavens!—

ascended, concluding the song, the same sound, but having leapt to the very heavens, it stopped short, and fell at once to earth. . . . The nasal, jaded tenor of the composer, for which he would not have been accepted as a chorister, spilled forth such magic of expression that even the most sweet-voiced singer would not have dared to sing after him what he had sung . . .

> Luxuriant star of love,
> You have set forever! . . .

he almost cried out immediately after this—the aria, about which he spoke: 'this is my anguish!' And even though it was written for a female voice, after him it was impossible to listen to it, whoever the singer might have been. . . . At the bachelors' dinner he did not fall behind the young people in jokes, witticisms, and tricks of every sort, but 'got his share of the fun' every time a well-aimed comparison at someone's expense succeeded or he told an amusing anecdote. He delivered such 'portions' himself more than anyone." At the same party Glinka performed his *Kamarinskaya,* indicating how it was to sound when performed by an orchestra. "He accompanied with his lips, struck the keyboard with all ten fingers in tutti passages, tapped his heels, sang and whistled along, and with striking picturesqueness conveyed the movement and colors of the instruments. . . . Whenever I heard this piece later on in concerts, so inimitable in its purely Russian recklessness, the orchestral performance added almost nothing and even diminished a little the fire and impetuousness of its transmission." At the end of the evening, "before he left, they sat him down again at the piano, and he said farewell to us with the romance:

> Farewell, dear friends!
> Life will scatter us in all directions . . .

and then he concluded:

> This family I shall not betray,
> I shall not trade it for childish dreams;
> To you I sing my final song,—
> And break my lyre's strings!!!

with a stupefying outburst on the final word and cut it short with a chord in both hands. Taking us all in with the fervor in his eyes, he encountered tears in the eyes of everyone. . . . Such evenings happen but rarely in life!" Some of the things which Glinka said at Novoselsky's include: "Brilliant, and particularly clamorous pianists, he could not bear. 'Phonious,' he said, 'but not euphonious.' When they tried to provoke him to say something about Liszt, Kolmakov spoke for him: "I would say, he has a thin face, and long, fair hair. He sat down: in one hand, brimstone, in the other, staves. He leapt. The hall rocked, and many pregnant women nearly had miscarriages! Enough, he said!" (Kovalevsky, *Vosp.*, p. 253).

Glinka visited at Nikolay and Olga Pavlishchevs' (L. Pavlishchev, *Vosp.*, p. 248).

The second edition of Dargomyzhsky's and Nikolay Stepanov's *Musical Album with Caricatures* was published by Bernard.

End of the Year

Glinka's romance *"Rozmowa"* to words by Adam Mickiewicz was published in Warsaw (inscription by Glinka on the music; cf. 18 and 19 January 1850).

"He had a nervous disorder, he spoke of nothing but his nerves ('Look how sick they make me, do you see? I see this clearly!'), he was depressed and neither sang, nor played, and especially did not compose. *C'est un génie manqué,* the fashionable priests of art intoned. But the youth did not agree. With them he forgot about being depressed . . . he sang again, and played, even improvised on the piano. . . . 'Gentlemen, with you I grow young again!' he said" (Kovalevsky, *Vosp.*, p. 251).

Season of 1849/1850

"The winter . . . was extremely severe, and I caught cold" (*Zap.*).

In the theater in Nizhny Novgorod there were repeated performances of the first act of *A Life for the Tsar* (*Nizhegor. gub. ved.*, 1856, no. 36).

1850

1 January

In *Otech. zap.*, vol. 68, nos. 1–2, "Musical Chronicle," Vasily Botkin writes about a performance of a symphony by Anton Rubinstein at a University Concert on 8 February and about his work on the opera *Dmitry Donskoy:* "Mr. Rubinstein has easily mastered fugal style. . . . We therefore recommend that he direct his attention to the combination of free and fugal styles, which M. I. Glinka utilized so masterfully in his opera, *A Life for the Tsar.* Among present-day composers, he has solved the problem of what these forms mean in an operatic medium better than most anyone. [Rubinstein] should . . . pay attention chiefly to Glinka's brilliant idea of treating Russian national tunes in fugato, for which they are so suitable. They take on such a wonderful coloration from contrapuntal treatment. What a powerful effect is created by the fugue for soloists, chorus, and orchestra in the first act of *A Life for the Tsar*" (d.c.a.).

In the January literary supp. to *Le Nouvelliste,* under "Petersburg Chronicle," it reports that "our gifted composer has once again left Petersburg and is living in Warsaw, where the climate is more agreeable to his fragile health. We are awaiting several new romances from him. . . . Speaking of his romances, we have to say something about an extremely important circumstance, namely, that our singers, including charming salon songstresses, are no longer limited as they once were to only Italian music. Now one finds few amateur evenings where the beautiful romances or duets of Glinka, Alyabiev, Varlamov, Dargomyzhsky, and Gurilev are not performed. Russian music has finally become independent, and it is fully worthy of this. . . . Glinka and Verstovsky initiated this effort" (d.c.a.).

18/30 January

On the Warsaw edition of the romance *"Rozmowa. Fantazya do śpiewu muzyka Michata Glinki"* there is this dedicatory inscription: "To Nikolay Ivanovich Pavlishchev, as a token of our friendship, from the composer. Warsaw, 18/30 January 1850."

19/31 January

On the manuscript of the romance *"Rozmowa. Fantazya do śpiewu muzyka Michata Glinka ofiorowana pannie E***** O** Warzawa"* is this inscription: *"A Monsieur Freyer de la part du compositeur Varsovie le 19/31 janvier 1850"* (*Sov. muzyka*, 1954, no. 12; there is facsimile in I. Belza's book *Iz istorii russko-pol' skikh muzykal' nykh sviazei* [From the history of Russo-Polish musical relations], Moscow, 1955, between pp. 16 and 17).

Before 20 January

A letter from Dargomyzhsky to Stanislaw Moniuszko dates from this period: "Glinka is in Warsaw. I received two new works from him yesterday, which were very well done" (*Sov. muzyka*, 1963, no. 2, p. 51; Fr. original).

20 January

In Petersburg, Matvey Bernard informs Engelgardt that he will agree to publish Glinka's third romance on the same conditions under which he published the first two (G 2-A, p. 299).
[The first two romances were "Mary" and "Adèle," the third was *"Dubrava shumit."*]

22 January

Evgenia Andreevna Glinka (from Novospasskoe) writes to Maria Stuneeva: "Michel promises to come home in the spring, God willing. It's so sad that I've not seen him for so long" (*L.*, p. 367).

23 January

Censor's authorization for the publication of the romance "Adèle."

25 January

Andrey Lodi (from Petersburg) writes to Karl Bryullov: "Glinka is in Warsaw . . . and is doing well. . . . Dargomyzhsky whines, writes trifling little duets, and tries to convince the world that his talent is far greater than Glinka's" (Archives of the Bryullovs, St. Petersburg, 1900, p. 178).
[The letter was erroneously dated 1849 by the editor. The date here is based upon Glinka's stay in Warsaw in January of 1850.]

26 January

Glinka tells Viktor Fleury that he has sent two romances to Odoevsky for Engelgardt to pass on to the publisher Bernard.

Censor's authorization for Bernard's publication of the romance "Mary. Song from a dramatic scene by A. S. Pushkin. . . . Dedicated to M . . . S . . . K."

Publication of the romance *"Dubrava shumit"* also belongs to this period (the year of publication has been established according to the number on the engraving plates).

13 February

In *Ved. Mosk. gor. politsii*, no. 35, there is an article by "F. P." entitled "Moscow Observations," which says that *"Askold's Tomb* and *A Life for the Tsar* will outlive us and our descendants and will be listened to with the same enthusiasm as they are now, because every note in them and every sound are a part of our hearing."

21 February

In a supplement to *Mosk. ved.*, no. 22, under "Musical News," there is an advertisement for new music, including the romance *"Dubrava shumit."*

25 February

In *Voronezhsk. gub. ved.*, no. 8, in an article entitled "Social Entertainment in Voronezh," a philanthropic concert is mentioned in which the trio from *A Life for the Tsar* is to be performed.

28 February

In *Sovremennik*, vol. 20, no. 3, under "New Musical Works," there is an announcement about romances by Glinka for sale at Bernard's: *"Dubrava shumit,"* "Mary," *"Milochka,"* and *"Pesn' Margarity,"* as well as the *Album with Caricatures*, which includes *"Ty skoro menia pozabudesh'."* Also mentioned here is a forthcoming concert of works by Russian composers, including the first performances of pieces by Glinka (d.c.a.).

1 March

In *Nizhegorodsk. gub. ved.*, no. 11, in an article by "V. V." entitled "Theatrical Chronicle: Several Words on Behalf of Mme Strelkova I," mention is made of a performance of excerpts from *A Life for the Tsar*.

Beginning of March

In the March literary supplement to *Le Nouvelliste*, Berthold Damcke's article "Concerts in the Provinces" reports of a concert in Kostroma where A. Shilov and N. Pogozheva performed Susanin's and Vanya's "famous duet" from the third act of *A Life for the Tsar*.

Beginning of March, before the 10th

In a philanthropic concert in Voronezh, local amateur singers E. Baturina, D. Korsakov, and Ya. Saveliev performed the trio from *A Life for the Tsar* (*Voronezh. gub. ved.*, 25 February and 11 March 1850).

11 March

In *Voronezh. gub. ved.*, no. 10, there is an article called "Philanthropic Concert in Voronezh," signed by "A frequenter of the theater," about the performance of the trio from *A Life for the Tsar*.

12 March

There is a notice in *Rus. invalid*, no. 57, about a concert on 15 March for the "Society for Visitation to the Poor, established by His Majesty," in the Hall of Nobility, for which as yet unperformed works by Vielgorsky, Glinka, Dargomyzhsky, et al., were being rehearsed.

In *Journal de St.-Petersbourg*, no. 1063, there is a notice about the 15 March concert, at which the "Spanish Overture" and *Kamarinskaya* are to be performed for the first time.

13 March

In *Sev. pchela*, no. 57, in the section called *"Pchelka"* [Little bee], there is an announcement of the concert on 15 March.

14 March

In *SPb. ved.*, no. 59, there is a feuilleton entitled "Petersburg Annals," signed "X. X." [Odoevsky], which is devoted to the forthcoming first Russian concert on the 15th of March for the Society for Visitation to the Poor. Works to be performed include "a new composition by M. I. Glinka called *"Ispanskie vospominaniia"* [Spanish memories], written expressly by him for this concert, and *Kamarinskaya*. The orchestra will be made up of 80 of the finest musicians under the direction of Kapellmeister Albrecht."

In *Ved. SPb. gor. politsii*, no. 58, there is an announcement of the 15 March concert in an article by Platon Smirnovsky called "Journal of the News of St. Petersburg."

The full program for the concert on 15 March is printed in *Journal de St.-Petersbourg*, no. 1064.

15 March

The program for the coming concert is included in *SPb. ved.*, no. 60, in a feuilleton entitled "Music and Philanthropy" (signed "V. G."). In the first part of the program, works by Glinka mentioned include *Recuerdos de Castilla*, and in the second part, the "Spanish Overture," *Jota aragonesa*, and a Russian dance song, *Kamarinskaya*, fantasy for orchestra, all performed for the first time. "Incidentally, we recommend paying attention to the 'Spanish Overture' (*Jota aragonesa*) and to *Kamarinskaya*, fantasy for orchestra. Both are among Glinka's best works, disregarding their contrapuntal perfection. It is a pity that the composer is now in Warsaw and will not hear his music performed by such a full and well-balanced orchestra as this one made up of the Italian opera orchestra supplemented by many amateurs. Not long ago he sent to one of his Petersburg friends three more new works, which the public will get to know during the course of Lent. He himself will probably arrive here in the fall."

First performance of the *Jota aragonesa*, *Kamarinskaya*, and *Recuerdos de Castilla* under the direction of Karl Albrecht in the first Russian concert for the benefit of the Society for Visitation to the Poor in the Hall of Nobility in Petersburg (*SPb. ved.*, 14 March 1850). The *Kamarinskaya* "was incredibly funny, original, so masterfully finished, and the audience enjoyed it so much that it had to be repeated. The musicians themselves played and laughed with emotion, and the servants in the halls left their masters' coats and listened open-mouthed to the familiar tune, tapped their feet, and looked at each other, their faces beaming with satisfaction. . . . Next to me [Aralov] there sat a French-man who could not sit still, he was so caught up in the music. When the piece was over, he turned to me and asked, 'Who is it who wrote such wonderfully cheerful music, what's the piece called?' And when I had satisfied his curiosity, he repeated over and over: 'Glinka, Glinka, "Komarnitski," "Komarnitski,'" in an effort to remember the name of the piece and its composer" (ltr. from F. Aralov to N. Ramazanov, 7 April 1850, in *Sov. muzyka,* 1954, no. 6, p. 33).

17 March

In *Journal de St.-Petersbourg,* no. 1067, in a section headed *"St.-Petersbourg, 16 mars,"* there is a report of the great success of "the Russian concert."

18 March

In *Sev. pchela,* no. 62, Bulgarin writes in a review of the concert on 15 March: "What the public masses liked most was the Russian dance song [*bychok*], a fantasy for orchestra by M. I. Glinka. The orchestration and interlacing of musical ideas in this fantasy are perfectly marvelous."

21 March

There is a review of the Russian concert on 15 March in *SPb. ved.,* no. 65, in a feuilleton entitled "Petersburg Annals," signed "I. M." [Mann]. "We will point out four pieces which most won the audience's favor. These are the overture from the opera *Torzhestvo Vakkha* [Triumph of Bacchus] by A. S. Dargomyzhsky, the overture to the opera *Starosta* [The elder] by A. F. Lvov, and Aragon melodies and a Russian dance song arranged for orchestra by M. I. Glinka. The first two of these pieces are well considered and distinctive works. So far as the last two are concerned, here the main interest is concentrated on the musical exposition and development of the existing ideas and likewise on the instrumentation. These superior qualities are primarily expressed in the Russian dance song, arranged for orchestra. The composer has artfully devel-oped the modest tune of this song through various combinations of musical lines and has created an exceptionally nice piece, which the audience, hearing it once, demanded a second time."

Ca. 26 March/7 April

Glinka received news of the success of his pieces in Petersburg. "Either the public, which up to now has hated instrumental music, has completely changed, or, actually, these pieces, which were written *con amore,* have succeeded beyond my expectations. However that may be, this completely unexpected success has cheered me up extremely."

26 March/7 April

Glinka writes to Engelgardt: "I am happy to leave the overture *Jota* and *Kamarinskaya* with you for concerts by the Philharmonic Society and others as you think best. So far as the *Recuerdos de Castilla* is concerned, this piece is only an experiment, and I intend to take two themes from it for a second Spanish overture: *"Souvenir d'une nuit d'été à Madrid,"* for which reason I ask you not to perform this piece anywhere nor to give it to anyone." He gives permission to Bernard "for separate publication of the romance '*Ty skoro menia pozabudesh*'' with the condition, however, that it be in the same format as the other romances already published [by Bernard]." Further on he writes: "This year marks the twenty-fifth year of my service, within my limitations, in the field of Russian national music. Many reproach me for laziness. But if these gentlemen were to take my place for a while, they would be convinced that with a continuous nervous disorder and the strict view toward art which has always led me, it is impossible to write much. Those worthless romances which gushed forth on their own in a moment of inspiration often cost me severe effort. *Not to repeat* oneself is more difficult that you can imagine. This year I have decided to close the factory of Russian romances and to dedicate the remainder of my strength and sight to more important work."

[Glinka reckoned 1825 as the beginning of his creative activity, when the romance *"Ne iskusshai menia"* was composed. In fact, the beginning of the composer's creative activity dates to an earlier time, not later than 1822.]

In a concert in Nizhny Novgorod, "Mme Schmidthof, and Messrs. Leonov and Rubtsev" performed the trio *"Ne tomi, rodimyi"* from *A Life for the Tsar* (*Nizhegorod. gub. ved.,* 29 March 1850).

27 March

In "The First Week of Concerts" in *Sev. pchela,* no. 68, "R. Z." [Zotov] mentions the Russian concert on 15 March.

29 March

In *Nizhegorod. gub. ved.,* no. 17, a performance of the trio from *A Life for the Tsar* is referred to in an article called "Concerts in the Nizhny Novgorod Theater" by Andrey Pechersky.

31 March

In *Sovremennik,* vol. 20, no. 4, under "Contemporary Notes," there is this notice: "We have heard that during the second week of Lent a magnificient concert is to be given comprised of the works of Russian composers. . . . First place is occupied by the newest compositions by M. I. Glinka" (d.c.a.).

In *Otech. zap.,* vol. 69, no. 4, under "Musical Chronicle," there is a review (unsigned) of Glinka's newest works: "M. I. Glinka's 'Spanish Memories' is an outstanding orchestral work, though we did not altogether like the choice of melodies. The composer hampered himself with local color. . . . M. I. Glinka's second Spanish fantasy (in A major) is even better than the first. Of particular interest here are the outstanding introduction, fugal devices, and the original, intricate rhythm. After the fantasy followed Glinka's third work, the *Kamarinskaya,* fantasy for orchestra, a beautiful and rather ingenious musical jest. After a small introduction, the well-known Kamarinskaya tune begins and continues uninterrupted until the end. All instruments present the tune, combining it in the most complicated and difficult contrapuntal interlacings. Every instrument expresses its own individuality and demands attention, but without destroying the overall effect. A masterful jest! Let us turn our attention to two devices: the violas' opening and the persistent, sharp note of the trumpets which intersects the melody. Also noteworthy is the tune's transition to the minor mode. . . . People who understand what contrapuntal development in music means probably appreciated M. I. Glinka's fantasy for its merits. There is also a homophonic, operatic style, but it does not answer the needs of symphonic music. . . . *Kamarinskaya* will be recognized as a work which satisfies all the requirements of strict symphonic style. Above all, direct your attention to the way grace and playfulness are combined with the most profound contrapuntal combinations. This is a masterful piece, and extremely difficult!" (d.c.a.).

March or April (?)

In Petersburg, in the hall of Kushelev-Bezborodko, the trio from *A Life for the Tsar* is performed in Mikhaylov's concert (*Otech. zap.,* 1850, vol. 70, no. 5, p. 60).

2 April

In the Bolshoi Theater in Moscow, Petrova-Vorobieva performs "an aria composed by Glinka" in a concert "with tableaux vivants" (*Mosk. ved.,* 1 April 1850).

6 April

In *Journal de St.-Petersbourg,* no. 1083, under "Concerts," there is an announcement of the second "Russian concert" on 9 April.

7 April

F. Aralov (from Petersburg) writes to Nikolay Ramazanov: "The Russian concert [15 March] made up of works by Russian composers was very remarkable. Among other works, it included three pieces by M. I. Glinka, two of which were on Spanish themes and one on the purely Russian tune of the Kamarinskaya. This last work was simply a delight! At first the simple tune of the song is played by the violins, and then it is interlaced and gets involved with other instruments, including the strings which play pizzicato in imitation of the balalaika. Suddenly, at the height of this cunning trick, some bassoon or bass plays a long note that covers the entire orchestra. Thus it seems that in the midst of the dancing a drunken peasant suddenly cries out in a burst of excitement: 'Hey you, well?' The tune becomes more lively, the entire mass of the orchestra participates, and again some trumpet blares several solitary notes in time with the kettledrums. All are drunk, tired, the rhythm hobbles, many instruments, as if from exhaustion, are unable to keep up with the pace and little by little fall behind. Only the winds lazily sustain the tune, and everything, apparently, ends, dies down, the orchestra's strength gives out like that of a tireless dancer, when suddenly the entire orchestra *jumps in*! A chord sounds, and the jest is over." After describing how enthusiastic both the orchestral musicians and the servants in the halls were, Aralov concludes: "This testifies to Glinka's genius!" (*Sov. muzyka,* 1954, no. 6, p. 33).

8 April

In *SPb. ved.,* no. 80, there is a feuilleton by Odoevsky (signed "A Passerby") entitled "The Russian Concerts of the Society for Visitation to the Poor, with Respect to the Music." It contains an enthusiastic assessment of the *Jota aragonesa* and *Kamarinskaya.* "Where in music of recent years will you find anything worthy to stand alongside the *Jota aragonesa,* which Glinka was inspired by Spanish melodies to write? How fresh these tunes are, what ardent coloring sets off the changes in them, what original and masterful instrumentation! The miracle worker leads you unwittingly into the warm southern night and surrounds you with all its attractions. . . . The 'Russian Dance Song,' or more simply, *Kamarinskaya,* is one of those fanciful but profound compositions by our musician of genius accessible only to Glinka and Berlioz, with the difference, however, that Berlioz would have found it difficult to bear its unremittingly Russian character (which does not betray itself once), despite the splendor of the instrumentation or the artistic linkage of the melodies, which are permeated by profound musical knowledge. However, you are not nearly so impressed by its technical refinement as the depth of its content. Russian character is fully expressed in it in all its freedom, good nature, light heartedness, and cheerfulness. . . . Initially the motif is heard alone, without any décor, as a Russian would sing it, unconcernedly amusing himself. The tune is repeated for a long time, while the songster discovers other thoughts and feelings which are reflected in it. First he is cheerful, then doleful, then wild. Perhaps this convivial fellow recalls a distant sweetheart, then a subsequent spirited squabble, and then his orphanhood, hapless, in a foreign land. The musician has noticed these transient feelings, just like a painter notices the fleeting expressions of a face and the effects of light. . . . For us they might disappear, but the artist preserves them from oblivion. . . . Glinka's *Kamarinskaya* is at once a marvelous musical composition, a picture, and a profound psychological observation." He reports on the forthcoming second Russian concert on 9 April, for which "Alyabiev from Moscow and Glinka from Warsaw have sent their compositions."

In *Ved. SPb. gor. politsii,* no. 79, in "Diary of Petersburg News Items," there is an announcement about the forthcoming second concert on 9 April of compositions by Russian composers.

9 April

Second Russian concert in the Hall of Nobility in Petersburg for the benefit of the Society for Visitation to the Poor. Of Glinka's compositions, they performed the *Tarantella* for orchestra, Gorislava's aria (Shilovskaya), and *Kamarinskaya* (*SPb. ved.,* 11 April; *Sev. pchela,* 7 April 1850).

In a philanthropic concert in Kharkov the amateurs Prasolova, Osipova, and Shukevich performed the trio from *A Life for the Tsar* (*Khar'k. gub. ved.,* 15 April 1850).

10 April

In Moscow, E. A. Varlamova (daughter of the composer) appeared in a performance of "Glinka's trio from the opera *A Life for the Tsar,* which has become a popular work" (*Ved. Mosk. gor. politsii,* 6 April 1850).

11 April

Review of the second Russian concert in *SPb. ved.*, no. 82, in a feuilleton by "I. M." [Mann] entitled "Petersburg Chronicle." It mentions the *Tarantella* by Glinka, "who by his skillful orchestration is able to masterfully impart character and meaning to any little trifle."

12 April

In the Hall of Nobility in Petersburg, Vera Bunina performs *"Ty ne plach', sirotinushka"* [Do not cry, little orphan] from *A Life for the Tsar* in a concert for the benefit of the family of the deceased Varlamov. (*SPb. ved.*, 12 April 1850).

15 April

There is a review signed "B. N. K." in *Khar'k. gub. ved.*, no. 15, entitled "Amateur Concert, Given in the City of Kharkov on 9 April 1850, for the Benefit of the Philanthropic Society." (The trio from *A Life for the Tsar* was performed.)

20 April

In *Syn otechestva*, no. 4, in the "Russian Literature" section, there is a story by M. Tatkov entitled "Adventures of a Musician (A True Story)," in which the hero of the story hears *A Life for the Tsar* in the theater (d.c.a.).

24 April

Elizaveta Fleury dies in St. Petersburg (Petersburg Necropolis).

28 April

In the May literary supplement to *Le Nouvelliste*, under "Survey of Petersburg Concerts," there is a report saying that in the Russian concerts "many remarkable new works for orchestra have been performed. The most distinctive among these have been a symphony by M. Vielgorsky; the *Jota aragonesa* and *Kamarinskaya*, composed by the famous M. I. Glinka"; the overture to the opera *Triumph of Bacchus* by Dargomyzhsky; and the overture to the opera *Dmitry Donskoy* by Rubinstein (d.c.a.).

2 May

In the "Musical Chronicle" section of *Otech. zap.*, vol. 70, no. 5, there is a review of the second concert for the Society for Visitation to the Poor. It reports that Neukomm, former director of the German opera in Petersburg, "has created a new type of orchestral work, the *fantasy for orchestra*. He has included within the framework of these fantasies free flights of imagination not permitted in the symphony with its strictly determined character and subordination of everything to the main idea. M. I. Glinka has taken advantage of Neukomm's idea, and with the help of his tremendous talent he has given us several exemplary works in this genre. The *Tarantella* and *Kamarinskaya* are already known to audiences." It remarks that in this concert Shilovskaya performed the "beautiful, and about the best of Glinka's vocal compositions, Gorislava's aria from *Ruslan and Lyudmila*" (d.c.a.).

10 May

In *SPb. ved.*, no. 103, in an article signed "I. M." [Mann] entitled "Petersburg Chronicle," it mentions the overture to *Ruslan and Lyudmila* performed in the Russian concert.

20 May

In *Syn otechestva*, no. 5, under "Miscellany," "Adventures of a Provincial in the Capital" is printed, which mentions *Kamarinskaya* and the *Tarantella* (d.c.a.).

May

Glinka's meeting with Avdotya Panaeva, who had travelled abroad. "I could not hide my surprise at Glinka's appearance: he was a completely different person. He looked stout, and his face was puffy and of a yellow-bluish color. He had an apathetic look, his hair was cut differently and laid straight, and he had grown a moustache. There was no trace of his former liveliness. His breathing was difficult when he had to come up a few steps to my hotel room. His voice was hollow, hoarse, and he no longer tossed his head with his former ardor." Panaeva and Sergey Golitsyn took Glinka to the theater, where the mazurka from *A Life for the Tsar* was performed after the conclusion of the drama. The audience, to whom Golitsyn had given advance notice of the composer's presence, gave Glinka an ovation (A. Panaeva, *Vosp.*, pp. 257–58).

First Half of the Year

Publication by Bernard of Glinka's romance *"Ty skoro menia pozabudesh'"* [date established from the number on the engraver's plates].

1 June

In the "Miscellany" section of *Bib-ka dlia chteniia*, no. 101, there is an announcement (signed, "N. N.") of the publication of the third edition of *Musical Album with Caricatures* (d.c.a.).

18 July

An unknown author [perhaps Dubrovsky?] composed this "Acrostic to M. I. Glinka":

> *Gimn rodnogo solov'ia,*
> *Lepet list'ev, shum ruch'ia,*
> *Iz grudi garmon'ei l'iutsia.*
> *Ne mechty li vkrug nas v'iutsia?*
> *Kto zhe milyi nash Orfei?*
> *Akh zaglavnye skorei*
> >> *Prochitaite*
> >> *I uznaite.*

> [Hymn of the native nightingale,
> Rustling of leaves, the sound of the brook,
> Pour from the breast in harmony.
> Is it not dreams which hover around us?
> Who is our dear Orpheus?
> Just quickly the capital letters
> >> Read
> >> And you will find out.]

18 July

Warsaw. Alexander Citadel (*Rus. starina*, 1876, vol. 16, no. 5, p. 204).

Summer (June–July)

Glinka "met frequently" with Dubrovsky, Rimsky-Korsak, Daniel Rozenberg (brother of Mme Grünberg), Sobolevsky, and Grigorovsky (a civil servant) (*Zap.*).

End of July

From Ivan Cavos, Glinka received the poem by the Inspector of the Smolny Institute, Matvey Timaev, for the graduation chorus. ". . . the words were awkward and silly." "Because of the time it was impossible to send them back to Piter to be changed. All I could do was shorten the poem" (ltr. to V. Engelgardt, 12/24 May 1851; *Zap.*).

[In the letter accompanying the poem, Cavos asked Glinka "to write as lightly as possible for the orchestra, and he suggested using piano . . . harp, and several wind instruments" (*Zap.*).]

8/20 August

Composer's dating on the title page of the manuscript score of the "Farewell Song" for the pupils of the Society of Genteel Maidens, "Warsaw, 8/20 August 1850."

24 August/5 September

In a letter to Viktor Fleury, Glinka conveys his condolences on the death of his sister Elizaveta Ivanovna: "Happiness appears on earth only to be followed by more acute misery." He complains about his health. "I have not been out of the house in a month. . . . From the time of my unfortunate return (despite the ridiculous fame, which concerns me less than anything on earth) my life has been a tissue of subtle and constant torments." He writes that because of the poor condition of his health he has decided not to return (Fr. original).

30 August/11 September

Rimsky-Korsak writes to Sobolevsky: "In the public library here there is a 60-volume lexicon of natural history (*Dict. d'hist. nat.*). His Excellency Pavel Aleksandrovich has been gracious enough to allow our friend Glinka to take books home from this library. Because of illness Glinka will surely stay at home. His head so hurts from music that he is unable to write you himself, and he has entrusted me to ask you to request of His Excellency Pavel Aleksandrovich when you see him . . . if it might be permitted to loan Glinka five or, better, ten books at once from the above-mentioned lexicon. Don Pedro's fastidiousness and Glinka's signature will serve as a guarantee that the books will be returned in good condition" (*L.*, p. 372).

[Pavel Aleksandrovich Mukhanov was vice president of the council of public education for the Warsaw educational district.]

Between 8/20 August and 31 August/12 September

Glinka worked on the "Farewell Song." "Knowing from experience . . . that it is impossible to expect a tidy performance from the woodwinds, along with the fortepiano and harp I utilized the entire orchestra, orchestrating the piece as transparently and lightly as possible, so as to display the girls' voices to greatest advantage" (*Zap.*).

31 August/12 September

Composition of the "Farewell Song" is completed. The composer's dating on the manuscript reads "Completed 31 August/12 September 50, Warsaw."

31 August

Performance of *A Life for the Tsar* in the Bolshoi Theater in Moscow (*Mosk. ved.*, 29 August 1850).

Beginning of September

Glinka forwards the "Farewell Song" to Cavos "with detailed instructions regarding the distribution of the orchestra and the girls" (*Zap.*).

11 September

In *Bib-ka dlia chteniia,* vol. 103, in the section "Miscellany," there is an announcement stating that the Petersburg music store *Musée Musical* has available Cherlitsky's Fantasy on Glinka's Romance *"Kto ona i gde ona"* [Who is she, and where is she] (d.c.a.).

21 September

Serov (from Simferopol) writes to Dmitry Stasov: "Not long ago a certain Andreev, the well-known dilettante tenor and friend of Glinka, who was passing through Simferopol, said to me that Glinka is doing nothing at all in Warsaw" (*MN* III, p. 67).

September

Glinka asks his mother to send him "the fugues of Bach, entitled *Le clavecin bien tempéré*" as well as provisions. In the same letter, he thanks Shestakova for caring for their mother and for him.

[The beginning of the letter, to his mother, and the conclusion, directed to Shestakova, have not been preserved. It has been dated by comparison with a letter from 18/30 October, in which Glinka thanks his mother for sending various things, including a cook, as well as saying that the music she has sent has been delayed in route.]

Beginning of October

Glinka and Don Pedro move "to Natanson's house on Nalevki."

8/20 October

Composer's dating on the manuscript of the romance *"Finskii zaliv"* [The Gulf of Finland] to the words of Obodovsky's "Palermo": "Finished 8/20 October 50, Warsaw."

14/26 October

Glinka sends Barteneva a copy of the romance *"Finskii zaliv"* and thanks her for the invitation to him and the young ladies Grünberg and Negroni. "With all the zeal of an old and devoted friend I shall try to enliven the party arranged in your honor" (Fr. original).
[14 October. Barteneva's nameday.]

Glinka is at Barteneva's (ltrs. to P. Barteneva of 14/26 October and to his mother of 18/30 October 1850).

16/28 October

Glinka is again at Barteneva's (ltr. to his mother, 18/30 October 1850).

17/29 October

Glinka writes to Barteneva of his desire to dedicate the romance *"Finskii zaliv"* to the Empress Aleksandra Fedorovna.

18/30 October

Glinka writes to his mother that he has been at Barteneva's twice and that "in several days" he and his students and acquaintances will "entertain her" with music. He asks that she come to Warsaw with his sister Lyudmila. "Besides bread and salt, I can entertain you as you wish with music which is not all that bad. . . . If I were in Petersburg or Moscow, there is no doubt that my colleagues would have arranged a dinner or something similar in honor of my *jubilee* (i.e., my twenty-fifth anniversary as a composer), though I do not desire all these honors and don't even like them."

Second Half of October

In a letter to Shestakova, Glinka asks her to persuade their mother to come to Warsaw. "We are on friendly, very friendly terms, it seems, yet we live apart. Also consider that Mother and I are not young. Do we have much time left on this earth? I still have not been able to recover, especially after the attack which you witnessed [in Smolensk]. . . . My companion Pedrusha . . . is sometimes difficult for hours. . . . It is a fault of character and upbringing, not at all of his heart, for Pedrusha is a good, noble man who loves me very much. I am probably in Warsaw for the last winter. Living here is getting more and more noticeably expensive." He thanks his sister for her sympathetic attention to him and their mother.
[Dated by comparison with his letter to his mother on 18/30 October.]

After 19/31 October

Glinka attended a party given by the Empress, for which it was required that one shave his moustache and beard. "When I entered the hall where the guests were assembled . . . Prince Paskevich, having before that seen me in moustache and beard, bowed to me with a smirk, and I gave him a pompous bow, also smirking, but in an opposite way, after which the prince bowed to me normally, and I to him. The prince and I did not meet again after this." Mme Grünberg and her daughters were at the party. Glinka and his students sang.

20 October

In *Rus. invalid*, no. 229, there is a translation of Berlioz's article on Russian church music (from *Journal des débats*). Glinka is mentioned in this article (cf. 24 October).

24 October

In an article by "I. M." [Mann] entitled "Petersburg Chronicle" in *SPb. ved.*, no. 240, there is a quotation from Berlioz's article about the court chapel choir with a reference to Glinka: "Among Russian composers who followed . . . [Bortnyansky] in this position and who preserved the style of his performance, one must mention Mr. Glinka, whose compositions—distinctive for their originality—we heard in Paris about five years ago."

28 October/9 November

Glinka promises Barteneva to write a duet as soon as she sends the words and tells him of her sister's range. He writes that he became ill the day after their last meeting.

[Reference is to the duet *"Vy ne priidete vnov' "* [You will not return again], composed at the request of Barteneva, who gave Glinka the French words with the request that he "see to their translation" and set them to music. Dubrovsky did the translation (Shestakova, *"Moi vechera"* [My evenings]; quoted according to the manuscript in GPB, coll. 857, no. 1). Dubrovsky, however, was unable to make a Russian translation in Warsaw and sent it to Glinka in Petersburg, whence he had moved before the composer. Probably Glinka composed the music for the duet in Warsaw, i.e., in 1850, but wrote it down later.]

28 October

In *SPb. ved.*, no. 244, under "Correspondent—The Moscow Theater," it says in reference to the revival of the opera *Vadim,* that Verstovsky "established the beginning of Russian national opera, which was subsequently developed and confirmed in his compositions and those of Glinka."

1 November

Dargomyzhsky (from Petersburg) informs Kastrioto-Skanderbek that Glinka is remaining in Warsaw for the winter (coll. *Dargomyzhsky,* p. 33).

28 November

In the "Petersburg Chronicle" section of the December literary supplement to *Le Nouvelliste,* there appear these remarks: "Ever since Italian opera became firmly established in Petersburg, salon singing has become very popular. . . . Italian music is sung in great quantities, but mostly they sing Russian romances. One should congratulate the amateurs on their choice, because the works of Count M. Yu. Vielgorsky, M. I. Glinka, A. A. Alyabiev, A. S. Dargomyzhsky, M. L. Yakovlev, A. E. Varlamov, A. L. Gurilev, and others have to be preferred to the monotonous French romances. . . . We can confidently assert that the character of the Russian romance is completely distinctive from the character of music of the same type of other nations and that it stands on a high level of perfection for its melodicism, originality, and energetic liveliness." In the same issue the translation of Berlioz's article "On Ecclesiastical Music in Russia," is printed, with its reference to Glinka (cf. 20 and 24 October) (d.c.a.).

Beginning of December

A mazurka and the *Tarantella* for piano (based on *"Vo pole berezon'ka stoiala"* [In the field there stood a little birch tree], composed in 1843) are printed in *Le Nouvelliste*, no. 12.

6 December

Performance of *A Life for the Tsar* in the Bolshoi Theater in Moscow (*Mosk. ved.*, 5 December 1850).

Performance of the epilog from *A Life for the Tsar* in a mixed concert in the Aleksandrinsky Theater in St. Petersburg (*Rus. invalid*, 6 December 1850).

Performance in Odessa of Gervasi's overture on themes from *A Life for the Tsar* and folk songs (*Odessk. vestnik*, 13 December 1850).

10 December

Censor's authorization for Bernard to publish the romance *"Finskii zaliv"* with a dedication to the Empress Aleksandra Fedorovna.

12 December

On p. 76 of an essay by Arapov on the theater in "Dramatic Album with Portraits of Russian Artists and Prints from Their Manuscripts" (a publication by P. N. Arapov and August Rappolt) it says this: "M. I. Glinka occupies one of the places of honor as the composer of the opera *A Life for the Tsar*, which is distinctive from other similar compositions due to the music's rhythm. It is marvelous native poetry which penetrates directly to one's soul. He also wrote the music for the opera *Ruslan and Lyudmila*" (d.c.a.).

13 December

In *Odessk. vestnik*, no. 99, in an article signed "K. Z." and entitled "Theatrical Festival in Odessa on 6 December," Gervasi's overture on themes from *A Life for the Tsar* and folk songs is mentioned as one of the works performed.

23 December

Glinka sends Sobolevsky a humorous invitation in the guise of a menu, the last item of which runs: "Friendly conversation, provided it succeeds. N. B. Glinka is sick, but with a healthy stomach that doesn't prevent him from eating with an excellent appetite."

28 December

Announcement in the January literary supplement to *Le Nouvelliste* (for 1851) that the romance *"Finskii zaliv"* is available in Bernard's music store.

End of the 1840s–Beginning of the 1850s

Andrey Sikhra presented Stellovsky with duets, almost all of which involved treatment of themes from *A Life for the Tsar* and *Ruslan and Lyudmila,* which Sikhra had worked on "utilizing Glinka's advice and directions," but "the publisher callously declined them" (V. Rusanov, *Gitara i gitaristy. Istoricheskie ocherki* [Guitars and guitarists. Historical essays], Moscow, 1901, p. 40).

1851

3 January

In *Sev. pchela,* no. 2, "Notes, Excerpts and Correspondence," preparation is announced of a musical album "To the Memory of Varlamov," in which Glinka's romance *"Razocharovanie"* [Disenchantment] is to be included.

9 January

In *SPb. ved.,* no. 5, in a feuilleton entitled "Petersburg Chronicle" (signed "I. M." [Mann]), it says that "not long ago M. Glinka's beautiful romance '*Finskii zaliv*' was published. A pleasantly melancholy tune harmonizes with the words of the romance in this new composition by our gifted composer. Generally we like M. Glinka's music, and it gives us great satisfaction to encounter similar sentiments in other writing about music."

12 January

In the "Miscellany" section of *Bib-ka dlia chteniia,* no. 105, there is a notice about the publication of the romances *"Finskii zaliv," "Adèle," "Mary," "Dubrava shumit,"* and *"Ty skoro menia pozabudesh'"* (d.c.a.).

25 January

The first act of *A Life for the Tsar* is performed in a mixed concert (for Stepanova's benefit) in the Aleksandrinsky Theater in Petersburg (from a poster).

End of Winter

Glinka's health "began to seriously deteriorate . . . in part from smoking cigarettes . . . in part from Hungarian wine, which did serious damage to my nerves. I subsequently gave them both up completely" (*Zap.*).

12 March

Concert of classical music under the direction of Iogannis in the Bolshoi Theater in Moscow. "The classical concert was comprised of three parts . . . in the third part there were assembled several pieces of various sorts, for the selection of which one must thank Mr. Iogannis. In this, the third part, he gave us an overture by Beethoven, a march by Mendelssohn-Bartholdy, and two new works by our national composer Glinka. . . . We venture to think that there were people in the audience who came only for the third part of the concert and that the concert's success was the result of the variety of this part, due mostly to the music by our dear national composer Glinka. The section began with Beethoven's overture to 'Egmont' . . . after which followed Glinka's capriccio on the Spanish dance *Jota aragonesa*. After an original introduction, the lively and passionate sounds of this southern dance were spread before the audience, accompanied by the gay clacking of castanettes. . . . Finally the audience heard the promised *Kamarinskaya*. It cannot be said, however, that the entire audience impatiently awaited this display of Russian cheerfulness, comprehensible to any ear. . . . Many left before the beginning of *Kamarinskaya*. We do not wish to guess about the cause of such indifference, or what is worse, embarrassment over a Russian national composition. We will only say that, unfortunately, we have on occasion seen not just coldness toward Russian song, whose worth, by the way, has long ago been established and which should have no fear of such coldness, but even a certain fear that somehow they might be moved by the simplicity of this song or the artistry of its performance" (*Mosk. ved.*, 15 March 1851).

15 March

In *Mosk. ved.*, no. 32, there is a review (unsigned) entitled "Classical Concert" [12 March]. It says of the *Jota aragonesa:* "A Russian meditated on a lively and impassioned southern tune and put his heart into its sounds; their gracefulness gives him little immediate pleasure, rather he attempts to extract from them all the delights of southern gaiety." Of the *Kamarinskaya* it says: "We will not expatiate either on Glinka's piece or its performance. We only wish to say that we were pleasantly struck by the skillful use of the wedding tune '*Kak vo sade sadike*' [In the garden] with which the introduction begins. If the rumor is right that these works of Glinka's are not going to be repeated, we feel sorry for those who were unable to hear them in Mr. Iogannis's classical concert."

26 March

At a musical gathering of students and musical amateurs in Moscow, S. A. Ladyzhensky performed a romance by Glinka (*Mosk. ved.*, 24 March 1851).

30 March

In "A Letter from Moscow" (unsigned) in *SPb. ved.*, no. 72, there is a report about the performance of the *Jota aragonesa* and *Kamarinskaya* under Iogannis's direction.

31 March

In *Ved. Mosk. gor. politsii*, no. 73, there is an announcement that the romances "Adèle," "*Finskii zaliv*," and "*Ty skoro menia pozabudesh'*" are available at the "Odeum."

Beginning of April

Performance of the "Farewell Song" at the graduation ceremonies of the Smolny Institute in Petersburg. "[Ivan] Cavos, in his characteristic absentmindedness, disregarded my instructions. The chorus did not have the hoped for effect" (*Zap.*).

7 April

Ivan Cavos (from Petersburg) writes to Glinka: "This beautiful music was performed quite well by my pupils. Connoisseurs found the composition charming. The only reproach which could be made of it, dear friend, is that it is long. . . . His Majesty found that the orchestration of the piece was somewhat weak. I believe that this opinion is correct, which is why I am convinced that somewhat stronger forces would produce a bigger effect, since the voices predominate too much, though I had them sing very softly" (*L.*, p. 375; Fr. original).

In *Sev. pchela,* no. 79, "Journalistic Odds and Ends," there is a report about the publication of a "Musical Anthology in Memory of A. E. Varlamov," which includes the romance *"Razocharovanie"* ("Where are you, first desire") to words of Sergey Golitsyn.

12 April

In an article by Vladimir Stasov in *SPb. ved.,* no. 79, there is a report about a concert on 18 April for the benefit of the Optical Clinic, at which the march from "Prince Kholmsky" is to be played—"an excellent piece by M. I. Glinka, which is little known to the public," and an aria from *Ruslan and Lyudmila* (performed by Shilovskaya).

15 or 16 April

Glinka received Cavos's letter of 7 April. *"Cavos partage l'opinion de S. M.!!"* (making this remark in the manuscript of his *Zapiski,* Glinka drew a picture of an ass's head and wrote, "bravo, bravissimo.") "In the future I will be smarter and flatly turn down all commissions" (*Zap.;* ltr. to V. Engelgardt, 12/24 May 1851).

16 April

In *Sev. pchela,* no. 83, there is an article by *"C."* about the forthcoming concert for the benefit of the Optical Clinic, whose program is to include "the brilliant and splendid march from *Prince Kholmsky.* This march is stylistically close to the charming march from Beethoven's 'Egmont' and indisputably belongs among the best dramatic marches."
[The concert was postponed until 29 April, and the march from "Kholmsky" was not performed (*SPb. ved.,* 2 May 1851; ltr. from A. Serov to M. Bakunin, 31 May 1851, in EIT, 1893/94, appendix, book 3).]

Ca. 17 April

Shilovskaya performs romances by Glinka in a concert given by the violinist Afanasiev in Benardaki Hall in Petersburg (*SPb. ved.,* 17 April 1851).

17 April

In *SPb. ved.,* no. 83, there is a review of Shilovskaya's performance of romances by Glinka in Afanasiev's concert (the date of the concert is not indicated).

In *Mosk. ved.*, no. 46, there is an article by Vasily Botkin entitled "An Evening of Classical Music . . ." which also refers to the concert on 12 March directed by Iogannis: "Nowhere do science and fantasy require such an inseparable merging as in music, and the less the science is noticed by the listener, in other words, contrapuntal form, the more the composer has mastered it. Theoretical knowledge has great significance, but only when the composer is gifted with musical fantasy. Unfortunately musicians do not clearly realize this, just as they are unaware of the application of the words, 'classical music.' Why, for example, have Glinka's fantasies on the *Kamarinskaya* and the *Jota aragonesa* and Preyer's symphony been promoted recently to the rank of classical music? . . . What could be classical about these pieces of Mr. Glinka's, which are distinctive for their weak counterpoint, indeterminate form, and poverty of imagination?"

27 April

In *Ved. SPb. gor. politsii,* no. 92, "Diary of the News of Petersburg," there is a report about the upcoming concert on 29 April of classical music, including works by Glinka.

28 April

In *Rus. invalid,* no. 90, there is an announcement concerning performance of the march from the music to *Prince Kholmsky* and an aria from *Ruslan and Lyudmila* in the concert on 29 April for the benefit of the Optical Clinic.

29 April

Shilovskaya performs an aria from *Ruslan and Lyudmila* in a concert for the benefit of the Optical Clinic in Petersburg (*Rus. invalid,* 28 April 1851).

In a letter to Bakunin, Serov (from St. Petersburg) describes the 29 April concert for the benefit of the Optical Clinic and tells of the obstacles which prevented him and V. Stasov from including projected works in the program (EIT, 1893/94, appendix, book 3).
[He has in mind the march from *Prince Kholmsky*.]

1 May

In *Rus. invalid,* no. 93, in the section "Miscellany," there is a notice of a forthcoming Russian concert on 2 May.

2 May

Russian concert in the Hall of Nobility in Petersburg. The hall "was a monotonous picture of endless rows of seats, which, instead of listeners, were occupied
by huge posters. Besides Glinka's famous overture to *Ruslan and Lyudmila,* the
audience enjoyed a concerto for violin composed by Bakhmetiev" (*SPb. ved.,*
10 May 1851). "There were very few in attendance" (*Sev. pchela,* 5 May 1851).

12/24 May

In a letter to Engelgardt, Glinka complains about his health: "A liver ailment
has completely changed me—I go nowhere, I see no one. . . . If, however,
inspiration pays me another visit, I will gladly write for you whatever God
grants my heart to write."

19 May

In *Mosk. ved.,* no. 60, there is a notice entitled "Russian Concert (Sunday, 20
May)" about the upcoming performance in a charity concert of works by Russian
composers, including Glinka.

20 May

In a charity concert "for the benefit of the families of soldiers killed in the
Caucasus" in the Hall of Nobility in Moscow, S. Ryabinina performed two arias
from *A Life for the Tsar* and *Ruslan and Lyudmila,* and the orchestra under the
direction of Iogannis performed *Kamarinskaya* (*Mosk. ved.,* 19 May 1851).

31 May

Evgenia Andreevna Glinka died in Novospasskoe (date on the tombstone).

In *SPb. ved.,* no. 119, there is an article (signed "Correspondent") entitled
"Overview of the Activities of the Moscow Theaters during the 1850/51 Season," in which it is reported that *A Life for the Tsar* was performed twice during
the course of the season.

Beginning of June

Glinka learned of the death of his mother. "The news disturbed me, but I did
not cry. The next day . . . I felt a weakness . . . in the thumb and forefinger of
my right hand . . . and after a few minutes my right hand became so weak that

I could not control it." The doctor consoled Glinka by telling him that it was "a temporary nervous disorder, and his words later proved to be true."

June

For the first time, Glinka "could not write and could sign [my] name only with the greatest difficulty" (*Zap.*). To Shestakova's request that he come to Novospasskoe "to deal with the estate," he "pointedly refused: [He] could not write [himself], but had Don Pedro write . . . that he felt very bad and without Mother would never again come to Novospasskoe" (Shestakova, *Vosp.*, p. 42). Glinka "gave power of attorney" for the administration of the estate to his sister Shestakova and her husband (*Zap.*).

1 July

In *Moskvityanin,* book 1, part 4, no. 13, "Criticism and Bibliography," there is this observation: "Certain gentlemen, who are completely uneducated in the arts, often allow themselves extremely harsh verdicts of artists and composers who have stature in the arts. . . . Not long ago we read such a judgment in an article which had been placed in the *Moskovskie vedomosti*. The article concerned Glinka's *Kamarinskaya* and was very censorious toward the composer" (d.c.a.).
[The reference is to Botkin's article, which was published on 17 April 1851.]

18 July

Mixed performance for the benefit of Artemovsky in the Aleksandrinsky Theater in Petersburg, which, in the first performance in the revival of the opera *Ivan Susanin* by Cavos, included a scene from the second act of *Ruslan and Lyudmila* and "Ukrainian Wedding" (*SPb. ved.,* 18 July 1851).

Before 21 July/2 August

Glinka sent the score of the "Farewell Song" to Engelgardt.

Glinka received "warm greetings from Meyerbeer, with the request to acquaint him" with his operas.

Glinka was still "very sick. [My] right hand still will not obey. I somehow still play the piano, but I write with such difficulty that I must dictate my letters."

21 July/2 August

Glinka writes to Engelgardt: "In the course of this year I will see to it, so as to bring your music library up to strength, that you are sent all my unknown pieces, completed and uncompleted, and studies from the country. I must ask you that when you see Dargomyzhsky (to whom I give my warmest regards), find out from him about the green notebook, where there are three fugues which I composed for piano and a sort of cantata, which I wrote at the beginning of 1826 on the death of the Emperor Alexander I and the accession to the throne of Nikolay Pavlovich." He asks that he temporarily "provide" Meyerbeer with *A Life for the Tsar,* translated into German. He intends to send Meyerbeer *Kamarinskaya* himself, but he does not have the scores of the operas with him.

23 July

A scene from the second act of *Ruslan and Lyudmila* is performed in a mixed concert in the Aleksandrinsky Theater in Petersburg (*SPb. ved.,* 22 July 1851).

26 July

Performance of *Kamarinskaya* under the direction of Schindler at the dacha "Aleksandria" in Petersburg (*SPb. ved.,* 26 July 1851).

20–29 July

Shestakova went to Warsaw. "Her attentiveness consoled me. My spirits were somewhat lifted. We dealt with our affairs, so far as it was possible" (*Zap.*).

8 August

In *Sovremennik,* vol. 28, no. 8, there is an announcement stating that Glinka's romances *"Finskii zaliv," "Dubrava shumit,"* and *"Ty skoro menia pozabudesh'"* are on sale at Bernard's.

Petrov, Bulakhov, and Stepanova perform the trio from *A Life for the Tsar* in the Krasnoselsky Military Theater (*Moskvityanin,* 1851, part 5, no. 18, book 2).

Mid-August

Shestakova's departure. "On my sister's departure . . . I reworked the potpourri of Spanish melodies called *Recuerdos de Castilla,* developed the piece, and called it Second Spanish Overture. Writing the music cost me less effort than writing my name."

Glinka "began to work on getting a foreign passport and sent a doctor's certificate to St. Petersburg with his application" (*Zap.*).

22 August

Performance of *A Life for the Tsar* in the Aleksandrinsky Theater in Petersburg (*SPb. ved.*, 22 August 1851).

1 September (?)

A transcription by Theodor Kullak of Glinka's romance *"Ia pomniu chudnoe mgnoven'e"* is printed in *Le Nouvelliste*, no. 9.

2 September

Performance of *A Life for the Tsar* in the Aleksandrinsky Theater in Petersburg (*SPb. ved.*, 2 September 1851).

4 September

In *Bib-ka dlia chteniia*, no. 108, under the section "Miscellany," it reports that the ninth issue of the journal *Le Nouvelliste* contains Kullak's transcription of *"Ia pomniu chudnoe mgnoven'e"* (d.c.a.).

Beginning of September

"Since I did not get permission for a passport and saw from my sister Lyudmila's letters that the papers we had drawn up after carefully thought-out plans would have to be redone, I decided to go to Petersburg myself" (*Zap.*).

13 September

In *Moskvityanin*, part 5, no. 18, book 2, there is a notice by P. Netanov about the performance of the trio from *A Life for the Tsar* in the Krasnoselsky Military Theater on 8 August (d.c.a.).

Second Half of September

Glinka, Don Pedro, their cook Vasily, and Daniel Rozenberg leave for Petersburg by post-chaise (*Zap.*).

24 September

Petersburg. Arrival from Warsaw. Stayed in the Hotel Volkov on Bolshaya Konyushennaya.

24 or 25 September

Glinka met with Dargomyzhsky, who "talked a lot" about Serov's opera *Maiskaia noch'* [May night].

25 September

At the Bilibinas' Serov learned from Dargomyzhsky about Glinka's arrival (ltr. from A. Serov to V. Stasov, 3 October 1851, in *MN* III, p. 93).

25 or 26 September

Glinka sends his address to Sobolevsky: Bolshaya Konyushennaya, Hotel Volkov, No. 24.

26 September

Serov "in the morning . . . hurried to Bolshaya Konyushennaya . . . and found him at home (he went out *very little,* because he was not well—his right hand was nearly paralyzed). He embraced and kissed me: 'I'm very glad that you're here, dear sir, and not in the Crimea. It is quite opportune. I congratulate you on your success in our matter. . . . Is it on Gogol's *"Utoplennitsa"* [The drowned woman]? I remember the story well. The plot is incomparable, and I sincerely wish you everything necessary for its performance!' Then he continued to speak of this and that, musical and not musical. . . . Glinka asked about *you,* where you are now, and was *a little bit* surprised that you are in Florence. He asked me to *immediately* send you his regards and ask his apologies for not writing, since now, if he takes up the pen, it's to write *music* rather than letters. (I feel it would be very pleasant for him if *you* would write him from Florence, for he *likes* such attention. For example, he *obviously* liked it that I was one of the *first* to visit him after his arrival). What pleases me extremely is Glinka's keen *enthusiasm* for everything excellent in art. It's like he *gets younger* and acquires a *glow of health* in this respect (in part because in Warsaw he hardly heard any good music at all, and the craving in *such* a person for *good things* has to be strong). Besides this, he talked with me a lot about purely technical matters (for example, what he heard in my orchestration of his 'Prayer.' It turned out all right, but it was *dead,* since the piece was not *composed* for orchestra. In general he said one *should not* rewrite for orchestra things written for piano, that they're *only* good as studies). He said to me that he *would like* to have an influence on Petersburg concerts (those of Lvov and the Philharmonic). 'Do you remember, sir, the chorus from Gluck's *Armide,* how "the birds speak with their singing of love . . ." Lvov could give us that, and for the Philharmonic I would order the Eighth or Fourth Symphony of Beethoven. Both are *marvelous*! Then, sir, I would ask you, if you could, to bring me some scores in a few days, first Méhul's *Joseph* and then Mozart's *Tito*. We'll *read through* these scores, and I'll show you some things in them. I simply adore *Joseph*—*j'ai un culte pour cette musique-là.*'"

27 September

"I [Serov] brought *Joseph* to him. . . . I found him at dinner (he dined in a tavern at 2 o'clock), but he was so curious to look at this score, which he had not seen for so long, that he could hardly eat. He jumped up from the table and began to scrutinize every line (the overture, romance, Simeon's aria). We were soon disturbed, however, and he kept the score with him and *assured* me, that if I came back (I already visited his apartment often), 'I will get myself a piano so we can play the score four-hands, and I will show you something which I dashed off in Warsaw.' He had reworked as a *complete* overture the fantasy on Spanish themes (which you heard along with the *Jota* and *Kamarinskaya*), with a new head and tail—*pas trop méchant*—you will like the crescendo at the end."

1 October

Glinka moved to Mokhovaya Street, house of Melikhov (ltr. from A. Serov to V. Stasov, 3 October 1851, in *MN* III, p. 93; *Zap.*.).
[Dated 1 October, since apartments were usually taken on the first of the month. Moreover, on the third of October, Serov writes that Glinka is "now in his own apartment on Mokhovaya."]

3 October

Serov writes to V. Stasov: "I hasten to convey an entertaining bit of news to you and *personal* regards from M. I. Glinka." He tells about the proposed concerts, which in part are connected with Glinka's arrival: "He still has not personally heard his *Kamarinskaya* with orchestra, which means that it will *certainly* be performed here, and not just once. The same for the *Jota*. Glinka has asked [Konstantin] Lyadov to do *Joseph* one of these days and also [*Les deux journées*]. . . . Lyadov will be giving the third, "Pastorale," and ninth [symphonies of Beethoven]. Engelgardt is also arranging some quartet performances *for Glinka,* where they will do primarily Haydn quartets." He writes that he is not showing Glinka his opera *May Night,* "even though Glinka himself has time to take an interest in my opera. He is too proud to ask me directly to show him something already finished, though I have often noticed that he *wants* to (for example, he asks to have the libretto read to him—he sends Engelgardt to me). I am going to wait, however, until he asks *himself.*" He writes that he is going to Glinka again to show him "a *curious* thing which will certainly interest him, the '*Marche marocaine*' by Meier-Berlioz. . . . Berlioz's arrangements of piano works might help to refute Glinka's idea that this *won't work,* though one must acknowledge that everything here depends upon the *particularities* of Berlioz's effects and gimmicks . . . but Glinka admires him." He tells of his acquaintance with Lenz, who has an excellent musical memory: "He might vie with Glinka so far as memory goes (*un memoire atroce,* as Mikhail Ivanovich himself puts it)" (*MN* III, p. 93).

4 October

In *Sovremennik,* vol. 29, no. 10, in "Contemporary Notes," there is an unsigned article [by Serov] called "Notes on the Theaters of St. Petersburg," which is about Cavos's opera *Ivan Susanin,* performed for Artemovsky's benefit in the Aleksandrinsky Theater. "*Ivan Susanin* (on a libretto by Prince Shakhovskoy) . . . has the same subject as M. I. Glinka's opera *A Life for the Tsar,* with the difference that 'at that time' (the second decade of our century) it was considered an essential condition of opera that the dénouement without fail be happy (!). In Cavos's opera, contrary to history, Susanin does not die. . . . The identity of subject and even the identity of the leading singer (Petrov sings the role of Ivan Susanin in both *A Life for the Tsar* and in Cavos's opera) have involuntarily caused audiences to continually compare the two operas. . . . Comparison of this opera with M. I. Glinka's opera . . . is not entirely appropriate. Similar things are being compared, but in this case on the one hand there is a large, four-act opera with recitatives and dances, and in the other instance something like a popular vaudeville, with no pretense of breadth of lyrical forms, and the singing and orchestra are given just as much space as would be given to them in the small German popular pieces known by the designation of *Singspiel*" (d.c.a.).

Beginning of October

Glinka is taken ill. Heydenreich's treatment was ineffective, and he turned to homeopathy, which helped him.

Glinka visited Engelgardt, who "ingratiated himself with music, and soon we began to play duets" (*Zap.*).

13 October

In *Sev. pchela,* no. 228, there is an announcement that the romances *"Slyshu li golos tvoi"* and *"Kogda v chas veselyi"* are available in Stellovsky's store.

Mid-October

Glinka dictated to Engelgardt a note to Odoevsky: "M. I. Glinka, who sends Count V. F. Odoevsky his humblest regards, forwards his new composition herewith and humbly requests that His Honor look it over, and if there be in it any unevenness, that is to say, deficiency, that he make note of it with a black or red pencil, at his discretion. Glinka is living on Mokhovaya, in the house of Melikhova, facing the courtyard."

Shestakova arrived and moved in with Viktor Fleury (*Zap.*).

21 October

Glinka received the score of *Médée* from Odoevsky and a letter (21 October) in which Odoevsky thanks him for his "Spanish jest." "What can I say to you about it? It's beautiful, like everything that comes from your lazy pen, for you have become wretchedly lazy! It really is a sin! Because of this you produce wonderful little dwarfs, the tiny head, the torso—a miracle, but the legs are unsteady! In all there are 480 bars to your Spanish mistress, which is far, far too little. . . . The audience will barely have begun to listen, and it will all be over! Realize that they want to hear you, that they are ready to listen for a long time, and that audiences have to be fed something already digested. . . . For God's sake, be a little more lengthy. I look upon your Spanish mistress as the first movement . . . and I am waiting for the second . . . why not write a *Spanish Symphony,* where, for example, the '*Jota aragonesa*' (is this what it is called?) might occupy the place of an intermezzo, if you have not already wished to expand it?" (*Rus. arkhiv,* 1890, part 2, p. 317).

[In the known edition of *Night in Madrid* (the Second Spanish Overture) there are 458 bars, and not 480. One must assume that either Odoevsky determined the number "by sight" (and erred by 22 bars), or that there was an earlier edition, unknown to us, which Glinka not only did not expand but shortened.]

23 October

On the title page of a copy of the score there is an inscription by Glinka: "Scherzo on the theme of the Russian dance tune *Kamarinskaya*. 1851, 23 October. Printing rights I turn over to Fedor Timofeevich Stellovsky in perpetuity as his own hereditary property. Mikhail Glinka" (GTsMMK, coll. 49).

Serov writes to V. Stasov: "Today I am going to see Glinka. It has been more than a week since I have seen him" (*MN* III, p. 98).

25 October

Glinka wrote his last will and testament.

27 October

Glinka's signed and legally registered will leaves all property, personal and real, to Shestakova, "as a token of true . . . brotherly favor toward her for her . . . love and kindred friendship."

29 October

As a keepsake Glinka gave Odoevsky's letter (of 21 October 1851) to Dubrovsky and wrote this dedicatory inscription: "To my good and dear partner in life in token of good will and memory, Mikhail Glinka, 29 October 1851. St. Petersburg" (*Rus. arkhiv,* 1890, part 2, p. 317).

30 October

Glinka writes to Odoevsky that because of his worsening health he is unable to visit him.

Autograph of Glinka's, dated 30 October in the collection of Nikolay Rubinstein (Facsimile publication of autographs of musicians, performers, and composers in the collection of N. Rubinstein, without place and year of publication, GTsMMK).

October

Serov and Engelgardt, under Glinka's guidance, transcribe the *Jota aragonesa* and *Night in Madrid* for two pianos, eight-hands (ltr. from L. Shestakova to P. Jurgenson, 8 April 1887, in *L.,* p. 383; ltr. from A. Serov to V. Stasov, 6 November 1851, in *MN* III, p. 102).

2 November

"A musical group gathered at Glinka's (where I almost always go once a week). (Engelgardt wanted to treat Glinka to his *Jota,* which Engelgardt had arranged for two pianos, four hands each.) There was Engelgardt's relative Ryndina, there was the director of the Russian Opera and my current friend K. Lyadov, there was the violist (and generally fine musician, a German) Meier, as well as I and Dmitry (whom Engelgardt had long ago invited to Glinka's). . . . Besides the *Jota* (which initially did not go very well, although that very morning we had *played well* together for this lady at Meltsel's), we played 'Coriolan,' and two *excellent* overtures by Cherubini, to *Faniska* (F major) and *Lodoiska* (D major). Lyadov brought his 'Melusine' with him (all for eight hands), and we played it to *everyone's* general dissatisfaction. To *everyone* it seemed like what it in fact is, sour and long-winded in the extreme. Glinka described Mendelssohn's music as '*un calmant contre la musique*'" (ltr. from A. Serov to V. Stasov, 6/28 November 1851, in *MN* III, p. 102).
[Musical gatherings occurred at Glinka's on Fridays. (The Friday before Serov's letter was 2 November.)]

Engelgardt introduced Dmitry Stasov, "a very well-educated young man and fine musician," to Glinka at this party (*Zap.*).

5 November

In *Panteon i repertuar russkoi stseny,* vol. 5, part 10, in the "Theatrical Chronicle," it says this of Artemovsky's benefit: "Nowhere else does Mr. Artemovsky's beautiful talent display itself so clearly as in the opera *Ruslan and Lyudmila.* On this occasion he performed his outstanding aria from the second act of the opera, 'O field, who has sown you with these dead bones?' etc. Mr. Artemovsky is able to give this aria a particular coloration. His every word embodies thought-out feeling and remarkable clarity of sound" (d.c.a.).

7 November

Glinka invites Maria Krzhisevich to visit him: "My *kukona* and patroness, my sister Lyudmila, is visiting me. We will be home tomorrow. . . . Our friendly gatherings usually begin at six o'clock in the afternoon; there will hardly be any guests."

Serov writes to Vladimir Stasov that every week he is a guest of Stasov's relatives in their box at the Italian Opera and rarely receives his "portion of satisfaction" (quoting Glinka) (*MN* III, p. 104).

8 November

Glinka asks Engelgardt to send the tuner for their planned musical gathering "tomorrow."

9 November

Musical "Friday" at Glinka's (ltr. to V. Engelgardt, 8 November 1851).

17 November

At a party arranged for Shestakova's birthday, she announced to Glinka that she would spend the entire winter with him and that an apartment for them was already rented. "This friendly concern from my sister touched me to the depths of my heart."

20 November

Performance of *A Life for the Tsar* in the Aleksandrinsky Theater (*SPb. ved.*, 20 November 1851).

21 November

In a letter to Mikhail Vielgorsky, Glinka petitioned for the appointment of an acquaintance of his at the Aleksandrovsky Orphans' Institute. Her parents "have treated me as their own son . . . since 1824."
[It has not been established for whom Glinka petitioned. In any case it was not Ekaterina Kern, as suggested by the first publishers of the letter (G 2-A, p. 317), since Glinka met her mother, Anna Kern, in 1826 (she was about his same age), and he did not know Ekaterina Kern's father personally. Moreover, she was the god-daughter of Alexander I and the daughter of a decorated general, and with such connections had no need of Glinka's assistance.]

22 November

Glinka returned to Serov the 29 volumes of the *Naturalists Library* he had borrowed from him and said that "Friday's musical academy must be postponed for an indefinite time." He asks Serov to tell him if he has available "perhaps one evening between Sunday and Thursday."
[The letter is written in Shestakova's handwriting and was dictated by Glinka.]

24 November

Composer's dating on the manuscript of the romance *"Ne iskushai menia bez nuzhdy"*: "St. Petersburg, 24 November 1851, corrected and transcribed by the composer for dear M. S."
["M. S." is Maria Krzhisevich.]

29 November

In *Rus. khudozh. listok* [Russian art leaflet], no. 35, Vasilko-Petrov writes in an article entitled "Petersburg Theaters for the Year 1851": "There is also noticeable in Russian opera a striving toward independence, and what is surprising is that this is connected to the Italian Opera. Since the time when a regular Italian troupe was established in Petersburg with European celebrities, Russian singers understood that they could not withstand the rivalry, and they began to withdraw from contact with it. That is to say, they limited their own repertoire to a small number of operas, primarily by Russian composers. But the contemporary repertoire of Russian opera is poor: two or three operas by Glinka, two or three operas by Verstovsky, and no more. It should therefore come as no surprise that the performances of the Russian Opera troupe occurred quite seldom" (d.c.a.).

Fall

Darya Leonova, on the advice of her teacher Vitelyaro, visited Glinka and performed *"Akh, ne mne bednomu"* for him. "Alas, he did not like my singing. He found it so bad that he said to me: 'The only singers who sing with such a tremolo are those who are ending [their careers], not those who are just beginning.' He explained to me why this was so bad . . . and gave me some direction on how to rid myself of it" (Leonova, *Vosp.*, p. 268).

1 December

Glinka and Shestakova moved to Zhukov's house on the corner of Nevsky Prospect and Vladimirskaya Street (today, number 49/2).

Serov writes to V. Stasov that "for several Fridays now in succession . . . Glinka has held his gatherings (now they will not be on Friday but on some other day)." He talks about his work on the opera *May Night* and mentions that "melodically, both in the voice parts and orchestra, I now am very positively indebted to the operas of Rossini . . . and negatively to Dargomyzhsky's opera [*Esmeralda*]." Of the latter he says that "the opera is trash, but it was a surprise to me that it is so bad. I did not think that he would give us good music, but I did expect *polished workmanship,* the same as we admire in Glinka" (*MN* III, p. 108).

4 December

Glinka asks Barteneva to help find a position for his nephew. He invites her to visit at any time except Tuesdays and Fridays, which are reserved for family affairs.
[It has not been determined which nephew Glinka is referring to.]

Beginning of December

"We rented two pianos from Meltsel, after which Engelgardt had his own piano brought to us. We began playing things for eight hands, and then for twelve."

Dubrovsky, who had been transferred from Warsaw as a professor of Polish language at the Pedagogical Institute prior to Glinka's arrival, introduced Glinka to De Santis, "a wonderful pianist and very nice man" (*Zap.*).

3–7 December

Serov spent this time at his sister's in Lisino and told her "besides all the theatrical and musical news, everything about Glinka that might interest Sonechka."

7 December

Glinka held his usual musical gathering on "Friday, which was his day" (ltr. from A. Serov to V. Stasov, 12 December 1851, in *MN* III, p. 114).
[Since he had just returned from Lisino, Serov was not at this gathering, even though he had received an invitation.]

12 December

Serov writes to V. Stasov: "Glinka is not well. He is not drinking, and consequently he never sings for anyone!! He likes very much to listen; we are not the better for it" (*MN* III, p. 114).

28 December

Glinka invites Bilibina to see him. "You may feel comfortable, for I live with my sister . . . and she sincerely wishes to make your acquaintance."

December

Glinka rewrote and edited anew his Sonata in D Minor for Viola and Piano (composed in 1825).
[Two movements of the Sonata were published under the editorship of V. Borisovsky in 1932.]

1851/1852

Winter

In order to play 12-hands, Engelgardt provided the necessary musicians and industriously arranged things for 12-hands, primarily from my operas. In general I was living pleasantly, though my health got worse and worse."

1852

1 January

In *Moskvityanin*, vol. I, no. 2, part 2, under the section "Miscellany," there is a reference to Glinka in an article by "N. Z." [Zakharov] entitled "A few words about music and the method of musical study in Russia": "The year 1836, which gave Russia *A Life for the Tsar* . . . established an epoch in our national music. *A Life for the Tsar* triumphantly demonstrated and proved what might be expected from national music and what our national opera in essence should be. *A Life for the Tsar* is a pure, natural, and powerful reproduction of original Russian melodies. . . . Even though Verstovsky and Alyabiev appeared with their works earlier than Glinka, this has not prevented the composer of *A Life for the Tsar* from being the Columbus of Russian music, who pioneered a completely new path without imitating anyone and created the model for Russian opera. For himself he acquired the enviable status of being an example to others" (d.c.a.).

10 January

The fourth act of *A Life for the Tsar* is presented in a mixed performance "for the benefit of the director of the opera troupe, Mr. Sokolov" in the Aleksandrinsky Theater (*Sev. pchela,* 10 January 1852).

10/22 January

Vladimir Stasov (from Florence) writes to Dmitry Stasov: "Aleksandr Nikolaevich [Serov] tried to persuade me to write Glinka, but I was angry with him, because he didn't answer me from Warsaw when I had written him cordially, wanting and hoping to do something nice for him. . . . For some reason or another I don't believe I'm interesting to him—so he speaks about me in conversation—otherwise he'd have taken up with me long before this. Therefore, thank him, etc., and tell him fifty times that I was glad and appreciative of his consideration (but not of anything else) and for his courtesy, and that's all. . . . Such as him are not what I need right now. I need the whole man, not just that he take me up and remember me some other time" (SPR I, part I, p. 117).

19 January

In *Panteon,* vol. 1, part 1, in an article about Dargomyzhsky's *Esmeralda,* Yury Arnold provides an appraisal of all Russian composers writing for the theater: "Without question, M. I. Glinka is superior to all our maestros, as much for the originality of his music as for his musical knowledge. Glinka has thoroughly, and principally, studied the human voice . . . although even he, as if attracted by the pernicious efforts of contemporary composers, often requires unnecessary exertion from his singers. His orchestration, which is full of brilliance and vitality and is always deeply thought-out, is consistent with musical laws and is distinctive for its charm and taste. Although Glinka is a fine contrapuntist, his bass parts are sometimes awkward, which is why his most beautiful musical ideas sometimes lose their energy of expression. In Glinka's last work, *Ruslan and Lyudmila,* the lyricism in particular proves everything I have said, though with respect to drama, one must favor his first opera, *A Life for the Tsar.* Here one still encounters dramatic truth, whereas it is entirely lacking in *Ruslan and Lyudmila.* This opera is not a musical drama, but a disconnected series of beautiful lyrical fantasies, or rather, a dramatic concert. One can admire each number sung separately, but one cannot help being bored hearing the *entire* opera on the stage. Even the clever instrumentation, worked out to a fault, does not always match the dramatic action on the stage and goes unnoticed in the general mass. Likewise in this opera Glinka betrayed his customary and characteristic natural singing. However, as a purely lyrical composer, there can be no doubt that Glinka is one of the finest in the world. The trio of the first act, Susanin's aria before he dies, and the final trio in the epilog of the opera *A Life for the Tsar* definitely will immortalize his name" (d.c.a.).

21 January

Glinka became seriously ill (*Zap.*).

23 January

Performance of the *Tarantella* in a mixed concert for the benefit of Samoylova II in the Aleksandrinsky Theater (*SPb. ved.*, 23 January 1852).

26 January

Performance of the *Tarantella* in a mixed performance in the Aleksandrinsky Theater (*SPb. ved.*, 26 January 1852).

21–28 January

"Heydenreich, who was called in to assist Jal [a homeopath] . . . saved me within a week" (*Zap.*).

Beginning (?) of February

Shestakova invited Karl Shubert to visit and asked him to organize a concert of the Philharmonic Society and include performances of *Kamarinskaya* and *Night in Madrid* (Shestakova, *Vosp.*, p. 49).

On Lvov's request, Glinka "undertook the preparation of the singers (the men) for a performance of Pergolesi's *Stabat Mater* arranged by Lvov (*Zap.*).

5 February

Glinka presented to the SPb. Philharmonic Society a manuscript score of *Night in Madrid* with the inscription: *"Ouverture Espagnol No. 2. Souvenir de Castilla (Recuerdos de Castilla) sur des thèmes de l'Espagne centrale dediée à la Société Philarmonique de St.-Pétersbourg par M. Glinka, le 5 février 1852"* (E. Albrecht, *Obshchii obzor deiatel'nosti SPb. filarmonicheskogo obshchestva* [General overview of the activity of the SPb. Philharmonic Society], SPb., 1884, p. 16).

[The manuscript has not been discovered. *Night in Madrid* exists only in authorized copies.]

11 February

Glinka writes in a joking note to Shestakova, "Misha to Lyudmila, the music still won't work."

15 February

Glinka congratulates Engelgardt on the birth of a baby, sending from Shestakova things for the baby's layette, and from himself, various good wishes, which end as follows: "I do not believe in happiness, but may the great Allah protect my *namesake* from *misfortune* in his life. I will pass over music, for on the basis of experience *I am unable* to regard it as a guide to happiness."

[When the letter was first published (*RMG*, 1894, no. 1), N. Findeyzen indicated that it was addressed to one of Glinka's friends. When it was next published in a collection of Glinka's letters (1907), Findeyzen named Vasily Engelgardt. In G 2-A, Findeyzen's assertion is refuted on the basis that Engelgardt was not married at the time and that the very tone of the letter departs from the usual style of Glinka's letters to Engelgardt. However, the very familiar and joking tone, possibly to hide a decidedly awkard situation, is entirely characteristic of Glinka. The reference is apparently to a child of Engelgardt's born out of wedlock, which is also why the child's mother is facetiously referred to as the general's wife. Glinka would have hardly congratulated any known general in such a tone. The gifts of a blanket and other things for the newborn also put in doubt the fact that the addressee was a general whom he knew. It is likewise important to point out that Engelgardt himself, who was extremely sensitive to the slightest inaccuracy about himself in publications concerning Glinka (in part, those of Findeyzen), did not refute the claim that the letter was addressed to him. (In 1894, Findeyzen, and certainly Engelgardt himself, might have considered it awkward for certain reasons to indicate the name of the addressee, but subsequently the awkwardness faded).]

Glinka held his regular "Friday" gathering.

16 February

In a letter to Dmitry Stasov, Glinka gives advice on how to arrange arias from Gluck's operas *Armide* and *Iphigénie en Tauride*. He invites him to visit instead of attending a concert, so as not to condemn himself "to all those awful torments, which ... charlatans and even (excuse me) soloists prepare so cunningly."

18 February

In *Sev. pchela,* no. 38, in an article by Rostislav [Feofil Tolstoy] entitled "*Sardanapale:* Opera in Five Acts, Music by Allari," there is also a short characterization of *A Life for the Tsar.*

19 February

In *Panteon,* vol. 1, part 2, in the section "Theatrical Chronicle," there is an article by Fedor Koni entitled "The Russian Theater in Petersburg," which mentions the performance of the *Tarantella* in the Aleksandrinsky Theater. In the same issue there is a notice entitled "New Music at Mr. Bernard's," which refers to Kullak's piece for piano, *"Illustrations russes* No. 2, *'Ia pomniu chudnoe mgnoven'e,'* Romance de Glinka transcrite" (d.c.a.).

24 February

Dargomyzhsky writes to Kastrioto-Skanderbek: "Glinka is spending the winter in Petersburg. At the beginning of the season he was quite healthy and in wonderfully high spirits, but he ended it badly. His health has deteriorated more than ever, and his frame of mind, as you know, is always connected to his health. Music occupies him very little. He likes to listen to Gluck and Cherubini, but other composers interest him very little. I like him as before, but so far as art is concerned, I no longer find him to be the artist and master of expression and feeling which made him such a splendid adviser before. This is a pity, because with his outstanding talent, when his own artistic career is over, he could still be beneficial as a critic. Meanwhile, one must attribute his strangeness (*bizarrerie*) and in particular the capriciousness of his opinions to his physical deterioration" (coll. *Dargomyzhsky,* p. 34).

28 February

Glinka invites Heydenreich to a musical "Friday," "tomorrow evening . . . classical arias of Gluck, Cherubini, and others . . . will be performed. We'll have *pipes*—two oboes and a bassoon, and a quartet will replace the piano. As you can see, the thing is a little strange. . . . Do not say a word to anyone. Otherwise there will be a crowd, and in such cases an extra person is worse than a Tatar." He complains about his health.

In *Ved. Mosk. gor. politsii,* no. 48, in a feuilleton called "The Moscow Theater," there is reference to *A Life for the Tsar* performed in September 1842.

29 February

Glinka had "a large musical evening. Arias by Gluck in particular were performed. . . . At that time Gluck made an even greater impression on me" (*Zap.*).
[In the *Zapiski* the evening is mistakenly dated 28 February.]

29 February/12 March

Vladimir Stasov (from Florence) writes to Dmitry Stasov: "Glinka turned out to be not at all like he had appeared to be—quite cool to anything that didn't concern himself, in fact, to anything at all, even in art" (*L.*, p. 387).

4 March

In *Moskvityanin,* vol. 2, no. 6, in an article entitled "Some Words on Singing in Russia," "N. Z." [Zakharov] expresses regret that Russian composers (among them Glinka) do not write articles about music, especially since they would be the best judges of musical questions (d.c.a.).

13 March

Songs and romances by Glinka are performed in a concert by the Malchugin brothers (*Sev. pchela,* 12 March 1852).

14 March

Composer's dating on the manuscript of a polka: "Completed on 14 March 52. SPb., in the house of Zhukov on Nevsky, in the apartment of lieutenant Liud. Iv. Shestakova, in a closet assigned in the above-named apartment for M. I. Glinka."
[Glinka wrote this polka "because of [my] sister's wishes" and had played it since 1840 as a duet. In print "it was called" *"Pervonachal'naia pol'ka"* [Primary polka] (*Zap.*).]

19 March

Composer's dating on the manuscript of an excerpt from Lyudmila's scene (Act IV of *Ruslan and Lyudmila*): "Mikhail Glinka. S.P.burg, 19 March '52" (ITMK, coll. 6).

21 March

Gorbunova performs an aria by Glinka in a concert given by the Dulken sisters in the Maly Theater in Moscow (*Ved. Mosk. gor. politsii,* 21 March 1852).

22 March

Composer's dating on a manuscript excerpt of the Head's scene (from the second act of *Ruslan and Lyudmila*): "S.P.burg 22 March '52."

24 March

On behalf of Memel, Glinka asks Dmitry Stasov to persuade Vera Bunina to participate in a Philharmonic Concert with any piece "from the latest school of Italian compositions."

[The letter, which is undated, is written in Shestakova's hand and is only signed by Glinka. On the envelope there is a postmark with an effaced first number of a two-digit number, but on the inside of the envelope the impression of the number two is visible. In G 2-A, it is incorrectly dated 4 March.]

March

Glinka, Engelgardt, and Heydenreich visit the orangerie on Apothecary Island (the Botanical Garden), which he liked more than the Botanical Garden in Paris (*Zap.*).

March–April

"During the spring, [Karl] Shubert visited us twice and played quartets."

1 April

Glinka was present at a rehearsal for a concert of the Philharmonic Society. The orchestra players gave him an ovation, regarding which he said to his sister: "You must understand that the opinion of performers of my music is dearer to me than the opinions and ovations of the entire world" (Shestakova, *Vosp.*, p. 49). At this rehearsal, Glinka met Feofil Tolstoy, who said that he had explained to the Empress "the meaning of the pedal point on F-sharp and C in the conclusion [of *Kamarinskaya*]. Our outstanding (!) critic, in his profound (!) and imaginative opinion was unable to find anything better or more intelligent to say than that some drunk was knocking at the door" (*Zap.*).

[In the manuscript of the *Zapiski,* together with this phrase, Glinka has drawn a cat with long whiskers and tail as well as the contour of a face with a long nose and whiskers.]

2 April

Glinka attends the second jubilee concert of the SPb. Philharmonic Society in the Hall of Nobility. Works of Glinka's which were performed included two romances (Shilovskaya), *Kamarinskaya, Night in Madrid,* and an aria from *Ruslan and Lyudmila* (Shilovskaya). The conductor was Karl Shubert (E. Albrecht, *Obshchii obzor deiatel'nosti SPb. filarmonicheskogo obshchestva*, SPb., 1884, p 16; ltr. to K. Shubert, 4 April 1852). Glinka sat in the gallery behind columns, but he was seen. "The composer was given a brilliant reception by the audience. This little triumph together with the satisfaction which his instrumental works gave him—which he heard here for the first time—so excited him that he became completely pale and tears flickered in his eyes" (V. Stasov, *Izbr. soch.*, vol. I, p. 505).

[Vladimir Stasov was himself at this time in Italy. He could have learned about the Philharmonic Society's concert and Glinka's reaction only later from his brother Dmitry, Engelgardt, or Shestakova.]

4 April

Glinka thanks Karl Shubert for his efforts in arranging the Philharmonic concert: "My compositions were performed perfectly, surpassing anything which I could have imagined, knowing what an outstanding conductor you are and relying on the justly deserved reputation of our musicians. Nor will I hide the fact that in my opinion you and Berlioz are the best conductors I know, and in truth I am obliged to you both for the greatest musical pleasures." He asks that his gratitude be conveyed to the orchestra members (Fr. original).

5 April

In *Sev. pchela,* no. 75, in the section "Journalistic Odds and Ends," there is a notice by Bulgarin about the concert on 2 April in the Hall of Nobility.

10 April

In *Zakavkazskii vestnik* [Transcaucasian Herald], no. 15, in an article signed "I. Evl.," entitled "Adventures in the Gallery of the Tiflis Theater," the performance of an aria from *A Life for the Tsar* is mentioned.

13 April

Glinka informs V. Stasov of his imminent departure abroad. "Despite illness, I did not spend the winter here all that badly, and your dear brother was of no little assistance in that." It suggests meetings "on the banks of the Guadalquivir."

14 April

Glinka visited Dmitry Stasov and left with him a letter for Vladimir Stasov (footnote of D. Stasov, 14 April 1852, on Glinka's ltr. to V. Stasov of 13 April 1852).

Between the Second Half of March and the First Half of April

Glinka asks Odoevsky (?) about the publication of the Polka before he and Shestakova depart from Petersburg.

[Reference is to the polka composed on 14 March and published by K. Golts under the title "Primary Polka" for the benefit of the Society for Visitation to the Poor. Odoevsky was president of the society. Nestor Zagorny determined the addressee and date of the letter on this basis. Still the tone of the letter (employing the polite "you" and a somewhat elevated style) was not used by Glinka in his letters to Odoevsky and prevents one from making a conclusive identification of the addressee. However, it is possible that Glinka did not just have in mind Odoevsky but also his wife (N. Zagorny also made this suggestion, in coll. *Pamiati Glinki,* p. 566).]

18 April

In a note to Maria Krzhisevich, Glinka expresses his chagrin over Krzhisevich's refusal to visit the "museum" with him, since Krzhisevich prefered Anton Rubinstein's opera *Dmitry Donskoy* to the museum.

[The "museum" is the Hermitage or Rumyantsev Museum. The letter is dated according to the premiere of Rubinstein's opera.]

19 April

In *Mosk. ved.,* no. 48, in the section "Petersburg News," it mentions the Philharmonic Society's concert on 2 April.

22 April

Glinka made this inscription on a copy of the score of the *Ouverture Espagnol No. 2 (Recuerdos de Castilla) sur des thèmes de l'Espagne centrale par M. Glinka:* "To my dear and kind colleague Al. Lvov in token of true friendship, Mikhail Glinka. S.P.burg, 22 April 1852."

Glinka recorded 16 bars from the score of the *Jota aragonesa* in someone's album with this inscription: *"St.-Petersbourg, Le 22 avril 1852. Michel Glinka."* (The autograph is in the State Szechin Library in Budapest. *Sov. muzyka,* 1955, no. 12).

24 April

Dedicatory inscription by Glinka in an album: "To my dear little sister Lyudmila Ivanovna Shestakova, Mikhail Glinka, 24 April 1852."

25 April

Glinka visited Lvov. On his return he "caught a very bad cold."

26 April

Glinka informs Dmitry Stasov that he has gotten sick and therefore is unable "to be at the Hermitage today."
[The picture gallery and sculpture collection in the Hermitage were opened to the public on 5 February 1852.]

Glinka receives an official letter from the SPb. Philharmonic Society, which is "proud to include you among its most celebrated and esteemed members" and which thanks him for the dedication of *Night in Madrid* (Fr. original).
[Glinka was named an honorary member of the Philharmonic Society in 1837 (*100-letnii iubilei S.-Peterburgskogo filarmonicheskogo obshchestva. 1802–1902* [100-Year jubilee of the St. Petersburg Philharmonic Society. 1802–1902], SPb., 1902, p. 3).]

April

Odoevsky arranged a musical evening for Glinka which was attended by many of Glinka's acquaintances. In their presence Mikhail Vielgorsky "began to make fun of me, but I cleverly avoided him."

End of April

Party at Novoselsky's in Glinka's honor. "Some of the pieces performed at our evening [on 29 February] were repeated at this one with bassoon and oboe" (*Zap.*).

1 May

Glinka invites Maria Krzhisevich for 2 May and asks her to get tickets for the Hermitage.

2 May

During the day Glinka and Shestakova attended a concert in the Court Chapel (ltr. to M. Krzhisevich, 1 May 1852).

8 May

Glinka attended a performance of *A Life for the Tsar* in the Aleksandrinsky Theater (*SPb. ved.*, 8 and 11 May 1852). "After the first performances in 1836, he had not seen his old lady, as he called *A Life for the Tsar*, and . . . since then it had not been updated at all: the same costumes, the same sets, the Polish ball illuminated by four candles. My brother remarked to me about this that soon it would be lighted by two tallow candle butts. But the things the orchestra manufactured. the tempos that were taken, were awful! I know what a sacrifice he made for me in not leaving the theater immediately. However, he admired Petrov, and it was then that he noticed Leonova's voice in the part of Vanya. . . . During one of the intermissions Prince Odoevsky came to our box and whispered to me that they wanted to call my brother out, but he whispered so loudly that my brother heard it and got up from his seat, left the box, and said to me: 'Please come to the director's rooms, and let them send someone for me. . . .' In fact he was called for, but from the stage it was announced that he had gone" (Shestakova, *Vosp.*, p. 299).
[Shestakova mistakenly dates this event to the year 1855.]

"The Moscow singer Semyonova performed the role of Antonida . . . the role of Vanya, a certain Leonova (not a true *contralto*, but not unpleasant). It couldn't have gone better. Glinka was in the theater himself, and the orchestra of the Bolshoi Theater, which I had forewarned of his presence, made a valiant effort (they even used an *English horn* instead of the usual oboe). I listened *very* intently as if I knew *neither* Glinka *nor* his opera, and I discovered such *incomparable* places in this music that I simply melted" (ltr. from A. Serov to V. Stasov, 15 May 1852, in *MN* III, p. 119).

9 May

In Shestakova's album Glinka inscribed an excerpt from Finn's ballad and a piano transcription of the chorus *"Mirnyi son uspokoi"* [Soothe my peaceful sleep] from *Ruslan and Lyudmila*. Composer's date: "S.P.burg. 9 May 1852, M. Glinka" (Album No. 2).

10 May

Glinka entered a transcription for piano of the Slavsya Chorus in Shestakova's album. The composer's date: "From the epilog of the opera *A Life for the Tsar*, SPburg 10 May 1852. M. Glinka" (Album No. 2).

Entry (with an indecipherable signature) in Glinka's album:

> With him blushed the first dawn of Russian opera,
> Never will he be forgotten, like his *A Life for the Tsar*.

On the same page there is the signature of another person: "Ya. Dovgolevsky, 10 May 1852." (Glinka's Spanish Album, in *L.*, p. 393).

11 May

In a letter to Dehn, Glinka asks that he patronize the pianist Ivan Neylisov. He writes of his intentions of stopping off in Dresden for a visit with Dehn on his way to Spain.

In *SPb. ved.*, no. 105, in "Notices," over the signature of "I. M.," there is a report about the performance of *A Life for the Tsar* on 8 May in which Semyonova debuted in the role of Antonida. "The entire opera went very well. We cannot remember such a performance since the time when Mme Petrova sang the role of Vanya. Petrov in the part of Susanin, Bulakhov in the role of Sobinin, Semyonova as Antonida, and Leonova as Vanya performed their roles excellently, and all the *morceaux d'ensemble* and arias drew loud applause. It was like the opera was being given for the first time. M. I. Glinka was himself in the theater, but, unfortunately, he left prior to the end and could not acknowledge the ovation unanimously given him."

13 May

Composer's dating on the manuscript of the vocal part of the romance *"Rozmowa"* (*"O milaia deva"*): "M. Glinka, May 13, 1852, SP.burg."

14 May

Composer's dating and dedicatory inscription on the manuscript of the romance *"Rozmowa"* (the music is written in an unknown hand, the Polish text is written by Glinka, the Russian by Serov): "To Aleksandra Yakovlevna Bilibina, in token of true friendship and respect from the composer. S.P.burg, 14 May 1852" (*L.*, p. 393).

First Half of May

Evening in honor of Glinka at Mikhail Volkonsky's. "They played quartets. [Karl] Shubert, Schering, and Beling were at the gathering" (*Zap.*).

Glinka "read a sort of *lecture* on instrumentation" to Serov and Dmitry Stasov. Serov then recorded his "Notes on Instrumentation" from Glinka's dictation.

Serov showed Glinka the serenade, duet, and quartet from *May Night:* "I am getting stricter with myself and therefore find it *impossible* to compose anything much *new* quickly. I complained of this to Glinka, who takes a serious interest in my development as someone *close* to me and as an expert. He gave me wonderful advice: continue the opera without hurrying or forcing myself, but at the same time to compose *operatic* things on completely different subjects, i.e., individual scenes (arias, duets, trios, *ensembles, etc.*) on mythological or chivalrous subjects, or anything that occurs to me; to plan it out and write it directly in full score (or in piano-score with orchestral *indications*); and to make every effort to finish these individual numbers from my 'imagined' operas *as if* they were going to be performed *tomorrow.* 'This,' Glinka said, 'will take the place for you of the *huge number* of operas that *every* respectable composer wrote while searching for his real path. I worked like this prior to *A Life for the Tsar.* . . .' He was *very* complimentary of the serenade. The duet he found *'un peu diffus,* but there are good things. . . . The same *good* but somewhat one-sided text doesn't allow you to learn everything you need for opera at once. When you're able to do individual numbers in various styles, doing *one* entire thing will no longer be difficult for you at all'" (ltr. from A. Serov to V. Stasov, 15 May 1852, in *MN* III, p. 119).

Shestakova tried to persuade Glinka to go to the country with her, but Glinka "emphatically disagreed, and he was right. Having lived almost continuously abroad, to be suddenly confronted with the disgrace of rural peasant life at that time would have been startling for him and even impossible" (Shestakova, *Vosp.,* p. 50).

15 May

Serov writes to V. Stasov: "Since I have gotten to know Glinka well, I believe in him more and more. All the outstanding aspects of his immense talent were made vividly evident to me not long ago in a performance of *A Life for the Tsar* (8 May, at the Aleksandrinsky). . . . Recall how when we were together we admired the fugue *à la Händel* in the introduction, yet how many similar beautiful moments throughout the opera! And if you look at *A Life for the Tsar* like a special kind of music, somewhat oratorio-like (similar in part to *Fidelio*), then there's even a wealth of drama. And what an orchestra! You, of course, know to what extent we hear things differently from before. Our ears have changed completely. Perhaps, still *par contraste,* they presented *A Life for the Tsar* especially brilliantly, because not long ago they gave Rubinstein's opera

The Battle of Kulikova at the Bolshoi Theater (18 April). . . . I wrote . . . at one time about Dargomyzhsky's *Esmeralda*. Imagine that *Dmitry Donskoy* is *worse!*" In the same letter he writes: "Glinka is going on May 23 . . . we were not with him for long. . . . I am *sick* that he is going! I am going to see him now to do his picture. This is a great *kindness* on his part, *parce qu'il déteste poser*" (*MN* III, p. 119).
[Serov's portrait of Glinka is not extant.]

16 May

Glinka tells Odoevsky that he has sent him the score of *Médée* and asks him to send him the manuscript of the "Canon in Jest" (*Shutochnyi kanon*), which he had composed in 1836 at breakfast at Aleksandr Vsevolozhsky's after a performance of *A Life for the Tsar*.

17 May

Dedicatory inscription by Glinka on a geographical atlas: "To Vasily Pavlovich Engelgardt for a successful journey over lands and seas. Sincerely presented by Glinka. S.P.burg, 17 May 1852."

18 May

Glinka had his picture taken alone and with Shestakova by the daguerrotypist Levitsky.

19 May

Dubrovsky wrote in Shestakova's album "Verses written by [means of] the wisdom of glasses on the occasion of the delivery of swan quills to Mikhail Ivanovich Glinka" (Album No. 2).

20 May

Glinka inscribed Shestakova's album with the *"Zazdravnaia pesn'; Pie Kuba do Yakuba"* [Toasting song]). The composer's dating: "20 May 1852, S.P.burg, Michel Glinka" (Album No. 2).

On his birthday, Glinka went with Shestakova, Serov, and Dmitry Shestakov to the *Birzha* (the spit of Vasilievsky Island).

21 May

In the morning Glinka released two of his birds in the Summer Garden and then together with Shestakova ate breakfast at Donon's and went to Tsarskoe Selo.

Tsarskoe Selo. Glinka spent the entire day walking with his sister.

Petersburg. Toward evening they returned home. "Friends gathered . . . by dinnertime, i.e., our company" (*Zap.*).

Before 22 May

Glinka's "Biography of Ivan Ekimovich Kolmakov" comes from the period of his stay in Petersburg (ltr. to L. Shestakova, 18/30 October 1852).

[At the beginning of the "Biography" there is an excerpt from a poem by Batyushkov entitled *"Na razvalinakh zamka v Shvetsii"* [On the ruins of a castle in Sweden] ("The light of day still burns in the west"). In G 1 (pp. 13, 363) authorship is mistakenly attributed to Glinka.]

22 May

Glinka inscribed the title page of Shestakova's album: "Whenever you feel melancholy, take this little book and remember me and the pleasant moments we have spent together, which with the help of the Almighty I will somehow try to restore, so to say, to return to you. Michel, 22 May 1852."

In *Panteon*, vol. 3, no. 5, under "Theatrical Chronicle—Russian Opera in Petersburg," there is an unsigned review [by Serov] of Anton Rubinstein's opera *The Battle of Kulikova,* which provides a survey of the activity of Russian composers. "After *Askold's Tomb,* there appeared *A Life for the Tsar,* which gave the composer a tremendous reputation and abounds in exceptional melodies and musical drama. . . . It appears that the composer exhausted all the riches of our native tunes in it. After this it even seems to us impossible that another one in a purely folk spirit could be written. At the very least, a musician must appear whose talent is the equal of Glinka's. In the future, of course, such people might appear, but at the present time we do not know them. Musical connoisseurs chastised Glinka for several offences against melodic construction and the rules of harmony in the instrumentation of this opera. The composer answered them with the composition of *Ruslan and Lyudmila,* which is learned in the highest degree. Despite splendid conditions and several beautiful numbers, this opera did not have a brilliant success. Actually, on the whole, as an opera the work is inconsistent, for it is devoid of the essential principle of drama. Educated musicians found a great number of outstanding things in the score of *Ruslan and Lyudmila* and a wealth of originality in its orchestration. We are completely in agreement with this, but we repeat again that opera, like any artistic work, is written for the public at large, which makes no pretense to knowledge of counterpoint, and it must not be either a symphony or an oratorio or a concerto, but simply an opera. Individual numbers of *Ruslan and Lyudmila* are outstanding, but the entire work leaves a most confused impression in one's mind, a mixture of striking tunes with the most obscure passages and of ravishing melodies with mannered and affected places which are remarkable only for their originality. The libretto of the opera, which is inept and lacks any kind of dramatic interest, also aids in dampening enthusiasm and tiring the public. Since *Ruslan and Lyudmila*, Glinka has been quiet, which is sincerely regretted by everyone who loves Russian opera and admires this gift from Russia's indisputably finest composer." With respect to *The Battle of Kulikova*, it says that "the question of what Russian music on a Russian folk subject should be like was already decided 16 years ago with the opera *A Life for the Tsar*, which aroused the general enthusiasm of both public and connoisseurs. Connoisseurs and everyone who has studied art still admire every line of this score. The outstanding orchestra of our Bolshoi Theater always performs this opera with rare enthusiasm, and the audience continues to call for the composer as warmly and unanimously 16 years later (a performance on 8 May at the Aleksandrinsky Theater) as on the evening of its first performance (27 November 1836). We would prefer not to believe that the gifted Mr. Rubinstein had the idea of writing a Russian *patriotic folk* opera only in order to compete with such an artist as M. I. Glinka. However . . . the thought involuntarily occurs to us: perhaps the young composer too arrogantly wished to 'outdo' M. I. Glinka!" Later on it says that Rubinstein tried to capture the spirit of folk music by imitating the style of Glinka, but "one must be born like M. I. Glinka in order to display the ability to work out ideas so close to the style of Handel, Haydn, and Cherubini in one's first work for the theater. Think of the fugue in the introduction to *A Life for the Tsar*, the chorus '*My na rabotu, v les*' in the third act, the entr'acte before the fourth act, the scene with the Poles and Susanin in the forest, the last entr'acte, the concluding chorus of the epilog: here is the style of a master, the richest working-out of musical ideas!" He refers to the inconsistency of the folk style: "We still do not see any great offence in this. After *A Life for the Tsar* it is difficult to write an entire opera in a purely folk style" (d.c.a.).

Before 23 May

Glinka presented Engelgardt with a collection of quartets by Haydn and quartets, quintets, and trios by Mozart, in which he himself played the violin part. He wrote the following inscription: "To V. P. Engelgardt, in remembrance, from M. I. Glinka. 1852, S.-Petersburg."

23 May

Accompanied by Don Pedro, Glinka goes abroad, "to Warsaw by post-chaise," with the intention of visiting Paris and Spain (*Zap.;* ltr. from A. Serov to V. Stasov, 15 May 1852, in *MN* III, p. 120).

In the *SPb. ved.* of 27 May, under "Leaving St. Petersburg, 24 May," it names "Retired Collegiate Assessor, Glinka, to Kovno."

27 May

In "V. P.'s" [Vasilko-Petrov's] Theater Chronicle in *SPb. ved.*, no. 117, there is a reference to Semyonova's performance in the role of Antonida in *A Life for the Tsar* on 8 May: "We have never heard such a successful performance of M. I. Glinka's beautiful opera."

23–29 May

The road from Petersburg to Warsaw. Glinka composed "a little mazurka in the manner of Chopin. This mazurka pleased people in Warsaw and Paris" (*Zap.*). Composer's dating: *"Mazurka, comp. à la fin de mai 1852 en diligence"* (Album No. 2). On a manuscript copy are the composer's signature and date: *"Cette mazurka a été composée à la fin de mai 1852 en diligence. M. Glinka."*

29 May

Warsaw. The trip lasted "six days and nights . . . I have found many friends and acquaintances here. Lvov in particular was ecstatic to see me again" (ltr. to L. Shestakova, 2 June 1852).

30 May

In the "Petersburg Letters" of *Ved. Mosk. gor. politsii*, no. 120, there is a report of Semyonova's recent successful debut in the role of Antonida.

2/14 June

Glinka presented the organist Freyer with an autograph copy of the first 16 bars of the Slavsya Chorus from *A Life for the Tsar* transcribed for piano, with the inscription: *"Marche-Hymne—thème principal de l'épilogue de l'opera "La vie pour le Zsar" Varsovie, le 12/24 juin 1852. Michel Glinka."* (The original is in

Warsaw in the Library of the Moniuszko Musical Society, *Sov. muzyka,* 1954, no. 12).

Composer's dating on an autograph copy of two musical lines from the chorus *"Mirnyi son, uspokoi serdtse devy"* [Sweet sleep, calm a maiden's heart] from the fourth act of the opera *Ruslan and Lyudmila:* "Warsaw, 2/14 June 1852. M. Glinka."
[It was located in the Findeyzen archives; its present location is not known (G 2-A, p. 14).]

In a letter to Shestakova, Glinka tells about his trip from Petersburg.

3/15 June

Glinka and Lvov heard the organist Freyer.

4/16 June

Departure for Berlin (ltr. to L. Shestakova, 2 June 1852).

5/17 June

Chenstokhov. They passed through Chenstokhov (*Zap.*).

Breslau. Arrival. After dinner they took a walk and at 6 o'clock in the evening left by train for Berlin (Don Pedro's footnote to a ltr. to L. Shestakova, 8/20 June 1852).

7/19 June

Berlin. Arrival at 5 o'clock in the morning. They stayed at the Römischer Hotel (ltr. to L. Shestakova, 8/20 June 1852; *Zap.*).

Dehn visited Glinka. "My teacher of composition, Dehn, was ecstatic to see me." Afterwards Glinka had dinner at Dehn's and listened to music there. "Three quartets were played—and very well" (ltr. to L. Shestakova, 8/20 June 1852).

Glinka and Dehn visited the music publisher Heinrich Schlesinger (*Briefe hervorragender Zeitgenossen an Franz Liszt. Hrsg. von* La Mara, Leipzig, 1885, vol. 1, p. 233).

Glinka added a note to a collective letter from Schlesinger, Peter Lindpaintner, and Dehn to Liszt in Weimar: *"Mille saluts à l'excellentissime ami."*

8/20 June

Meyerbeer visited Glinka. "Among other things he said to me: *'Comment se fait-il, M-r Glinka, que nous vous connaissons tout de réputation, mais nous ne connaissons pas vos oeuvres? Cela est très naturel,—lui ai-je répondu,—je n'ai pas l'habitude de colporter mes productions.'* Meyerbeer was incidentally extremely pleasant and courteous" (*Zap.*; footnote by Don Pedro to a ltr. to L. Shestakova, 8/20 June 1852). That same day Dehn visited Glinka.

Glinka informs Shestakova of his arrival the day before in Berlin and of his further plans and adds: "Yes, my friend, I am not what I was before; once you race around like a bird, and your heart sings—but now the bones are weary and things are somehow boring."

11/23 June

Glinka asks the General Director of the Royal Museums in Berlin, Ignaz von Olfers, to issue him a ticket allowing him repeated visits to the Kunstkammer. [Written by an unknown hand (perhaps a copy?).]

8/20–12/24 June

"S. Dehn showed me everything noteworthy. I got a good look at the museum and the menagerie. Dehn also entertained me with quartets and Mosel wine" (*Zap.*).

13/25 June

At 11 o'clock in the morning Glinka and Don Pedro left by train.

Hannover. In the evening they arrived in Hannover, where they spent the night.

14/26 June

Departure in the morning for Cologne.

Night of 14/26–15/27 June.

Arrival in Cologne.

From the Morning of 15/27 to the Evening of 16/28 June

On the Rhine from Cologne to Strasbourg. "A pleasant trip" by steamship (ltr. to L. Shestakova, 20 June/2 July 1852; *Zap.*).

From the Night of 17/29 to the Morning of 18/30 June

Strasbourg. They spent a day and two nights in Strasbourg. "We saw the outstanding cathedral."

18/30 June

Departure in the morning by coach (ltr. to L. Shestakova, 20 June/2 July 1852).

Nancy. That same day they stopped in Nancy, where they spent a few hours and left by train for Paris.

19 June/1 July

Paris. At 5 o'clock in the morning "I arrived in Paris, not without pleasure, for many, many things from the past were called up in my mind" (*Zap.*). "A wonderful city! An outstanding city! An excellent city! The little town of Paris" (ltr. to L. Shestakova, 20 June/2 July 1852). They stayed in the Hôtel de la Marine Française, where Glinka "had stayed before" (*Zap.*). "We spent the evening on the Champs Elysées with my friend Henry Mérimée. You [Shestakova] saw his portrait in my Spanish Album."

20 June/2 July

Glinka "looked for [my] old friend Volkov, whom I have known since 1824. I have not yet seen him."

In a letter to Shestakova, Glinka tells of his trip from Berlin to Paris and writes that in five weeks he intends to leave for Madrid.

20 June

Censor's authorization for the romance *"O milaia deva"* [O lovely maid] (translated from the Polish, *"Rozmowa,"* words by Mickiewicz) published by Bernard.

22 June

In *Panteon,* vol. 3, no. 6, Serov recalls in an article entitled "Letters about Music to A. D. Ulybyshev, Occasioned by Our Talks about Mozart and Beethoven," how in 1843 he took the score for *A Life for the Tsar* from Glinka to Ulybyshev (d.c.a.).

30 June

Serov (from Pargolovo) writes to V. Stasov: "I cannot . . . but complain to you about the 'sourness' of my present life, especially sensitive for me after Glinka's departure. His stay in Petersburg, all the trouble for him . . . was for me a most delightful oasis." He reminisces about Glinka "and our evenings with him, my conversations with him, which were so beneficial to me, especially with respect to the operas of Cherubini . . . and about Glinka's incomparable observations about the orchestra and instrumentation (you will recognize this, by the way, in the lectures I have written) . . . about *our* concert, i.e., the Glinka concert with the new Spanish overture, and about *Kamarinskaya.*" And further: "Regarding the news that you have recently become fascinated with the ancient masters after all this time . . . I am vividly reminded . . . what happens with you that you should disavow your extremely amusing blunders. . . . Take Glinka— he never denies it, but with the greatest naivete admits that he was wrong, and stupid, because he did not know the thing itself or at the time had not yet attained i is present level of understanding. . . . How many things there still are to *study.* . . . What marvels in Cherubini's operas! And what is remarkable is that it is a kind of opera completely unlike Mozart, and everywhere one sees prototypes of *Fidelio* and *A Life for the Tsar*" (*MN* III, p. 120, 124).

4/16–5/17 July

"D. A. Shestakov arrived for a short time. . . . For two days he and I were inseparable, and cheerful and carefree as children we surrendered ourselves to the various pleasures of Paris" (*Zap.;* ltr. to L. Shestakova, 5/17 July 1852).

5/17 July

Glinka reports to Shestakova that he intends to leave for Madrid on 20 or 22 July.
[There are footnotes to the letter from Dmitry Shestakov and Don Pedro.]

Before 12/24 July

With Henry Mérimée Glinka saw the museums and "the ancient streets of Paris" (*Zap.*).

12/24 July

Informing Shestakova of his departure for Spain that same evening, Glinka writes: "Paris is a dear little spot. *It would be a sin if we can't live a while here together, my incomparable little cuckoo. . . .*" In a footnote Don Pedro writes of their departure from Paris to Lyons, etc.).

At 8 o'clock in the evening Glinka and Don Pedro left by train for Chalon (ltr. to L. Shestakova, 12/24 July 1852; *Zap.*).

Night before 13/25 July

Route from Paris to Chalon along the Seine. In the train Glinka "suffered . . . for several hours from a nervous feeling of sinking with fear, like what [I] had experienced in 1847 in Novospasskoe and Smolensk. Toward morning the suffering abated."

13/25 July

Chalon. In the morning "we travelled by steamship on the Saône to Lyons."

Lyons. In the evening they arrived in Lyons, "where we spent the night" (*Zap.*).

"As we got farther and farther from Paris, Miguelito's suffering and repetition of the word 'boring' increased to an astonishing degree" (ltr. from Don Pedro to L. Shestakova, 5/17 August 1852; Fr. original).

14/26 July

Lyons–Avignon. Journey by steamship on the Rhône. "The banks of the Rhône are not nearly so picturesque as the Rhine."

Avignon. Arrival at five o'clock in the morning, after which Glinka and Don Pedro saw the sights of the city. They spent the night.

15/27 July

In the morning Glinka's nervous condition resumed "with terrible force." He received homeopathic treatment and was somewhat calmed. After breakfast Glinka and Don Pedro "set out . . . by rail for Beaucaire, where there was a fair."

Beaucaire. Arrival and departure for Montpellier.

Montpellier. Arrival. Glinka "did not like" the city "at all" (*Zap.*).

16/28 July

Departure by coach for Toulouse.

Toulouse. They arrived the same day and stayed at the Hôtel Casset.

17/29 July–28 July/9 August

During the time Glinka and Don Pedro spent in Toulouse, Glinka "suffered daily." Here he made the acquaintance of Emile Delile. "Incessant suffering deterred me from my intention of travelling to Spain, and I decided to return to Paris."

29 July/10 August

Departure for Paris in a covered carriage by post-chaise.

31 July/12 August

Poitiers. Arrival and departure the same day for Tours by rail.

Tours. Arrival and departure for Orleans the same day.

2/14 August

Orleans. Arrival and departure the same day for Paris (*Zap.*).

Between 12/24 July and 3/15 August

Glinka "travelled over almost all of France with the exception of seaside locales. In picturesqueness France cannot compare with her neighbors, Spain and Italy.

On the other hand, the cities are wonderful, and you can't read all the historical monuments. . . . However, Paris is still the best with its pleasant environs" (ltr. to A. Serov, 22 August/3 September 1852). "The banks of the Loire seemed less picturesque to me than those of the Seine."

3/15 August

Paris. Arrival. They stopped at the Hôtel de la Marine Française, where there were no rooms, "and we spent the night in the dining room, one of us on the couch, the other on a table" (*Zap.*).

5/17 August

After telling Shestakova in a letter of the aborted trip to Spain and his intention of spending the winter in Paris, Glinka adds: "I can say honestly that *cheerful Spain* is out of season for me. Here, in Paris, I can find new untried *intellectual* pleasures."

7 August

In *Mosk. ved.*, no. 95, in a piece of correspondence from Danilevsky (signed "D.") entitled "Petersburg Life," Leonova's debut in the part of Vanya in the opera *A Life for the Tsar* is mentioned.

15/27 (?) August

Glinka and Don Pedro moved from their hotel to a small apartment "in the very center of fashionable Paris . . . i.e., in a very cheerful area next to the theater of the *Grand Opéra, rue Rossini, au bel étage*, #26."

19/31 August

Glinka writes to Shestakova that he has decided to stay in Paris, since he cannot travel: the railroad "upsets me and wrenches my soul with its unbearably malignant stench," and the stagecoach "is unbearable because of the crowding and inordinate jolting." Glinka refers to both means of transportation as instruments of torture: "they cram you into a compartment or carriage, close the door, and you're done for. Add to this the fact that my *hypochondria* has reached such a pitch that in everyone sitting near me I imagine someone sick or infected with some contagious disease, which is why a trip for me is not pleasure but profound, excrutiating torture. . . . I have given up Spain—it is not the right time for this happy place. . . . Paris is a marvelous city. You can find everything, and for all ages."

19 August

In *SPb. ved.*, no. 135, in Vasilko-Petrov's "Theatrical Chronicle" (signed "V. P."), the author writes that "our Russian Opera offers many beautiful hopes. We believe, thanks to the attentions given it by the enlightened Directorate and the public after the most recent performances of *A Life for the Tsar, The Battle of Kulikova,* and *L'elisir d'amore,* that it will fullfil these hopes." Later the Chronicle reports: "They say that M. I. Glinka is going abroad and will visit Spain again."

Second Half of August

Glinka makes the acquaintance of Mme Beaucé, who lived in the same building. "She was extremely lively and cheerful of disposition; she studied music, and was not at all bad. Her daughter, Mme Ugolde, was the leading singer in the Opéra-Comique" (*Zap.*).

21 August/2 September

Glinka obtained a quire of music paper, "somewhat longer and a little bit narrower than an arshin. Sixteen very wide lines."

22 August/3 September

Glinka writes to Serov that he has sent him a book by Dehn on 'General-Bass' for translation, and he says that Dehn has decided to have a translation done "of the notebook written for me" in 1833/34. He shares his impressions of Paris: "I will tell you the most important things. The Louvre is *comme toiles et marbres.* Among the best painters, the beauty of Veronese is inconceivable. *Les noces de Cana* is in my opinion the pearl of the museum. The picture is almost the size of *Pompeii* and *The Serpent,* both of which are laid in the dust by it. I had already made friends with Correggio in Berlin. The *Jupiter and Io* there is surpassingly graceful. Here he is the thunderer in the form of a Satyr before the sleeping Antiope. It's a marvel! The Raphaels, Titians, Poussins, et al, are, in a word, outstanding examples of the finest artists of all schools. Without leaving the gallery one can study the history of painting. Among the statues, the *Venus de Milo, Polimnie,* and *Le Tibre* are quite remarkable. (I forgot about Murillo's *Conception.* I am very glad that Bruni did not buy it. The picture is large but creased . . . it is drawn like the drawings on Sèvres porcelain. The Madonna's ecstasy resembles a grimace . . .) All the museums, libraries, and courses in the sciences are free of charge. One could not study all the historical antiquities in a year." He describes how he is spending his time and states that he has visited the botanical garden, the menagerie, and the Champs Elysées. "I do not attend the theaters. I frequently attend the *bals champêtres*. . . . The dance orchestras are exceptionally good: *cornets à pistons* and the brass play a big part, but this, incidentally, anyone can hear. Now everyone is out of town . . . and consequently there is no music. In the winter an excellent quartet is promised." Concerning his domestic life Glinka writes: "We have acquired a cook. He, namely Pedro, goes to the market every day and has supplied the kitchen in excellent fashion." At the end of the letter he states: "With this very pen I will begin a symphony tomorrow."

[*"Pompeii"* is the *Last Day of Pompeii*, a picture by Karl Bryullov; *"The Serpent"* is the *Bronze Serpent*, a picture by Bruni (both of which are now in the Russian Museum in Leningrad).]

23 August/4 September

Glinka began to write a symphony based on Gogol's "Taras Bulba" (ltr. to A. Serov, 22 August/3 September 1852).

23 August

In *Sev. pchela*, no. 188, in "Livonian Letters" by Bulgarin (signed "F. B."), he mentions *Kamarinskaya*, "on the theme of an ancient folk melody, which is known among the peasants by the name of *bychok* [the steer]." Reference is made to Glinka's success with this piece in a Philharmonic concert. "What a delight!" Likewise, "in *A Life for the Tsar* . . . one can feel the folk tunes which imbue it with a folklike character."

27 August

In *Moskvityanin*, vol. 4, no. 16, part 2, under "Criticism and Bibliography," there is a notice by Zakharov (signed "N. Z.") entitled "Things occasioned by Russian song, collected and transcribed for voice and piano by Mr. Gurilev, and published in Moscow by Mr. Gresser," which says: "Our dramatic poetry in the person of Pushkin and our dramatic music in the person of Glinka are the result of the development of modern Russian society" (d.c.a.).

End of August

Mme Beaucé "gathered several of her students in our hall one evening. Subsequently, in the fall and winter, they constantly came to me to study singing, particularly Italian singing" (*Zap.*).

Between 23 August/4 September and 7/19 September

Glinka "had begun to work on *Taras* and was writing well when a cold interfered with [my] work, though I hope to get back to work soon" (ltr. to L. Shestakova, 7/19 September 1852).

Beginning of September

"I had written the first part of the allegro and the beginning of the second part of [my] Cossack Symphony in C Minor (*Taras Bulba*). I was unable to continue with the second part, which I found unsatisfactory. When I thought about it, I found that the development of the allegro (*Durchführung, développement*) I had begun in the German manner, while the general character of the piece was Little Russian. I discarded the score, and Pedro destroyed it" (ltr. to N. Kukolnik, 12 November 1854).
[There is a note in the *Zapiski* regarding Don Pedro's destruction of *Taras Bulba:* "He wasn't a bad sort." Engelgardt and Balakirev recollected excerpts of the symphony from memory (V. Stasov, *M. I. Glinka. Novye materialy dlia ego biografii. Simfoniia "Taras Bul'ba"* [M. I. Glinka. New materials for his biography. The symphony *Taras Bulba*], in *Rus. starina*, 1889, vol. 61, no. 2, p. 387).]

Between 31 August/12 September and 7/19 September

Glinka attended the Opéra-Comique for a performance of Méhul's *Joseph* (*Zap.; G 1*, p. 417).

Before 7/19 September

Glinka "saw the daguerrotypist Levitsky several times. He even had dinner with me. He was a pleasant and obliging man."

7/19 September

Glinka writes to Shestakova and tells her about his life and further plans: "I'm not bad, generally speaking, but sometimes off and on I'm unwell with a cold or stomach upset (my vomiting has let up noticeably), though an unbearable hypochondria comes over me sometimes (depression) and I painfully yearn for my own people, most of all you, *kukonushka*. Where and when might we meet? I sincerely wish for this, only not in Russia. I suffer too cruelly there. . . . I am thinking of going to Milan at the beginning of May, where I can easily find a little house and garden in the environs. . . . I will see Florence, where I have never been, and Rome . . . and then to Warsaw. . . . I can only say that loafing about the world bores me already and doesn't appeal to me." He considers that for the birth of Shestakova's child it would be best to go to Moscow, "because there are neither relatives nor acquaintances." Moreover "it is necessary to set out *in good time*—this is more important than you think. There are few of us, so we must love and look after each other."

9 September

In *Mosk. ved.*, no. 109, in correspondence by "D." [Danilevsky] called "Petersburg Life," a rumor is reported that Glinka is composing an opera called *Taras Bulba*.

10/22 September

Glinka thanks Shestakova for sending him money. He gives her advice on how to behave during her pregnancy: "in particular . . . avoid anger, disappointment, grief, colds, and unnecessary movement."

16 September

Serov (from Petersburg) writes to Vladimir Stasov that he has received a letter from Paris from Glinka. "It was very nice of him that he thought to write to me, and so much. I remember well his reluctance to write and, naturally, I value his attention *very* much and also that he wrote to me *before* I had written him. . . . He writes that he is beginning a symphony. It will be *Taras Bulba*, from which he played me the principal ideas several times. It will be *splendid*, one can vouch for this in advance, and, as always with him, original in the highest degree, because he follows his own special path. Naturally, in *A Life for the Tsar* there is much in common with Cherubini, even in the *style* of individual parts, but there is a vast difference also, for everything is changed by the preponderance of the *national* element. If you are in Paris for even a short while, you should of course look him up. I am sorry about one thing: apparently he talked with you sufficiently about all kinds of things (1849), but so far as I could tell, you did not become particularly close. Whenever he recalled you, it was almost always your superficial side, for example that you 'shout louder than any trombones and enjoy quarreling.' I would very much like for him to get to know you *more intimately,* as, for example, he now knows Dmitry and me so well.

Dehn . . . has commissioned him to ask me . . . to translate his *Harmonielehre* into Russian. . . . I have already written to Glinka that I regard this as very flattering . . . though *pointless,* because there are certain trifles missing here— such as readers and buyers" (*MN* III, p. 132).

18 September

In *SPb. ved.,* no. 208, under "St. Petersburg Chronicle," there is an article called "News of M. I. Glinka" signed "D." [Danilevsky]: "News from Rome! We have just received news that our esteemed composer M. I. Glinka, surrounded by Italian melody and the inspiring sky of Raphael and Rossini, has again found the life-giving key to his own musical voice. What would you think . . . his travels around Italy have elicited? . . . He informs us that a new symphony has come from his pen, the topic for which is the poetic tale 'Taras Bulba.'" In the same section: "Stepanov," who has attained great fame here with his caricature statues of Russian literary figures . . . is now working on elegant busts of our celebrities . . . out of ivory-colored alabaster at one-quarter the natural size of the face, and on filling out his collection of small statues." In counting those portrayed by the statues, he includes Glinka.

23 September

In *Mosk. ved.,* no. 115, in correspondence from "D." [Danilevsky] headed "Life in Petersburg," mention is made of a letter of Glinka from Rome (?!) with the statement that he has purportedly written a symphony called *Taras Bulba.*

25 September

In *Syn otechestva,* no. 8, there is an announcement stating that a piano arrangement of *Kamarinskaya* is available in Denotkin's store (d.c.a.).

27 September/9 October

For the second time Glinka heard Méhul's *Joseph* at the Opéra-Comique. "It was very well performed, that is without any mannerisms and so neatly that despite the fact that Joseph and Simeon were rather weak, the performance of the opera brought tears to my eyes. Bussine was outstanding in the part of Jacob."

28 September

In *SPb. ved.*, no. 217, there is a notice that a four-hand arrangement of *Kamarinskaya* is available at Denotkin's store.

2/14 October

Glinka writes to Shestakova: "Everything is going very well for us in the little town of Paris. . . . It's a wonderful season, though the mornings are cold, and Pedro is busying himself preparing for the bad weather to come. . . . My life, or rather, ours, is quiet and modest—as before I am a convinced sit-at-home. I have gotten lazy, I lie around, eat (and eat a lot), read, etc. My friend Henry Mérimée has gotten me involved with the *ancient Greeks*—I have consumed all of Homer (of course in French translation) and now am reading the tragedian Sophocles. I console myself that they, i.e. these gentlemen, were robbed of more than I. I only employ music to entertain my neighbors and friends. The symphony has come to a halt. It hasn't ripened, but God permitting, I will live long enough to finish it. I include my schoolfellow Melgunov among my friends and the two Volkovs . . . they have been friends *since the time of the Flood,* i.e., my acquaintances since 1824." Regarding his distant plans: "I would like to visit Italy and at the end of next summer, Warsaw. *A little house with a garden, a quiet life.* This is my only desire."

"At the end of October the weather began to get bad, and so to dispel the boredom, with Don Pedro's help, a nice-looking young nurse by the name of Leonie, known as Ninie, turned up. . . . She was quiet and submissive but not very good" (*Zap.*).

14 October

In *Sovremennik,* vol. 35, no. 10, the following appears in an article called "Chronicle of News and Entertainment in Petersburg": "Our maestro Glinka writes from Rome that he has been inspired again and has written a new symphony, the subject for which is Gogol's story 'Taras Bulba.'" It also reports that Leonova has debuted in the role of Vanya in *A Life for the Tsar* and "has become famous . . . only since Easter of this year" (d.c.a.).

18/30 October

Glinka writes to Shestakova: "I'm living quietly and modestly in noisy Paris, and if time permits I walk, though mainly I sit at home. I have stopped working on 'Taras.' It hasn't ripened yet, but then I am reading, reading the ancient classics: Homer, Sophocles, and now Ovid, who is mentioned in the biography of Ivan Ekimovich, which I ask you to keep." In reference to Shestakova's will, he writes: "It would be desirable to take care of everything while you are *alive,* so that Novospasskoe and Pochinok do not fall into others' hands. I consider family (even if the others become angry) to include you and Olga and your husbands. And don't forget Pedrusha."

27 October

Serov writes to Dmitry Stasov (from Priyut Burluk, Anastasieva's estate in the Crimea) that he has received a daguerreotype of Glinka, which arrived "complete and undamaged, as if it came straight from Levitsky" (*MN* III, p. 140).

30 October/11 November

In a letter to Shestakova Glinka reports on his health and how he is spending his time.

31 October

In *Sev. pchela,* no. 244, "R. Z." [Zotov] reports in the "Theatrical Chronicle" that at Orlova's benefit in the Aleksandrinsky Theater, Leonova performed an aria from *A Life for the Tsar* in a divertissement.

16/28 November

The portraitist Nikolay Volkov was a guest of Glinka and "after dinner he did a pencil drawing (because of nothing better to do) . . . which turned out very nicely and incomparably better than Stepanov's" (ltr. to L. Shestakova, 18/30 November 1852).

16 November

It says in *Panteon,* vol. 5, no. 10, in the section "Petersburg Herald—Music": "In general our music does not have a folklike character. The primary exception to this are our romances. Composers of the latter who are well known include Varlamov, Gurilev, Dargomyzhsky, Verstovsky, Titov, and others. Nothing need be said about Glinka. These composers have dedicated themselves to the study of folk tunes and occupy a respected place in the history of Russian music. Their works, which breathe Russian spirit, have become national works and with their native sounds awaken in everyone's hearts a feeling of participation. They have become a part of our spiritual world. Regrettably, national character has still been inadequately studied, and knowledge of it has not yet become the property of all our composers. This is the main reason why the efforts of our composers to say something folklike on a large scale up to now still cause us to wish for something better. Glinka's *A Life for the Tsar,* from the first note to the last, bears a folklike imprint and breathes something native to the Russian heart. How many attempts of this sort, however, have been unsuccessful? *Ruslan and Lyudmila, Olga, the Russian Orphan* [*Ol'ga russkaia sirota*], *The Battle of Kulikova.*" And further: "Several days ago news was received from Rome that Glinka has written a symphony, whose topic is the poetic Russian story 'Taras Bulba'" (d.c.a.).

18/30 November

Glinka writes to Shestakova in Moscow: "Thank you, my incomparable little cuckoo, for petitioning for *Ruslan.* I would not object should they give *Ruslan* (wanting also to have the financial arrangements in order). If you have occasion to see Verstovsky or write to him, give him my regards."

20 November

In a mixed performance in the Aleksandrinsky Theater in Petersburg, the epilog from *A Life for the Tsar* was presented (*Sev. pchela,* 20 November 1852).

22 November

In "Journalistic Odds and Ends" in *Sev. pchela,* no. 262, it says that working with folk music in Russia began recently. "Enough has been said already about the two folk operas, Verstovsky's *Askold's Tomb* and M. I. Glinka's *A Life for the Tsar.*"

28 November/10 December

Glinka writes to Shestakova: "Thanks for the excerpt from the life of I. E. [Kolmakov]. Now I am unable to continue either it or *Taras,* and, strangely, I have written very little while abroad. Now I feel sure that I can still be fit for something only in my homeland. I somehow feel awkward here . . . I *think* there should be nothing wrong with trying to live *with you* in Moscow. . . . A little garden and a place for pheasants, pigeons, rabbits, etc., are important for me, to say nothing of *private* rooms for each of us. . . . *Even the hope of this is already pleasant to me.* . . . Here, as everywhere else abroad, I feel at my age a heavy solitude."

Fall

Henry Mérimée introduced Glinka to the Duport family. "Sometimes musical amateurs gathered there and sang various *morceaux d'ensemble* very capably."

9/21 December

Volkov got Glinka a box at the Opéra-Comique for the premiere of Auber's opera *Marco Spada*. "The beginning of the overture was extremely nice and promised *many fine things,* but the allegro of the overture and the music of the opera turned out to be very unsatisfactory" (*Zap.*).

9 December

Performance of the third act of *A Life for the Tsar* in a mixed concert in the Aleksandrinsky Theater in Petersburg at a benefit for the director of the opera troupe Sokolov (*Sev. pchela,* 9 December 1852).

In *Mosk. ved.,* no. 138, in correspondence entitled "Life in Petersburg" by "D." [Danilevsky], Glinka's opera (?!) *Taras Bulba* is mentioned again.

11/23 December

Glinka thanks Shestakova for looking after him and asks that she not be distressed "by the letters from our sister Masha." He agrees to be godfather to "the little one."

15 December

In *Sev. pchela,* no. 280, in an article by Rostislav [Feofil Tolstoy] called "Letter to the editors . . . occasioned by a new Handbook on the study of harmony, published by Iosif Hunke," it says that Hunke "sincerely respects Glinka's talent."

Between 11/23 and 19/31 December

Nikolay Volkov begins to do an engraving of Glinka: "Judging from its beginning, the likeness will be remarkable. The work is outstanding and may be printed, if there is a demand, in an edition of up to 1000 copies and more."

19/31 December

Glinka writes to Shestakova: "We're living quietly, well, and warmly. My health is so-so. . . . I leave the house very little."

23 December/4 January 1853

After wishing Dmitry Stasov a happy New Year, Glinka writes about himself: "I am not sick, though I've gotten lazy, have aged villainously, and have run to fat, that is to say, I've gotten disgracefully fat. . . . My music is slumbering, but it is not asleep. I sit at home and warm myself at the fireplace. I have read Homer, Sophocles, and Ovid (in translation), and now I just eat and sleep and nothing more."

In a letter to Bilibina he asks for her assistance in getting the young Aleksandr Efimov accepted in a military academy.

29 December/11 January

Glinka attended the theater "Vaudeville" for a performance of *La Dame aux camélias* by Dumas-fils. "It was played extremely well . . . I even shed a few tears myself during the last act."

Between 23 December/4 January and 30 December/11 January

Ivan Alekseevich Shestakov visited Glinka "three times, had dinner, and spent the evening."

30 December/11 January

Glinka reports to Shestakova about his life and his meetings with his schoolmate Boris Glinka and his wife: "They are visiting me, and I am spending the time pleasantly with them. I am teaching the lady to sing. The gentleman is a very intelligent and knowledgeable man." He writes that he would like to remain in Paris until the spring of 1854, "because there is to be a huge exposition here in 1854, and then, for the balance of my life, among my own people."

Beginning of the 1850s

Fedor Stellovsky published the Variations on a Scottish Theme for Piano.

Winter of 1852/53

That winter Glinka "spent sitting at home quietly and very pleasantly. In the morning we had a fire in the fireplace in the hall, and before lunch it was like a *cabinet de lecture* with each of us sitting behind his own book. Almost every day after lunch one of Mme Beaucé's pupils would come . . . sometimes friends came to have dinner, nor did we spend the evenings alone." Glinka read a lot. Besides classical writers he read Ariosto's *Orlando furioso,* which he "liked very much." He was "provided" with books by Emile Delile as well as Henry Mérimée.

1853

7 January

Serov (from Priyut Burluk) informs V. Stasov that he has brought to the Crimea with him a number of orchestral and piano scores and "everything that . . . I need is at hand for reference (excerpts from Berlioz, from Glinka, the '*Marche marocaine,*' from *Faniska, Lodoiska,* etc."). He writes further that Glinka "does not know the sacred works of Palestrina at all" (*MN* III, pp. 145 and 147).
[Later V. Stasov makes a note at this point: "This is totally incorrect. In *Ruslan* he uses the church modes many times" (*MN* III, p. 200).]

9/21 January

"Volkov . . . spent nearly the entire day" at Glinka's, "and the portrait . . . moved ahead significantly—the likeness is striking, the work marvelous."

10/22 January

In a letter to Shestakova Glinka tells of his life and financial affairs. Don Pedro reports in a footnote: "There are almost always people in the house whose company is quite pleasant. Thus your dear brother kills the time without getting too bored" (Fr. original).

11/23 January

Glinka writes to Dubrovsky: "I am living quietly, alone, and quite well and warmly (so far as is possible). I suffer incomparably less than in Russia. Still nostalgia often overcomes me, which has happened ever since I left Warsaw. . . . The winter has stopped everything—the Ukrainian symphony and my reading."

Glinka at the Piano in 1853
Drawing by Vasily Samoylov.

18/30 January

Glinka writes to Shestakova: "To tell the truth, even if I am suffering a great deal less, on the other hand my life here is completely colorless. If you ask, why am I here, I myself do not honestly know. . . . Today all of Paris is on its feet for the emperor's wedding. Pedrusha has gone to see the procession. . . . I of course am completely indifferent to all such events."

30 January/11 February

Glinka writes to Shestakova: "I am living as before: I sit at home busy with music, i.e., I teach singing and sometimes read. That's all, so that in reality my life is just the same as always."

12 February

In *SPb. ved.*, no. 34, "Petersburg Chronicle" (signed "r"), it reports that the "Primary Polka" for piano four-hands is available in Golts's store. "According to the composer's wish the sales from this polka are to go to the benefit of the needy supported by the Society for Visitation to the Poor. . . . This polka, like everything coming from the pen of our Glinka, is beautiful."

19 February/3 March

Several proofs of the lithograph portrait of Glinka by Volkov were prepared. The portrait, "to everyone's surprise, did not turn out well at all and was not a good likeness. I will not consider printing them."
[Apparently the proofs were destroyed. Volkov's work is unknown.]

Glinka writes to Shestakova: "It's rather cold in the room, which is difficult for Mishka. Thank heaven, however, I am not sick, but I am very bored and much drawn toward my homeland!"

1/13 March

Glinka informs Shestakova that on 2/14 April the "lease on the apartment" expires and he would like to leave for Warsaw, but he does not know if he "will be able to carry out [my] intention this year."

8/20 March

Glinka reports to Shestakova of his intention of leaving Paris not later than 15 April (O.S.). "In the event that *circumstances independent of my wishes and my sincere desire to return* do not allow me to leave during the first half or at the beginning of April, then, contrary to my own desires, I will have to stay here."

10 March

In *Rus. khudozh. listok,* no. 8, in an article by "X. X." called "Italian Opera in St. Petersburg in 1852/53," the first performance of *A Life for the Tsar* at the opening of the Bolshoi Theater after its remodelling is mentioned.

15/27 March

Glinka receives from Shestakova news of the birth of her daughter: "This joyous news moved me to tears (which does not happen often to me now), and the same day Pedro, our guests, and I each drank a glass of champagne to your health" (ltr. to L. Shestakova, 17/29 March 1853, and Don Pedro's footnote).
[The daughter, Olga, of Shestakova and Dmitry Stasov was born in Moscow during the first half of March, 1853 (the exact date has not been established). She was very musical. The young Balakirev gave her lessons. She died ten years later in Petersburg.]

17/29 March

Glinka congratulates Shestakova on the birth of her daughter.

22 March/3 April

Volkov gave Glinka his season ticket for a concert of the Paris Conservatory "solely for me to verify my earlier impression," i.e., an unfavorable one. "Incidentally, they performed Beethoven's Fifth Symphony (C minor) at this concert, and I found the performance to be just the same as before, i.e., very mannered: the pianissimos approached an absurd Rubini-like level, and wherever the woodwinds played at all they appeared affected. In a word, it was not a Beethoven symphony at all (*elle a été complètement escamotée*). The other pieces, like the chorus of dervishes from Beethoven's *Ruins of Athens* and a Mozart symphony, were performed clearly and quite satisfactorily."
[The Mozart symphony was the C major; besides the works named, they performed the "Turkish March" from Beethoven's *Ruins of Athens,* excerpts from the second act of Spontini's *Vestale,* and Auber's *Plaisir d'amour.* The reviewer of the *Revue et gazette musicale* commented on the poor performance of the Beethoven symphony. The conductor was not named (G 1, p. 417).]

31 March/12 April

Humorous entry in Glinka's album by several of his French friends (Glinka's Spanish Album, in ITMK, coll. 6).

March

"Ninie left for her parents'. I likewise planned for my return . . . I was beginning to get bored in Paris. The Eastern Question arose; these circumstances increased my desire to return home even more, and there is no doubt that I would have left Paris if my colleague Don Pedro had shared my intentions, but he had taken a definite liking to Paris and already offered resistance. . . . Meanwhile a rather nice-looking and young grisette who was lively and peppery turned up from Bordeaux" [Amalia] (*Zap.*).

2/14 April

Glinka moved from his old apartment into a new, temporary one in the same building, "involving a lot of trouble." The apartment was "on the fifth floor, by our reckoning, the sixth."

4/16 April

Glinka informs Shestakova of his decision to prolong his stay in Paris until 1854. Next year he will come back, but to Moscow: "I cannot agree to Piter, but in Moscow, perhaps, we can try." In a note Don Pedro says that Glinka's decision to remain in Paris "is perhaps for the better because of your dear Michel's health, which over the past year has improved to the extent that so far there has been no occasion to turn to doctors" (Fr. original).

4 April

In *Sev. pchela*, no. 75, "Journalistic Odds and Ends," Bulgarin reports Anton Rubinstein's refusal to perform Dargomyzhsky's Fantasy on Themes from *A Life for the Tsar* in a concert (on 9 April).

5 April

Performance of the romance *"Somnenie"* in a concert of amateurs in Ekaterinoslav (*Sev. pchela,* 16 June 1853).

8/20 April

Glinka writes to Shestakova, "I am definitely staying here."

9/21 April

Glinka and Don Pedro "moved to rue Richer," no. 43, into an "extremely comfortable" apartment on the second floor, which was "recently very nicely furnished." Next to them they found "a little apartment for Amalia also" (*Zap.;* ltr. to L. Shestakova, 8/20 April).

9 April

Performance of Dargomyzhsky's Fantasy on Themes from *A Life for the Tsar* for piano four-hands at his concert for the benefit of the Society for Visitation to the Poor in the Hall of Nobility in Petersburg (*Sev. pchela,* 15 April 1853).

13 April

In *Sev. pchela,* no. 82, in an article by Rostislav called "Musical Conversations: Mme Viardot's Concert," there is an enthusiastic review of Glinka's romances.

In *Sev. pchela,* no. 84, in "Remarks, Notes, and Correspondence" signed by "F. B." [Bulgarin], concerning Dargomyzhsky's Fantasy on Themes from *A Life for the Tsar* (performed on 9 April), it says that it was first written for solo piano but was so difficult that Anton Rubinstein refused to play it. Only after this did Dargomyzhsky rework it for piano four-hands.

15 April

In *Panteon,* vol. 8, no. 4, "Petersburg Herald: New Musical Works," there is a notice of the publication of a new edition of *Kamarinskaya* in a transcription for piano four-hands, of the romances *"Slyshu li golos tvoi," "Ne iskushai," "Khodit veter u vorot," "Somnenie"* (new edition), *"Zhavoronok"* (new edition), *"Golos s togo sveta,"* and all the numbers from *A Life for the Tsar* and *Ruslan and Lyudmila* (d.c.a.).

17 April

In connection with the tenth anniversary of the Italian Opera in Petersburg, in *SPb. ved.,* no. 86, the company and repertoire of the Russian Opera, beginning in 1841, are mentioned. Of operas performed earlier it refers to *A Life for the Tsar,* and among the premieres (1842) it names *Ruslan and Lyudmila.*

19 April/1 May

Glinka writes to Shestakova, "Everything is going favorably with us, thank God, and the new apartment is lovely."

23 April

Serov (from Priyut Burluk) asks Dmitry Stasov: "How is our 'Michel' doing in Paris? Is he really bored? This, by the way, is opportune for us: he'll *return home* sooner. The winter would be interesting if by then *everyone* could be together in Petersburg who ought to be. There might then be a variety of musical undertakings *so important* for us all" (*MN* III, p. 158).

26 April

In Petersburg, in a farewell concert before her departure abroad, Pauline Viardot performed "Glinka's inspired melody *'Akh, ne mne bednomu'*" with the assistance of Leonard and Bulakhov (*Sev. pchela,* 4 May 1853).

From the End of April

Glinka met with Aleksey Saltykov, who had arrived from Egypt, and "made a friendly trip . . . to Bois de Boulogne. Later, in the summer, we often had dinner and spent the time together. At heart he is an artist, in his behavior (too polite) a diplomat."

Glinka often visited the Tuilleries gardens, which "are wonderful in the spring— the bright green of the chestnuts (*marroniers*), the lilacs in full bloom, and especially the swarm of attractive and smartly well-dressed children, the little girls especially, are pleasing and attractive."

1/13 May

Glinka writes Shestakova: "There is nothing to say about our quiet and modest life. I will only say that in the evenings Mishka entertains himself with singing and conversation. Most of all, though, I have become good friends with Prince Aleksey Saltykov, the famous traveller. . . . He often visits me and gives me extremely nice drawings which he has done." In a footnote Don Pedro informs her of *"le pauvre Miguelito's"* illness.

3 May

Performance of *Kamarinskaya* at Maurer's musical matinee in Petersburg (*Sev. pchela,* 6 May 1853).

4 May

In *Sev. pchela,* no. 79, there is a review by Rostislav of a performance with Viardot's participation of the "concluding trio" from *A Life for the Tsar,* "the inspiring melody to the words '*Akh, ne mne, bednomu.*' Let the learned gentlemen explain why the audience's enthusiasm is different after an aria from *A Life for the Tsar* than after Italian arias."

In the Aleksandrinsky Theater in Petersburg, a mixed performance (Petrov's benefit) in which the fourth act of *A Life for the Tsar* was performed (*Sev. pchela,* 4 May 1853).

7 May

In *Mosk. ved.,* no. 55, in a review of a concert given by Viardot, regret is expressed over the substitution for an aria by Glinka: "We would have liked very much to hear the music of the brilliant Russian composer sung by the famous artist."

14 May

In *Mosk ved.,* no. 58, there is a "Letter from Petersburg of 2 May" by "B." [Bulgarin] concerning the enthusiastic reception of the trio from *A Life for the Tsar* performed by Viardot, Leonard, and Bulakhov on 26 April.

15/27 May

Glinka writes to Shestakova that his health "has improved noticeably." In answer to one of her letters he writes: "You call me . . . *clever.* How am I *clever*? Isn't it true that clever people seek something better of what's good? Wouldn't it be smarter for me to live with you, my dear little cuckoo? Judge for yourself about this: it suits neither me nor my age [*mne ne k litsu i ne po letam*] to wander about in distant lands! . . . 'But [your] friends, and Pedrusha,' you say; friends are there more in good weather . . . but Pedrusha is just as good and obliging and, so far as one can judge, just as devoted to me and our family as before. But neither our stay in Paris nor his courses in language and declamation, which he attends daily, have changed him. . . . He is a *difficult* person, especially

when I am sick, for he neither had, has, nor will he ever have any understanding about *delicacy*. Most of all . . . he is stubborn and secretive."
["It suits neither me nor my age" is a quotation from Pushkin's poem *"Ia vas liubil"* [I loved you].]

15 May

In *Sev. pchela,* no. 107, there are comments about the recitatives in *A Life for the Tsar* in Rostislav's "Musical Conversations."

20 May/1 June

Glinka writes to Shestakova: "I am 49 today, 50 approaches, and what will it be like? . . . I am tired of being in foreign places. I often reproach myself for undertaking this ridiculous and unfortunate trip."

21 May

In a mixed performance in memory of Vasily Karatygin in the Aleksandrinsky Theater in Petersburg, "In the divertissement . . . Petrov and Leonova sang the doleful, heartfelt Russian songs of M. I. Glinka" (*Sev. pchela,* 21 May 1853).

In *Panteon,* vol. 9, part 5, under "Petersburg Herald: New Musical Composi-tions," among romances performed "by Mme Viardot-Garcia with great suc-cess," "the song and trio from *A Life for the Tsar,* '*Akh, ne mne [bednomu], sirotinushke"* is named (d.c.a.).

In *Panteon,* vol. 9, part 6, in the section "Repertory of the Russian Stage," there is a drama by Vonlyarsky entitled *Liubov' artista* [The artist's love], in which, during the course of the action, the orchestra performs Glinka's *Kamarinskaya* (d.c.a.).

Serov (from Priyut Burluk) writes to Dmitry Stasov and expresses his regret that Viardot will no longer be coming to Petersburg. "Let's assume that when Mikhail Ivanovich is there, Woldemar can have his sensible concerts fairly often and Gluck's marvels will not be lost to me for long." He reports: "I'm soon going to begin a new series of articles. . . . *Their subject will be* opera in our time (anger toward Meyerbeer) and the operatic ideal in general. . . . I will also include a pragmatic history of opera . . . and analysis of the newest works (including, perhaps, both Wagner and Glinka)" (*MN* III, pp. 160, 163).

Spring

"Even though the Eastern Question flared up more and more and I saw even then that it would lead to war; despite the fact that I suffered frequently from stomach and nervous ailments; despite this, I must add, that my suffering and sad thoughts caused me homesickness (*nostalgie*), there were some gratifying moments."

"Sometimes Amalia was amusing, but more often she plagued me with her excessive liveliness. She left for Bordeaux sometime around the beginning of June. By chance before her departure a Spanish acquaintance of ours turned up. . . . Antonia was a very pretty, playful, and cheerful Andalusian girl. Unfortunately she soon left" (*Zap.*).

1 June

In *Rus. khudozh. listok,* no. 16, in an article called "A. S. Dargomyzhsky's Concert," it refers to Dargomyzhsky's and Santis's performance of Dargomyzhsky's Fantasy on Themes from *A Life for the Tsar.*

3/15 June

Glinka writes to Shestakova: "Boredom and melancholy are quickly consuming me. I am drawn homeward like I was in 1833. . . . With the exception of my melancholy, or rather nostalgia, my health is improving. Still I am not of an age to enjoy myself in Paris . . . my ideas and feelings have changed. All the things that are called the pleasures of life here offer me no comfort. . . . Paris strikes one with its false splendor, and living here as I have lived . . . you see that everything is vanity, vanity, and vanity."

3 June

In *Sev. pchela,* no. 122, Rostislav writes in his "Petersburg Letters": "Petersburg audiences judge musical works with great care, observing first the musical *horizon,* especially the works of native composers. Of course they have gone to hear M. I. Glinka's most famous works, *A Life for the Tsar* and *Ruslan and Lyudmila.* Not many, however, offered to express a candidly favorable opinion, and only now, while Glinka is silent and his operas are almost never produced, have they begun to judge them justly and admire what was artistically beautiful even then."

6 June

In *Bib-ka dlia chteniia,* no. 119, the following romances by Glinka are cited in an announcement of new music: *"O, milaia deva," "Finskii zaliv,"* and Yakovlev's *"Elegiia,"* arranged by Glinka for two voices.

14/26 June

Aleksey Saltykov has dinner at Glinka's. "The prince was simply a godsend to me: he was good, pleasant, and *delicate* to a fault."

16/28 June

Glinka writes to Shestakova that each month he is putting away 200 francs to buy a carriage in order to return to Russia.

Ca. 25 June/7 July

Glinka received "a long, friendly, and amusing message from Vasily Pavlovich Engelgardt. Among other things he informed me that the singer Viardot got a tremendous response with my trio *'Akh, ne mne bednomu sirotinushke,'* which she sang in Russian."

Meyerbeer visited Glinka. "I had always been very close to him. He was a pleasant and well-mannered man. He promised to arrange some performances of Gluck's operas for me in Berlin if I gave him and my teacher Dehn a month's advance notice" (ltr. to L. Shestakova, 26 June/8 July 1853). "From Gluck we moved to other classical composers, and I expressed my views on art. *'Mais vous êtes très difficile,'* Meyerbeer said to me. *'J'en ai complètement le droit,'* I answered him, *'Je commence par mes propres oeuvres, dont je suis rarement content'* " (*Zap.*).

26 June/8 July

Glinka tells Shestakova: "Your Polka is very fashionable here, and the Parisians, especially the ladies, find it very moving."
[The polka is the "Primary Polka."]

3 July

Dargomyzhsky writes to Odoevsky (from Petersburg): "The more I study our musical folk elements, the more variety I discover in them. Glinka, who is the only one so far to give Russian music broad dimensions, still, in my opinion, has only touched one aspect of it, the lyrical side. His drama is too doleful, and the comic side loses its national quality. I am talking about the character of his music, because his style is always impeccable. Insofar as I am capable, in my *Rusalka* I am working on the development of our dramatic elements. I will be happy if I succeed in this to half the extent that Mikhail Ivanovich Glinka has" (coll. *Dargomyzhsky,* p. 41).

12/24 July

Glinka complains to Shestakova about the poor condition of his health, particularly his "nerves" and homesickness. He writes further: 'The romance *"Ia liubliu, ty mne tverdila'* [*Te souviens-tu*], I recommend you find and entrust to Dubrovsky."

Ca. 23 July/4 August

Ivan Shestakov visited Glinka. "[He was] a dear and practical man."

23 July/4 August

Glinka writes to Shestakova that in Paris "I miss my own people, and you are perhaps right in preferring Petersburg to Moscow, where you will not find such company as we have kept." In a footnote Don Pedro writes of his upcoming walks with *"petit Michel"* in the Botannical Gardens, Luxembourg, and the Champs Elysées.

June–July

"Besides visiting the Jardin des Plantes and walking in the environs, I sometimes liked to entertain my countrymen at dinner. Every newly arrived friend, on my insistent demands, came to my place for dinner. With Zoë [an Indian servant] I myself went to select fruits and was able to manage very nicely" (*Zap.*).

End of July

Glinka's Warsaw acquaintance A. K. Kazachkovsky arrived: "I was extremely glad to see him. He is a dear and very *delicate* man, in a word, he is a colleague to my liking. My other friends have all left town now, and you could not track them down with dogs" (ltr. to L. Shestakova, 2/14 August 1853).

June? July?

The dressmaker Adelina visited Amalia before the latter's departure. "Adeline H. . . . on my invitation often visited me and during the summer moved in with me in the capacity of nurse. She was approaching 30, was pleasant, rather well educated, and a very literate lady" (*Zap.*).

July?

In a park near the Forestry Institute in Petersburg there was a concert for Schindler's benefit in which 16 German performers "jauntily dashed off Glinka's *Kamarinskaya*" (*Panteon*, 1853, vol. 10, no. 8, p. 50).

2/14 August

Glinka advises Shestakova to put their relations with their sister Olga aright: "I even hope that her feelings for us will return. To this end I recommend that you *not try to ingratiate yourself* . . . but . . . let her know that we are prepared to forget the past."
[Apparently the cause of the quarrel between Shestakova and her sisters stemmed from Glinka's will and the division of the estates.]

6 August

In *SPb. ved.*, no. 172, "Petersburg Chronicle," signed "V. G.," it reports that compositions for guitar by Vladimir Morkov are available in Stellovsky's store. The works named include *Kamarinskaya*, "borrowed from M. I. Glinka's work for full orchestra; a grand fantasy from the opera *A Life for the Tsar* . . . and the Cavatina from the opera *Ruslan and Lyudmila* for two guitars."

9/21 August

Glinka sent Shestakova the romance *"Ia liubliu, ty mne tverdila,"* and in an accompanying letter he includes the French text of the romance (*Te souviens-tu*). He writes that Saltykov and Kazachkovsky visit him "oftener than anyone else."

11 August

In *Sev. pchela*, no. 176, Ulybyshev's "Letter to Mr. Rostislav" is printed, which mentions Glinka's letter of recommendation concerning Serov, addressed to Ulybyshev "some ten years prior to this."

22 August/3 September

Glinka writes to Shestakova: "I am drawn to our motherland, and if I do not follow my heart's strong inclination, it is because I know from experience how much my health depends upon the climate. It is not unfounded that I am afraid of an abrupt move from the very moderate climate here to our harsh one. However, there is no bad without good, and you cannot imagine the extent to which I cherish and am devoted to our country and how devotedly I love you and our dear, good countrymen. This is all because I have had sufficient time to study Paris. Everything here is superficial brilliance, in essence egotism, self-interest, and indifference, to the extent that I cannot avoid yearning for and recalling Russia and its cordiality, hospitality, and friendliness, often very sincere." He writes that he is reading Rousseau's *Emile*. "There is much about it that is good. In his opinion there is nothing which can replace a mother and education."

25 August

In Petersburg, at the mineral waters bottling works in Novaya Derevnya, a chorus of Moscow gypsies gave a performance. "When Liza and Masha sang '*Khodit veter u vorot*' and '*Bez uma, bez razuma*' [Without sense, without reason] (a romance by Prince Trubetskoy), the music lovers went out of their minds with excitement" (*Panteon*, 1853, vol. 11, part 9, p. 31).

1/13 September

Glinka writes to Shestakova that he hopes to return to his homeland in the spring. "For a long time, for a very long time now I have dreamed of a little house with a *little garden*, but with the garden *behind* the house, so that it cannot be seen from the street. This is because I am an unsociable person, and the presence of strangers is alien to me and can poison everything. . . . Above all, besides rooms for my bedroom and study, I would like to have an adjoining room for birds, so that the room for the birds separates my bedroom from that of Pedrusha. . . . This Pedrusha is very much given to mechanical exercises, and in the morning he often scrubs, saws, scrapes, etc., which grates on my nerves and offends my ears."

5 September

In *Panteon*, vol. 10, part 8, under "New Musical Works," publications available in Stellovsky's store are enumerated as follows: in the section headed "Russian romances for voice and piano, newly published," the following are cited: *"O, milaia deva," "Ia zdes', Inezil'ia," "Kogda v chas veselyi," "Somnenie," "Slyshu li golos tvoi," "Esli vstrechus' s toboi," "Khodit veter u vorot," "Ne iskushai menia bez nuzhdy," "Golos s togo sveta," "Ne nazyvai ee nebesnoi," "Tol'ko uznal ia tebia," "Sto krasavits," "O, deva chudnaia moia," "Davno li rosko-shno," "Spi, moi angel, pochivai," "Stoi, moi vernyi burnyi kon',"* and *"Mezhdu nebom i zemlei."* Also cited are all numbers from the operas *A Life for the Tsar* and *Ruslan and Lyudmila.*

In the same issue there is an account of Schindler's benefit concert in the park near the Forestry Institute (d.c.a.).

11 September

In Petersburg, a performance of the first and second acts of *A Life for the Tsar* in a mixed performance in the Aleksandrinsky Theater "for the benefit of the actress Mme Lavrova" (*Sev. pchela,* 11 September 1853).

First Half of September

"Michel is less bored than before, thanks to the frequent visits of his country-men, among them the actor Samoylov, who has already done portraits of Michel and Zoya, our maid" (Don Pedro's note in Glinka's ltr. to Shestakova, 17/29 September 1853; Fr. original).
[Two portraits of Glinka by V. V. Samoylov are known: a full length one (GPB, coll. 190, no. 241) and one of Glinka sitting at the piano (ITMK, coll. 6, inventory [*opis'*] 2, no. 21), both of them published.]

17/29 September

Glinka asks Shestakova to "save up" about 20 tropical trees from her orangerie for his "aviary" in Petersburg, where he dreams of acquiring his own little house.

22 September

In the Aleksandrinsky Theater in Petersburg, a mixed performance at which the first and second acts of *A Life for the Tsar* were given (*Sev. pchela,* 22 September 1853).

30 September

In *Panteon,* vol. 11, part 9, "Petersburg Herald: New Musical Compositions," there is an announcement that Stellovsky has works for two guitars by Morkov: a grand fantasy from *A Life for the Tsar* and the cavatina from *Ruslan and Lyudmila* (d.c.a.).

6/18 October

Glinka gives Shestakova some domestic advice: "It would be advisable when opportune to acquire some good linen for shirts and other things. In my opinion, linen, not only for myself and the servants, but also for the beds and the kitchen table, is one of the most important things in housekeeping, for cleanliness is more important than luxury." He shares his impressions of Rousseau's *Emile:* "The book is long and boring, though one does find good ideas in it."

8 October

In a mixed performance in the Aleksandrinsky Theater in Petersburg (for Lileeva's benefit), a scene and aria from *Ruslan and Lyudmila* are performed (*SPb. ved.,* 8 October 1853).

11 October

Performance of a scene and aria from *Ruslan and Lyudmila* in a mixed performance in the Aleksandrinsky Theater in Petersburg (*SPb. ved.,* 11 October 1853).

17/29 October

Glinka agrees to Shestakova's suggestion of spending the summer of 1854 in Tsarskoe Selo, since "first, it is a sublime, healthy, and beautiful place; second, the railroad makes it convenient to get to Piter; third, it reminds me of the happiest days of my youth when I was a guest there of Princess Khovanskaya, whose son was a friend of mine. . . . Finally, fourth, it is not superfluous that it is at most seven to ten minutes to Pavlovsk, which is very pleasant to visit in good weather." He asks that Dmitry Stasov or Maria Krzhisevich be entrusted to seek out a little house. "I would very much like that there be a little garden behind the house." He gives domestic instructions: "Be so kind as to attend to matters in the kitchen, that is, the cook's clothing, and primarily the *washing*— the most important thing from them is cleanliness . . . have clothing made for the people, especially so that there is enough linen. Contented people will make it happier for us."

22 October

Serov (from Sevastopol) complains to Dmitry Stasov that he is tired from writing out the score to *May Night,* that is, from "the actual 'writing' of the notes! And Glinka floundered through such huge five-act operas! (In *Ruslan,* there are probably far more than 1000 pages, and I'll only have about 600)!..." He laments the death from cholera in Petersburg "of our dear mutual acquaintance, the young sailor Shestakov.... Who would have thought, when we shared a bottle of ale with this fine young man and Mikhail Ivanovich at the *Birzha* that this youth was fated to only live another year!!" He writes further that the part of the Head in *May Night* is intended for Osip Petrov, "just as Glinka ... could not find a better singer for Susanin," although the part of Susanin only shows a "hint" of "profound comedy." "There, however, there could be no more than a trace of the actual elements of *burlesque* and *grotesque* because of the seriousness of the subject" (*MN* III, p. 171).
[Dmitry Alekseevich Shestakov (1821–53) was a relative of Lyudmila Shestakova's husband.]

Between October and the Beginning of November (?)

Glinka gave the artist Mikhail Zheleznov his calling card to carry to "Vladimir Vasilievich Stasov in Florence."
[Dated approximately in reference to V. Stasov's letter of 18/30 November (q.v.).]

4/16 November

Glinka recommends to Shestakova that she read *A Thousand and One Nights,* which "is not a silly thing for children to read but a collection of thoughtful and clever tales." He writes that he intends to return to Russia by 15 May 1854.

15/27 November

To Shestakova's question if he has seen Rachel, he answers: "I have not seen Rachel—*depression* has not permitted me and still does not allow me to go to the theaters. Pedrusha will describe her to you—this is his province." He writes that he has received a letter from their sister Olga—"*very* touching and tender— not a word about you or about the past."

18/30 November

Vladimir Stasov (from Florence) thanks Glinka for sending his visiting card by way of Zheleznov: "What a joy . . . it was for me to suddenly see after such a terribly long break that you had not forgotten me, even in Paris." He invites Glinka to Rome, where "among the *genuine* talents" only Aleksandr Ivanov and Moller remain. "What if another famous Russian name were to be added to their's, one who all of a sudden has taken the notion of falling asleep somewhere, or, at least, of dozing off in a corner!" (Collection of the Pushkin House for 1923, Petrograd, 1922, p. 196).

20 November

Performance in a mixed concert in the Aleksandrinsky Theater in Petersburg of the epilog from *A Life for the Tsar* (a poster).

3/15 December

Glinka sends Shestakova V. Stasov's letter from Florence, which "made me very happy . . . perhaps you can forward it to our company in Piter."

4/16 December

Glinka thanks V. Stasov for his "cordial and touching message." In response to Stasov's enthusiastic opinion of Rossini, Glinka writes: "Your opinion of him does not surprise me . . . Dehn in Berlin, and before him (in 1832) Pollini in Milan could not speak about him without enthusiasm. However, we are all more or less *egoists,* and I admit that your abundant harvest of ancient Italian music is closer to my heart than all Rossini's perfection." He urges Stasov to travel to Petersburg for the winter of 1854. "You will hardly find anywhere such fervent admirers of classical music: your brother, Serov, a certain Engelgardt, I, and others during the winter of 1851–52, amused ourselves a great deal with everything we could, but we know the old Italians poorly. We do not have their music."
[In Florence Stasov had copies made of the works of old Italian composers from the collection of Abbot Santini.]

4 December

In *Sev. pchela,* no. 270, there is an announcement that Vladimir Morkov's transcriptions for guitar of *Kamarinskaya,* a fantasy on motives from *A Life for the Tsar,* and Gorislava's cavatina from *Ruslan and Lyudmila* are for sale in Stellovsky's store.

6/18 December

Glinka writes to Dubrovsky: "I am in the most disgusting city, especially for an artist. . . . Soon I hope to tear myself away from this cursed Babylon."

6 December

"Successful performance of *A Life for the Tsar*" in the Aleksandrinsky Theater in Petersburg (ltr. to L. Shestakova, 1/13 January 1854).

8/20 December

Glinka asks Shestakova to entrust Dmitry Stasov with finding a dacha for them in Tsarskoe Selo—"a separate little house (without other tenants) with a little garden to the rear."

12/24 December

Glinka asks Dmitry Stasov to write Vladimir Stasov and request that he forward to Petersburg "several individual pieces, especially a capella works" by the Italian classics. He refers to his request to locate a dacha in Tsarskoe Selo and indicates his own requirements regarding its location. "From the onset of spring this year I have been overcome by *nostalgia,* but now the thought of returning soon to my native land and of meeting you have somewhat calmed me."

Glinka informs Engelgardt of his impending return, complains of his homesickness, and shares his impressions of Paris.

22 December/3 January 1854

In a letter to Shestakova, Glinka projects the time of his return to Russia and writes that he will stay in Berlin only in the event "that, as Meyerbeer promised, they perform Gluck in the theater. . . . A week will be sufficient for meeting with my teacher, Dehn."

23 December

In *Sev. pchela,* no. 286, "Observations, Notes, and Correspondence" by Bulgarin, Glinka is named along with Vielgorsky, Lvov, and others as one of "the outstanding Russian composers."

Last Days of December

Glinka receives a letter from Engelgardt "with a detailed description of the successful performance of *A Life for the Tsar*" on 6 December (ltr. to L. Shestakova, 1/13 January 1854).

31 December

Under "Musical News" in *Sovremennik,* vol. 43, part 1 (1854), there is an announcement that new pieces arranged by Vladimir Morkov for guitar are available in Stellovsky's store: a fantasy on motifs from *A Life for the Tsar, Kamarinskaya,* and Gorislava's cavatina from *Ruslan and Lyudmila* (d.c.a.).

1853/54

Winter

During the winter Glinka read "almost all of of Paul de Kock, *A Thousand and One Nights* (what a shame that I did not read these tales before I composed my opera *Ruslan!*), and Boccaccio's *Decameron*. I did not feel like doing serious reading or work."

1854

1/13 January

Glinka writes to Shestakova: "Here it is a new year, the year of our reunion." He sends a list of stories from *A Thousand and One Nights* which he particularly recommends she read and explains in addition that the story of the two sisters who envy the younger sister "was read to me in days of old by [my nurse] Avdotya." He also recommends that she read Boccaccio's *Decameron*. "There are 100 tales of various sorts, including indecent ones that are simply delectable."

16/28 January

Glinka thanks Shestakova for her letter and money. "Your sincere and sensitive friendship and care for me are such that it would take me a century to thank you." He writes that he received "friendly and pleasant" letters from Dubrovsky, Engelgardt, and Vladimir and Dmitry Stasov. He acknowledges that she has "guessed . . . intuitively" that he would like to visit Italy with her, since he was only "in Rome a total of two weeks and did not see the environs of Rome and Florence at all." For a trip to Italy one should "need 1) an understanding of art, and 2) not to travel alone but with someone genuinely receptive to poetry. Who could be better suited to these conditions?"

End of January

Glinka received a letter from Kukolnik which was "very cordial. Incidentally, he beckons me to return to Piter quickly and promises to get up an opera for me. However, he does not have my permission for this. All of these things I hate—the noise of the world, theaters, and even travelling. I thirst for a quiet life in the circle of my family."

2/14 February

Glinka writes to Shestakova: "Winter, thank heaven, is coming to an end, and with it, I hope, my wearying stay abroad." Of himself he writes: "My health . . . is so-so. . . . I can't complain, only I've gotten so obese."

3/15 February

Vladimir Stasov (from Florence) writes to Aleksandr and Dmitry Stasov: "Hunke . . . also says that I will do well if I write my history of music later and establish the music society in Petersburg as I wish to do. I always say to him that in this society he and Glinka will serve as directors (Glinka for everything, and he for financial affairs), Serov as conductor, and I as secretary" (SPR I, p. 251).

4/16 February

Meyerbeer "performed the opera *L'étoile du nord* at the Opéra-Comique. I did not hear it and was indignant because Peter I was portrayed very disrespectfully in it."

4 February

Serov (from Moscow) writes to Dmitry Stasov: "How splendid this summer will be for us when Mikhail Ivanovich returns and my opera will be performed!" (*MN* III, p. 179).

16/28 February

In a letter to Shestakova, Glinka expresses his joy over their forthcoming reunion and reports that he hopes to arrive in Warsaw "by the 15th of April our style."

2/14 March

Glinka asks Shestakova to send to him in Warsaw "one of the dressing gowns she has had made" in care of Kazachkovsky by 15 April. "I should be able to manage (if things turn out as I wish) to spend about three weeks in Warsaw." In a note Don Pedro adds: *"A la maison* everything is very good."

4/16 March

Glinka writes to Maria Krzhisevich: "One finds everything . . . in Paris, everything for the senses and imagination, but for the heart, what can replace one's own people and homeland!" He expresses his condolences over the deaths of Grigory and Anna Dmitrievna Tarnovsky. "I was sorry for them, but more so for you. My pen cannot find words, and do not demand them of me."

5 March

In *Sev. pchela*, no. 52, there is a notice (signed "***") entitled "Two or three words on Russian singing and the concert on 7 March," which is an announcement of Leonova's forthcoming performance of romances by Glinka.

7 March

"Among other pieces" Leonova performs *"Ne nazyvai ee nebesnoi," "V krovi gorit ogon' zhelan'ia,"* and *"Ne o tom skorbliu, podruzhen'ki"* in "a large vocal and instrumental concert with tableaux vivants" done by the decorators Serkov and Valts "for the benefit of D. M. Leonova, artiste of the Imperial Theaters . . ." in Petersburg (*Panteon,* 1854, vol. 14, part 3, p. 93).

10 March

Performance of *Kamarinskaya* under the direction of Shtutsman in Moscow (*Mosk. ved.*, 18 March 1854).

14/26 March

Glinka informs Shestakova that he will be leaving Paris no later than 19 or 23 March "our style."

15/27–16/28 March

England and France, in coalition with Turkey and Sardinia, declare war on Russia.

16 March

Concert in the Hall of Nobility in Tsarskoe Selo for the benefit of the families of those on indefinite furlough, in which Leonova performed *"Akh, ne mne, bednomu sirotinushke"* "to unanimous applause" (*Panteon*, 1854, vol. 14, part 3, p. 93; *Sev. pchela*, 15 March 1854).

February–March

Glinka spent the last months of his stay in Paris playing the violin and "acquired after a fashion a certain *vélocité*" (ltr. to V. Engelgardt, 2 June 1854). "Soon after the announcement of war between Russia and France, Pedro and I left Paris."

Night of 23 March/4 April

Glinka fell ill the night prior to their departure (*Zap.*).

23 March/4 April

Glinka and Don Pedro left Paris in the morning. "Adelina accompanied me to the train" (ltr. to L. Shestakova, 24 March/5 April 1854; *Zap.*).

Brussels. That evening they arrived in Brussels and stayed in the Hôtel de Suède (*Zap.*).

24 March/5 April

Glinka describes his trip in a letter to Shestakova.

Glinka and Don Pedro are invited to dinner by the brother of Henri Beaucé (a Parisian acquaintance, the son of Mme Beaucé). They spent the evening in the theater "and had a rather good laugh. They were performing a play pertaining to the political situation at the time."

25 March/6 April

Glinka visited the Feygen family, one of whose daughters was the fiancée of Berthold Damcke. Afterwards he was in the studio of "a very talented but extremely audacious painter" named Antoine-Josef Wirtz. "His pictures made a very unpleasant impression on me." In the evening Glinka and the Feygens visited "a certain Belgian musical amateur. The violinist Léonard and his wife and Servais were at the party. At my request they performed Beethoven's D-major trio. The host himself played the piano very well, that is, simply (unmannered) and distinctly. Léonard played the violin. The cello was played by I do not know whom, only it was not Servais, who did not play at all but put on airs" (*Zap.*).
[The violinist Léonard was married to the singer Antonia Siches di Mendi, a cousin of Pauline Viardot.]

Damcke "saw Glinka for the last time in the spring of 1854. On his trip from Paris to Petersburg, he stopped in Brussels and spent two days there. . . . He complained more than once that his music was rather coldly received in other countries, whereas in Russia it stirred such lively interest." Damcke explained this by the fact that there were no editions of Glinka's works abroad and tried to persuade him to prepare an edition of *Kamarinskaya*. "Before his departure from Brussels, Glinka gave me the score of his *Kamarinskaya,* which he called *Scherzo Russe*" (Damcke, *Vosp.*, p. 266).

Glinka's inscription on a copy of the score of *Kamarinskaya: "J'autorise Monsieur B. Damcke à faire imprimer cette oeuvre aux conditions que lui paraîtront convenables.*" A note reads, *"L'auteur supplie de ne pas employer les instruments à pistons.*" (*Sov. muzyka,* 1971, no. 10, p. 124).

In Kursk, in a concert "for the benefit of wounded members of the lower ranks . . . S. A. Ladyzhensky sang M. Glinka's very lovely little romance '*Inezil'ia*'" (*Kursk. gub. ved.*, 8 May 1854).

26 March/7 April

Glinka's departure for Berlin by rail via Cologne and Hannover (ltr. to L. Shestakova, 24 March/5 April 1854; *Zap.*).

28 March

Concert of the Philharmonic Society in the Hall of Nobility in St. Petersburg "for the benefit of the hospitals for front-line forces." Among other things arias from *Ruslan and Lyudmila* (Shilovskaya) and *A Life for the Tsar* (Shashina) were performed with Dargomyzhsky accompanying on the piano (Albrecht, *Obshchii obzor deiatel'nosti S.-Peterburgskogo Filarmonicheskogo obshchestva* [Overview of the activities of the St. Petersburg Philharmonic Society], p. 17; *Panteon*, 1854, vol. 14, part 4, p. 53).

30 March/11 April

Berlin. Arrival of Glinka and Don Pedro in Berlin. Glinka felt as if he "had been ground to powder by the train."

31 March/12 April

Glinka writes to Shestakova that he will be detained in Berlin, since his "friend and teacher Dehn . . . intends to entertain [me] . . . with some good music," and furthermore he may succeed in hearing "one of Gluck's operas in the theater here."

1 April

In *Panteon*, vol. 14, part 3, "Petersburg Herald—Social Life," there is a reference to Leonova's success with her performance in Tsarskoe Selo of *"Akh, ne mne, bednomu."* The article discusses the large vocal and instrumental concert for Leonova's benefit, where she performed romances by Glinka (d.c.a.).

2/14 April

Glinka attended a *Singverein*, where "they performed Graun's *Tod Jesu*. The singing was not bad, but the orchestra was weak, and the music even weaker" (*Zap.*).

6/18 April

Glinka heard "the great organist, perhaps the greatest in the world," Haupt, who played Bach. "He worked such amazing things with his feet that I simply doff my hat to him."

Between 31 March/12 April and 7/19 April

"Dehn entertained" Glinka "continuously with every possible treat," namely quartets by Beethoven and Haydn. "I prefer Haydn . . . to all others in this type of music" (ltrs. to L. Shestakova, 7/19 April, and N. Kukolnik, 12 November 1854).

Upon the advice of the publisher Schlesinger, Glinka paid a visit to the prima donna Koester, with the request that she promote the performance of one of Gluck's operas during his stay in Berlin (*Zap.*).

7/19 April

Glinka writes to Shestakova: "Despite the plaintive promises, I have little hope of hearing any Gluck. If so, *fine;* if not, we'll still be leaving here on the twenty-fifth, that is, 13 April, like all the others, that is to say, *by train.* We will not hire a carriage." He writes of his Berlin impressions: "After Paris everywhere else seems *provincial.* I will not say boring."

8/20 April

Glinka again heard "a quartet and the organ" (ltr. to L. Shestakova, 7/19 April 1854).

13/25 April

Glinka writes to Dubrovsky that he was "entertained" in Berlin with classical music. He asks that two rooms be found for him in Petersburg before Shestakova's arrival.

"On the King's orders . . . they gave *Gluck's Armide for me* in a most splendid performance. Such a portion of satisfaction I have never received. All of this I arranged myself, without Meyerbeer's assistance" (ltr. to L. Shestakova, 20 April/2 May 1854). "The effect of this music on the stage exceeded my expectations. The D-major scene with mutes in the magic forest was fascinating. The *hatred* scene in the third act (the 'great scene,' as the Germans call it) was exceptionally majestic. Mme Koester, in my opinion, was fine, sang accurately, and acted intelligently. . . . In my opinion the orchestra was incomparably better than in the Paris Conservatory. They played without affectation and distinctly. . . . The sets were very good . . . the gardens from landscapes by Claude Lorraine, the ballet, etc." (*Zap.*).

13 April

In a concert in Petersburg, Leonova performed a "Russian Song" by Glinka, orchestrated by Konstantin Lyadov (*Sev. pchela,* 22 April 1854).

14/26 April

Glinka departs for Warsaw via Breslau and Chenstokhov (ltr. to P. Dubrovsky, 13/25 April 1854).

16/28 April

Warsaw. Arrival by train.

20 April/2 May

Glinka tells Shestakova of his arrival and thanks her for the parcel.

28 April/10 May

Note to Krzhisevich: "In these gloomy old squares of Warsaw, my orphaned heart has come to life with the recognition that you have preserved a memory of poor me."

Glinka applies to the director of the Warsaw Post Office "to reserve . . . a small post-chaise by 10 May."

Glinka writes to Shestakova about his ill health: "You say that I am clever. If this were in fact true, would I have forsaken you, my little dove? Would I have decided, heaven knows why, to wander around about infidel lands? Now the Lord has ordered me home, and I live with the single thought of my imminent reunion with you and ours."

4 May

In *Panteon*, vol. 14, part 4, in the section "Petersburg Herald—Music," the performance of vocal works by Glinka in a concert of the Philharmonic Society on 28 March is mentioned (d.c.a.).

5 May

In *Sev. pchela*, no. 92, "Survey of the Activities of the St. Petersburg Theaters during the Years 1853/54," R. Zotov cites *A Life for the Tsar* as one of the operas which were performed.

End of April–Beginning of May (?)

In a note to Nikolay Pavlishchev, Glinka writes that he is sick and is not going out.

8 May

In *Kursk. gub. ved.*, no. 19, a performance of the romance *"Ia zdes', Inezil'ia"* in a concert on 25 March is mentioned.

11/23 May

Glinka and Don Pedro leave for Petersburg by post-chaise.

16 May

Petersburg. Early in the morning they pass through Petersburg to Tsarskoe Selo.

Tsarskoe Selo. Arrival with Don Pedro. They find Shestakova and "my little god-child Olinka in perfect health" (*Zap.*).
[The address was *Malaya ulitsa*, number 45, Meyer's house. (The common name of the street is *Griaznaia ulitsa*.) The building has not been preserved. Glinka concludes his *Zapiski* with the description of his arrival in Tsarskoe Selo.]

"Our dacha was . . . very comfortable, with a nice balcony and a small garden. Both parks were very close to us. . . . The orangeries were also not far from us" (Shestakova, *Vosp.*, p. 296).

18 May

In the Aleksandrinsky Theater in Petersburg a performance of *"A Life for the Tsar* for the benefit of Mme Stepanova," and after the performance, a divertissement "of dances and singing" (*Sev. pchela,* 18 May 1854).

21 May

A large company gathered to celebrate Glinka's nameday, and Glinka "was cheerful" (Shestakova, *Vosp.,* p. 297).

27 May

In the June literary supplement to *Le Nouvelliste,* in the section "Internal News," the results of the winter season are reckoned up. The article states that "Mme Stepanova selected the opera *A Life for the Tsar* for her benefit, an opera which audiences consistently enjoy" (d.c.a.).

Spring

Damcke tried to publish *Kamarinskaya* abroad with Breitkopf and Härtel in Leipzig, Schott in Mainz, and other publishers, and was turned down everywhere. "Leaving the publishers alone, I turned to conductors and performers. Alas . . . in everyone's eyes, Glinka was guilty of the fact that he was still alive" (Damcke, *Vosp.,* p. 266).

2 June

Glinka asks Krzhisevich to come and get Ekaterina Kern's letters, which he has "carefully preserved . . . my sister now has them. Come quickly for them, for I am sure that by returning these letters, you will calm our friend no little." In a note Shestakova also invites Krzhisevich to visit, "the sooner to console her."
[In 1854, on the insistence of relatives, Ekaterina Kern married Mikhail Shokalsky. According to her son, Yuly Shokalsky, his mother burned her correspondence with Glinka shortly before her death in 1904.]

Glinka asks Engelgardt to send him a violin. "The desire to saw on the violin nags at me . . . if I can continue my practice here, in time I might be able to play *second* part (not in quartets), but in accompaniments to the vocal music of Handel, Bach, and other similar works." He asks Dmitry Stasov to give him the addresses of Bilibina and Lomakin. He writes further: "I hurry to inform you that tomorrow I will begin my biography according to your outline, as my sister Lyudmila instructed me."

3 June

Glinka began to write his *Zapiski*. The author's date is "Tsarskoe Selo, 3 June 1854."

4 June

Glinka invites Bilibina to Tsarskoe Selo and gives her his address. "I cannot be in Petersburg myself because of an ailment in my leg."

22 June

Glinka asks Dmitry Stasov to order a gift for Olya for her nameday, a silver saucepan. "I cannot stand to give those I love finery, sweets, and other things which are soon destroyed."

End of June

"In looking over the score of *Ruslan,* I found it necessary and beneficial for effect to make changes in several places in the score" (ltr. to L. Heydenreich, 3 June 1854).

June, July

"Overall we lived well. My brother was healthy and satisfied. Generally his day was spent as follows: he got up rather early and covered an entire page of his *Zapiski* with his small script. At about ten o'clock he came in for tea . . . and read to me what he had written that morning. After talking a little while, we went out on the balcony. Sometimes he wrote something or another . . . but more often he read alone or I read to him aloud. For a break he would lie around or play with my little girl . . . on the carpet spread out there on the balcony. When, as often happened, the kitten was brought to them, he was contented. At one o'clock we had lunch, after which acquaintances from Petersburg normally arrived. In the evening we took a walk in one of the parks or the orangerie" (Shestakova, *Vosp.,* p. 296).

3 July

Glinka asks Dmitry Stasov about Kologrivov: "Where is he?" He requests that an invitation be extended to Levitsky: "I would awfully much like to see him."

In an invitation to Heydenreich to come for Olya's nameday on 11 July, Glinka asks him to request Pavel Fedorov to arrange a meeting with Konstantin Lyadov for the purpose of making changes in several places in the score of *Ruslan and Lyudmila*. "In this matter I cannot and should not proceed without K. Lyadov."
[Konstantin Lyadov was at the time conductor of the Russian Opera in St. Petersburg.]

11 July

Celebration of Olya's nameday (ltr. to L. Heydenreich, 3 July 1854).

27 July

Glinka began to teach Shestakova German. An inscription on the book *Lehren der Weisheit und Tugend* (Stuttgart, 1853) reads: "Begun on 27 July 1854. *Schön*!!!" (ITMK, coll. 6).

May–July

"At the time we were visited most frequently by A. F. Lvov, V. P. Engelgardt, I. A. Shestakov, A. N. Serov, D. V. Stasov, K. P. Villebois, and P. P. Ryndin and his wife. Vasily Pavlovich Engelgardt was extremely fond of my brother and always afforded him every possible musical pleasure and even in Tsarskoe arranged quartet evenings with Pikkel and others. Among other things they performed one of my brother's youthful works, and he did not recognize his own quartet. . . . Ivan Alekseevich Shestakov and Aleksandr Nikolaevich Serov visited us" (Shestakov, *Vosp.*, p. 297).

Before 31 July

Glinka wrote "Notes for V. P. Engelgardt's Travels" in Italy: "To be able to use one's time well is the first condition of prudent travelling." There follows advice on just what should be seen and in what order.

31 July

Via the departing Engelgardt, Glinka sends to Dehn a gift for the royal library of his compositions for orchestra and also asked that the library be given the variant of his *Jota aragonesa,* which he had left in Berlin. As a gift to Dehn he sends an antique snuff-box. He recommends Engelgardt as one of his best friends and writes that he is a fine musician and that he has the perseverance to assemble all of Glinka's manuscripts which time has not destroyed.

Glinka gave Engelgardt several calling cards. Among those preserved are ones addressed to Karl Meier, Lipiński, and Dr. Moritz Wolf.

2 August

In *Otech. zap.,* vol. 96, part 8, under "New Musical Works," there is an announcement of new publications, among them romances by Glinka: *"Ne nazyvai ee nebesnoi," "Tol'ko uznal ia tebia," "Sto krasavits svetlookikh," "O, deva chudnaia moia," "Mezhdu nebom i zemlei," "Prosti! korabl' vzmakhnul krylom"* [Farewell! The ship's sails have unfurled], *"Ne trebui pesen ot pevtsa"* [Do not demand songs from the singer], as well as *A Life for the Tsar* for voice and piano, and Vollweiler's transcriptions for piano of the romances *"Somnenie"* and *"Ne trebui pesen ot pevtsa"* (d.c.a.).

Beginning of August

Glinka asks Dmitry Stasov to send him Weber's *Invitation to the Dance* and music paper, and he requests that he try to persuade Serov "to hurry up and visit us." He writes that he has completed his *Zapiski* to the point of the first performance of *A Life for the Tsar.* He invites Dmitry Stasov to come visit with his brother in order to read through what he has written.

"So the time passed until August. We did not go anywhere. My brother did not like to go out. One time we were in Pavlovsk for the music, and that at my request. In the beginning of August, Engelgardt went abroad. I noticed that his departure told upon my brother, and that together with the fact that autumn was approaching, and it was beginning to get cold and rainy and the nights darker— all this together made my brother eager to hurry our return to the city" (Shestakova, *Vosp.,* p. 297).

13 August

In *Sev. pchela*, no. 180, the first article of Rostislav's (Feofil Tolstoy's) "Musical Conversations: On the Artistic Activity of M. I. Glinka—Detailed Critique of the Opera *A Life for the Tsar*." "The most important and, so to say, genuine cause of my entrance into the thankless field of music criticism is none other . . . than my sincere interest in the works of our native composers. The thought that M. I. Glinka's works of genius have still not been analyzed, studied, and evaluated according to their merits has pursued me relentlessly."

Second Half of August

"An apartment had already been located and taken . . . in Tomilova's house on Ertelev Lane. . . . It was strange to move from Tsarskoe in the month of August when the fall there is so beautiful, but to my brother it was cold. . . . Because of the bad weather our guests were fewer, and he was getting bored" (Shestakova, *Vosp.*, p. 297).
[The present address of Glinka's last apartment is Chekhov Street no. 7. There is a memorial plaque on the house (thanks to the efforts of Vladimir Stasov).]

19 August

In *Sev. pchela*, no. 185, Rostislav's second article on *A Life for the Tsar*. He cites brief biographical facts about Glinka and discusses the creation "of that immense sea of harmony and melody known by the name of *A Life for the Tsar*."

25 August

Petersburg. Glinka moved to Petersburg "with [my] sister, the baby, and domestics." "Our apartment was simply charming." The address was Ertelev Lane, Tomilova's house, no. 7 (ltrs. to V. Engelgardt, 16 September, and to N. Kukolnik, 12 November 1854).

In *Sev. pchela*, no. 190, Rostislav's third article on *A Life for the Tsar*, this one including an analysis of the overture, introduction, cavatina, and Antonida's rondo.

26 August

Performance for Bulakhov's benefit in the Aleksandrinsky Theater of *A Life for the Tsar* and a divertissement of dances (*Sev. pchela*, 26 August 1854).

After 25 August, Beginning of September (?)

Serov asks Dmitry Stasov to take Serov's compositions to Kologrivov's, if he should have occasion to be there, but "under no condition to tell anyone, not even Glinka, who their author is. Invent some kind of story. . . . I will be sincerely glad and grateful to you if they were all played at Kologrivov's, even in Mikhail Ivanovich's presence" (*MN* III, p. 179).

[The beginning of the letter and date are missing. The dating here is conditionally established after Glinka's move from Tsarskoe Selo to Petersburg, when he might have been at musical evenings at Kologrivov's. In published editions the letter is dated "not earlier than August."]

3 September

In *Sev. pchela*, no. 197, there is a letter to the editor from Rozen titled "On a strange theft of authorship." Rozen points out to Rostislav, who had not mentioned the librettist, that Glinka could not have been the author of the text for *A Life for the Tsar.* "Who might think that a young man . . . could accomplish what Zhukovsky could not do!" Later he provides examples of his verses, "distorted" by Glinka, and asks the question: "Could M. I. Glinka have been the author of the *poetic part* of our opera?"

6 September

In *Sev. pchela*, no. 199, the fourth of Rostislav's articles on *A Life for the Tsar* (a continuation of his critique of the first act).

7 September

In *Otech. zap.*, vol. 96, part 9, "Miscellany: Petersburg Notes," the "news" is reported that "one of Russia's most well-known composers is preparing a symphony on 'Taras Bulba.' Those who value everything Russian rejoice with us of course, both for the appearance of a new piece of music by one of our compatriots as well as for the title of the symphony" (d.c.a.).

9 September

Rostislav's answer to Rozen appears in *Sev. pchela*, no. 201, as a "letter to the editor" and includes a harsh critique of the libretto. "In *A Life for the Tsar* . . . only M. I. Glinka's musical ability . . . was able to smooth out all the unevenness and conceal the roughness of the verse."

Glinka held a musical evening, "which we enjoyed pleasantly together in the company of our friends and artists." At this party Glinka presented Dmitry Stasov with "the greater part" of his romances bound in one volume (dedicatory inscription to D. Stasov, 17 March 1855).

10 September

A Life for the Tsar is performed in a mixed concert in the Maly Theater in Moscow (for the benefit of Kurov) (*Mosk. ved.,* 9 September 1854).

12 September

Announcement of new music in Stellovsky's store, in *Panteon,* vol. 16, part 8. Among the works for piano are *Privet otchizne. Muzykal'nye ocherki* [A greeting to my native land. Musical sketches]. No. 1, *"Souvenir d'une mazurka."* No. 2, *"La Barcarolle."* Among the vocal works are *"K nei"* [To her], *"Tol'ko uznal ia tebia," "Sto krasavits svetlookikh," "O, deva chudnaia moia," "Ne trebui pesen ot pevtsa,"* and *"Ne nazyvai ee nebesnoi"* (d.c.a.).

13 September

In *Sev. pchela,* no. 204, the fifth of Rostislav's articles on *A Life for the Tsar* (continuation, analysis of act II).

15 September

In *Sev. pchela,* no. 206, Rostislav publishes an excerpt from chapter 1 of Ulybyshev's unpublished book *Betkhoven i ego tolkovateli* [Beethoven and his interpreters], where an evaluation of *A Life for the Tsar* appears: "The opera . . . is one of the greatest artistic works of the current century. It embodies visible progress with respect to both composition and music. M. I. Glinka has remained entirely true to Russian character, and for the first time in his opera there is national music appropriate to the greatness of the Russian people." The article continues with the polemic with Rozen over the libretto.

Between the Beginning of August and 16 September

Glinka "orchestrated" Weber's *Invitation to the Dance.*

By 16 September

Glinka completed his *Zapiski* "to Little Russia." He works on the orchestration of Hummel's Nocturne in F Major.

16 September

Glinka writes to Engelgardt: *"Just as a wolf must always return to the forest, so it is with me. Despite my sister's care, I am uncomfortable in the north."*

17 September

Glinka received Dehn's letter of 21 August/2 September, which expresses thanks for the snuff-box and scores, "which have great significance not only for me but for all the connoisseurs to whom I have showed them. They represent a great stride in art, thanks to the felicitous selection and inventive originality of the thematic material; to the careful and effective arrangement of the whole; and, finally, to the brilliant economy of means in carrying it out, as well as the formal perfection of individual numbers, and the clarity of the whole. . . . You have created a a unique new direction in art." Concerning Glinka's work on the *Zapiski:* "Not only will it be interesting for me and musical biographers to read your memoirs, but with them you will render the history of art a serious favor" (*RMG*, 1911, no. 48; German original).

Glinka asks Dmitry Stasov to obtain a box at the French Theater and invites him to accompany them. He writes that he has received a letter from Dehn, "which I can only make out with difficulty; it is written in German."
[Because of his poor eyesight Glinka had difficulty making out Dehn's handwriting, since the letter is written in Gothic script. Glinka knew German well.].

Censor's authorization for Stellovsky's edition of Glinka's romance *"Ia liubliu, ty mne tverdila."*

21 September

In *Sev. pchela*, no. 211, Rostislav's sixth article on *A Life for the Tsar* (analysis of the third act).

A Life for the Tsar is presented in a mixed performance in the Maly Theater in Moscow for the benefit of Kurov (*Mosk. ved.,* 21 September 1854).

24 September

In *Rus. invalid,* no. 214, among correspondence from Moscow, there is this report: "The Russian Theater is preparing many new things. Benefits have already begun, and thanks to Mr. Kurov, several days ago we heard the finest Russian opera, *A Life for the Tsar.* We have not had the pleasure of hearing this opera for a long time now. The greater the attention we paid to it now, the greater was our enjoyment."

27 September

Rostislav's seventh (and final) article on *A Life for the Tsar* (an analysis of the fourth act) appears in *Sev. pchela,* no. 216. In conclusion the author compares *A Life for the Tsar* with *Ruslan:* "Although in many respects it [the second opera] is not inferior to the first opera, it is unfortunately no less perceptibly removed from the folk-melodic character of the music."

1 October

In *Otech. zap.,* vol. 96, part 10, under "New Musical Works," there is an announcement that Kullak's piano transcription of *"Ia pomniu chudnoe mgnoven'e"* is available.

Beginning of October, Before the 5th

Glinka writes to Dmitry Stasov: "Come to see us, we are bored, Olenka is sick, and my sister is so distraught there's no helping her. . . . As you wished . . . Dr. Person has been called in. Good sir, friends get visited when they are despondent, and therefore I expect you as soon as possible."

5 October

Writing to Vladimir Stasov of Olya's improvement, Glinka wishes the ailing Stasov "a speedy recovery."

7 October

Censor's authorization for Stellovsky to publish a new edition of the romance *"Ne iskushai"* for voice with transpositions for soprano and tenor.

9 October

Composer's dating on the manuscript score of Glinka's orchestration of Hummel's Nocturne *Souvenir d'amitié: "Arrangé pour l'orchestre par M. Glinka. Dédiée à sa soeur Loudmila de Schestakoff,* St. Petersburg, 9 October 1854." "I will not be answerable for the success of the first piece [*Invitation to the Dance*]; the second [the nocturne], it seems to me, should be better" (ltr. to V. Engelgardt, 2 November 1854).
[The manuscript of the orchestration of the Weber has not been discovered.]

10 October

Performance in the Aleksandrinsky Theater for Stepanova's "last benefit before her retirement" of *A Life for the Tsar,* and afterwards a divertissement "of dances and singing" (*Sev. pchela,* 9 October 1854). "On the very day that Ivan Susanin's heroic deed was recalled to the public for more than the hundredth time by M. I. Glinka's beautiful opera, we encountered on one of Petersburg's streets a descendant of the renowned citizen of Kostroma. He was a tall, handsome man with a beard. He wore the usual merchant's hat and coat, and on his hat band in gold letters was written: 'descendant of Ivan Susanin'" (*Otech. zap.,* 1854, vol 97, part 11, p. 40).

12 October

Glinka writes to Dmitry Stasov: "I have written a Russian song, but I cannot write the romance '*Venetsianskaia noch*' [Venetian night] because I do not remember the words." He asks Stasov to provide him with Kozlov's poetry. "I would also like to see you and play my Variations on a Scottish Theme for you."
[Glinka dated this letter "Tuesday, the 12th," to which V. Stasov added the note, "12 March 1856." By its content and the calendar, the letter should be dated 12 October 1854.]

Censor's authorization for a brochure entitled "Detailed analysis of the opera *A Life for the Tsar,* dedicated to admirers of Mikhail Ivanovich Glinka's talent by Rostislav" (St. Petersburg, printing house of N. Grech, 1854). Published in the introduction are excerpts from [Glinka's] *Zapiski* (dealing with the composition of *A Life for the Tsar*). Also included in the brochure is Wilhelm Lenz's opinion of *Kamarinskaya:* "If the majestic shade of Beethoven, called from the other world by the sounds of this fantasy, had hands, it [i.e., the shade] would take satisfaction in signing the immortal name of the creator of the Ninth Symphony to Glinka's *Kamarinskaya* with both hands."

19 October

Performance in the Aleksandrinsky Theater, in a mixed concert for the benefit of the director of the opera troupe Sokolov, of the second act of *Ruslan and Lyudmila* "for the first time since its revival" (*Sev. pchela* and *SPb. ved.*, 19 October 1854).

22 October

With Glinka's permission, Stellovsky acquired from "Odeum" the right to print a piano score of *A Life for the Tsar*. "Villebois is arranging for piano those numbers which have not yet been transcribed. Even though he is working conscientiously and neatly, I am carefully overseeing everything myself. This will be a complete edition with Russian and German texts" (ltr. to V. Engelgardt, 2 November 1854).

23 October

Glinka made the following dedicatory inscription on the reverse side of the cover of the first edition of the piano score of Bayan's second song, *"Est' pustynnyi krai"* [There is a deserted place], published by "Odeum" [1840]: "To Fedor Ivanovich Buslaev as a token of respect from Glinka, who has taken pleasure in reading his article on 'Female types in the statues of Greek goddesses.'" There is also a line of music from the Slavsya Chorus with this text underneath: "'*Slavsya, slavsya, sviataia Rus'*!' 23 October 1854, St. Petersburg, *A Life for the Tsar*, Epilog" (facsimile first published by Aleksandr Ilyinsky in *Biografii kompozitorov s IV–XX vekov* [Biographies of composers from the 4th–20th centuries], Moscow 1904, p. 454).

Between 17 September and the End of October

Glinka answered the letter from Dehn (ltr. to V. Engelgardt, 2 November 1854).

28 October

Glinka informs Grigory Kuzminsky that "the singing of Italian pieces at Lomakin's will be on Saturday, the 30th of this month, at half-past ten."

30 October

In the morning Glinka attended a performance "of Italian pieces" by Sheremetiev's choir under the direction of Lomakin. "The pieces of church music by ancient Italian masters" which Glinka had brought back from abroad "they sang quite neatly" (ltr. to V. Engelgardt, 2 November 1854).

1 November

In *Otech. zap.,* vol. 97, part 11, it states under "Petersburg Notes" that "The honored operatic performer Mme Stepanova said farewell to the public at her benefit performance in the role of Antonida in Glinka's well-known work *A Life for the Tsar*" (d.c.a.).

Between 16 September and 2 November

"The Germans entertained me with music several times, at my apartment, at the Stasovs', and at my neighbor Charukovsky's."

By 2 November

Glinka "completed [my] *Zapiski* [up to] 1840; I am also dictating a short autobiography for Dehn."

2 November

Glinka writes to Engelgardt: "I am bringing to completion the complete edition of my romances." Regarding his violin playing: "Little by little and with effort I am playing excerpts from the Bach sonatas, and several days ago I played through the entire E-flat major sonata of Beethoven with Serov." Of his plans for the future: "One cannot expect anything as a sit-at-home in Petersburg. And under the present circumstances I cannot guess what lies ahead." He writes that Shestakova "agreed to allow" Engelgardt "to have the manuscript of the score of the Hummel Nocturne," which Glinka had dedicated to her.
[The "present circumstances" refers to the Crimean War.]

Shestakova writes to Engelgardt of plans to settle with Glinka next year in Paris. She says that recently Glinka has been visited by Dubelt, Dubrovsky, Heydenreich, Villebois, and Dmitry Stasov. "Sometimes we hear quartets, singing, and other fare of this sort, but things are not cheerful, and my brother and I are waiting for spring with great impatience" (*L.,* p. 434).

Beginning of November

Glinka completes the dictation of his autobiography in French for Fétis's *Biographie universelle des musiciens*. He gave it to V. Stasov to look over, who found such a biography too short. Glinka decided not to send it abroad and turned it over to V. Stasov (ltr. to N. Kukolnik, 12 November 1854).

11 November

Dubrovsky writes to Sobolevsky: "Neither at the Pavlishchevs' nor at Glinka's, where I visit frequently, do I ever meet you. . . . On Fridays at Glinka's there are beautiful musical evenings, and there are even women present (his sister has arrived from the country). By the way, various artists gather at his house almost every day" (*L.*, p. 433).

Before 12 November

Glinka completed his *Zapiski* up to 1842. "Insofar as I have been able to, I have described our fraternity."

Glinka visited Nestor Kukolnik's wife Amalia Ivanovna. He read to her his "description" of the fraternity from the *Zapiski,* "and she said that everything was actually like I had described it."

12 November

Glinka writes to Kukolnik: "In accordance with my sister Lyudmila Ivanovna's wish (with whom I am now living for the third time), I began in June and have persisted continuously to write my memoirs from the time of my birth, i.e., from 1804, to the time of my current return to Russia, i.e., to 1854. My sister does not know about my life prior to 1847. I cannot foresee how my life from here on may lend itself to narration. I am writing these memoirs without any attempt at beautiful style. I am simply writing what happened and how it happened in chronological order, excluding all that did not have a direct or indirect relation to my artistic life. . . . Additionally I am putting together an edition of my romances. Part of them are with Bernard and are in tidy condition. Almost all the rest were printed singly by Stellovsky in similar format. . . . My muse has grown quiet, I believe because I have changed a great deal. I have grown serious and quiet and am very rarely in an enthusiastic state. Above all, little by little a critical attitude toward art has evolved, and now, other than *classical* music, I cannot listen to any other kind of music without boredom. In regard to this last circumstance, if I am strict toward others, I am even stricter toward myself." He recalls how he spent two years in Paris, of his conversation with Meyerbeer, and of his musical impressions of Paris and Berlin. He tells of his life in Petersburg: "Now and then we have quartets at home (primarily Haydn). The principal participants are Shubert (cello), a friend of ours, and Pikkel, a young and very talented artist. . . . Out of nothing to do I orchestrated Weber's *Invitation to the Dance* and Hummel's Nocturne in F Major, opus 99. The latter, it seems to me, is better than the first. For my sister I am arranging a children's polka, which is intended for my goddaughter and niece."

Censor's authorization for Stellovsky's publication of the romances *"Gor'ko, gor'ko mne"* [I am grieved, beautiful maid] and *"Venetsianskaia noch'."*

13 November

This report appears in *Panteon*, vol. 17, part 10, under "Petersburg Herald— Society": "Also on 10 October was Mme Stepanova's farewell benefit, for which she chose the opera *A Life for the Tsar*. . . . Despite the fact that her natural gifts do not fully match her extreme conscientiousness and inordinate love of work, one must nonetheless regret that with her our opera troupe has lost a diligent performer of many roles." In the same issue there is a notice that Stellovsky has available the piano score to *A Life for the Tsar* as well as romances and the songs *"Elegiia: Ne iskushai menia bez nuzhdy"* (for two voices), *"Net ego, na tom on svete," "O krasnyi mir," "Ne poi, krasavitsa, pri mne,"* and *"Ia liubliu, ty mne tverdila."* The following announcement is also printed there: "Shortly two- and four-hand arrangements done by the composer himself, as well as the orchestral score, of M. I. Glinka's favorite scherzo on the Russian dance tune 'Kamarinskaya' will be published. This piece has been successfully performed by many orchestras." There is also an announcement that Vollweiler's piano pieces *"Somnenie. Romance de Glinka," "K Molli"* [To Molly], and *"Barcarolle de Glinka"* are on sale (d.c.a.).

15 November

Glinka invites Charukovsky "to spend the evening with us" on 18 November.

In a letter to Engelgardt, Shestakova tells of their life in Petersburg and of Glinka's intention of going abroad. She enumerates those who most often visit them. She writes of V. Stasov's serious illness. In a note to the letter, Glinka asks Engelgardt to wait for him in Italy.

17 November

In *Sev. pchela*, no. 259, there is a notice of the publication of Rostislav's "Detailed analysis of Glinka's opera *A Life for the Tsar*," with excerpts from Glinka's memoirs.

18 November

Composer's dating on the score of some verses ("Now I will get married") of an Englishman from the vaudeville *Kuplennyi vystrel* [The hired shot]: "Completed on 18 November 1854, in St. Petersburg" and the dedicatory inscription "To Vasily Vasilievich Samoylov, a sincere offering from M. I. Glinka" (LGK, no. 1630).

Evening at Glinka's (ltr. to A. Charukovsky, 15 November 1854).

19 November

Censor's authorization for the duettino *"Vy ne priidete vnov'"* [You will not return again], published by Stellovsky.

In *Moskvityanin*, vol. 6, no. 23, part 1, under "Miscellany. Musical Criticism," there is an article by Serov entitled "Some Lines about Rostislav's Brochure 'Detailed Critique of M. I. Glinka's Opera *A Life for the Tsar*,'" with harsh criticism and this conclusion: "This is no analysis and certainly not a detailed one" (d.c.a.).

26 November

Censor's date and number on the title page of a copy of the romance *"Za mig odin"* (*Pour un moment*): "No. 1174, November 26, 1854."

30 November

Censor's authorization for Stellovsky's edition of the romance *"Chto, krasotka molodaia"* [Why do you cry, young beauty].

November

Glinka gives as a gift to Dmitry Stasov the duettino *"Vy ne priidete vnov'"* with the inscription: "To D. V. Stasov from the composer." On the cover of a copy of the duettino *"Vy ne priidete vnov',"* included in the "Collection of Musical Pieces" assembled by Andrey Lodi, there is a dedicatory inscription by Glinka: "To His Highness Prince V. Odoevsky as a token of remembrance and respect from the Composer."

Not Later than November

Feofil Tolstoy read through his critique of *A Life for the Tsar* to Glinka. "When I had finished reading," Glinka "expressed the following opinion, worthy of note: 'Thank you for your good intentions, but I find that your critique does not hit the mark. While you carry certain technical details to excess, you explain nothing by them. Meanwhile you overlook the very things which ought to be pointed out as useful warnings for other Russian composers. For example, why did you not say that it is inappropriate to introduce an Italian caballeta into Russian style, as at *Menia ty na Rusi*?' 'But pardon me,' I exclaimed in horror, 'this melody is saturated with Russian flavor!' 'Yes! but the form is Italianate. Is it probable that a man such as Susanin would have thought to repeat word for word, just a fifth lower, the naive effusions of the orphan Vanya? Why did you not point out the irrelevance of a coda in that same duet, *Na velikoe nam delo tol'ko put' nam ukazhi*? It just reeks of Italianateness! Do you understand?' Glinka became agitated and continued to point out the digressions he had made in *A Life for the Tsar* from a fundamental, rational (according to him) Russian operatic style. 'No, dearest friend,' he finally said, 'you should not write such reviews if you are going to take on the work of a critic. You should write the naked truth; you won't amaze anyone by praise" (F. Tolstoy, *Vosp.*, p. 115). "I was *not* delighted when, with a smile of self-satisfaction and smugness, he read me his critique of my opera *A Life for the Tsar*. What's one to do when each is free to think as he wishes? I have never considered Rostislav a serious musician. His critique not only did not convince me to think otherwise but clearly pointed out that his views on music have remained just as superficial as they've always been. What is he compared to N. N. Norov and Count M. Yu. Vielgorsky?" (ltr. to K. Bulgakov, 8 June 1855).

"In a conversation with me, Glinka became terribly indignant with Feofil Tolstoy over the fact that when analyzing the opera *A Life for the Tsar* he found no blunders in it at all. Glinka's noble, artistic spirit expressed itself in the following amusing words: 'What kind of reviewer is he when he does not smell out the fact that the entire opera is permeated with cadences which weary the listener to the point of exhaustion. He's only read one book in his entire life, and he came upon the very one he shouldn't have read.'" The book spoken of is one of the works of Reicha (A. Dargomyzhsky, "Notes and Anecdotes," coll. *Dargomyzhsky*, p. 9).

November–December

To this period belongs Glinka's request to Aleksandra Bilibina to visit him: "We will sing and chat a little."

5 December

In *Panteon,* vol. 18, part 11, under "Petersburg Herald—Society," it says in connection with the Weimar success of Rubinstein's opera *Sibirskie okhotniki* [The Siberian hunters]: "One must hope for further successes for our Russian music, with which Europe is already familiar through the outstanding compositions of M. I. Glinka" (d.c.a.).

In *SPb. ved.,* no. 272, in an article signed "I. M." [Mann] entitled "New Books . . . A Detailed Critique of the Opera *A Life for the Tsar,*" there is a positive review of Rostislav's brochure.

6 December

Performance in the Maly Theater in Moscow of *A Life for the Tsar,* a hymn, and divertissement (*Mosk. ved.,* 4 December 1854).

8 December

In *Sev. pchela,* no. 275, under "Notices, Notes, and Correspondence," Bulgarin disputes the high evaluation of the Polish scene from *A Life for the Tsar* given by Rostislav and contrasts Glinka's music to the polonaises of Ogiński.

10 December

In the manuscript of the *Zapiski,* after the description of his departure abroad in 1844, there is the date: "Completed on 10 December 1854."

13 December

In *Ved. Mosk. gor. politsii,* no. 275, under "Petersburg Chronicle—Feuilleton," there is an announcement of the publication of Rostislav's brochure "Critique of the Opera *A Life for the Tsar,*" with excerpts from the *Zapiski.*

First Half of December

Darya Leonova visited Glinka for the second time and again performed *"Akh, ne mne bednomu"* (cf. fall 1851). On this occasion "the effect of my singing was completely the reverse of the first time. M. I. Glinka, when he had heard me through, rushed off to his study, and when he returned there were tears in his eyes. . . . From that day M. I. Glinka rewarded me by taking me on as his student" (Leonova, *Vosp.*, p. 268). Glinka began to give voice lessons to Leonova (ltr. to V. Engelgardt, 22 January 1855).

15 December

Composer's dating on the manuscript of the "Children's Polka," composed for Olya Shestakova: "Completed in St. Petersburg, 15 December 1854."

18 December

At an artists' dinner in the Hall of the Chess Club in celebration of Feofil Tolstoy's 50 years of activity, Petrova-Vorobieva "performed all her best, well-known songs, with which she had once enthralled all of Petersburg. . . . Among others, she sang M. I. Glinka's chivalrous romance '*Sto krasavits svetlookikh*'" (*SPb. ved.*, 8 February 1855).
[Reference is to the romance "*Pobeditel'*" [The victor].]

29 December

In *Panteon*, vol. 18, part 12, there is a notice of the publication of the romances "*Venetsianskaia noch'*," "*Chto, krasotka molodaia*," "*Ia liubliu, ty mne tverdila*," "*Ne poi, krasavitsa, pri mne*," "*Gor'ko, gor'ko mne*," "*Odin lish' mig*" (*Za odin mig*), and "*O, krasnyi mir*" (d.c.a.).

30 December

Composer's dating on the first aria from Handel's *Jephtha: "arrangé pour M. Isabella de Grünberg par Michel de Glinka, 30 décembre 1854."*

End of December

Kukolnik (from Taganrog) sends Glinka his music for his own drama *Azovskoe siden'e* [The seat of Azov] and writes: "Misha, you know me. I will not take offense at anything if it is bad, since I have crawled into someone else's garden. If I get chased out, it serves me right. If *c'est chien*, then put up a cross, brother, and it's over; then take pen in hand and mark up *Azov* however you like" (Kukolnik's ltr. is quoted by him in "In place of a preface to the drama *The Seat of Azov*," in LGK, the Papers of N. Kukolnik).

December

In answer to Dubrovsky's inquiry whether the music for the song *"Gude viter"* [The wind blows] really belongs to him, Glinka answers: "The music to the song *'Gude viter'* (words by Zabella) was written by me, but if it has any resemblance to a Little Russian tune, I am not guilty."

End of the Year

Glinka rewrote his Variations on a Theme of Mozart (E-flat major) for harp or piano, one of his first compositions (composed in 1822).

1854/1855

Winter

Glinka "went out very little," but he "was at the Princes' Odoevsky and Volkonsky's for musical evenings and was very satisfied to hear the good music and excellent performances there. He continued to visit Lomakin, where he heard Sheremetev's singers perform pieces by early Italian and German composers." At this time Glinka "was more enthusiastic about Gluck than anyone else."

Glinka often arranged for musical evenings at home. "Sometimes the playing involved up to 12 hands. At that time P.A. Barteneva, M. V. Shilovskaya, and A. Y. Bilibina visited us." Glinka also was visited by Dargomyzhsky and played excerpts from *Rusalka*. "My brother was enthusiastic about many things in this opera, but when Dargomyzhsky sang for him the princess's aria . . . *"Dnei minuvshikh naslazhden'ia"* [Days of vanishing pleasures], my brother said: 'It looks a lot like Gorislava's aria from the third act of *Ruslan*.' Dargomyzhsky . . . laughed it off very nicely: 'Well, brother, everyone else robs from you, why shouldn't I pinch off a little?' Then my brother tried to persuade Dargomyzhsky to immediately begin a comic opera once he had finished this one and said that he was already convinced that it would be a *chef d'oeuvre*. It is strange though that Dargomyzhsky always seemed to take offense at this and one time even said to him: 'Do you really think that I am unable to do anything besides comic pieces?' My brother said to him that, of course . . . in *Rusalka* the serious parts were also excellent, but that, in his opinion, writing a comic opera was no easier and that such writing required a special talent, which he had only seen in him" (Shestakova, *Vosp.*, p. 298).

One time the conversation turned to Dargomyzhsky's small pieces, and the song *"Kaius', diadia"* [I confess it, Uncle] was referred to. "Glinka said then that if

Dargomyzhsky decided to write an opera *buffa,* he would immediately establish himself as superior to any other composers who had written in this style" (P. Stepanov, *Vosp.,* p. 311).

"My brother liked to advise others to write, but when someone tried to persuade *him* to write he ordinarily was angered" or "he brushed their efforts aside with a joke. Thus once, when Dargomyzhsky started to tell him that it was shameful for someone with his talent not to be writing, my brother, instead of answering, sang to him his romance 'I confess it, uncle, it's the devil's work,' in his squeaky discant. . . . The more A. S. tried to persuade my brother, the louder he squeaked out '*Diadia,*' until finally A. S. said: 'How schoolboyish you are, brother!' and began talking about something else" (Shestakova, *Vosp.,* p. 298).

1855

1 January

Glinka congratulates Vladimir Stasov on his upcoming birthday and the New Year and invites him to come visit.

4 January

In *Moskvityanin,* vol. 1, no. 1, part 1, in the section under "Petersburg News and Rumors" (signed "Z*Z*") the following appears: "Many curious things have accumulated in the musical world. M. I. Glinka has arrived in Petersburg from abroad with a store of new romances and a symphony called *Taras Bulba.* Now he is busy arranging various pieces which society favors, and he is preparing, with the assistance of the Smirdin of music publishing, Mr. Stellovsky, an edition of the remaining, scholarly parts of his opera *A Life for the Tsar,* which will finally complete Mr. Snegirev's earlier edition. . . . We haven't the strength to express what profound respect and sincere sympathy is aroused in us by the activities on behalf of art and Russian national music of Glinka, Verstovsky, Dargomyzhsky, and Lvov" (d.c.a.).
[Smirdin was a well-known book publisher.]

5 January

In *Otech. zap.,* vol. 98, part 1, the following romances are named as being for sale: *"Venetsianskaia noch',"* *"Chto, krasotka molodaia,"* *"Ia liubliu, ty mne tverdila,"* *"Ne poi, krasavitsa, pri mne,"* *"Uimites' volneniia strasti"* (with violin), *"Gor'ko, gor'ko mne,"* *"Pour un moment,"* *"O, krasnyi mir,"* and *"Net ego! Na tom on svete"* (d.c.a.).

6 January

Composer's dating on Iphis's aria from Handel's oratorio *Jephtha: "À made-moiselle Isabelle Grünberg arrangé et copié par Michel de Glinka le 6 janvier 1855 S-P.bourg."*

12 January

Glinka gave Maria Krzhisevich several of his romances as a gift: *"Slyshu li golos tvoi,"* with the inscription "To my dearest lady, Maria Stepanovna, SPb 12 January 18 [date clipped off by the bookbinder]; *"Zazdravnyi kubok,"* with the inscription "To the inimitable lady Maria Stepanovna"; the duettino for two sopranos *"Vy ne priidete vnov',"* with the inscription "To my dear Mary from Mimosa, 12 January 1855"; and *"Pesn' Margarity"* [Gretchen's song], "To my dear lady Maria Stepanovna, a heartfelt gift" (ITMK, coll. 6).

In his concert in Nizhny Novgorod, Mily Balakirev performed his Fantasy on Themes from *A Life for the Tsar* (from the program for the concert, in *Letopis Balakireva* [Balakirev Chronicle], p. 21).

The following notice appears in the newspaper *Kavkaz* (Tiflis), no. 4: "The day after tomorrow we are promised a benefit performance by Mme Schening. . . . She has selected *Il barbiere de Siviglia*. . . . Additionally we may look forward to the satisfaction of hearing two excerpts from the opera *A Life for the Tsar*. We are sure that Glinka's music will lose nothing even alongside that of Rossini. For us, Russians, it has the incalculable quality of conveying the feeling of Russian folk life, which is somehow close and familiar to the soul. Mlle Vazoli will perform the romance *'Ne o tom skorbliu, podruzhen'ki'* with chorus, and Mme Schening, in the role of Vanya, will sing the leading part in the well-known [trio] *'Akh, ne mne, bednomu.'* Finally the corps de ballet will perform the Mazurka from the opera *A Life for the Tsar,* and to conclude the spectacle for the benefit of connoisseurs there will be a genuine lezghinka in Georgian costumes."

14 January

In a benefit performance in Tiflis, Schening performed in the same evening *Il barbiere de Siviglia* and three excerpts from *A Life for the Tsar* (*Kavkaz,* 12 January 1855).

16 January

Kukolnik's nephew Ilya Puzyrevsky and his wife and Sofia Aleksandrova spent the evening with Glinka. Puzyrevsky presented Glinka with Kukolnik's music to his drama *The Seat of Azov*.

19 January

Having looked over and corrected Kukolnik's music, Glinka returned the manuscript. "My desire to please you notwithstanding, I will not undertake to orchestrate your melodies. . . . You should turn to some experienced regimental Kapellmeister. . . . Tell him that he should orchestrate your music literally and *en masse,* i.e., with the violins and winds all together, which is more reliable than my difficult, *transparent* orchestration in which every *fool* must stand on his own and not yawn. I remind you of your own words. When you heard Keller's oratorio, you said that this was the *diligence of solid German work*. I advise you once again to have your tunes orchestrated without frills but respectably." In response to the accusation that he had stopped composing, Glinka writes: "I never was a Hercules in art. I wrote when I felt like writing. I loved music then and still love it sincerely. The fact of the matter is that for some time now I have not felt a calling and urge to write. What am I to do if, when I compare myself to the great maestros, I become so keen on them that I convince myself that I cannot and do not wish to write? If my muse unexpectedly awoke, I would write for orchestra without text. I would give up Russian music as well as the Russian winter. I am not interested in Russian drama; I have fiddled around enough with it. I am now orchestrating '*Molitva*' [Prayer], which I wrote for piano without words. Lermontov's words *"V minutu zhizni trudnuiu"* [In a difficult moment of life] fit this prayer remarkably. I am preparing this piece for Leonova's concert. She is studying diligently with me, and quite successfully." [Villebois advised Glinka in adapting Lermontov's verses to *"Molitva"* (ltr. to V. Engelgardt, 7 April 1855).]

In *Sev. pchela,* no. 14, under "Remarks, Notes, and Correspondence," Bulgarin comments on Lodi's publication of a musical album containing "compositions of our famous composers M. I. Glinka and A. S. Dargomyzhsky."

20 January

Composer's dating on the title page of the manuscript of the score of *"Molitva"* to words by Lermontov: "S.-P.burg, 20 January 1855." "Since I did not know whether her voice [Leonova's] (though it was clear and sonorous) could adequately perform the '*Molitva*,' I first wrote out the most difficult places on a little scrap of paper as a test. Since it went so well, I wrote the score for orchestra, adding a chorus to enhance the effect and to allow the soloist to rest" (ltr. to Bulgakov, 23 June 1855).

In *Panteon,* vol. 19, part 1, in the section "Petersburg Herald—Musical Chronicle," Serov comments on the similarity of several phrases from the witches' scene in Verdi's opera *Macbeth* to phrases sung by Naina in *Ruslan and Lyudmila* (d.c.a.).

21 January

Composer's dating on the manuscript of *"Starinnaia tsyganskaia pesnia 'Akh! kogda b ia prezhde znala'"* [An old gypsy song, 'Oh, if I had known before,'] sung by the famous Styoshka:" "To my dear pupil Olga Vladimirovna Lykoshina, M. Glinka, S.-P.burg, 21 January 1855." On another copy of the manuscript there is the inscription, "To Darya Mikhailovna Leonova, S.-P.burg, 21 January 1855, M. Glinka" (GTsMMK, coll. 49).

22 January

Glinka gives advice and makes recommendations to Engelgardt on what to see first of all in Spain, which cities to visit, and names some of his Spanish friends. "Do not joke about my recommendations: there is a particular type of hospitality in Spain." He recommends that Engelgardt pay special attention to the canvases of Murillo and Zurbaran. He writes that he has begun procedures to acquire a foreign passport.

25 January

Composer's dating at the beginning of the fourth part of the *Zapiski:* "S.P.burg, 25 January 1855."

26 January

Glinka asks Hunke to come quickly: "You can help me in an embarrassing matter pertaining to our favorite art, that is, music."

30 January

Matinee concert of the Philharmonic Society in the Hall of Nobility, which included a performance of Hummel's nocturne *"V pamiat' druzhby"* [In memory of friendship], orchestrated by Glinka. The conductor was Baveri (E. Albrecht,

"General Overview of the Activities of the St. Petersburg Philharmonic Society," p. 18).

Censor's authorization for Stellovsky's publication of the romances *"Pour un moment," "Zhavoronok"* (arranged for two voices), and *"Molitva."*

31 January

The opera *Ruslan and Lyudmila* is purchased from Glinka by Stellovsky "by a deed executed in the presence of a broker" (I. Bocharov, *The Case of F. Stellovsky and L. I. Shestakova,* SPb., 1867, p. 11).

Censor's authorization for Stellovsky's edition of *"Kolybel'naia pesnia"* [Lullaby] arranged for two voices.

1 February

Glinka promises to send Ludwig Maurer a recently orchestrated romance in several days and asks Maurer to provide one of his charming overtures for Leonova's concert.

3 February

In a note to Charukovsky, Glinka asks to be informed "if I can expect that Mr. Dütsch will orchestrate my romance *'Ne nazyvai ee nebesnoi,'* or, if because of this misunderstanding, he does not wish to be bothered with this matter?"
[It is not known what the misunderstanding referred to is.]

8 February

In *SPb. ved.,* no. 28, in an article by "G. D." [Danilevsky] entitled "A private dinner in honor of the fiftieth anniversary of the career of Count F. P. Tolstoy (letter to the artist I. I. Sokolov in a Kursk village)," mention is made of a performance of the *"Rytsarskii romans"* [Knight's romance] on 18 December 1854 by Petrova-Vorobieva.

9 February

Composer's dating on the title page of the manuscript of the score of *"Nochnoi smotr"* [Night watch]: "S.P.burg, 9 February 55, *house of Tomilova."*
[Only the title page is written in Glinka's hand. The music is in another handwriting (perhaps Villebois's?).]

10 February

Censor's authorization for Stellovsky's publication of the gypsy song *"Kosa"* [The tress], arranged by Glinka for voice and chorus.

11 February

Glinka tells Dmitry Stasov about preparations for Leonova's concert and asks that he obtain the *Jota aragonesa* from the copyist Westphal.

[The letter was written on Friday, 11 February. The year has been established according to the calendar and the letter's contents.]

12 February

Composer's dating on the title page of the manuscript of the score "*'Ne nazyvai ee nebesnoi,'* romance, words by N. F. Pavlov, music by M. I. Glinka, orchestrated 12 February 1855, S.P.burg."

13 February

In *SPb. ved.*, no. 33, in a feuilleton called "Petersburg Chronicle," there is mention of Glinka's intention of writing an opera on the subject of Shakhovskoy's drama *Dvumuzhnitsa* [The bigamist]. "It is a very good idea, and we sincerely hope that the rumor we hear is true. . . . Only Glinka is silent, but we would love to hear his songs." The article reports that in her forthcoming concert Leonova will perform "new music by M. I. Glinka on words by M. Y. Lermontov, 'In a difficult moment of life.'"

Second Half of January–First Half of February

"For the greater part of my romances and songs in their orchestral arrangements, my assistant was Villebois, who lately has become such a practiced hand that he could orchestrate as I dictated. . . . In order to provide an incentive to the publisher Stellovsky and my lieutenant [Villebois], I *allowed* two of my romances to be arranged for two voices: '*Zhavoronok*' and '*Kolybel'naia pesnia*'" (ltr. to V. Engelgardt, 7 April 1855).

16 February

Glinka asks Kraevsky to place "an announcement of Mme Leonova's concert written by my good friend Mr. Serov" in a feuilleton in *SPb. ved.*

17 February

Glinka was in the chapel for a rehearsal of the Crucifixus of Bach's *"Hohe Messe,"* which he heard "for the second time" (ltr. to D. Stasov, 18 February 1855).

Glinka invites Aleksandra Bilibina and her sister Yulia to Leonova's concert. Shestakova sends Bilibina works by Glinka: "three new romances and the promised polka."

In *Mosk. ved.*, no. 21, in a notice called "Moscow Municipal Chronicle," it is indicated that *A Life for the Tsar* was played twice during the winter season. It mentions Semyonova's performance of the part of Antonida.

18 February

In a letter to Dmitry Stasov, Glinka gives directions for the performance of the Crucifixus from Bach's *"Hohe Messe"*: "The strings must play piano, even pianissimo, the flutes—dolce, the boys' voices *mf,* and the men's—*p*. Special attention must be paid to the last measures of the chorus. And it would not be bad if eight, ten, or however many of the last measures were to be repeated by the chorus. Be so kind as to communicate these thoughts of mine to Lomakin and to Aleksey Fedorovich himself. I hope that A. F. will not take offence at the genuine interest which I take in his exceptional concerts."

Glinka is present at a choral rehearsal at 12 a.m. in the theater school for Leonova's concert, scheduled for 20 February. At the rehearsal's conclusion Glinka was introduced to Vasilko-Petrov. Glinka "extended his hand cordially. 'I have wanted to meet you for a long time; thank you for your review of me in the *SPb. ved.* and for the favor you have shown me.'" This initiated a conversation which ended with Glinka inviting Vasilko-Petrov to his house to discuss the new opera. "He wanted to do an opera on Prince A. A. Shakhovskoy's drama *The Bigamist*" (*SPb. ved.*, 3 March 1857; ltr. to D. Stasov, 18 February 1855). [On this day Nicholas I died. Leonova's concert, and all others as well, were cancelled because of official mourning.]

Censor's authorization for Brandus's edition of the romance *"Razocharovanie"* ["Where are you, first desire"].

19 February

Glinka rewrote from memory his youthful romance *"Moia arfa"* [My harp]. The composer's dating reads "N.B. This romance was written by me in 1824 before the flood. It was my first effort in composition with a text. M. Glinka. 19 February 1855. S.P.burg."
["The flood" is the Petersburg flood of November 1824.]

After 19 February

Glinka visited Vasilko-Petrov. "Glinka talked about Prince Shakhovskoy's drama and about those qualities which it presented for a purely Russian folk opera. . . . Glinka began . . . to develop the plan of the poem with clarity and enthusiasm" (*SPb. ved.*, 3 March 1857).

Once he had gotten the idea of writing *The Bigamist,* Glinka "was always making witticisms about how appropriate it was for him to be writing this opera, because his wife was a woman with two husbands" (Shestakova, *Vosp.*, p. 299).

20 February

Composer's dating on the title page of the manuscript of the score: "*'Ty skoro menia pozabudesh'*,' romance, words by Yulia Zhadovskaya, music by M. I. Glinka, SP.burg, 20 February 1855."

25 February

In the March literary supplement to *Le Nouvelliste,* Glinka's intention of writing an opera entitled *The Bigamist* is reported in an article by A. Chapellon entitled "Internal News" (d.c.a.).

2 March

In a note to Dmitry Stasov, Glinka invites him, Vladimir Stasov, and Serov "to come to dinner" on 3 March. He asks Dmitry Stasov to meet with the censor Nikolay Peyker and convey to him that Glinka needed to meet with him very soon.
[The letter is dated "Wednesday, 2 March." The year has been established according to the calendar.]

4 March

In *Otech. zap.*, vol. 99, part 3, the following romances are named among new music recently published: *"Elegiia"* [Elegy], *"Somnenie," "Kolybel' naia pesnia," "Zhavoronok," "Usnuli golubye," "Vy ne priidete vnov',"* as well as *"Kak mat' ubili"* from *A Life for the Tsar* and *"Uspokoisia, minet vremia"* [Be calm, time passes] from *Ruslan and Lyudmilla* (d.c.a.).

13 March

In *SPb. ved.*, no. 57, in "Petersburg Chronicle" "V. P." [Vasilko-Petrov] discusses Nikolay Stepanov's collection of portraits and busts of Russian composers.

14 March

In *Sev. pchela,* no. 51, "Musical Conversations," Rostislav polemicizes with Serov over Serov's critical review of the "Critique of *A Life for the Tsar.*"

First Half of March

Glinka's *"Molitva,"* arranged by Villebois, appeared in print, "sold to Stellovsky for an insignificant amount." "Instead of simply calling it 'Prayer' [*Molitva*] (although in size and character it was entitled to be called a *cantata* or *hymn*)" Stellovsky published it "under the general rubric of romances and songs by M. I. Glinka. This was not all: written for Leonova, that is, for contralto with chorus, it was designated by him as being for *soprano and chorus.* Moreover, the publisher promises the public the same 'Prayer' for *contralto* without chorus! One wonders, when a 'Prayer' with chorus extends two octaves from a low 'a' to the upper one . . . which notes will the contralto sing, Mr. Publisher? This disrespect exasperated me. On my first meeting with *Vil* [Villebois] I clearly explained to him that I was dissatisfied with the publisher and that I demanded the title 'Prayer' be changed. Furthermore, *he no longer had my permission* to arrange *any more of my romances* for two voices."

Several days later Shestakova "purchased from the publisher-swindler two complete collections of romances and songs with the *disgraceful 'Prayer.'* In these two collections *'Somnenie'* and *'Usnuli golubye'* also turned up, arranged in the most disgusting fashion (the craftsmanship, no doubt, of [my] lieutenant), despite my lack of permission, and what is even better, over *my name"* (ltr. to V. Engelgardt, 7 April 1855).

15 March

In the periodical *Moda,* under "Herald of New Things," it speaks of Glinka's work on the opera *The Bigamist.*

16 March

In *SPb. ved.,* no. 59, Glinka published "A Necessary Explanation" to inform the public and "to forestall misunderstanding." He wrote that he had only composed one duet, *"Vy ne priidete vnov'"* and had only arranged two romances for two voices, *"Ne iskushai"* and *"Kogda dusha prosilas' ty."* Under his direction *"Zhavoronok"* and *"Kolybel'naia pesnia"* were arranged for two voices. "I neither composed nor arranged other romances for two voices, and therefore I cannot and do not desire to answer for the accuracy of my romances which are now appearing from Stellovsky's, arranged for two voices, by whom I do not know, but published over my name. . . . I do not recognize and will not recognize any kind of arrangement of my music without the indication that they were done by me, because I do not wish to take upon myself responsibility for others' work."

17 March

Glinka presented Dmitry Stasov with a collection of his romances with this inscription: "The greater part of these romances I brought to my good sir Dmitry Vasilievich Stasov on the evening of 9 September 1854, which we spent so pleasantly in the company of mutual friends and artists. Now this book includes a complete collection of my romances. The French words 'Le baiser' and 'Pour un moment' were written with my own hand, as was my first effort in vocal music, the romance 'Moia arfa,' to words by Bakhturin. With that said, accept it. Mikhail Glinka. S.P.burg, 1855, 17 March."

19 March

Glinka presented Leonova with a collection of his romances. In a letter attached to the music it says: "As a token of my respect for you and your beautiful voice I ask you to accept this complete collection of my romances and to preserve them in memory of your teacher." He asks that she send Kukolnik's drama.

Glinka's dedicatory inscription on the romance *"Ne iskushai"*: "To Darya Mikhaylovna Leonova, a sincere offering from the composer, M. I. Glinka. S.P.burg, March 19, 1855" (*Sov. muzyka,* 1954, no. 6, p. 71).

[Apparently the volume which Glinka presented to Leonova opened with this romance. The volume has not been preserved in its entirety.]

Ca. 20 March

Glinka had harsh words with Villebois and made a complete break with him (ltr. to V. Engelgardt, 7 April 1855).

24 March

On a copy of the score of the *Jota aragonesa* there is a title page and this dedicatory inscription by Glinka: *"Ouverture Espagnol No. 1 (Jota Aragonesa) à grand orchestre (partition) composé par M. Glinka (comp. à Madrid l'an 1845) à Don Pedro Fernandez, S.P.bourg le 24 mars 1855"* (*Sov. muzyka*, 1971, no. 10, p. 125).

End of March

Glinka finished "the last part" of his *Zapiski* (ltr. to V. Engelgardt, 7 April 1855).

3 April

Glinka began to write the "Solemn Polonaise for the Coronation of Alexander II," "six weeks after the death" of Nicholas I, "following my own bent" (ibid.).
[The official date of Nicholas I's death was 20 February. The expiration of six weeks occurs on 3 April.]

For the Polonaise Glinka "had invented three trios, and playing them for me [Shestakova], he allowed me to choose which one I liked the best. Perhaps the other two were better, I do not know, but he definitely wanted to keep the one which I chose" (ltr. from L. Shestakova to E. Napravnik, 20 January 1880, in *L.*, p. 445.) "The main theme was borrowed from a real Spanish bolero. The trio is my own. It causes tender-hearted tears of emotion, since it is made in a very Russian way" (ltr. to V. Engelgardt, 7 April 1855).

Beginning of April

Glinka was in Engelgardt's apartment and listened to the organ "distractedly. I involuntarily thought of you. . . . Moreover, when I am keen on work, I listen unwillingly to others' music—it detracts me from my business" (ibid.).

6 April

Composer's dating on the title page of the manuscript of the score of the "Solemn Polonaise" on the theme of a *"Bolero Espagnol"*: "S.P.burg, 6 April 1855."

7 April

Glinka reports to Engelgardt that the Polonaise was "finished yesterday" and that Leonova's concert did not take place because of the official mourning. He writes that he is keeping all his original manuscripts for Engelgardt. He says that he is considering writing an opera called *The Bigamist,* since his "relations with the Directorate of the St. Petersburg theaters is growing more amicable by the hour." He tells about his break with Villebois.

Glinka inscribes a volume in which his romances are bound: "This book contains a collection of romances and songs by M. I. Glinka, carefully collected and organized by L. I. Shestakova, to whom this book belongs. K. A. M. I. Glinka. S.P.burg, 7 April 1855."
[At the bottom of the page is Shestakova's inscription certifying Glinka's autograph and affirming that Glinka sang from this copy (his notes appear in several of the romances). "K. A." is Collegiate Assessor [*Kollezhskii assesor*], the rank at which Glinka retired from the civil service. In this instance it is intended as a joke.]

After 7 April

"On the instructions of Mr. Fedorov" they performed the Polonaise and *Molitva* at the theater school. "The Polonaise needed to be reinforced, that is, I needed to add two trombones and two cornets *à pistons,* which I did. '*Molitva,*' sung by Mme Leonova with orchestra and chorus, had a powerful and profound effect on the audience and went excellently from the start" (ltr. to N. Kukolnik, second half of April, 1855).

13 April

On a copy of a score of *Kamarinskaya,* there is a title page and Glinka's dedicatory inscription: *"Scherzo Russe (Kamarinskaya) partition d'orchestre musique de Michel Glinka. A son ami Don Pedro Fernandez de la part du compositeur. S.P.bourg le 13/25 avril 1855"* (*Sov. muzyka,* 1971, no. 10, p. 125).
[This was the second edition of *Kamarinskaya.*]

The title page of a copy of the score of *Night in Madrid* reads: *"Recuerdos de Castilla. Ouverture Espagnol No. 2 (Potpourri) partition d'orchestre musique de Michel Glinka. A Don Pedro Fernandez par le compositeur. S-P.bourg. Le 13/25 avril 1855"* (*Sov. muzyka*, 1971, no. 10, p. 125).

Glinka asks Dmitry Stasov to obtain a copy for him of *"Molitva"* "abbreviated and without chorus" and also to find out from Stellovsky "if '*Molitva*' (for solo piano) and the Variations on a Scottish Theme were printed."
[The year has been established according to the calendar: the letter was written on Wednesday, 13 April.]

Before the Beginning of the Second Half of April

Glinka looked through and corrected Kukolnik's music to *The Seat of Azov,* "without touching the ideas themselves" and "making note of his own ideas regarding orchestration" (ltr. to N. Kukolnik, second half of April, 1855).

15 April

Glinka writes on the title page of a copy of the score of the *Jota aragonesa: "Ouverture Espagnol No 1 (La Jota Aragonese) (partition) par M. Glinka.* N.B. I made some changes in the beginning of the Allegro, but after the middle of the ninth page some parts have been corrected, others not. Mikhail Glinka, 15 April 1855" (LGK).

22 April

Composer's dating on the manuscript of an arrangement: " '*Prosti menia, prosti*' [Pardon me], romance sung by Mme Leonova and M. Bulakhov, words by A. I. Bulgakov, music by P. S. Fedorov, arranged for two voices and dedicated to the composer by M. Glinka. S.P.burg, 22 April 1855." On one side is Glinka's inscription in pencil, "To Vasily Pavlovich Engelgardt."

23 April

Glinka inscribes Fedorov's romance *"Prosti menia, prosti"* in Shestakova's album. Date of the entry: "S.P.burg, 23 April 1855" (Album no. 2).

24 April

Glinka was at Fedorov's, where he sang a lot and "the ladies wore [me] out" (apparently from requiring him to sing so much).

25 April

Glinka asks V. Stasov "to prepare music" for Tuesday, 26 April. He invites him for dinner and asks that he convey the invitation to Serov. "We will laugh and eat together."

26 April

Musical gathering at Glinka's—"something like an *ensemble*," in which Leonova and the amateur singer Bok sang (ltr. to V. Stasov, 25 April 1855).

28 April

Glinka asks Dargomyzhsky to tell him Shilovskaya's correct address. Glinka and Shestakova intend to visit her "tomorrow."

29 April

Glinka and Shestakova visit Shilovskaya, "but we did not find her at home." In a letter to Dargomyzhsky, Glinka asks him to invite Shilovskaya for the first of May—"to sing your music."

Second Half of April

Glinka sends Kukolnik his observations on the musical parts of *The Seat of Azov*. "In general, I would advise you to base everything (more or less) on the strings. The winds, especially the woodwinds (the fools, as you called them), although they're beautiful, they're also extremely capricious and require great experience." He writes about his intentions of writing an opera called *The Bigamist*. "The plot . . . has been turning around in my mind for a long time already. Several preliminary ideas are already done, but what's been recruited, that is, the motives, I'm not writing down, since I am waiting for the libretto for the first two acts, which have already been tentatively thought out."

1 May

Musical evening at Glinka's, at which Shilovskaya sang romances by Dargomyzhsky (ltr. to A. Dargomyzhsky, 29 April 1855).

In *Otech. zap.*, vol. 100, part 5, among newly published music the following romances are named: *"Ne nazyvai ee nebesnoi," "Tol'ko uznal ia tebia," "Sto krasavits," "Esli vstrechus' s toboi," "V dvenadtsat' chasov po nocham"* [At midnight], *"Pamiat' serdtsa,"* and a new edition of *"Venetsianskaia noch'"* (d.c.a.).

10 May

In *Odessk. vestnik,* no. 53, "Notices and News," there is mention of Stepanov's statuettes (among them, Glinka's).

13 May

In a letter to Charukovsky, Glinka asks him to get a carriage for Shestakova for 14 May.

The title page of a copy of the score of *"Molitva"* is inscribed by Glinka as follows: "'Prayer' to Lermontov's words 'In a difficult moment of life.' Music by M. I. Glinka (*partition d'orchestre avec choeur et chant*), *S.P.bourg le 13/25 mai 1855"* (*Sov. muzyka,* 1971, no. 10, p. 125).

14 May

Shestakova and Olya leave for the country. Having accompanied them to the gates and returned home, Glinka worked with Leonova and then "got busy," that is, cleaning the apartment and preparing a room for his birds (ltrs. to A. Charukovsky, 13 May, and to L. Shestakova, 15 May 1855).

15 May

Glinka rewrote the duet and added a part for violin to the romance *"Somnenie."* He wrote to Kologrivov. Vladimir and Dmitry Stasov had dinner with Glinka. Dovgolevsky was there and sent a bluethroat prior to his arrival (ltrs. to L. Shestakova, 15 and 22 May 1855).
[Kologrivov's letter is not known.]

In a letter to Shestakova, Glinka tells her how he has been spending his time since her departure and about the changes he has made in the apartment.

16 May

"The weather was abominable—it was snowing. I was bored, but I was not suffering from my nerves very much."

17 May

In the evening at Glinka's apartment there was "a partial rehearsal of Leonova's concert. Besides the splendid person of our prima donna (as Olya calls her), there were Vitelyaro, Grigoriev, Zeyfert, and . . . a neat general [Kuzminsky?]. Grigoriev is a very talented violinist, and I regret that you were not here (ltr. to L. Shestakova, 22 May 1855).

Between 10 and 20 May

In a letter to Glinka (from Voronezh) Kukolnik outlines the program for his music to his drama *The Seat of Azov*. He is glad that Glinka has settled on the subject of *The Bigamist* (*Bayan,* 1888, no. 5, p. 44).
[The dating of Kukolnik's letter is established in G 2-B, p. 326.]

20 May

In *Sev. pchela,* no. 108, there is an article by Rostislav entitled "Musical Conversations": "On the virtues of Mr. Stellovsky, proprietor of the music store and publisher of the works of Russian composers. Complete edition of the works of M. I. Glinka. Analysis of the romance *'Ne iskushai menia bez nuzhdy.'* Doubts aroused by the romance *'Somnenie'* [Doubt]. M. I. Glinka's first and last compositions."

In the evening Glinka celebrated his birthday. "Bouquet [Leonova] arranged everything to my complete satisfaction. . . . The evening passed extremely pleasantly. I was in voice and sang very well without shouting. On the spot Fedorov concocted some congratulatory couplets for me, which Bulakhov sang splendidly to the tune of *'Proshchai, korabl' vzmakhnul krylom.'* . . . After supper we sang the 'Farewell Song' again with chorus, and we again regretted that you [Shestakova] were not here" (ltr. to L. Shestakova, 22 May 1855). To express his gratitude for the performance in his honor of Fedorov's couplets, Glinka "sang his amazing song *'Proshchaite, dobrye druz'ia'* [Farewell, dear friends] with profound inspiration and emotion. Tears of enthusiasm and applause were the response of everyone present" (V. Stasov, *Izbr. soch.,* vol. 1, p. 517).

21 May

In *SPb. ved.,* no. 109, there is a notice of Leonova's forthcoming concert on 22 May. "The direct participation of M. I. Glinka, who has written many new things for this concert after a long and sustained silence, lends a special interest to Mme Leonova's musical matinee."

In *Sev. pchela,* no. 109, in Bulgarin's "Journalistic Odds and Ends," there is a notice of Leonova's forthcoming concert, in which she, Petrov, and Bulakhov are to sing several works by Glinka.

At 12 noon Dubrovsky arrived "with the vilest article on Mr. Stellovsky's virtues. This article by Rostislav, which fully demonstrates his disgusting impertinence, is in no. 108 of the *Severnaia pchela.* . . . Petersburg is a cesspool" (ltr. to L. Shestakova, 22 May 1855).

At 6 o'clock Don Pedro left via Berlin for Paris (to get married there). Glinka sent several compositions to Dehn via him.

Night of 21 May

Glinka slept poorly because Rostislav's article "had so exasperated" him (ltr. to L. Shestakova, 22 May 1855).

22 May

In *SPb. ved.,* no. 110, there is a feuilleton entitled "Petersburg Chronicle" about Leonova's concert that day which includes an assessment of her voice and gifts. "She is much indebted to the advice of our famous composer M. I. Glinka."

Leonova's concert took place that day. Glinka "did not go . . . out of fear of meeting some scoundrel. The concert was very successful" (ltrs. to L. Shestakova, 22 and 29 May 1855).

Glinka writes to Shestakova: "In response to his vile article [Rostislav's], I am going to have my new duet *'Prosti menia, prosti'* printed by Bernard."

26 May

Glinka invites Charukovsky for 27 May: "The Maurers will be here and intend to play Beethoven trios. . . . Do not broadcast my invitation, for I fear *uninvited* guests."

Leonova was at Glinka's and sang. While she was singing, Vladimir Zhemchuzhnikov arrived. He sang Susanin's aria "in a somewhat weak but very pleasant voice (baritone)." Maria Krzhisevich was also there.

27 May

Glinka had "one of the most remarkable evenings. The Maurers were here, Kologrivov declined, Andrey Bogdanovich Memel arranged the evening. The Maurers played enchantingly. . . . I invited all four Stasovs, though Nikolay didn't come" (ltr. to L. Shestakova, 29 May 1855).

29 May

There is a notice about Leonova's concert on 22 May in a feuilleton entitled "Petersburg Chronicle" in *SPb. ved.*, no. 116.

Glinka writes to Shestakova: "V.-Petrov promises the libretto after 29 May. Vladimir Stasov affirms that he genuinely wishes to be my collaborator. In that case, I will see to it myself and ask Fedorov directly, despite the fact that there are already those who wish to write for my new opera."

May

In the Viennese paper *Blätter für Musik, Theater und Kunst* there is an article by Anton Rubinstein entitled "Russian Composers." While he appraises Glinka's music highly, Rubinstein asserts that the establishment of Russian national opera is impossible and that Glinka "came to ruin" in this aspiration.
[Glinka found out about this article in November (cf. 29 November).]

"Rubinstein undertook to acquaint Germany with our music and wrote an article in which he soiled us all and wounded my old lady *A Life for the Tsar* rather impertinently" (ltr. to V. Engelgardt, 29 November 1855).
[Rubinstein's article bears witness to the lack of understanding on the part of the young musician at that time about the character and significance of the work of the majority of Russian composers. In his autobiography (1889) Rubinstein admitted that "the article I wrote . . . was total nonsense" (*Rus. starina*, 1889, November).]

End of May–Beginning of June (?)

In a note to August Freyer, Glinka asks that Mme [Krzhisevich (?)] be permitted to hear him play.
[Dated in G 2-B, p. 74.]

2 June

Glinka asks Heydenreich to come, since he is sick and "suffering from my stomach and liver."

2 and 4 June

Heydenreich attended Glinka two times.

4 June

Glinka received a letter from Vasilko-Petrov with the promise to bring the completed libretto for the first act of *The Bigamist* on 7 June and "that for the remainder there will be no delays."

29 May–5 June

Glinka was visited by the Stasovs, two times by Serov and Leonova, by Memel, Dargomyzhsky, and Dubrovsky. Glinka's ill health continued. "In part I am sick because of the way he [Dubrovsky] handled Tolstoy's article on my name-day."

5 June

Glinka writes to Shestakova: "If the malady passes and I return to my activities, I will hardly decide to go see anyone. What haven't I seen in this nasty place? Those places which I remember favorably are associated with my wasted youth. Those with which I associate grief are not worth seeing. It is better to stay at home." He asks that a letter be sent to his pupil Olga Lykoshina.
[The letter to Lykoshina is not extant.]

7 June

Composer's dating on the manuscript of the Mazurka composed in the stage-coach: "This Mazurka (*genre Chopin*) was composed by me toward the end of May in 1852 in a post-chaise during a trip from S.-P.burg to Warsaw. I have reworked it again now for K. A. Bulgakov. M. I. Glinka, 7 June 1855. S-Petersburg" (Bulgakov, *Vosp.*, p. 235).

In a note to Charukovsky, Glinka requests that he send to Bulgakov in Moscow a portrait of Beethoven and the manuscript of the Mazurka "(still unknown to you) of my composition, which has been completed for Bulgakov" and "my *Children's Polka* with commentary." He reports that he has been sick for the entire time. "Today I am promised the libretto for the first act of *The Bigamist*."

Glinka was visited by Dmitry Stasov, Serov, and the "neat general" [Kuzminsky]: "To please them I sang (without shouting) Spanish songs and played *Taras*

Bulba, which I will probably include in *The Bigamist.* The general devoured me with his eyes and listened very attentively. The others, it would seem, were also very satisfied" (ltr. to L. Shestakova, 12 June 1855).

8 June

In a letter to Konstantin Bulgakov, Glinka tells about the recent years of his life and writes that he has completed the *Zapiski* and collected his romances. He writes: "I am taking up a new work, an opera in three acts and five scenes: *The Bigamist.*"

Heydenreich attended Glinka. "I played *Taras* for him and said that I would like to make an entr'acte from it. 'What kind of entr'acte?' he exclaimed. . . . 'No,' he said, 'it's such a lady. It would make a most outstanding overture.' V. Stasov protested, saying that the music was too Ukrainian. Time will tell, I suppose!"

9 June

Lodi visited Glinka.

10 June

Leonova arrived in the morning. Then "V.-Petrov appeared with a trial scene for the second act. Although it was necessary to rework it (to which V.-Petrov agreed), its overall style pleased me—Russian and intimate. Having eaten breakfast, Leonova and I left in a splendid carriage. We drove to the Summer Garden. The monument to Krylov was intolerably disgusting. Before dinner Leonova declaimed Tanya's last conversation with Onegin to me so skillfully that I felt faint. At four o'clock V.-Petrov appeared [for the second time] for dinner, and after dinner the three of us went for a drive on the islands. On Krestovsky we went to the coast, and there we were faced with such a splendid view that I became truly ecstatic. Generally, the islands are fascinating. On our return trip I asked V.-Petrov to drop in on A. A. Kraevsky for a minute on my behalf. Learning of my presence, he himself cordially rushed to meet us. He provided such a welcome that I recalled your words that nowhere in the world am I so loved as in Piter." At Kraevsky's, "Leonova's singing ('*Akh, ne mne sirotinushke*' and '*Likhoradushka*' [Fever]) moved both him and his guests to tears. The evening and part of the night we spent at Lodi's, who undertook to teach Leonova a little" (ltr. to L. Shestakova, 12 June 1855).

11 June

Glinka asks Serov to come—"I have many interesting things for you"—and to bring *The Barber of Seville*. "I very much need it."

12 June

Glinka tells Shestakova about how he is spending his time: "This week had greater variety than last."

In *SPb. ved.,* no. 128, in the section "Petersburg Chronicle" there is a notice by Vasilko-Petrov which mentions Glinka. "We are happy with all our heart for the respect which Mr. Puñi feels toward our great composer."

13 June

Glinka was visited by Dmitry Stasov and after him by Vladimir Stasov.

14 June

In the morning Leonova came by and "took her lesson. In the evening there was Yakov Dovgolevsky, who drank tea with me and told me about his sister Olga and her children . . . whom he saw last year in Mogilev."

15 June

"The weather was damp and cold, just like in the fall. In the morning Dubrovsky dropped in."

16 June

Vasilko-Petrov had dinner with Glinka "and promised . . . to bring the second act next week. Illness prevented me from discussing the third act. Instead, V.-Petrov entertained me with humorous stories."

17 June

After dinner "Dargomyzhsky . . . dropped by and stayed for about two hours."

18 June

At 11 o'clock a.m. Leonova arrived and took her lesson. "We had dinner together," went to her dacha, and then to Lodi. "He taught her singing," while Glinka "strolled with Mme Lodi in their little garden." At 8 o'clock in the evening they "set out for a new establishment, the Villa Borghese, where there was a garden, an orchestra, and a station." Glinka encountered Feofil Tolstoy there: "He bowed, gave me his hand, and spoke to me cordially; and I answered him likewise, without any anger or sarcasm. At 9 o'clock I returned home" (ltr. to L. Shestakova, 19 June 1855). "Several people in the audience, when they noticed the presence of the famous composer of *A Life for the Tsar* and *Ruslan,* asked the Kapellmeister to perform *Kamarinskaya,* but he kept out of sight, apparently not wishing to be the object of attention and applause. . . . That evening the orchestra was led by Mr. Ferrero, and one must say that they performed this masterfully orchestrated piece not badly at all" (*SPb. ved.,* 26 June 1855).

Between 13 and 19 June

Glinka had "a slight fever and cold."

19 June

In the morning Heydenreich attended Glinka and "found . . . [his] pulse improved and promised that in several days" he would be fully returned to health.

Glinka writes to Shestakova about the work he plans on *The Bigamist:* "During this week I suppose I will receive the entire second act from V.-Petrov. Questions remain about the first act, and the third we must think about together. Since he is free and we see each other often, there will be a libretto. But to write down the music so soon, as you and I wish it, will hardly be possible, because 1) I cannot write except when I am feeling well, and my health is intermittently beginning to cause me more and more trouble; 2) you know how strict I am toward my musical work. *Il ne faut pas se dépêcher pour bien faire.*" He writes that he has been "for some time in pleasant correspondence with Bulgakov, a friend of long standing. . . . He is a pleasant rake who likes me and appreciates my music better than almost anyone. This correspondence affords me many pleasant minutes."

In *SPb. ved.,* no. 134, under "Musical News from M. Bernard," new music listed includes piano pieces by Döhler—Variations on the Trio from *A Life for the Tsar,* and Glinka's Variations on Alyabiev's Song *"Solovei."*

20 June

Vasilko-Petrov and Lodi had dinner with Glinka. The former brought the second scene of the opera (in draft). I fed Lodi, because he teaches Leonova Italian-style singing twice a week. He was a master at this. In the evening D. Stasov came and stayed about two hours."

21 June

Glinka "began to look over the libretto. In the evening V. Stasov and Serov came and carefully read through what V.-Petrov had written and made pertinent observations" (ltr. to L. Shestakova, 26 June 1855).

22 June

New music mentioned under "Musical News from M. Bernard" in *SPb. ved.,* no. 136, includes Glinka's romances *"Adel'"* [Adèle] and *"Meri"* [Mary].

In the evening Daniel Rozenberg and Dargomyzhsky came to see Glinka (ltr. to L. Shestakova, 26 June 1855).

23 June

In a letter to Bulgakov, Glinka expresses his ideas concerning Sergey Shtuts-man's forthcoming Glinka concert in Moscow and recommends that Leonova participate in the concert (performing *"Molitva"*). "Having worked with me vocally for over half a year with exemplary constancy, she has made remarkable progress. I torment her with despicable Italian music in order to develop her voice. She is a native Russian talent and sings Russian songs particularly well, with a certain gypsy chic which Russian audiences instinctively like. Overall she performs Russian music well, particularly my 'Molitva,' which I have adapted to her voice." And about himself: "I have no new pieces. Now I am completely immersed in the libretto for my new labor. Heat and illness still do not permit me to work on the thing. Your little piece is interesting, despite a few clumsy places. It is still better than the long drawn-out proceedings of F. Tolstoy."

Vasilko-Petrov had dinner with Glinka and "made all the necessary changes" in the libretto of the second scene of *The Bigamist*. "Heat and insomnia keep me from concentrating on work, but I am not losing time and have thought out many things."

24 June

He obtained "a little bracelet for Olya, which is apparently nice. Darya Mikhaylovna [Leonova] was good enough to compliment me on it."

25 June

Glinka spent the day with Leonova. They called on Fedorov, who gave Glinka the couplets he had composed on 20 May and which Bulakhov had performed. After this "for an hour's time" they drove about the islands, and at 8:30 Glinka returned home.

26 June

In a letter to Shestakova, Glinka complains about his health: "The fever has passed and my stomach feels better, but I am still overcome by sleeplessness. . . . There is no night at all, and that irritates my nerves." He describes how he is spending his time.

In *SPb. ved.,* no. 140, in "Petersburg Chronicle," "V.-P." [Petrov] reports on Glinka's visit to the Villa Borghese on 18 June and the performance of *Kamarinskaya*.

30 June

For her nameday, Glinka sent his niece Olya "a gold bracelet with an appropriate inscription" (ltr. to L. Shestakova, 3 July 1855).

In a feuilleton entitled "Moscow Chronicle" in *Ved. Mosk. gor. politsii,* no. 142, it says that the restored Bolshoi Theater was opened on 9 September 1843 with *A Life for the Tsar*.

End of June

The Overture and Mazurka from *A Life for the Tsar* are performed at the Villa Borghese (*SPb. ved.,* 3 July 1855).

Between 27 June and 1 July

Aleksandr Serov and Dmitry and Vladimir Stasov visited Glinka. "V.-Petrov has only come once and in general has been lazy this week. I have done the musical program for the entire opera. Perhaps something is beginning to stir in my imagination."

2 July

Glinka "spent the time very pleasantly" with Leonova on the islands and at Lodi's.

3 July

Glinka writes to Shestakova about how he is spending his time and reports that he has been invited to Kraevsky's on the fourth of July. "Whether I will go, I do not know, because I have been overcome by insomnia."

Glinka writes to Kraevsky that he will try to be at his nameday party on 4 July, "if not for dinner . . . then in the evening and will try to show you how much I value your good favor."

In *SPb. ved.*, no. 144, "Petersburg Chronicle," on the occasion of the performance "last week" of the Overture and Mazurka from *A Life for the Tsar* at the Villa Borghese, Vasilko-Petrov writes: "At the Villa Borghese . . . the Kapellmeisters managed very skillfully and intelligently. We are already tired of waltzes, polkas, and galops. These Kapellmeisters understood this and tried to provide concerts of more serious music . . . they have begun to perform music of our Russian composers." In the section "Musical News at M. Bernard's," Kullak's piano transcription of the romance *"Ia pomniu chudnoe mgnoven'e"* is named.

4 July

In the evening Glinka attended Kraevsky's nameday party (ltr. to A. Kraevsky, 3 July 1855).

Bulgakov (from Moscow) thanks Glinka for his letter and for "the excellent music, that is to say, the *'Molitva'* with chorus," which he received from Glinka. He promises to assist Leonova in the organization of her concert in Moscow, despite the fact that "Verstovsky does not like anything that comes from you. All his 'Askold's Tombs,' 'Devil's Valleys,' and 'Longings for the Opera' are thin as water compared to the harmony in your music" (*Rus. starina*, 1883, vol. 37, no. 2, p. 478).
[Bulgakov jestingly distorts the names of Verstovsky's operas, which should read *Churova dolina* [Chur Valley] and *Toska po rodine* [Longing for the homeland].]

10 July

In *SPb. ved.*, no. 150, in a notice about Puñi's musico-dramatic poem entitled "June 6, 1855, at the Walls of Sevastopol," it says that it is comprised of various Russian works, among which in the first part there are several bars from *Kamarinskaya*.

11 July

Glinka celebrated the nameday of his niece. "All who love you, Olya, and me, congregated like God's little birds. We spent the time marvelously, pleasantly."

12 July

Glinka was visited by Dmitry Stasov, who brought money from Shestakova and "also brought me good news" (ltr. to L. Shestakova, 14 July 1855).

13 July

Bulgakov (from Moscow) sent Glinka his romance *"Ispoved'"* [Confession] to words of Matvey Bibikov. On the manuscript is this inscription: "To Mikhail Ivanovich Glinka. Moscow, 13 July 1855. Taken down from my sinful hands and impious voice in 1851 by the deceased A. A. Alyabiev" (*L.*, p. 457).

14 July

In a letter to Shestakova, Glinka complains about his "awful general condition because of the heat." Of his work with Leonova he says: "I gave her over to Lodi, who in eight lessons (free of charge) has taught her to sing so that . . . you would not recognize her. She will be a prima donna, just as our angel Olinka predicted."

Vasilko-Petrov visited Glinka (ltr. to L. Shestakova, 14 July 1855).

By 19 July

"All numbers of the second act were planned by Glinka at the piano," but "they were not written down on paper" (*SPb. ved.*, 3 March 1857).

19 July

In the morning Glinka was visited by Heydenreich and Leonova. "Heydenreich was amazed with Leonova's progress and called her a prima donna."

Glinka writes to Shestakova: "The heat, insomnia, and then persistent nausea have completely exhausted me. . . . I often spend entire days at home alone. Sometimes a group of people will gather, all of them nice people. . . . Occasionally one or two friends eat dinner with me, always by invitation. Vasilko-Petrov is sick." He expresses his desire to travel to Warsaw in the fall. He reports that "they still enjoy [*Kamarinskaya*] and perform it daily."

In a note to Charukovsky he asks him to assist Shestakova in getting a family coach in Moscow.

20 July

Glinka reports to Barteneva about the results of hearing the singer V. K. Filatova, for whom she had pulled strings. About himself he says, "I am quite sick and do little with music."

Between 20 and 24 July

In a letter to Shestakova, Glinka complains about his health and regrets that because of military events he cannot "leave our disgusting city for Warsaw. . . . The opera is not progressing: V.-Petrov slumbers, and I with my paunch am really not in the mood for music."

24 July

Dmitry Stasov visited Glinka. "I said to him that I intended to travel to Warsaw, and he responded: 'So? Then go.' 'But what will the Minister of Finance say,' I responded. 'Minister of Finance?' he said with surprise. 'Yes, I answered, the Minister of Finance, Lyudmila Ivanovna.' And he laughed very heartily" (ltr. to L. Shestakova, 28 July 1855).

26 July

Glinka sends Dmitry Stasov the *"corrected* duet, with a request to forward it to Bernard."
[The duet is *"Prosti menia, prosti."*]

On the holiday at the Villa Borghese they performed the Lezghinka from *Ruslan and Lyudmila* (*SPb. ved.*, 31 July 1855).

28 July

Glinka writes to Shestakova: "My health is improving a little, I can eat without aversion, but I still sleep poorly, and generally my spirits have fallen, and one feeling prevails: an irresistible desire to get out of this detestable Petersburg. The climate here is decidedly harmful to me, but perhaps the gossips here do even more damage to my health. They all have at least a drop of poison on the tips of their tongues. Regarding this, I'll give you details when we meet." He asks that she make him an "allowance" to live on in Warsaw. "I love Warsaw . . . no less than you love Elnya. I can live quietly, comfortably, and freely there, and no one tries to offend me there."

Glinka is visited by Vladimir Stasov, who "sticks painfully close, so that I will work—it doesn't matter to them whether I'm well or not. Just write and write and nothing else. I cannot agree to that!"

29 July

Andrey Memel visited Glinka.

Glinka writes to Shestakova: "Here in Piter there is *nothing at all* for me to do. Besides boredom and suffering I have nothing to expect. V.-Petrov has promised the opera by fall. I do not know if he will keep his word, but if he does write it, I not only have not begun, but illness has blotted from my memory all the ideas which I have had. In any event, the opera will be put off, and I do not intend to be a *prisoner* because of it in this repulsive city. The public is not worth it. . . . I have turned Leonova over to Lodi for voice lessons and to Hunke (a master of his craft and a friend of ours) for accompanying and coaching. She has progressed incredibly and can manage without me. On account of her, they're starting to nibble at me, which goes against the grain. Don't tread on me—that's my motto."

4 August

Glinka had "Arkasha" as a dinner guest. "In the evening there was good music."
["Arkasha" is Arkady Golenishchev-Kutuzov.]

5 August

Glinka "became ill early in the morning" (ltr. to K. Bulgakov, 28 August 1855).

22 August/3 September

Dehn (from Berlin) thanks Glinka for sending his compositions "via your Spanish Pedrillo. . . . Every day your works pass from hand to hand. I had them bound in two volumes and gave them to the royal library as a cherished gift. Although we cannot understand their texts, your melodies, besides the charm of profound feeling and noble simplicity, possess an attractive and even magical quality, thanks to certain brilliant turns. Thus both these volumes have become favorites among educated musicians and have created a demand for other works of yours. Send me everything which has come from your pen and, if possible, one of your operas in score as well." He asks Glinka to send him biographical information to place in a projected (though not established) music journal (*RMG*, 1911, no. 48; German original).

26 August

Balakirev performs his Fantasy on Themes from *A Life for the Tsar* at his concert in Nizhny Novgorod (program of the concert, in *Letopis' Balakireva,* p. 23).

5–27 August

Glinka is sick.

27 August

Glinka writes to the Archimandrite Ignaty that he has been sick and that he "wished to communicate to you some of my ideas regarding Russian church music, though now I am reserving this for the arrival of Ivan Grigorievich Tatarinov."
[Tatarinov was a tenor and novice in the St. Sergius Monastery.]

28 August

Glinka writes to Bulgakov: "I am just now beginning to recover. . . . There is no doubt that the principal cause of my cruel sufferings is this harsh climate. In the fall I had intended to go to Warsaw, but conditions have not allowed it. I will spend the winter here."

End of August

Glinka had a section of the apartment separated off from Shestakova for himself.

30 August

Glinka invites Dargomyzhsky to come visit him in the early part of September and reports: "My sister and I are going to be living differently, that is to say, my sister and I are going to have separate living quarters."

Performance of *A Life for the Tsar* in the Circus Theater (*Otech. zap.*, 1855, vol. 102, part 10, p. 97).

1 September

Glinka started to live separately from Shestakova (ltr. to A. Dargomyzhsky, 30 August 1855). "My brother had the fantasy of closing up the door between the living room and hall. . . . I did not oppose it, because I knew quite well that given my brother's persistent character it would lead nowhere, and he would rather do as he pleased. Normally it was necessary to give in to him and let him in time think over and analyze the matter. . . . So it was now . . . the door was sealed up, wallpaper was hung on his side, and no trace of the door remained. Initially my brother was satisfied, but then he began to discover the inconvenience of it, and it all ended with the wallpaper being torn off after two weeks and the door unsealed so that everything was as it had been before" (Shestakova, *Vosp.*, p. 302).

On a manuscript of Glinka's: " '*Sleza*' [Tears], romance, words by V. Vasilko-Petrov, music by D. Leonova," dated "1 September 1855."

Performance of *A Life for the Tsar* in the Circus Theater (*Sev. pchela*, 1 September 1855).

2 September

In a note to Dmitry Stasov, Glinka asks him to forward the enclosed letter to Dehn and "to petition" Bernard, who would be returning to Petersburg in several days, "about the duet."
[This letter to Dehn has not been discovered.]

9 September

Glinka writes to Bulgakov: "I am spending the winter in Petersburg, and if there is the slightest possibility, early in the spring I will leave for Germany. . . . Nothing has come of my musical mischief for a long time. I have a beautiful hall for quartets and other musical fare, but I am not undertaking anything. I have a distaste for music."

12 September

Performance of *A Life for the Tsar* in the Maly Theater in Moscow for the benefit of the tenor Petrov, with the following performers: Kurov—Susanin; Semyonova—Antonida; Legoshina—Vanya; Petrov—Sobinin. The opera was given "without the last act, which is necessary both for the sense of the play and for the sense of the music. One must regret such a cut. Because of this we were deprived of the satisfaction of hearing many beautiful things, including the famous contralto aria '*Ne mne bednomu*.' This, however, has been the fate of M. I. Glinka's music in the Moscow theaters. Every time here the best and foremost Russian composer somehow gets cut" (*Panteon*, 1855, vol. 23, part 9, p. 11).

23 September

In *Sev. pchela*, no. 208, there is an article by A. Kresin called "Letter from Nizhny Novgorod" about Balakirev's concert on 26 August: "The piece *A Life for the Tsar* which he played was a perfect example of its kind."

24 September

In *Otech. zap.*, vol. 102, part 10, "Miscellany—Petersburg Notes," there is a note about the opening of the season in the Circus Theater on 30 August with *A Life for the Tsar* (d.c.a.).

27 September

In *Sev. pchela*, no. 211, Rostislav's "Musical Conversations" refer to events of the past 20 years: "The Russian Opera troupe of that time rendered significant services: it acquainted Petersburg music lovers with the best works of Meyerbeer. . . . But its most important and valuable service, which will always serve as a monument to these Russian dilettantes, was their presentation of M. I. Glinka's *A Life for the Tsar* and *Ruslan and Lyudmila*. . . . The very perfection of *A Life for the Tsar* had . . . a powerful influence on Russian opera. . . . Once they had savored the charm of Russian melodies presented in mature artistic form, the majority of people became indifferent to foreign operas performed in the Russian language. Audiences waited for new native music, which the appearance of *Ruslan and Lyudmila* did not fully satisfy. They were waiting for the complete development of national opera, whose character and method Glinka had brilliantly demonstrated in his first work. The music of *Ruslan and Lyudmila*, although it is inimitable, does not bear the imprint of nationality [*narodnost'*]. In the meantime Glinka has been silent, and other composers have not decided to follow in his footsteps, fearing unfavorable comparison and the virtual impossibility of equal status." Rostislav considers that if there were a conservatory in Russia, then "the beginning established by Glinka would bear plentiful fruit." But our composers are separated, and each of them works apart, "following individual interests. . . . This is why we believe that the very perfection, or rather genius, evident in *A Life for the Tsar* is an obstacle to new experiments in this genre. The consequence of this was that the Russian Opera troupe's prosperity came to a halt. *A Life for the Tsar* did not disappear from posters for a long time, because this was the only opera that attracted audiences. *Ruslan and Lyudmila*, as we have already said, did not meet general expectations. Rubini's arrival in Petersburg completed the reversal, and for a time the Russian Opera suspended its existence. So it was until last year. . . . The present season of the Russian Opera began on 30 August with a performance of the opera *A Life for the Tsar*."

Beginning of Fall and Later

Glinka's acquaintance with the Belenitsyn family. "The oldest daughter . . . Lyubov Ivanovna . . . was a very nice, educated girl with great musical talent and an excellent ability to sing from sight . . . as if she had always known the piece. My brother was very enthusiastic about such talent, and she often sang at our house with my brother accompanying" (Shestakova, *Vosp.*, p. 301).

4 October

Glinka writes to Serov: "I am expecting another piano today, but the main thing we wish is to make up our minds about *A Life for the Tsar*, so that your work and the copying go independently of one another." He asks Serov to come by "if only for a minute today."

[Reference is to Serov's arrangement of *A Life for the Tsar*.]

6 October

In a mixed performance for Petrov's benefit in the Circus Theater, the first act of *A Life for the Tsar* (*Sev. pchela*, 7 October 1855).

21 October

Glinka gives his pencil drawing as a gift to Mikhail Mikeshin (composer's dating).
[The drawing was in Findeyzen's archives. Its location now is unknown (G 2-A, p. 14).]

27 October

In *Sev. pchela*, no. 236, Rostislav complains in his "Musical Conversations" about the lot of music critics, who cannot avoid offending someone, always because of misunderstanding. "Thus, in speaking of the influence of the opera *A Life for the Tsar* on the productivity of Russian composers, I said: 'In the meantime Glinka has been silent, and other composers have not decided to follow in his footsteps, fearing unfavorable comparison.' These words provoked the indignation of many of our composers. 'What was Rostislav thinking of, they said, when he claimed that after Glinka writing music was impossible!' This was not at all what I said, however. When I said that other composers had not decided to follow in Glinka's footsteps, I implied in this that they did not wish to write national operas like *A Life for the Tsar*, fearing unfavorable comparison and the accusation of imitation. And I feel that this observation is completely justified, because no one has written in this manner, but to construe these words in an *absolute* sense is totally strange. . . . If they wrote after Mozart, Haydn, Gluck, and others, then there is no reason not to write after Glinka."

28 October

Glinka asks Dmitry Stasov to come by "if only for several minutes," and also to convey to Vladimir Stasov and Serov "that I very much want to see them."

4 November

In *SPb. ved.*, no. 242, under "Musical News from M. Bernard," Fedorov's romance *"Prosti menia, prosti,"* transcribed by Glinka for two voices is named along with other new music.

8 November

Glinka is surprised that in Bulgakov's letter he "encountered the names Spohr and Bortnyansky. . . . I. E. Kolmakov would ask: 'Why Spohr?' Spohr is the reliable stagecoach of German work [in music], in my opinion, a hard-working mule—idol of German mediocrity. What about Bortnyansky? Mr. Sugar Son-of-Honey Syrup—enough!!! . . . To purge you I'm sending the following prescription: No. 1. For theatrical music: Gluck, first and last, who is scandalously fleeced by Mozart, Beethoven, etc., etc. No. 2. For church and organ music: Seb. Bach: the B-minor mass and *Passion-Musik*. No. 3. For concert music: Handel, Handel, and Handel. A chorus of Bortnyansky's, for example, is so *schwach* in comparison to Handel, that Bortnyansky's 80 people with Handel *représentent au moins* 200. Of Handel I recommend *Messiah* and *Samson* (In this there is a soprano aria with chorus in B minor, when Delilah lulls Samson to dupe him, similar to mine in *Ruslan*, 'O my Ratmir, love and peace,' only a hundred times brighter, more intelligent, and racier). *Jephtha*. I hope that after such a *cure radicale*, Spohr and Bortnyansky will not be encountered again in your letters. *Pour dorer la pilule*, in several days I'm sending you Leonova's romance 'Tears.' She composed the melody and I worked it out. And then the duet '*Prosti, prosti*,' etc., music by Fedorov, the arrangement mine."

17 November

For her birthday Glinka gives Shestakova a collection of the works of Zhukovsky with this inscription: "I ask you, dear sister, Lyudmila Ivanova, to accept this my sincere gift graciously. I am indebted to V. A. Zhukovsky for many, many pleasant poetic moments in life. He in fact led me to the opera *A Life for the Tsar*. V. A.'s pure, noble soul is clearly reflected in his creations. I am sure that reading these will afford you many pleasant and gratifying moments. Your friend and brother Mikhail Glinka, 17 November 1855. S.P.burg." (*Rus. starina*, 1884, vol. 41, no. 1, p. 194).

Between Mid-October and the Last Week of November

"Not long ago we played six-hands on three pianos and eight-hands on two. The participants were the two Stasovs, Serov, Santis and two ladies, as well as Serov's sister Mme Dyutur. Serov has arranged the Polish act of *A Life for the Tsar* very well, especially the Krakowiak and the Polonaise. We also played the finale to *A Life for the Tsar* which you arranged, the introduction to *Ruslan* and the overture to *Ruslan*. The first two went quite neatly, but in the overture the performers got mixed up" (ltr. to V. Engelgardt, 29 November 1855).

22 November

Composer's inscription on a copy of a manuscript: *" 'Las Mollares,' air de danse Andaloux transcrit pour piano par M. Glinka.* To Bulgakov from Glinka, 22 November 1855" (*L.* p. 461).

24 November

In *St.-Petersburger Zeitung,* no. 258, there is an article by Theodor Berthold called *"M. I. Glinka and His Opera* A Life for the Tsar," a polemical response to Rubinstein's article (cf. May). Drawing upon examples from the history of music, Berthold refutes Rubinstein's position and emphasizes that genuine works of art, in reproducing noteworthy national details . . . acquire, because of this folk character, a universal character, and thanks to style and originality belong to world history and become immortal.

Dedicatory inscription on the title page of the "Primary Polka": "To K. A. Bulgakov from Glinka, 24 November 1855."

25 and 26 November

The continuation and conclusion of Berthold's article appears in *St. Petersburger Zeitung,* nos. 259 and 260. "In the St. Petersburg German paper . . . a feuilleton in defense of the scolding my old lady got from Rubinstein has been printed. The feuilleton was written by a certain Berthold . . . it's written dispassionately and in a businesslike manner, but Rubinstein gets put in his place."

26 November

Glinka asks Dmitry Stasov to get a copy of the couplets written "in the winter of 1836–37 by Pushkin, Zhukovsky, and Prince Vyazemsky from Odoevsky."

29 November

Glinka writes to Engelgardt: "Since *sometime,* though hardly *soon,* Stellovsky's edition of *A Life for the Tsar* will be coming out, it would be good if on your return trip through Germany you could find time for the publication of Serov's arrangement abroad. Surely the swindler Stellovsky's influence does not extend to Germany. . . . I have long since given up on *The Bigamist.* My poet Vasilko-Petrov, who visited me twice a week during the summer, has disappeared in August, and as is the custom in Piter, he has begun to spread stupid rumors about me around the city. I am sincerely grateful to him, as I am to Villebois. I do not have to associate with the nasty public. And I am glad that the opera has come to end, 1) because it is strange and nearly impossible to write an opera in Russian style without borrowing on the character of my old lady, 2) I do not have to blind myself, for I see poorly, and 3) in the event of success I would have to remain longer than necessary in this despicable Piter. Disappointment, distress, and suffering have ruined me. My spirits have fallen (*démoralisé*). I'm waiting for spring in order to make off to somewhere away from here. Berlin and Italy . . . would be best. Incidentally, it would be sensible for me to work with Dehn on the old church modes (*Kirchen-Tonarten*). It would yield good results."

1 December

In *Otech. zap.,* vol. 103, part 12, in Apollon Mokritsky's "Memoirs of Bryullov" there appear Bryullov's words about Petrova-Vorobieva's singing, accompanied by Glinka (d.c.a.).

2 December

Glinka asks Dmitry Stasov to take a good box on the second tier or in the stalls for tomorrow's performance of *The Barber of Seville.*
[Dated according to its contents (a poster) and the calendar: the letter is dated "Friday."]

3 December

Glinka and Shestakova attend a performance of *The Barber of Seville* in the Bolshoi Theater (ltr. to D. Stasov, 2 December 1855; *SPb. ved.,* 3 December 1855).

14 December

In *Rus. invalid,* no. 272, "Musical News," there is a report of the forthcoming publication of a transcription of *A Life for the Tsar* for piano solo by Karl Meier and Konstantin Villebois.

24 December

In *SPb. ved.,* no. 283, in the "Petersburg Chronicle" section, there is an announcement of the publication of Stellovsky's edition of *A Life for the Tsar,* transcribed for piano solo by Meier and Villebois, and of the publication by Denotkin of the Andalusian dance *"Las Mollares,"* transcribed by Glinka for piano.

26 December

Glinka has a Christmas tree. "It will be my Christmas tree party and I will invite whom I wish," he said to Shestakova. "He invited the Belenitsyn family, Dargomyzhsky, his sister Sofia Sergeevna and her husband, and no one else. He lit the tree and had the idea of dancing a mazurka around the tree. He got me to play a mazurka, and they began to dance. . . . At first all went well. They did various figures, and my brother managed well for his age and stoutness, but Dargomyzhsky decided to tease my brother, and he . . . ventured a figure in which the men must kneel." Glinka could not get to his feet, "all the ladies rushed to help him up, there was general laughter . . . my brother said [to Dargomyzhsky] . . . 'You have really played a malicious trick on me.' . . . Of course, the mazurka ended then, and the Christmas tree party with it. Music began: my brother and Dargomyzhsky played duets. Then everyone sang in turn and together. Thanks to my brother's idea, we all spent the evening very pleasantly" (Shestakova, *Vosp.,* p. 302). Later Ulybyshev and Balakirev arrived. "I was bold enough to play . . . for Glinka himself my transcription of the trio '*Ne tomi, rodimyi.*' Glinka was very lenient toward it and even praised the transcription. Subsequently he often had me play it before others" (M. Balakirev's ltr. to M. Gurskalina, 15 July 1899, in *Letopis' Balakireva,* p. 24).

End of December

Petr Stepanov and his wife had dinner with Glinka (ltr. to K. Bulgakov, 2 January 1856). "We spent that day very pleasantly, the last in our lives as friends. . . . After dinner Glinka sang a great deal. He acquainted us with many of the numbers from *The Bigamist.* . . . At my request he sang '*Kak sladko s toboiu mne byt',*' but he sang unwillingly and very sluggishly, because he did not like this romance. Toward the end of the evening he said to me that he was leaving for Berlin very soon and that he wanted to devote himself exclusively to sacred music" (P. Stepanov, *Vosp.,* p. 65).

30 December

In *Panteon,* vol. 23, part 9, under "Moscow Herald—Moscow Theater" (signed "A correspondent"), there is a review of the performance of *A Life for the Tsar* on 12 September in Moscow, which lacked the entire epilog. It particularly mentions Legoshina's successful performance in the role of Vanya.

31 December

In the "Miscellany" section of *Bib-ka dlia chteniia*, vol. 135, there is an article by "E. M." [Moller] entitled "Essay on the Development of Russian Dramatic Music." Making note of Glinka's exclusive role and *A Life for the Tsar* in the development of Russian opera, the author writes: "M. I. Glinka . . . stands on the same pinnacle with those artists of genius who are beyond imitation, who by their originality established a new path for art. His service in relation to our music may be compared to that of Lomonosov's to literature" (d.c.a.).

December

Glinka inscribed in Shestakova's album a mazurka to which he danced in his childhood (Album No. 2).

End of the Year

Glinka informs Nikolay Stepanov that he is sick and that he is sending him and Petr Stepanov "eight rings of homemade sausage."

Glinka's arrangement for piano of the second scene from the fourth act of Gluck's *Armide* and the sacrificial chorus from *Iphigénie en Aulide* date from this year.

Glinka's last meeting with Anna Kern dates from this year. "He avoided talking about himself and turned the conversation to my then unenviable position, asking about my affairs with lively concern, and only in passing did he touch on his own circumstances and intentions. . . . In this regard he told me that he was busy with sacred music. He played, incidentally, a 'Cherubim's Song' and even sang something reminiscent of past times. Despite the danger of agitating him too much, I could not restrain myself and asked . . . him to sing Pushkin's romance '*Ia pomniu chudnoe mgnoven'e*.' He played it with pleasure, and I was ecstatic!" (A. Kern, *Vosp.*, p. 158).
[In Pavel Annenkov's book, *A. S. Pushkin. Materialy dlia ego biografii i otsenki proizvedenii* [A. S. Pushkin. Material for his biography and evaluations of the works], SPb., 1855, p. 249, there is a history of the creation of the poem *"Ne poi, krasavitsa, pri mne."*]

The firm of Brandus published a second edition of the romance *"Razocharova-nie"* ["Where are you, first desire"].

1855/1856

Winter

At Glinka's "this winter, as last, people gathered and made music, and the Belenytsyns reinforced those who always came. Dargomyzhsky was there quite often," as well as Balakirev. "My brother predicted a brilliant musical future for Balakirev." Glinka himself "went out even less . . . once or twice he visited Prince Odoevsky" (Shestakova, *Vosp.*, p. 301).

End of December–Beginning of January

"While putting my compositions in as much order as possible, I found the Bolero, and in several days I hope to find the *Valse-fantaisie,* which were played in Pavlovsk in 1840" (ltr. to K. Bulgakov, 2 January 1856).

1856

1 January

In *Muz. i teatr. vestnik* [Musical and Theatrical Bulletin], no. 1, there is an article by Serov called "Music and Talk about It," where he promises to print a critical study of Glinka's romances.

2 January

Glinka writes to Bulgakov about his decision to leave for Germany in the spring: "I intend to take this trip not only for the improvement of my poor health but also for some musical instruction. In Berlin, where I intend to spend the winter, I can hear Gluck, Bach, and Handel."

3 January

In *Mosk. ved.*, no. 1, there is an announcement of the availability in music stores of a transcription for piano of *A Life for the Tsar,* "which has just appeared."

4 January

Shestakova writes to Dargomyzhsky: "The Belenitsyns have decided to have dinner with us on Friday, the sixth of January. You are so genuinely close to both them and us that it would be a great pleasure for us to see you that day. . . .

Besides the Belenitsyns there will be no one else with us that day. My brother instructed me to give you his regards and to say that he is trying to restrain his jealousy" (IRLI, coll. Stepanov, 4267, XXII, b. 44).
[The year has been established according to the letter's contents and the calendar.]

5 January

In *Rus. invalid,* no. 4, "Musical News," there is a notice about the publication of a transcription for piano solo of *A Life for the Tsar*.

6 January

Dargomyzhsky and the Belenitsyns had dinner with Glinka (ltr. from L. Shestakova to A. Dargomyzhsky, 4 January 1856. IRLI, coll. Stepanov).

In *Journal d'Odessa,* no. 3, in an article signed "R." and entitled *"Théâtre d'Odessa,"* there is a notice about the performance of excerpts from *A Life for the Tsar* for the benefit of the conductor Bouffé (the date of the concert is not indicated).

8 January

Musical inscription by Glinka in Stepanov's album: "I recall the wonderful moment [*Ia pomniu chudnoe mgnoven'e*] when you first appeared before me (Pushkin). Mikhail Glinka. S.P.burg, 8 January 1856" (IRLI, coll. Stepanov).

Glinka annotated Grigory Danilevsky's album with an excerpt from the song *"Gude viter":* "S.P.burg, 8 January 1856 (composed in Little Russia in the summer of 1838)" (GPB, coll. 236).

In *Muz. i teatr. vestnik,* no. 2, the beginning of an article written by Serov in 1852, "M. I. Glinka's comments on instrumentation," part 1, is printed. "Tonality and the character of the orchestral instruments: the characteristics of kettledrums and brass, woodwinds, strings, and the other instruments." In the same number there is an announcement that Stellovsky's store has available a transcription for piano solo of *A Life for the Tsar*.

9 January

Serov informs Balakirev that "the music intended for today at Glinka's will not take place for various reasons" (*Ocherki po istorii i teorii muzyki* [Notes on the history and theory of music], inst. 2, Leningrad, 1940, p. 289).

11 January

In *SPb. ved.*, no. 8, in an announcement under "Musical News from M. Bernard." Fedorov's romance *"Prosti menia, prosti,"* arranged by Glinka for two voices, is named along with Glinka's romances *"Finskii zaliv," "O milaia deva," "Dubrava shumit,"* and *"Ty skoro menia pozabudesh'."*

Dedicatory inscription on the cover of an edition of *"Las Mollares":* "To Dmitry Vasilievich Stasov from M. Glinka. S.P.burg, 11 January 1856."

13 January

Glinka asks Obodovsky to bring or send the score of the Graduation chorus for the Ekaterininsky Institute and makes a commitment to get it back by 1 February (for a performance on graduation evening). "Poor health again causes me to go abroad in the early spring. I am using my stay here to put my compositions in as much order as possible."

15 January

In *Muz. i teatr. vestnik*, no. 3, there is an article by Serov (signed "Modest Z-n") entitled *"A Life for the Tsar,* opera by M. I. Glinka, arranged for solo piano (without voices) by K. Meier and K. Villebois. St. Petersburg, published by F. Stellovsky." He comments on the importance of this edition, which for the first time makes it possible for a broad public to acquaint itself with the entire opera.

20 January

While congratulating Dmitry Stasov on his birthday, Glinka writes: "I hope that in the not too distant future . . . we can cook up some pleasant musical fare either at your place or at ours."

22 January

In *Muz. i teatr. vestnik*, no. 4, in Serov's article (signed "Modest Z-n") "Newly Published Musical Compositions," he refers to the similarity of Kazhinsky's "Lullaby" with Glinka's "Lullaby" and of a melody from Kazhinsky's *"Shutki"* [Jokes] with a phrase from an aria of Lyudmila's in *Ruslan and Lyudmila*.

23 January

In a note to an unknown person Glinka expresses regret that he "did not find him at home."

25 January

In *SPb. ved.,* no. 20, in an announcement entitled "Musical Novelties from M. Bernard," reference is made to a "Musical Caricature Album," in which Glinka's romance *"Ty skoro menia pozabudesh'"* appears.

27 January

Vasily Samoylov's benefit performance of S. Boykov's vaudeville *The Hired Shot* with couplets by Glinka in the Aleksandrinsky Theater (*Muz. i teatr. vestnik,* 1857, no. 16, p. 272).

29 January

In *Muz. i teatr. vestnik,* no. 5, there is a review by Serov ("Modest Z-n") of "two little things with the name of M. I. Glinka," namely the two-part arrangement of Fedorov's romance *"Prosti menia, prosti"* and the Andalusian dance *"Las Mollares,"* transcribed for piano. There is an announcement in the same number of the availability in Denotkin's store of *"Las Mollares"* and the publication of "Ferdinand Hiller's 'Conversations about Russia'" (translated by Serov). In a footnote Serov remarks on Glinka's indifference to the fate of his manuscripts.

31 January

In *Otech. zap.,* vol. 104, part 2, in the section "New Musical Compositions at Bernard's," there is an announcement of the sale of Fedorov's romance *"Prosti menia, prosti,"* arranged for two voices by Glinka (d.c.a.).

January

Lev Golitsyn was at Glinka's, where he heard Leonova sing and "was quite pleased with her."

Glinka "spent [the evening] very pleasantly" at Dmitry Ivanovich Naryshkin's with Sergey and Lev Golitsyn: "all the Bartenevs were there; they sang and played the zither, etc. I played several of my studies (*essais*) in Russian church music for them, and they were quite satisfied with them" (ltr. to K. Bulgakov, 2 February 1856).

Balakirev played the allegro from his Concerto in F-Sharp Minor for piano and orchestra for Glinka, and Glinka "was sympathetic" to the concerto. *Letopis' Balakireva* [Balakirev Chronicle], p. 26).

End of January

From Anna Kern, Glinka received a chapter from the novel *Ne shuti s gorem* [Do not trifle with grief], which she had translated, and a letter with the request to assist her in the publication of the translation.

1 February

In a letter to Anna Kern, Glinka speaks approvingly of her translation, which "seems very natural . . . although I am no sorcerer in literature (especially the newest literature, which I do not care for at all)" and promises to speak with Kraevsky about obtaining steady work for Kern. "I cannot answer for our success in advance. Kraevsky is a difficult person and something of a pedant."

2 February

Glinka asks Bulgakov to assist with Leonova's performance in Moscow and to get permission from Nikolay Pavlov to print the romance written by Kuzminsky, *"Ne govori, chto serdtsu bol'no"* [Do not say that it grieves your heart]. Glinka writes that he himself promised Pavlov to write music to these words, "but here in Piter the cold, gossip, and boredom have gotten the better of me, and my inspiration has vanished." He says: "I am searching for many of my pieces for piano, but the *Valse-fantaisie* . . . [cannot be found]. I am earnestly looking for this piece, and when I find it, I will give you a copy."

5 February

In *Muz. i teatr. vestnik*, no. 6, conclusion, second article, of "Notes on Instrumentation": "The application of instrumentation to musical composition: 1) [Normal] application. 2) [Abuse]. 3) Coquetry." "The beauty of a musical idea *stimulates* orchestral beauty. Let us assume that we did not know the orchestral versions of Handel's, Bach's, and Gluck's music. . . . If we only studied their music at the piano, the marvelous beauty of their thoughts would certainly guarantee us of the inimitable beauty of their orchestration. And in fact, their orchestration is amazing, despite the poverty of instrumental means at that time

compared to our own post-Beethoven era. The capabilities of musical architec-
tonics and the inviolable proportionality of the whole and parts in Haydn's
music are reflected in his orchestration, which is always elegant as a result of
these qualities. Nowhere is there noise or overstatement. Beethoven's orchestration expresses power first of all, the powerful grandeur of his fantasy. . . . One
should pay attention to how the great masters of orchestration command gradual-
ness, the *gradation* of orchestral powers, and never forget that power in music,
as everywhere, is often a relative quality. . . . Instrumentation, just like counterpoint and harmonic treatment in general, must *supplement* and enhance melodic
thought. . . . The obligation of harmony (four-part as infrequently as possible,
since it is always somewhat opaque and confusing) and orchestration (as transparent as possible) is to supplement for the listener the depiction of those
characteristics which do not and cannot exist in vocal melody (which is always
un peu vague in relation to dramatic thought). Orchestration (together with
harmony) must give a musical thought definite meaning and coloration, in a
word, must give it character and life. With orchestration being so significant,
it is clear that the choice of instrument in any case is extremely important and
that it has a very significant influence on music's effect, but the secret of such
choice is only suggested by *talent*. Theory is of no avail here. *Abuse* is the
antithesis of *use*, so it follows that here too there will be just as few specific
rules. Any exaggeration, or excessive orchestral noise, as well as dull insuffi-
ciency, deliberate poverty, or restriction of the means of each instrument's
characteristic effect or means of expression are all abuse. . . . It is rather difficult
to draw a line between *coquetry* in orchestration and certain *truly graceful* uses
of the orchestra in cases of *élégance*. The criterion here must be a *flaunting* of
orchestral effects to the detriment of higher aesthetic meaning and proportionality. . . . The composer who understands art seriously, the thinker in the realm
of sounds, never allows himself to use the orchestra too *elegantly,* nor does he
tolerate the flaunting of certain combinations of instruments or devices, even
though they may be extremely effective. . . . One may observe . . . that the
partiality of composers for well-known forms or well-known orchestral devices
are just as harmfully one-sided as mannerisms are in performance."

In the same number there is a review by Serov entitled "Concert in the Hall of
the Imperial St. Petersburg University," which mentions Balakirev's Fantasy
on Themes from *A Life for the Tsar*.

In *SPb. ved.,* no. 29, there is an announcement that Glinka's Variations for
Piano on the Theme of Alyabiev's romance *"Solovei"* is available at Bernard's.

Beginning of February

Glinka wrote a series of sacred compositions in three and four parts for the monks of the Sergievsky Monastery (ltr. to V. Engelgardt, 29 June/11 July 1856).

6 February

In *Sev. pchela,* no. 20, "Musical Conversations," Rostislav writes in connection with the production of Meyerbeer's opera *L'étoile du nord:* "The introduction begins with a beautiful phrase very reminiscent of a melody by M. I. Glinka (in the introduction to *A Life for the Tsar*)."

7 February

Glinka wrote *"Da ispravitsia"* [Let my prayer be fulfilled], a canticle for three solo voices and chorus. Composer's dating: "1856, 7 February," on a copy made by Kashperov. "Copied from the manuscript given to me by Mikhail Ivanovich on 5 March 1856 in St. Petersburg. V. Kashperov" (GBL, coll. 380. D. V. Razumovsky, carton 21, no. 5]).

Glinka informs Kuzminsky that he has received permission from Nikolay Pavlov to print Kuzminsky's romance *"Ne govori, chto serdtsu bol'no."*

8 February

Composer's dating and dedication on the title page of the manuscript of the score of the *Valse-fantaisie: "Scherzo (Valse-Fantaisie) instrumenté pour la 3-me fois par M. Glinka l'auteur.* Sincerely dedicated to my old friend K. A. Bulgakov." At the top is the inscription: "Begun on 8 February 1856."

9 February

Censor's authorization for the arrangement for voice and piano (published by Stellovsky) of *Ruslan and Lyudmila.*

13 February

In *Sev. pchela,* no. 35, in Rostislav's feuilleton "Musical Conversations," there is an announcement of the publication of "Notes on Instrumentation" in the paper *Muz. i teatr. vestnik* and of the publication (by Stellovsky) of a complete edition of *A Life for the Tsar.*

Before 14 February

Glinka suggested to Balakirev that he "compose a little piece for piano on a Spanish theme written down by Don Pedro" and recommended that in the title he mention that the theme had been given to him by Glinka (*Letopis' Balakireva*, p. 37).

[Composer's dating at the end of Balakirev's manuscript: *"Fandango-étude, sur un thème donné par M. Glinka*, 14 February" (*ibid.*).]

19 February

In *Muz. i teatr. vestnik*, no. 68, there is a review by Serov called "*'Uzkie bashmaki'* [Tight shoes]—an Operetta by Otto Dütsch": "Not long ago in our 'Bulletin,' in 'Notes of M. I. Glinka on Instrumentation,' it was said how contemporary composers have lost all sense of measure in orchestral effects and any sense of aesthetic propriety. . . . Mr. Dütsch's operetta is living confirmation of Glinka's remarks." In the same review: "Not long ago in *Library for Reading* (in the February issue), in an article entitled 'A note on the development of dramatic music,' it was said explicitly that now performance of *A Life for the Tsar* would be acceptable only if a new Russian tenor participated in it (!)—not Mr. Bulakhov—and furthermore that they placed hopes on the new tenor for some changes in tempo and dynamics!! Meanwhile Mr. Bulakhov's performance of the role of Sobinin was perfectly impeccable in a musical sense. His ample, inspiring voice projects marvelously—a better Sobinin one could not wish to have. Take note that the opera's composer is in full agreement with this opinion. An authority, I would suppose, of no little importance!" (d.c.a.).

[Reference is to an article by Moller (cf. 31 December 1855).]

Performance in a mixed concert in the Maly Theater in Moscow of the first act of *A Life for the Tsar* (*Mosk. ved.*, 18 February 1856).

1 March

In *Otech. zap.*, part 3, in the section "News," mention is made of the performance at Vasily Samoylov's benefit concert of the vaudeville *The Hired Shot*, with music by Glinka (d.c.a.).

In *Bib-ka dlia chteniia*, vol. 136, in the section "Miscellany," there is a notice about Samoylov's benefit, in which he participated, "of three translated pieces, one drama, and two vaudevilles." The vaudeville *The Hired Shot* was "noteworthy for the fact that he [Samoylov] portrayed the Englishman very entertainingly" (d.c.a.).

4 March

In *SPb. ved.,* no. 51, there is an announcement of the availability at Bernard's of the third edition of "Musical Album with Caricatures," in which the romance *"Ty skoro menia pozabudesh'"* is printed along with Stepanov's caricature of Glinka, "The composer, returned to his homeland."

5 March

Glinka gave Kashperov *"Da ispravitsia"* to copy down (V. Kashperov's annotation on the copy. GBL, coll. 380, carton 21, no. 5).

Beginning of March

Glinka wrote a letter to Bulgakov about Leonova: "Her talent can stand for itself, and I ask you, as an old and true friend, to take her into your patronage." In the same letter: "I am sick as a dog, but nonetheless I am little by little trying to finish the instrumentation of the *Valse-fantaisie,* which I am dedicating to you."

6 March

In *Sev. pchela,* no. 52, "Musical Conversations," Rostislav writes, speaking of Balakirev, that "in Russia the best representative of melodic giftedness is unquestionably M. I. Glinka, and . . . Balakirev has followed in his footsteps." He mentions compositions by Glinka given by him to Leonova for performance in her concerts.

In *Ved. Mosk. gor. politsii,* no. 53, "Musical News," it reports the arrival in Moscow of Latysheva, who appeared with great success in the soprano part of Esmeralda in Dargomyzhsky's opera and in the part of Vanya in *A Life for the Tsar.*

8 March

In *Ved. Mosk. gor. politsii,* no. 56, "Musical News," there is a report that in Kapellmeister Shtutsman's concert on 12 March in the Maly Theater they will perform *Kamarinskaya* and premiere *"Molitva"* (with Yakovleva as soloist), orchestrated by Shtutsman.

9 March

Glinka completed the orchestration of the *Valse-fantaisie*. On the last page of the manuscript of the score is the composer's dating: *"Completed on 9 March 1856.* N.B. In this score there are many corrections, because I wrote it while I was sick. M. Glinka." "I have reorchestrated it for the third time with the most studied sophistication and devilish contrivance. I dedicate my work to you, but I am turning the score over to Mme Leonova" (ltr. to K. Bulgakov, 10 March 1856). "The cellos remain. I changed (i.e., refined) the orchestration only in the forte and in the last crescendo (ltr. to K. Bulgakov, 17 March 1856).

10 March

After informing Bulgakov of the completion of the *Valse-fantaisie,* Glinka asks that the piece be performed in Leonova's concert in Moscow.

In *Mosk. ved.,* no. 30, there is a notice reading "Several words about the forthcoming concert by Mme Latysheva, who, among other works, will perform an aria from *A Life for the Tsar.*"

Before or on 11 March

In Gatchina pupils of the Gatchina Orphanage performed a chorus from *A Life for the Tsar* under the direction of Albrecht.

11 March

In *Muz. i teatr. vestnik,* no. 11, in "Survey of Last Week's Concerts," Serov points out the similarity between Karl Shubert's Fantasy on Russian Themes and Melodies from *A Life for the Tsar* and *Kamarinskaya* and also the use of the same motif in Félicien David's symphony *Le désert* and Ratmir's aria in *Ruslan and Lyudmila.* In the same issue: "Response to Mr. Rostislav's review of the *Musical and Theatrical Bulletin* in no. 35 of *Sev. pchela.*" Mention is made of Rostislav's brochure "Analysis of the Opera *A Life for the Tsar*" and a polemic with Rostislav occasioned by several expressions in Glinka's "Notes on Instrumentation."

In her concert in Moscow, prima donna of the Petersburg Russian Opera Latysheva performs an aria from *A Life for the Tsar* (*Mosk. ved.,* 10 March 1856).

12 March

Kamarinskaya is performed under the direction of Shtutsman in a concert in Moscow (*Mosk. ved.,* 12 March 1856).
[*"Molitva,"* announced on 8 March, was not performed.]

Before 17 March

Glinka's inscription on a copy of the score of the *Valse-fantaisie: "Valse-fantaisie,* composed in 1839, reorchestrated for the third time in March of 1856. M. Glinka."

17 March

Glinka completed the romance *"Ne govori, chto serdtsu bol'no"* to words by Pavlov. "Pavlov begged me on his knees to write music for the words he had composed. In them the world is cursed, meaning the public also, and this was very consistent with the way I felt" (ltr. to N. Kukolnik, 18 March 1856).

Glinka sent Bulgakov a copy of the score of the *Valse-fantaisie* with a request "to write out the parts as soon as possible. . . . Although I do not count on Verstovsky's cooperation at all, I nonetheless would like to see this *Valse-fantaisie* performed in Mme Leonova's concert, as much for her benefit as, or even more so, because this music will remind you of days of love and youth." He writes further: "I am happy that my 'Prayer' was not performed by Shtutsman: 1) Leonova sings it as I like, 2) I stand by my own orchestration. I heard it in performance and am myself very satisfied with it. You mistakenly think that I prefer the woodwinds to the strings. On the contrary, I am deliberately stingy with the winds."

In honor of the visiting 32nd Naval Crew in Yaroslavl, a concert with tableaux vivants took place. "In conclusion Mme Soboleva sang an aria from the opera *A Life for the Tsar" Yaroslav. gub. ved.* [Yaroslavl Regional News], 24 March 1856).

18 March

Date on a copy of the romance *"Ne govori, chto serdtsu bol'no"*: "1856, March 18."

Glinka asks Kukolnik to return the *Zapiski,* which Kukolnik had taken "with the intention of removing everything cruel and improper. . . . If you have not finished the whole thing, there is no problem. I will ponder the corrections you have made and how I can improve it, and I will correct it all at my leisure abroad." He says that he is putting his compositions in order. "Thus, for example, the *Valse-fantaisie, h-moll,* which I composed in your apartment in Merts's house (on Fonarny Lane) in the summer of 1839, and which was played with considerable success in Pavlovsk, has been lost. I have orchestrated it again from memory with devilish contrivance." He says that he is planning to go abroad in the spring and that he is busy getting a foreign passport.

In *Muz. i teatr. vestnik,* no. 12, "Concerts," it is said in Serov's note to Mavriky Rapaport's article that Glinka's name is unknown in Europe.

In a concert in the Aleksandrinsky Theater, Bulakhova, Bulakhov, and Petrov performed the trio from *A Life for the Tsar* (*Muz. i teatr. vestnik,* 1856, no. 12, p. 233).

20 March

Glinka invites Charukovsky: "Besides my sincere desire to see you, I need your advice and probably your assistance as well" in obtaining a carriage for the trip.

Glinka asks Bulgakov to write about the day of Leonova's concert in Moscow and to send the program. He writes that he has "received the draft article, but am unable to make it out. Moreover, I am not at all familiar with your Moscow audiences."

20 March

In her concert in Moscow Leonova performed Vanya's song from *A Life for the Tsar* (*Ved. Mosk. gor. politsii,* 24 March 1856).

Bulgakov (from Moscow) writes to Glinka: "Well done, Mikhaylo Ivanovich! You've let me have it and God knows for what. . . . I dared to praise Spohr [Shpor]—having the right to it, after all, since I once wore spurs [*shpory*], having served in the Moscow regiment—and then old man Bortnyansky, whose Cherubic hymns really are quite good. But you lash out. So what's Handel to me? I never even nuzzled up to *Samson,* so as to fully understand it. . . . Still, I'm very glad to know your opinion" (coll. *Pamiati Glinki,* p. 486).
[This letter is an answer to Glinka's letter of 8 November 1855. It is hard to understand why Bulgakov was so late in reacting to Glinka's statements, since at that time they corresponded regularly.]

22 March

Glinka sends Barteneva romances for her, her sister, and Zinaida Yusupova. He writes of his impending departure abroad and asks that she assist him in the dedication of his Polonaise to Alexander II for the coronation.

In his "matinée" in Myatleva's hall, Balakirev performed pieces by Glinka (which ones is not known) and his own Fantasy on Themes from *A Life for the Tsar* (*Letopis' Balakireva*, p. 29).

In the Hall of Nobility, in the violinist Apolinary Kontski's concert, *Kamarinskaya* is performed by the orchestra of the Italian Opera under the direction of Kazhinsky (*Muz. i teatr. vestnik*, 1856, no. 12, p. 233; *Sev. pchela*, 17 March 1856).

In a concert for the benefit of the poor in the home of A. Nelidov in Kursk, S. Postnikova performed *"Somnenie"* (*Kursk. gub. ved.*, 31 March 1856).

22 March/3 April

Dehn writes to Glinka from Berlin: "After many, many years, I have finally had the good fortune of taking on a talented student, and even greater good fortune that he has completed the entire course. How often, dear friend, have I been reminded at his lessons of you, for even if he does not possess your melodically productive talent, [he is aided by his innate sense of good taste]."
[It is not known to whom Dehn is referring.]

23 March

Glinka congratulates Leonova on her successful concert in Moscow and expresses the hope that the next concert with Ferzing participating will also go well.

In a letter to Bulgakov, Glinka gives instructions for the performance of the *Valse-fantaisie* and *"Molitva,"* which "are newly orchestrated. Nothing is to be gained from virtuosity (which I definitely cannot abide) nor from a huge mass of orchestral players. In all from 27 to 31 players . . . are required. A note. In the *'Molitva'* the first bassoon and trombone should be considered (*considérés*) soloists, although they have no complicated passages at all. In the *Valse-fantaisie* particular attention must be given to the *corni*, which are not tuned the same, i.e., the first is tuned in one and the other in another key. The 'Prayer' requires a strict (*sévère*) performance, and the *Valse-fantaisie* should be mannered (*un peu exagéré*) . . . 16 voices in the chorus are sufficient: 3 basses, 3 tenors, and 5 boys on each of the other parts. You can also use the regimentals." He expresses pleasure that Leonova's first concert came off successfully, especially "taking into account the flood of concerts during the present Lent and the vileness of that notorious son-of-a-bitch" [Verstovsky].

The pianist Ingeborg Stark, in her own concert in the Mikhaylovsky Theater, performed Glinka's Cavatina, transcribed for piano by Henselt.

24 March

In *Ved. Mosk. gor. politsii,* no. 69, in the section "Diary," it is reported that in her concert on 20 March, Leonova performed Vanya's song from *A Life for the Tsar* and that in her concert on 26 March she will sing *"Molitva,"* with organ accompaniment, and Vanya's song.

In *Yarosl. gub. ved.,* no. 11/12, there is mention of the performance in a concert on 17 March of an aria from *A Life for the Tsar.*

26 March

Leonova's concert in the Maly Theater in Moscow. " '*Molitva,*' a new composition by the renowned M. I. Glinka, performed by her [Leonova] to organ accompaniment, was received by the audience with great enthusiasm" (*Muz. i teatr. vestnik,* 1856, no. 16, p. 305).

27 March

Glinka asks Krzhisevich "to put in . . . a word about . . . my foreign passport." He reports that he intends to leave between 20 and 30 April.

In *Ved. Mosk. gor. politsii,* no. 71, "Musical News," there is information about the new journal *Muz. i teatr. vestnik,* in the literary section of which "we encounter some of the brilliant names in our musical literature—M. I. Glinka, Ulybyshev, Serov, and others."

30 March

Composer's dating on an authorized copy: "Farewell song for the students of the Ekaterininsky Institute, composed in 1841 by M. I. Glinka" ("Here, friends, we proceed on one path to a wordly goal," words by Obodovsky; text set by

Glinka): Certified true copy. Mikhail Glinka. 30 March 1856. S.P.burg" (facsimile published by Jurgenson, 1903).

Shestakova invites Charukovsky for Wednesday, 4 April, at seven o'clock in the evening to hear the singing of Lyubov Belenitsyna, who has "a great talent. . . . I add that seeing you is always a great pleasure for my brother, who is terribly depressed and is rushed by his trip." She asks that he pacify Glinka by "letting him know something about the carriage" (ITMK, coll. 6).

Glinka thanks Charukovsky for his efforts and asks that he reserve a post-chaise for him for 26 April.

31 March

In *Kursk. gub. ved.*, no. 13, there is an account of the concert on 22 March in which S. Postnikova performed *"Somnenie"*: "Having once heard this singing, you will not forget it for a long time."

March

At the end of the manuscript of an arrangement for piano of *Duo du 3-me acte de l'opéra "Joseph" de Méhul* is the composer's dating: *"Arrangé par M. Glinka, mars 1856."*

In *Panteon*, vol. 26, part 3, in the section "Petersburg Herald—the Petersburg Theaters in 1855," there is a reference to Petrov's performance of the role of Susanin in *A Life for the Tsar*.

1 April

In *Muz. i teatr. vestnik*, no. 14, in Serov's article ("Modest Z-n") "The Musical Compositions of Stanislaw Moniuszko," Serov places Moniuszko's romances on a level with those of Glinka and Dargomyzhsky. He calls his orchestration transparent "like M. I. Glinka's . . . just as interesting and masterful." In the same number an announcement is printed regarding the availability of Meltser's fantasy on Glinka's romance *"Zhavoronok."* There is also news of Leonova's concert on 5 April, in which "M. I. Glinka's *'Molitva'* will be performed for the first time" (d.c.a.).

3 April

In the Hall of Nobility in a concert "of the Shashin girls for the benefit of a poor orphan," A. Shashina performs *"Akh, ne mne, bednomu"* from *A Life for the Tsar* (*Sev. pchela*, 3 April 1856).

4 April

Glinka writes to Barteneva that he is not well and that at the end of the month he is leaving for abroad. He sends his new romance to words by Pavlov. He writes concerning the dedication of the Polonaise to Alexander II: "I am sincere in reporting to you that I (a sick man) am not trying to ingratiate myself."

5 April

Barteneva visits Glinka and says regarding the polonaise that "she has already dealt with the young Count Adlerberg, who will see that everything is arranged through his father, Minister of the Court."

In a letter to Dmitry Stasov, Glinka asks him to come by and help him compose an official letter about the dedication of the Polonaise.

In *Sev. pchela*, no. 78, there is an announcement of Leonova's concert, in which she will perform *"Molitva"* for the first time. A review is attached from the Moscow press about Leonova's concert in Moscow on 20 March.

First public performance in the Aleksandrinsky Theater in Petersburg of *"Molitva"* and the third version of the *Valse-fantaisie* in Leonova's concert under the direction of Konstantin Lyadov. Additionally Leonova performed *"Kosa"* [The tress] and "Ilyinishna's song" (*Sev. pchela*, 5 April 1856). Glinka did not attend the concert, but Shestakova did. "The concert . . . went very well. . . . The orchestra performed excellently" (ltr. to V. Kashperov, 13 April 1856). The concert "was a complete success. The orchestra did its job like never before, though the chorus members spoiled the effect somewhat in the chorus from *Ruslan.* . . . The audience applauded '*Molitva*' and the 'Valse' enthusiastically" (ltr. to K. Bulgakov, 10 April 1856).
[The chorus from *Ruslan* was the Persian chorus.]

6 April

In a note to Charukovsky, Glinka complains about his health. He requests that he notify "the appropriate person so that the necessary sum for the post-chaise may be deposited." He sends Charukovsky a reading desk and expresses the hope that "the lost musical fare" might "be arranged during Holy Week."

7 April

Glinka tells Barteneva that Shestakova will forward to her the required official letters concerning the dedication of the Polonaise.

8 April

In *Muz. i teatr. vestnik,* no. 15, in Serov's ("Modest Z-n") article "Concerts," he mentions the proximity of Moniuszko's orchestration to the orchestration of Glinka and the similarity of Moniuszko's cantata "Undine" with Glinka's style in *Ruslan and Lyudmila.*

10 April

Glinka tells Bulgakov about the success of Leonova's concert and complains about his health.

In *Zakavkazskii vestnik* [Transcaucasian Herald], no. 15, in an article signed "I. Evl." entitled "Adventures in the Gallery," there is a reference to the performance of an aria from *A Life for the Tsar* (which aria, the date, or the name of the performer are not indicated).

March–Beginning of April (?)

Serov writes to V. Stasov: "Mikhail Ivanovich was so visibly satisfied with the good bit of news that he again grew pale with pleasant emotion." He also writes about his work on an eight-hand arrangement of the Polonaise and Mazurka from *A Life for the Tsar (MN* III, p. 180).
[The letter is undated. V. Stasov indicated "spring." "The good bit of news" is either about Leonova's concert, a decision on the dedication of the Polonaise, or a favorable decision concerning his foreign passport. One must assume that a performance of Serov's arrangement took place at one of Glinka's evenings before his departure.]

March–11 April

Glinka received two letters from Dehn and wrote him an answer (ltr. to V. Engelgardt, 11 April 1856).

11 April

Glinka complains to Engelgardt about his physical and emotional condition: "I have sunk into a profound apathy. . . . There have been concerts, and good ones, but I could not attend them. Of my few musical labors you will find out upon your return from my manuscripts, which are being kept for you."

Memorandum from the Minister of the Imperial Court to the Directorate of Imperial Theaters with notification that Glinka "solicits" permission to dedicate a polonaise to Alexander II (G 2-B, p. 122).

13/25 April

Glinka invites Kashperov "to meet . . . in Paris" in the summer.

March–Before 15 April

During Lent the monks of the Sergievsky Monastery (near Petersburg) perform "with great success" the First Litany and *"Da ispravitsia,"* arranged by Glinka for three parts. Glinka was not well and did not go. Shestakova attended. From this period Glinka "began to think seriously about church music and began to work a little with the church modes" (Shestakova, *Vosp.*, p. 299).
[Shestakova mistakenly dates this event in 1855 (the dating here corresponds to the period of Glinka's composition of the indicated works).]

18 April

Glinka invites Barteneva "to spend an evening with us . . ." on any day she prefers. "Perhaps we can sing some, and we will try to see that there are other good musical amateurs present."

Glinka thanks Barteneva for her consent to visit him "tomorrow at 7 o'clock along with dearest" Dmitry Ivanovich Naryshkin (Barteneva's brother-in-law).

19 April

Glinka "had a light musical evening" (ltrs. to Praskovya Barteneva, 18 April, and Konstantin Bulgakov, 24 April 1856). Dargomyzhsky and Lyubov Belenitsyna performed a duet from *Rusalka* for Glinka and "made him cry" (ltr. from A. Dargomyzhsky to L. Karmalina, 9 December 1857; coll. *Dargomyzhsky,* p. 55). Serov and Dmitry Stasov played Bach's B-minor mass (ltr. to [A.] Stasov, 15/27 August 1856).

20 April

Censor's authorization for the romance *"Ne govori, chto serdtsu bol'no,"* published by Denotkin.

22 April

In *Muz. i teatr. vestnik,* no. 16, there is an article by Serov (signed "Modest
Z-n") entitled "The opera *Ruslan and Lyudmila* in full piano score with voices.
St. Petersburg, published by Stellovsky": "It hurts to think that the name of such
an uncommonly gifted, original artist as M. I. Glinka is still almost unknown
in Europe, while here we are obliged to know and remember the names of
various tenth-rank talents whose ephemeral reputations are founded on the boast-
ful exclamations of bribed newspapers! Can it really be that such a state of
musical affairs will never be changed? No, they must be changed. We only
have to work together toward such a goal. In this respect Mr. Stellovsky has
taken a very important step." In the same number, in an article by Antoni
Kontski entitled "On Teaching Piano Playing," there is reference to Glinka as
"one of the premiere artistic celebrities of the fatherland." Under correspondence headed "A Muscovite, Letter from Moscow," there is reference to Leonova's performance of Vanya's song on 20 March and *"Molitva"* on 26 March.

Ca. 24 April

Glinka received the manuscript of his *Zapiski* from Kukolnik (ltr. to N. Kukolnik,
23 June/5 July 1856).

24 April

Glinka reports to Bulgakov: "In three days I am travelling abroad. The passport
and carriage are already here." He writes that he intends to stay in Berlin "for
about two weeks. From there I plan to go to a certain little place called Paris."

Glinka inscribes a note in Lyubov Karmalina's (née Belenitsyna) album: "I, the
undersigned, promise (with the help of the Almighty) to write a piece for L. I.
Belenitsyna in this album which is worthy of her beautiful talent. Mikhail
Glinka, 24 April 1856. Petersburg."

V. Stasov advises Shestakova to have a photograph made of Glinka (Shestakova, *Vosp.,* p. 303).

25 April

Glinka had his photograph taken by Levitsky, who, according to Glinka's words, "made an amazing portrait of my mug" (ltr. to K. Bulgakov, 10/22 September 1856). "The portrait is an extremely good likeness" (*SPb. ved.*, 3 March 1857).

Before 26 April

The "Register of Glinka's Scores" for Engelgardt dates from this period (included in this list are Glinka's most recent works, ending with the Polonaise).

January–26 April

"Glinka was cordial toward me. I came to see him primarily in the mornings and showed him my compositions of that time. . . . Glinka accepted them graciously and gave me helpful advice regarding instrumentation. . . . He did not talk to me about *The Bigamist,* but once he played two themes from the first part of his symphony *Taras Bulba,* which was to portray the Ukrainian steppe with its feather grass." Additionally, Glinka expressed his thoughts on Liszt's and Berlioz's work to Balakirev (M. Balakirev's ltr. to N. Findeyzen, 5 October 1903, in *RMG,* 1910, no. 41).

26 April

Glinka wrote out the theme of a Spanish folk march for Balakirev. Beneath is Balakirev's note: "Theme for an overture, given by Mikhail Ivanovich Glinka, 26 April 1856. Its first appearance in the orchestra should be unisono, according to his instructions." Glinka presented Balakirev with his photograph with the beginning of the trio *"Ne tomi, rodimyi"* written on it and with the following inscription: "To Mily Alekseevich Balakirev, in remembrance, from a true admirer of his talent. Mikhail Glinka. 26 April 1856. S.P.burg" (*L.,* p. 474).

Composer's inscription on a copy of the Polonaise ("Solemn Polonaise") with interpolations and corrections by Glinka: "I present this entirely to Mr. Denotkin with the right to do with it as he wishes. Collegiate Assessor Mikhail Glinka, 28 [26] April 1856. S.P.burg."

The following appears under Bulgarin's "Remarks, Notes, and Correspondence" in *Sev. pchela,* no. 92: "We have very few composers of dramatic music. . . . In our time we have added the names deserving of praise in dramatic music of Aleksey Nikolaevich Verstovsky and Mikhail Ivanovich Glinka and their authentic Russian nationalist operas *Askold's Tomb* and *A Life for the Tsar.*"

Before 27 April

In conversation with Serov, sometime after 1842, Glinka said: "The people create music. We, the artists, just arrange it" (Serov *Izbr. stat'i,* vol. 1, M.-L., 1950, p. 111).

Before 27 April

Vladimir Sollogub visited Glinka in the 1850s "on some matter or another. He frightened me with his look full of suffering and gloomy cynicism" (Sollogub, *Vosp.,* p. 627).

"Remarks by M. I. Glinka" on the manuscript of the chorus "The Sea of Life," dictated by him to the author of the chorus (who has not been identified), dates from the end of Glinka's stay in Petersburg. The advice includes: "Avoid as much as possible difficult harmonization which is uncomfortable for voices to perform. . . . Take the example of the old Italian composers, who held to a strict liturgical style. Bortnyansky is overindulgent and allows himself a secular style. . . . For the most part in classical music the chord of the fourth [second inversion] and its related chords are reserved for the end of a piece. There is a special charm in this chord. I explain this by the fact that its use forms a full cadence and the most satisfactory conclusion with the fundamental key, the tonic. . . . For the sake of symmetry, which is individual to the different arts, you should repeat the initial musical phrases ('The Sea of Life') at the end of the piece, that is, end it with these phrases" (coll. *Pamiati Glinki,* p. 458, and facsimile).

27 April

At one o'clock in the afternoon Glinka departs for Berlin accompanied by the contrabass player Memel. V. Stasov. Shestakova accompanied him to the gates. "At the gates he [Glinka] got out of the carriage, bid farewell to us, and then spat, saying: 'May I never see this vile country again.'" (Shestakova, *Vosp.,* p. 303).

1 May

In *Otech. zap.,* vol. 106, part 5, under "Bibliographical lists, Russian publications received in the Imperial Public Library between 1 January and 15 March 1856," Glinka's *"Kolybel'naia pesnia"* is cited (d.c.a.).

3 May

Censor's authorization for the romance *"Ne govori, chto serdtsu bol'no"* (in Moscow, typeset by T. Volkov).

4 May

In *SPb. ved.*, no. 98, in an announcement under "Musical Novelties at M. Bernard's," there is a reference to the "Musical and Caricature Album," which includes "very good likenesses" of the composers. The volume includes the romance *"Ty skoro menia pozabudesh'."*

5 May

Report to the Ministry of the Imperial Court from the Directorate of Imperial Theaters forwarding the score of the Polonaise with the opinion of the Inspector of Music, Maurer (G 2-B, p. 122).

6 May

In *SPb. ved.*, no. 100, there is the notice of Glinka's departure abroad.

13 May

In *Syn otetchestva*, no. 6, Serov's article *"Rusalka*, opera by A. S. Dargomyzhsky"* appears. Serov greets the appearance of a new Russian opera, "written in the independent character of the Russian operatic school, i.e., which was established by the two operas of M. I. Glinka." However "the overture does not make a strong impression. . . . It is strange that the overtures in both of M. I. Glinka's operas were unsuccessful! Perhaps composers of Slavic stock are not natural symphonists." In the tercet from the first act "in many phrase endings the music reminds one in part of the style of M. I. Glinka, a composer, of course, who can very easily be avoided. But perhaps he wished for the similarity for the sake of the unity of the school. . . . This new opera is an extremely important thing for the reason that our Russian opera school, founded by M. I. Glinka, has finally found a worthy successor" (d.c.a.).

15 May

In *Sev. pchela*, no. 108, in Rostislav's article entitled "Several words on A. S. Dargomyzhsky's *Rusalka*," it says that Dargomyzhsky is a worthy successor to Glinka and mentions the similarity between *Rusalka* and *A Life for the Tsar*.

16/28 May

Berlin. Arrival. Address: *"Hôtel de Rome"* on *Unter den Linden* (ltrs. to K. Bulgakov, 25 May/6 June, and to an unknown woman, July 1856).

In a jesting note, Dehn reports to Shestakova that he has received Mikhail Glinka in beautiful condition from Memel, who delivered him from Petersburg to Berlin.

Before 19/31 May

Glinka moved to a private apartment at *Marienstrasse,* No. 6 (ltr. to K. Bulgakov, 16/28 May 1856).

19/31 May

Glinka writes to Shestakova that he has decided to stay in Berlin "for an indefinite period. . . . 1) I am very, very tired from the prolonged trip. 2) I do not have the desire to go to Paris. 3) . . . but the most important thing is that with Dehn I have already begun to work with the liturgy, and, it seems, the work has potential, since the ancient Greek modes, with which I worked so much in vain in Petersburg, still possess rich resources and are almost the same as our church modes."

20 May/1 June

In honor of Glinka's birthday, his servant, Gustav, arranged a serenade for him in the early morning: "Seven regimental trumpeters played quite nicely, and at 4 o'clock in the afternoon Dehn arranged a quartet for me. I spent the evening with Dehn also, at his apartment, most pleasantly" (ltr. to L. Shestakova, 4/16 June 1856).

20 May

In *Muz. i teatr. vestnik,* no. 20, in the continuation of Serov's article *"Rusalka, an opera by A. S. Dargomyzhsky,"* there is a reference to Glinka.

22 May/3 June

In a note to Dehn's letter to Dmitry Stasov, Glinka complains that he "still" cannot "recover from the fatigue. Instead of Paris I am staying in Berlin."

25 May/6 June

Glinka writes to Bulgakov that "despite terrible fatigue," he is working "diligently already" with Dehn, "the premiere sorcerer in the world." He sends Bulgakov contrapuntal exercises written by Dehn in the hope of giving Bulgakov "a few pleasurable moments. These harmonies, which are incomprehensible to an orangutan, you'll catch in your gizzard."

27 May

In *Syn otechestva*, no. 8, "Musical Chronicle," Serov's "More on New Russian Opera. A Moscow Guest" appears. In connection with the performance of *Rusalka* he writes that whenever "a new Russian opera appears, a determination of the character of its style is somehow very difficult . . . because we have very few points of comparison and very few Russian operatic composers of note." Serov speaks further about Verstovsky: "Lack of seriousness in development and the 'singing' tendency of this composer . . . have prevented him from creating such works as would have laid the foundation for a Russian school of operatic music. By all rights this honor goes to M. I. Glinka. The importance of his two operas in relation to the further development of our operatic music no one would think of disputing. As the founder of a school, the significance of M. I. Glinka is felt unconsciously by everyone who either works in the arts or talks about them seriously. . . . The influence of Glinka's music is so strong that, as they say, 'it's impossible to get away from it. . . .' The influence has, so to say, entered our art's atmosphere. But the question remains, why should one avoid this influence? Why should one not 'swim with the current'? Glinka was the founder of a school, but after 'founders' normally come 'followers,' otherwise there would be no school, for one artist does not make a school. . . . Some hold it against the composer for the similarity between several turns in the music of *Rusalka* and certain phrases in *A Life for the Tsar*. On the other hand, others complain that the style of *Rusalka* is not similar enough to Glinka's style, not lyrical enough, not melancholy enough! . . . The fact of the matter is that the composer of *Rusalka*, once he had selected a Russian folk subject for his opera, necessarily had to submit in many ways to the influence of the school's founder. Not to write in the spirit of this school was impossible, and every effort to disengage oneself from this influence would have only expressed lack of taste and misunderstanding of the general laws of art. But as a musician with uncommon gifts, A. S. Dargomyzhsky looks at art with his own eyes and sometimes is not in complete agreement with M. I. Glinka, for whom the predominant element is lyricism. In places a family resemblance to the music of Chopin and Moniuszko flashes through . . . as much as with M. I. Glinka's music." Regarding the "Moscow Guest," Semyonova: "From her very first appearance on the operatic stage, Mme Semyonova had to take on performance of the difficult part of Lyudmila in Glinka's opera, which had just been written. At that time Mme Semyonova considered the role of Antonida beyond her abilities. . . . On this trip Semyonova is making her debut in the opera *A Life for the Tsar*." Serov expresses regret that "Mme Semyonova did not have the fitting thought of singing her two big arias from *Ruslan and Lyudmila,* the cavatina from the first act with women's chorus, and the large scene from the fourth act, also with women's chorus, if only as separate, excerpted scenes. In its entirety we have little occasion to hear M. I. Glinka's second opera, which includes so many marvelous things! We would be glad to hear even a part of it" (d.c.a.).

In *SPb. ved.,* no. 117, in the section "Petersburg Chronicle . . . Russian musicians . . . New compositions by M. I. Glinka and Mr. Rubinstein," there is a note about the Polonaise. There is a reference to the situation of Russian musicians, among them Glinka.

28 May

In *Sev. pchela,* no. 118, Rostislav's first article entitled "Analysis of A. S. Dargomyzhsky's *Rusalka*" appears. Rostislav designates Glinka in speaking of efforts to elevate national melody to the level of dramatic music: "In the opera *A Life for the Tsar* he made masterful use of the national element and embellished musical thoughts taken from the fund of folk melodies with all the splendor of contrapuntal art. One might ask: did M. I. Glinka's inimitable classical work lay a solid foundation for Russian national dramatic music?" Rostislav answers this question in the negative, "first, because Glinka himself turned aside in his last work (*Ruslan and Lyudmila*) from the path he had first established, and second, the very reasons for his turning aside were apparently quite well-founded. By avoiding recitatives with Italian forms, which in the mouths of Russians seemed entirely inappropriate, Glinka intended to exchange them for melodic phrases carefully worked out in both the vocal and orchestral parts. Such richness of musical thought, it would seem, should have served to embellish the opera, but in fact it turned out otherwise. The continual strain on the listener's attention leads to exhaustion, and as a result of this, an opera, which is full of first class merits, seems endlessly long. Another discomforting thing (noticed, by the way, by the composer of *A Life for the Tsar* himself) consists in the monotony of the turns of national melody, which in Russian melodies, as is known, for the most part revolve around minor keys. From this stems an inevitable monotony and a certain gloominess, which lends dramatic composition the character of oratorio, despite the element of Polish music, so aptly contrasted by the composer to the Russian element. Hence a solid basis for Russian dramatic music which answers all the conditions of artistic and dramatic production has still not been established, but to completely avoid the expression of Russian musical speech suggested by Glinka in drama based on a national plot is almost impossible." There follows an analysis of *Rusalka*. Rostislav believes that in the composition of the opera Dargomyzhsky "had in mind all these considerations." Rostislav points to a number of pieces written under Glinka's influence, although in a number of instances "the melody itself does not have a positive similarity to any melody by M. I. Glinka."

In *Ved. Mosk. gor. politsii,* no. 118, "Moscow Chronicle," the romance *"Ne govori, chto serdtsu bol'no"* is named with other music published in Moscow.

End of May or Beginning of June, before 3/15

Meyerbeer was at Glinka's. "Naturally I did not say anything to him about [Rubinstein's] article and so forth. On the contrary, we conversed in the friendliest fashion, and he even asked me to let him know if any of my pieces were to be performed here" (ltr. to L. Shestakova, 4/16 June 1856).

3 June

In *Muz. i teatr. vestnik,* no. 22, Serov's article "The Theater-Circus. A Moscow Guest on the Petersburg Operatic Stage" is printed, in which he mentions Semyonova's performance of the part of Lyudmila. In the section "Petersburg Herald" there is mention of a new composition by Glinka, "Solemn Polonaise for Large Orchestra."

In *Otech. zap.,* vol. 106, part 6, it says in a review (unsigned) of Dargomyzhsky's *Rusalka* that "excessive striving for national color caused the composer to revolve in a rather narrow sphere of musical invention and somewhat trite modulations. . . . We are told that a composer who wishes to write music in Russian style can never escape the well-known modulations of folk song. In that case we might ask how Glinka, if you like, without escaping accepted forms, was able to carry them to artistry. The answer to this, of course, is in the degree of the composer's creative capabilities." In the same number, in the section "Bibliographic Leaflet, publications appearing in Russia and received in the Imperial Public Library between 15 March and 15 May," the piano score of the opera *Ruslan and Lyudmila* is listed (d.c.a.).

4/16 June

Glinka complains to Shestakova about his health: "I still have not succeeded in recovering from the exhausting trip . . . my nerves are upset and my stomach refuses food." He describes how he is spending his time and says that every evening he drives through the environs of Berlin with Dehn and Gustav. "In general, one can live here. . . . Dehn takes care of everything. It could be said that I am living under his wing."

10 June

In *Muz. i teatr. vestnik,* no. 23, in the section "Petersburg Herald," *A Life for the Tsar* is mentioned among productions of the past season.

14 June

At Strauss's benefit concert in Pavlovsk, which he conducted, "in the third part of the concert . . . we heard M. I. Glinka's inimitable *Kamarinskaya*. This capricious fantasy of purely Russian character was performed precisely and, of course, with great success" (*Muz. i teatr. vestnik,* 1856, no. 25, p. 459).

15/27 June

Glinka writes to Shestakova: "I am still suffering, though the vomiting has stopped. . . . I have already begun to work with Dehn, for, despite my nerves, my head is clear. Probably I will not spend a full two years abroad, and I will not go farther than Germany. . . . It would be better . . . once I have finished my business, to retrace my steps home."
[A note by an unidentified person was written on Glinka's letter and carefully torn off.]

15 June

In *Moda,* no. 12, in the section "News," Glinka's Polonaise is mentioned.

19 June/1 July

Glinka's autograph with two canons: *"À M. J. Hunke de la part de M. Glinka. Berlin le 1 juillet/19 juin 1856. M. Glinka"* (*RMG,* 1897, no. 12).

In *Odessk. vestnik,* no. 69, "Petersburg News," a report from the 27 May issue of *SPb. ved.* is printed concerning Glinka's "Solemn Polonaise." "Together with Rubinstein's solemn overture, both these pieces were intended for the celebrations prepared in Moscow for the coronation."

Between 15/27 June and 21 June/3 July

In a letter to "my dear, kind fraternity," Dmitry, Aleksandr, and Vladimir Stasov and Aleksandr Serov, Glinka describes his life and work with Dehn. Concerning the success of *Rusalka,* he asks Serov to convey the following to Dargomyzhsky: "I beg his pardon for my *unintentional* offense. . . . The poor production of his opera to Pushkin's libretto exasperated me. . . . Also say to him that I love and respect him, as always, and am sincerely glad for his success." He writes that on 23 June/5 July, Memel is leaving for Petersburg and can tell them about him. He asks Dmitry Stasov "to send as soon as possible" the piano score of *Ruslan and Lyudmila,* Levitsky's 3 photographs "without decoration," and a copy of the score of the *Valse-fantaisie.*
[The "offense" against Dargomyzhsky was Glinka's departure not long before the premiere of *Rusalka.* The letter was written several days before Memel's departure for Petersburg but after the letter to Shestakova on 15/27 June.]

23 June/5 July

Glinka's note at the end of the manuscript of part 2 of the *Zapiski:* "Good Dmitry Vasilievich Stasov, I entreat you, as I assume you are sincerely devoted to me, to acquire a copy of these verses from Prince Odoevsky. Once you have received them, I ask you to attach them to the *Zapiski.*"
[He is speaking of the canon *"Poi v vostorge russkii khor"* [Sing in ecstasy, Russian chorus].

Glinka congratulates Kukolnik with having attained the rank of Actual State Councillor and wishes "Your Excellency every possible success in service, since, in the words of Amalia Ivanovna . . . literature does not feed one (which in Russia, for the present, it is almost beyond doubt)." He thanks him for returning the *Zapiski.* "I won't start redoing them, so you can put your mind at rest. In the fall I will send them to Piter into trusted hands, that is to say, my *factotum* D. V. Stasov. . . . When I die these comforting notes may serve as detailed material for my biography."

24 June/6 July

Composer's dating at the beginning of the manuscript of the score of Alyabiev's *"Solovei":* "Air russe: Solovei (Rossignol), comp. A. Alabieff, instrumenté pour Madem. Valentine Bianchi par Glinka, 6 juli, Berlin, 1856."

24 June

In *Muz. i teatr. vestnik,* no. 25, in the section "Petersburg Herald," there is an article by Serov entitled "On the Occasion of Strauss's Benefit Concert" about the performance of *Kamarinskaya* in Pavlovsk on 14 June. In the same section, in a list of music appearing between 15 March and 15 May, the publication of the piano score of the opera *Ruslan and Lyudmila* is mentioned.

In *Syn otechestva,* no. 12, in the section "Journalism," there is an article entitled *"Muz. i teatr. vestnik,* weekly newspaper, published by Mavriky Rapaport." It sorts out the contents of the paper, which included Glinka's "Notes on Instrumentation," and remarks that "the name of M. I. Glinka alone . . . has created much interest in the 'Messenger'" (d.c.a.).

27 June/9 July

Glinka writes to Bulgakov: "I am fine here, free and calm. *Fine* because there is work. *Free* because the food is good. . . . *Calm* because I am living as a stay-at-home and am not looking for new acquaintances. . . . With Dehn I am struggling with the church modes and with canons of various sorts—a difficult business, but intentionally diverting, and God willing, very beneficial for Russian music."

28 June/10 July

For a projected performance in Berlin, Glinka asks Aleksandr Stasov to order a copy of the score of the Polonaise, which Glinka gave to the publisher Denotkin to be printed.

Completion of the orchestration of Alyabiev's *"Solovei."* Composer's dating on the manuscript of the score: *"Terminé le 10 juillet/28 juin à Berlin 1856."*

29 June/11 July

Upon completion of the orchestration of *"Solovei"* "for small orchestra" for Valentina Bianchi, Glinka writes to Vasily Engelgardt: "I am sending a copy to the lady, but the manuscript is for you." He reports that he is working with Dehn so that "later I can write an *exercise* (though not a model) *in Russian-Slavic Orthodox style* (neatly) from the liturgy of Ioann Zlatoust, not for chorus, but for three and two voices, for the *junior deacons*." Of music in Berlin he writes: "Without mentioning quartets and Haupt's organ playing, the *Dom-Chor* here performs old Italian works very precisely and old German music excellently. Above all . . . operas, including: five by Gluck, Beethoven's *Fidelio,* several by Cherubini and Méhul, much Mozart, and even *Entführung,* etc." He invites Engelgardt to complete his joint trip to the Harz and then to come to Berlin.

30 June

In *Sovremennik,* vol. 58, no. 7, in the section "Petersburg Life. Notes of a New Poet" [Ivan Panaev], there is a reference to the performance of *Kamarinskaya* in Pavlovsk on 14 June at Strauss's benefit concert (d.c.a.).

1/13 July

Glinka writes to Shestakova that his health "is improving little by little" and that he has decided, "if nothing prevents it," to stay in Berlin "until next May." "I am used to the quiet life here and do not wish to be torn away from my difficult but very engaging exercises with Dehn." He reports that he has sent via Memel some children's books for Olya and a gift for Heydenreich, a "geographical atlas with historical and statistical tables."

1 July

In *Otech. zap.,* vol. 107, no. 7, in the section "Bibliographical Leaflets"— "Publications appearing in Russia and received in the Imperial Public Library between 15 May and 15 June 1856," the entr'acte and aria (no. 13) and recitative and song (no. 14) from *Ruslan and Lyudmila* and the romance *"Ne govori, chto serdtsu bol'no"* are cited (d.c.a.).

In *Syn otechestva,* no. 13, "Musical Chronicle," Serov writes in reference to orchestras that perform outdoors in the public parks: "A piece which always has a big effect and is appropriate for outdoor orchestras, despite the seriousness of its workmanship, is M. I. Glinka's *Kamarinskaya.* What orchestral charm there is in this original, capricious fantasy! The horns' escapade and then the trumpet on notes which form a dissonance with the violins where the principal motif is constantly heard (the 'Kamarinskaya' song) always provoke a smile. It would pay, toward the end of *Kamarinskaya,* to take up front near the orchestra those who remain unconvinced of the comic force of some sounds—as sounds, independent of poetic content or meaning—and let them watch the expressions on the faces of the audience" (d.c.a.).

In *Muz. i teatr. vestnik,* no. 26, in the continuation of his article "Dargomyzhsky's *Rusalka,*" Serov compares, to Dargomyzhsky's opera's benefit, the libretto and plots of *Ruslan* and *Rusalka*. Comparing the work of Dargomyzhsky and Glinka, Serov writes that as Russians both composers are incomparably closer to the elements of Russian melody than Moniuszko is to Polish folk melody, but "in M. I. Glinka's music, on the one hand, there is the influence of the purely Italian school, which conforms to the predominantly lyrical character of this composer, and on the other hand, in the music's development, the influence not so much of the Germans as of Cherubini. In A. S. Dargomyzhsky there is hardly a trace of Italianateness, but there is a very noticeable influence of the models of the French school and even of that aspect which M. I. Glinka did not touch, the light comic style. . . . In the opera *A Life for the Tsar* (of course, *unpremeditated* on the part of the composer) a Slavic operatic style appeared fully armed for the first time. A plot from Russian peasant life and a patriotic plot moreover, elicited tunes as close as possible to our native songs. Nationalism reveals itself in all music. The Russian peasant element had to be balanced by another element, but what should it be? Polish, and consequently *again* Slavic, which directly evoked Chopin's forms. All of this, but first of all of course the composer's immense gifts, made it possible to create a type of new operatic style with his first opera, which is the forefather of Russian opera. The entire opera was conceived in the broadest, most serious style: consequently he chose the form of *continuous* operatic music, i.e., without conversational intervals and also without the recitatives which exist in Italian comic opera under the name of recitativi secchi. . . . M. I. Glinka's second opera, *Ruslan and Lyudmila,* was in many respects not as successful. The choice of plot was a fortunate one, but the entire plan of the opera was very poorly thought out and clumsily coordinated. The libretto . . . could not bear up to even the most indulgent criticism. All the scenes (beginning with the second act) are awkward, devoid of action and dramatic interest, and are pale and cold in their progress, because of which the entire opera, though it is remarkable to the highest degree as music and as a *score,* is entirely unsatisfactory *as opera,* i.e. on the stage. One can also raise many criticisms of the music of this piece, especially with respect to local color, to which the composer attached too much importance. . . . But, besides the marvelous, original beauty of the music, this not entirely successful opera is extremely remarkable from a critical standpoint. Excluding several places (in the first and fifth acts), there are almost no strictly Russian *folk* melodies in this opera, while throughout the entire work one hears music which is special, Slavic, and has its own *unique* style. Thus it appears clear that musical nationalism is in no way obligated to the plot and does not consist in the copying and working out of folk songs (as some 'experts' think and even print). Glinka's music, whatever he writes, on whatever subject, will always be *Russian* music, because he is *Russian* and his talent is so original that novel, unique forms flow from him, in part related to those of Chopin, in part eclectic. However, *Ruslan's* subject is entirely Russian, and the music is strongly subject to local color.

Given the immense power of his talent, with experience it would have been easy for him to avoid both a certain monotony and *gloominess* which perforce hang over the music of *A Life for the Tsar* and several superfluous 'baroque places' in *Ruslan*." In conclusion Serov says that he is not analyzing Glinka's operas here, but that "the matter concerns only operatic style, for which Glinka's two works have established such a broad course." Further, in analyzing *Rusalka*, Serov writes that it is "the *first Russian* opera since *Ruslan and Lyudmila*." In a number-by-number analysis Serov remarks that the countess's phrase to the words "Has he really vanished forever, the magical dream of living love," "is very reminiscent in its entire character and even shape to Gorislava's aria" (d.c.a.).

[Serov's article was printed between 17 July (no. 24) and 30 September (no. 39). All his opinions concerning Glinka I have collected in one place, omitting his evaluation of *Rusalka*.]

3 July

In *Mosk. ved.*, no. 79, in correspondence from Vilno from 22 June concerning a musical evening by Moniuszko, Glinka is named among famous Slavic composers.

4/16 July

Glinka asks Dehn to send him "the *Jota* for examination."

7 July

Bulgakov (from Moscow) informs Glinka that he has received the piano score of *Ruslan and Lyudmila* published by Stellovsky and that it "is saturated with mistakes." He writes of Mikhail Vielgorsky's illness (*RMG*, 1896, no. 12).

8/20 July

Glinka writes to Shestakova that he has finally decided to stay in Berlin until spring: *"Do not seek something better from what is already good! . . .* It is *good* because there is *business* here. My work with Dehn is *difficult, very difficult,* but extremely diverting, and most importantly, may be beneficial." Of his life he writes: "For the time being Dehn has settled me with a very nice, kind family named Müller. . . . At the end of August, 1 September here, I have already rented an apartment so that I can live as I am accustomed. . . . Dehn has my papers and money. He is not only my minister of finances, but in fact I live under his wing . . . my finances are in order. . . . It is *quiet* for me in Berlin because my male acquaintances are all *specialized* people—Dehn, Meyerbeer, *etc*. No one with poison on the end of his tongue visits me." He laments the death of Viktor Fleury, "which we had predicted."

10/22 July

Glinka invites Kashperov to come to Berlin "to study a little but also to hear good, sensible music." He answers Kashperov's questions: "I would have liked to write you an entire dissertation about music, of Russian science, etc., but since I still have not given up the hope of seeing you in Berlin . . . and I prefer living conversation to dead, written words, I will limit myself here to a few aphorisms. All art, and consequently music, demands: 1) *Feeling* (*L'art, c'est le sentiment*)—this comes from inspiration, from above. 2) *Form. Forme*—it means beauty, i.e., proportionality of the parts for the formation of an *orderly* whole. Feeling creates—it provides the fundamental idea; *form* clothes the idea in proper, *suitable* garments. The *conventional* forms, like canons, fugues, waltzes, quadrilles, etc., all have a *historical* basis. *Feeling and form*—these are the soul and the body. The first is a gift of grace, the second is acquired by work. Moreover, an experienced and intelligent leader is not at all something superfluous. *Ergo,* it would be a good idea for you *to see me* in Berlin."

Ca. 11/23 July

Glinka received "a flattering epistle" from Vladimir Stasov, who compared Glinka "in music with Peter the Great."
[Stasov's letter is not extant.]

Glinka received a letter from Engelgardt cancelling his trip to the Harz, since it was necessary for him to return to Petersburg.
[Engelgardt's letter is not extant.]

11/23 July

Glinka celebrated his niece's nameday: "There are happy days in one's life . . . our angel Olya's nameday I spent in *near* total pleasure. . . . The festivities opened: 1) With dances, in which I participated. 2) Some *small* fireworks. . . . 3) When dinner time arrived (about 9 o'clock in the evening), my servant Gustav managed things excellently. . . . 4) I stood Olya's portrait on the table, and everyone present drank a glass of Malaga to the health of the dear honored one. 5) Drinking songs were performed adequately (German fare, which, by the way, were often performed in Petersburg after dinner at the Vielgorskys). 6) Several songs and dances in my hall concluded the evening." That day, while passing through Berlin, *"Marie* [Krzhisevich] turned up, but she flitted past. . . .

Taras was not there but *promised* to be on the return trip. She laughed heartily at my efforts to persuade her" (ltr. to L. Shestakova, 15/27 July 1856).

[In the context in which Glinka refers to Maria Krzhisevich here and later, "Taras" must apparently be understood as an allegorical expression for a romantic relation (by analogy with "Ilyinishna's song": "I fell in love with Taras"). Glinka devised the expression in conversation and correspondence with Shestakova.]

14/26 July

Glinka tells Heydenreich about his life in Berlin and reports on his health. "My prescription is as little medicine as possible and as much activity as possible. I can stand several versts a day walking without strain."

Glinka asks Engelgardt to stop in Berlin on his way to Petersburg. He writes that "my work . . . with Dehn has stopped for the time being. A sirocco rages through here periodically, which is bad for Mimosa."

15/27 July

Glinka thanks Shestakova for her concern for him: "Perhaps your labors will be beneficial." Krzhisevich prefaces the letter with: "As you see, my dear Lyudmila Ivanova, I made it to Berlin just in time for our dear Olya's name-day. . . . I am very pleased with Mimosa, he looks fine." A postscript by an unknown person is appended to the letter: "I am sending you this letter, since I'm sure it will please you. I'm no longer in the midwife's house. The little girl is well, but I'm not. Please send me a letter as soon as possible telling me how you are" (G 2-B, p. 153).

[These lines were carefully crossed out by Shestakova, but it is still possible to read them. According to information from Anastasia Lyapunova (for which there is no documentary confirmation), in the summer of 1856 Leonova gave birth to Glinka's daughter. Allusions to their relationship appear in Glinka's letters to his sister after 1855. It is also known, from Dehn's remarks in a letter to Shestakova (February–March 1857), that not long before his death, Glinka repeatedly sent large sums of money, to whom, Dehn did not know. Cf. *Vosp.*, pp. 306–7.]

22 July

The third and fourth acts of *A Life for the Tsar* are presented in a mixed performance in the Kammeny Ostrov Theater in Petersburg (poster).

In *SPb. ved.*, no. 163, in the section "Petersburg Chronicle," there is a reference to Glinka's stay in Berlin.

23 July

Viktor Fleury's obituary appears in *Sev. pchela,* no. 164.

25 July

In the Mikhaylovsky Theater in Petersburg there is a performance of the vaude-ville *The Hired Shot,* the music for the final couplets of which Glinka arranged (poster).

22–29 July

In *Muz. i teatr. vestnik,* no. 29, in the section "Petersburg Herald," Glinka's romance *"Ne govori, chto serdtsu bol'no"* is cited in a list of compositions published between 15 May and 15 June.

30 July/12 August

Glinka tells Shestakova that he recently received a letter "from Dodo" [V. Stasov], who praises him "to the skies, but all the same can't help himself and writes crap." He also writes: "I regret very much that our poor peasants have suffered a bad harvest, but I hope that *you do not lose your head.*"

To this month dates Glinka's letter to Valentina Bianchi with the news that he is sending her the orchestration of Alyabiev's romance *"Solovei."* "This arrange-ment was intentionally done for small orchestra . . . a romance is not a bravura aria and consequently does not require the brilliance of an operatic scene. Be so kind, I ask, as to turn your attention to the third verse, where there is a flute solo. It will do no damage to your beautiful voice but, on the contrary, will give it a greater brightness of sound. . . . All the fermatas are done just as you sang them for me" (Fr. original).

A letter from Glinka to an unknown woman was written during this month. In it he reports that he is staying in Berlin and hopes to meet her on her return trip to England.

A letter from Kukolnik to Glinka was written during this month: "I rarely read the present-day gentlemen. . . . It's extremely entertaining to watch the cock fights of someone like Serov with Rostislav, Ulybyshev, and in fact anyone who is bold enough to write about music. He shoots from the hip, and sometimes he hits, sometimes, not . . . Here you understand all the humiliation a man seeking fame subjects himself to." He thanks Glinka for the "mirror waltz" sent in a letter of 23 June/5 July and writes that he has "inserted it in his wife's album" (*L.*, pp. 483–84).

4/16 August

Glinka writes to Bulgakov that the "Solemn Polonaise" is to be performed in the Berlin Opera Theater, where "the orchestra is marvelous. . . . They are even talking about staging a production of *A Life for the Tsar.*" He asks that Bulgakov "beat into the heads" of all their acquaintances "that Glinka is *not in Paris* as they say but *in Berlin.* . . . As it turns out, work with Dehn is harder than I had imagined."

5 August

In *Muz. i teatr. vestnik,* no. 31, in the section "Newly Published Music," Serov ("Modest Z-n") speaks about the romances of Dargomyzhsky: "A. S. Dargomyzhsky, along with M. I. Glinka and a few others, has brought this type of music in Russia to such a flowering that only in the profoundly musical land of Germany can one find minor vocal pieces which might rival ours *in all respects.* . . . [Concerning Dargomyzhsky's romance] *'Odelas' tumanom Grenada'* [Grenada clothed in mist]. . . . In the design of the refrain there is even something closely reminiscent of the *Jota aragonesa,* which M. I. Glinka inimitably developed in the form of a fantasy for orchestra. . . . However, '*O, milaia deva,*' a romance in Polish style, in the character of a mazurka, is not particularly remarkable, especially in comparison with M. I. Glinka's outstanding music to the same words."

Beginning of August

Engelgardt visited Glinka while en route to Petersburg.

10/22 August

Glinka received "music and three photographs" from Dmitry Stasov. "The photographs are actually excellent. Dehn was amazed with them. I gave him two copies, one for himself, the other for the Royal Library, where my portrait will hang next to Gluck's, for the portraits are arranged alphabetically. This is very much to my liking!" (ltr. to D. Stasov, 11/23 August 1856).

Glinka presented Dehn with a printed edition of the piano score of *Ruslan and Lyudmila* with the inscription: *"A son ami et maestro S. W. Dehn M. Glinka.*

Le 22 août 1856. Berlin" (preserved in Berlin in the Public Scientific Library. coll. *Pamiati Glinki,* p. 579).

11/23 August

Glinka reports to Dmitry Stasov that the summer heat has temporarily halted his work with Dehn. "Meanwhile I am not wasting time unnecessarily. I am reading, or, more correctly, I am finishing Kiesewetter and little by little supplementing my historical knowledge: I read *Richard Coeur de Lion* of Gretry and recommend this piece to you, it's a good work. Now I have two operas by Philidor, also remarkable. Dehn checks out scores for me from the Royal Library."

In a letter to V. Stasov, Glinka thanks him for his letter of praise: "Almost your entire letter consists of undeserved praise for me. What am I to answer? . . . The business which I undertook with Dehn, the more it reveals of itself, the more work it demands, persistent and prolonged work. . . . I will consider myself fortunate if I can succeed in laying a path to our church music." He reports: "Rubinstein and Gungl are here, but I seem them seldom and do not intend to become familiar with them."

12 August

In *Muz. i teatr. vestnik,* no. 32, in the section "Newly Published Music," is Serov's ("Modest Z-n") review of a French quadrille from *A Life for the Tsar,* arranged for piano by Villebois and published by Stellovsky. "From the famous opera of our famous composer there is already a well-known French quadrille arranged *by the composer himself,* which is very suitable for dancing and easy of execution. K. P. Villebois, who has just transcribed both of M. I. Glinka's important scores for piano, had the thought of making one more quadrille from the opera *A Life for the Tsar.* His desire was praiseworthy, and the effort is interesting. But alas! It is not very successful!"

In *SPb. ved.,* no. 179, in an announcement of "Musical Novelties," Glinka's Variations on Alyabiev's Romance *"Solovei"* (*Air russe varié*) is mentioned.

14/26 August

"Doctor of Philosophy Haupt played as many as six pieces by Bach for us, all different."

15/27 August

Glinka writes to Aleksandr Stasov that with the approach of fall he has "begun to improve significantly." He reports of forthcoming concerts: "In addition to classical operas we may look forward to Bach's B-minor mass with orchestra in the *Singverein*."

Dehn writes to Shestakova about his friendly relations with Glinka and reports that Glinka is not well (GPB, coll. 190).

15 August

Bulgakov (from Moscow) writes to Glinka: "Koko Dolgoruky sang your last piece on Pavlov's text quite well, and also '*Milochka*,' but everything came to an abrupt end with me, decrepit old man. They always make me sing '*Kak sladko s toboiu mne byt*'" (*RMG*, 1896, no. 12).

16/28 August

Glinka congratulates Kashperov on his marriage and expresses his happiness over his forthcoming trip to Berlin. "I will not write a dissertation about music, for I prefer the living word to paper . . . when you come to see us here, I will be at your service."

18 August

In Pavlovsk, *Kamarinskaya* is performed in a concert under the direction of Strauss (*Bib-ka dlia chteniia*, 1856, vol. 139, September, "Miscellany").

19 August

Glinka's Polonaise is cited in *SPb. ved.*, no. 184, in the section "Petersburg Chronicle."

22 August

Vladimir Stasov reports to Dmitry Stasov: "Glinka writes me commonplaces. Dehn does not answer at all. It appears that they have quarreled and that Glinka has moved to another apartment" (SPR I, p. 269).

27 August

In *Muz. i teatr. vestnik,* no. 34, there is an announcement of the publication of the "Solemn Polonaise" in score as well as in solo and four-hand piano versions. In the section "Musical Novelties" it is reported that in the next issue there will be an analysis of the "Solemn Polonaise." In the same number, in the section "Newly Published Music," there is a critique of "I. Setov's Cherkasskian Song to words by Lermontov," in which Serov ("Modest Z-n") says concerning "this wild eastern poetry" that "to capture the musical expression *approximating* such a text would be a very difficult matter even for M. I. Glinka or A. S. Dargomyzhsky."

The "Solemn Polonaise" is performed in Moscow during the coronation ceremonies at a ball in the Granovitaya Palace (*Muz. i teatr. vestnik,* 1856, no. 36, p. 647).

28 August

Mikhail Vielgorsky dies in Moscow.

31 August

Bulgakov (from Moscow) reports to Glinka about the death "of our old friend Count Mikhaylo Yurievich Vielgorsky, who passed away on the night of the 27th. . . . This loss is irreplaceable for all who knew him. . . . I am sure that you share my feelings, for although the deceased envied you a little, he nonetheless loved and admired you sincerely. Often our conversation was about you" (*RMG,* 1896, no. 12).

Summer

Kamarinskaya and the "Solemn Polonaise" are performed in Spa (ltr. to L. Shestakova, 1/13 December 1856).

1/13 September

Glinka moved into a winter apartment at *Französische Strasse,* no. 8 (ltrs. to K. Shestakova, 8/20 July and 2/14 September 1856).

2/14 September

Kashperov arrived with "his young wife, who appears to be a very nice person."
Glinka complains to Shestakova about his health. He asks her to come to Berlin,
and requests that she "arm [herself] with patience, character, and intelligence;
take care of yourself and time will remove everything little by little."

[Attached to Glinka's letter are notes from Dehn and Kashperov. The latter promises "to warm if
needed your dear, kind brother, my papa." Glinka jestingly referred to Kashperov as his little son.]

2 September

In *Muz. i teatr. vestnik,* no. 35, in the section "Newly published Music," is
Serov's ("Modest Z-n") review of the "Solemn Polonaise," published by Denotkin. "In two important thoughts, M. I. Glinka's Polonaise (F major) breathes
an open, vital joy and a sort of knightly spirit. In the second half of the Polonaise
there is a very beautiful harmonic development of both primary thoughts. From
time to time something majestic and formidable flashes past in the orchestra.
But unquestionably the best part of this Polonaise is the melodic idea in the trio
(B-flat major). It resembles an echo of the well-known Russian folk melody
(*'Slava'*) with unusually appropriate inflection. The cellos on high notes accompany the melody of the uppermost part in marvelous counterpoint. In these
tender, gratifying sounds much is expressed which of all the arts only music is
able to pour into the soul at once, in one fleeting impression. . . . From such a
master as M. I. Glinka, one might wish for greater power and brilliant solemnity, as well as, perhaps, greater originality in the first parts of the piece, but
the melody in the trio makes this Polonaise a remarkable composition. Its entire
form and expression are naturally full of grace. In our time and in the entire
world of music there are very few artists who can rival M. I. Glinka. In Russia
there are even fewer." In evaluating Bernard's "Solemn March," written for the
coronation, Serov says: "In the second half of the march the composer introduced the same Russian melody ('Praise God on High') to which M. I. Glinka
'alluded' in the trio of his Polonaise."

After 2/14 September

Kashperov brought to Berlin with him a small library of Russian authors—
"Gogol, Ostrovsky, Turgenev, Grigorovich, Belinsky, Kudryavtsev, and others. Glinka eagerly tried to grasp their meaning, and then was moved to tears
by them. Only there in Berlin did I notice that he did not know the literature of
the forties at all, because he moved in a milieu where, besides Pushkin,
Zhukovsky, Karamzin, and a few others, no one else was recognized as a writer,
and they subsisted more on foreign literature" (V. Kashperov, *Vosp.,* p. 315).

"Being a responsive person, he laid hold of me, a very simple person, like a life-saving anchor" (ltr. from V. Kashperov to I. Turgenev, 25 February/9 March 1857, in *L.*, p. 486).

4 September

P. Radonezhsky's concert in Yaroslavl, in which the artist performed Susanin's aria and scene from *A Life for the Tsar* (*Yarosl. gub. ved.*, 8 September 1856).

Beginning of September

Glinka's Polonaise is performed under the direction of Johann Strauss in Petersburg during the coronation ceremonies at a ball in the Hall of Nobility (*Bib-ka dlia chteniia*, 1856, vol. 140, p. 100).

6/18 September

Glinka writes to Leonova that he is happy for her successes and often thinks about her. "What can one do if in society, especially in Petersburg, there are people who love mud slinging and intrigue?" He promises to send her his photograph with an inscription. "I cannot tell you when you will receive the portrait . . ."

6 September

Vladimir Stasov writes to Dmitry Stasov that "through Serov [I] had Dargomyzhsky donate to the Public Library several autographs of Glinka, Struysky, Alyabiev, and a letter of Fétis" (SPR I, p. 273).

7/19 September

Glinka writes to Shestakova in regard to her will: "In having authorized the letters of enfranchisement [to be given to the serfs to be freed], you have fulfilled one of my heart's long-standing desires and calmed me inexpressibly." Of his life he says: "The Kashperovs are my neighbors and we see each other daily. They often read to me and read well. Dehn is just as good, obliging, and attentive as he has always been. One thing is annoying, and that is that I am often sick, despite the fact that I avoid overindulgence *en femme et vin*."

8 September

In *SPb. ved.*, no. 198, in the section "Petersburg Chronicle," there is an announcement of the sale of the "Solemn Polonaise" in score and in transcriptions for piano solo and piano four-hands.

In *Mosk. ved.*, no. 108, in an article entitled "Petersburg Mail" and signed ". . . sky," there is an announcement of the publication of the "Solemn Polonaise."

In *Yarosl. gub. ved.*, no. 36, in the section "Internal News," there is an account of P. Radonezhsky's concert on 4 September.

10/22 September

Upon hearing from Bulgakov of the death of Mikhail Vielgorsky, Glinka writes: "Count M. Yu. is one of the few people who should never die. I do not wish to remember our petty misunderstandings but only his friendship and benevolence toward me." Of Kashperov: "I believe that he has musical talent."

After 10/22 September

Quartet evening at Glinka's (ltr. to K. Bulgakov, 10/22 September 1856).

14 September

In *Rus. invalid*, no. 201, there is an announcement of the sale of the "Solemn Polonaise" in score and in transcription for piano solo and piano four-hands. "The name of the composer of this music needs no recommendation."

17/29 September

At Dehn's sister-in-law's there were performances of a piano trio by Haydn and two Beethoven trios: "Among other things, the big trio in E-flat, a good piece" (ltr. to D. Stasov, 18/30 September 1856).

17 September

Performance of the *Slavsya* chorus from *A Life for the Tsar* in Moscow during the coronation ceremonies (*SPb. ved.*, 21 September 1856).

18/30 September

Glinka writes to Dmitry Stasov about his life in Berlin. In a letter to Engelgardt, Glinka tells about the singing lessons he is giving the nieces of his landlord, the Schultz girls. He writes that for him Petersburg, "after the divorce affair . . . is vile," and he cannot think of it "without an especially profound loathing."

After 18/30 September

Glinka hears Gluck's *Orfeo* in the opera theater.

19 September/1 October

After a one-and-one-half-month interval, Glinka resumed his work with Dehn. "Dehn intends to work with me twice a week in the following fashion: to continually get me to compose double fugues (*à deux sujets*), the themes for which are based on the church modes, about which I still do not have a clear understanding. In general I can say that I still have never studied *real* church music, since I do not hope to achieve in a short time what took several centuries to build up. As examples Dehn recommends Palestrina and Orlando Lasso to me" (ltr. to D. Stasov, 18/30 September 1856).

21 September/1 October

Glinka thanks Shestakova for her concern about him, for the "letters of enfran-chisement" for the serfs, and for "putting an end to the family squabbling." He writes about his distrust of the servant Yakov Ulyanych. "The Kashperovs and I are living hearts-in-tune and without inconveniencing one another; we see each other every day."

21 September

In *Ved. Mosk. gor. politsii,* no. 207, there is an announcement of the sale in the music store Lira of the "Solemn Polonaise."

In *SPb. ved.,* no. 207, in an article entitled "Moscow Chronicle" and signed "Delta" [A. E. Nadezhdin], a performance of excerpts from *A Life for the Tsar* is mentioned.

In *Muz. i teatr. vestnik,* no. 37, there is an article called "New Debuts," signed "Correspondent," about Yakovleva's debut in *A Life for the Tsar.*

22 September/ 3 October

Composer's dating on pp. 23–24 of the manuscript of his exercises in the church modes: *"Fin (enfin!) 3 Octobre 1856."*

24 September

In *Sev. pchela,* no. 211, in the section "Journalistic Odds and Ends," Bulgarin is indignant with writers "of the naturalist school," especially Gogol, who "make good, honest, and industrious Russian peasants play a pitiful role in their stories." He feels that the Russian peasant "in his true aspect" is portrayed in *A Life for the Tsar.*

30 September

In *Muz. i teatr. vestnik,* no. 39, Serov ("Modest Z-n") reports the subscription opening at Stellovsky's "in several days" for the complete edition of *A Life for the Tsar* for piano and voice with Russian and German texts. "M. I. Glinka's first opera has waited exactly 20 years for its complete publication by Russian publishers. This was great negligence on their part. In the West, any however remarkable opera is published in a full vocal score (*Clavierauszug*) immediately after it appears on the stage. If anybody in our age wrote a score like *A Life for the Tsar* in Germany or France, the music publishers there would mob the composer and argue among themselves for the honor, and the profit, of printing such a work. As I have already had occasion to remark when talking about the solo piano (without voices) edition of the opera *A Life for the Tsar,* a piano-vocal score is an *absolutely necessary* aid and most important means for providing the music lover with the opportunity to study an opera *thoroughly.* A transcription for piano solo (without voices) is also a very helpful thing, and proof of the public's sympathy for it is that Mr. Stellovsky has already sold nearly 200 copies of such a transcription. How much *more* beneficial, more important, is a *full* piano-vocal score! For such an undertaking everyone should be sincerely grateful to Mr. Stellovsky, that is, everyone who values national music and appreciates the great worth of M. I. Glinka's music. . . . Here I consider it essential to draw the public's attention to what it can expect from this new edition. Several numbers from the opera *A Life for the Tsar* were published by Snegirev for *piano and voice.* The same transcriptions of these several numbers are still around, but carefully corrected and enriched with indications of the instrumentation, etc. All the remaining vocal numbers will be printed in K. Villebois's transcription, which is an accurate, careful transcription, and, most importantly, reviewed and corrected *by the composer him-*

self. Among numbers published by Snegirev, some belonged to the purely instrumental part of the opera, i.e., one of the three entr'actes and the dances (in Karl Meier's transcription, which was subsequently included in Mr. Stellovsky's edition of a complete arrangement of the opera *for solo piano*.) Meanwhile the overture was published for four-hands, the form in which it was first composed by the composer. (He wrote the overture for piano four-hands before he began to orchestrate it.) In order to reconcile all the instrumental parts of the opera with the edition of the overture and to give the new edition new interest, Mr. Stellovsky printed all *three entr'actes* (before the second act, before the third, and before the epilog), as well as the *dance numbers,* in *four-hand* transcription, prepared by a contributor to our journal, A. N. Serov. Besides the overture, not a single number from the opera *A Life for the Tsar* has been published in *four-hand transcription* before. This aspect of the edition, like the full transcription of *all the numbers for voice,* will be a complete novelty in printed musical literature and, so that Mr. Stellovsky's service might be truly meaningful, only one thing remains to be wished for: that the exterior appearance of the edition matches the care of the transcription."

30 September

In *Sovremennik,* vol. 59, no. 10, in "A Letter from Moscow" (signed "A Muscovite"), it mentions that on 17 September at the coronation ceremonies the "marvelous, solemn chorus from the epilog of *A Life for the Tsar* was performed" (d.c.a.).

End of September

In a note to Shestakova, sent via Krzhisevich, Glinka writes: ". . . our Marie arrived and departed today. God give her happiness, but apparently there will be no Taras. . . . I am living quitely, my health is improving, and I'm working hard with Dehn on church music of the XVII century."

Between 20 September/1 October and 2/14 October

"Besides quartets and trios with piano and the organ, Kashperov and I have already heard Beethoven's *Fidelio*. Mme Koester sang and acted well. The orchestra played the E-major overture marvelously at the beginning, and instead of the entr'acte they played the famous 'Leonore' overture in C-major. . . . We have heard Gluck's *Orfeo*. Although it is his weakest opera, it works wonderfully on the stage."

2/14 October

In a letter to Shestakova, Glinka describes in detail how he is living. "My health has significantly improved . . . and my head is always disposed toward work." He tells her that he is giving singing lessons to Kashperov's wife and to two German girls. He writes that by his account he must stay in Berlin until 20 May in order to complete his work with Dehn. "My work with Dehn is moving right ahead, I have bitten into my work *with a vengeance.*"

To this period belongs the "School of Singing" for soprano, exercises which Glinka wrote for Adel Kashperov (*LNG* 2, p. 726; *Sov. muzyka,* 1953, no. 9, p. 40).

Composer's dating on pp. 27–28 of the manuscript of Glinka's exercises in the church modes: *"14 octobre 1856. Berlin."*

2 October

In a letter to Glinka, Bulgakov (from Moscow) expresses his enthusiasm for the Polonaise and writes that "to the shame of Moscow" the music is not available in stores (*RMG,* 1896, no. 12).

3 October

On the day after the "solemn entrance of the sovereign from Moscow" in Petersburg . . . there was a ball . . . in the Hall of Nobility. . . ." At the appearance of Alexander II, "the orchestra under the direction of Strauss played Glinka's polonaise from the opera *A Life for the Tsar*" (*SPb. ved.,* 7 October 1856).

14 October

In *Muz. i teatr. vestnik,* no. 41, in the section "Newly Published Music," there is a review of *Kamarinskaya* by Serov ("Modest Z-n") in Stellovsky's new edition arranged by Villebois for piano four-hands and on sale in Stellovsky's store. "The fantasy for orchestra on the tune of the well-known dance song 'Kamarinskaya' is one of the best works by Russian composers and has justifiably acquired considerable fame and even a certain popularity. This fantasy is frequently performed not only in concerts but even by summer garden orchestras and in entr'actes of various performances. However, among Kapellmeisters and orchestral musicians manuscript copies of this well-known score are afloat which are not entirely accurate and are even distorted, particularly by *arbitrary* changes of tempo (allegro piu mosso andante), which the composer never dreamed of.

Above all, there is a four-hand arrangement of *Kamarinskaya* on sale which is very inept. Consequently Mr. Stellovsky has done a service in having the piece transcribed completely anew from a copy of the score proofread by the composer himself and published a new transcription which is not only correct but even elegant. . . . The arrangement is complete, correct, and not difficult to play. Detailed references to the instrumentation and trueness to the original score give this transcription interest even for connoisseurs. Having praised the merits of this beautiful edition, we note its one significant flaw. On page 4, in the left part at the beginning of the allegro moderato in D major, 2/4, there is a pause of 12 bars. In these bars small notes should have been placed to signify what the right part (primo) was playing. Lacking this cue it is very easy for the secondo to err in counting and enter at the wrong time, and the entry of the second part (as a counterpoint to the theme) at this particular moment, in the delicacy and transparency of the combination, makes for great charm and is extremely noteworthy. After the word 'Kamarinskaya' in the title, 'Scherzo' is placed in brackets. Does this name belong to the pen of the composer? Formerly this composition was called 'Fantasy for Orchestra.' This is more accurate."

16/28 October

Glinka tells Shestakova about his life and friendship with the Kashperovs: "We are neighbors, we see each other every day, we almost always attend the theater and concerts together, and above all, in case of the slightest disorder in my health, they stop by to read and chat. In short, I am always getting from them proof of their genuine affection."

17 October

In *SPb. ved.*, no. 227, in the section "Musical News," there is an announcement of the sale of the romances *"Prosti menia, prosti"* by Fedorov, arranged by Glinka for two voices, and *"O, milaia deva."*

18 October

Dütsch (from Petersburg) writes to Glinka about the performance of *Rusalka*, the completion of his opera *Kroatka* [The Croatian girl], the subscription edition of the piano score of *A Life for the Tsar*, Verdi operas on the Italian stage, and about the "three" performances at court of the "Solemn Polonaise" (coll. *Pamiati Glinki*, p. 499).

Before 19/31 October

Glinka "was happy to hear" Beethoven's *Fidelio* and Mozart's *La Clemenza di Tito* ("there are very interesting places"), Gluck's *Orfeo* ("on the stage it works marvelously, the second act in particular"), and Bach's B-minor mass ("in which there are marvels of poetry and invention.") "It is a colossal work, and long. There are wonderful places, like the Crucifixus. On the whole I found the performance satisfactory. The orchestra played beautifully and the chorus precisely, but the soloists, with the exception of Mme Koester, were pretty poor" (ltrs. to V. Engelgardt, 19/31 October, and to K. Bulgakov, 3/15 November 1856).

19/31 October

Glinka writes to Engelgardt and says that his exercises with Dehn "have been going successfully, but my health is changing a little."

27 October/8 November

Composer's dating on pp. 29–30 of the manuscript of Glinka's exercises in the church modes: *"Berlin, 8 novembre 1856."*

28 October

In *Muz. i teatr. vestnik*, no. 43, in an article on Flotow's opera *Martha*, Serov observes that "the Scottish folk tune which Lady Martha sings at Lionel's request . . . was arranged for piano by M. I. Glinka and published by Mr. Stellovsky about three years ago (*Variations pour le piano sur un thème écossais*). . . . These variations, excellent in themselves . . . now have special significance because of their theme, which is repeated so many times in the opera *Martha*. It should also be noted that M. I. Glinka selected this tune for his variations long before Flotow's opera, and for the true music lover it will be interesting to compare the development of one and the same melody by two such different composers. They even correspond in key (both are in F major), but, without regard to the variations invented by the Russian composer, the preponderance of worth with respect to the harmonization of the existent melody lies with M. I. Glinka. How one must regret that our musical public still values the work of native artists so little."

Before 31 October/12 November

Glinka heard Mozart's *Marriage of Figaro* and *The Magic Flute*. "The orchestra and chorus were wonderful."

31 October/12 November

Concerning his activities with Dehn, Glinka writes to Shestakova that they "are not going quickly but steadily and successfully. Not long ago I wrote a double fugue (*fugue à deux sujets*) for three parts with which Dehn was very satisfied. When I am dealing with a four-part fugue and cook up something better, I will let you know."

1 November

The first volume of the complete piano score of *A Life for the Tsar* appears in Petersburg in Stellovsky's edition (*Muz. i teatr. vestnik,* 1856, no. 45, p. 821).

3/15 November

Glinka writes to Bulgakov: "Besides various types of fare, and in particular the simple, quiet life which is very much to my liking, the *musical* pleasures alone are enough to chain me to Berlin for the winter months." Of his activities: "Slowly but surely my work with Dehn goes on, always fighting with fugues. I am nearly convinced that it is possible to combine the western fugue *with the properties of our music* by bonds of legitimate marriage."

3 November

In *Bib-ka dlia chteniia,* vol. 140, in the section "Miscellany," there is a reference to a performance of the Polonaise under the direction of Strauss during the coronation festivities (d.c.a.).

4 November

In *Syn otechestva,* no. 31, in the section "Musical Chronicle," Serov, speaking about Flotow's opera *Martha,* makes reference to Glinka's "excellent" Variations on a Scottish Theme for Piano (d.c.a.).

After 5/17 November

Glinka heard Gluck's *Alceste* in the opera theater (ltr. to K. Bulgakov, 3/15 November 1856).

11/23 November

Glinka attends a concert of the *Singverein:* "150 amateurs (the chorus) and upwards of 50 orchestral players performed a Bach cantata and Cherubini's *Requiem* very, very well" (ltr. to L. Shestakova, 14/26 November 1856).

11 November

In *Muz. i teatr. vestnik,* no. 45, in the section "Newly Published Music," there is a review by Serov ("Modest Z-n") of the first volume of the piano score of *A Life for the Tsar.* "The recently published first volume (containing no. 1, Introduction and chorus '*V buriu, vo grozu*' [In the storm] and no. 2, Antonida's aria '*V pole chistoe gliazhu*' [I gaze upon the open field]) completely fulfills the publisher's promise regarding the subscription and will satisfy the most discerning demands of connoisseurs for exterior beauty (paper, printing), which equals many of the best German editions of operas (*Clavierauszüge*), and thoroughness of transcription (with detailed indications of instrumentation). This is the first example of a totally acceptable full Russian edition of a Russian opera." Serov expresses uneasiness that even given the inexpensiveness of the edition it may not obtain a large number of subscribers. . . . "Perhaps it is possible that the taste for good music and good editions is still not particularly extensive among people here. I repeat that in elegance and accuracy this edition is absolutely the first of its kind in Russia. Of all the 13 plates which have come from the press so far, I have only noticed one misprint (and it not very significant): in Antonida's aria, on page 52, in the third line from the top, in the voice part, a natural has not been printed before the 'B' in the first bar." In the same issue, in an article entitled "*La Traviata,* Opera by Verdi," Serov refers to Glinka's romances.

Before 14/26 November

Glinka gave a dinner "for Dehn, his wife, his sister-in-law, and the Kashperovs. . . . Everyone was satisfied except my stomach, which is just getting better."

Between 31 October/12 November and 14/26 November

Glinka heard Mozart's *The Magic Flute:* "A delicious thing, what a piece!" and Gluck's *Iphigénie en Aulide:* "My lord! What a work on the stage! . . . Mme Koester (Iphigenia) and Mme Wagner (Clytemnestra) were *inimitable,* both as singers and as actresses. I simply *sobbed* from profound emotion. . . . In fact, the entire work is strongly dramatic, but Clytemnestra's scene . . . in the third act, when the off-stage chorus sings something similar to the Cherubic Hymn I wrote in your album, and Clytemnestra tries to tear herself from her mistresses' hands to rush to the aid of her daughter—this scene simply tears one's heart out."

14/26 November

In a letter to Shestakova, Glinka tells about his life and musical impressions, and conveys regards to his Petersburg friends. In the same letter: "I sincerely wish Leonova happiness (I am not jealous). Mustard after dinner doesn't work, and so with Taras. I am too keen on church music and have no taste for Cossack revelry. Nonetheless I love, sincerely love dear, kind, playful Mary."

14 November

Bulgakov (from Moscow) writes Glinka that he has received an edition of the *Valse-fantaisie* for piano from an unknown person (*RMG,* 1896, no. 12).

15/27 November

Composer's dating on pp. 37–39 of the manuscript of exercises in the church modes: *"Le 27/15 novembre 1856, Berlin."*

Glinka attends a performance of Gluck's *Iphigénie en Tauride* in the opera theater. On the eve of the performance (14/26 November), Glinka writes to Shestakova: "I am indescribably happy." Gluck's opera "is exceptionally rich in invention. Mme Koester (prima donna) and the orchestra were excellent, though the production was not altogether satisfactory." At the performance Glinka met Meyerbeer, "who heard *Kamarinskaya* and the Polonaise during the summer in Spa and was quite pleased." During Glinka's conversation with Meyerbeer *"he offered his services"* to see that excerpts from *A Life for the Tsar* might be performed in Berlin "this winter at the court" (ltrs. to S. Dehn, 16/28 November, and L. Shestakova, 1/13 December 1856).

16/28 November

Glinka asks Dehn to send "the entire score of my opera *A Life for the Tsar,* so that after thorough review and thought I can present my thoughts concerning selection of excerpts for your judgement." He returns the *Requiem* "with the request that I be given *Iphigénie en Tauride:* to my shame I confess that I did not understand the plot very well. I completed my fugue yesterday and am impatient to find out what you will say about it."

18 November

In *Muz. i teatr. vestnik,* no. 46, in the section "Newly Published Music," while commenting on the publication of an album with romances by E. Cavallini, Serov ("Modest Z-n") remarks: "And in the small, even miniature framework of the romance, a song may be significant and even great, but for that one must be a Franz Schubert, Schumann, Rossini, or Glinka."

20 November

In *Sev. pchela,* no. 258, in Rostislav's "Musical Conversations," Serov's ("Modest Z-n") opinion of the "Solemn Polonaise" in F major is cited.

21 November

Vaudevilles were performed in Yaroslavl, and "during the entr'actes music of the Third Infantry Regiment was played. All the pieces they played were listened to with great pleasure, particularly the 'Steamship Polka' and *Kamarinskaya,* a work, of course, by the gifted Glinka" (*Yarosl. gub. ved.,* 15 December 1856).

23 and 24 November/6 and 7 December

For two days in succession Glinka attended concerts of the Royal Cathedral Choir, "which corresponds to our chapel choir: the first two pieces (a 'Sanctus' by Palestrina and 'Miserere' by Orlando Lasso) went excellently, the other things were rather poor." On the second occasion in the same hall Glinka heard Haydn's *The Seasons,* "but the unbearable heat did not permit me to stay till the end of the concert. I listened only to Spring and Summer, i.e., the first two parts."
[The program of the first concert on 23 November/6 December was enclosed with a letter to Shestakova on 1/13 December. Works by Palestrina, Orlando Lasso, Lotti, Mendelssohn, Fioroni, Eccard, Bach, and Beethoven were performed (G 2-B, p. 185).]

End of November

Glinka sent Meyerbeer to choose from "as he wished . . . five pieces from *A Life for the Tsar:* the trio *'Ne tomi, rodimyi,'* the chorus *'My na rabotu v les,'* the quartet *'Vremia k devishniku,'* the chorus of Poles *'Ustali my,'* and the episode from the epilog *'Akh, ne mne bednomu.'* What will come of it, I do not know, but I will not plead for anything."

"While passing through, Count Matvey Yurievich Vielgorsky stopped here. I visited him. I was received like a relative. He was alone, and we talked for about an hour. By the way, he was with Meyerbeer in Spa and said to me: *qu'après avoir entendu ma musique il en a été ébahi!"*

1/13 December

Glinka writes to Shestakova that he is working "moderately." He promises to send her his two fugues when he gets them back from Dehn.

1 December

In *Otech. zap.,* vol. 109, part 12, in "Bibliographic Leaflets," the first installment of *A Life for the Tsar* is listed among publications received in the Public Library between 15 October and 15 November 1856 (d.c.a.).

2 December

In *Muz. i teatr. vestnik,* no. 48, in the section "Newly Published Music," Serov ("Modest Z-n") responds to Rostislav's remarks about Serov's article on the "Solemn Polonaise": "There are no contradictions at all in my review of the polonaise, because 'open, vital joy and knightly mettle' are in no way a synonym for 'strength and solemnity' (moreover it is all in the degree of these qualities)." In analyzing Olga Smirnitskaya's romance *"Slyshu li golos tvoi"* [When I hear your voice] to Lermontov's words, Serov remarks: "The melody is not at all bad (in its gracefulness it is even a little like M. I. Glinka's romance on the same words)."

6 December

Vladimir Zotov's Prolog "30 August 1856, or the Centenary Jubilee of the Russian Theater" is performed in the Bolshoi Theater in Petersburg. It included a tableau vivant from *A Life for the Tsar (Muz. i teatr. vestnik,* 1856, no. 50, p. 900; *Rus. invalid,* 14 December 1856).

Dargomyzhsky (from Petersburg) writes to Lyubov Belenitsyna about *Rusalka:* "Several critics place it beneath other Russian operas. I myself am ready to yield to the mastery of Moniuszko and Glinka and to the effectiveness of Verstovsky, but on the other hand the boxes are full at all its performances" (coll. *Dargomyzhsky*, p. 46).

Before 11 December

A Life for the Tsar is performed in Penza (*Sev. pchela*, 13 December 1856).

12 December

Latysheva, Bulakhova, Petrov, and Bulakhov performed the quartet from *A Life for the Tsar* "excellently" in a divertissement in a benefit performance for the singer Orlova in Petersburg (*Muz. i teatr. vestnik*, 1856, no. 51, p. 923).

13 December

In *Sev. pchela*, no. 276, in an article signed "Ar." and entitled "Theatrical Performances in Penza," there is a report of the performance of *A Life for the Tsar*.

14/26 December

Glinka writes to Shestakova that he has been sick recently and therefore has not answered her letters. "You yourself have said that if I am just alive, that is news. Report this fact to everyone from Ispolin [D. Stasov] to little Serov, and do not exclude our Marie, who sent me Gluck's overtures as a gift."

14 December

In *Rus. invalid*, no. 273, there is a description of the performance in the Bolshoi Theater on 6 December.

15 December

In *Yarosl. gub. ved.*, no. 50, in an article signed "V. I." and entitled "The Yaroslavl Theater," there is a reference to a performance on 21 November of *Kamarinskaya*.

16 December

In *Muz. i teatr. vestnik,* no. 50, in an article by P. Shpilevsky entitled "Russian Performances, I. The Bolshoi Theater," there is a reference to the performance in Vladimir Zotov's Prolog of a tableau vivant from *A Life for the Tsar* (d.c.a.).

23 December

In *Muz. i teatr. vestnik,* no. 51, the conclusion of Wilhelm Lenz's article "Count Mikhail Yurievich Vielgorsky" is printed (translated from German by Serov). In the translator's concluding remarks, M. I. Glinka is named among those who enjoyed "the humanitarian hospitality" of the Vielgorskys' home, which served "as the finest shelter for all musical celebrities" of the time. In the same issue is P. Shpilevsky's article "Russian Performances. The Aleksandrinsky Theater. Mme Orlova's Benefit on 12 December" (d.c.a.).

24 December

Konstantin Bulgakov (from Moscow) tells Glinka about the musical news (*RMG,* 1896, no. 12).

28 December

Performance in the Theater-Circus in Petersburg of *A Life for the Tsar* (Bulakhova, Latysheva, Petrov, Bulakhov). Dargomyzhsky attended this performance (*Sev. pchela,* 28 December 1856; ltr. from A. Dargomyzhsky to V. Kastrioto-Skanderbek, 2 January 1857, in coll. *Dargomyzhsky,* p. 50).

30 December

In *Muz. i teatr. vestnik,* no. 52, in Serov's article entitled "Something about the Contrast to 'Profundity' in the Realm of Musical Polemics," there is a reference to Rostislav's brochure on *A Life for the Tsar.*

End of the Year

Letter from Dehn to Odoevsky with a composition by Glinka recopied for him: *"Primo saggio d'una fuga nel primo tono ecclesiastico"* (*L.,* p. 492).

From Glinka's conversations Kashperov "noted down the characteristics of the orchestra in general and each instrument in particular. I kept it as a valuable remembrance" (Kashperov, *Vosp.*, p. 316).
[These notes have not been located.]

Rubinstein visited Glinka: "He was . . . sick and short-tempered. . . . He received me dryly and showered me with reproaches and admonitions for the very article in which I spoke of his work and talent with great respect and even enthusiasm. . . . Thus I left him with a dislike for me" (A. Rubinstein, *Vosp.*, in *Rus. starina*, 1889, vol. 64, no. 11).

Note from Glinka to Dehn with a request to send Beethoven's Fourth Symphony.

To this year belongs Glinka's letter of recommendation to Engelgardt concerning the appointment of his Berlin students Malvina and Francisca Schultz as members of the chorus at the SPb. Italian Opera.

The romance *"Dubrava shumit,"* composed in Berlin in the winter of 1833/34, is published for the first time by Bernard.
[This edition does not agree with the autograph redaction of 1843 (which has not been preserved in its entirety).]

During this year the romance *"Il desiderio"* ("the words are an imitation of the poetry of Romani") was published in Russian translation under the title *"Zhelanie"* [Desire].
[This is the second version of the romance. The translator could be Glinka himself (which has been suggested by Nestor Zagorny).]

1857

1/13 January

Glinka asks Shestakova "not to hurry in sending *Ruslan*. . . . Despite my genuinely cordial relations with Meyerbeer . . . so far nothing is known about the production of *A Life for the Tsar,* which is for me, however, *ni chaud, ni froid!*" He asks her to order a copy of the *Jota aragonesa,* the nocturne *Souvenir d'amitié* (Hummel's nocturne in Glinka's orchestration for symphony orchestra), and to order from Levitsky "two photographs taken of the snuff box known to you that shows our deceased mother, our deceased sister Pauline, and me at age 13." He asks her to petition through Fedorov regarding acceptance in the Russian Opera chorus of his two students.

2 January

Dargomyzhsky (from Petersburg) writes to Kastrioto-Skanderbek that several days ago he heard *A Life for the Tsar*. "It is a masterful, original work. There are so many beautiful things that one does not even want to notice the blunders. One thing in this opera is dissatisfying: there is little dramatic truth" (coll. *Dargomyzhsky*, p. 50).

Beginning of January

Glinka "must have received . . . some kind of unpleasant news . . . he has become irritable. . . . He intended to explain everything . . . something important, but he excused himself on grounds" that the time was not right. At Glinka's request, Dehn provided him "repeatedly with large sums of money, which he said he sent off" (ltr. from S. Dehn to L. Shestakova, February or March 1857 [extract]; Shestakova, *Vosp.*, p. 306).

5/17 January

Ivan Turgenev (from Paris) writes to Kashperov: "Give Glinka my regards; probably he does not remember me, but I remember him very well. He visited us while I was living with my brother, whom he apparently loved" (*Rus. obozrenie*, 1895, vol. 36, p. 927).

Meyerbeer writes to Glinka: "Yesterday I played your splendid trio for Mlle Wagner. She was delighted with it and gladly agrees to sing the contralto part." Meyerbeer invites Glinka to Johanna Wagner's to listen to her sing (Fr. original).

7/19 January

Glinka writes to Kashperov that he is unable to arrange for him to attend today's rehearsal of the concert at court. "Besides, the rehearsal is *au piano; et le jeu ne vaut pas la chandelle*."

Meyerbeer invites Glinka to a piano rehearsal of the trio *"Akh, ne mne bednomu."*

9/21 January

At a court concert in the White Hall of the Royal Palace, the trio, *"Akh, ne mne bednomu,"* from *A Life for the Tsar* is performed. The performers were Leopoldine Tuczek-Ehrenburg (soprano), Johanna Wagner (mezzo-soprano), and Mantius (tenor) (from a poster). "Mlle Wagner, understandably a favorite of audiences here, sang Petrova's part. She was in good form and sang very, very competently. Meyerbeer conducted the orchestra, and one has to admit that he is an excellent conductor in all respects. I was also invited to the court, where I spent more than four hours. In order to understand the importance of this event for me, you must realize that this is the only concert of the year . . . there were about 500 to 700 people in the audience. . . . If I am not mistaken, I believe that I am the first Russian to have achieved such an honor" (ltr. to L. Shestakova, 15/27 January 1857). "After leaving the hot rooms of the Royal Palace where Glinka suffered from the heat, he caught a bad cold."

10/22 January

Glinka was visited by Dr. Busse, who prescribed warm baths, after which Glinka improved (ltr. from S. Dehn to L. Shestakova, February or March 1857; Shestakova, *Vosp.*, p. 306).

In *Neue Preussische Zeitung*, no. 19, there is an account of the concert at court. Of all the works played (Beethoven, Glinka, Meyerbeer, Rossini, Verdi, et al.), the only work which received an enthusiastic review was a new composition by the amateur Count von Redern.

10 January

A Life for the Tsar is performed in the Theater-Circus in Petersburg (*Sev. pchela*, 10 January 1857).

13 January

In *SPb. ved.*, no. 11, in the feuilleton "Petersburg Chronicle," there is a notice entitled "A Russian Musician in Berlin." "What in particular Glinka has done for his art during his stay in Berlin, we do not know. His cordial relations with Dehn, Meyerbeer, and other Berlin musicians, who have developed a profound respect for our famous countryman, could not but awaken him to activity! . . . We have heard, by the way, that he has written two large works of symphonic character and that he plans to produce *A Life for the Tsar* in Berlin." It reports of the improvement of Glinka's health.

Before 15/27 January

Through the priest at the Russian embassy, Vasily Polisadov, Glinka sent Shestakova "a little Chinese box done very nicely in mother-of-pearl and two little silk scarves" for Olya.

15/27 January

Glinka writes Shestakova about the concert at court on 9/21 January. "Meyerbeer's letter is proof that I did not intrude myself, and I'll supply you with newspaper articles as soon as possible. The fugues will also soon be recopied and sent." He reports: "I have a very bad cold or influenza."

After 15/27 January

Glinka "began to complain of sharp pain near his liver and of his complete loss of appetite." He demanded the dismissal of his servant Gustav, declaring to Dehn that "he had his reasons for not being pleased with him. At this he was overcome by anger and even rage." On the day after Gustav's discharge Glinka became ill. "During the night he vomited without stopping" (ltr. from S. Dehn to L. Shestakova, February or March 1857; Shestakova, *Vosp.*, p. 307).

Glinka "got Dehn's word that if he were to die, an autopsy would be performed immediately" (N. Kukolnik, *Vosp.*, p. 317).

23 January/4 February

Odoevsky visited Glinka: "He was in bed. *He had made friends with Meyerbeer.* Excerpts from *A Life for the Tsar* were performed here. . . . At the rehearsals Glinka caught a cold and now is sick" (from V. Odoevsky's diary, in *Rus. arkhiv*, 1869, inst. 2, p. 348). Glinka's last meeting with Odoevsky. "He was already sick . . . but he roused himself when he heard Russian being spoken." Glinka thanked Odoevsky for his advice to study the church modes with Dehn. Then "he got up from bed, assuring me that he was only mildly ill, and played me a small, new piece in strict sacred style—western, of course" (V. Odoevsky, "Notes to Glinka's Letters to K. Bulgakov," in *Rus. arkhiv*, 1869, inst. 2, p. 347).

27 January

In *SPb. ved.,* no. 23, in the feuilleton "Petersburg Chronicle," it speaks of Glinka's life in Berlin and of his activities with Dehn: "He has written two fugues, and not two symphonies." There is a reference to the court concert on 9/21 January.

29 January

In *Sev. pchela,* no. 24, in Rostislav's "Musical Conversations," there is a notice about the publication of Villebois's transcription for solo piano of *A Life for the Tsar* (published by Stellovsky) and of Seymour-Schiff's fantasies for piano on themes of Mozart, Beethoven, and Glinka (published by Brandus).

30 January/11 February

Kashperov reports to Shestakova that Glinka "has taken a severe chill . . . the illness has gotten much worse, but . . . everyone thinks . . . that life will hold its own" (Shestakova, *Vosp.,* p. 305).

Glinka "did not know that he was seriously ill. On the contrary he thought that he was improving, although he had not eaten or drunk anything for the past three weeks, because his stomach was extremely weak and was crowded by the liver, which had almost filled the entire abdominal cavity. Under such conditions digestion was impossible" (ltr. from V. Engelgardt to L. Shestakova, 16/28 May 1857; *RMG,* 1898, no. 12).

1/13 February

The serious condition continued until 1/13 February. That day Glinka joked while talking with Dehn about his fugues. Dehn spent the entire day with him (ltr. from S. Dehn to L. Shestakova, February or March 1857; Shestakova, *Vosp.,* p. 307). Glinka was fully conscious except for a few hours. He dictated a fugue subject to Kashperov and asked him to finish the *Zapiski.* "He said that he would like to live about two more years and show what could be done for the Russian fugue. Toward evening he began to speak about eternity and added that it was nonsense and that he did not believe in eternity. Later he was seen praying before a small icon which had been given to him by his mother."

2/14 February

Glinka was in the same condition all day as he had been the day before (ltr. from
V. Kashperov to I. Turgenev, 25 February/9 March 1857, in *L.*, p. 496). In the
morning Dehn "found [Glinka] exhausted and . . . apathetic. . . . The doctor . . .
announced that the illness had suddenly taken a new turn and that the patient's
life was in danger, but because of his unusually strong physical condition he
would not die suddenly. He prescribed some more medicine, which Glinka took
willingly."

3/15 February

At 5 o'clock in the morning Glinka "died suddenly but peacefully" (ltr. from
S. Dehn to L. Shestakova, February or March 1857; Shestakova, *Vosp.*, p.
307). Glinka "died peacefully without any visible signs of suffering" (ltr. from
V. Kashperov to I. Turgenev, 25 February/9 March 1857, in *L.*, p. 496).

4/16 February

Odoevsky learned of Glinka's death in Weimar. "Thinking about this irreplaceable loss, one cannot help but be reminded that with his death also died,
perhaps, an entirely new period in our church music, for which Glinka was
preparing himself" (V. Odoevsky, *Vosp.*, p. 105).

5/17 February

"A postmortem in compliance with all legalities was performed" on Glinka's
body "in the doctor's presence. Glinka had often and insistently demanded that
this be done. . . . The autopsy indicated that Glinka had died as a consequence
of a radical development, a so-called adipose liver, and that under such conditions he would not have been able to live long in any case" (ltr. from S. Dehn
to L. Shestakova, February or March 1857; Shestakova, *Vosp.*, p. 307). During
the autopsy "they found a grossly enlarged liver and a shrunken stomach. Glinka
died of hunger. For two weeks he was unable to receive food. . . . It is doubtful
that his illness would inevitably have been fatal. Karlsbad successfully cures
enlargement of the liver, which the doctors had even counseled" (N. Kukolnik,
Vosp., p. 317).

6/18 February

Glinka's burial in the presence of Meyerbeer, Kashperov, the violinist Grünwald,
the conductor Beyer, his landlord, and Dehn, as well as the wives of the two

Russian priests and an official from the Russian embassy. A marker was placed on the grave with the inscription: *"Michael von Glinka. Kaiserlicher russischer Kapellmeister. Geb. 20 Mai 1804 zu Spasskoe, Guv. Smolensk. Gest. 15 Februar 1857 zu Berlin"* (ltr. from S. Dehn to L. Shestakova, February or March 1857; Shestakova, *Vosp.,* p. 308). "I do not know why they buried him so far away, painfully far away, in the Trinity cemetery, in the rows, like a common soldier, and the eighth one at that" (in Russian military tradition, the eighth soldier in a row was the one traditionally picked for unpleasant or dangerous assignments) (N. Kukolnik, *Vosp.,* p. 317).

12 February

Shestakova received the news of Glinka's death (Shestakova, *Vosp.,* p. 305).

13 February

Obituary notice in *SPb. ved.,* no. 36. "We have just received the news, the sorrowful meaning of which will be understood by everyone to whom Russian art and Russian glory are dear."

Kukolnik writes to Lvov of the necessity of organizing a public requiem mass for Glinka in the Kazan Cathedral with the participation of the court singers: "A feeling of conscious national pride demands a solemn public expression of the common sentiment of respect for the dignity and service of an unforgettable singer of the Russian land" (*L.,* p. 498).

Serov writes to Albert Starchevsky: *"Do not refuse* to publish the *obituary* of our famous composer Mikhail Ivanovich Glinka which I am preparing. . . . A biographical sketch and survey of his most important works will provide material for two articles for *Syn otechestva,* and I believe that they will be read with interest, especially given the sad news. I will send the first article next week, but tomorrow, if it is convenient, you will receive a little article called 'Chronicle.' I await your answer. P.S. If you think fit to accept *Glinka's obituary* from someone other than myself, this will be a signal for severing relations" (A. Starchevsky, "The composer A. N. Serov (from his memoirs)," *Nabliudatel',* 1888, no. 3, p. 160).

14 February

Lvov's report to the Minister of the Imperial Court: "Having learned of the death of our famous composer Glinka, who served as Kapellmeister to the court chapel choir, upon the request of all the gentlemen of the chapel choir I take the liberty

Extract of the Year 1857, Sent from Berlin by Archpriest Maltsev

Register Number		Month & Day		Name & Rank	Age	Cause of Death	Who Heard Confession and Administered the Sacrament	Who Officiated at the Burial
M	F	of death	of burial					
1		3	February 6	Collegiate Counselor Mikhail Ivanovich Glinka the composer [entered in] pencil	53	enlargement of the liver	without confession and Holy Communion Archpriest Stefan Sabinin Chorister Petr Kazansky Chorister Mstislav Tikhonravov	Archpriest of the Orthodox Church in Weimar, Stefan Sabinin with choristers Petr Kazansky and Mstislav Tikhonravov

"Extracted from a bound volume having the inscription 1841–1859, preserved in the archives of the Russian embassy church in Berlin. Archpriest A. Maltsev" (RMG, 1898, no. 12).

to most humbly request Your Excellency's permission to perform a requiem mass in memory of our most valued colleague and through the newspapers to inform everyone who like ourselves loved him as a man and honored him as a famous artist" (*L.,* p. 498).

Vladimir Stasov's "News on the Death of M. I. Glinka (ltr. to the editor)" appears in *Rus. vestnik,* vol. 7, February, part 1: "My brother and I were very close to Mikhail Ivanovich. We stayed in constant correspondence with him, and therefore we received the sad news before anyone else. We also received the last pieces which he had written before his death, two fugues, written in the so-called church, or Greek, modes. During his last trip abroad, M. I. . . . had the serious aim of studying the system of the above-mentioned modes, which are forgotten by almost everyone today except a few very learned musicians and theoreticians, though they are essential for one wishing to write church music in its authentic ancient style. Glinka created Russian national opera, national instrumental music, a Russian national scherzo (his *Kamarinskaya,* etc.), the Russian national romance, and he wanted to create a national harmony (which we have been missing till now) for the melodies of our church. For this he dedicated the last days of his life to the necessary study, and undoubtedly he would have been just as original an initiator in this style as in all other styles. He left behind an autobiography written in 1854–55 and a small biography in French which he had reviewed and which was intended for a foreign musical journal at the request of his friend Professor of Music Dehn (written in 1854, but not printed)" (d.c.a.).

15 February

In *Rus. invalid,* no. 38, and *Muz. i teatr. vestnik,* no. 7, there is a notice of Glinka's death (reprinted from the 13 February issue of *SPb. ved.*).

16 February

In *Syn otechestva,* no. 70, in the section headed "Internal News," there is a notice of Glinka's death.

17 February

Memorandum from the Minister of the Imperial Court to Lvov granting permission to the chapel singers to sing a memorial service for Glinka (*L.,* p. 498).

18 February

Kukolnik put together a plan for invitational cards to Glinka's memorial service and sent the text to Lvov. The text reads: "With His Majesty's consent, a requiem will be performed in the church of the Imperial Stables for the repose of the soul of the renowned Russian composer Mikhail Ivanovich Glinka, who passed away in Berlin following a short illness on the third of this instant February. [His work to the glory of Russian art is so well known to every Russian that to give an account of it here would be inappropriate.] The Messrs. Choristers of the Imperial Court Chapel, honoring the memory of their former Kapellmeister [and esteemed artist, expressed a unanimous desire] to accompany this sorrowful sacrament with their singing. Admirers of the talent and spiritual attributes of the deceased who wish to pay their last respects to [the precious memory of the deceased] his memory will be gratefully welcomed on Saturday the twenty-third of this instant February to the church of the Imperial Stables at half past 2 o'clock in the afternoon." The erasures (marked in brackets) and corrections were made by Lvov, who wrote the final version of the invitation: "The gentlemen of the Imperial Chapel Choir, with His Majesty's consent, will perform a memorial service in memory of their former Kapellmeister Mikhail Ivanovich Glinka, who passed away in Berlin on the third of this instant February. The service will be held on Saturday, the 23rd of this February, in the church of the Imperial Stables, at half past 2 o'clock in the afternoon. May all be informed who by their presence wish to honor his memory as a renowned composer of our land." One ticket each was sent to the editors of *Sev. pchela, Rus. invalid, SPb. ved.*, and *Journal de St.-Pétersbourg (L.,* p. 499).

19 February

Dargomyzhsky informs Kastrioto-Skanderbek of Glinka's death: "Now we are bustling around preparing to give a large concert in his memory for the benefit of widows and orphans of the Philharmonic Society. The concert will consist of his works exclusively" (coll. *Dargomyzhsky*, p. 50).

21 February

In *Rus. invalid*, no. 40, a notice of Glinka's death and the text of the invitation to the memorial service are printed.

G. Kuzminsky's poem "In Memory of Mikhail Ivanovich Glinka" (ITMK, coll. 6).

22 February

In *SPb. ved.,* no. 41, in the section "Internal News," there is a report: "The Imperial Chapel Choir will perform a service to the memory of M. I. Glinka on 23 February in the church of the Imperial Stables."

23 February

In the church of the Imperial Stables, a memorial service for Glinka, "whom the Imperial Chapel singers served . . . while he was their Kapellmeister. . . . Many carriages bearing coats of arms stood at the entrance to the cathedral . . . but the majority of the celebrants arrived on foot, many from the opposite end of the city, and this was gratifying proof to us that Glinka's works were understood even among this segment of Russian society and that they have already become part of our national heritage" (*SPb. ved.,* 3 March 1857). "During the requiem service for Mikhail Ivanovich, Lvov learned that they wanted to deliver a sermon, and he immediately went up to the altar to prevent it, saying that a sermon was absolutely out of place, and that in any case it couldn't be delivered without his censoring it, besides, he'd left his glasses at home. As a consequence of that [i.e., despite that], the archpriest ordered Polisadov to deliver the sermon" (ltr. from V. Engelgardt to L. Shestakova, 16/28 May 1857; *RMG,* 1896, no. 12).

24 February

A notice from *SPb. ved.* is reprinted in the March literary supplement to *Le Nouvelliste* in the section "Internal News." This issue also includes the program for the court concert in Berlin on 9/21 January (d.c.a.).

After 24 February

At a musical evening at Shilovskaya's, Petrov, Andreev, and Shilovskaya performed the trio, and Shilovskaya performed Vanya's scene, *"Bednyi kon' v pole pal"* [The poor steed fell in the field] from *A Life for the Tsar* (*Muz. i teatr. vestnik,* 1857, no. 9, p. 158).

25 February/9 March

Letter from Kashperov to Ivan Turgenev with details of Glinka's death (*L.,* p. 500).
[The letter bears the character of an "open" letter, and along with valuable factual information (cf. 1/13, 2/14, and 3/15 February), it contains a series of lurid insinuations. Kashperov's version was

widely disseminated, which Kukolnik found out about when he travelled to Berlin at the end of March. Kashperov attempts to slander the character of the composer in the minds of his countrymen (for example, claiming that the nurses who looked after Glinka were prostitutes).]

27 February

Glinka's obituary appears in *Moda,* no. 5, in the section "News Herald and Anecdotes" (reprinted from *SPb. ved.,* 13 February 1857). In the same issue and section there is a report of the January concert in Berlin under the direction of Meyerbeer.

Serov asks Vladimir Stasov to send "the rough draft" of his sketch of Glinka's life, written by Stasov for Dehn and Fétis, with essential biographical data, for an article in *Syn otechestva (MN* III, p. 181).
[Stasov composed a biography of Glinka for Fétis's *Biographie universelle de musiciens et bibliographie générale de la musique* (second edition, 1860–62).]

28 February

Glinka's obituary is printed in *Sovremennik,* vol. 59, no. 3, in the section "Petersburg Life in the Notes of a New Poet [Ivan Panaev]: "Glinka's name has reached the most obscure and distant corners of Russia, along with his melodic, pensive, and passionate music. . . . It is a shame that Glinka's activity, which was never extensive, completely ceased recently and that he left behind so few works. . . . Glinka's death is a great loss for the Russian musical world. . . . Meanwhile, in its annals he will indisputably occupy first place" (d.c.a.).

Beginning of March

Serov returns Vladimir Stasov's draft copy of comments about Glinka and writes: "With respect to the Glinka concert, I find that you still have said too little about the general *baseness* and *indifference* to affairs of this sort. Is it really this way everywhere or only in our blessed fatherland? Everything that I've learned during the evening at Shilovskaya's and yesterday at Leonid's [Lvov] goes beyond the bounds of disgust. 1) Shilovskaya refuses to sing, without the slightest real reason, and besides, I know that she deeply loves Glinka's music. . . . 2) The directors of the Philharmonic Society try to avoid having a military orchestra so they can pay less. 3) Not only do the *parts* of the military music for *Ruslan* not exist in the music office, but even the *score* for military orchestra (marvelously arranged by Ral under Glinka's personal supervision) is also lost. . . . To better explain the matter" Serov describes the full complexity of Ral's work: "even on posters of the time Ral's name appeared, as Glinka wished. *No one* in the audience understood what was meant when it said 'arranged by someone else,' when the music was Glinka's. And they had to lose these scores!! Meanwhile without it, *it is impossible to play* either the *introduction,* the *march,* or the *lezghinka.* . . . What a concert and well-thought-out program!" (*MN* III, p. 182).

[The letter is undated. It was written several days after 27 February, since Serov returned Stasov's notice about Glinka after the evening at Shilovskaya's.]

3 March

In *Muz. i teatr. vestnik,* no. 9, in the section "Petersburg Herald," there is a review by Mavriky Rapaport about Shilovskaya's musical evening, where excerpts were performed from *A Life for the Tsar* "by our inimitable Glinka, who, alas, is no longer among us!" In the same issue there is an announcement about a forthcoming concert by Leonova on 5 March, in which "we will hear several works by the unforgettable Russian composer M. I. Glinka." The notice also announces the publication of Pavel Fedorov's romance *"Prosti menia, prosti,"* arranged by Glinka for two voices.

In *SPb. ved.,* no. 49, there is a feuilleton [by Vasilko-Petrov] entitled "Petersburg Chronicle. Memorial Service for M. I. Glinka. Articles about Him in German Newspapers. Our Acquaintance with Glinka. Project for a New Opera. Glinka the Singer. Glinka the Listener. Glinka's Teachers. His Portrait. A Concert in Memory of Glinka. . . ." It also includes a description of the memorial service and the author's reminiscences of Glinka. At the end it says: "No disciples of Glinka have emerged, his work has still not been evaluated according to its merits, but even during his life his works were already recognized for their nationality and had acquired European fame and the respect of all musical authorities. For us Russians, the death of Glinka, the creator of Russian opera, has a solemn significance."

4 March

In *Otech. zap.,* vol. 111, part 3, in the section called "Contemporary Chronicle of Russia," there appears an obituary of Glinka (unsigned): "Glinka's name is one which requires no elaboration to clarify its significance. His name has acquired great renown not only in Russia but abroad. To say that Glinka has died, the composer of the opera *A Life for the Tsar,* means to express all the bitterness and importance of a loss which, in his person, Russian art and Russian music have suffered. . . . May he who honestly fulfills his calling for the good of all rest in peace, who moreover brings glory to his native land by virtue of his gifts." In the same issue there is an account of the memorial service on 23 February (d.c.a.).

5 March

In *SPb. ved.*, no. 50, there is an announcement from Shestakova about Glinka's death and a request to all who were indebted to him and to whom he was indebted to report to Shestakova for settlement.

In *Bib-ka dlia chteniia*, vol. 142, in the section "Miscellany—Petersburg Chronicle," there is an obituary of Glinka—"the famous and well-loved composer." There is a reference to the two fugues he had written and to the concert in Berlin on 9/21 January (d.c.a.).

Dargomyzhsky informs Lyubov Belenitsyna about Glinka's death "after a brief illness, as the consequence of a bad cold. I won't pass along petty gossip about the reasons that hastened his death, because I'd rather let idle chatter in one ear and out the other; but I will tell you something that may be some consolation in such a situation. While Glinka's death did not make much of an impression on the world at large, his fame in the press grows and resounds by the day. The choristers of the Imperial Chapel, on A. F. Lvov's initiative, sang the requiem for him, and the church of the Imperial Stables could not accommodate the masses of people who came by carriage and on foot to pay their last respects to our composer. The public's sympathy toward his lofty talent should be expressed even more strongly in the concert which the Philharmonic Society will give in his memory. The concert will consist exclusively of his music. . . . I hope sincerely that the audience will confirm Glinka's fame, which has been preached in the papers. Without the people's grief, the noise in the papers is empty and sickening, like all venality" (coll. *Dargomyzhsky*, p. 51).

Leonova's concert in the Aleksandrinsky Theater. With chorus, she performed "for the second time '*V minutu zhizni trudnuiu*,' words by Lermontov, music composed and orchestrated by M. I. Glinka." The orchestra, under the direction of Otto Dütsch, performed the *Valse-fantaisie*, and Leonova sang "Gretchen's Song" (*Muz. i teatr. vestnik*, 1857, no. 9, p. 151).

First Week of March

"A curious thing: Dehn, who sent me all the things I asked about, did not send the dressing gown. 'I am not sending the dressing gown,' Mr. Dehn wrote with a totally German quickness, 'because the gown is too old and *you will not be able to make any use of it*'" (Shestakova, *Vosp.*, p. 308).

6 March

Grech writes to Aleksandr Vasilievich (Nikitenko?): "This past Saturday the Imperial Chapel Choir performed a memorial service in the church of the Imperial Stables for their former professor Mikhail Ivanovich Glinka. The Philharmonic Society here also intends to honor his memory with a selection of his best music for their annual concert for the benefit of musicians' widows. This is a beautiful tribute to this great native talent! I am sure that the hall will be full" (coll. *Shukinsky*, inst. 8, Moscow, 1909, p. 449).

[Grech expressed himself inaccurately. The concert was on 23 February, not "this past Saturday."]

8 March

In *Sev. pchela*, no. 53, Rostislav in "Musical Conversations" announces the concert of the Philharmonic Society planned for 8 March "in memory of the unforgettable Mikhail Ivanovich Glinka. The impression produced by the sorrowful news of this loss when it reached the Russian music world is still so strong that words fail us, and our grief, society's grief, and Russian grief still remain inexpressible."

At eight o'clock in the evening in the Hall of Nobility, a concert by the Philharmonic Society "in memory of the deceased and honored member of the Philharmonic Society, Mikhail Ivanovich Glinka, the program for which consists exclusively of his music: Part I: 1) Overture from the opera *Ruslan and Lyudmila;* 2) Introduction from the same opera (Mme Leonova, Messrs. Bulakhov, Artemovsky, Zakharov)—a) the chorus *'Dela davno minuvshikh dnei'* [Things of days long past], b) Bayan's song (Mr. Bulakhov), c) the chorus *'Mir i blazhenstvo'* [Peace and bliss]; 3) aria from the opera *Ruslan, 'O pole, pole'* (Mr. Artemovsky); 4) *'Molitva'* with chorus (Mme Leonova); 5) *Valse-fantaisie,* for orchestra; 6) Farlaf's aria from the opera *Ruslan* (Mr. Zakharov); 7) Lyudmila's aria *'Vdali ot milogo'* [Far from my love] from the same opera (Mme Tiefensee, Signora Pexatori); 8) chorus and Chernomor's march with military band and ballet (lezghinka) from the fourth act of the opera *Ruslan and Lyudmila*. Part II: 9) the overture *Jota aragonesa* for orchestra; 10) Ratmir's romance from the opera *Ruslan* (Mme Leshetitskaya); 11) improvisations on themes by Glinka (performed on the piano by Mr. Seymour-Schiff); 12) aria *'Liubvi roskoshnaia zvezda'* [Radiant star of love] from the opera *Ruslan* (Mme Kochetova); 13) finale from the opera *A Life for the Tsar* for orchestra, chorus, and military band. Conducted by Mr. K. Shubert" (E. Albrecht, "Survey of the Activities of the St. Petersburg Philharmonic Society," p. 19).

"A rather large audience attended the concert. At the center of the platform built for the musicians, a bust of our renowned composer had been placed, decorated with a laurel wreath and surrounded by garlands of flowers. The audience listened quietly to excerpts from *Ruslan and Lyudmila* and received the soloists Mme Leonova, and Messrs. Zakharov, and Artemovsky very approvingly, especially the amateurs Mme Kochetova, Leshetitskaya, and the newly arrived singer Tiefensee (Pexatori). Mme Leshetitskaya, a sincere and unusually polished contralto, made a very pleasant impression on everyone. Then the music subsided, and there before us, so to say, Glinka towered in all the variety, uniqueness, and capriciousness of his genius. The orchestra conducted by Shubert performed the Lezghinka, *Kamarinskaya,* finale from *A Life for the Tsar,* and the Waltz, and the bitter native sounds stirred everyone. With unanimous applause the audience greeted the performers capable of conveying the inimitable and, for a non-Russian, elusive beauty of our native composer with such artistry. To this, perhaps, should be added mention of the chilliness with which they listened to Seymour-Schiff's improvisations on Glinka's themes" (*Rus. invalid,* 17 March 1857). The concert "was attended by a large audience. On the stage stood a bust of the deceased decorated with a wreath" (*Sovremennik,* 1857, vol. 62, no. 4, p. 302).

In a concert in the Great Hall of the Nobility in Moscow given by the guitarist Sokolovsky, there was a performance of "the outstanding fantasy on 'Kamarinskaya,' composed by our recently deceased operatic composer . . . Glinka" (*Mosk. ved.,* 21 March 1857).

9 March

In *Sev. pchela,* no. 54, in a notice entitled "Portrait of M. I. Glinka," there is a report about the sale of a portrait engraved on stone by M. Baryshev from a photograph by Levitsky (1856).

10 March

In *Muz. i teatr. vestnik,* no. 10, in the section "Petersburg Herald," Mavriky Rapaport writes in a survey of concerts during the past week that in her concert of 5 March, Leonova performed "several works by the unforgettable M. I. Glinka and rendered the thoughts of the great Russian composer with enthusiasm and imagination."

In *Rus. invalid,* no. 55, a significant portion of the Sunday feuilleton is dedicated to Glinka's memory: "We spoke of this subject under the influence of our impressions after the concert given . . . by the Philharmonic Society in memory of our composer Mikhail Ivanovich Glinka, who was stolen so early by death. When we heard his profound, genuinely Russian music, we were reminded of how much hostile talk was aroused by the appearance of each of his works. . . . And now this radiant genius, who called forth the unearthly sounds of the Russian heart from the depths of his soul, is no longer among us. Death, speaking in the words of one of . . . his romances, 'tore out his harp's strings.' At his grave admirers and enemies gathered and now begin to understand his love and vital sympathy toward Russian man and what a perished treasure the spirit of this man contained. In his tightly knit circle of friends he was outwardly unsociable and reserved. Ruslan's aria made a sorrowful impression on us, for both poet and composer seemed to ask from the depths of their graves,

> Oh, this field, this field,
> Who has sown you with dead men's bones . . .

The reverential attention of all, followed by loud, unceasing applause, served as proof that now the time has come for Glinka's true appreciation. May musical experts understand his marvelous works and, on the basis of the theory of art, establish his place among great composers. Russian people will not forget him. Glinka expressed an intimate popular thought in *A Life for the Tsar,* and in *Ruslan and Lyudmila* he immortalized the first poem of our dearest writer. Henceforth Pushkin and Glinka will live inseparably in our legends."

In a concert the pianist Jean Vogt performed his piano fantasy *Hommage à Glinka (SPb. ved.,* 5 March 1857).

14 March

In *Rus. vestnik,* vol. 8, March, part 3/4, there is a poem by Maykov entitled "On the Death of M. I. Glinka." In the same issue are Dubrovsky's "Memories of Glinka" (d.c.a.).

In *SPb. ved.,* no. 58, there is review of a concert by Ludwig Maurer, in which he performed his own composition entitled *Une larme sur la tombe de Glinka.*

15 March

Meeting of Vladimir Stasov with Minister of Foreign Affairs Illarion Tolstoy concerning moving Glinka's remains to Petersburg (ltr. from V. Stasov to L. Shestakova, 15 March 1857; *RMG,* 1898, no. 12).

17 March

In *Muz. i teatr. vestnik,* no. 11, in the section "Petersburg Herald—Review of the Concerts of the Past Week," Yury Arnold writes about Glinka and the Philharmonic Society concert on 8 March. "Glinka is gone! The founder of our national opera has died. A truly great composer has died, one whose genius was remarkable, not just to his countrymen, but it also far, far surpassed many so-called European celebrities. *'Ne stony rodnykh'* ['Twas not the laments of kinsmen] that resounded at the death bed of our great composer, but indifferent mumbling in a foreign tongue. He did not die in his native land, but in foreign parts, dispirited not by age but by sadness and grief which had long burdened his sorely wounded heart! Who among us was not struck by the news of Glinka's death? Whoever truly loves music will value the genius of Glinka's work. If not everyone mourned the loss of a friend, then certainly they all mourned for the glory and fame of our native land! The best confirmation of this was the large assembly on 8 March (including all our musical celebrities without exception) and the reverence with which they listened to the music of our prematurely departed composer. . . . Glinka's accomplishments and the importance of his work should not be spoken about in the ephemeral observations of a feuilleton, but in a more wide-ranging and serious article. Who in art occupies a position as high as Glinka's is a question posterity will pose to the last breath of life; opinions on such matters must be subject to historical analysis."

Concerning the concert, it says that Karl Shubert, as well as "Messrs. Bulakhov and Artemovsky and Mme Leonova, fully deserved the audience's resounding, unanimous recognition." It gives a negative account of Seymour-Schiff's improvisations on themes from *A Life for the Tsar* and *Ruslan.*

In *SPb. ved.,* no. 61, there is an account (unsigned) of the Philharmonic Society's concert in memory of Glinka. "Every piece in the concert was greeted with ringing applause. . . . The performances were intelligible despite the difficulty of preparing for such a concert and the scarcity among us of singers able to display their talent at such a musical festival." It especially mentions Kochetova's performance of Lyudmila's aria: "She elicited a very enthusiastic response. Mme Leshetitskaya likewise enjoyed great success," as did Tiefensee, whom "the audience received very cordially. . . . The singer was only able to prepare for the concert for several days. . . . Despite the difficulty of singing in Russian and her unfamiliarity with the character of Russian music . . . she performed her piece very distinctly. . . . The orchestra and chorus played well together under the direction of Mr. Shubert. Mr. Seymour-Schiff successfully improvised on themes of Glinka's."

In *Rus. invalid,* no. 61 (in an unsigned feuilleton), there is a comparison of the characteristics of Glinka's and Dargomyzhsky's music: "We are ready to say, judging from our own feelings, that one wants to listen to *Rusalka* when the mind is looking for stunning and powerful sensations. Glinka's music, however, whatever one's state of mind, finds a string to touch in the spirit and heart. . . . The mention of Glinka's name brings to mind the dear names of those who were so prematurely lost to us for poetry and pleasure: Gogol, Lermontov, and especially Pushkin." It reports details of the concert on 8 March and criticizes Seymour-Schiff's improvisations on themes by Glinka: "Improvising on Glinka's music means attempting to demonstrate what he did not demonstrate, but one must ask, 'What did our marvelous composer not demonstrate?'"

20 March

In a concert in the Mikhaylovsky Theater, Maurer performed his elegy for orchestra, *Une larme sur la tombe de Glinka.* "The piece was repeated by unanimous demand" (*Sev. pchela,* 26 March 1857).

21 March

In *Mosk. ved.,* no. 35, in an article entitled "Moscow Municipal Chronicle," there is a report of the Petersburg memorial service on 23 February and the concert of the Philharmonic Society on 8 March. "The death of the great Russian composer M. I. Glinka made a painful impression on everyone, of whatever walk in life, to whom national glory is near and dear." Also included is an account of the guitarist Sokolovsky's concert on 8 March, where *Kamarinskaya* was performed.

24 March

In *Syn otechestva,* no. 12, in the section "Musical Chronicle," Serov's obituary remarks, "Mikhail Ivanovich Glinka," appear. "Russia mourns a great national artist, the founder of a Russian school of music, and one of the foremost representatives of contemporary musical art. . . . Now, just after the sad news, readers are not yet entitled to ask for either a detailed biography of M. I. Glinka . . . or a detailed evaluation of all or even his most outstanding pieces (for this, time and much careful planning are needed)." There follows a short "overview of the most important facts about his life and artistic activity," which Serov based on Glinka's autobiographical sketch. In the same issue there is a review of the concert on 8 March.
[This obituary was printed in shortened form in the journal *Severnyi tsvetok,* no. 11 (unsigned).]

26 March

In *Sev. pchela,* no. 67, in a notice about the concert in Glinka's memory, Rostislav writes: "It is terrible to think that even death itself . . . sometimes lacks the power to soften the verdict of a hostile circle! Is the meaning of this sad loss which struck the Russian artistic family on 3 February of this year really comprehensible to everyone without exception? Did everyone respond to the Philharmonic Society's appeal the day of the solemn concert in memory of our unforgettable countryman Mikhail Ivanovich Glinka? The Hall of Nobility was nearly full. True, but it was not difficult to persuade oneself, with profound regret, that a circle which did not appreciate M. I. Glinka's music during his lifetime protested even now by its absence!"

In the April literary supplement to *Le Nouvelliste,* it is reported that the news in Moscow of Glinka's death had "a profoundly distressing effect on all true music lovers" (d.c.a.).

End of March

Upon his arrival in Berlin, Kukolnik "hoped to gather information about Glinka . . . especially from Dehn. But this upright German spoke reluctantly about Glinka, and what he did say did not console me. Instead of telling me stories, Dehn referred to a detailed letter to Engelgardt, where, as he asserted, he had described the last days of Glinka's life in detail. I merely learned that Glinka's death had been very bad and that two weeks before he died he had gotten Dehn's word that, if he died, a postmortem be performed immediately, which Dehn had done. . . . Dehn was not present at the very moment of death." Having told Kukolnik who was present at Glinka's funeral, "Dehn passed it off . . . as a great honor rendered to Glinka. Another honor was that in his library he had a quasi-complete collection of Glinka's music in a cheap binding, which he did not overlook drawing my attention to. I gathered that this binding represented the third honor rendered to Glinka. I took a dislike to Dehn. . . . Poor Glinka! Such a friend could not save him!" (N. Kukolnik, *Vosp.,* p. 317).

[Dehn's letter to Engelgardt is not extant. His letter to Shestakova is known only through her transmission. The original of the letter has not been found.]

31 March

In *Sovremennik,* vol. 62, no. 4, in the section "Petersburg Life: Notes of a New Poet," Panaev mentions, among the concerts during Lent, Glinka's memorial service in the church of the Imperial Stables and the Philharmonic Society's concert (d.c.a.).

In *Syn otechestva,* no. 13, in "Survey of the Activities of the Petersburg Theaters During the 1856–1857 Season," it says: "Russian opera has sustained . . . an irreparable loss. M. I. Glinka, our only Russian composer in every sense of the word, died in Berlin, and all music lovers will feel this loss for a long time, even though he had not written for some time and scarcely wrote anything for the stage" (d.c.a.).

March

A concert during Lent took place in Moscow in Glinka's memory. "The program was the same as . . . in Petersburg: several numbers from the opera *Ruslan and Lyudmila,* '*Molitva,*' and Glinka's romances" (*Muz. i teatr. vestnik,* 1857, no. 15, p. 248).
[The date of the concert or the names of the performers are not indicated.]

12 April

In a sacred concert in the Hall of Nobility (at which the *Stabat Mater* by Pergolesi-Lvov was performed), Servais, who participated, performed his own transcription of Glinka's *"Somnenie."* "There was such intimacy and expressiveness in his playing that the audience demanded he repeat the piece, which reminded us of the great Russian artist M. I. Glinka" (*Muz. i teatr. vestnik,* 1857, no. 15, p. 244).

13 April

In *Mosk. ved.,* no. 45, there is a notice of the sale in Moscow of portraits of Glinka received from Petersburg (from Levitsky's photographs).

16 and 17 April

In *SPb. ved.,* nos. 81 & 82, in an article by Berthold Damcke entitled "Liszt and Virtuosos in General," it says that in the news "there are only three things worthy of note: the success of Weber's *Oberon* in Paris, Glinka's death, and Mr. Ulybyshev's new book. With respect to Glinka, the great, celebrated musician of whom Russia has been deprived, it is not for me to describe his life and evaluate his beautiful music. This is a matter for his countrymen, who, of course, will not delay in rendering the greatest composer which Russia has ever had the necessary tribute of respect."

21 April

Matinee concert for the benefit of the poor in the Hall of Nobility under the direction of Karl Shubert, at which Ludwig Maurer's *Une larme sur la tombe de Glinka* was performed (*SPb. ved.,* 19 April 1857).

In *Muz. i teatr. vestnik,* no. 15, under "Theatrical and Musical News from Various Russian Cities," there is a reference to the memorial service performed by the Imperial Chapel singers for Glinka, the concert of 8 March, and the concert in Glinka's memory in Moscow. The *SPb. ved.* reports on Servais's performance in his transcription of Glinka's *"Somnenie"* and about performances of *A Life for the Tsar* at the benefit concerts by Mme Perine and Mme Latysheva (in articles by M. Rapaport, "Resumption of Performances after Lent . . . *A Life for the Tsar*" and "Mme Latysheva's Benefit").

26 April

In the May literary supplement to *Le Nouvelliste,* in an account of the concert season in Petersburg, there is a report about the Philharmonic Society's concert in memory of Glinka, "a composer whose memory will never be effaced" (d.c.a.).

1 May

In *Moda,* no. 9, in the section "News Herald and Anecdotes," there is discussion of the reaction of Muscovites to Glinka's death: "The passing of the Russian composer M. I. Glinka made a sorrowful impression on everyone to whom national glory is valuable. . . . A large crowd filled the Hall of Nobility. The chorus was dressed in mourning. The program of the concert was the same as here in Petersburg" (d.c.a.).

4 May

In *Sev. pchela,* no. 96, there is an article by V. Stasov entitled "Return to Mr. Damcke's Article" (cf. 16 and 17 April): "Damcke refers to Glinka's death as significant musical news. To us it is a sad and bitter event."

13/25 May

Engelgardt's arrival in Berlin to move Glinka's body to Russia.

14/26 May

Disinterment of Glinka's remains at 4 o'clock in the morning in the presence of Engelgardt, Dehn, the priest Polisadov, and Glinka's landlord. "There was no odor at all, but no one wanted to raise the sheet to look at the body. Only the grave digger had such courage and said: '*Das Gesicht sieht böse aus.*' According to his words, it was already impossible to distinguish any characteristics, for the entire face was covered with some kind of white substance like a layer of cotton wool" (ltr. from V. Engelgardt to L. Shestakova, 16/28 May 1857; *RMG,* 1898, no. 12).

17/29 May

Glinka's remains were transported to Stettin (*SPb. ved.,* 19 May 1857). At the station, Mstislav Tikhonravov, who had accompanied the remains from Berlin to Stettin, handed over the box with the coffin for personal baggage, "explaining that the box contained china." Otherwise it would have been necessary "to take a separate coach and to be provided in advance with the accompanying certificate for such an event . . . from the police. This would have incurred significant expense and would have caused lost time."

18/30 May

In Stettin, Tikhonravov "hired a wagon to deliver the box to the pier," where the postal steamer *Vladimir* awaited. He informed "the captain of the steamer confidentially what precious cargo there was in the box" after giving him "the box and all official correspondence and a parcel" (ltr. from M. Tikhonravov to N. Findeyzen, 18/30 July 1898, in *L.,* p. 508). That morning the steamship *Vladimir* with Glinka's body departed for Kronstadt (ltr. from V. Engelgardt to L. Shestakova, 16/28 May 1857, in *RMG,* 1898, no. 12).

19 May

In *SPb. ved.,* no. 107, under the heading "Petersburg Chronicle. M. I. Glinka's Mortal Remains," it says that Glinka's remains were transferred from Berlin on 17 May and that a burial service will be conducted on 24 May in the Alexander Nevsky Monastery.

21 May

Shestakova booked herself "on a steamer and travelled . . . to meet my brother's body," accompanied by Balakirev, Dmitry and Vladimir Stasov, and Serov (ltr.

from L. Shestakova to E. Nápravnik, 19 November 1893, in *L.*, p. 509; ltr. from M. Balakirev to N. Findeyzen, 30 September 1903, in GPB, coll. 816; Shestakova, *Vosp.*, p. 308).

22 May

The steamship *Vladimir* with Glinka's remains arrives in Kronstadt (Shestakova, *Vosp.*, p. 308; *SPb. ved.*, 23 May 1857). On her return to Petersburg, Shestakova was met by an official with an order to transfer the box as hand baggage by night to a cart" (ltr. from L. Shestakova to Nápravnik, 19 November 1893, in *L.*, p. 509). Until 11 o'clock in the evening "we had to leave his body . . . on the pier. . . . But his body did not remain alone on the pier for a minute, for we who had served him were vying with each other to be near him. That night, without any parades, my brother's body was transferred to the Nevsky Monastery into the Church of Lazarus. There they took the box and replaced it with a high, dark grey or black wooden coffin without any decoration" (Shestakova, *Vosp.*, p. 309).

[In a letter to Nápravnik on 19 November 1893, Shestakova says that Glinka's remains were transferred to the Alexander Nevsky Monastery on the night of 22 May.]

23 May

"Early in the morning I saw to it that the coffin was upholstered with brocade" (Shestakova, *Vosp.*, p. 309).

An invitation: "Lyudmila Ivanovna Shestakova, reporting the removal here from Berlin of the body of her deceased brother Mikhail Ivanovich Glinka, humbly requests your presence at his memorial service and burial in the Alexander Nevsky Monastery, Church of the Holy Spirit, on Friday the 24th of May, at 10:30 in the morning" (*L.*, p. 510).

In *SPb. ved.*, no. 110, Aleksandr Elkan's article entitled "Glinka's Burial Service" appears.

"At the vesper service many of those close to my brother moved him into the Church of the Holy Spirit. . . . In the church, as on the pier, my brother was not left alone for a moment."

24 May

Early in the morning Shestakova "went to the Nevsky [Monastery] in order to decorate the coffin and grave of my brother with flowers. I had not even begun my task when Osip Afanasievich Petrov entered the church, and we hung the garlands together" (Shestakova, *Vosp.*, p. 309). "At ten o'clock in the morning the Church of the Holy Spirit filled up with a crowd of people who esteemed the great talent of the gifted Glinka . . . it was a large, a very large gathering. Among those who appeared *for the final kiss* of the deceased were many scholars, famous writers, composers, performers, artists, and even the proprietors of music stores. Particularly significant was that among those assembled there were performers from the Russian Opera troupe who were indebted for their fame and artistic perfection to the immortal composer of *A Life for the Tsar*. . . . It should not be overlooked that among the company of these people were many women who were indebted to the famous Glinka for their musical education. . . . At the conclusion of the memorial service everyone hastened to bid the deceased farewell, and the flowers, which were strewn about his tomb, were snatched up as remembrances of the terrible loss. Afterwards Glinka's body was borne by writers and performers of the Russian Opera to the cemetery of the Nevsky Monastery. The location of his grave had been selected for its proximity to the graves of famous Russian writers: Zhukovsky, Karamzin, Krylov, and Gnedich. Glinka's grave is very close to the cemetery gates" (*Syn otechestva*, no. 22, p. 521). At 10:30 in the morning "after the liturgy and requiem," the burial of Glinka's remains took place in the Tikhvinskoe cemetery of the Alexander Nevsky Monastery. "A small number of his friends and admirers gathered at Glinka's open grave" (Shestakova, *Vosp.*, p. 309; V. Sollogub, *Vosp.* p. 627).

"Today we buried M. I. Glinka, our gifted national artist, our musical glory. In the Nevsky Monastery, not far from the graves of Karamzin and Zhukovsky, a fresh grave now rises up, near which every Russian ought to pause in grief and veneration. . . . Despite newspaper announcements and special notification by cards, the number who showed up to pay last respects to the deceased was quite limited. *Personages of both sexes* did not appear at all, and there were few from the public and fewer still of *common folk*. The deceased belonged to no particular officialdom, which explains this sad occurrence. Many were vainly hoping at Glinka's burial service to hear the polished singing of the [Imperial Chapel] Choir, which had formerly been under his direction, and mistakenly thought they would see representatives from the Academy of Arts and Theater; only a few performers from the Russian Opera troupe came to pay their final respects to their gifted teacher. Doubtless, sympathy for the deceased would have been expressed more strongly in Moscow." (*Molva*, 1857, no. 9, p. 104).
["Personages" implies members of the aristocracy.]

1 June

In *Moda,* no. 11, there is an account of Glinka's burial "in the Nevsky Monastery in the presence of a large gathering of admirers of his talent" (d.c.a.).

In *Sovremennik,* vol. 63, no. 6, in "Notes of a New Poet [Ivan Panaev]—On Glinka's Funeral": "Relatives, friends, and admirers of his talent (Who did not love his beautiful talent!) were at his funeral. Many people gathered to pay respect to one of their most talented countrymen" (d.c.a.).

2 June

In *Syn otechestva,* no. 22, in an unsigned article [Senkovsky] entitled "Diary of a Familiar Man" there is a description of the arrival of Glinka's remains from Stettin, their reception in Kronstadt, and burial on 24 May in the Alexander Nevsky Monastery. "It is sad! . . . that I must speak of the burial of a great Russian composer, the author of the immortal work *A Life for the Tsar,* Mikhail Ivanovich Glinka. . . . Death put a halt to his new and absorbing work. . . . The news of the great composer's death echoes bitterly in the hearts of all Russians. Who among Russians did not have a reverential attitude toward Glinka's genius? . . . Only Glinka's body died, however. His music lives and will live eternally not only in Russia but also abroad. Glinka's last published work was a polonaise for the coronation of His Majesty the emperor, published by V. D. Denotkin. It is said that in Petersburg a big subscription is being established for the erection of a worthy monument to the famous Russian composer. It would be sinful for a Russian not to support such a worthy undertaking. . . . It is time finally for us also to learn to appreciate our native talents, our men of genius" (d.c.a.).

[A monument "executed by the master monument maker Denneis from a design by Academician I. I. Gornostaev" was erected in 1858. "The medallion with [Glinka's] portrait in profile, which was set into the monument, was made from a silhouette drawn [of Glinka] . . . in 1842 from his shadow on a piece of paper [Sofia Dyutur]. This medallion was executed . . . by the talented sculptor Lavretsky and installed by the sculptor Pimenov at the request of V. V. Stasov (who was in charge of the monument's construction)" (Shestakova, *Vosp.*, p. 309).]

8 June

"A Letter from Petersburg" (signed "O.") appears in *Molva,* no. 9. "After the brilliant work of M. I. Glinka, the question concerning nationalism in art can no longer be raised. Glinka solved it and by the power of his genius not only created a new Russian school of music but also immediatly established an honored place for it in the realm of art. Glinka's services are far from being appreciated in Russia. He shared the fate of all the men of genius who have appeared among us in recent times and whom Providence has taken away from us so early. Our society's indifference toward all manifestations and questions of life, learning, and art is the bulwark against which one after another all the inspired impulses of our poets, artists, performers, and scholars have been crushed. Glinka's poetic nature suffered in like measure, struggled and was exhausted in the midst of contemporary society. We will of course find out about this from the deceased's memoirs, which, we hear, are being prepared for publication by one of his closest friends" (d.c.a.).

[At that time Glinka's *Zapiski* were not being prepared for publication. Vladimir Stasov included excerpts from them in the monograph which he was writing at the time. The author, apparently, has in mind Stasov's work.]

10 June

In *Rus. khudozh. listok,* no. 17, there is a notice "Concerning a Portrait of M. I. Glinka," with his last portrait and a sketch of his room in Berlin on the day of his death attached.

In *Zhivopisnaia russkaia biblioteka* [Library of Russian Painting], no. 23, vol. 2, published by Ksenofont Polevoy, there is an unsigned article entitled "The Composer M. I. Glinka." It refers to the comparatively greater success of *A Life for the Tsar* than *Ruslan and Lyudmila,* despite the fact that in the second opera "experts find . . . beautiful things of the first order. . . . In all the known pieces of the later years of his life inspiration appears incidental—moments of rest in a constant melancholy. Nonetheless there is apparent in these works a mature gift, rich both in thought and musical experience. *A Life for the Tsar* remains the most lasting momument to M. I. Glinka's ability. It is one of the most successful efforts to create a *Russian* opera. We do not share the opinion of those who assert that Glinka created it [Russian opera]. First of all, one should not forget the beautiful folk operas of A. N. Verstovsky, who even before Glinka tried to establish the idea of Russian opera. Secondly, the ideal and personal character of both of Glinka's operas cannot be a complete expression of the character of Russian music, just as Pushkin's poem, which serves as the basis for one of Glinka's operas, cannot be called a complete and accurate echo of Russian poetry. For us it is a fortunate and precious attempt. Is this really not enough to bring glory for such a great gift? Perhaps the time to create Russian opera has not even arrived, because generally the full character of Russian poetry has not expressed itself. What is Russian music? Certainly it lies in more than the melodies of folk songs. Such exceptional practitioners, gifted with creativity like M. I. Glinka deserve the love and gratitude of their countrymen for their noble efforts and successes in expressing Russian poetry and Russian genius" (d.c.a.).

16, 18, and 19 June

Translation of Serov's article from *Syn otechestva* in nos. 130–32 of *St.-Petersburger Zeitung*. It is entitled "Michael Ivanovitch Glinka."

27 June

In *SPb. ved.*, no. 139, there is a "Musical Review" by Berthold Damcke in which he tells about the failure he encountered when he tried to publish *Kamarinskaya* or give it to performers abroad in the spring of 1854. "Nowadays it is necessary to die in order to live in classical concerts. Glinka has died. His death was profoundly deplorable." Still efforts to perform *Kamarinskaya* in Brussels failed. "Thus I continue to seek out orchestras which will agree to play and publishers who will decide to print one of the most remarkable works of our time, a composition which would occupy an honored place and elicit enthusiastic applause if under it stood the name of Beethoven or Mendelssohn" (*Vosp.*, p. 265).

18 August

In *Muz. i teatr. vestnik*, no. 32, in the section "Foreign Herald," there is this report: "Several pieces of music of M. I. Glinka in the possession of Professor Dehn, according to the deceased's final instructions, will be published shortly in Berlin."

25 October

In *SPb. ved.*, no. 231, there is an article by Vladimir Stasov "On the Performance of a Little-Known Work by M. I. Glinka" in a University Concert on 27 October, i.e., Glinka's music to the tragedy *Prince Kholmsky* (the overture and entr'actes): "This is a work of genius which belongs to the full flowering of Glinka's talent." There follows a detailed analysis and the conclusion: "The beauties and perfection of artistic style of this great composition . . . provide inexhaustible pleasure for those ready to understand real music. We hope that there will be many such among us and that thanks to them Glinka's music to 'Kholmsky' will finally come to occupy a place in their minds which in the eyes of all musicians Beethoven's overture and entr'actes to 'Egmont' occupy." Serov writes to V. Stasov: "I read your article about 'Kholmsky' in the *SPb. ved.* today with great pleasure. Good, and correct!" (*MN* III, p. 187).

27 October

The overture and entr'actes to *Prince Kholmsky*, on the initiative of Vasily Engelgardt and Aleksandr Serov, were performed at a University Concert under the direction of Karl Shubert after an interval of many years (*SPb. ved.*, 25 October 1857).

10 and 17 November, 8 and 15 December

In *Muz. i teatr. vestnik*, nos. 44, 45, 48, and 49, Serov's article about the music to *Prince Kholmsky* is printed under the title "A Little-Known Work by M. I. Glinka": "This is a powerful work from the time of *Ruslan* . . . when Glinka's genius . . . had entered a new phase of its development and opened new horizons for art. . . . The music to the tragedy *Prince Kholmsky* belongs among Glinka's most remarkable creations, both in inspiration and planning and in the maturity and strictness of its style. A brilliant future awaits this piece in an enlightened musical world." Further on there is a detailed analysis and account of the content of Nestor Kukolnik's tragedy.

14 September–14 November

Publication of Vladimir Stasov's work "Mikhail Ivanovich Glinka" in *Rus. vestnik*, vol. 11, October, part 2 (no. 20); vol. 12, November, parts 1 and 2 (nos. 21 and 22); December, part 2 (no. 24). This was the first monograph on Glinka, based on his *Zapiski* and letters, and for many years remained the fundamental work on the composer.

Index of Persons

A., reviewer for the *Odessa Herald* [*Odesskii vestnik*], 487

A., author of the welcoming speech for Glinka in Smolensk, 489

Abbondio, Giuseppa, Glinka's landlady in Milan, 64

Achard, French comic actor, 419

Adam, Adolphe (Charles) (1803–1856), French composer, 234, 264, 312, 316, 437
Giselle, 370

Adeliade (Didina), friend of Glinka in Milan during the period 1830–1833, 64

Adelina (Adeline H.), milliner who lived with Glinka in Paris from the summer of 1853 to the beginning of April 1854, 617, 627

Adlerberg, Aleksandr Vladimirovich (1818–1888), son of V. F. Adlerberg, 705

Adlerberg, Vladimir Fedorovich (1790/1–1884), general, minister of the Imperial court, member of the State Council, 705

Afanasiev, Vasily Matveevich (? after 1920), curator of the Glinka Museum of the SPb. Conservatory, 412

Afanasiev, A., correspondent of A. F. Veltman, 301

Afanasiev, Nikolay Yakovlevich (1821–98), violinist and composer, 556

Afanasy, Glinka's cook, 26

Akhmatova, Elizaveta Nikolaevna (1820–1904), writer and translator, 356, 357, 378

Aksakov, Ivan Sergeevich (1823–1886), journalist, son of S. T. Aksakov, 407, 408, 515

Aksakov, Sergey Timofeevich (1791–1859), writer, 46, 407

Aksel, writer of vaudevilles, 380, 381, 382

Albrecht, Karl Frantsevich (1807–1863), violinist and conductor; from 1833, violinist, and from 1840, conductor with the SPb. Imperial Opera orchestra, 276, 304, 308, 332, 349, 360, 371, 372, 538, 699

Aledinskaya, Sofia Aleksandrovna. *See* Zybina, S. A.

Aledinsky, Nikolay Aleksandrovich (1813–1868), Glinka's colleague at the Boarding School, 174

Aleksandra Fedorovna (1798–1860), Prussian princess, from 1817 wife of Nicholas I and Russian empress, 524, 549, 552

Aleksandrov, Timofey Aleksandrovich, member of the Board of Deans, Glinka's attorney during his divorce proceedings, 296, 297

Aleksandrova, Vera Timofeevna, amateur singer at the beginning of the 1840s; student of Glinka, daughter of T. A. Aleksandrov, 241

Aleksandrova, Sofia Timofeevna, amateur singer, student of Glinka, daughter of T. A. Aleksandrov, 654

Aleksandrova-Kochetova, Aleksandra Dermidontovna (née Sokolova), married name Kochetova, stage name Aleksandrova (1833–1902), soprano and teacher, 759, 760, 762

Aleksandroviches, the, acquaintances of Glinka in Warsaw in 1848, 509

Aleksey. *See* Netoev, Aleksey Ulyanych

Alexander I (1777–1825), Russian emperor from 1801, 12, 20, 560, 568

Alexander II (1818–1881), Russian emperor from 1825, 560, 702, 705, 707, 735

Alferiev, S., medical student in Paris, 444

Allari, composer
Sardanapale, opera, 574

Álvarez, Castoma, acquaintance of Glinka in Madrid, 474

Álvarez, José, music lover, flutist, and acquaintance of Glinka in Madrid, 460, 473, 477

Álvarez-Gonzáles, José, acquaintance of Glinka in Murcia, 477

Alyabiev, Aleksandr Aleksandrovich (1787–

"Confession" [*Ispoved'*], romance (words by M. Bibikov), 677
"Gypsy Song, The Braid" [*Kosa*] Russian Galop
Bulgarin, Faddey Benediktovich (1789–1859), writer and critic; editor of the *Northern Bee* [*Severnaia pchela*], 43, 137, 147, 148, 176, 186, 188, 252, 277, 279, 304, 306, 335, 345, 347, 349, 351, 352, 355, 356, 358, 374, 378, 389, 399, 404, 430, 461, 475, 499, 503, 578, 596, 609, 610, 624, 649, 654, 668, 709, 733
Bull, Ole (1810–1880), Norwegian violinist and composer, 188, 489
Military Polonaise for violin, 188
Siciliana, 188
Bunina, Vera Ivanovna, amateur singer, 514, 521, 544, 577
Buryanov, Viktor, economist(?), 163
Buslaev, Fedor Ivanovich (1818–1897), philologist and academician, 643
Busse (?), physician who treated Glinka in Berlin, 747
Bussine, Prosper Alfonse (1821–1881), French baritone, soloist with the Paris Opéra Comique, 599
Bussine, Romono (1830–1899), French bass and teacher, 599
Butashevich-Petrashevsky, Mikhail Vasilievich (1821–1866), leader of a political circle in the 1840s, 464, 520
Butu, 163
Byron, George Gordon, Lord (1788–1824), English poet, 13

Calderón de la Barca, Pedro (1600–1681), Spanish dramatist and librettist, 474
Cambiaggio, Cyrilla, née Branca, amateur pianist; daughter of Branca the lawyer and wife of Isidoro Cambiaggio, 78
Cantù, Italian bassoonist and orchestral player, 84
Carlini, Carlo. *See* Arnold, Yury
Carozzi, Enrico, 40
Casado-Diez, Mariano, acquaintance of Glinka's in Madrid, 474
Cassera, Angiola, Italian amateur singer (contralto), 77
Castilla, Felix, guitarist in Valladolid, 451
Catherine II, (1729–1796), Russian empress from 1762, 4
Cavallini, E., composer, 741
Cavos, Catterino Albertovich (1775–1840), Italian composer and conductor who lived and worked in SPb. from 1798, 15, 122, 128, 145, 152, 355, 372, 374, 375, 381, 392

"My Darling, My Dear" [*Dusha l' moia, dushen'ka*], aria, 12
Ivan Susanin, opera, 122, 253, 263, 268, 559, 564
Overtures
Rusalka, opera (possibly by Davdov)
Cavos, Ivan Catterinovich (1805–1863), director of the chorus of the SPb. Imp. Opera; singing teacher in the Smolny and Ekaterininsky Institutes; son of Caterino Cavos, 145, 152, 525, 547, 555, 556
Cervantes Saavedra, Miguel de (1547–1616), Spanish author, 421, 428
Chachkov, Vasily Vasilievich, journalist, collaborator on the *SPb. vedomosti*, 505
Chapellon, A., collaborator on *Le Nouvelliste*, 659
Chaplin, owner of a house in SPb., 156
Charlitsky, 172
Fantasy for piano on the romance "Who is she, and where is she" [*Kto ona i gde ona*], 548
"La murmure," nocturne for piano
Charpentier, Leon Ivanovich. *See* Leonov, L. I.
Charukovsky, Aleksey Prokhorovich (1825–1889), official in the Council for Communications, music lover, bibliophile, 644, 646, 656, 666, 668, 670, 678, 701, 704, 705–6
Chekka, teacher of singing in the SPb. Theater School, 365
Châteauneuf, A., acquaintance of Glinka in Paris, 439
Cherepnin, N., author of a book about the Smolny Institute, 215
Cherlitsky, Ivan Karlovich (1799–1865), organist, pianist, and composer, 172
Chernikov, V. V., amateur musician, 179, 182, 184, 185
Chernyshev, Fedor S. (1805–1869), military figure and author known in his time for his *Tales of the Two Tsars* [*Skazki pro dvukh tsarei*], 174
Chernyshev, N., 198
Chernyshevsky, Nikolay Gavrilovich (1828–1889), journalist, philosopher, literary critic, and writer, 374
Cherubini, Luigi (1760–1842), Italian composer who lived and worked in Paris from 1786, 19, 21, 31, 575, 586, 591, 598, 719, 720
Les deux journées, opera, 20–21, 28
Faniska, opera, 28, 40, 220, 567, 605
L'hôtellerie portugaise, opera, 28
Lodoiska, opera, 28, 567, 605
Médée, opera, 28, 64, 584
Requiem Mass, 739

75, 136, 184

Makovskaya, amateur singer, 191

Malchugin brothers, the, singers(?), 576

Malfatti, Johann (1775–1859), Italian physician who worked in Vienna, 88, 89

Malkov, violinist, 291

Malov, Aleksey Ivanovich (?–1855), priest at the Engineering Castle and archpriest of the Cathedral of St. Isaac, 110, 235

Maltsev, A. I., archpriest, priest of the orthodox church at the embassy in Berlin, 751

Maltsev, I., Sergey Sobolevsky's partner in the Samson textile mill in SPb., 160

Malyshev, chorister with the Imp. Chapel Choir, 187

Mamonova, SPb. landlady, 315

Mann, Ippolit Aleksandrovich (1823/4–1894), dramatist and music critic, 529, 538, 544, 545, 550, 553, 582, 649

Mantius, German tenor, 747

Marcel (née Rykalova), Elizaveta (?–1850), mezzo-soprano with the SPb. Imp. Opera during the period 1822–1844, 349

Maria ("with the madonna's face"), German singer who was Glinka's student in Berlin, 91, 92, 98, 110

Maria Nikolaevna (1819–1876), daughter of Nicholas I, wife of Duke Maximilian Lichtenberg, 228

Maria Stepanovna. *See* Krzhisevich, M. S.

Mario, Giovanni Matteo (1810–1883), Italian tenor who sang with the Italian Opera in SPb. from 1849–1853, 419

Markevich, Nikolay Andreevich (1804–1860), historian and ethnographer; Glinka's companion at the Boarding School, 13, 197, 198, 199, 202, 203, 204, 208, 210, 247, 248, 250, 251, 252, 253, 269, 274

Markov-Vinogradsky, Aleksandr Vasilievich (1820–1879), Anna Kern's second husband, 251, 257, 258, 293

Marochetti, Mikhail Petrovich (1782–?), surgeon; from 1827 physician at the Theater School; Glinka studied Italian with him, 51

Marras, French tenor, 434, 435, 436

Masalsky, Konstantin Petrovich, journalist; pupil at the SPb. Boarding School, 179

Mathieu, Pierre (1797–1866), costumier with the SPb. Imp. Theaters during the period 1837–1850, 349, 362

Maurer, Aleksandr Vasilievich, cellist; son of Ludwig Wilhelm Maurer, 668, 669

Maurer, Ludwig Wilhelm (1789–1878), violinist, conductor, and composer who served in the orchestras of the SPb. and Moscow Imp. Theaters; from 1841 music inspector

with the SPb. Imp. Theaters, 111, 312, 316, 435, 439, 612, 656, 668, 669, 711

Overture in E-flat for orchestra, 28

"Une larme sur la tombe de Glinka," elegy for orchestra, 761, 763, 766

Maurer, Vsevolod Vasilievich (1819–1892), violinist, member of Aleksey Lvov's quartet; concertmaster of first the French and then the Italian Opera orchestras; son of Ludwig Maurer, 668, 669

Maykov, Apollon Nikolaevich (1821–1897), poet, 761

Mayer, Desirée, acquaintance of Glinka in Paris, 424

M-ch. *See* Mezhevich, V. S.

Medici, Sofia Marchesa di Marignano de', Sofia, Italian amateur pianist, 82, 83

Medvedovsky, P. *See* Yurkevich, P. I.

Mego, apothecary in Smolensk, 497

Méhul, Etienne-Nicolas (1763–1817), French composer, 19, 719

Les deux aveugles de Tolède, opera, 7

L'irato, opera, 28

Joseph, opera, 21, 28, 563, 564, 597, 599, 704

Le trésor supposé, opera, 28

Meier, Karl (1799–1862), pianist and pedagogue; settled in Russia at the beginning of the 1800s, where he studied with Field; lived in SPb. during the period 1819–1845, 17, 23, 24, 25, 31, 32, 40, 116, 117, 131, 150, 252, 256, 328, 636, 692, 734

Toccata in D-flat for piano

Waltz for piano, 100

Meier, Leopold (1816–1883), Austrian pianist and composer, 269, 434, 567, 687

"Marche marrocaine" for piano, 426, 564, 605

"La Prière des âmes du purgatoire" for chorus and orchestra, 434

Triumphal March for piano, 435

Meier, landlord in Tsarskoe Selo, 632

Melety, archbishop of Kharkov and Akhtyrsk, 200

Melgunov, Aleksandr Nikolaevich (1766–1847), father of N. A. Melgunov, 12

Melgunov, Nikolay Aleksandrovich (1804–1867), literary figure and music critic; colleague of Glinka at the Boarding School, 12, 13, 29, 39, 40, 46, 71, 75, 83, 93, 96, 97, 101, 111, 112, 118, 125, 126, 130, 134, 149, 155, 169, 173, 187, 218, 239, 417, 420, 425, 430, 439, 443, 490, 600

Melikhova, proprietor of a house on Mokhovaya Street in SPb., 563, 565

Melnikov, Pavel Ivanovich, pseudonym Andrey

Index of Glinka's Works